RESEARCH HANDBOOK ON FUNDAMENTAL CONCEPTS OF ENVIRONMENTAL LAW

RESEARCH HANDBOOKS IN ENVIRONMENTAL LAW

This highly topical series addresses some of the most important questions and areas of research in Environmental Law. Each volume is designed by a leading expert to appraise the current state of thinking and probe the key questions for future research on a particular topic. The series encompasses some of the most pressing issues in the field, ranging from climate change, biodiversity and the marine environment through to the impacts of trade, regulation, and sustainable development.

Each *Research Handbook* comprises specially-commissioned chapters from leading academics, and sometimes practitioners, as well as those with an emerging reputation and is written with a global readership in mind. Equally useful as reference tools or high-level introductions to specific topics, issues and debates, these *Handbooks* will be used by academic researchers, post-graduate students, practising lawyers and lawyers in policy circles.

Titles in the series include:

Research Handbook on Climate Change Adaptation Law
Edited by Jonathan Verschuuren

Research Handbook on Climate Change Mitigation Law
Edited by Geert Van Calster, Wim Vandenberghe and Leonie Reins

Handbook of Chinese Environmental Law
Edited by Qin Tianbao

Research Handbook on International Marine Environmental Law
Edited by Rosemary Rayfuse

Research Handbook on Biodiversity and Law
Edited by Michael Bowman, Peter Davies and Edward Goodwin

Research Handbook on Fundamental Concepts of Environmental Law
Edited by Douglas Fisher

Research Handbook on Fundamental Concepts of Environmental Law

Edited by

Douglas Fisher

Emeritus Professor, Queensland University of Technology, Australia

RESEARCH HANDBOOKS IN ENVIRONMENTAL LAW

Edward Elgar PUBLISHING

Cheltenham, UK • Northampton, MA, USA

Published by
Edward Elgar Publishing Limited
The Lypiatts
15 Lansdown Road
Cheltenham
Glos GL50 2JA
UK

Edward Elgar Publishing, Inc.
William Pratt House
9 Dewey Court
Northampton
Massachusetts 01060
USA

A catalogue record for this book
is available from the British Library

Library of Congress Control Number: 2016942184

This book is available electronically in the **Elgar**online
Law subject collection
DOI 10.4337/9781784714659

MIX
Paper from
responsible sources
FSC® C013056

ISBN 978 1 78471 464 2 (cased)
ISBN 978 1 78471 465 9 (eBook)

Typeset by Columns Design XML Ltd, Reading

Printed and bound in Great Britain by
TJ International Ltd, Padstow, Cornwall

PUBLISHER'S NOTE

Contents

Contributors

Afshin Akhtar-Khavari is an Associate Professor in the Griffith Law School, Griffith University, Australia. He is a former Deputy Head and (acting) Head of the Griffith Law School. He is currently a member of the World Commission on Environmental Law for the International Union for the Conservation of Nature and a lead author for the Intergovernmental Platform on Biodiversity and Ecosystem Services on a report dealing with land degradation and restoration. He is on the editorial board of the Griffith Law Review. He publishes in the general area of international law and environmental humanities. He recently completed a co-authored monograph with Routledge on *Ecological Restoration in International Environmental Law* and is currently working on a co-edited collection in the Griffith Law Review dealing with law and ecological recovery. He is also writing his next book dealing with fear in the law and ecological recovery discourse.

Klaus Bosselmann is a Professor of Law and Founding Director of the New Zealand Centre for Environmental Law at the University of Auckland. He has provided consultancy for the OECD, UN, EU, and the governments of Germany and New Zealand. He was a delegate at the Earth Summits in Rio de Janeiro (1992 and 2012), is an executive member of several global sustainability organisations and is Chair of the IUCN World Commission on Environmental Law Ethics Specialist Group.

Nicholas Bryner is an Emmett/Frankel Fellow in Environmental Law and Policy at UCLA School of Law in Los Angeles, California. Prior to his current position, he worked as a Visiting Associate Professor of Law and Environmental Program Fellow at The George Washington University Law School and has also served as Executive Officer for the International Union for Conservation of Nature's World Commission on Environmental Law (WCEL).

Peter Burdon is an Associate Professor in the Adelaide Law School at Adelaide University in Australia and deputy chair of the International Union for the Conservation of Nature Ethics Specialist Group. He has published several books including *Earth Jurisprudence: Private Property and the Environment* (Routledge, 2014) and he is currently completing a book on Hannah Arendt and the Eichmann trial for the Routledge Nomikoi Critical Legal Thinkers series.

Michael Faure is the academic director of the Maastricht European Institute for Transnational Legal Research (METRO) and Professor of Comparative and International Environmental Law in the Law Faculty at Maastricht University. In addition, he is the academic director of the Ius Commune Research School, a member of the board of directors of Ectil, a half time Professor of Comparative Private Law and Economics at the Rotterdam Institute of Law and Economics (RILE) of the Erasmus University in Rotterdam and academic director of the European Doctorate in Law and Economics (EDLE) programme.

Douglas Fisher is Emeritus Professor of Law at the Queensland University of Technology in Australia. His involvement in environmental law began in 1970 and he has engaged in both professional and academic activities related to environmental law since then in Scotland, Australia and New Zealand. His most recent publications include *Legal Reasoning in Environmental Law: a Study of Structure, Form and Language* (Edward Elgar, 2013).

Elizabeth Fisher is Professor of Environmental Law in the Faculty of Law at the University of Oxford. She is General Editor of the *Journal of Environmental Law* and lead author of Fisher, Lange and Scotford, *Environmental Law* (Oxford University Press, 2013).

Anna Grear is Professor of Law and Theory in the Cardiff Law School and School of Law and Politics at Cardiff University in the United Kingdom. She is the founder and Director of the Global Network for the Study of Human Rights and the Environment (http://www.gnhre.org) and the Editor in Chief of the *Journal of Human Rights and Environment* (Edward Elgar).

David Grinlinton is an Associate Professor of Law in the Faculty of Law at the University of Auckland in New Zealand and a Visiting Professor of Law at Western Law School at the University of Western Ontario. His areas of research include the role of property rights in environmental and natural resources law, facilitating the greater uptake of renewable energy, and legal processes and regulation to encourage greater sustainability in the extractive industries. He is a member of the IUCN's CEL Specialist Group on Energy Law and a founding member of the 'Sustainable Energy for All' global community of practice.

Jørgen K. Knudsen is a political scientist graduated from the University of Oslo in Norway. He obtained his Doctoral degree at the University of

Twente in the Netherlands. He has been a research scientist at SINTEF Energy Research, Norway and is currently working on environmental research for the Norwegian Management of Public Constructions and Properties.

Louis Kotzé is Research Professor of Law in the Faculty of Law at North-West University (Potchefstroom Campus) in South Africa and Visiting Professor of Environmental Law at the University of Lincoln in the United Kingdom. He is co-editor of the *Journal of Human Rights and the Environment* (Edward Elgar) and Deputy-director of the Global Network for Human Rights and the Environment. His recent publications include *Global Environmental Governance: Law and Regulation for the 21st Century* (Edward Elgar, 2012) and *Research Handbook on Human Rights and the Environment* (with Anna Grear) (Edward Elgar, 2015).

William M. Lafferty is a retired Professor of Political Science at the University of Oslo where he was Director of the Program for Research and Documentation for a Sustainable Society (ProSus). He is Professor Emeritus of Strategic Research for Sustainable Development in Europe at the Center for Clean Technology and Environmental Policy at the University of Twente in the Netherlands. In recent years he has also served as a senior advisor on governance and policy for SINTEF Energy Research, Norway.

Chris McGrath is a senior lecturer in environmental regulation in the School of Geography, Planning and Environmental Management at the University of Queensland in Australia. He is a barrister and has been involved in many of the most significant environmental law cases to have been decided in Australia over recent years.

Brian J. Preston has been the Chief Judge of the Land and Environment Court of New South Wales in Australia since 2005. He is a member of a number of national, regional and international organisations whose focus is environmental law. He has contributed significantly over many years to an understanding of environmental law and to its development through his judicial and extrajudicial writings and commentary.

Niko Soininen is a lecturer in environmental law and jurisprudence at the University of Eastern Finland School of Law. He has a keen interest in environmental law, administrative law and jurisprudence. He is co-editor of a book entitled *Transboundary Marine Spatial Planning and International Law* (Earthscan/Routledge, 2015) and author of several articles and book chapters on water law, marine environmental law and legal theory. In September 2016 he defended his LL.D. thesis entitled *Transparencies in Legality: A Legal Analysis of the Reason-giving Requirement* *in Water Management Permitting in Finland.* Outside of academia Niko has worked as an adviser for HELCOM and the Ministry of Agriculture and Forestry and the Ministry of the Environment in Finland.

Caiphas Soyapi is a doctoral candidate in the Faculty of Law at North-West University in South Africa. His thesis focuses on the emergence of transnational environmental rights law in Africa. Research interests include international environmental law, transnationalism in law and socio-legal studies.

Tim Stephens is Professor of International Law and an Australian Research Council Future Fellow in the Sydney Law School at the University of Sydney in Australia. He has written extensively on international environmental dispute settlement including *International Courts and Environmental Protection* (Cambridge University Press, 2009).

Prue Taylor teaches environmental and planning law to graduate and undergraduate students in the School of Architecture and Planning at the University of Auckland in New Zealand. She is the Deputy Director of the New Zealand Centre for Environmental Law and a member of the IUCN Commission of Environmental Law and its Ethics Specialist Group. Her specialist research interests are in the areas of climate change, human rights, environmental and commons governance, ocean law and policy, property rights and environmental ethics. Prue has co-authored *Common Heritage of Mankind: A Bibliography of Legal Writing* (Fondation de Malte, 2013) with Lucy Stroud.

Anastasia Telesetsky is an Associate Professor of Law at the University of Idaho School of Law in the Natural Resources and Environmental Law program. She is currently the co-chair of the International Environmental Law Committee of the American Bar Association Section of International Law and an editorial board member of the Asia-Pacific *Journal for Ocean Law and Policy*. In 2016, she was the Ian Axford Public Policy Fellow at the New Zealand Ministry of Primary Industries focusing on fisheries sustainability issues.

Jonathan Verschuuren is Professor of International and European Environmental Law at Tilburg University in the Netherlands, a faculty member of the Tilburg Sustainability Center and an EU Marie Sklodowska-Curie Fellow. He has been a visiting professor at a number of universities outside the Netherlands. His extensive list of publications includes *Research Handbook on Climate Change Adaptation Law* (Edward Elgar, 2013).

Annecoos Wiersema is a Professor of Law at the University of Denver Sturm College of Law. She was the Director of the International Legal Studies Program at the Sturm College of Law from 2013 to 2015 and former Ved P. Nanda Chair. Prior to joining the faculty at the University of Denver Sturm College of Law, she was an Assistant Professor at the Ohio State University Michael E. Moritz College of Law and worked in the Denver office of Arnold and Porter LLP as a litigation associate. Annecoos was the George W. Foley, Jr. Fellow in Environmental Law at Harvard Law School from 1999 to 2000 and spent time as a Visiting Scholar at the International Monetary Fund (IMF) in 2001.

Claire Williams holds degrees in law, legal practice, science and climate science. She specialised in international law and human rights at Masaryk University in the Czech Republic. Claire is now undertaking a PhD which examines the disconnection between our scientific understanding of human impact and the laws and policies governing our behaviour. Claire has just been awarded an Endeavour Scholarship to complete her PhD at New York University.

PART 1

THE OVERARCHING FRAMEWORK FOR ENVIRONMENTAL GOVERNANCE

1. The jurisprudential structure of environmental law

Douglas Fisher

INTRODUCTION[1]

A legal system traditionally comprises a set of protectable rights and a correlative set of enforceable duties together with a range of institutional processes for their recognition, creation, implementation, compliance and enforcement. Such a system operates within the framework of the values and norms acceptable to the society which it serves. These arrangements manifest themselves in the form of rules that perform a range of different functions and disclose a variety of characteristics. Here are three examples. First, on the one hand there is the substantive right to own and to use land and the procedural right to vindicate this right in a court, while on the other hand there is the duty imposed on all persons not to interfere with or harm this right and supported by the procedural right to ensure compliance with this duty. Second, on the one hand there is the administrative right conferred on a public institution to make a decision affecting an individual, while on the other hand there is the duty imposed on the public institution to make the decision according to the relevant legal rules and supported by the procedural right of the individual to ensure compliance with these legal rules. Third, on the one hand there is the substantive right of the individual not to be assaulted, injured or damaged, while on the other hand there is the duty imposed on all persons not to assault, injure or damage an individual and supported by the procedural right of the individual and, in certain circumstances, of the state to ensure compliance with these rules.

Traditionally, these rules-based arrangements have been designed to protect the interests of the individual vis-à-vis those of other individuals and, more recently, to advance the broader interests of the society of which the individuals are a part. Over the last few decades, the broader interests advanced and protected by the law have expanded to include the public interest in how the natural resources of the environment are managed and how the environment is protected. This has introduced into the legal system at all levels – international, regional and national – not only new approaches to governance but also distinctive paradigms of governance. Accordingly, the context within which the rules have effect has become as important as the formal text – a treaty, a constitution, a statute or a judicial decision – within which they are expressed. Arguably, an innovative jurisprudential structure has begun to emerge in response to these ideological and doctrinal developments.

THE DOCTRINAL DILEMMAS FACING ENVIRONMENTAL LAW

The watershed of contemporary environmental law has often been taken to be the acceptance by the international community of the values incorporated in the Stockholm Declaration of 1972. Although it is an international instrument, it recognises the inherent relationship between individuals within the community and the states of which these communities are a part. Articles 1 and 21 acknowledge – at least by implication – this relationship. Article 1 recognises three specific fundamental rights of man 'in an environment of a quality that permits a life of dignity and well-being' and at the same time 'a solemn responsibility to protect and improve the environment for present and future generations'. Consistently with this from a structural perspective, article 21 recognises the sovereign right of states 'to exploit their own resources' and at the same time 'the responsibility to ensure' that damage is not caused to the environment beyond their territorial boundaries. There could be no clearer acknowledgment of the relationship between rights and responsibilities in relation to states and individuals. The emerging arrangements for environmental governance are an example of this relationship but they reveal a much more complex matrix of relationships.

The provenance of the Stockholm Declaration as a statement of principles declared at an international conference of nation states indicates that its provisions, while not strictly binding as a matter of law, represent the values favoured by the international community and the contexts in which they are intended to have effect. Articles 1 and 21 talk about rights and responsibilities at a structurally normative level. Multilateral environmental agreements similarly formulate rights and responsibilities at a structurally normative level. For example, article 2 of the Geneva Convention on Long-Range Transboundary Air Pollution 1979 states, first, that 'the contracting parties … are determined to protect man and his environment against air pollution'. This is an expression of an intention linked to a value. Article 2, however, goes on to state, second, that parties 'shall endeavour to limit and, as far as possible, gradually reduce and prevent air pollution'. This is structurally different. It is an obligation to endeavour to achieve a stated objective. Although it is formulated as an obligation in a legal instrument, it probably does not constitute an enforceable obligation. Nevertheless it is part of the normative context within which the obligation has effect. Thus norms, rights and obligations perform different but not independent functions within these sets of arrangements. Again the question is their relationship.

Similar issues arise in relation to national arrangements for environmental governance. Section 2 of the National Environmental Management Act 1998 of South Africa states the principles that apply to the administration of the Act. Section 2(3) states: 'Development must be socially, environmentally and economically sustainable'. This is an obligation imposed not on any particular person. It is owed *erga omnes*. Its capacity to be enforced is perhaps unclear at this stage but its normative force is quite clear. Section 2(4)(o) is similarly structured as a normative rather than as a strictly legal obligation. It states:

> The environment is held in public trust for the people, the beneficial use of environmental resources must serve the public interest and the environment must be protected as the people's common heritage.

These provisions are not only to assist in the performance of the range of functions created by the Act but also to guide the interpretation of the Act. These examples indicate that, both internationally and nationally, the normative and legal arrangements for environmental governance are interdependent and that the range of rights and responsibilities associated with them are equally dependent on each other. In practice this means that the interpretation, the application and the implementation of an instrument for environmental governance are a response to its status, structure, form and language.

THE FUNCTIONS OF RIGHTS AND OBLIGATIONS IN ENVIRONMENTAL LAW

It may be useful to put these perspectives into their jurisprudential context. A right recognised by international or national law may perform a range of different functions. A right may be formulated as a normative value – to freedom or to a healthy environment. Alternatively a right may be operational or administrative – to engage in a particular activity or to permit a person to engage in a particular activity, for example, to exploit resources, to use land for a particular purpose, to extract water from a particular source or to mine for specific minerals. The first is usually described as a right, while the second is usually described as a power. Then there are responsibilities. A responsibility is a general description of an obligation to engage in or not to engage in a particular activity. An example of the former is to take measures to reduce greenhouse gas emissions, to conserve biodiversity or to protect the environment. Examples of the latter are not to cause pollution, not to harm the environment and not to injure or damage the interests of a group of persons or of a particular person. A right formulated as a normative value remains in common parlance a right – usually a human right but increasingly as an environmental right. Powers and responsibilities – obligations or duties – are described respectively in this chapter as rules of competence and rules of limitation.

It has been suggested that rules of competence and rules of limitation have effect within the wider framework of the normative values that are part of the overall system of environmental governance. The part played by these rules is critical. Rules of competence enable decisions to be made and describe what can be done in these circumstances:

- In the exercise of a right of sovereignty in the case of a state
- In the exercise of a right of property in the case of an individual or a private or public institution within a state including the state itself
- In the exercise of a right of administration by a public institution within a state.

The exercise of these rights is subject to a range of rules of limitation. There are in particular four:

- Strategic rules
- Regulatory rules
- Liability rules
- Market rules.

These have been described in these words:

> Strategic rules point out the substantive direction of decision-making and of operational activity. Regulatory rules describe what cannot be done and what can be done through the involvement of the executive branch. Liability rules describe what can be done and what cannot be done in accordance with clearly stated and defined sets of rights and duties. Market rules provide for the administration of existing markets or the creation of new markets when

economic instruments of this kind are seen to be a way of managing the environment.[2]

The rules of environmental law are both reactive and proactive in nature. Traditionally, legal rules have been reactive: determining what has happened in the past and deciding whether a rule has been breached and a liability incurred. Essentially these are liability rules. Here is an example. Has the person in question caused pollution of the waters of the river or caused the damage sustained by the injured party? The sanction may be civil or criminal. Although the sanction may look to the future – an injunction, a fine or imprisonment – the initial stage of these proceedings is reactive.

Then there are proactive rules. Much of environmental law is now concerned with affording access to the resources of the environment and with protecting the environment. Although the private sector plays a part in these arrangements, for the most part these functions are performed by the public sector. The matters to be determined include:

- Should mining be permitted?
- Should land be reserved from development?
- For what purposes should land be used?
- How should biodiversity be conserved?
- How should this element of the environment be protected?

Significantly, the word 'should' is used. It connotes an element of discretion in addressing these issues and points to what should be the future outcome of the process. This is a proactive approach in the sense that it looks to the future rather than the past. The result, depending on the evidence and how it is analysed, may be the approval of the request and hence the grant of an interest in the resource or it may be the protection of an element of the environment. New rights and obligations have been created by this process and they have been created by the application of strategic rules.

The provisions – usually statutory – designed to protect the environment have mostly been regulatory in nature. The controlled activity is prohibited without an administrative grant of approval. The regulatory process of approval is governed by rules that are either substantive or methodological or both. In this way the rules explain not only what the objective or the outcome of the approval process is intended to achieve – strategic rules – but also how the decision is to be made – methodological rules. A failure to comply with a strategic rule may in certain circumstances be justiciable. A failure to comply with a methodological rule will almost certainly be justiciable. Thus all involved parties – those engaging in activities impacting on the environment, those proposing to engage in activities likely to impact on the environment and those determining whether to grant administrative approval to such activities – are subject to the relevant rules of law.

The policy objectives of the public sector are able to be achieved not only by these strategic, regulatory and liability rules but also by the use of economic instruments such as financial incentives or disincentives. The use of economic instruments places the responsibility for deciding what to do and how to do it upon the entrepreneur rather than upon the public sector as is the case with regulation. This is the most significant distinction between these two sets of arrangements – regulatory instruments and economic instruments.

The use of economic instruments, however, is not an example of a laissez-faire approach. Markets do not operate in a legal vacuum. Their operation depends upon rules of competence – a right of property and a right to enter into a contract – and upon rules of limitation such as those dealing with contractual, tortious or delictual liability and even liability under taxation rules. In addition, the operation of markets is sometimes regulated by sets of strategic and liability rules created by legislation. Environmental governance overall is thus a combination in all respects of strategic, regulatory, liability and market rules. Each set of rules plays an important but distinctive part in the overall system. Significantly, in theory and in practice they frequently operate in tandem with each other.

THE EVOLUTION OF POLYCENTRIC GOVERNANCE

To return to the fundamental values underpinning the system of environmental governance and implemented – at least in theory – by these sets of rules. Environmental law has a long history but not with that nomenclature:

- Medieval regimes of building regulation
- Nineteenth-century regimes for pollution control
- Establishment of national parks at the beginning of the twentieth century
- More sophisticated land use planning arrangements during the twentieth century
- Air and water pollution control during the second half of the twentieth century

- The emphasis on the protection and improvement of the environment after the Stockholm Declaration.

These developments created a very fragmented and sectoral approach to environmental governance. The Stockholm Declaration provided the opportunity for a new approach. It emerged over the next 20 years in the shape of sustainability. Whatever it means in practical and operational terms and whatever its status as a matter of law, it is now the fundamental concept upon which the system of governance is based. It embraces these three dimensions – the economic, the social and the ecological – but each in the context of development. Development is a proactive notion – whether it is the development of the economy or of the society. But the economic, social and ecological dimensions operate to limit the way in which the notion of development operates. Perhaps in these words:

> If a development is to satisfy the standard of ecologically sustainable development, then it must satisfy these three conditions. It must be sustainable in terms of the long-term and continuous use of the resource itself. It must be sustainable in terms of the long-term integrity and stability of the human resources that comprise the society in question. And it must be sustainable in terms of the ecological integrity of the environment out of which the resource is taken.[3]

If this is a credible analysis, it is a major challenge for all parties involved in environmental governance: nation states, legislatures, executive governments, judicial institutions, corporate institutions, non-government organisations and individual members of the community. A critical element is the simple idea of integration – not only of process and procedure but also of substance. There is one and only one intended outcome – sustainable development. The approach is neither anthropocentric (a focus on humans), nor ecocentric (a focus on nature), nor monocentric (a focus on one specific issue) but polycentric. This connotes a new conception of decision-making. There are fundamentally two challenges:

- The complex methodology of decision-making in environmental governance
- The substantive content of the notion of sustainable development.

The nature of polycentricity has been described in these words:

> The range of interests affected, the complexity of the issues and the interdependence of the issues means that decision-making involves a polycentric problem. A polycentric problem involves a complex network of relationships, with interacting points of influence. Each decision made communicates itself to other centres of decision, changing the conditions, so that a new basis must be found for the next decision.[4]

Against this background it is now relevant to review the way the jurisprudential structure of environmental law is revealed by the text of a range of international and national instruments and by their interpretation and application by judicial institutions.

INTERNATIONAL PERSPECTIVES

The United Nations Convention on the Law of the Sea 1982 provides for the governance by coastal states of the natural resources – living and non-living – of their exclusive economic zones. The first proposition in article 193 confers upon states 'the sovereign right to exploit their natural resources'. This is a rule of competence. The exercise of this right is regulated by a series of rules of limitation related to the objective of the optimum utilisation of these resources and the determination of the allowable catch. These are essentially strategic and regulatory rules. There is a generally formulated obligation in article 192: 'States have the obligation to protect and preserve the marine environment'.

This obligation is supported by the obligation in article 194(1) to take all measures necessary to reduce and control pollution of the marine environment and by the obligation in article 194(2) to take all measures necessary to ensure that damage by pollution is not caused to other states and their environment. Neither the right to exploit nor the obligation to protect is absolute. Their relationship is governed by the second proposition in article 193. In its entirety it provides:

> States have the sovereign right to exploit their natural resources pursuant to their environmental policies and in accordance with their duty to protect and preserve the marine environment.

There is thus the juxtaposition of a rule of competence and a rule of limitation. The Convention – in the context of sustainable development – discloses arrangements for the conservation – sustainable use – of the living resources of the sea as well as the protection of the marine environment itself.

Article 2 of the Vienna Convention for the Protection of the Ozone Layer 1985 is structured in a way reflective of article 194 of the United Nations Convention on the Law of the Sea 1982. Thus:

> The parties shall take all appropriate measures in accordance with the provisions of this Convention and of those protocols to which they are a party to protect human health and the environment against adverse effects resulting or likely to result from human activities which modify or are likely to modify the ozone layer.

The obligation to take measures – to an extent discretionary in nature – is linked to a strategic rule: the objective of protection. The Montreal Protocol 1987 to the Vienna Convention is structurally different. The rules of limitation in the Protocol are regulatory rather than strategic. The standards incorporated in the regulatory rules are stated to be the levels of consumption and production of controlled substances by each state. According to article 2A(1) each state is required to ensure that for the relevant period its calculated level of consumption of the controlled substance does not exceed its calculated level of consumption in the year of commencement of these arrangements. It is a regulatory rule rather than a strategic rule because of the imposition of quantitative limitations.

The approach adopted by the United Nations Convention on the Law of the Non-navigational Uses of International Watercourses 1997 is again different. More than one state has – by definition – an interest in how international watercourses are managed. There is accordingly an obligation in article 8 to cooperate:

> Watercourse states shall cooperate on the basis of sovereign equality, territorial integrity, mutual benefit and good faith in order to attain optimal utilization and adequate protection of an international watercourse.

This recognises the complementarity of rules of competence – sovereignty – and rules of limitation – utilisation and protection. This anticipates the notion of sustainable development. This notion is further reflected in the fundamental principle set out in article 5(1):

> Watercourse states shall in their respective territories utilize an international watercourse in an equitable and reasonable manner. In particular an international watercourse shall be used and developed by watercourse states with a view to attaining optimal and sustainable utilization thereof and benefits therefrom, taking into account the interests of the watercourse states concerned, consistent with adequate protection of the watercourse.

The first sentence states an obligation coupled with the relevant standard. This comes close to its formulation as a liability rule in the sense that a failure to comply with the standard may lead to a determination of liability. The second sentence states an obligation linked to a strategic rule – attaining optimal and sustainable utilisation – coupled with a methodological rule – taking the stated interests into account. The standards stated are clear:

- Equitable and reasonable
- Optimal and sustainable
- Adequate.

These are relatively subjective standards. It is likely, however, that in particular sets of circumstances they will be interpreted and applied in the context of the strategic and liability rules in the Convention. For example, what is an equitable use in the context of optimal utilization and what is adequate protection of the watercourse are determined from the perspective of all states. In any event, the general direction of these arrangements is sustainable use.

CONSTITUTIONAL PERSPECTIVES

It has become increasingly common for constitutions to include provisions about the environment. Article 11 of the Constitution of the State of Illinois in the United States is an interesting example. Section 1 of article 11 states: 'The public policy of the state and the duty of each person is to provide and maintain a healthful environment for the benefit of this and future generations'. Clearly, this is not only a statement of public policy but also the imposition of a duty on all persons. It seems to have been assumed that the provision is not enforceable – at least in relation to the public policy – because it goes on to indicate that legislation is required 'for the implementation and enforcement of this public policy'. Section 2 states that 'each person has the right to a healthy environment'. This similarly requires legislation to enable it to be enforced. On the face of it, therefore, the policy, the duty and the right are unenforceable unless supported by relevant statutory provisions. A court is unlikely to proceed in the absence of legislation. Nevertheless, article 11 clearly states the normative framework within which the state is expected to perform its statutory functions.

Not all courts are limited in this way. One example is India. There is no fundamental right to an environment of a particular quality in the

Constitution of India. However, article 21 confers a fundamental right to life and article 32 confers a fundamental right to invite the Supreme Court to enforce this right. Articles 48-A and 51-A address the quality of the environment. The directive principles of state policy acknowledge the function of the state and the duty of every citizen in protecting and improving the environment. These provisions in the Constitution together with the developing rules and principles of international law – in particular the importance of sustainable development – led the Supreme Court to provide remedies for protection of the environment and to recognise the existence of a right to a healthy environment. Thus:

> It is now an accepted social principle that all human beings have a fundamental right to a healthy environment, commensurate with their well-being, coupled with a corresponding duty of ensuring that resources are conserved and preserved in such a way that present as well as future generations are aware of them equally.[5]

Although described as a 'social' principle, the right to a healthy environment is couched in legal as well as normative language and supported by the international and constitutional sources relied on by the Supreme Court. Accordingly it has perhaps been transformed into a legal principle and a legal rule.

The Supreme Court of Costa Rica has been equally creative. The Political Constitution of Costa Rica includes provisions to this effect:

- Human life is inviolable
- Every individual has the right to a healthy and ecologically balanced environment
- The state guarantees this right.

In this way a right to life and a right in relation to the environment are brought together. The Supreme Court has noted that the improvement of the quality of life is the main objective of development: 'The latter must however be linked to the environment so that it is harmonious and sustainable'.[6] In addition, 'environmental quality is a fundamental condition of the quality of life'. However, there is a wider normative perspective that is relevant:

> Even more important is to understand that although man has the right to use the environment for his development, he also has a duty to protect and preserve it for the use of future generations. This is not a great novelty, it is no more than conveying in this specific context the principle against injury. This is well established in the common law (*derecho comun*), according to

> which the lawful exercise of a right finds two limitations: on the one hand the rights of others and, on the other hand, reasonableness in the exercise and the positive use of the right.[7]

This approach comes close to acknowledging the existence of liability rules in the context of damage to the environment – based on the rules of the common law and no doubt of the civil law. There are, accordingly, on the one hand rules of competence and on the other hand rules of limitation. The criterion accepted by the common law is reasonableness: a concept inherently flexible and responsive to circumstances and one not unknown in international law.

These judicial comments are important because the concept of providing a remedy for an injury has been extended beyond an injury sustained by a person to an injury sustained by the environment. Importantly, the notion of an injury sustained by the environment is juristically linked to the concept that the quality of life is dependent upon the quality of the environment. This represents a complex web of relationships between humans and the environment, between rules of competence and rules of limitation, between human rights and environmental rights, and between constitutional rights and common law or civil law rights – all set in the context of sustainable development.

STATUTORY PERSPECTIVES

The arrangements enacted by legislatures in many jurisdictions reveal examples of strategic, regulatory and liability rules. Strategic and regulatory rules are largely the province of the public sector. Often they are supported by liability rules. There is an interesting example of liability rules as the principal mechanism for achieving their objectives. The US Comprehensive Environmental Response, Compensation and Liability Act (CERCLA) creates a liability regime in two sets of circumstances. Here is one: the person responsible for the release or a threatened release of a hazardous substance is liable for the costs of removal or the costs of remedial action incurred by the US government or other agencies and for any other necessary costs of response incurred by other persons.[8] Here is the other: where there is injury to, destruction of or loss of natural resources resulting from the release or a threatened release of a hazardous substance, a liability arises to pay damages.[9] For this purpose natural resources include wildlife, biota, air and water.[10] Significantly this liability is owed to the US government and other prescribed agencies.[11] In this respect the President of the United States is required to act on behalf of the public as trustee of the resources to enable the recovery of these damages.[12] This liability regime comprises a set of rules of limitation. It is for the potentially liable persons – not the public sector – to take action to prevent the release or threatened release of a hazardous substance. But this is supported by a rule of competence – the power and perhaps the duty of the President to enforce these rules[13] and through the judicial system if necessary.

The Resource Management Act of New Zealand is a combination of strategic, regulatory, methodological and liability rules. A range of activities is prohibited without authorisation – the foundation of regulation. These include the use of land, the use of water and the discharge of substances impacting on the environment. This regulatory system is directed at the achievement of the purpose of the Act. According to section 5 this is to promote the sustainable management of natural resources. The lengthy definition of sustainable management brings together the functions of the use, development and protection of natural and physical resources in the context of their conservation and preservation and the protection of the environment.

The Act explains the methodology according to which the purpose of the Act is to be achieved. There is an obligation to recognise and provide for the matters of national importance stated in section 6. These include:

- The preservation of the natural character of the coastal environment
- The protection of outstanding natural features and landscapes
- The protection of historic heritage.

Particularly important is the inclusion in section 6 of the relationship of Maori and their culture and traditions with their ancestral lands, water, sites, waahi tapu and other taonga. Section 7 imposes an obligation to have particular regard to a number of factors. These are both ecocentric and anthropocentric. The former includes the intrinsic values of ecosystems and the maintenance and enhancement of the quality of the environment; and the latter includes the efficiency of the end use of energy and the efficient use and development of natural and physical resources. Addressing both perspectives is the obligation to have particular regard to the effects of climate change.

The Environment Court of New Zealand has stressed the importance of the statutory methodology in making decisions under the Act and particularly the relationship between section 5 – the purpose – and sections 6 and 7 – the mandatory factors for consideration. These are all in Part 2 of the Act. The court explained the methodology in three succinct propositions. Here is the first:

> The cardinal and pivotal matter for us to bear in mind in weighing and evaluating the evidence and exercising our discretion is the Act's single purpose set out in s 5.[14]

Here is the second:

> The remaining sections in Part 2, subsequent to s 5, inform and assist the purpose of the Act. We may accord such weight as we think fit to any competing consideration under Part 2, bearing in mind the purpose of the Act. These subsequent sections must not be allowed to obscure the sustainable management purpose of the Act. Rather, they should be approached as factors in the overall balancing exercise to be conducted by the court.[15]

Here is the third:

> We thus propose to consider the relevant evidential matters, make decisions on the facts, and then apply a balancing and weighing process to determine what best achieves the single purpose of the Act.[16]

This is one judicial response to what has been described as a polycentric problem. The methodology is complex but the outcome is clear. Four features essential to solving this problem have emerged from this judicial analysis:

- The Act states its purpose
- It is one single purpose
- The objective is to achieve this single purpose
- To achieve this purpose the best alternative way of doing so must be selected.

The courts in the United States have on occasion directed their attention to the relationship between strategic and methodological rules. An early example is the *Calvert Cliffs* case which required an analysis of the US National Environmental Policy Act.

The Act contained a lengthy and detailed declaration of national environmental policy together with the imposition of a duty upon all agencies of the federal government to undertake an environmental impact assessment of all proposals for major federal actions significantly affecting the quality of the human environment. The judicial analysis of the Act began with this proposition: 'Our duty, in short, is to see that important legislative purposes, heralded in the halls of Congress, are not lost or misdirected in the vast hallways of the federal bureaucracy'.[17]

The strategic – in this case the substantive – provisions were distinguished from the methodological – in this case the procedural –

provisions. The substance of the Act was stated in the declaration of policy and the procedural provisions included the obligation to consider the environmental issues that had been identified by the required environmental impact assessment. The relationship between them was described in these words:

> The general substantive policy of the Act is a flexible one. It leaves room for a responsible exercise of discretion and may not require particular substantive results in particular problematic instances. However, the Act also contains very important 'procedural' provisions – provisions which are designed to see that all federal agencies do in fact exercise the substantive discretion given to them. These provisions are not highly flexible. Indeed, they establish a strict standard of compliance.[18]

Although the strategic provisions stating the policy objectives of the Act were probably not taken to be enforceable, there was no doubt that the procedural provisions were enforceable. After a careful analysis of the Act as a whole, this was the conclusion:

> Section102 ... mandates a particular sort of careful and informed decision-making process and creates judicially enforceable duties. The reviewing courts probably cannot reverse a substantive decision on its merits under section 101 unless it be shown that the actual balance of costs and benefits that was struck was arbitrary or clearly gave insufficient weight to environmental values. But if the decision was reached procedurally without individualised consideration and balancing of environmental factors – conducted fully and in good faith – it is the responsibility of the courts to reverse.[19]

It was to this extent that the court was able to ensure that 'important legislative purposes were not lost or misdirected' in the administration of the legislation. There would seem little doubt that the declaration of national environmental policy in the Act was a critical part of the methodology of decision-making required by the Act. The clearly stated 'legislative purposes' were almost mandatorily relevant.

The rules about environmental governance in Sweden are almost entirely contained in the Environmental Code of Sweden. The purpose of the Code stated in section 1 of chapter 1 is to promote sustainable development which will assure a healthy and sound environment for present and future generations. Sustainable development is underpinned by three concepts:

- Nature is worthy of protection
- Nature is capable of being modified and exploited

- The exploitation of nature is conditional upon the wise management of natural resources.

The application of the Code requires a number of outcomes to be ensured. These include the protection of the environment and the preservation of biological diversity. The mechanisms for implementing the Code are traditional: for example, setting standards, managing protected areas, licensing prescribed activities, environmental impact assessment, liability regimes, and civil and criminal sanctions.

It is the range of obligations set out in chapter 2 of the Code and their substance that sets these arrangements apart from others. Some of the obligations are quite specific:

- To possess the knowledge necessary to protect human health and the environment
- To implement protective measures to protect the environment
- To select sites for land and water use so as to reduce damage to the environment
- To conserve raw materials and energy and to reuse and recycle them
- To avoid using chemical products or biological organisms involving risks to the environment.

The general obligation stated in section 1 of chapter 2 and linked to the more specific obligations is critical:

> Persons who pursue an activity or take a measure, or intend to do so, shall show that the obligations arising out of this chapter have been complied with. This shall also apply to persons who have pursued activities that may have caused damage or detriment to the environment.

This applies to all measures that are not of negligible significance. It is important because it places the obligation upon the person who is pursuing an activity or intends to do so. It is not absolute. This is because, according to section 7 of chapter 2, these rules 'shall be applicable where compliance cannot be deemed unreasonable'. In other words, if there is no reason to justify non-compliance, there must be compliance.

The effect of these provisions has been summarised in this way:

> Everybody must observe the rules of consideration, irrespective of any intervention on the part of a public authority. The rules lay down common requirements for all activities that involve a risk of harm to the environment.

> The party exercising the activity is, through the consideration of permits and similar procedures and supervision, liable to prove that the general rules of consideration of the Environmental Code are complied with. Thus, the burden of proof is reversed.[20]

The effectiveness of the Code is supported by the capacity of the Environmental Court of Sweden to ensure compliance. The strength of the Code is the extensive range of interrelated rules – strategic, regulatory and liability – designed to achieve the clearly stated purpose of sustainable development.

CONCLUSION

This review of international, constitutional and statutory instruments in a number of jurisdictions together with some examples of their judicial interpretation and application indicates that the arrangements for environmental governance disclose a number of common features. The standards set for behaviour and decision-making tend to be relatively general – fair, equitable, reasonable, appropriate, necessary, significant, rational, even wise. Much more significant have been the statements of value and of objectives or outcomes. These have become part not only of the regulatory systems that have been put in place but also of the liability regimes that exist alongside these regulatory systems or independently of them. These objectives have traditionally been sectoral – prevention of pollution, conservation of biodiversity, preservation of cultural heritage, protection of the environment – all set in the context of development of natural resources. The contemporary approach has become much more integrated through the influence of sustainable development.

The jurisprudential architecture has adapted to these changes. It has become almost common practice to incorporate values and fundamental norms in legal instruments; to give them effect through the formulation of strategic rules; to provide for their implementation directly by the public sector through sets of regulatory rules including methodological rules; and ultimately to ensure compliance with them by those engaged in operational activities through the automatic application of liability rules which in some cases complement the use of economic instruments supported by market rules. It has become a complex and interrelated web or matrix of rules of competence and rules of limitation. Rights and duties perform a range of different functions within this set of arrangements. Environmental governance seeks to move consistently in the direction of sustainable development – a controversial and structurally challenging vision for the future. The law has traditionally set standards of behaviour and of decision-making that are public knowledge. The community could therefore determine in advance whether or not their activities complied with the relevant rules. This remains so for environmental law. The processes of adjudication to determine whether there has been compliance with individual rights and duties are critical. But environmental law is now focused as much on promoting and protecting the wider public or community interest in how the resources of the environment are developed and how the environment is protected. The range of relevant interests has expanded exponentially and so has the range of relevant norms and rules. The following chapters review in detail many of these conceptual developments.

NOTES

1. See generally Fisher (2010) and Fisher (2013).
2. Fisher (2014, p. 11).
3. Ibid. (p. 162).
4. *Bulga* case (2013, para.31).
5. *Tirupathi* case (2006, p. 322).
6. *Mejia* case (1993, p. 180).
7. Ibid. (pp. 180–181).
8. CERCLA, s.9607(a)(4)(A) and (B).
9. Ibid. s.9607(a)(4)(c) and 9607(f)(1).
10. Ibid. s.9601(16).
11. Ibid. s.9607(f)(1).
12. Ibid.
13. Ibid.
14. *Genesis Power* case (2005, p. 553).
15. Ibid. (p. 554).
16. Ibid. (p. 555).
17. *Calvert Cliffs* case (1971, p. 1111).
18. Ibid. (p. 1112).
19. Ibid. (p. 1115).
20. Silten (1999, p. 530).

REFERENCES

Fisher, D.E. (2010), 'A view of jurisprudential architecture for sustainable governance', *Environmental Liability* 3, 83–103.

Fisher, D.E. (2013), *Legal Reasoning in Environmental Law* (Cheltenham, Edward Elgar).

Fisher, D.E. (2014), *Australian Environmental Law – Norms, Principles and Rules* (Sydney, Lawbook Co. Thomson Reuters).

Silten M.S. (1999), 'Environmental Law in Sweden' in N.S.J. Koeman (ed.), *Environmental Law in Europe* (London, Kluwer).

INSTRUMENTS

CERCLA: Comprehensive Environmental Response, Compensation and Liability Act Title 42 United States Code Annotated
Constitution of India
Constitution of the State of Illinois (United States)
Environmental Code of Sweden
Geneva Convention on Long-Range Transboundary Air Pollution: (1979) *International Legal Materials* 18, 1442.
Montreal Protocol: Montreal Protocol on Substances that Deplete the Ozone Layer: (1987) *International Legal Materials* 26, 1550.
National Environmental Management Act (South Africa)
Political Constitution of Costa Rica
Resource Management Act (New Zealand)
Stockholm Declaration: Declaration of the United Nations Conference on the Human Environment: (1972) *International Legal Materials* 11, 1416
United Nations Convention on the Law of the Non-navigational Uses of International Watercourses 1997: (1998) *International Legal Materials* 36, 700.
United Nations Convention on the Law of the Sea: (1982) *International Legal Materials* 21, 1261.
Vienna Convention for the Protection of the Ozone Layer 1985: (1987) *International Legal Materials* 26, 1529.

CASES

Bulga case: *Bulga Mibrodale Progress Association Inc v Minister for Planning and Infrastructue* (2013) New South Wales Land and Environment Court 48.
Calvert Cliffs case: *Calvert Cliffs Coordinating Committee v United States Atomic Energy Commission* (1971) *Federal Reporter* 2nd Series 449, 1109.
Genesis Power case: *Genesis Power Ltd v Franklin District Council* (2005) *New Zealand Resource Management Appeals* 541.
Mejia Chaeon case: *Mejia Chaeon v Ministry of Health* (1993) *International Environmental Law Reports* 4, 131.
Tirupathi case: *Intellectuals Forum Tirupathi v State of Andhra Pradesh* (2006) *Supreme Court Journal* 2, 293.

2. A normative approach to environmental governance: sustainability at the apex of environmental law

Klaus Bosselmann

INTRODUCTION[1]

Norms, governance, sustainability and law are complex concepts. These concepts lie at the foundations of environmental law. The legal system comprises a set of interrelated rules. These rules are a reflection of the norms and principles that drive the legal system. Environmental law in particular has become an amalgam of these norms, principles and rules. The critical questions include the relationship between these norms, principles and rules and the extent to which sustainability as a norm not only underpins the legal system but also functions as a rule. This chapter seeks to answer these questions. It does so by following this structure:

- sustainability in the context of environmental law
- sustainability from an historical perspective
- the emergence of sustainability in the context of sustainable development
- instrumental responses to sustainability
- ecological integrity and sustainability
- the legal nature of sustainability
- the future need for sustainability.

SUSTAINABILITY IN THE CONTEXT OF ENVIRONMENTAL LAW

Despite the long history of sets of legal rules relating to activities that impact on the environment – especially in relation to the ownership and the use of land and resources closely associated with land – it was not until 1972 that the modern era of environmental law emerged. The watershed was the Declaration of the United Nations Conference on the Human Environment of that year – the 1972 Stockholm Declaration.

The reference to the 'human environment' was significant because it pointed to an essentially anthropocentric approach to the protection of the environment. Although this has changed – largely as a result of the recognition of the concept of sustainability – it remains the point of commencement of any analysis of contemporary environmental law.

Since 1972 the world's population has nearly doubled to more than seven billion with a daily increase of over 200,000. During the same period the Earth's regenerative capacity – described as biocapacity – has suffered substantially from an ever-increasing human demand. If measured as the amount of biologically productive land and of marine areas required for human consumption – the ecological footprint of humans – 50 per cent more of the Earth's biocapacity is required to satisfy human demand in 2016 than in 1972. This discrepancy means that it would take 1.5 years for the Earth to regenerate fully the resources that humans are using in 2016. Clearly, humanity is living unsustainably and is running out of time.

If humans are to retain their capacity to exist – at least according to their current expectations – the only option left for humanity is to learn to live within the limits of the Earth's biocapacity. This requires a profound shift in the way societies and economies are organised. In particular it involves the incorporation of sustainability in the methodology of environmental governance. Nothing short of transforming law and governance is needed to make such a shift happen. No country will ever be able to bring about the shift on its own. Nations need to find ways of cooperating in the pursuit of sustainability. However, each country – especially in the developed world – has a responsibility to ensure its own transition to sustainable forms of development. This has been the core message of the first and the most influential report in this context: namely, the 1987 Report of the World Commission on Environment and Development, *Our Common Future* ('the Brundtland Report'). The term 'sustainability' in the report established a direct relationship between the concept of human need and the idea of limitations in accordance with this definition: 'Sustainable development is development that meets the needs of the present without compromising the ability of future generations to meet their own needs'. In this way, it placed the concept of sustainability on the agenda of international law and it continues to provide the contours of 'law for sustainability' or 'sustainability law'.[2]

In the past environmental law was perceived to be for the most part reactive and fragmentary in character.[3] It responded to specific environmental risks without regard to cumulative effects and in isolation from social and economic issues. Hence it focused on environmental protection. The notion of sustainability, on the other hand, calls for a proactive and comprehensive approach. If implemented in law, sustainability would require social and economic development to conform with ecological realities. Conceptually, environmental law needs to change its character from its current specialist discipline at the periphery of the legal system to become the driving force for a greening of the entire legal system. Eventually, all laws must be informed by the principle of sustainability.

SUSTAINABILITY FROM AN HISTORICAL PERSPECTIVE

Often, sustainability has been understood as a mere ethical or political ambition. However, it has now begun to shape the development of law. All levels of law – local, national or international – are now, in some ways, informed by the principle of sustainability.[4] There is now considerable agreement that sustainability is a legal principle. Although it has emerged recently in modern environmental law, it has its origins in the history of many cultures, including that of Europe. Despite the relative novelty of the definition in the Brundtland Report, neither the concept nor the term is new.[5] The origins of sustainability reach back to the first time when humans were able to reflect on the impact of their activities on the environment and thus to alter their behaviour. Ancient tribal cultures – for example North American Indians and Australian Aborigines – understood that the human and natural spheres complemented those of humans in their roles of husbandry and custodianship.[6] Living in harmony with nature was fundamental to their value system.[7] Long before 1987 the idea of 'sustainability' described a physical balance between human settlements and their natural surroundings.[8]

There is a wealth of sustainability wisdom in the history of all cultures.[9] European culture is no exception. The experience of pre-industrial Europe, for example, is worth noting. By the mid-1800s Europe's forests had all but gone. Deforestation had reached a degree that threatened the entire economy of Europe.[10] This opened up two possibilities for the future. One was to look for a new energy source to refuel the economy. The other was to look for an alternative economy. Coal replaced wood and fired up the industrial revolution. But the alternative was available too: namely the rediscovery of sustainability.

Forest management scholars in Germany proclaimed the wisdom of replacing every tree felled with planting a new one. They cited the medieval land use system –'Allmende'– as the mother of sustainable economies. The Allmende system recognised public ownership of the land to guide any form of private land use. Thus, the substance of the land could be protected from overuse and thereby preserved for future generations. In 1714 this effect was termed 'Nachhaltigkeit' by German accountant and administrator Hans Carl von Carlowitz.[11] The first law based on the sustainability principle was the Weimar Forestry Statute of 1775. The term and concept eventually dominated forest economic theory and were exported, for example, to the French Forest Academy where, in 1837, its director, Adolphe Parade, translated it to 'soutenir'. This reflected its Latin roots: 'sustinere' – to keep, preserve, sustain. From there it reached the English terminological version – sustainability. By the early 1800s the notion 'living from the yield, not from the substance' was widespread among forest academies and indeed science faculties throughout Europe.

The Industrial Revolution of the nineteenth century and its global impact did not render the idea of sustainability redundant.[12] On the contrary, dormant until its international debut in the 1980s, the idea of sustainability had been alive for hundreds of years in the culture of Europe. Given the current global crisis concerning ecological, economic and social structures in equal measure, it is more topical than ever before. This paradoxically seems like an irony of history. The substitution of the use of wood with an excessive use of non-renewable fossil resources in the nineteenth century prevented the economic and social breakdown of Europe. But it turned into a burden. As the result of unrestrained emissions of carbon dioxide due to combustion processes, climate change became a sad reality with its tremendous detrimental effects on the economy and society. At the same time, this prime example reveals how crucial has become the realisation that ecology is the core of the concept of sustainability. This is so notwithstanding that the framing conditions have fundamentally changed.[13] The industrialised and commercialised world of 2017 has reached a level of complexity that impedes quick solutions. As the financial and economic systems seem to be completely detached from their natural resource base, the challenges are systemic. They require a review of the relationships between, on the one hand, the ecological spheres and, on the other hand, the social and economic spheres in which all human activities operate.

If the history of the basic idea of sustainability and its semantic origin are set aside for the moment, an elucidated understanding of the extensively used, melodious and catchy notion[14] of 'sustainability' emerges. Although the use of the notion has been emancipated from its exclusive application in the area of forestry, it – metaphorically speaking – can still be grounded in this idea: 'living from the yield, not from the substance'.[15] In sharp contrast to the blind exploitation of natural resources during the Industrial Revolution, with its pivotal upheavals in land use and its changes to property rights, this strategic approach allows the preservation of nature as the basis of life for future generations. Taking care of the environment has to be regarded as an inevitable prerequisite for economic and social prosperity. There is ecologically sustainable development or there is no sustainable development at all.[16] It cannot be reduced to the simple necessity of balancing between competing interests. It has to be admitted, however, that the formation of a 'sustainability law' remains at the embryonic stage of development. Future conceptual innovations are going to challenge continuously this dynamic process in multipolar areas. How that challenge has been managed so far at the international level and which deficiences justify criticism are now addressed.

THE EMERGENCE OF SUSTAINABILITY IN THE CONTEXT OF SUSTAINABLE DEVELOPMENT

1. Institutional Responses

The notion of sustainability entered the modern legal arena in 1987 on the publication of the Brundtland Report. Sustainability found its expression in the composite term 'sustainable development' described as 'development that meets the needs of the present without compromising the ability of future generations to meet their own needs'. This focuses on the objective of sustainable development with little reference to its actual content. However, the next sentence must be considered:

> it [sustainable development] contains within it two key concepts:
>
> - the concept of 'needs', in particular the essential needs of the world's poor, to which overriding priority should be given; and
> - the idea of limitations imposed by the state of technology and social organization on the environment's ability to meet present and future needs.

The term 'environment's ability' seems to be the forgotten part of the definition. Some sense of what the needs of future generations might be is required to operationalise the basic concern behind the idea of sustainable development. The first key concept of this description refers to the development problem – 'needs'. The second key concept refers to the sustainability problem – 'environment's ability'. What do 'needs' and 'environment's ability' mean?

There is no obvious reason to assume that only basic material needs are included – healthy living conditions or protection from poverty. With equal justification immaterial needs could be included – such as freedom, security, education or justice. What about protection from the ever-increasing debts that the countries are presently assuming? All of these and many other activities currently undertaken to meet 'needs' have the potential effect of 'compromising the ability of future generations to meet their own needs'. What does matter, however, is the distinction between these forms of development that perceivably do not compromise the ability of future generations and those that do. The former group includes developments towards healthier living conditions, freedom from poverty, access to education and material security. In the latter group are the very same developments but without their unsustainable nature. What is crucial is *how* needs are being met. This puts the focus on the sustainability of ecological systems. Nothing can ever be developed for the benefit of humanity, either now or in the future, if it threatens the very living conditions on which all humanity depends.

Critically this means that human needs – 'development' – and the 'environment's ability' are intrinsically linked: in other words, no development without keeping the planet's ecological systems sustainable. If the sustainability of ecological systems is paramount, it sets a non-negotiable absolute negative to any form of development. This interpretation prohibits compromises or trade-offs between the 'economy' and the 'environment'. This interpretation is usually referred to as 'strong' – as opposed to 'weak' – sustainable development. It is more correct, however, to think of genuine sustainable development as opposed to watered-down versions merely promoting an undefined 'integration' of social, economic and environmental concerns. The origins, history and conceptualisation of sustainability prior to the Brundtland Report[17] clearly show that there can be only one meaning of sustainable development. There are not two to choose from. Can this be justified conceptually?

2. Conceptual Responses

These institutional responses indicate the extent to which anthropocentric approaches to sustainable development are severely hampered. They attempt the impossible. How could a future-oriented concept of needs ever be practical if it is based on anything other than respect and care for ecological sustainability? Anthropocentric motivations are riddled with uncertainties with respect to what human needs are; what the needs of future generations may be; and what the needs of the non-human world may be. The unqualified focus on human needs leaves speculation about the future wide open: it could range from a planet without nature to a planet without humans. In the current age of the Anthropocene, it is not beyond imagination that humans may, one day in the future, aim for an artificial environment as a complete substitute for the natural environment. Such a view spells ecological suicide – 'ecocide'.[18] It overlooks a simple truth: namely the interrelatedness of all life across the boundaries between humans and non-humans.

Respect for Earth and life in all its diversity[19] is a far better guide for the future. It allows for a more practical focus on essentials that are common to all life: namely the ability to exist, reproduce and evolve. These essentials call for the preservation of conditions that have proved to be favourable in the past. While predictions of such conditions for future life are far from reliable, it is wise to preserve what has proved successful rather than to create unknown new conditions.

From an ecological point of view, anthropocentric conceptions of the future are difficult to justify. Edith Brown Weiss, the eminent proponent of intergenerational equity,[20] has never attempted to exclude the welfare of nature from thinking about future generations. Her three principles of intergenerational equity involve the preservation of options, quality and access.[21] The first principle is 'to conserve the diversity of the natural and cultural resource base'; the second is 'to maintain the quality of the planet'; and the third is to provide 'equitable rights of access to the legacy of the past'.[22] While the third principle is essentially anthropocentric, the first two describe duties towards the community of life. There is certainly no suggestion in Brown Weiss' concept to be concerned only with the welfare of humans.[23] According to Ulrich Beyerlin, 'much speaks in favour of conceiving the intergenerational component of sustainable development in eco-centric terms'.[24] He concludes in these words: 'As intergenerational equity is inseparably intertwined with intragenerational equity, the concept of sustainable development in its entirety must be perceived as both anthropocentric and eco-centric in nature.'[25]

Other commentators have made the same point and this challenges the widely held view that sustainable development reflects anthropocentrism and trade-offs between environmental, economic and social interests.[26] The fundamental importance of the environment is not contingent on an ecological approach to sustainable development. An economic approach may emphasise material prosperity. It can nevertheless be formulated on the basis of ecological sustainability. World Bank economist Roberto Repetto has presented this argument: 'The core idea of sustainability is that current decisions should not impair the prospects for maintaining or improving future living standards. This implies that our economic systems should be managed so that we can live off the dividends of our resources.'[27] Two other economists from the World Bank, Mohan Munasinghe and Ernst Lutz, define 'sustainable development as an approach that will permit continuing improvements in the quality of life with a lower intensity of resource use, thereby leaving behind for future generations an undiminished or even enhanced stock of natural resources and other assets'.[28] Accordingly it is clear that the preservation of the natural stock determines the ability to meet the needs of present and future generations.

The ecocentric component of sustainable development is crucial for making this concept operable. If human needs are perceived without regard to ecological reality, there is a risk that humans will lose the ground under their feet. If this is the reality, any talk about the equal importance of development and environment, about the two-scale model, about a 'three-pillar model' or about a 'magic triangle' reveals outdated and ideologically motivated thinking. Concerns for social justice and economic prosperity are vital. However they are secondary compared to the functioning of the Earth's ecological systems as the basis of any human prosperity. Ecological sustainability is the fundament for development and not a mere 'pillar'. As a consequence, despite the ambiguity of the Brundtland Report's reception in the literature and in international instruments, it would be wrong to conclude that the principle of sustainability has lost its contours. On the contrary, international environmental law has always been informed by it. This points to a brief review of the principal instruments.

INSTRUMENTAL RESPONSES TO SUSTAINABILITY

A few years after the publication of the Brundtland Report, a number of initiatives at the international level recognised the relevance of sustainability and referred to it in a range of instruments.[29] These include:

- Caring for the Earth, which describes the purpose of sustainable development as improving the quality of human life while living within the carrying capacity of the Earth's ecosystems and requires a commitment to a new ethic based on respect and care for one another and for the Earth and to the integration of conservation and development[30]
- The Rio Declaration and Agenda 21, which stressed the interconnectedness of environmental, social and economic concerns

- The Earth Charter, which was negotiated as an unofficial alternative to the Rio Declaration and which defines the principle of sustainability as preserving the integrity of ecological systems[31]
- The Millennium Declaration, which reaffirmed the principle of 'respect for nature' as among the 'fundamental values essential to international relations'
- The Johannesburg Declaration on Sustainable Development, which, although it failed to define sustainable development, made a commitment to sustainable development and to building a humane, equitable and caring global society cognisant of the need for human dignity for all
- The New Delhi Declaration on the Principles of International Law Related to Sustainable Development, which stated seven key principles in this context.

In many respects the New Delhi Declaration represents the culmination of these developments. These are the seven principles which have emerged:

- the duty of states to ensure sustainable use of natural resources
- the principle of equity and the eradication of poverty
- the principle of common but differentiated responsibilities
- the principle of the precautionary approach to human health, natural resources and ecosystems
- the principle of public participation and access to information and justice
- the principle of good governance
- the principle of integration and interrelationship, in particular in relation to human rights and social, economic and environmental objectives.

The Rio Declaration, however, remains the foundational instrument in the move towards sustainability. It is therefore worth analysing in more detail. A careful interpretation shows that the Declaration did not promote the three pillars model that was heralded by many post-Rio commentators. Principle 4 states 'that in order to achieve sustainable development, environmental protection shall constitute an integral part of the development process and cannot be considered in isolation from it'. On the one hand, a mere undefined idea of integration can be perceived as a sufficient modus operandi of sustainable development – a weak interpretation. On the other hand, principle 4 can be interpreted in a strong sense: the development process can be pursued only through preserving its ecological basis.[32]

The Declaration incorporates other concepts as key aspects of sustainable development:

- the right to development in principle 3
- the integrative approach in principle 4
- the indispensable task of poverty alleviation in principle 5.

The relative prominence of the right to development and of poverty alleviation is clearly meant to acknowledge the special needs of developing countries. However, this does not diminish the importance of ecological sustainability. The Declaration does not allow industrialised states to compromise the principle of sustainability for the sake of pursuing their economic prosperity and their social development.[33] The developing states participating in the Conference did not insist that their right to development would allow the multinational corporations of rich states to develop more quickly and effectively. The political implication is not to expect sustainability measures from developing states with the same urgency as can be expected from developed states that have affected the Earth's ecological integrity to a much higher degree.

Essentially, the Rio Declaration attempted to find a solution to the distribution problem that the global ecological crisis had created. This attempt may have been incomplete and not very satisfactory. However, it can hardly be argued that the principle of sustainability had been dismissed or replaced by something else.[34] On the contrary, principles 3 and 4 confirm its existence. Even economic development in developing countries must not compromise the ability of future generations to meet their needs.[35] If the right to development could only be exercised by violating this principle of sustainability because of developed countries' overburdening of the environment, then *these* countries need to reduce their overburdening in order to preserve the development opportunities of developing countries. It follows that ecological sustainability is paramount in the developing world and even more so in the developed world.

It has already been suggested that the New Delhi Declaration in many respects synthesised the underlying principles of sustainability. In this respect it is perhaps the last – the seventh – of these principles that is critical. That is the principle of integration and the principle of interrelationship in relation to human rights and to social, economic and environmental objectives. The distinction between rights and objectives is likely to prove critical. With respect to this last principle, the Declaration explains that it 'reflects the interdependence of social, economic, financial, environmental and human rights aspects of principles and rules of international law'. It explains further that 'states should strive to resolve apparent conflict between competing economic, financial, social and environmental considerations' and finally that 'the above principles are interrelated and each of them should be construed in the context of the other principles of this Declaration'. This suggests that there is no paramount or prime principle to guide the others. However, the first principle of sustainable use could be seen as having such a function, but only if it is interpreted as a reflection of the principle of sustainability.

It may be concluded in general that sustainability is a fundamental norm of international environmental law and hence of environmental law generally. The content and the limitations of the principle of sustainable use are, however, uncertain in international law. If sustainability is to be implemented in practice, ecological sustainability or, more specifically, ecological integrity would need to be at its core. In this respect, much depends upon the text which incorporates the concept in the relevant instrument. A well-defined concept of sustainable development would have to be modeled around ecological sustainability at its core.[36] Attention now turns to this important aspect of the environmental legal system.

ECOLOGICAL INTEGRITY AS THE CORE OF SUSTAINABILITY

1. International Instruments

The concept of ecological integrity is central to a wide range of disciplines of environmental study including science, public health, philosophy, anthropology and law.[37] It has already been noted that the Earth Charter defines the principle of sustainability as preserving the integrity of ecological systems. The meaning of ecological integrity has been well defined not only in the literature but also in a range of legal instruments. It is useful to begin with a transnational example: the Great Lakes Water Quality Agreement[38] between Canada and the United States.

As a matter of law, the concept of integrity had its origin in the US 1972 Clean Water Act. It was then used in North America in the Great Lakes Water Quality Agreement. The Preamble states:

> The purpose of the Parties is to restore and maintain the chemical, physical and biological integrity of the waters of the Great Lake Basin Ecosystem …

> where the latter is defined as … the interacting components of air, land, water and living organisms including humans.

This acknowledges the characteristics of an ecosystem. Like the Great Lake Basin, each ecosystem has certain characteristics. Ecosystems exist in infinite variation. Like snowflakes, no two systems are identical. But, again like snowflakes, all ecosystems have a number of characteristics in common. For example, they:

- contain living and non-living elements
- have a measurable degree of diversity – species, genes, chemicals
- have some degree of resilience – defined as the system's ability to maintain relationships between system elements in the presence of disturbances
- have a one-way net flow of energy – from outside to inside
- have a carrying capacity for particular kinds of organisms
- exist in a state of non-equilibrium – that is, they change through time
- changes are irreversible – that is, ecosystems do not return to a previous state but evolve to a new form.

Taken together, these characteristics can be seen as the integrity of an ecosystem. In the biological and ecological sciences, a common and tangible concept is, therefore, ecological integrity.

Against this background the text of a number of international instruments can be considered. The idea of ecological integrity is well known internationally and often referred to in international environmental agreements. The first of such agreements to include the notion was the Convention on the Conservation of Antarctic Marine Living Resources adopted in 1980. It recognised in its preamble 'the importance of safeguarding the environment and protecting the integrity of the ecosystem of the seas surrounding Antarctica'. Since then, more than a dozen international environmental agreements have been adopted with some reference to the integrity of ecosystems in the preamble or the operative part. Here are some examples.

First, there are two examples of a general reference to the norm of ecosystem integrity. Article I (4) of the World Charter for Nature 1982 includes as one of the principles:

> Ecosystems and organisms, as well as the land, marine and atmospheric resources that are utilized by man, shall be managed to achieve and maintain optimum sustainable productivity, but not in such a way as to endanger the

> *integrity* of those other ecosystems or species with which they coexist. (emphasis added)

Ecosystem integrity, accordingly, has effect as a condition on the achievement of optimum sustainable productivity. The preamble to the Rio Declaration 1992 refers to protection of the integrity of the global environmental and developmental system. Principle 7 imposes a duty to cooperate in ecosystem integrity in these words: 'States shall cooperate in a spirit of global partnership to conserve, protect and restore the health and *integrity* of the Earth's ecosystem' (emphasis added).

Second, there are more specific references to ecosystem integrity in Agenda 21 – the plan associated with the implementation of the Rio Declaration. It applies the concept of ecosystem integrity in three ways. First, it applies the concept to the planning and management of land resources. Section 10.1 acknowledges the variety of services provided by ecosystems and essential to the maintenance of the integrity of life-support systems and the productive capacity of the environment. Second, it applies the concept to the environmentally sound management of biotechnology. Section I6.4 requires particular attention to be paid to how the use of biotechnology will impact on the maintenance of environmental integrity and section I6.22 states that a specific target of an associated programme is to apply biotechnologies and their products to protect environmental integrity with a view to long-term ecology security. Third, it applies the concept to the protection of the quality and supply of freshwater resources. Section I8.38 states as an objective the maintenance of ecosystem integrity according to a management principle of preserving aquatic ecosystems.

Third, the concept of ecosystem integrity has become an important element in the management of marine fisheries resources. It has been included in the preamble to two relevant conventions. The preamble to the South Pacific Living Marine Resources Framework Agreement of 2000 states:

> With these goals in mind, the coastal states in question agreed to establish the South Pacific Permanent Commission (SPPC), to coordinate their maritime policies and to promote the adoption of measures to preserve the environment and protect the integrity of the South Pacific's marine ecosystem.

The preamble to the South Pacific Fishery Resources Convention of 2009 states:

> Conscious of the need to avoid adverse impacts on the marine environment, preserve biodiversity, maintain the integrity of marine ecosystems and minimise the risk of long term or irreversible effects on fishing.

These two examples from the text of the preamble are structured, as it would be expected, as statements of politically ambitious objectives. Finally, more recently, and on a much more general level directed at political commitment, the instrument of 2012 with the intriguing title *The Future We Want* has included in section II.40 this statement:

> We call for holistic and integrated approaches to sustainable development which will guide humanity to live in harmony with nature and lead to efforts to restore the health and integrity of the Earth's ecosystem.

Although this is very much an aspirational statement, it captures the spirit of the concept of ecosystem integrity as the core of sustainable development.

2. National Instruments

The legislation of nation states from time to time refers directly or indirectly to ecological integrity. Two examples may be considered: one from Canada and one from New Zealand. The Canada National Parks Act 2000 provides this definition of ecological integrity:

> 'ecological integrity' means, with respect to a park, a condition that is determined to be characteristic of its natural region and likely to persist, including abiotic components and the composition and abundance of native species and biological communities, rates of change and supporting processes.

Section 8(2) goes on to provide:

> Maintenance or restoration of ecological integrity, through the protection of natural resources and natural processes, shall be the first priority of the Minister when considering all aspects of the management of parks.

The relevant Minister is assisted by an expert Panel on Ecological Integrity. It defined ecological integrity as follows:

> An ecosystem has integrity when it is deemed characteristic for its natural region, including the composition and abundance of native species and biological communities, rates of change and supporting processes. In plain language, ecosystems have integrity when they have their native components (plants, animals and other organisms) and processes (such as growth and reproduction) intact.

The Panel has, among other activities, developed a set of indicators to measure the ecological integrity of parks. This approach is a useful foundation for future developments. First, Canada should expand its sustainability approach beyond the confined space of national parks to include the entire country. Second, other countries should follow the Canadian example.

In the case of New Zealand, the Resource Management Act 1991 does not refer expressly to ecological integrity. But it captures the content of the concept. Conceptualising it as 'sustainable management', section 5(c) defines its purpose as follows:

> In this Act, 'sustainable management' means managing the use, development, and protection of natural and physical resources in a way, or at a rate, which enables people and communities to provide for their social, economic, and cultural wellbeing and for their health and safety while –
>
> a. Sustaining the potential of natural and physical resources (excluding minerals) to meet the reasonable foreseeable needs of future generations; and
> b. Safeguarding the life-supporting capacity of air, water, soil, and ecosystems; and
> c. Avoiding, remedying, or mitigating any adverse effects on activities on the environment.

During the development of its environmental jurisprudence, the Environment Court developed two different approaches to the interpretation of section 5 of the Act – the 'environmental bottom line approach' and the 'overall judgment approach'.[39] They reflect the two competing concepts of 'strong' and 'weak' sustainability.[40] Perhaps the legislature should decide which is intended rather than leave it to the judiciary. It is suggested that the statutory purpose could be: 'The purpose of this Act is to achieve ecological sustainability'. The meaning of ecological sustainability could be: 'The absence of damage to ecological integrity caused by human impact in an ecosystem of any size within which the impact is found'. The meaning of ecological integrity could be: 'The ability of an ecosystem to recover from disturbance and re-establish its stability, diversity and resilience'.

These textual examples could easily be extrapolated to any legal system.

3. Conclusion

Whatever examples and texts are considered, environmental law and the implementation and interpretation of the relevant instruments are for the most part ineffective and inefficient. There is at the same time a growing body of evidence that environmental law fails to prevent inequity. In the context of food prices, for example, the issue of environmental justice becomes ever more urgent. But environmental justice cannot be isolated from ecological justice as the broader concept embracing humans and nature alike.[41]

A law based on sustainability will further incorporate legal norms such as the precautionary principle, the polluter pays principle, the principle of common but differentiated responsibility and the concept of intra-generational, intergenerational and interspecies equity. Some of these have been acknowledged as principles of law: others are only evolving. In their significance and mutual reinforcement they are most poignantly expressed in the Earth Charter. The Earth Charter should serve, therefore, as the overall ethical and legal framework for achieving a sustainable society.[42] The increasing number of references to ecological integrity in international and national instruments suggests that the notion of integrity of Earth's ecological systems has emerged as a common denominator of many of these instruments – particularly those at the international level. The protection of global ecological integrity can, therefore, be seen as the emerging raison d'être or grundnorm of international environmental law[43] but at the same time of a growing corpus of national law.

The functionality of the concept of ecological integrity comes from not only the concept's ethical and scientific heritages but also its strength as an emergent legal concept. Ecological integrity originates as an ethical concept in the wake of Aldo Leopold, who famously proclaimed that: 'A thing is right when it tends to preserve the integrity, stability and beauty of the biotic community. It is wrong when it tends otherwise'.[44]

Here, ecological integrity was presented as an ethical maxim. This ethical approach resolves a moral dilemma arising from the relationship between the preservation of ecological integrity and the social and economic demands of humanity by way of prioritising ecological integrity. To what extent does the law reflect this ethical approach?

THE LEGAL NATURE OF SUSTAINABILITY

It has been argued throughout this chapter that sustainability is a legal principle.[45] This means that it has a number of legal consequences and it is potentially enforceable. There is no doubt that sustainability is directly enforceable when used in the context of a specific legal provision, for example, in a statute or a treaty. When legal consequences follow automatically once the factual circumstances it stipulates are present, lawyers normally speak of a rule. According to Ronald Dworkin, a legal rule applies in 'an all or nothing fashion', while a legal principle 'states a reason that argues in one direction, but does not necessitate a particular decision'.[46] In this sense, sustainability can function as a rule leading to a specific consequence. This is particularly so when sustainability has been clearly defined.

Apart from its capacity to function as a rule in positive law, sustainability functions as a legal principle. This means that it provides direction without prescribing a particular decision. It can be said that sustainability points in one direction and prevents going 'backwards'. In this way, it postulates a fundamental norm for all society and for all humanity: namely, do not destroy any further the integrity of ecological systems. What this means in the circumstances of a certain region or activity is the task of decision-making according to law either through implementation or adjudication. Decisions may go one way or another but must broadly point into one direction.

With respect to the further development of law, a process is needed that establishes sustainability alongside other fundamental principles such as freedom, equity or justice. Law makers can promote this process appropriately by acknowledging sustainability as a 'grundnorm'.[47] Such a grundnorm will not necessarily manifest itself as legally defined. It will rather inform the making of positive law. As a consequence, any positive law will be reflective of the principle of sustainability.

To consider sustainability as a grundnorm *stricto sensu* is problematic in the context of Hans Kelsen's pure theory of law with which the concept of a grundnorm is commonly associated. In Kelsen's theory, the status and meaning of grundnorm – in English 'basic norm' – are not a matter of actual content.[48] Kelsen does not provide the basic norm with an ethical or political function, rather with only an epistemological function.[49] Following Kelsen, who emphasised the separation of law and morality, the normativity of sustainability could be understood as a *moral* basic norm – given that there can be a variety of basic norms in a system of moral norms – but not as a *legal* grundnorm. There can only be one legal grundnorm. It provides unity to the legal system. The basic norm of a legal system addresses the question of legal validity in terms of authorisation. It is not a question of content.[50] Kelsen observes that a constitution may contain substantive limits to law making. But for Kelsen, a constitution itself is not a grundnorm.[51] The grundnorm is a hypothetical construct about a constitution, by functioning to give validity to an order of legal norms.

A grundnorm *can* provide the foundation for the legal quality of a norm, provided proper constitutional processes are followed. Alternatively a grundnorm may change.[52] For example, there may be a revolution, as a result of which an older constitution is displaced and a new 'sustainable constitution' put in place by revolutionary forces – but with substantive limits to law making in terms of preserving ecological integrity. If the new constitution becomes efficacious to the requisite degree, the *new* grundnorm of the society would then be 'the sustainable constitution is to be obeyed'. However, environmental law can find more robust normative reasoning in other jurisprudential concepts. According to Kelsen's theory, sustainability can hardly be a legal grundnorm.

Kant formulated the idea of a 'basic norm' – although he did not use this specific term – as a source of the validity of positive law in his 1797 work entitled *The Metaphysics of Morals*, which commenced with a treatise on the philosophy of law.[53] In contrast to Kelsen, who postulated that the basic norm is simply an epistemological premise, for Kant the basic norm is a natural law – recognised by means of reason. For Kant, a legal system can consist entirely of positive law. But it must be 'preceded by a natural law that establishe[s] the legislator's authority … to bind others simply by his arbitrary action'.[54]

Unlike classical natural law, which defines the content of positive law in terms of reason and justice, in Kant's attenuated version of natural law – the natural law basic norm – reason *dictates* that people leave a state of nature and move into a civil or legal state of affairs, by 'subjecting oneself to a publicly lawful, external coercion'.[55] According to Kant, any positive law must be grounded in a 'natural' norm of general acceptance and reasonableness – *Vernunft* – to prevent pure arbitrariness – *blosse Willkür*. Preserving the integrity of Earth's ecological systems – the core of sustainability – could therefore be seen as a dictate of reason – *Gebot der Vernunft* – demanding general acceptance – *allgemeine Gültigkeit*.

German legal philosopher Robert Alexy follows Kant in the sense that the legal 'grundnorm' should include 'content'.[56] He reinterprets Kelsen's basic norm by making a claim to substantive justice with respect to the content of the laws it purports to authorise. The basic norm 'may include moral elements that take the argument of injustice into consideration … [the basic norm] needs grounding'.[57]

From the perspective of natural law, sustainability appears – at least potentially – as a requirement of practical reasonableness. As John Finnis explains, 'the principal concern of a theory of natural law is to explore the requirements of practical reasonableness in relation to the good of human being'.[58] He lists seven 'basic goods' as equally important components of human flourishing – life, knowledge, play, aesthetic experience, sociability or friendship, practical reasonableness and 'religion'.[59] Protection of the life-supporting capacity of the natural environment most obviously relates to the first 'good' on the list – life. Finnis observes that all societies in some sense are concerned with 'life' in the sense of survival. Thus, the argument for the fundamental importance of sustainability in natural law terms is fairly straightforward. It is reasonable to sustain the natural conditions upon which life depends.

Practical reasonableness refers to 'bringing intelligence to bear on problems, choosing one's actions'.[60] One of the nine requirements of practical reasonableness is that the good of one's community be advanced. One's view of what reason and natural law require will vary, depending on which 'community' is perceived to be relevant and on the time horizon within which the good of one's community is viewed. The Earth Charter's emphasis on respect for the 'community of life' is perhaps one of the broadest and non-anthropocentric articulations of community. However, to varying degrees, all local communities are linked to the Earth Charter's global community of life. Due to the borderless nature of many ecological systems, it becomes apparent that laws facilitating, or even encouraging, the disintegration of ecological systems put the good of one's community at risk. As such, these laws may be assessed ultimately as contrary to reason and thus contrary to natural law.

Classical natural law holds that positive law can be derived from natural law by deduction or determination. Although the importance of sustainability has not been explicitly at the fore of the natural law tradition in the law of nations throughout history, it can arguably be arrived at through rational deduction. Alternatively, through determination, reason ascertains 'law' appropriate from its historical context. In doing so, the congruence of positive law with reason will be within a specific range of parameters. In the current age of the Anthropocene, laws that violate ecological integrity are unlikely to be within the reasonable range of determination and can therefore be said to be inconsistent with natural law.

In light of this analysis the notion of a grundnorm can be likened to 'basic' or 'fundamental' norms or norms of natural law. Leaving aside Kelsen's definition, a grundnorm can reflect content according to Alexy, and reasonableness according to Kant and Finnis. This makes it possible to use the term with respect to foundational norms that no positive law can ignore. Differences between grundnorms and norms of natural law are more terminological rather than conceptual. What matters is the foundational character that certain concepts or ideas have for the law. Sustainability is one such concept; justice is another; and so are human rights. With respect to norms of natural law, discernable by reason and universally applicable, Finnis explains:

> Any sound theory or philosophy of law will need to attend to two broad kinds of principle, norm and standard: those applicable by persons of practical reasonableness only because they are standards chosen or otherwise factually established by past choices of their community, and those that are applicable whether or not so chosen or ratified. For the latter, the history of our civilisation has chosen the name 'natural law' ... [It] has been decisive for our vocabulary, making its way through Aristotle, the Stoics, Cicero, St Paul, Gaius and Aquinas and their successors down to the United Nations Charter and today.[61]

In this way, sustainability can be perceived as foundational for society and rooted in natural law. To appreciate this, a parallel to human rights can be drawn.

Comparable to human rights law, environmental law as a discipline has its roots in natural law.[62] With regard to human rights law, nobody seriously doubts that humans are born free and equal. The adequate normative protection of their rights is a matter of discourse, although there is no scientific evidence supporting that postulation. By contrast, environmental law can be justified by reference to many sources that scientifically prove ecological interdependencies. Human beings are inevitably and unescapably embedded in ecosystems. By arguing a fortiori, this shall ultimately require governments and states to incorporate an absolute acceptance of ecological interdependencies in their strategies and to enact laws correspondingly.

Concurrently, however, purely anthropological traditions continue to impede a compatible organisation of legal norms. Throughout history, humans placed themselves on the superior hierarchy level above all non-human components of their natural surroundings. This dualistic approach results in a vision of the world that allows a merely utilitarian view towards all elements not constituting a human being. But the misconception of this approach is revealed by taking into account that humans are no different from other natural beings and by realising the intimate interconnection of the spheres.

However, humans as 'cultural beings' in unison are able to generate a sphere which is independent from the natural world and which consists of cultural achievements. One of the ladders is the organisation of the lives of humans by laws. The creation of norms in turn takes place in a multipolar field of tensions between the mental models promulgated by the political-economic ideology of the West and those of the political-ecological world view of the Globe. The Western view, for instance, assumes that resources are unlimited. But the alternative interpretation of reality accepts the limitation of natural goods.

The mere recognition of the existence and of the development of cultural achievements does not necessarily envisage their efficacy for long-term sustainability. Rather, the prediction of an all-embracing crisis demands a rejuvenation of the system in the form of the expansion of existing or the creation of new cultural achievements. Accordingly, the established, valuable and indispensable cultural achievements of the rule of law, the idea of human rights and the ideal of democratic governance need to be accompanied by an environmental grundnorm.[63] Thereby, the principle of sustainability serves as the central element of such a grundnorm in order to underpin and supplement these maxims. As the principle advocates the preservation of nature as the basis of life for future generations, it provides an effective instrument to counter the detrimental development stimulated by the Western political-economic view of the world in ecological, social and economic terms. This approach advocates an ecologically reasonable culture of self-constraint because it limits the use of resources, requires cooperation instead of competition, combines emotion and rationality, sets property rights into a wider perspective, and dismisses ideas like the ultimate criterion of monetary value.

If these ideas are placed in their broader jurisprudential context, it results in the assumption that the grounding of the rule of law in nature requires fundamental changes to the legal systems in international and national terms. Legal structures have to be modified so that they are constrained by ecological concerns in order, first, to prevent the further crossing of planetary boundaries and, second, to maintain environmental goods as a basis for a flourishing development of our posterity.[64] Legal regimes have to be pervaded on a systematic and interdisciplinary basis by a 'greening' process that creates bounded and coherent systems.

Such a greening of the systems of law and governance can be accomplished, for example, by adopting the notion of the eco-constitutional state – *Ökologischer Rechtsstaat*.[65] This type of state differs considerably from a state solely committed, on the one hand, to the rule of law – *Rechtsstaat* – and, on the one hand, to environmental protection – *Umweltstaat*. Rather, both must be seen as jointly underpinning and together defining the state. This allows the global implementation of environmental primacy in the interest of a fair sharing of common goods among present and future generations. At the same time, this method respects valuable principles constituting the classical rule of law. Such an integrating view, with its coinciding impact on non-state actors, is in sharp contrast to the traditional liberal idea of the state promoting neutrality of the state. While the liberal concept of the rule of law emphasises the well-being of humans, the ecological concept of the rule of law lays its focus on the well-being of both humans and nature in the same measure. The difference between these models is not only gradual but also paradigmatic. Commonalities and overlaps in practical law making are, however, possible.

THE FUTURE NEED FOR SUSTAINABILITY

Having reviewed the history, meaning and legal status of the principle of sustainability, it is now appropriate to suggest some conclusions. Due to the almost unlimited exploitation of natural resources under the prevailing system of private property rights detached from any common responsibility, the integrity of the Earth's ecological systems at global, regional and local levels is at a high risk of collapse. The current system of law and governance threatens the basis of human life now and in the future. Effective instruments to counteract this risk are indispensible simply because existing legal structures at all levels fail to provide adequate mechanisms. Simply enlarging the number of laws protecting environmental goods and sectors or improving their enforcement will not be enough.

One approach is for the principle of sustainability to pervade our laws in all areas and at all levels. As the rule of law is the most basic tool not only to control but also to ensure the responsibility of government, it needs to be considered here. It demands that the decisions of government are bound by law and that all citizens are subject to the law. But not any law can be taken as a measure of the true meaning of the rule of law. A purely 'formal' or 'thin' recognition of the rule of law[66] reflecting any value or content is doomed not only to fail again but also to perpetuate the flaws already identified in the design of legal norms – compartmentalisation, fragmentation and anthropocentric focus.

In addition, standards and principles of a certain qualitative substance have to be taken into account by states in creating laws. Thus, the proposed grounding of the rule of law in nature by implementing an environmental grundnorm appears as an appropriate contribution to a way out of the all-embracing crisis.[67] Against this backdrop, the rule of law calls for an expansion to include ecological responsibility. The supranational and over-arching creation of an eco-constitutional state – *Ökologischer Rechtsstaat* – unifying valuable aspects of the classical idea of the rule of law with environmental values and issues is well worth considering. This will be challenging given its ultimate roots in natural law. Furthermore, to overcome the anthropocentric approach of most current laws it is necessary to educate humans in environmental ethics and their importance for law making.

Designing laws around the principle of sustainability, as defined here, would ensure the kind of guidance that decision-makers so desperately need. Sustainability aims to preserve the potentially measurable integrity of ecosystems while at the same time acknowledging that humans are part of these ecosystems. In pursuing the protection of ecological integrity, sustainability reflects the most basic concern of human existence: namely the desire to live, survive and reproduce.

It would be too presumptuous to think that a fundamental concern such as the one described above has guided the legislators of laws or the drafters of international instruments such as the World Charter for Nature, the Rio Declaration or even the Earth Charter. More likely, there was no such conscious and coherent effort behind the various approaches to legislate for sustainability. It would be even more presumptuous to assume that these approaches were guided by merely balancing economic, social and environmental concerns. Ecological integrity is fundamental to any sustainability concerns including their social and economic dimensions.

NOTES

1. This chapter includes some of the material discussed in Bosselmann (2015a), but from a different perspective.
2. Bosselmann (2017, pp. 26–31).
3. Bosselmann (2010, pp. 2424–48).
4. Bosselmann (2017).
5. Spindler (2011, p. 2).
6. Ibid.
7. Bosselmann (2017, p. 11).
8. Ibid (pp. 12–14).
9. See Diamond (2005) and Bosselmann (2017, p. 3).
10. See Radkau (2008, p. 245).
11. Von Carlowitz (1713); Grober (2010, pp. 111–25); Grober (2007).
12. Bosselmann (2017, p. 14).
13. Ibid (p. 21).
14. Ibid (p. 15).
15. Bosselmann (2010, p. 2437); Bosselmann (2013, p. 75).
16. Bosselmann (2017, p. 21).
17. Spindler (2011, pp. 10–26); MacNeill (2007).
18. Higgins (2010).
19. Earth Charter, Principle 1.
20. Brown Weiss (1989, p. 17).
21. Brown Weiss (1990, p. 98).
22. Ibid.

23. Bosselmann (2013).
24. Beyerlin (2006, pp. 263–75); Beyerlin and Marauhn (2011, p. 77); Agius (1998, p. 87); Taylor (1998, pp. 281–2).
25. Beyerlin (2006).
26. Boer (1995, pp. 111–13); Taylor (1998, pp. 325–7, 348–9); Gillespie (1997, pp. 2–5, 127–8); Birnie and Boyle (2002, pp. 44–7).
27. Repetto (1986).
28. Munasinghe and Lutz (1991).
29. Bosselmann (2017, pp. 32–36).
30. Repetto (1986); Boer (1995, pp. 111–13).
31. For further analysis see Vilela (2005).
32. Kim and Bosselmann (2012, pp. 194–208).
33. Murswiek (2002, pp. 641–5).
34. Sands (2003, p. 259).
35. Beyerlin (1996, pp. 95, 104–105).
36. Bosselmann, Brown and Mackey (2012); Beyerlin and Marauhn (2011, pp. 78–9).
37. Global Ecological Integrity Group www.globalecointegrity.net.
38. Signed in 1978, ratified in 1988.
39. Bosselmann (2009, pp. 355–80).
40. Sustainable Aotearoa New Zealand (2009, pp. 8–9).
41. Bosselmann (2017, pp. 102–128).
42. Bosselmann (2004, pp. 62–75).
43. Kim and Bosselmann (2013, pp. 285–309); Kim and Bosselmann (2012, pp. 194–208).
44. Leopold (1949, p. 262).
45. Bosselmann (2017, pp. 54–101).
46. Dworkin (1977, p. 22).
47. Godden (2009, pp. 807–16).
48. Fisher (2013, pp. 7, 59).
49. Kelsen (1967, p. 218).
50. Ibid (p. 217).
51. Ibid (p. 223).
52. Harris (1971, p. 103).
53. Bindreiter (2002, p. 15).
54. Alexy (2002, p. 116 and fn 202) citing Kant.
55. Ibid (p. 118 and fn 206) citing Kant.
56. Vinx (2007, p. 58) citing Alexy (1994, pp. 154–97).
57. Alexy (2002, p. 147).
58. Finnis (2011, p. 351).
59. Ibid (p. 86).
60. Ibid (p. 87).
61. Finnis (2014, p. 139).
62. Morrow and Coyle (2004, pp. 9–58).
63. Garver (2013).
64. Ibid.
65. Bosselmann (1992).
66. Tamanaha (2004).
67. Bosselmann (2015b, pp. 266–7); Fisher (2013, p. 433).

REFERENCES

Agius, Emanuel (1998), 'Towards a relational theory of intergenerational ethics' in Salvino Busuttil, Emmanuel Agius, Peter Serracino Inglott and Tony Macelli (eds), *Our Responsibilities to Future Generations* (Valletta, Malta Foundation for International Studies).

Alexy, Robert (1994), *Begriff und Geltung des Rechts* (Freiburg, Alber, 2nd edn) (English translation: *The Argument from Injustice*).

Alexy, Robert (2002), *The Argument from Injustice* (Oxford, Clarendon Press).

Beyerlin, Ulrich (2006), *Bridging the North-South-Divide in International Environmental Law* (Zeitschrift für ausländisches und öffentliches Recht).

Beyerlin, Ulrich and Thilo Marauhn (2011), *International Environmental Law* (Oxford, Hart).

Bindreiter, Uta (2002), *Why Grundnorm? A Treatise on the Implications of Kelsen's Doctrine* (The Hague, Kluwer).

Birnie, Pat and Alan Boyle (2002), *International law and the Environment* (Oxford, Oxford University Press, 2nd edn).

Boer, Ben (1995), 'Implementation of international sustainability at national levels' in Konrad Ginther, Erik Denters and Paul De Wart (eds), *Sustainable Development and Good Governance* (The Hague, Kluwer).

Bosselmann, Klaus (1992), *Im Namen der Natur: Der Weg zum ökologischen Rechtsstaat* (Bern, Scherz).

Bosselmann, Klaus (2004), 'In Search for Global Law: The Significance of the Earth Charter', *Worldviews: Environment, Culture, Religion* 8(1), 62–75.

Bosselmann, Klaus (2009), 'Judiciary and environmental governance in New Zealand' in Louis Kotzé and Alexander Paterson (2009), *The Role of the Judiciary in Environmental Governance: Comparative Perspectives* (The Hague, Kluwer).

Bosselmann, Klaus (2010), 'Losing the Forest for the Trees: Environmental reductionism in the law', *Sustainability* 2(8), 2424–48; http://www.mdpi.com/2071-1050/2/8/2424.

Bosselmann, Klaus (2013), 'Grounding the rule of law' in Hans Christian Bugge and Christina Voigt, *Rule of Law for Nature: Basic Issues and New Developments in Environmental Law* (Cambridge, Cambridge University Press).

Bosselmann, Klaus (2015a), 'Sustainability in the context of sustainability' in Peter Salmon and David Grinlinton (eds), *Environmental Law in New Zealand* (Wellington, Thomson Reuters NZ).

Bosselmann, Klaus (2015b), *Earth Governance: Trusteeship of Global Commons* (Cheltenham, Edward Elgar).

Bosselmann, Klaus (2017), *The Principle of Sustainability: Transforming Law and Governance* (Abingdon and New York: Routledge, 2nd edn).

Bosselmann, Klaus, Peter Brown and Brendan Mackey (2012), 'Enabling a Flourishing Earth: challenges for the green economy, opportunities for global governance', *Review of European Community and International Environmental Law* 21(1), 20–38.

Bosselmann, Klaus, David Grinlinton and Prue Taylor (2013), *Environmental Law for a Sustainable Society* (Auckland, New Zealand Centre for Environmental Law Monograph Series, 2nd edn).

Brown Weiss, Edith (1989), *In Fairness to Future Generations: International Law, Common Patrimony and Intergenerational Equity* (Japan, United Nations University Press).

Brown Weiss, Edith (1990), 'Intergenerational justice and international law' in Salvino Busuttil, Emmanuel Agius, Peter Serracino Inglott and Tony Macelli (eds), *Our Responsibilities to Future Generations* (Valletta, Malta Foundation for International Studies).

Bugge, Hans Christian and Voigt, Christina (2013), *Rule of Law for Nature: Basic Issues and New Developments in Environmental Law* (Cambridge, Cambridge University Press).
Busuttil, Salvino, Emmanuel Agius, Peter Serracino Inglott and Tony Macelli (eds) (1990), *Our Responsibilities to Future Generations* (Valletta, Malta Foundation for International Studies).
Corcoran, Peter Blaze (ed.) (2005), *Toward a Sustainable World: The Earth Charter in Action* (The Hague, Kluwer).
Diamond, Jared (2005), *Collapse: How Societies Choose to Fail or Succeed* (New York, Viking).
Dworkin, Ronald (1977), *Taking Rights Seriously* (Cambridge, Harvard University Press).
Finnis, John (2011), *Natural Law and Natural Rights* (Oxford, Oxford University Press).
Finnis, John (2014), 'What is the philosophy of Law?', *The American Journal of Jurisprudence* 59(2), 133–42.
Fisher, Douglas (2013), *Legal Reasoning in Environmental Law* (Cheltenham, Edward Elgar).
Garver, Geoffrey (2013), 'The Rule of Ecological Law: The Legal Complement to Degrowth Economics', *Sustainability* 5(1), 316–37; http://www.mdpi.com/2071-1050/5/1/316.
Gillespie, Alexander (1997), *International Law, Policy and Ethics* (Oxford, Oxford University Press).
Ginther, Konrad, Erik Denters and Paul De Wart (1995), *Sustainable Development and Good Governance* (The Hague, Kluwer).
Godden, Lee (2009), 'Book Review: The Principle of Sustainability: Translating Law and Governance, by Klaus Bosselmann', *Osgoode Hall Law Journal* 47(4), 807–808.
Grober, Ulrich (2007), *Deep Roots: A Conceptual History of Sustainable Development (Nachhaltigkeit)* (Wissenschaftzentrum Berlin für Sozialforschung).
Grober, Ulrich (2010), *Die Entdeckung der Nachhaltigkeit: Kulturgeschichte eines Begriffs* (Antje Kunstmann).
Harris, James (1971), 'When and why does the Grundnorm change?', *Cambridge Law Journal* 29(1), 102–33.
Higgins, Polly (2010), *Eradicating Ecocide: Laws and Governance to Stop the Destruction of the Planet* (London, Shepheard-Walwyn).
Kelsen, Hans (1967), *Pure Theory of Law* (Berkeley, UCLA Press).
Kim, Rakhyun and Klaus Bosselmann (2012), 'Operationalizing Sustainable Development: Ecological Integrity as a Grundnorm', *Review of European Comparative and International Environmental Law* 24(2), 194–208.
Kim, Rakhyun and Klaus Bosselmann (2013), 'Towards Environmental Law in the Anthropocene: Towards a Purposive System of Multilateral Environmental Agreements', *Transnational Environmental Law* 2(2), 285–309.
Kotzé, Louis and Alexander Paterson (2009), *The Role of the Judiciary in Environmental Governance: Comparative Perspectives* (The Hague, Kluwer).
Leopold, Aldo (1949), *A Sand County Almanac* (Oxford, Oxford University Press).
MacNeill, Jim (2007), *Our Common Future: Advance or Retreat? Sustainable Development: A New Urgency* (Ottawa, EcoLomics Occasional Papers Series 2007-3).
Martin, Paul, Sadeq Z. Bigdeli, Trevor Daya-Winterbottom, Willemien du Plessis and Amanda Kennedy (2015), *The Search for Environmental Justice* (Cheltenham, Edward Elgar).
Morrow, Karen and Sean Coyle (2004), *A Philosophical Foundation for Environmental Law* (Oxford, Hart).
Munasinghe, Mohan and Lutz, Ernst (1991), *Environmental-Economic Evaluation of Projects and Policies for Sustainable Development* (Environment Working Paper No. 42, The World Bank).

Murswiek, Dietrich (2002), *Nachhaltigkeit – Probleme der rechtlichen Umsetzung eines umweltpolitischen Leitbildes* (Natur und Recht).
Radkau, Joachim (2008), *Nature and Power: A Global History of the Environment* (Cambridge, Cambridge University Press).
Repetto, Robert (1986), *World Enough and Time* (New Haven, Yale University Press).
Sands, Phillippe (2003), *Principles of Internationale Environmental Law* (Cambridge, Cambridge University Press, 2nd edn).
Smith, Michael, Karlson Hargroves and Cheryl Desha (2010), *Cents and Sustainability: Securing Our Common Future by Decoupling Economic Growth from Environmental Pressures* (London, Earthscan).
Spindler, Edmund (2011), *Geschichte der Nachhaltigkeit. Vom Werden und Wirken eines beliebten Begriffs*, 1-21; http://www.nachhaltigkeit.info/media/1326279587phpeJPyvC.pdf.
Sustainable Aotearoa New Zealand (2009), *Strong Sustainability for New Zealand: principles and scenarios* (Auckland, Nakedize).
Tamanaha, Brian (2004), *On the Rule of Law: History, Politics, Theory* (Cambridge, Cambridge University Press).
Taylor, Prue (1998), *An Ecological Approach to International Law* (London, Routledge).
Vilela, Mirian (2005), 'Building consensus on shared values. History and provenance of the Earth Charter' in Peter Blaze Corcoran (ed.), *Toward a Sustainable World: The Earth Charter in Action* (The Hague, Kluwer).
Vinx, Lars (2007), *Hans Kelsen's Pure Theory of Law: Legacy and Legitimacy* (Oxford, Oxford University Press).
Von Carlowitz, Hans Carl (2000), *Sylvicultura Oeconomica, Anweisung zur Wilden Baum Zucht* [*Forest Economy or Guide to Tree Cultivation Conforming with Nature*] (reprint of 1st edn 1713, TU Bergakademie Freiburg und Akademische Buchhandlung).
Wolfrum, Rüdiger (1996), *Enforcing Environmental Standards: Economic Mechanisms as Viable Means?* (Berlin, Springer).

INSTRUMENTS

Agenda 21: *Agenda 21 – Programme of Action for Sustainable Development* A/Conf/151/26 (1992).
Brundtland Report: World Commission on Environment and Development (1987), *Our Common Future* (Oxford: Oxford University Press).
Caring for the Earth: International Union for the Conservation of Nature and Natural Resources (IUCN), World Wide Fund for Nature (WWF) and United Nations Environment Programme (UNEP) (1991), *Caring for the Earth: A Strategy for Sustainable Living.*
Convention on the Conservation of Antarctic Marine Living Resources: Convention on the Conservation of Antarctic Marine Living Resources 1329 UNTS 47 (signed 20 May 1980, entered into force 7 April 1982).
Earth Charter: Earth Charter Commission, *The Earth Charter* (29 June 2000).
Great Lakes Water Quality Agreement: Agreement on Great Lakes Water Quality, Canada–United States of America 1153 UNTS 187 (signed 22 November 1978, entered into force 22 November 1978).
Johannesburg Declaration on Sustainable Development A/CONF199/20 (2002).
Millennium Declaration: United Nations Millennium Declaration GA Res. 55/2, UN GAOR, 55th sess., 8th plen. mtg., UN Doc. A/Res/55/2 (2000).
National Parks Act 2000 (Canada): Canada National Parks Act (SC 2000 c32).

New Delhi Declaration on the Principles of International Law Related to Sustainable Development: International Law Association, *New Delhi Declaration of Principles of International Law Relating to Sustainable Development* (ILA resolution 3/2002, London, 2002).

Resource Management Act 1991 (New Zealand); http://www.legislation.govt.nz/act/public/1991/0069/latest/DLM230265.html.

Rio Declaration: Rio Declaration on Environment and Development A/Conf/151/26 (1992).

South Pacific Fishery Resources Convention: Convention on the Conservation and Management of High Seas Fishery Resources in the South Pacific Ocean ('SPRFMO Convention'), South Pacific Regional Fisheries Management Organisation (SPRFMO, Wellington, 2015; http://www.sprfmo.int).

South Pacific Living Marine Resources Framework Agreement: Framework Agreement for the Conservation of the Living Resources ('Galapagos Agreement'), Law of the Sea Bulletin No.45, DOALOS, United Nations (2001), 70–78.

The Future We Want GA Res 66/288, A/Res/66/288 (2012).

World Charter for Nature: *World Charter for Nature* GA Res 37/7, A/Res/37/7 (1982).

3. From protection to restoration: a challenge for environmental governance

Afshin Akhtar-Khavari and Anastasia Telesetsky

INTRODUCTION

It has often been argued that environmental principles assist in the coherent development of international environmental law.[1] While the legal status of environmental principles is often debated, the ideas they support and the concepts they introduce into the debate continue to influence the development of environmental law deeply and persistently. They give meaning to certain developments and influence the shape and design of environmental law over time. It has been suggested that environmental principles not only direct behaviour[2] but also help states to understand issues in multilateral engagements and fora.[3] The principles prohibiting transboundary harm, seeking intergenerational equity and applying the precautionary principle are examples of significant environmental principles that continue to play a variety of complex roles in global governance. But principles like these continue to support protection and conservation measures rather than the 'recovery' and 'restoration' of ecosystems as a whole.

This is not to suggest that existing environmental principles directed at protection totally ignore efforts designed to restore ecosystems. Allowing nature to recover on its own – passive restoration – is a central feature of much of existing environmental law. The concept of sustainability presumes that nature will recover on its own and that the impact of human activities will not negatively influence its resilience. Over recent years, ideas like the Anthropocene and the tipping points in the earth systems have prompted questions about the carrying capacity of planet earth itself and about the value of relying on passive restoration without the active involvement of human beings in that process.[4] Similarly, global environmental problems – such as climate change and invasive species – are examples of the influences the human species has brought to bear on the potential value of passive restoration in the elements of the natural world.[5] International environmental protection measures in the context of arrangements that support passive restoration are unlikely to continue to be effective.

Protection of the environment is critical. It remains a fundamental driver of normative developments in environmental law. But in the Anthropocene it needs to be complemented increasingly by restoration goals and ideals. It is accordingly important to discuss the idea of ecological restoration as an approach requiring a shift away from the protection paradigm in environmental law. Although international environmental law contains rules acknowledging the idea of restoration, the question is whether a restoration-focused approach is indicated for the management of ecosystems by a set of broader and more general soft law instruments.[6] Environmental principles commonly emerge through soft law instruments. It is important to determine, by examining a number of such instruments, whether there is any evidence that restoration is seen as important or significant in environmental governance. Accordingly, this chapter is structured as follows:

- A review of the concept of ecological restoration
- An assessment of the need for ecological restoration
- A prediction of how the legal system should respond to ecological restoration in the Anthropocene
- A review of the incorporation of ecological restoration in these relevant instruments
- The Stockholm Declaration
- The World Charter for Nature
- The Rio Declaration
- Agenda 21
- The Johannesburg Plan
- Rio+20 and *The Future We Want*
- The 2015 Sustainable Development Goals
- The Sendai Declaration.

THE CONCEPT OF ECOLOGICAL RESTORATION

1. Introduction

The idea that humans can restore or help with the recovery of nature is not a new idea. Going as far back as the middle of the nineteenth century, the popular conservationist George Perkins Marsh, whose *Man and Nature*[7] helped change how humans react to degradation and the human effect on earth systems, spoke about and vigorously promoted the idea of restoration.[8] In the opening sentence in the preface to his book first published in 1864, he wrote that 'the object of the present volume is … to suggest the possibility and the importance of the restoration of disturbed harmonies and the material improvement of waste and exhausted regions'.[9] The inclusion of restoration in his book was not accidental. Hall has highlighted how Marsh's time in Italy in 1861 helped him recognise the importance of restoration for understanding the differences between the approaches of the Italians and the United States to nature.[10] During his time in Italy he drew upon concepts developed by Italian scholars to understand better the importance of human agency in either repairing or improving the existing capacities of the natural environment.[11] Hall has written how, when 'reading Marsh, one realizes that environmental restoration is an old pursuit, much older than a few decades'.[12]

Despite the age-old concern with restoration, global governance instruments have rarely concerned themselves with it. The term is not defined in any international law instruments – not even in agreements that use the term.[13] Restoration is an idea that encourages different thinking about how human beings can experience and relate to the natural world.[14] As such it is a big idea that is not easily defined without compromising on some important matters. An essential and defining purpose or goal of restoration is, despite the reasons for doing so, to assist with the 'recovery' of an ecosystem. Traditionally, restoration is viewed as repairing an ecosystem after human beings have done some kind of damage to it.[15] It will be seen that the concept of the Anthropocene encourages broader thinking about the causes of harm done to the natural environment. The current conception of degradation and restoration needs to broaden as well.

2. The Goals of Recovery Activities

The important question most restorationists have to think about is what the goal of the recovery activities should be. There are varying schools of thought on the idea of restoration, ranging from scholars who are deep ecologists to those who recognise that nature is potentially meaningless without the value that human beings have come to ascribe to it. The Society for Ecological Restoration (SER) is a pre-eminent international society that brings together a vast group of ecologists and a host of others from various disciplinary backgrounds interested in environmental or ecological restoration.[16] It adopted a definition of restoration in the SER Primer which describes restoration as the 'process of assisting the recovery of an ecosystem that has been degraded, damaged, or destroyed'.[17] The terms 'assist' and 'recovery' both need further discussion.[18] This is because the term 'recovery' is general and can support activities aimed at ecosystems regaining their health, integrity or some of their functions. The SER Primer defines these terms with more precision by indicating that:

> Ecological restoration is an intentional activity that initiates or accelerates the recovery of an ecosystem with respect to its health, integrity and sustainability … Restoration attempts to return an ecosystem to its historic trajectory.[19]

The idea in the SER Primer that ecological restoration has to 'return an ecosystem to its historic trajectory' is not an uncontroversial assumption. In contrast, the Intergovernmental Panel on Biodiversity and Ecosystem Services (IPBES) in its second plenary meeting in 2015 adopted a definition of restoration that refers only to the 'recovery of an ecosystem from a degraded state'.[20] What is common to each of these definitions is that they set the natural state of an ecosystem as the baseline against which degradation is measured. According to the SER Primer, returning an ecosystem to its historical trajectory is restoration. For IPBES it is returning an ecosystem back to its pre-degradation state. This requires agreement on the difficult question of what kind of degradation is relevant and significant. The pre-degradation state could be 10, 20 or 100 years in the past but this may or may not be the same as having to assist with recovery that restarts the historical trajectory of the ecosystem.

The IPBES definition of 'rehabilitation' adds another dimension to the broader recovery process. The definition recognises it as restoration. It defines rehabilitation as the 'activities that may fall short of fully restoring the biotic community to its pre-degradation state'.[21] In other words, restoration goes further than rehabilitation. Rehabilitation does not have to be as holistic in terms of the recovery process involved. The differences between the SER Primer and the IPBES definition are a matter of judgment. The IPBES definition is simpler to implement because it requires only the identification of a pre-degradation natural state. Neither definition is explicit about the requirement to achieve 'ecological integrity' because it probably presumes that this quality already exists in any kind of pre-degradation natural state.[22]

A range of other restoration-type activities focuses attention on the recovery of an ecosystem or of some of its function. But they do so with a variety of different purposes and goals in mind – such as making a landscape more beautiful, healthy or simply more productive for food production. The creation of 'novel ecosystems' and the 'rewilding' of an area are two concepts that describe different approaches to the recovery processes. A sustainable forestry initiative or revegetation project that reduces soil erosion would help to create a 'novel ecosystem' by replacing historical features of an ecosystem with new alternatives and sometimes more productive natural features.[23] The concept of rewilding describes a process whereby one species is introduced into an environment to build complexity back into an ecosystem where usual conservation efforts have been adversely affected.[24] Both these recovery efforts are a form of natural geo-engineering. Although they support the active involvement of human beings in the recovery of ecosystems, they fall short of some of the ambitions inherent in the SER Primer's definition of restoration that connects humanity with nature by actively involving humans in taking an ecosystem back to its historical trajectory.

3. The Historical Trajectory Approach to Ecological Restoration

The focus on returning the functioning of an ecosystem back to its historical trajectory is an important feature of the concept of ecological restoration. It narrows the approach that SER takes to restoration by focusing the activities of humans purely on the holistic ecological features of an ecosystem rather than by trying to balance them with the cultural, social and importantly the economic interests humans have in ecosystems. Human interests in an ecosystem generally have to be weighed against the holistic ecological value of the recovery process itself – not only for regional and local biodiversity but increasingly in terms of their contributions to the health and integrity of the various earth systems, such as that of the climate system. If so, the idea that restoration is recovery that seeks to 'return an ecosystem to its historic trajectory' raises some complex challenges about how to think about restoration ecology.[25]

The historical trajectory of an ecosystem is not an easy concept or idea to define because of the number of possibilities to be taken into account. For instance, if the intention were to restore an Australian landscape, would the aim be to restore an ecosystem to its trajectory from pre-European settlement days? The alternative would be to restore the same ecosystem back to its pre-degradation stage, even if the area of concern had simply been used for agriculture. Rackham has suggested that the best way to account for the historical trajectory of an ecosystem is to identify the losses that accompany the degradation. Important losses for him include the loss of historical vegetation and wildlife and also the loss of meaning from the degradation.[26] The problem with this view is that restoration has to be about ecological recovery and, by focusing on loss, there is a tendency to complicate the decision-making process by asking human beings about what they see as valuable.

A significant challenge for returning an ecosystem to its historical trajectory is that ecosystems are dynamic and respond to both internal and external influences. Returning nature to some untouched or wild state before human beings had influenced it is almost impossible. Current temperatures, pollution levels and soil conditions, for instance, may not make the achievement of a pre-degradation natural state a possibility. A requirement to identify a natural baseline would be difficult to include in projects because of the uncertainty about having to define it in some way.[27]

Nevertheless, there are several arguments to support the view that this narrower version of the idea of restoration – as compared for instance to novel ecosystems – is useful and is likely to give important direction to restoration efforts and ideas. The first is that restoration managers do not have to make choices about what to leave in and out of the management of the restoration process. There is no room to interpret creatively the potential or capacity of an ecosystem to survive as long as the goal of the project is to take an ecosystem back to some natural state baseline.[28] One of the challenges in selecting what to restore in an ecosystem is the possibility of ignoring the influences of 'minor' species or 'inconspicuous processes'.[29] Gross has argued that restoration has to help with the recovery of the ecosystem along pathways that are not controlled by human beings.[30] Restorationists have argued that, with climate change and the spread of invasive species, there could be increasing domestication and homogenisation of landscapes around the world.[31] Ecological restoration is seen as a solution to avoiding such challenges because it focuses on recovery that is not always driven by what is immediately beneficial for human beings. This leads to an important question. Why is ecological restoration necessary at all?

THE NEED FOR ECOLOGICAL RESTORATION

Is it enough to preserve and protect existing ecosystem health and functions? If preservation is enough, then all that is needed are approaches to restoration that seek to rehabilitate and remediate degraded ecosystems. On this assumption, once the wrongs of humans are corrected, nature will continue to support the ecosystem beyond simple efforts to rehabilitate and remediate it. Any activity in addition to these simple restoration efforts is to make an ethical choice in one direction compared to another. As such, it is useful to discuss whether environmental law is actually able to confront the question why humans should engage in ecological restoration.

When introduced to the idea of restoration, some people may assume that the practice is intended to reintroduce wild nature into urban areas and take landscapes back to a time before human beings had begun to exploit them for economic gains. The reasons for engaging in restoration can vary. Whether it is to rewild or engage in ecological restoration, it will require choices to be made and options to be evaluated according to criteria about what is right, preferable or wrong in relation to degrees of degradation. Much scholarly time has been spent discussing how these choices are framed in terms of understanding the relationship between humans and the natural world and whether humans are engineering nature for their needs or doing what is perceived as serving some 'natural' purpose – whatever that may be.[32] For instance, in 2001 Vietnam decided to restore its mangroves around coastal areas because of its increasing vulnerability to natural disasters – including tropical cyclones.[33] Engineering a recovery process that is designed to serve a particular purpose is one of the significant benefits of engaging in restoration.

The reason for invoking the environmental legal system in efforts to restore has to be found in the potential of the law to support the effective management of the natural world. Environmental law can help coordinate, systematise and regulate conduct to avoid harm and damage at the global level. At the same time this has collective impacts on human beings. Environmental law, much like other disciplines, is built on certain foundations and principles that propel it in particular directions. This means that certain new concepts and ideas relating to protection of the environment are likely to be more easily adopted and developed because the foundations already exist in environmental law. For instance, it would be relatively easy to create rules relating to the rehabilitation or remediation of parts of nature that have been intentionally destroyed. These activities would remedy the adverse effects of failed earlier attempts to protect or preserve elements of the environment.

Similarly, because of the prominence of concepts and ideas that inadvertently support passive restoration, it would be difficult to argue – in the context of environmental law – that active restoration is a necessary feature and a blind spot of the discipline. Conservation, protection or preservation efforts are about restoration of the natural world. But this is on the assumption that nature can recover by itself only when it is less vulnerable to damage as a result of certain kinds of human activities.[34] For example, restoration initiatives around coastal zones can include protecting mangroves from further deterioration and allowing the ecosystem to heal itself gradually.[35] Sustainability as a concept relies on the notion that, once consumed, the natural world is capable by itself of replenishing, renewing or maintaining viable and healthy ecosystems. More active forms of helping nature to recover are seen by many as being the hallmark of the idea or process of restoration. However, the conceptual language of environmental law – such as preservation and conservation – is built on assumptions that nature will recover on its own if it is consumed sustainably. The arguments for and against restoration indicate a blind spot for environmental law in ways similar to the arguments about the limits of the discipline in dealing with ecosystems as a whole.[36]

THE CAPACITY OF THE LAW TO RESPOND TO THE ANTHROPOCENE

In the past decade the idea of the Anthropocene has become a popular concept, a linguistic term and a metaphor to describe the general impact of human beings as a geological force on planet earth.[37] Paul Crutzen in 2000 suggested the term as a new geological epoch which described the profound impact of human activities on planet earth.[38] In the geological sciences, the Anthropocene describes the variety of stratigraphical signals that human beings leave behind by building cities, dams, roads and similar constructions. During the Holocene – the precursor to the proposed Anthropocene – major changes to planet earth and its various subsystems came about as a result of subsystem activities such as shifts in plate tectonics, the weight of glaciers or the melting of ice. Human species in the Anthropocene are significant in geological and morphological ways not just because of the size of the human population but in terms of its anthropogenic impact on earth's subsystems. These impacts have come from increased carbon and nitrogen oxide levels in the atmosphere, biodiversity loss and a range of other conditions that place pressure on one of the earth's subsystems. In terms of changes to the biosphere as a result of the release of carbon and nitrogen, humans are as powerful as the forces of the climate itself – perhaps more powerful.

The Anthropocene may have emerged during the industrial age or perhaps even as far back as the time when humans cleared trees, cultivated land for the purposes of agriculture or domesticated animals. Some scientists have argued that, from the 1850s onwards, the increased levels of carbon dioxide in the atmosphere as a result of increased fossil fuel usage in urbanised areas have contributed significantly to the human impact on earth systems. These explain the onset of the Anthropocene. In previous geological epochs, particularly the Holocene, human species flourished because of stable and clement conditions that allowed them to build communities and societies to flourish. In 2016, the International Commission of Stratigraphy, which has set up a Working Group on the Anthropocene, is expected to decide whether planet earth has officially entered the Anthropocene.[39]

The significance of the concept of the Anthropocene for the humanities and social sciences is yet to be adequately researched and discussed.[40] Scholars are only just starting to explore its relevance for environmental law and justice issues.[41] The idea of the Anthropocene has, however, given earth-system scientists the language to encapsulate what they have observed as the 'radical anthropogenic alteration of the planet's natural cycles and systems'.[42] One consequence of this observation for environmental law is that it has to adapt and develop towards a new reality: namely a reality that can no longer rely simply on the protection and preservation of the environment as its underlying paradigm for dealing with the natural world. Galaz uses the term 'Anthropocene gap'[43] to refer to the idea that in this epoch there is a need to respond to 'gaps in our political lives' because of the uncertainty and the state of chaos potentially created by the 'alteration of the planet's natural cycles and systems'.

The normative consequences for humans of the existence of the Anthropocene will be difficult to assess because of the significance of the global impact of the idea that, as a collective, humans are geologically significant for planet earth. The responses need to be radical. On the one hand, it has been suggested that in the Anthropocene there is a need to conserve nature not for nature's sake but only for human survival.[44] On the other hand, according to another group a better use of existing concepts such as sustainability is required.[45] These suggestions are based on the presumption that the natural world will retain its capacity to restore itself passively and to continue being resilient in the face of 'radical' earth-systems changes. The challenge in drawing on these more traditional views of the carrying capacity of planet earth is that some events are likely to be more unpredictable and uncertain in nature and consequence.

An example of these normative challenges is the number of very extensive and severe fires that have devastated large ecosystems. These have been described as 'megafires' – such as the fires in Tasmania in Australia during 2015 and 2016.[46] Fire has always played an important role in the management by nature of its own affairs. It has been noted that 'fire in the Anthropocene has … shifted dramatically, from an ecological phenomenon driven by natural factors to a spatially and temporally variable hazard strongly associated with humans'.[47] Megafires are now very common around the world. As a consequence of the increasing frequency of megafires, governance structures have to adapt to protect not only humans but also critical ecosystems from fires of immense magnitude. There is nothing new about this idea. It is important to plan for the recovery of the ecosystem and for the containment of the consequences of the fire for ecosystems connected to the areas impacted by the fires. This is because megafires impact not only on ecosystems directly destroyed by the fires but also on ecosystems in other parts of the world.[48]

This conclusion does not suggest that the only normative and governance response to megafires is to restore areas after they have been damaged or destroyed by fire. Research suggests that humans light over 90 per cent of all fires and that they start and spread as a consequence of the land use policies formulated by humans and of other human activities.[49] If there is more emphasis on restoration, one consequence would be a modification of land use policies by returning a greater percentage of ecosystems to their historical trajectories that may be sufficiently complex and resilient, with the potential to cope with fires. Connecting more people with the natural environment through restoration efforts – large or small – will ensure that their relationship with nature develops in a more caring rather than managerial way.[50] This cultural shift will not only change how humans approach the governance of megafires by protecting forests; it will also be significant by indicating how environmental law can adapt to the Anthropocene.

THE CONCEPT OF ECOLOGICAL RESTORATION IN INTERNATIONAL INSTRUMENTS

1. Introduction

The discussion in the preceding paragraphs of why the law should adapt to the Anthropocene indicates the importance of dealing systematically with ecological issues in general by drawing on the practices and principles that have developed in the context of ecological restoration. What are some of the practices and principles that have emerged in governance arrangements to realise such approaches to restoration? They are revealed in an analysis of the range of soft law instruments that have, over recent years, begun to recognise the value of restoration and which can enable the adoption of policies and approaches to the natural world that do not have human beings as central to their effective functioning. A discussion of restoration in global governance necessarily involves a careful and detailed analysis of the text of the instruments and of the discussions that led to their acceptance by the international community. It is an enquiry into whether there are principles or ideas that are important for informing the implementation of national and international ecological restoration efforts. While it will identify a number of legal and normatively important texts that include the term 'restoration' in the operative language, it is worth noting at the outset that the concept of restoration is rarely defined in any of the legal texts. The idea of restoration is increasingly supported by the language adopted in these instruments but it has not developed sufficiently or been articulated to the point that it could be concluded that environmental law is moving in a different direction.

2. The Stockholm Declaration

One of the earliest direct references to the concept of 'restoration' is in the Stockholm Declaration. While it is non-binding in terms of its legal provenance, the 26 negotiated principles reflect the consensus of 114 states and it provides international evidence to support the application of several international environmental law principles.[51] As a follow up to the Biosphere Conference organised by UNESCO in 1968,[52] the Stockholm Conference was the product of four years of preparatory meetings designed to integrate environmental concerns into human decision-making.[53] In 1969, the UN General Assembly directed the Conference 'to serve as a practical means to encourage, and to provide guidelines for, action by Governments and international organizations designed to protect and improve the human environment and to remedy and prevent its impairment'.[54]

Principle 3 of the Stockholm Declaration states that 'the capacity of the earth to produce vital renewable resources must be maintained and wherever practicable, restored, or improved'. Statements prepared throughout the negotiating history covering the convening of the Stockholm Conference support a desire for states to pursue restoration as a priority remedial action. Some of these statements represent extreme optimism about the potential for restoration. In November 1969, the diplomatic representative from the Byelorussian Socialist Soviet Republic commented that his country attached 'great importance to the problem of protecting and rehabilitating the environment'.[55] The representative went on to indicate that 'natural resources were unlimited, but they must be protected, used rationally, increased and constantly replenished'.[56] For this representative at least, restoration seems to be linked directly to preserving a capacity for resource production.

This idea of 'restoration' and the improvement of natural resources seemed to have found favour with the Preparatory Committee that was formed in advance of the Stockholm Conference. This Committee understood the Draft Declaration to be a document that:

> would serve to stimulate public opinion and community participation for the protection and betterment of the human environment and, where appropriate, for the restoration of its primitive harmony etc. in the interest of present and future generations. It would also provide guiding principles for Governments in their formulation of policy and set objectives for future international cooperation.[57]

At the Second Preparatory Meeting, state representatives indicated that the Declaration was intended to be formulated as 'a document of universally recognized fundamental principles recommended for action by individuals, States and the international community'.[58] An Intergovernmental Working Group was formed which eventually produced a set of draft principles for the Stockholm Declaration. The original version of principle 3 – the only principle eventually to mention restoration – in the form proposed by Sweden did not include an explicit reference to restoration. Rather, it stated that 'the productive basis of renewable resources of the earth such as farmland, forests, crops and fish, which in many cases and places have been threatened or destroyed, must be maintained and enhanced'.[59] The Netherlands proposed this alternative urging that 'each State shall do its utmost to restore and improve the productive capacity of renewable resources of the earth, such as farmland, forests, crops and fish for the proper supply of future generations with food and other material products'.[60] Brazil, Egypt and Yugoslavia narrowed the proposal by suggesting that states should 'restore, wherever possible, the productive capacity of those renewable resources that have been unnecessarily depleted'.[61] A later version of the text called on states to 'maintain and wherever practicable, restore or improve, the capacity of the earth to produce vital renewable resources'.[62]

The final draft by the Intergovernmental Working Group included the following language for principle 3. States share 'common conviction' that 'the capacity of the earth to produce vital renewable resources must be maintained and wherever practicable, restored, or improved'.[63] This language was ultimately adopted as one of the principles of the Stockholm Declaration. Arguably, this principle can be interpreted to stand for the proposition that 'restoration' of vital renewable resources that humans need for survival – such as food – is a matter of common concern for the international community. The final version of principle 3 included the word 'must'. This suggests a recognition by states that investments in restoration may be essential for long-term human well-being.

While there was no negotiated set of definitions at the Stockholm Conference,[64] it can be assumed that 'renewable resources' referred to those components of nature that states considered to have some inherent economic values for humans. At that time, this would have been tradeable commodities such as fish stocks and timber since the focus of the Stockholm Declaration was squarely on the 'enhancement of the human environment'.[65] This reading is supported by previous proposed versions of the text of principle 3. This emphasis on restoring resources of value is not surprising given the focus of the Conference on acknowledging directly the interconnectedness between humanity and nature with man as 'creature and molder of his environment'.[66] As the preamble observed, the 'improvement of the human environment is a major issue which affects the well-being of peoples and economic development throughout the world'.[67] Restoration as a form of enhancement of the human environment is offered as one antidote to 'massive and irreversible harm to the earthly environment on which our life and well-being depend'.[68]

The Stockholm Declaration is informative in terms of contemporary attitudes towards restoration, many of which continue to define discussions by national and international policymakers. Principle 3 is limited to natural resource management, suggesting that restoration in 1972 was understood as serving primarily human production ends. As the principle also indicates, restoration will only be pursued 'wherever practicable', suggesting that states were aware of both the financial obstacles to reviving certain 'vital renewable resources' as well as the technical challenges of restoring degraded sites. The difference between the terms 'restored' and 'improved' in principle 3 is worth noting because the Declaration is one of the only international legal instruments to make a distinction between these two terms. The use of the term 'improved' may have been included in the text in order to allay state concerns over how much they might be expected to do to achieve a condition of restoration. The use of the term 'restored' in principle 3 would have set a high bar for state performance at the time the Declaration was negotiated. The definition of restoration in the 1971 *Oxford English Dictionary* referred to 'the act of restoring to a former state or position … or to an unimpaired or perfect condition' and restore meant 'to bring back to the original state … or to a healthy or vigorous state'. Given this definition, it suggests that state negotiators would have used the term 'restored' as a reference to bringing back a resource to some former condition of plentitude or perhaps ecological autonomy. For those resources where this would simply not be possible – such as salmon runs in a river whose headwaters had been dammed – the states could instead seek to create 'improved' capacity through programs such as aquaculture or timber plantations.

The form in which a principle is drafted is important. Principle 3, like several others in the Stockholm Declaration, is drafted in the passive voice. Who is responsible for achieving the goals of principle 3? In the preamble, states agreed that the 'protection and improvement of the human environment is … the duty of all Governments'.[69] In particular 'local and national governments will bear the greatest burden for large-scale environmental policy and action within their jurisdictions'.[70] But the preamble also suggests that restoration triggers 'the acceptance and responsibility by citizens and communities and by enterprises and institutions at every level, all sharing equitably in common efforts'.[71] This preambular language signals the contributions to be made by both state and non-state actors in 'environmental protection and improvement'.

Based on the language of the Declaration, states appear to have committed at least to the idea that they may have some obligation to participate in 'restoration' of vital natural commodities as long as such efforts are financially and technically practical. While this does not reflect a legally cognisable restoration ethos, it does signal the potential start of a larger international dialogue about the role of humanity in mediating nature. Having collectively rejected the idea that humanity serves as an overseer of nature, the states who attended the Stockholm Conference understood that humanity depended on nature and to some extent nature depended on humanity. As expressed in the Declaration, humans must 'for the purpose of attaining freedom in the world of nature … use knowledge to build, in collaboration with nature, a better environment'.[72]

Although principle 3 is the only principle to refer explicitly to restoration, other principles provide context for the type of restoration work that is currently being pursued through organisations such as the Global Partnership for Forest Landscape Restoration.[73] For example, principle 24 offers international cooperation as a leveling mechanism where 'international matters concerning the protection and improvement of the environment should be handled in a cooperative spirit by all countries, big and small, on an equal footing'.[74] States should enter into bilateral and multilateral cooperative arrangements 'to effectively control, prevent, reduce and eliminate adverse environmental effects resulting from activities conducted in all spheres'.[75] States can also act collectively through their active membership of international organisations. The

Stockholm Declaration suggests that states should ensure that international organizations 'play a coordinated, efficient and dynamic role for the protection and improvement of the environment'.[76]

States understood that 'political will' was essential to achieving the norms embodied in the principles.[77] In the spirit of cooperation and the recognition of the power of 'political will' that can be accessed at a world conference, the states attending the Conference also negotiated a number of recommendations as an action plan. While there was no specific effort to highlight broader concepts of ecological restoration in the recommendations, states did agree to promote 'soil restoration' by recommending that the UN Secretary General in conjunction with appropriate UN bodies provide capacity training in support of soil 'restoration'.[78]

When the state representatives made the decision to move forward with the Stockholm Conference, the representative from Sweden observed that 'the preparations for the Conference, the Conference itself, and the follow-up to the Conference should be considered as parts of one single continuing process'.[79] While this observation was intended to apply broadly to the emerging practice of international environmental policy-making, it can be applied more specifically to emerging attitudes about 'restoration' as part of 'one single continuing process' in mediating how people interact with the natural environment and with each other. Fundamentally, principle 3 of the Stockholm Declaration can be regarded as setting the stage for subsequent multilateral negotiations that would recognise restoration as an appropriate policy choice where resource management by conservation was no longer viable.

3. The World Charter for Nature

After the adoption of the Stockholm Declaration and the creation of the United Nations Environmental Programme, environmental protection and particularly conservation were becoming mainstreamed. Restoration was becoming popularised as a last resort option to address degraded or impacted areas. The World Charter for Nature reflected an effort by states and civil society to enhance cooperation on protecting the natural environment. In 1975, the President of Zaire made the proposal for a Charter and requested the International Union for the Conservation of Nature and Natural Resources (IUCN) to draft a Charter for negotiation by the UN General Assembly. The result was a document modelled in part on the Universal Declaration of Human Rights in the sense that the Charter assigns 'each person' a duty to act in accordance with the terms of the Charter and to 'strive to ensure that the objectives and requirements of the present Charter are met'.[80] Of the 154 voting members of the United Nations, 112 endorsed the Charter. These included all of the European Community States and all of the NATO nations except the United States. The Charter is not a legally binding instrument. It reflects an important joint political statement and a potential basis for the evolution of customary international law.

The term 'restoration' is not used in the Charter. The drafters referred to rehabilitation as one of many 'principles of conservation'.[81] Specifically, the drafters urged persons to control activities with impacts on nature and provided that 'areas degraded by human activities shall be rehabilitated for purposes in accord with their natural potential and compatible with the well-being of affected populations'.[82] The language in article 11 raises some questions about what the intent of the states might have been in adopting this provision of the Charter. There is no indication whether the 'well-being of affected populations' refers to populations of animals and plants or merely to human communities. It is fair to assume that the term 'populations' is intended to refer to human communities because the term 'well-being' is not typically used to refer to the non-human environment.

While an interest in safeguarding human community values can be assumed, the concept of rehabilitation 'for purposes in accord with their natural potential' in article 11 remains vague. One possible reading of the term 'rehabilitation' suggests a twenty-first-century concept of ecological restoration. In this case actors re-establish environmental values for a given ecosystem that restore the development of an ecosystem on to a historical trajectory. A second interpretation of this term is more pragmatic. It focuses instead on what potential there is to recover any 'natural potential' after human degradation. Under this second interpretation, a formerly forested region that has been heavily quarried might be appropriately rehabilitated into an area with lakes that may or may not have forest values. The first interpretation captures a progressive understanding of human obligations for environmental intervention. The second interpretation more closely reflects practice at the time the Charter was endorsed. This is revealed by national laws and practices such as the UK National Parks and Access to the Country Act 1949, which enables land made derelict by underground mining operations to be transformed for potential reuse.[83]

While the World Charter for Nature remains an aspirational document rather than an operational agreement, it was important in establishing general principles focused on conserving the ecological functions of natural systems. In particular, it formally introduced to the international community an environmental interaction hierarchy with the emphasis on avoiding environmental impacts, minimising environmental impacts and, but only as a final resort, rehabilitating after environmental impacts.[84]

4. The Rio Declaration

Twenty years after the Stockholm Conference, states gathered in Rio de Janiero in 1992 at the United Nations Conference on Environment and Development to refine the principles that states should apply to 'respect the interests of all and protect the integrity of the global environmental and developmental system'.[85] The final meeting was a public relations success attracting the attendance of hundreds of heads of state and securing active participation from a large sector of civil society. During the meeting, two treaties – the Convention to Combat Desertification and the Convention on Biodiversity – with substantive obligations involving restoration were adopted. The other major output of the Conference was the Rio Declaration, negotiated as an extension to the Stockholm Declaration to reflect concerns over mainstreaming human development into environmental management.

The negotiating history of the Rio Declaration was markedly different from that of the Stockholm Declaration. To bring together disparate thinking proved challenging. At an early meeting, 136 separate proposals were made by states offering potential principles.[86] At the final meeting of the Preparatory Committee, there was no working draft. Seven representatives from the Global North and seven representatives from the Global South collaborated on a text that was ultimately adopted at the Conference.[87]

Of the 27 principles in the Rio Declaration, only one specifically mentions restoration.[88] Principle 7 reflects an amalgam of ideas. The first element of the principle provides that 'States shall cooperate in a spirit of global partnership to conserve, protect, and restore the health and integrity of the Earth's ecosystem'. The remainder of principle 7 introduced the concept of common but differentiated responsibilities. Linking these two elements of principle 7 together suggests that 'developed countries' have special obligations to help other states to 'conserve, protect and restore' by providing technological assistance and financial resources. While it is not stated in principle 7, developed countries may have a 'differentiated responsibility' to support restoration efforts particularly within former colonies where large amounts of timber, biodiversity or minerals were extracted in the pre-colonial era. Even if legitimate post-colonial concerns to right past environmental wrongs motivated the drafting of principle 7, the final language of principle 7 reflects curious drafting choices.

Here is the first. Principle 7 refers to 'the Earth's ecosystem', which is an incorrect usage of the term 'ecosystem' as understood by ecologists. To use the definition of ecosystem in the Convention on Biological Diversity drafted contemporaneously with the Rio Declaration, an ecosystem is understood to be 'a dynamic complex of plant, animal and micro-organism communities and their non-living environment interacting as a functional unit'.[89] The earth does not have a single 'ecosystem' but rather a multitude of ecosystems. It may have been that the intention was to emphasise a 'one world' or a 'all for one, one for all' approach in order to bolster the common but differentiated responsibilities principle.[90] But the choice of the earth as the unit to be restored ultimately provided no particularly helpful guidance to states seeking new environmental policy directions.

Here is the second. This was the suggestion that states shall cooperate to 'conserve, protect, and restore'. It is unclear why there is an 'and' in this expression. The use of 'conserve' and 'protect' suggest a redundancy since conserve in the context of the principle fundamentally requires some degree of legal protection. The choice of the phrase 'conserve … and restore' rather than 'conserve … or restore' is similarly an interesting choice of words because it seems to imply unintentionally that a state would conserve and protect 'Earth's ecosystem' up to a certain point before the ecosystem would presumably be exhausted. After the 'Earth's ecosystem' had been exhausted by the various states, then the states would collectively and cooperatively restore it to some condition of 'health and integrity'.

Even though the principles were adopted as aspirational measures rather than as binding obligations, the lack of attention given to the text of the first half of principle 7 remains important. States in the Global South regularly cite and rely upon a now legalised concept of 'common but differentiated responsibilities' to explain why their states should be given additional time to comply with an international obligation or to urge states in the Global North to provide adequate resources to support states in the Global South in their pursuit of sustainable development.[91] In contrast to the attention given to the second half of principle 7, there has been far less effort over the past two decades dedicated to pursuing cooperation through global partnerships for conservation or restoration of ecosystems.[92]

In spite of the confusing language of principle 7, the evolution of the principle from the initial reference to restoration in the Stockholm Declaration is remarkable. In 20 years, the emphasis on restoration has shifted from a narrow focus on restoring ecosystem provisioning services to a focus on much broader holistic concepts of undertaking restoration for the purpose of ecosystem health and integrity. This is a notable normative change in light of the criticisms by some that the Rio Conference was taking the international community attention away from environmental protection.[93]

5. Agenda 21

In addition to subscribing to the Rio Declaration, states agreed to an action plan similar to the one formulated at the Stockholm Conference. This 40-chapter document – Agenda 21 – was drafted on the basis of 'global consensus and political commitment at the highest level' to further development and environmental cooperation.[94] Designed to be a practical document, the Agenda includes specific shared objectives and proposals for activities and implementation means. The concept of ecological restoration is threaded throughout the various chapters as an action item. For example, in the chapter on combatting deforestation, states share the goal of 'enhancing the protection, sustainable management and conservation of all forests, and the greening of degraded areas, through forest rehabilitation, afforestation, reforestation and other rehabilitative means'.[95] In order to achieve this goal, 'rehabilitation' activities should be designed to:

> restore productivity and environmental contributions, giving particular attention to human needs for economic and ecological services, wood-based energy, agroforestry, non-timber forest products and services, watershed and soil protection, wildlife management, and forest genetic resources.

While this strongly anthropocentric perspective of the goals for forest rehabilitation can be criticised, the same ecosystem service motivations continue to drive many contemporary projects that are labelled instead as forest restoration.[96]

In the chapter on combatting desertification and drought, states agreed to the goal of 'combating land degradation through, inter alia, intensified soil conservation, afforestation and reforestation activities'.[97] To achieve this goal, states 'at the appropriate level and with the support of the relevant international and regional organizations, should' take corrective measures to restore the productivity of drylands.[98] Governments should promote 'integrated research programmes on the protection, restoration and conservation of water and land resources'.[99] Both of these examples demonstrate that a core driver for restoration is human dependency on the environment. Typical investments in restoration efforts are investments in human development to revive resource productivity. A similar type of commitment to productivity for human ends is made in the chapter on oceans. This calls on states in relation to the resources of the high seas and within waters under their national jurisdiction to 'restore populations of marine species at levels that can produce the maximum sustainable yield as qualified by relevant environmental and economic factors'.[100]

In the chapter on conservation of biodiversity, states called upon each other to 'promote the rehabilitation and restoration of damaged ecosystems'.[101] This is almost exactly the language in the Convention on Biological Diversity (CBD).[102] But unlike the CBD, which speaks primarily to states, Agenda 21 provides that the state 'with the support of indigenous people and their communities, non-governmental organizations and other groups, including the business and scientific communities' should pursue restoration of damaged ecosystems. This multi-stakeholder approach to restoration embedded in Agenda 21 is critical to the success of effective restoration for any country where there is a patchwork of land tenure.

A similar multi-stakeholder coordination approach is proposed in the chapter on protection of the oceans. Coastal states are encouraged to develop integrated management for the sustainable development of the coastal regions by drawing on support from 'the academic and private sectors, non-governmental organizations, local communities, resource user groups, and indigenous peoples'.[103] Part of any proposed integrated coastal zone plan is 'restoration of altered critical habitats'.[104]

The year 1992 was a landmark year for the recognition of restoration of ecosystems. Agenda 21 took special notice of restoration in its chapter detailing the role of science to support environmental management and sustainable development. Specifically, the states need to 'develop further restoration ecology' to enhance scientific understanding to respond better to 'short- and long-term perturbations' to terrestrial, freshwater, coastal and marine ecosystems.[105]

The Rio Declaration in conjunction with Agenda 21 suggests the presence of dual policy attitudes to restoration. On the one hand, restoration, as indicated in the forest and ocean chapters of Agenda 21, is regarded as a utilitarian exercise to recover vital human commodities. On the other hand, restoration is designated as a therapeutic exercise for purposes of recovering global 'health and integrity'. These arguments in support of restoration continue to be relevant.

6. The Johannesburg Plan of Implementation

Ten years after the Rio Conference, states convened in Johannesburg in South Africa for the World Summit on Sustainable Development. This meeting did not produce sets of principles like the Stockholm and Rio meetings but it did negotiate a plan of implementation.[106] Focused on reducing poverty, on changing consumption and production patterns, and on protecting natural resource bases for economic and social development, the Plan did not set new goals. It reinforced Agenda 21 goals with – in some cases – additional specificity. For example, states agreed to work 'at all levels' to 'maintain or restore [marine] stocks to levels that can produce the maximum sustainable yield' by 2015.[107]

The Plan identified two additional developments that have become increasingly relevant in assessing the costs and benefits of restoration. First, in relation to freshwater allocation, the Plan suggested that states should develop by 2005 integrated water resources management plans and water efficiency plans that balance 'the requirement of preserving or restoring ecosystems and their functions, in particular in fragile environments, with human domestic, industrial and agriculture needs, including safeguarding drinking water quality'.[108] The issue of restoring in-stream riparian rights in over-allocated water basins remains a sensitive issue. Second, the Plan proposed ecosystem restoration work to reduce disaster risks for communities where environmental degradation has increased vulnerability. Under the Plan, states 'at all levels' are expected to take action to 'reduce the risks of flooding and drought in vulnerable countries by, inter alia, promoting wetland and watershed protection and restoration'.[109] The Plan was intended to accelerate the efforts of states in achieving sustainable development. While many of the implementation targets were missed, the Plan is still an interesting negotiated document in terms of highlighting a global need to restore not only individually useful species such as fish stocks, but also complex systems such as wetlands.

7. Rio+20 and *The Future We Want*

Twenty years after the UN Conference on Environment and Development and ten years after the UN Summit on Sustainable Development, states organised another multilateral meeting to take stock of the progress made and the challenges remaining in greening the economy and implementing sustainable development.[110] The outcome of the meeting was a single document entitled *The Future We Want*. This was generally regarded as a disappointment because it failed to elicit any new commitments from states beyond an agreement to develop sustainable development goals to be adopted by the UN General Assembly. Perhaps the failure to take on new commitments should not have been surprising in light of the number of unmet commitments under existing treaty regimes and other international agreements such as the Johannesburg Implementation Plan. Even so, *The Future We Want* reflects important normative developments in how restoration is regarded.

To a greater extent than previous internationally negotiated documents, *The Future We Want* explicitly recognised restoration as a key environmental management strategy that could be mainstreamed into economic decision-making. On the first page of the document, the authors wrote about the need to achieve sustainable development by 'promoting integrated and sustainable management of natural resources and ecosystems that supports *inter alia* economic, social and human development while facilitating ecosystem conservation, regeneration and restoration and resilience in the face of new and emerging challenges'.[111] This language indicates a shared commitment to 'ecosystem restoration' and not only to restoration of vital commodities. The term 'regeneration' has replaced the former use of 'improve' in the Stockholm Declaration. It might have been included to distinguish holistic restoration efforts from ecological rehabilitation efforts such as afforestation. States have thus recognised a new condition for environmental management with implications for economic decision-making: namely that conservation, regeneration and restoration should be resilient. While the term 'resilience' was never explained in the document, it can be assumed that the intention of the state was to undertake restoration projects which would be capable of responding to or adapting to external stressors such as climate change.

Acknowledging directly principle 7 of the Rio Declaration, sustainable development was identified as a complex process requiring 'holistic and integrated approaches … which will … lead to efforts to restore the health and integrity of the Earth's ecosystem'.[112] Restoration activities were also recognised by states as a public works job generator and as essential for the recovery of certain industries such as the fishing industry.[113] While most of *The Future We Want* is drafted in general aspirational language, the section on restoration of fish stocks is specific. Building on the commitments under the Johannesburg Implementation Plan, the Rio+20 outcomes document defines specific action items for states. These include implementing science-based management plans, reducing or suspending fishing catch and effort, better managing by-catch and discards, and effectively using impact assessments.[114]

8. The Sustainable Development Goals

Three years after the conclusion of Rio+20, states through the UN General Assembly adopted the Sustainable Development Goals (SDGs) as a set of goals and targets to continue measuring progress towards internationally shared objectives.[115] The SDGs are not mandatory but reflect instead an expectation for states in cooperation with stakeholders to identify chronic challenges and to devise national strategies to address these challenges. One of the 17 goals and six of the 169 targets explicitly mention restoration. Goal 15 provides that states must 'protect, restore and promote sustainable use of terrestrial ecosystems, sustainably manage forests, combat desertification, and halt and reverse land degradation and halt biodiversity loss'.[116] In order to achieve this goal states agreed to three short-range targets involving restoration as an environmental management strategy:

> 15.1 By 2020, ensure the conservation, restoration and sustainable use of terrestrial and inland freshwater ecosystems and their services, in particular forests, wetlands, mountains and drylands, in line with obligations under international agreements
>
> 15.2 By 2020, promote the implementation of sustainable management of all types of forests, halt deforestation, restore degraded forests and substantially increase afforestation and reforestation globally
>
> 15.3 By 2030, combat desertification, restore degraded land and soil, including land affected by desertification, drought and floods, and strive to achieve a land degradation-neutral world.[117]

Two additional goals included restoration targets. Goal 6 provides that states must ensure availability and sustainable management of water and sanitation for all. Goal 6.6 calls upon states by 2020 to 'protect and restore water-related ecosystems, including mountains, forests, wetlands, rivers, aquifers and lakes'. Finally, goal 14 – on the conservation and sustainable use of the oceans, seas, and marine resources – includes two targets. One is to take action by 2020 for the restoration of coastal and marine areas 'in order to achieve healthy and productive oceans'. The second is to 'restore fish stocks in the shortest time feasible, at least to levels that can produce maximum sustainable yield as determined by their biological characteristics'.[118]

In order to measure achievement towards these goals and targets, states will adopt a set of indicators. While the indicators have not been finalised, the proposed indicators at 2015 suggest potentially recurring challenges of measuring the 'quality' of a restoration versus the 'quantity' of a restoration. For goal 6.6, the target will be the 'percentage of change in wetlands extent over time' that will be collected on the basis of self-reporting in national reports, scientific papers and analysis of remote sensing.[119] This could prove problematic where states such as the United

States identified an increase in wetlands acreage by counting man-made features such as golf course features that were not designed to increase wetland ecosystem functions.[120] For goal 14.2 on restoration of coastal and marine areas, the two proposed indicators are the measurement of the percentage of coastlines that have an integrated coastal management or marine spatial planning program and an 'ocean health index'.[121] It is unclear that having an integrated coastal management plan or a marine spatial planning program will by definition include restoration efforts. Thus, this indicator does not seem to be a useful proxy for measuring progress towards ecological restoration of degraded areas. The 'ocean health index' offers an interesting tool for measuring a variety of ecosystem services based on ten intersecting goals and a shared outcome of healthy oceans.[122] How the ocean health index might be used to evaluate the quality of restoration in a manner that would be useful for improving future restoration efforts is less clear. Finally, the indicators for terrestrial restoration seem to focus primarily on forests.[123] The proposed indicators that might be applied include the forest area as a percentage of the total land area, the forest cover that is under sustainable management, and the area of lands under sustainable management. While all of these indicators may provide some insight into forestry practices, they do not provide a means for distinguishing timber reforestation work from ecological restoration work.

9. The Sendai Framework

In 2015, states negotiated a non-binding but normative framework for disaster risk reduction.[124] The document was intended to continue the progress that had been made under the Hyogo Framework for Action, which encouraged states to develop effective disaster response plans.[125] The word 'restoration' is never mentioned in the text. But the concept of ecological restoration as a strategy for disaster risk reduction is implicitly included in the framework with the frequent references to 'environmental assets' and the need for investing in disaster risk reduction to protect these assets. The authors of the framework recognise that it is 'urgent and critical to anticipate, plan for and reduce disaster risk in order to more effectively protect persons, communities and countries, their livelihoods, health, cultural heritage, socioeconomic assets and ecosystems'.[126] States commit to achieving by 2030 'the substantial reduction of disaster risk and losses in lives, livelihoods and health and in the economic, physical, social, cultural and environmental assets of persons, businesses, communities and countries'.[127] One internationally agreed means of achieving disaster risk reduction is ecological restoration. Nationally funded projects such as mangrove restoration or mountain forest restoration are often regarded as disaster risk reduction projects.[128]

10. Conclusion

The instruments examined in the foregoing paragraphs – when assessed all together – reflect a gradual transition in community thinking about the role of restoration in international law. Although it has been recognised since 1972 that society at large has a role to play in restoration, it has been only since 1992 that ecological restoration at the ecosystem level has become the shared objective. The relationship between conservation and restoration has become clearer over the decades. Restoration as a legitimate but last-resort environmental management strategy to support the broader goals of conservation has emerged as a mainstream concept. The relationship between sustainable development and restoration has been clarified, with restoration playing an increasingly important role in commencing the recovery of socio-ecological systems. However, the soft law targets remain aimed at specific resources or landscapes. This gives the impression that, instead of ecosystems, the international community is concerned with restoration of the services that the natural world can provide. This is most evident in the Sustainable Development Goals. Goal 15.2 refers to restoring 'degraded forests'. While restoration of this kind is valuable, it ignores the broader dimension – namely why ecological restoration itself is valuable and necessary. It presumes that degraded forests when restored will achieve ancillary benefits for the ecosystem where it is located.

OVERALL CONCLUSION

It is evident from this analysis that the international community has yet to provide adequately for goals, objectives and principles that can drive restoration initiatives and obligations through relevant soft law instruments. This review of these instruments suggests that, although the term 'restoration' increasingly features in them, much more needs to be done to inject into them an approach to the recovery of ecosystems through relevant initiatives. Because there have been no disputes requiring the interpretation of restoration in any treaty or soft law instrument, the international community would benefit from refining its understanding of what constitutes 'restoration' for legal purposes if 'restoration' is to be a meaningful concept.

The Sustainable Development Goals of 2015 push the boundaries the furthest by requiring that states implement restoration goals and targets. The goals continue to reflect the spirit of the Stockholm Declaration and focus attention on restoration for the purpose of creating or assisting with the recovery of ecosystem services. More significantly, the restoration obligations aim to achieve a higher level goal or objective – whether to increase the potential of conservation or to protect from desertification. The goals are valuable aspirations. But, if global governance is to be developed more pervasively, restoration has to be an end in itself. This is because of its potential, first, to connect human beings with the natural world and, second, to contribute to the recovery of earth-systems. What is perhaps needed initially is a shift from thinking about restoration as remediation or rehabilitation. The idea of ecological restoration and its commitment to a recovery process that re-establishes the historical trajectory of an ecosystem may provide for this shift in thinking. Environmental governance must, first, contribute to a global cultural shift in the way agreements are conceived and, second, move from simply protecting the natural world to restoring it. This will be important if the approaches of international environmental law and governance are going to achieve their objectives in the Anthropocene.

NOTES

1. Akhtar-Khavari (2010).
2. de Sadeleer (2002).
3. Akhtar-Khavari (2010).
4. Biermann et al. (2015).
5. Allison (2012, ch.1).
6. A variety of scholarship exists on restoration and the law. See Craig and Benson (2013).
7. Marsh (1864).
8. For an example of a work discussing Marsh and his influence on restoration, see Hall (1998).
9. Marsh (1864, p.iii).
10. Hall (1998, 2005).
11. An example is the concept of 'bonifica', which, according to Hall, means 'improvement' and informed Marsh's view on the possibilities and potential of restoration. Hall (1998, pp. 96–7).
12. Hall (2005, p. 7).
13. For an exception, see the Protocol on Conservation and Sustainable Use of Biological Diversity to the Framework Convention on the Protection and the Sustainable Development of the Carpathians.
14. For prominent advocates of this idea, see Jordan III (2012) and Higgs (2003).
15. Allison (2012, p. 22).
16. See http://www.ser.org/ for more information on the work of the SER internationally and in some regions around the world.

17. SER Primer (2004, section 2).
18. Allison (2012, p. 5).
19. SER Primer (2004, section 2, p. 1).
20. IPBES Plenary (2005, p. 1).
21. Ibid.
22. Allison (2012, p. 13) sees 'ecological integrity' as a key element in ecological restoration alongside having to achieve the recovery of the historical trajectory of an ecosystem.
23. On novel ecosystems, see generally Hobbs et al. (2009).
24. Macdonald et al. (2013, ch.23).
25. SER Primer (2004, section 2, p. 1).
26. Rackham (1986).
27. Normander et al. (2008, p. 25).
28. Jordan III (2012, pp. 23–4).
29. Jordan III (2012, p. 23).
30. Gross (2006).
31. Allison (2012, p. 42); Kareiva (2007); and McKinney and Lockwood (1999).
32. Elliot (1982) and Katz (1992).
33. World Resources Institute (2006).
34. Although Hall (2005, p. 7) has argued that one of the interesting assumptions behind Marsh's views on restoration is that 'nature by itself could not adequately repair damage cause by humans'.
35. An example is the project in 2001 in Vietnam whereby mangrove protection measured in the Southern parts of the country were seen as a part of the restoration projects aimed at reducing the impact of natural disasters on human populations. See http://www.wri.org/blog/2016/02/crisis-response-when-trees-stop-storms-and-deserts-asia.
36. Keiter (1998).
37. Biermann et al. (2015).
38. Crutzen (2002).
39. Zalasiewicz et al. (2010).
40. Galaz (2014) and Baskin (2015).
41. Akhtar-Khavari (2015).
42. Bierman et al. (2015) and Zalasiewicz et al. (2010).
43. Galaz (2014).
44. Kareiva et al. (2012).
45. Kotze (2014, pp. 121–56).
46. See http://www.abc.net.au/radionational/programs/scienceshow/urban-areas-threatened-by-megafires-in-early-days-of-climate-ch/6939756.
47. Biermann et al. (2015, p. 6).
48. McConnell et al. (2007) and Biermann et al. (2015, p. 6).
49. Biermann et al. (2015, p. 6) referring to Dube (2013).
50. Allison (2012, p. 10).
51. J.A. Beesly, United Nations Representative of Canada, stated after the adoption of the Stockholm Principles that the principles were 'a first step towards the development of international environmental law': United Nations Doc. A/CONF.48/14 at 115.
52. UNESCO (1968, p. 31, recommendation 17).
53. Caldwell (1984).
54. UNGA 1969c (1969, Resolution 2581 (XXIV)).
55. UNGA 1969b (1969, para.35).
56. Ibid.
57. Stockholm Conference Report First Session (1970, p. 19, para.36).

58. Stockholm Conference Report Second Session (1971, p. 16, para.30).
59. United Nations Doc. (1971), A/CONF.48/WG.1(II)/CRP.2 at 3.
60. United Nations Doc. (1972), A/CONF.48/PC/WG.1(II)/CRP.5 at 3.
61. United Nations Doc. (1972), A/CONF.48/PC/WG.1(II)/CRP.3/Rev.3 at 3.
62. United Nations Doc. A/CONF.48/PC/WG.1(II)/CRP.3/Rev.4 at 3.
63. United Nations Conference on the Human Environment, A/CONF.48/4 Annex Draft Text of a Preamble and Principles of the Declaration of the Human Environment. The same non-controversial language was included in the second Intergovernmental Working Group reports at UN Doc. A/CONF.48/PC/16 (1972).
64. The term 'renewable resources' is not defined in the Declaration. The term 'natural resources' is defined in principle 2 to include 'air, water, land, flora and fauna and especially representative samples of natural ecosystems'.
65. Stockholm Declaration (1972, preamble).
66. Ibid. (preamble, para.1).
67. Ibid. (preamble, para.2).
68. Ibid. (preamble, para.6).
69. Ibid. (preamble, para.2).
70. Ibid. (preamble, para.7).
71. Ibid.
72. Ibid. (preamble, para.6).
73. For more on this organisation see http://www.forestlandscaperestoration.org/.
74. Stockholm Declaration (1972, principle 24).
75. Ibid.
76. Ibid. (principle 25).
77. See the Brief Report of the United Nations Conference on the Human Environment, Stockholm, 5–16 June 1972, A/Conf.48/14/Rev.1, pp. 49–50, available at http://www.un-documents.net/aconf48-14r1.pdf. In the section titled, 'Brief Summary of the General Debate' (para.64) it is noted that speakers at the Stockholm Conference 'often expressed' the view 'that man possessed the skills to foresee and avert ecological misfortunes and to create a much happier and richer world, but that no positive advances could be made without the political will'.
78. United Nations Doc. A/CONF.48/PC/16 (1972, recommendation 15).
79. UNGA 1969b (1969, para.87).
80. World Charter for Nature (art.24).
81. Ibid. (preamble).
82. Ibid. (art.11(e)).
83. Section 89 provides that for land that is derelict or likely to become derelict local authorities may 'carry out, for the purpose of reclaiming or improving that land or of enabling it to be brought into use, such works on that land or any other land as appear to them expedient'.
84. World Charter for Nature (1982, art.11(a), (c) and (e)).
85. Rio Declaration (1992, preamble).
86. General Principles (1991).
87. Mann (1992).
88. The initial text of principle 3 proposed by Japan included a specific reference to 'restoration' as an obligation of intergenerational equity. The text originally read 'Today and in the future, the individual has both a fundamental right to benefit from the common resources of humankind, which constitute the global environment, and at the same time a responsibility to protect, restore and improve for present and future generations': UN Doc. A/CONF.151/PC/WG.III/L.22, principle 4.
89. Convention on Biological Diversity (1992, art.2).
90. Rio Declaration (1992, preamble). The Conference agreed to 'Recognizing the integral and interdependent nature of the Earth, our home'.

91. See e.g. Statement by China on Behalf of Brazil, India, South Africa and China at the Opening Plenary of the Durban Platform, Warsaw Poland (12 November 2013): 'The process and outcome of the Durban Platform [to develop a new climate protocol] shall be under the [Climate Change] Convention and guided by its principles and provisions, in particular the principles of equity and common but differentiated responsibilities and respective capabilities'; http://unfccc.int/files/documentation/submissions_from_parties/adp/application/pdf/adp2.3_basic_20131112.pdf.
92. Since the negotiation of the UN Convention on the Law of the Sea in 1982, there still remain areas of the high seas that lack basic conservation and management measures. A paradigm shift may be beginning as individual countries recognise the need for greater external technical or financial involvement in conservation or restoration efforts and join multi-stakeholder conservation and restoration projects. Cf. Global Partnership on Forest Landscape Restoration (launched in 2003 by United Nations Environment Program) and the Global Partnership for Oceans (launched in 2012 by the World Bank).
93. Wirth (1995).
94. Agenda 21 (1992, ch.1, para.1.3).
95. Ibid. (ch.11(B)).
96. US Forest Service: the program described one of the goals of the landscape restoration to be managing woods for local community economic development and to reduce wildfire management costs.
97. Agenda 21(1992, ch.12(B).
98. Ibid. (ch.12, para.12.18).
99. Ibid. (ch.12, para.12.23(b)).
100. Ibid. (ch.17, para.17.46(b) and para.17.74(c)).
101. Ibid. (ch.15.5(h)).
102. Convention on Biological Diversity (1992, art. 8).
103. Agenda 21 (ch.17, para.17.6).
104. Ibid. (para.17.6(h)).
105. Ibid. (ch.35, para.35.12(e)).
106. Johannesburg Plan (2002).
107. Ibid. (para.31(a)).
108. Ibid. (para.26(c)).
109. Ibid. (para.37(d)).
110. This meeting was convened as the United Nations Conference on Sustainable Development.
111. *The Future We Want* (2012, para.4).
112. Ibid. (para.40).
113. Ibid. (paras 154 and 158).
114. Ibid. (para.168).
115. Sustainable Development Goals (2015).
116. Ibid.
117. Ibid.
118. Ibid. (targets 14.2 and 14.4).
119. Indicator Proposals List (2015).
120. Dahl (2011), noting that between 2004 and 2009 freshwater ponds increased by over 200,000 acres but that 'the functional characteristic of these water bodies continues to be debated': Barringer (2006).
121. Indicator Proposals List (2015).
122. See generally http://data.oceanhealthindex.org/anatomy-of-score: identifying the ten goals of the index as measuring improvements in food provision, artisanal fishing,

natural products, carbon storage, coastal protection, livelihood economics, recreation, sense of place, clean waters, and biodiversity – habitats and species.
123. Indicator Proposals List (2015).
124. Sendai Framework (2015).
125. Hyogo Framework (2005).
126. Sendai Framework (2015, para.5).
127. Ibid. (para.16).
128. Philippines Project: describing a program of reforestation designed for both economic benefits and reduction of disaster risks.

REFERENCES

Akhtar-Khavari, A. (2010), *Global Governance of the Environment: Environmental Principles and Change in International Law and Politics* (Cheltenham, Edward Elgar).

Akhtar-Khavari, A. (2015), 'Accessing Ecological Justice in the Anthropocene Epoch!' in P. Keyzer, V. Popovski and C. Sampford (eds), *Access to International Justice* (London, Routledge).

Allison, S. (2012), *Ecological Restoration and Environmental Change. Renewing Damaged Ecosystems* (London, Routledge).

Barringer, Felicity (2006), 'Fewer Marshes + More Man-Made Ponds = Increased Wetlands', *New York Times* (31 March 2006); http://www.nytimes.com/2006/03/31/washington/31wetlands.html?_r=0.

Baskin, J. (2015), 'Paradigm dressed as Epoch: the ideology of the Anthropocene', *Environmental Values* 24, 9–29.

Biermann, Frank, Xuemei Bai, Ninad Bondre, Wendy Broadgate, Chen-Tung Arthur Chen, Opha Pauline Dube, Jan Willem Erisman, Marion Glaser, Sandra van der Hel, Maria Carmen Lemos, Sybil Steitzinger and Karen C. Seto (2015), 'Down to Earth: Contextualizing The Anthropocene Epoch', *Global Environmental Change*; http://dx.doi.org/10/1016/j.gloenvcha/2015.11.004.

Caldwell, L. (1984), *International Environmental Policy: Emergence and Dimensions* (Durham, Duke University Press).

Cowell, C.M. (1993), 'Ecological Restoration and Environmental Ethics', *Environmental Ethics* Spring 15, 19–32.

Craig, R. and M. Benson (2013), 'Replacing Sustainability', *Akron Law Review* 46, 841.

Crutzen, P.J. (2002), 'Geology of mankind' (2002) *Nature* 415, 23.

de Sadeleer, N. (2002), *Environmental Principles: from Political Slogans to Legal Rules* (Oxford, Oxford University Press).

Dahl, T.E. (2011), *Status and Trends of Wetlands in the Conterminous United States 2004 to 2009*, Report to Congress, Department of Interior, US Fish and Wildlife Service 42.

Dube, O.P. (2013), 'Challenges of wildland fire management in Botswana; towards a community inclusive fire management approach', *Weather Climate Extremes* 1, 26–41.

Elliot, R. (1982), 'Faking Nature', *Inquiry* 25, 81–93.

Galaz, V. (2014), *Global Environmental Governance, Technology, and Politics: The Anthropocene Gap* (Cheltenham, Edward Elgar).

Gross, M. (2006), 'Beyond expertise: ecological science and the making of socially robust restoration strategies', *Journal for Nature Conservation* 14, 172–9.

Hall, M. (1998), 'Restoring the Countryside: George Perkins Marsh and the Italian Land Ethic' (1861–1882) *Environment and History* 4(1), 91–103.

Hall, M. (2005), *Earth Repair: A Transatlantic History of Environmental Restoration* (Charlottesville, University of Virginia Press).

Higgs, E. (2003), *Nature by Design: People, Natural Process, and Ecological Restoration* (Cambridge, Massachusetts Institute of Technology).
Hobbs, Richard J., Eric Higgs and James A. Harris (2009), 'Novel ecosystems; implications for conservation and restoration', *Trends in Ecology and Evolution* 24(11), 599–605.
Jordan III, William R. (2012), *The Sunflower Forest: Ecological Restoration and the New Communion with Nature* (Berkeley, University of California Press).
Kareiva, P. (2007), 'Domesticated nature: shaping landscapes and ecosystems for human welfare', *Science* 316, 1866–9.
Kareiva, P., M. Marvier and R. Lalasz (2012), 'Conservation in the Anthropocene: Beyond Solitude and Fragility', *The Breakthrough*; http://thebreakthrough.org/index.php/journal/past-issues/issue-2/conservation-in-the-anthropocene.
Katz, E. (1992), 'The big lie: human restoration of nature', *Research in Philosophy and Technology* 12, 231–41.
Keiter, R. (1998), 'Ecosystems and the Law: Toward an Integrated Approach', *Ecological Applications* 8(2), 332–41.
Kotze, L. (2014), 'Rethinking Global Environmental Law and Governance in the Anthropocene', *Journal of Energy and Natural Resources Law* 32(2), 121–56.
Macdonald, David and Katherine Willis (2013), 'Rewilding' in David Macdonald and Katherine Willis, *Key Topics in Conservation Biology 2* (Wiley-Blackwell), Chapter 23.
Mann, H. (1992), 'The Rio Declaration', *Proc. American Society of International Law* 86, 405–11.
Marsh, G.P. (1864), *Man and Nature* (New York, Scribner).
McConnell, Joseph R., Ross Edwards, Gregory L. Kok, Mark G. Flanner, Charles S. Zender, Eric S. Saltzman, J. Ryan Banta, Daniel R. Pasteris, Megan M. Carter and Jonathan D.W. Kahl (2007), '20th–century industrial black carbon emissions altered Arctic climate forcing', *Science* 17, 1381–4.
McKinney M.L. and J.L. Lockwood (1999), 'Biotic homogenization: a few winners replacing many losers in the next mass extinction', *Trends in Ecology and Evolution* 14, 450–53.
Normander, Bo, Gregor Levin, Ari-Pekka Auvinen, Harald Bratli, Odd Stabbetorp, Marcus Hedblom, Anders Glimskär and Gudmundur A. Gudmundsson (2008), *State of biodiversity in the Nordic countries* (Copenhagen, Norde Press).
Oxford English Dictionary (1971) (Oxford, Oxford University Press).
Rackham, O. (1986), *The History of the Countryside* (London, Phoenix).
Wirth, D. (1995), 'The Rio Declaration on Environment and Development: Two Steps Forward and One Back, or Vice Versa', *Georgia Law Review* 29, 599–653.
Zalasiewicz, J., M. Williams, W. Steffen and P. Crutzen (2010), 'The New World of the Anthropocene', *Environmental Science and Technology* 44, 2228–31.

INSTRUMENTS

Agenda 21: United Nations Agenda 21 (1992): Chapter 1, para.1.3; https://sustainabledevelopment.un.org/content/documents/Agenda21.pdf.
Convention on Biological Diversity1992: 5 June 1992, 1760 UNTS 79.
General Principles: Principles on General Rights and Obligations: Chairman's Consolidated Draft, UN Doc. A/CONF.151/PC/WG.III/L.8/Rev.1 (30 August 1991).
Hyogo Framework for Action, UN Doc. A/CONF.206/6 (22 January 2005).
Indicator Proposals List: Working Draft for List of Indicator Proposals for Sustainable Development Goals (August 2015); https://sustainabledevelopment.un.org/content/documents/7981List%20of%20Indicator%20Proposals%2011-8-2015.pdf.

IPBES Plenary: Plenary of the Intergovernmental Science-Policy Platform on Biodiversity and Ecosystem Services, 3/7 (12–17 January); http://esa.org/ipbes/wp-content/uploads/2015/02/landdegscoping.pdf.
Johannesburg Plan 2002: United Nations Doc. A/CONF.199/20 (2002).
National Parks and Access to the Country Act; http://www.legislation.gov.uk/ukpga/Geo6/12-13-14/97.
Philippines Project: Philippines Department of Environment and Natural Resources, Philippines National Greening Program; http://ngp.denr.gov.ph.
Protocol on Conservation and Sustainable Use of Biological Diversity to the Framework Convention on the Protection and the Sustainable Development of the Carpathians; http://www.carpathianconvention.org/tl_files/carpathiancon/Downloads/01%20The%20Convention/1.1.2.1%20BiodiversityProtocolFinalsigned.pdf.
Rio Declaration 1992: Declaration of the United Nations Conference on Environment and Development, UN Doc. A/CONF.151/26 (Vol.1) (13 June 1992), reprinted in 31 ILM 874 (1992).
Sendai Framework: Sendai Framework for Disaster Risk Reduction 2015–2030, UN Doc. A/CONF.224/L.2 (7 April 2015).
SER Primer: Society for Ecological Restoration, Science and Policy Working Group, SER International Primer on Ecological Restoration (Version 2, October, 2004); http://www.ser.org/resources/resources-detail-view/ser-international-primer-on-ecological-restoration.
Stockholm Conference Report First Session: Report of the Preparatory Committee for the United Nations Conference on the Human Environment, First Session, UN Doc. A.CONF.48/PC/6 (10–20 March 1970).
Stockholm Conference Report Second Session: Report of the Preparatory Committee for the United Nations Conference on the Human Environment, Second Session, UN Doc. A/CONF.48/PC/9 (8–19 February 1971).
Stockholm Declaration 1972: Declaration of the United Nations Conference on the Human Environment, UN Doc. A/CONF.48/14/Rev.1 at 3 (1973), reprinted in 11 ILM 1416 (5–16 June 1972).
Sustainable Development Goals: General Assembly of the United Nations, Transforming our world: the 2030 Agenda for Sustainable Development (2015) A/RES/70/1.
The Future We Want (2012, para.4); http://www.uncsd2012.org/content/documents/727The%20Future%20We%20Want%2019%20June%201230pm.pdf.
UNESCO: Intergovernmental Conference of Experts on the Scientific Basis for Rational Use and Conservation of the Resources of the Biosphere (1968); http://unesdoc.unesco.org/images/0001/000172/017269eb.pdf.
UNGA 1969a: United Nations General Assembly, A-C.2-SR.1276 (November 1969).
UNGA 1969b: United Nations General Assembly, A/PV.1834 (December 1969).
UNGA 1969c: United Nations General Assembly Resolution 2581 (XXIV) (1969).
United Nations Convention on the Law of the Sea 1982, (1982) ILM 33, 1261–354.
US Forest Service: United States Forest Service Collaborative Forest Landscape Restoration Program Overview; http://www.fs.fed.us/restoration/CFLRP/overview.shtml.
World Charter for Nature 1982: United Nations General Assembly, A/RES/37/7 (28 October 1982).
World Resources Institute; http://www.wri.org/blog/2016/02/crisis-response-when-trees-stop-storms-and-deserts-asia.

4. Transnational environmental law: the birth of a contemporary analytical perspective

Louis Kotzé and Caiphas Soyapi

INTRODUCTION

Environmental law is now a fully recognised and autonomous specialised field of law. It can broadly be considered to include the collection of all legal norms that aim to govern the human-environment interface. Domestic environmental law norms have developed in tandem with, and to a large extent predicated on, the body of environmental law norms that have gradually been developing in the international regulatory arena. Like its domestic counterpart, international environmental law (IEL) has come of age, at least since the Stockholm Conference on the Human Environment in 1972.[1] While much of the analytical focus of scholars has principally revolved around these two bodies of law, a new paradigm of analysis is evolving. It seeks environmental norms in transnational spaces within and beyond the axiomatic confines of domestic environmental law and IEL. This analytical approach focuses on the emergence of transnational environmental law (TEL). TEL is steadily becoming a burgeoning field of analytical inquiry but not yet a fully autonomous taxonomically independent body of law.[2]

TEL is defined to include the current body of pure juridical and non-legal but law-like norms. These norms are situated at various geographical levels ranging from the local to the international sphere. They are created by state and non-state actors in regulatory spaces within and beyond states. They aim to respond to complex and interconnected global environmental problems. The scope of TEL encompasses considerably more than either domestic environmental law or IEL; it transcends geographical and functional boundaries; and it includes a multifarious range of norms that are created and enforced by multiple actors. Notwithstanding these factors, TEL arguably remains an analytical approach or perspective that seeks to situate and to understand environmental law in contemporary global terms. While it may do so in the future, TEL has not yet developed taxonomically into a fully autonomous body of environmental law:

> [TEL] does not conjure into existence a new, previously unknown layer of jurisdiction that is untrammelled by either the geographical limitations of national/regional law or the legitimacy and authority deficits of international/global law. Nor does it gather and reconfigure legal principles and practices around a new substantive theme, as is currently happening in the field of climate change law. It does, however, offer a powerful new mode of understanding and engaging with environmental law. More than a domain, the concept of transnational environmental law embodies an approach to legal studies and practice.[3]

Fisher[4] has argued for a more rigorous understanding of TEL. This chapter addresses this challenge. Accordingly, it seeks to elaborate upon and to unpack the notion of TEL and to understand the steady emergence of TEL as the latest analytical approach focused on those legal norms that govern the human-environment interface in the global sphere. It does so in accordance with this structure:

- by reflecting on the various considerations that are driving the emergence of TEL including globalisation; the shift of focus from 'government to governance'; the issue of fragmentation of IEL and governance; and the 'radical' idea of the Anthropocene and the increasingly urgent need for enhanced global environmental governance that its imagery calls for
- by reviewing the conceptual state of the art by briefly investigating several descriptions of TEL
- by identifying and discussing the various processes of transnationalism that are creating TEL
- by applying the TEL framework to the global environmental rights sphere in an attempt to illustrate practically how, and the extent to which, TEL is emerging as a contemporary analytical approach in this specific domain.

THE TRANSNATIONALISATION OF ENVIRONMENTAL LAW

1. Introduction

A unique characteristic of law is its ability to respond to continuously changing socio-economic, environmental, cultural and political circumstances and regulatory realities. The following paragraphs reflect on some of the circumstances and regulatory realties that are driving the emergence of TEL.

2. Globalisation

The most evident consideration related to the rise of TEL is globalisation. This is essentially a process describing the intensification of global interdependence and, as a result, a concomitant increase in vulnerability to regulatory challenges that global governance actors, notably states, are experiencing. It can be understood to mean the exponential increase in the flow of people, capital, goods, services and ideas across the globe. Thus globalisation increases the number, reach and intensity of global institutions, including the law, that regulate these phenomena, while expanded legal and institutional arrangements, such as those apparent in trade law, conversely support and further extend the processes of globalisation.[5]

In these ways globalisation is a reciprocal and mutually re-enforcing process of regulatory growth that feeds upon itself and involves the collection of global norms that are evolving to address regulatory challenges beyond the reach of states.[6] While globalisation requires the adoption of a global regulatory focus, the effects of globalisation on traditional socio-legal and other systems of order have been and continue to be immense. This is because globalisation and its processes and consequences are not only putting the state and its domestic regulatory mechanisms under strain but also compelling states to cooperate globally and to provide for innovative normative arrangements and governance institutions in spaces beyond the state.[7]

Globalisation is essentially challenging age-old truths about the state, law and governance, visions of global order and anarchy, and ways to co-exist sustainably and peacefully. It has been suggested in this context that:

> globalization produces a serious challenge to conventional premises: the axiomatic notion of the nation-state as the cornerstone of the territorial sovereignty of the almost 200 states of the world as it developed over centuries, is rapidly losing definition; the state's perceived dominance as provider of the framework within which law is made, administered, adjudicated and enforced is increasingly being challenged; the potential for integration of legal norms across conventional national and international jurisdictions, is growing exponentially.[8]

In addition, globalisation is questioning the continued prevalence of geographically defined territorial dictates as a crucial consideration in the design and focus of environmental law and governance. Moreover it 'appears indeed characterized by a shift from territorial borders to functional boundaries'.[9] The world, current social reality, and current perceptions of reality are evidently changing. Lawyers especially require 'a fresh vocabulary, and expanded set of concepts, [and] alternative ways of framing the challenge [to govern and maintain order]'.[10] TEL is seen as one of the 'fresh' and 'expanded' ways of framing and responding to prevailing global challenges.

Climate change is a typical example of a global environmental problem that arises as a result of increased globalised human activities. In particular, it strains the regulatory machinery of a state to the extent that climate change cannot be governed only by a single state and its legal and governance order. It is an interconnected global problem that demands a collective global normative response by many states and a diverse range of non-state actors at multiple geographically and functionally defined governance levels.[11] This is clearly demonstrated by the current global climate law regime. It consists of multilateral environmental agreements such as the United Nations Framework Convention on Climate Change of 1992, its Kyoto Protocol of 1997, the more recent Paris Climate Agreement of 2015, the domestic climate laws of states,[12] regional climate norms and policies such as those of the European Union,[13] and non-state climate initiatives.[14] Keohane and Victor properly capture the disaggregated nature of the global climate regime through the term 'regime complex for climate change' which they describe as follows:

> When states invest resources in building regulatory regimes, the outcomes can vary along a continuum. At one extreme are fully integrated institutions that impose regulation through comprehensive, hierarchical rules. At the other extreme are highly fragmented collections of institutions with no identifiable core and weak or nonexistent linkages between regime elements. In between is a wide range that includes nested (semi-hierarchical) regimes with identifiable cores and non-hierarchical but loosely coupled systems of institutions. What we are calling 'regime complexes' are arrangements of the loosely coupled variety located somewhere in the middle of this continuum. Regime complexes are marked by connections between the specific and relatively narrow regimes but the absence of an overall architecture or hierarchy that structures the whole set.[15]

TEL is primarily concerned with the issue of 'regime complex'. Thus it focuses on the multitude of state and non-state actors, the various formal and informal institutions they create to govern this challenge, and the multiple state and non-state rules they produce to address environmental problems.

3. From 'Government to Governance'

Globalisation and the birth of the concept 'governance' go hand in hand. The state's historically central – even almost exclusive – role in regulation and its ability to perform many of its traditional regulatory functions are being significantly altered as a result of the steady emergence of new modes of regulation. These involve 'processes through which collective goals are defined and pursued in which the state (or government) is not necessarily the only or most important actor'.[16] The dwindling central importance of government as the only actor responsible for regulation is well documented.[17] It is now generally accepted that the regulatory landscape is shifting its focus from the overbearingly important role of a centralised, top-down government to more disaggregated, non-centralised and hierarchical regulatory forms of governance in which multiple state and non-state actors are involved.

This shift from 'government to governance' is being caused by the forces of globalisation. These include:

- significant advances in communication technology and social media that are connecting the world
- modes of travel that enable global connectivity
- systems of free trade
- the creation of regional and international superstructures of governance such as the European Union
- the rise of epistemic networks and non-governmental organisations as well as non-state, but law-like, rules
- the emergence of treaty regimes and international norm-producing, functional, non-state organisations such as the World Bank that enable inter-state cooperation around specific concerns
- the steady growth of economically dominant and politically influential multinational corporations that function in an intermeshed transnational setting
- the emergence of global regulatory problems such as climate change that require multi-stakeholder solutions and that are affecting everyone everywhere with scant regard for physical borders or for the sanctity of state sovereignty.

As a result of these impulses, the strict separation between public and private forms of regulation is increasingly blurred, while forms of public and private ordering overlap and become interchangeable.[18] 'Governance' is subsequently providing a new regulatory mind-set in the sense that it is more 'open' or flexible. This is because it takes up novel forms of permeability of the state that involve less formal bureaucratic government arrangements while relying on informal avenues for norm creation and enforcement. The governance mind-set also provides greater linkages between actors from different institutional levels. It involves a shift of power from orthodox and traditionally well-established actors situated at clearly defined hierarchical levels to organisations or individuals who now must link and coordinate different stakeholders in a non-hierarchical setting. The governance mind-set moves away from hierarchy towards more unstructured consultation, negotiation and 'softer' normative regulatory arrangements such as the Equator Principles.[19] While these new governance processes are not necessarily entirely unstructured, chaotic and non-hierarchical, they are conducive to facilitating more adaptive, responsive, productive, multi-actor and decentralised forms of regulation that do not exclusively depend on the state for their legitimacy and effectiveness.[20] These new governance arrangements assume increasingly autonomous forms of social orderings that constitute their own cognitive spaces in the regulatory arena.[21] The rise in particular of non-state entities in the governance realm is opening up hitherto prohibitive closures in government-dominant epistemologies to alternative understandings of regulation. In this way the state has a less pronounced role in promoting social welfare and non-state actors have the potential to assert themselves gradually as co-governors, in varying degrees, alongside the state. TEL essentially aims to respond to these developments and to provide alternative understandings of regulation.

4. Fragmentation

A third consideration that is contributing to the emergence of TEL is the fragmentation of IEL.[22] In short, international law is considered to be fragmented as a result of a highly decentralised process of normative and institutional development that responds to specific global problems; often through clustered regimes. These regimes exist in silos as they are centred on separate functional areas such as environment, trade, human rights and humanitarian law. In most instances these functional areas are themselves highly fragmented. IEL, with its separate tracks of climate law and governance, global biodiversity law and governance, and global oceans law and governance, clearly illustrates this functional fragmentation. Various governance institutions such as treaty secretariats – for example, the United Nations Framework Convention on Climate Change Secretariat – and international institutions such as the United Nations Environment Programme (UNEP) have been created to enforce the fragmented but burgeoning body of global normative arrangements that must address numerous global environmental problems.[23]

As Biermann has illustratively indicated:

> Since 1972, when UNEP was set up, the increase in international environmental regimes has led to ... considerable fragmentation of the entire system. Norms and standards in each area of environmental governance are created by distinct legislative bodies – the conferences of the parties to various conventions – with little respect for repercussions and links with other fields. While the decentralized negotiation of rules and standards in separate functional bodies may be defensible, this is less so regarding the organisational fragmentation of the various convention secretariats, which have evolved into quite independent bureaucracies with strong centrifugal tendencies.[24]

Collectively, in tandem with globalisation and the 'governance shift', fragmentation contributes to a continuously evolving and growing body of environmental law and governance rules and institutions that aim to address an entire range of global environmental problems. The end result is the steady growth of a highly complex, diversified and multifarious architecture of global environmental law norms, institutions and governance actors that could conveniently be situated under the umbrella of TEL.

5. The Anthropocene and Enhanced Regulation for Global Problems

Today, humanity is confronted by events that, according to various scientific accounts, are set to affect the continuation of life on Earth.[25] The climate is changing; biodiversity is being lost at alarming rates; inter-species and intra-species injustices are intensifying; and a host of ecological cycles are being flung into such disarray that the possibility for recovery seems remote. Similar events of ecological upheaval occurred during earlier stages in Earth's geological history. But there is one significant difference: the current socio-ecological crisis is being caused not by volcanoes or meteors but by humans. It is in this context that scientists have recently suggested that the Earth system might have entered a new geological epoch called the Anthropocene. The Anthropocene was first introduced in a 2000 publication by Paul Crutzen and

Eugene Stoermer as a term of art expressing the geological significance of anthropogenic change.[26] By emphasising the central role of mankind as a major driving force in modifying the biosphere, the term 'Anthropocene' suggests that the Earth is rapidly moving into a critically unstable state. Earth systems are gradually becoming less predictable, non-stationary and less harmonious as a result of the global human imprint on the biosphere.[27]

Globalisation and its impacts exacerbate the type and severity of socio-ecological conditions arising in the Anthropocene as a result of amplified human activity globally. These conditions increasingly impact upon an interconnected Earth system. The Anthropocene and its imagery, supported by evidence of its emergence today, serve as evidence that traditional modes of domestic environmental law and IEL have been unable either to preserve relatively stable Holocene conditions or to prevent human-induced Anthropocene events from affecting Earth system integrity. The deepening socio-ecological crisis requires a radical alternative to the business-as-usual approaches to environmental law and to the way these juridical interventions are perceived. For lawyers and juridical scientists, an alternative mindset is only possible if there is an opening-up of epistemological closures that currently prevent them from thinking differently about environmental law. A possible alternative regulatory mindset, such as TEL, must be directed at two outcomes: to think creatively about the potential of more contemporary juridical constructions to respond better to Anthropocene exigencies; and to counter human domination, create order, and strive for better regulatory outcomes in this new geological epoch.

But the link between the Anthropocene and its potential implications for TEL do not stop there. Part of the imagery that the Anthropocene offers requires an expanded spatial cognition of these factors:

- what the Earth and its systems are
- global Earth system transformations
- how Earth systems are connected globally
- how an increasingly integrated global human society is related to and dependent on the Earth system
- how such a human society impacts upon the Earth system.

The Anthropocene demands not only localised regulatory but also truly global interventions which transcend borders and which are sensitive to cause-and-effect relationships in the Earth system.

While the global imagery of the Anthropocene should not be generalised by implying that the same socio-ecological conditions occur and are experienced by everyone everywhere in exactly the same way,[28] the arrival of the Anthropocene arguably requires a novel way of thinking about law, politics and social ordering in planetary terms. As Dalby has suggested:

> Discussions of the Anthropocene necessarily require thinking at the scale of the biosphere and over the long term. This is a planetary issue, matters at the large scale require some consideration of ethical connection and, perhaps, the implicit invocation of a single polity, however inchoate.[29]

One way to think about environmental law revolving around a single global polity in planetary terms is through the lens of Earth system science and, more specifically, through the lens of Earth system governance. Recognising the connectivity, nonlinearity and complexity of socio-ecological processes, Earth system science is concerned with the 'study of the Earth's environment as an integrated system in order to understand how and why it is changing, and to explore the implications of these changes for global and regional sustainability'.[30] Fundamentally rooted in Earth system science, Earth system governance has been developed as a reactive counter-narrative to localised, state-based and narrowly focused regulatory approaches to environmental issues. These narrow approaches involve the trite application of an issue-specific environmental governance regime that focuses – among others – on pollution control, nature conservation and wildlife and that predominantly employs formal, state-based law and state institutions.

What is contemplated through Earth system governance is a more open, holistic, flexible, multi-scalar and multi-actor regulatory approach. Such an approach would be designed to capture and address, first, the many complex global developments that transform the bio-geophysical cycles and processes of Earth; second, the complex relations between global transformations of social and natural systems; and, third, the multi-scale consequences of ecological transformation. Such a system of Earth system governance has been defined as:

> The interrelated and increasingly integrated system of formal and informal rules, rule-making systems and actor networks at all levels of human society (from local to global) that are set up to steer societies towards preventing, mitigating and adapting to global and local environmental change and, in particular, earth system transformation.[31]

Earth system governance clearly is not only concerned with ways to influence and direct the Earth system (the governance of aspects of technological innovations that are able to change the Earth system might resort under its ambit): '[E]arth System governance is [also] about the human impact on planetary systems. It is about the societal steering of human activities with regard to the longterm stability of geobiophysical systems'.[32] Because law is particularly adept at steering human behaviour, it is a crucial aspect of Earth system governance. Any Earth system governance-based regulatory responses, including its juridical elements, must involve a range of functions:

- respond to persistent Earth system uncertainty
- nurture new responsibilities and modes of co-operation as a result of intergenerational and intragenerational, spatial and socio-ecological interdependence between people, countries, species and generations
- respond to the functional interdependence of the Earth system and Earth system transformations
- respond to the needs of an increasingly integrated globalised society
- respond to extraordinary degrees of socio-ecological harm.[33]

Because domestic environmental law and IEL on their own will be unable to respond to such complexity and because it takes a more holistic view of law and governance and of the regulatory problem it seeks to address, TEL arguably is a more likely and potentially useful approach to global environmental governance in the Anthropocene.

THE CONCEPTUAL STATE OF THE ART

As an 'emergent system',[34] TEL is no longer only an abstract idea but also a fast-developing analytical perspective on environmental law that increasingly demands the attention of scholars. There are various descriptions of this concept, although a generally accepted definition remains elusive. Reasons for this might be attributed to disagreements on what 'transnationality' means; what the parameters of 'environmental' concern could entail; and what 'law' could mean in the context of TEL. As Lin and Scott state, 'the language of the "transnational" is useful and appropriate, perhaps in part because its meaning is contested and its boundaries unclear'.[35] How, then, do scholars understand TEL?

Wiener[36] sees TEL – also referred to interchangeably as 'global environmental law' – as 'a marriage of international and national environmental law; something old, something new, something borrowed for something blue'. Yang and Percival[37] define global environmental law as an emergent system which comprises:

> the set of legal principles developed by national, international, and transnational environmental regulatory systems to protect the environment and manage natural resources. As a body of law, it is made up of a distinct set of substantive principles and procedural methods that are specifically important or unique to governance of the environment across the world. It includes: (1) public international environmental law … (2) national environmental law … and (3) transnational law, which describes the set of legal principles used to regulate the cross-border relationships between private individuals and organizations.

In terms of the latter description, one of the ways through which environmental law has become transnational is through the internationalisation of environmental law. The internationalisation of environmental law involves not only the actual creation of IEL but also the interactive political and diplomatic process through which state and non-state actors engage to create these laws.[38] Presumably, these processes present rich opportunities for cross-fertilisation that has the potential to influence the creation of some common global legal rules. These rules could at least be based on the same ideas and influences, if not on exactly the same content.

However, the internationalisation of environmental law is only part of a much larger project of the transnationalisation of environmental law. The *nationalisation* of IEL, the inter-jurisdictional transplantation of laws or the *inter*-nationalisation of laws, the regionalisation of national environmental laws and the nationalisation of regional environmental laws also play a part in environmental law becoming transnational. Transnationalisation in this context could thus be explained as the 'legal regulation of the full gamut of economic, cultural, social, and, in this context, environmental interaction between and across nations'.[39]

TEL could also be understood in terms of the geography of environmental law; an approach that corresponds with the idea that environmental law should respond to Earth system science and governance in the Anthropocene (see the discussion above). Kysar explains that 'law contains its own geography':

> the geography implicit in law will over time come to resemble that of the earth sciences. As the category of environmental pathways acknowledged by law expands and diversifies, and as the operations of those pathways come to be seen as hemispheric or global in scale rather than national or regional, then eventually, the claims of deep interconnection so prominent in environmental

> science, and so urgently pressed in environmental politics, also will find concrete expression in environmental law.[40]

Arguments for an expanded geography of law to fit more closely the expansive reach and interconnected global nature of the Earth system resonate particularly well with the concept of Earth system governance. Through the lens of Earth system governance, TEL has a more expansive geography and it has the potential to expand even further its geography to resemble more closely that of the Earth system.

More recently Shaffer and Bodansky[41] have explained that TEL is much broader than international environmental law and that it subsumes the latter legal sub-discipline. In their view, TEL most usually involves inter-state cooperation in a transboundary setting. Moreover it relates to the 'migration and impact of legal norms, rules and models across borders … [and] … encompasses all environmental law norms that apply to transboundary activities or that have effects in more than one jurisdiction'.[42] While their focus is on transboundary issues, they seem to imply that transnationalism involves trans-jurisdictionality: a possibility which is reinforced by their reliance on the idea of cross-nationality as used by Holzinger, Knill and Sommerer to study the cross-national convergence of environmental policies.[43]

As a result of the foregoing analysis of these descriptions of TEL, environmental law is becoming transnational horizontally – between the different national, regional and international levels – and transnational vertically – ranging between nations inter se and between regions inter se. It is becoming transnational in terms of its sources of authority to the extent that it is both private and public due to the numerous state and non-state actors involved. Finally, it is becoming transnational with respect to the expanded geography of law when juxtaposed to the interconnected Earth system to which it applies.

SOME PROCESSES OF TEL

1. Introduction

It is possible to identify a range of processes that contribute to the steady growth of TEL norms, and, more importantly for present purposes, to TEL's analytical agenda. Five of these processes justify a detailed analysis.

2. Transplantation

History is filled with evidence of the interaction of legal systems.[44] Legal developments in one country can serve as the basis upon which other countries develop their own legal systems through a process of borrowing or transplantation of laws from one country to another. This process of transplantation can happen in diverse ways. For instance, countries with less developed legal systems might import good practice rules or principles into their own legal systems.[45] Alternatively, scholars from one jurisdiction are exposed to other legal systems through research and other scholarly work and this interaction might result in knowledge transfer. Similarly, transplantation can occur when actors situated at the supranational level borrow from actors at the national level or when actors at the national level borrow from those situated at supranational levels. This is a form of vertical transplantation – also described as trans-echelon borrowing.[46]

Fisher explains that this form of legal transplantation in TEL involves processes of uploading and downloading. For instance, there are some elements of national environmental laws that have been uploaded into IEL and there are international legal norms that have been downloaded into national and regional systems.[47] One example is that of the development and implementation of environmental impact assessment which originated in the United States. Environmental impact assessment is now widely accepted and operational beyond the United States from where it evolved.[48] This includes its incorporation in IEL. Thus, environmental laws around the globe could become 'similar' because of copying or cross-pollination by one state of another's legal system, notably to the extent that these are shaped by regional and international law. Interestingly, Shaffer and Bodansky prefer the term 'mimicry'.[49]

3. Convergence

Convergence is a process whereby environmental laws of some states develop similarly not because of deliberate acts of transplantation or borrowing but as a result of similar external pressures and common functional demands to which these laws must respond.[50] It could involve the growth of expert networks and the spread of a type of 'universal' world culture.[51] Ultimately, convergence is an elaborate process that results in the increased similarity of policies in a certain field across a set of jurisdictions over a period of time in reaction to global regulatory problems such as climate change.[52] Processes of convergence will normally be driven by states but non-state actor initiatives might also play a part. The process of convergence allows a more harmonious global regulatory framework to be created when the self-interests of a state are aligned with those of other states or other global governance actors.[53] In other words, if there is a convergence of interests, a transnational emergence of norms and principles might occur along the lines of those interests.

An example of convergence is the Strategic Approach to International Chemicals Management (SAICM) that is partly being driven by UNEP. One of the objectives of SAICM is to respond to several regulatory challenges in the international chemicals governance regime. The challenges include these:

- the international law and policy framework for chemicals is fragmented and inadequate and needs to be further strengthened
- implementation of international laws and policies is uneven
- coherence and synergies between existing institutions and processes are not fully developed and should be improved
- several countries lack the capacity to govern chemicals adequately at the national, sub-regional, regional and global levels.[54]

The foregoing are problems shared by states and they result in various functional demands and regulatory challenges faced by them.

This initiative – SAICM – does not aim to create one multilateral environmental agreement with a single governing body that should be responsible for global chemical governance. What it does aim to do, in a bottom-up way, is to facilitate greater synergies between the normative and institutional machinery processes of a number of international arrangements such as:

- the Montreal Protocol on Substances that Deplete the Ozone Layer 1987
- the Basel Convention on the Control of Transboundary Movement of Hazardous Wastes and their Disposal 1989
- the Rotterdam Convention on the Prior Informed Consent Procedure for Certain Hazardous Chemicals and Pesticides in International Trade 1998
- the Stockholm Convention on Persistent Organic Pollutants 2001
- the International Labour Organization's Convention No.170, 1990, concerning safety in the use of chemicals at work.[55]

The approach that SAICM foresees in order to achieve its objectives is very much a 'softer' bottom-up one that includes, among others, an enabling phase to build necessary capacity; to develop a national strategic approach implementation plan for participating countries; and to develop regional strategic approach implementation plans. It also includes a drive to encourage intergovernmental organisations, international financial institutions and private actors to support these activities and to consider the development of their own action plans as appropriate.[56]

4. Integration and Harmonisation

Integration and harmonisation refer to multi-country efforts that result in similar approaches or regulatory diffusion to various regulatory issues such as transboundary water governance.[57] This might include cooperative action among states mutually to recognise each other's environmental permitting systems.[58] Integration and harmonisation usually play out at the regional governance level. Regional environmental governance is now a fully recognised manifestation or aspect of global environmental governance. It has emerged as a response from regionally grouped states to shared environmental problems and as a means to exert greater influence as a regional collective in global environmental diplomacy, law making and governance. To this end, regional environmental governance is especially desirable:

> when the global seems to fail (or, at least, is not an appropriate level to deal with collective action problems) and states simply cannot solve their own environmental problems through unilateral action or where scaling up has the potential to deliver more effective outcomes, then the 'goldilocks principle' kicks in; regionalism becomes attractive as it is neither 'too hot' nor 'too cold' but 'just right'.[59]

Other benefits are the potential for regional environmental governance to provide for enhanced commonalities to address a particular environmental challenge; greater familiarity with key actors; the ability to tailor mitigating and adaptation actions to a smaller global constituency; and the ability to focus on ecologically defined regions such as river basins rather than on political-administrative entities.[60]

There are various examples of regional organisations that have been constituted on the basis of the need for integration and harmonisation. For example, the African Union as a regional body seeks to foster regional integration. So too does the European Union with its elaborate environmental law and governance regime. There is usually a link between the desired goals and the harmonisation and integration efforts that drive the pursuit of those goals. However, in some instances one state takes the lead in the development of norms by adopting rules unilaterally that other states are forced to adopt. Hegemons like the United States and regional bodies like the European Union have been described sometimes as acting in such a manner as to require other states to adopt similar approaches to theirs.[61]

As an example of this approach, many countries had to improve their regulations regarding chemicals after 2006 in order to access the European market after the European Union introduced stringent measures in the form of Regulation (EC) No.1907/2006 of 18 December 2006 concerning the Registration, Evaluation, Authorisation and Restriction of Chemicals (REACH).[62] However, where processes of integration and harmonisation occur, it does not mean that the laws of states have become uniform or similar in every aspect.[63] States, as a result of sovereignty, will always have some leeway over the framing and implementation of rules, norms or laws within their jurisdictions.[64]

5. Networking

The creation, sharing and dissemination of ideas by networks of like-minded and influential individuals or groups are essential and significant to the development of TEL.[65] At a conceptual level, Benford prefers the term 'transnational social movements' to describe networks or groups of civil society that seek to impact the outcomes of global governance. Chirico and Larouche present a persuasive economic argument for networking. For them, 'network effects' occur when the value of certain products to individual users increases as the number of users also increases.[66] They apply this theory to law where they first lay out a general proposition that the market for legal ideas is also subject to network effects.[67] The result is that 'the more members of the legal epistemic community subscribe to a given opinion, the more attractive it becomes, sometimes irrespective of its inherent validity'.[68] As such, these epistemic communities are also perceived to contribute to the development of TEL by facilitating the exchange of knowledge that could indirectly affect normative development.[69] When these non-state actor networks are actively involved in environmental issues, they are able to influence legal processes by being 'transnational norm entrepreneurs'.[70]

Networking especially occurs through the work of transnational epistemic communities which are groupings of people around a specific issue such as environmental law. The IUCN Academy of Environmental Law is an example of a globally representative transnational epistemic community. Through regular interaction, research and capacity-building events, it seeks to develop environmental law norms in the global domain.[71] Non-governmental organisations play an equally important role in networking and in the 'creation' of TEL. Salamon and Anheier believe that the reason:

> these organizations have attracted so much attention in recent years is due in large part to the widespread 'crisis of the state' that has been underway for two decades or more in virtually every part of the world, a crisis that has manifested itself in a serious questioning of traditional social welfare policies in much of the developed North, in disappointments over the progress of state-led development in significant parts of the developing South, in the collapse of the experiment in state socialism in Central and Eastern Europe, and in concerns about the environmental degradation that continues to threaten human health and safety everywhere.[72]

The environment has clearly become a proper concern of global civil society actors and it is beginning to appeal gradually to social movement energies and to energetic global solidarities. Acting outside of the formal government setting, environmental non-governmental organisations 'affirm values that are universally recognized but politically manipulated in their own interest by political agencies'.[73] Aiming to 'undo evil or to do good',[74] non-governmental environmental organisations are popular and enjoy broad based public support. Their activities focus on practical and current matters, specific cases and concrete expressions of human solidarity. While global non-state actors remain unable to participate fully in global environmental law making and diplomacy as a result of their lack of international legal personality, these actors increasingly influence the outcomes of the more formal global juridical processes, thereby indirectly contributing to the development of global environmental norms and structures beyond the state.[75]

In addition to their broader global policy influence at a strategic political and advocacy level, global environmental civil society actors, through their respective networks, sometimes engage in the development of softer, law-like norms that aim to bolster environmental protection. One example is the voluntary ISO 14000 environmental standard that has been developed by the International Organization for Standardization (ISO) as a means to enhance the environmental performance of businesses. ISO is an independent, non-governmental international organisation with a membership of 162 national standards bodies.[76] Today there is little doubt that ISO 14001 'has become the international benchmark by which corporations can voluntarily develop and assess their environmental practices'.[77]

6. Judicial Comparative Borrowing

Judicial bodies play an important role in the emergence of TEL. Comparative judicial reliance on foreign and international law has been referred to as judicial cross-fertilisation, judicial dialogue, constitutional borrowing, judicial importation and judicial migration.[78] Through these processes, different legal systems are able more generally to mirror each other. This contributes, however minimally, to some normative uniformity either between two or more countries, in a region or across the globe. One particularly pertinent example of judicial borrowing in the environmental context is the South African Constitutional Court's significant reliance on the burgeoning body of international law pertaining to sustainable development that guided its interpretation of this environmental law concept in South Africa's domestic legal regime in a landmark decision in 2007 – namely the *Fuel Retailers* case.[79] The court ultimately concluded, first, that 'sustainable development is an evolving concept of international law' and, then, that it:

> has a significant role to play in the resolution of environmentally related disputes in our law. It offers an important principle for the resolution of tensions between the need to protect the environment on the one hand, and the need for socio-economic development on the other hand.[80]

TRANSNATIONAL ENVIRONMENTAL RIGHTS IN THE CONTEXT OF TEL

1. The Context

The emergence of TEL is evident in various focus areas of environmental law. One illustrative example is that of environmental rights.[81] These rights have emerged as a continuous and fast-developing body of law globally. This is evident because the environment was not a concern during the first significant global constitutional moment that saw the almost universal adoption of human rights following the Universal Declaration of Human Rights in 1948.[82] Environmental rights only began to feature in domestic constitutional orders following the United Nations Conference on the Human Environment in Stockholm in 1972. The text of principle 1[83] of the Stockholm Declaration provided the impetus for couching environmental concerns in rights terms. It took only a relatively short period of time for the current world-wide adoption of human rights to a healthy environment, of environmentally related procedural rights, of other substantive political and socio-economic human rights bearing on environmental interests and, more recently, of the right of nature.[84] Today, approximately three-quarters of the world's constitutions – 150 out of 193 – include some reference to environmental rights, to environmental responsibilities or to both.[85] This is a surprisingly large number given that the right to a healthy environment is one of the few rights widely recognised in constitutions today that have no 'ancestral claim' in the International Bill of Rights.[86]

Despite these domestic developments, there is neither a universally applicable global treaty that explicitly provides for an environmental right[87] nor has such a right been accepted into the corpus of customary international law.[88] Regionally, however, in addition to the environmental rights in the African Charter on Human and People's Rights and in the San Salvador Protocol to the American Convention on Human Rights, article 3(2) of the Asian Human Rights Charter 1998 provides for the right to a 'clean and healthy environment'.[89] The Arab Charter on Human Rights 2004 includes a right to a healthy environment as part of the right to an adequate standard of living that ensures well-being and a decent life.[90]

Surprisingly, none of the constituting treaties of the European Union provides for an explicit environmental right. Neither does the European Convention for the Protection of Human Rights and Fundamental Freedoms 1950 provide for an explicit environmental right.[91] Rather, environmental entitlements are raised and protected incidentally through the assertion of other rights.[92] The European Court of Human Rights has been very active in protecting environmental interests in the context of the right to privacy in article 8 of the 1950 Convention and its rich jurisprudence on human rights in the environmental context.[93] On the other hand, although the United Nations Economic Commission for Europe (UNECE) Convention on Access to Information, Public Participation in Decision-making and Access to Justice in Environmental Matters 1998 – the Aarhus Convention – provides an environmental right, this right is non-justiciable.[94] Despite this phenomenon, the Convention significantly strengthens the force of substantive regional environmental constitutional claims because it provides for communications to be brought before its Compliance Committee by one or more members of the public about compliance by any party to the Convention with the Convention.[95]

2. The Emergence of Transnational Juridical Processes

The development of environmental rights globally is not occurring in isolated spaces that are disconnected from one another. Processes of transplantation, convergence, regional integration and harmonization, networking and judicial comparative borrowing are collectively at play. This suggests the emergence of transnational juridical processes. Through these processes of cross-jurisdictional learning, comparative analysis and legal transplantation – including transnational migration, cross-pollination and sharing of ideas – it is possible to observe the emergence of transnationality in the environmental rights domain. Boyd has indicated that the 1976 Portuguese formulation of a 'healthy and ecologically balanced human living environment' is now found in 21 other constitutions and that the decisions on environmental rights by the Supreme Court of India have significantly influenced courts in Bangladesh, Pakistan, Sri Lanka, Uganda and Kenya.[96]

Regional judiciaries are also increasingly borrowing from one another. This suggests that these global judicial conversations are not the exclusive domain of domestic courts. In the *SERAC* case[97] the African Commission on Human and Peoples' Rights delivered the first substantive interpretation of a regional environmental right.[98] Recognising that certain provisions of the African Charter on Human and Peoples' Rights 1981 were adopted as a reaction to the 'aftermath of colonial exploitation [that] has left Africa's precious resources and people still vulnerable to foreign misappropriation',[99] the Commission, relying on European Court of Human Rights and Inter-American Court of Human Rights jurisprudence, confirmed that governments have a duty to protect their citizens not only through appropriate legislation and effective enforcement but also by protecting them from damaging acts that may be perpetrated by foreign oil companies.[100] Within an increasingly interconnected globalised world, it is to be expected that transnational comparative environmental conversations such as these will increase. It is clear that 'the increased citation of judgments and borrowing of legal doctrines from international and foreign courts by domestic judges is a concrete sign of a developing transnational legal culture'.[101]

These domestic and regional initiatives together with their relatively active judicial oversight bodies are set to be bolstered by the increasingly vocal and influential global civil society movements that champion environment-related rights protection. Working from their domestic jurisdictions and beyond, it is especially global civil society actors that indirectly contribute to cementing, strengthening and further expanding environment-related rights at the global level through their core functions.[102]

An example of a global non-state actor initiative that contributes to the transnational development of environmental rights is the International Rights of Nature Tribunal. In its own words, this people's tribunal:

> gives a vehicle for re-framing and adjudicating prominent environmental and social justice cases within the context of a Rights of Nature based earth jurisprudence. It gives people from all around the world the opportunity to testify publicly as to the destruction of the Earth – destruction that governments and corporations not only allow, but in some cases encourage.[103]

Civil society actors created the Tribunal in 2014. To date it has been convened thrice: in Ecuador, Peru, and more recently in Paris for the 2015 global climate negotiations. It is based on a methodology that allows concerned citizens to 'testify' even in the absence of an 'accused' party, such as a state, that has allegedly infringed the rights of nature. While it is by no means a traditional court, it serves an important educational and awareness-raising function.

A second example is the Permanent Peoples' Tribunal – the successor to the 1967 Bertrand Russell–Jean Paul Sartre Vietnam War Crimes Tribunal that exposed war crimes during the Vietnam War. Similarly, it functions as a public opinion tribunal because its judgments have no binding force. Nevertheless, it could significantly raise global awareness of environmental issues. In March 2017, the Permanent Peoples' Tribunal will hold a session on hydraulic fracturing. This is an initiative that was initiated by the Global Network for the Study of Human Rights and the Environment, the Environment and Human Rights Advisory, and the Human Rights Consortium.[104] Initiatives such as these, while they cannot strengthen or expand the more traditional global judicial functions, do provide a forum for global civil society actors not only to voice their concerns in non-state spaces but also to contribute, however minimally or indirectly, to the transnational development of environmental rights law.

CONCLUSION

It is relatively clear from the foregoing analysis that TEL is the most recent contemporary analytical tool to try and understand global environmental problems from a regulatory perspective. It is at once also an attempt to respond better to these challenges:

> The complexity of the governance landscape presents a challenge for both scholars and for policy-makers. This is a descriptive (or data) challenge and a normative (or legitimacy) challenge as well. For lawyers, the phenomenon of transnational governance is exciting but also destabilizing. We are not quite as certain today that we know what to count as law or that law is inherently tied to the state. Our methodologies for identifying and constructing law have also started to change. In the world of trans-national law and governance, we can

> no longer simply read law off the statute book or case report. We have to examine multifarious institutional practices as well.[105]

TEL provides an excitingly novel analytical lens for environmental lawyers in their attempts to address the increasingly urgent socio-ecological crisis of the Anthropocene in an interconnected and globalised world. It is suggested that, based on the foregoing analysis, there are sufficient reasons to believe that the TEL project will continue to mature as an alternative approach to scrutinising and to developing further the global panoply of norms that aim to mediate the human-environment interface.

NOTES

1. See for a detailed discussion, Beyerlin and Marauhn (2011, pp. 1–29).
2. In 2012 a specialized peer reviewed journal, *Transnational Environmental Law* (Cambridge University Press), was created that specifically focuses on contemporary developments in TEL.
3. Heyvaert and Etty (2012, p. 2).
4. Fisher (2012, p. 46).
5. Dunhoff and Trachtman (2009, pp. 5–6).
6. Fombad (2012, p. 440).
7. Peters (2005, p. 536).
8. Venter (2010, p. 20).
9. Paulus (2004, p. 1048).
10. Boyd (2010, p. 466).
11. See most recently, Lyster (2015).
12. Climate change is increasingly regulated by states through domestic laws. For an example of the burgeoning body of domestic laws and policies in the South African context, see Humby et al. (eds) (2016).
13. See, for a list of European Commission decisions, directives and regulations, European Commission (2016).
14. See, for example, the work that is being done by the International Council for Local Environmental Initiatives (ICLEI) in this regard at ICLEI Europe (2016). In the initial document, this was referenced http://www.iclei-europe.org/topics/climate-change-adaptation/.
15. Keohane and Victor (2011, p. 8).
16. Betsill and Bulkeley (2006, p. 144).
17. See Bellamy and Palumbo (eds) (2010).
18. Ladeur (2004, p. 17).
19. Coen and Thatcher (2008, p. 50).
20. Ladeur (2004, pp. 10–1).
21. Kjaer (2014, p. 4).
22. See, for a discussion of fragmentation of global environmental law and governance, Kotzé, 'Fragmentation Revisited' (2014, pp. 548–83).
23. See generally, Beyerlin and Marauhn (2011).
24. Biermann (2005, p. 120).
25. See for a detailed discussion, Kotzé (2016), especially ch.2.

26. Crutzen and Stoermer (2000, pp. 17–18).
27. Kotzé, 'Rethinking Global Environmental Law' (2014, pp. 121–56).
28. Whitehead (2014, pp. 4219/5354).
29. Dalby (2004).
30. Ignaciuk et al. (2012, p. 147).
31. Biermann et al. (2010, p. 203). See also for a more detailed conceptual analysis, Biermann (2007, p. 326); and more recently, Biermann, *Earth System Governance* (2014).
32. Biermann, 'The Anthropocene: A Governance Perspective' (2014, p. 59).
33. Biermann (2007, pp. 329–30).
34. Yang and Percival (2009, p. 617); Kotzé, 'Fragmentation Revisited' (2014, p. 566); Heyvaert and Etty (2012, p. 7).
35. Lin and Scott (2012, p. 23).
36. Wiener (2001, p. 1371).
37. Yang and Percival (2009, pp. 616–17, 619 et seq).
38. Ibid. (p. 646).
39. Ong (2010, p. 44).
40. Kysar (2010, pp. 123–4).
41. Shaffer and Bodansky (2011).
42. Ibid.
43. Holzinger, Knill and Sommerer (2008, pp. 553–87).
44. Twining (2009, p. 52).
45. Yang and Percival (2009, p. 617); Percival (2013, p. 2).
46. Wiener (2001, p. 1297).
47. Fisher (2012, p. 46).
48. Sand (1991, p. 256).
49. Shaffer and Bodansky (2011, p. 33).
50. Yang and Percival (2009, p. 627).
51. Shaffer and Bodansky (2011, p. 33).
52. Holzinger, Knill and Sommerer (2008, p. 556).
53. Cremades and Plehn (1984, p. 319).
54. UNEP (2007, p. 12).
55. Ibid. (p. 20).
56. Ibid. (p. 21).
57. Yang and Percival (2009, p. 627).
58. Shaffer and Bodansky (2011, p. 33).
59. Elliot and Breslin (2011, p. 4).
60. Balsiger and VanDeveer (2012, p. 3).
61. Shaffer and Bodansky (2011, p. 34); Yang and Percival (2009, p. 648).
62. Shaffer and Bodansky (2011, p. 34); Yang and Percival (2009, p. 620).
63. Fisher (2012, p. 48).
64. Holzinger, Knill and Sommerer (2008, p. 557).
65. Boyd (2011, p. 109); Kotzé (2012, p. 145).
66. Chirico and Larouche (2013, p. 13).
67. Ibid.
68. Ibid. (p. 14).
69. Young (1994, p. 96); Haas (2007, p. 792).
70. Shaffer and Bodansky (2011, p. 35).
71. IUCN Academy of Environmental Law (2016).
72. Salamon and Anheier (1999, p. 4).
73. Castells (2008, p. 84).
74. Ibid. (p. 85).

75. The number of non-governmental environmental organisations at global United Nations conferences has steadily increased, notably since the Stockholm Conference on the Human Environment in 1972. See United Nations (1972, p. 43).
76. See ISO (2016).
77. Rondinelli and Vastag (2002, p. 499).
78. Dupre (2009, p. 107).
79. *Fuel Retailers* case (paras 46–56).
80. Ibid. (paras 46, 57).
81. Environmental human rights are generally understood to include: rights to the environment; incidental substantive rights such as the rights to life and dignity that bear on the environment; and concomitant procedural rights such as rights of access to information and access to courts that are used to enforce substantive environment-related entitlements.
82. Kotzé (2015).
83. Principle 1 states, among others: '[M]an has the fundamental right to freedom, equality and adequate conditions of life, in an environment of a quality that permits a life of dignity and well-being.'
84. See articles 10, 71–74 of the Constitution of Ecuador (2008). Bolivia is similarly exploring the possibility to enact a 'Mother Earth Law', which draws on the indigenous concept of *Pachamama* (Mother Earth) and which aims to provide nature rights including the right to life, regeneration, biodiversity, water, clean air, balance and restoration. See Buxton (2016).
85. Boyd (2015, pp. 171–5).
86. May and Daly (2015, pp. 691/11268).
87. See generally, Turner (2013).
88. At most, environmental entitlements are inferred indirectly from the provisions of other human-focused but environment-related rights treaties, such as the International Covenant on Economic, Social and Cultural Rights (1966) (arts 7(b), 10(3), 12); the Convention on the Rights of the Child (1989) (art.24); and the International Labour Organization Convention Concerning Indigenous and Tribal Peoples in Independent Countries (1989) (arts 2, 6, 7, 15). See Shelton (2010, pp. 266–7).
89. Asian Human Rights Commission (1998).
90. Article 38. Notably, neither the Asian Human Rights Charter nor the Arab Charter on Human Rights has enforcement mechanisms.
91. Council of Europe (2006).
92. Pedersen (2008, pp. 73–111).
93. See for a summary of environment-related cases the summary in European Court of Human Rights (2015).
94. See generally, Kravchenko (2007, pp. 1–50).
95. UNECE (2016).
96. Boyd (2011, p. 108).
97. *SERAC* case.
98. See art.24 of the Charter.
99. *SERAC* case (para.56).
100. Ibid. (para.57); *Honduras* case; *Netherlands* case.
101. Ip (2010, p. 644).
102. Gemmill and Bamidele-Izu (2002, pp. 77–100).
103. Global Alliance for the Rights of Nature (2015).
104. See Short (2015).
105. Lin and Scott (2012, p. 24).

REFERENCES

Asian Human Rights Commission (1998), Asian Human Rights Charter; http://www.refworld.org/pdfid/452678304.pdf.

Balsiger, Jörg and Stacy VanDeveer (2012), 'Navigating Regional Environmental Governance', *Global Environmental Politics* 12(3), 1–17.

Bellamy, Richard and Antonino Palumbo (eds) (2010), *From Government to Governance* (Aldershot, Ashgate Publishing).

Betsill, Michelle and Harriet Bulkeley (2006), 'Cities and the Multilevel Governance of Global Climate Change', *Global Governance* 12, 141–58.

Beyerlin, Ulrich and Thilo Marauhn (2011), *International Environmental Law* (Oxford, Hart Publishing).

Biermann, Frank (2005), 'The Rationale for a World Environment Organization' in Frank Biermann and Steffen Bauer (eds), *A World Environment Organization: Solution or Threat for Effective International Environmental Governance?* (Aldershot, Ashgate Publishing), pp. 117–43.

Biermann, Frank (2007), '"Earth System Governance" as a Cross-cutting Theme of Global Change Research', *Global Environmental Change* 17(3–4), 326–37.

Biermann, Frank (2014), 'The Anthropocene: A Governance Perspective', *The Anthropocene Review* 1, 57–61.

Biermann, Frank (2014), *Earth System Governance: World Politics in the Anthropocene* (Cambridge, MIT Press).

Biermann, Frank, Michele M. Betsill, Susan C. Vieira, Joyeeta Gupta, Norichika Kanie, Louis Lebel, Diana Liverman, Heike Schroeder, Bernd Siebenhuner, Pius Z. Yanda and Ruben Zondervan (2010), 'Navigating the Anthropocene: The Earth System Governance Project Strategy Paper', *Current Opinion in Environmental Sustainability* 2(3), 202–208.

Boyd, David (2011), *The Environmental Rights Revolution: A Global Study of Constitutions, Human Rights, and the Environment* (Vancouver, UBC Press).

Boyd, David (2015), 'Constitutions, Human Rights, and the Environment: National Approaches' in Anna Grear and Louis J. Kotzé (eds), *Research Handbook on Human Rights and the Environment* (Cheltenham, Edward Elgar), pp. 170–99.

Boyd, William (2010), 'Climate Change, Fragmentation, and the Challenges of Global Environmental Law: Elements of a Post-Copenhagen Assemblage', *University of Pennsylvania Journal of International Law* 32, 457–550.

Buxton, Nick (2016), *The Law of Mother Earth: Behind Bolivia's Historic Bill*; http://therightsofnature.org/bolivia-law-of-mother-earth/.

Castells, Manuel (2008), 'The New Public Sphere: Global Civil Society, Communication Networks, and Global Governance', *The ANNALS of the American Academy of Political and Social Science* 616, 78–93.

Chirico, Filomena and Pierre Larouche (2013), 'Convergence and Divergence in Law and Economics and Comparative Law' in Pierre Larouche and Péter Cserne (eds), *National Legal Systems and Globalization* (The Hague, TMC Asser Press), pp. 9–33.

Coen, David and Mark Thatcher (2008), 'Network Governance and Multi-Level Delegation: European Networks of Regulatory Agencies', *Journal of Public Policy* 28(1), 49–71.

Council of Europe (2006), *Manual on Human Rights and the Environment* (Strasbourg, Council of Europe Publishing)

Cremades, Bernardo M. and Steven L. Plehn (1984), 'The New Lex Mercatoria and the Harmonization of the Laws of International Commercial Transactions', *Boston University International Law Journal* 2, 317–48.

Crutzen, Paul and Eugene Stoermer (2000), 'The "Anthropocene"', *IGBP Global Change Newsletter* 41, 17–18.

Dalby, Simon (2004), *Anthropocene Ethics: Rethinking 'The Political' after Environment*; http://www.yumpu.com/en/document/view/42485216/anthropocene-ethics-rethinking-the-political-after-environment/3.

Dunhoff, Jeffrey and Joel Trachtman (2009), 'A Functional Approach to International Constitutionalization' in Jeffrey Dunhoff and Joel Trachtman (eds), *Ruling the World: Constitutionalism, International Law, and Global Governance* (New York, Cambridge University Press), pp. 5–6.

Dupre, Catherine (2009), 'Globalisation and Judicial Reasoning: Building Blocks for a Method of Interpretation' in Andrew Halpin and Volker Roeben (eds), *Theorising the Global Legal Order* (Portland, Hart Publishing), pp. 107–123.

Elliot, Lorraine and Shaun Breslin (2011), 'Researching Comparative Regional Environmental Governance Causes, Cases and Consequences' in Lorraine Elliot and Shaun Breslin (eds), *Comparative Environmental Regionalism* (New York, Routledge), pp. 1–18.

European Commission (2016), *EU Law on Climate Change and Protection of the Ozone Layer*; http://ec.europa.eu/clima/about-us/climate-law/index_en.htm.

European Court of Human Rights (2015), *Factsheet – Environment and the European Convention on Human Rights*; http://www.echr.coe.int/Documents/FS_Environment_ENG.pdf.

Fisher, Elizabeth (2012), 'The Rise of Transnational Environmental Law and the Expertise of Environmental Lawyers', *Transnational Environmental Law* 1(1), 43–52.

Fombad, Charles (2012), 'Internationalization of Constitutional Law and Constitutionalism in Africa', *American Journal of Comparative Law* 60, 439–74.

Gemmill, Barbara and Abimbola Bamidele-Izu (2002), 'The Role of NGOs and Civil Society in Global Environmental Governance' in Daniel Esty and Maria Ivanova (eds), *Global Environmental Governance: Options and Opportunities* (Yale, Yale Centre for Environmental Law and Policy), pp. 77–100.

Global Alliance for the Rights of Nature (2015), *International Rights of Nature Tribunal*; http://therightsofnature.org/rights-of-nature-tribunal/.

Haas, Peter M. (2007), 'Epistemic Communities' in Daniel Bodansky, Jutta Brunnee and Ellen Hey (eds), *The Oxford Handbook of International Environmental Law* (Oxford, Oxford University Press), pp. 791–806.

Heyvaert, Veerle and Thijs Etty (2012), 'Introducing Transnational Environmental Law', *Transnational Environmental Law* 1(1), 1–11.

Holzinger, Katharina, Christopher Knill and Thomas Sommerer (2008), 'Environmental Policy Convergence: the Impact of International Harmonization, Transnational Communication, and Regulatory Competition', *International Organization* 62, 553–87.

Humby, Tracy, Louis Kotzé, Olivia Rumble and Andrew Gilder (eds) (to appear 2016), *Climate Law and Governance in South Africa* (Cape Town, Juta).

ICLEI Europe (2016), *Climate Change Adaptation*; http://www.iclei-europe.org/topics/climate-change-adaptation/.

Ignaciuk, Ada, Martin Rice, J. Bogardi, Josep G. Canadell, Shobhakar Dhakal, John Ingram, Rik Leemans and Mark Rosenberg (2012), 'Responding to Complex Societal Challenges: A Decade of Earth System Science Partnership (ESSP) Interdisciplinary Research', *Current Opinion in Environmental Sustainability* 4(1), 147–58.

Ip, Eric C. (2010), 'Globalization and the Future of the Law of the Sovereign State', *International Journal of Constitutional Law* 8(3), 636–55.

ISO (2016), *About ISO*; http://www.iso.org/iso/home/about.htm.

IUCN Academy of Environmental Law (2016), *Home Page*; http://www.iucnael.org/en/.

Keohane, Robert and David Victor (2011), 'The Regime Complex for Climate Change', *Perspectives on Politics* 9(1), 7–23.

Kjaer, Poul (2014), *Constitutionalism in the Global Realm* (Abingdon, Routledge).

Kotzé, Louis J. (2012), *Global Environmental Governance: Law and Regulation for the 21st Century* (Cheltenham, Edward Elgar).
Kotzé, Louis J. (2014), 'Fragmentation Revisited in the Context of Global Environmental Law and Governance', *South African Law Journal* 131(3), 548–83.
Kotzé, Louis J. (2014), 'Rethinking Global Environmental Law and Governance in the Anthropocene', *Journal of Energy and Natural Resources Law* 33(2), 121–56.
Kotzé, Louis J. (2015), 'The Anthropocene's Global Environmental Constitutional Moment', *Yearbook of International Environmental Law* 25(1), 24–60.
Kotzé, Louis J. (2016), *Global Environmental Constitutionalism in the Anthropocene* (Oxford, Hart Publishing, forthcoming).
Kravchenko, Svitlana (2007), 'The Aarhus Convention and Innovations in Compliance with Multilateral Environmental Agreements', *Colorado Journal of International Environmental Law and Policy* 18(1), 1–50.
Kysar, Douglas (2010), *Regulating from Nowhere: Environmental Law and the Search for Objectivity* (New Haven, Yale University Press).
Ladeur, Karl-Heinz (2004), 'Globalization and Public Governance: A Contradiction?' in Karl-Heinz Ladeur (ed.), *Public Governance in the Age of Globalization* (Aldershot, Ashgate Publishing), pp. 1–22.
Lin, Jolene and Joanne Scott (2012), 'Looking beyond the International: Key Themes and Approaches of Transnational Environmental Law', *Transnational Environmental Law* 1(1), 23–9.
Lyster, Rosemary (2015), *Climate Justice and Disaster Law* (Cambridge, Cambridge University Press).
May, James and Erin Daly (2015), *Global Environmental Constitutionalism*, Kindle edn 691/11268 (New York, Cambridge University Press).
Ong, David (2010), 'From "International" to "Transnational" Environmental Law? A Legal Assessment of the Contribution of the "Equator Principles" to International Environmental Law', *Nordic Journal of International Law* 79, 35–74.
Paulus, Andreas (2004), 'Commentary to Andreas Fischer-Lescano and Gunther Teubner: The Legitimacy of International Law and the Role of the State', *Michigan Journal of International Law* 25, 1047–73.
Pedersen, Ole (2008), 'European Environmental Human Rights and Environmental Rights: A Long Time Coming?', *Georgetown International Environmental Law Review* 21, 73–111.
Percival, Robert V. (2013), 'Human Rights and the Evolution of Global Environmental Law', *U of Maryland Legal Studies Research Paper No.*2012-66, pp. 1–16.
Peters, Anne (2005), 'Global Constitutionalism in a Nutshell' in Klaus Dicke, Stephan Hobe, Karl-Ulrich Meyn, Anne Peters, Eibe Riedel, Hans-Joachim Schütz and Christian Tietje (eds), *Weltinnenrecht: Liber Amicorum Jost Delbrück* (Berlin, Duncker and Humblot), pp. 535–50.
Rondinelli, Dennis and Gyula Vastag (2002), 'Panacea, Common Sense, or Just a Label? The Value of ISO 14001 Environmental Management Systems', *European Management Journal* 18(5), 499–510.
Salamon, Lester M. and Helmut Anheier and Associates (1999), 'Civil Society in Comparative Perspective' in Lester M. Salamon, Helmut K. Anheier, Regina List, Stefan Toepler, Wojciech S. Sokolowski and Associates (eds), *Global Civil Society Dimensions of the Nonprofit Sector* (Baltimore, The Johns Hopkins Center for Civil Society Studies), pp. 3–39.
Sand, Peter H. (1991), 'Lessons Learned in Global Environmental Governance', *Boston College Environmental Affairs Law Review* 18(2), 213–77.
Shaffer, Gregory and Daniel Bodansky (2011), 'Transnationalism, Unilateralism and International Law', *Transnational Environmental Law* 1(1), 31–41.

Shelton, Dinah (2010), 'Human Rights and the Environment: Substantive Rights' in Malgosia Fitzmaurice, David Ong and Panos Merkouris (eds), *Research Handbook on International Environmental Law* (Cheltenham, Edward Elgar), pp. 265–83.
Short, Damien (2015), *Media Release – Fracking Goes on Trial*; https://www.tribunalonfracking.org/news/media-release/.
Turner, Stephen (2013), *A Global Environmental Right* (Abingdon, Routledge).
Twining, William (2009), 'Implications of "Globalisation" for Law as a Discipline' in Halpin Andrew and Roeben Volker (eds), *Theorising the Global Legal Order* (Portland, Hart Publishing), pp. 39–59.
UNECE (2016), *Communications from the Public*; http://www.unece.org/env/pp/pubcom.html.
UNEP (2007), *Strategic Approach to International Chemicals Management: SAICM Texts and Resolutions of the International Conference on Chemicals Management* (Geneva, UNEP).
United Nations (1972), *Report of the United Nations Conference on the Human Environment*; http://www.un-documents.net/aconf48-14r1.pdf.
Venter, Francois (2010), *Global Features of Constitutional Law* (Nijmegen, Wolf Legal Publishers).
Whitehead, Mark (2014), *Environmental Transformations: A Geography of the Anthropocene*, Kindle edn 4219/5354 (New York, Routledge).
Wiener, Jonathan (2001), 'Something Borrowed for Something Blue: Legal Transplants and the Evolution of Global Environmental Law', *Ecology Law Quarterly* 271, 1295–372.
Yang, Tseming and Robert Percival (2009), 'The Emergence of Global Environmental Law', *Ecology Law Quarterly* 36, 615–64.
Young, Oran R. (1994), *International Governance: Protecting the Environment in a Stateless Society* (New York, Cornell University Press).

INSTRUMENTS

Additional Protocol to the American Convention on Human Rights 1988 (1988) *Organization of American States Treaty Series* A-52.
African Charter on Human and Peoples' Rights 1981, (1982) *International Legal Materials* 21, 58.
Arab Charter on Human Rights 2004, 22 May 2004, *reprinted in* (2005) 12 Int'l Hum. Rts. Rep. 893.
Asian Human Rights Charter 1998.
Basel Convention on the Control of Transboundary Movement of Hazardous Wastes and their Disposal 1989, (1989) *International Legal Materials* 28, 657.
Convention Concerning Indigenous and Tribal Peoples in Independent Countries 1989, (1989) *International Labour Organization* C169.
Convention on Access to Information, Public Participation in Decision-making and Access to Justice in Environmental Matters 1998, (1999) *International Legal Materials* 38, 517.
Convention on the Rights of the Child 1989, (1989) *United Nations Treaty Series* 1577, 3.
European Convention for the Protection of Human Rights and Fundamental Freedoms 1950, (1950) *European Treaty Series* 5.
International Covenant on Economic, Social and Cultural Rights 1966, (1967) *International Legal Materials* 6, 360.
International Labour Organization Convention No.170, 1990 (Entry into force 4 November 1993; Adoption: Geneva, 77th ILC session on 25 June 1990).

Kyoto Protocol to the United Nations Framework Convention on Climate Change 1997, (1997) *International Legal Materials* 37, 22.
Montreal Protocol on Substances that Deplete the Ozone Layer 1987, (1987) *International Legal Materials* 26, 1550.
Paris Climate Agreement: Conference of the Parties 21, (2015) FCCC/CP/2015/L.9/Rev.1.
Rotterdam Convention on the Prior Informed Consent Procedure for Certain Hazardous Chemicals and Pesticides in International Trade 1998, (1998) *International Legal Materials* 38, 1.
Stockholm Convention on Persistent Organic Pollutants 2001, (2001) *International Legal Materials* 40, 532.
United Nations Framework Convention on Climate Change 1992, (1992) *International Legal Materials* 37, 22.

CASES

Fuel Retailers case: *Fuel Retailers Association of Southern Africa v Director-General: Environmental Management, Department of Agriculture, Conservation and Environment, Mpumalanga Province and Others* (CCT67/06) [2007] ZACC 13.
Honduras case: Inter-American Court of Human Rights: *Velàsquez Rodríguez v Honduras* 19 July1988, Series C, No.4.14.
Netherlands case: European Court of Human Rights: *X and Y v Netherlands* (1985) 91 ECHR (Ser. A).
SERAC case: Communication 155/96: *Social and Economic Rights Action Center (SERAC) and Center for Economic and Social Rights (CESR).*

5. Economic approaches to environmental governance: a principled analysis

Michael Faure

INTRODUCTION

It is appropriate that a discussion of the fundamental concepts of environmental law includes an analysis of the economic approach to environmental governance. It is well recognized that environmental law – like other new fields of law such as consumer law – is one of the more 'multi-faceted' fields of the law. They involve not only administrative regulation but also civil liability and criminal liability, each at different levels of governance. In addition it is recognized that – like other fields of law touching upon technology – it is difficult to analyze the function of environmental law without understanding the goals of environmental policy more broadly. The question which goals environmental policy should achieve has given rise to much debate. It will undoubtedly be answered differently depending upon the relevant field of research in which one is engaged. Moreover, no matter how one defines the goals of environmental law, an important issue that will often arise is the existence of a price: in other words a cost involved in reaching a specific level of environmental protection. This is why an economic approach, indicating how a particular level of environmental protection could be reached at the lowest cost possible, may to some extent be an indispensable tool of environmental policy.

THE ISSUES IN CONTEXT

It is useful to begin by considering the literature which has indicated the relationship between environmental protection and environmental quality. This approach assumes the form of the 'environmental Kuznets curve'.[1] This describes a relationship whereby, in the first phase of economic development, more economic growth leads to more environmental degradation.[2] But there is a turning point in economic development when individual income levels increase and a demand for higher environmental quality emerges. At that moment increased economic welfare goes hand in hand with environmental improvement and hence with a reduction in pollution levels. This suggests on the face of it that the way to promote environmental protection is to promote economic growth. However, the literature has indicated that this relationship is by no means an automatic one. Pollution levels go down with increasing economic growth because at the same time those nations strengthen their institutions and hence their environmental law. In particular, it has been demonstrated that it is not only income levels but also the stringency of a nation's regulatory regime that influence environmental quality.[3]

Interestingly, two further conclusions have emerged. First, economic growth leads to improved environmental quality only when the growth is accompanied by institutional developments – more particularly environmental law. Second, nations that do adopt a stringent environmental regime were able to speed up economic growth rather than retard it.[4] There is accordingly clear support for a strong relationship between environmental law and environmental economics. The environmental Kuznets curve indicates that increased economic growth can lead to higher environmental quality but only if it is accompanied by strengthened regulatory structures which encourage the promotion of environmental quality.[5]

These analyses point to two conclusions. First, at this macro level, it is important to include legal institutional analysis in an economic approach. Second, the reverse is true: it is important to include economic analysis in a legal institutional approach. Accordingly, when defining their desired level of environmental quality, policy makers will undoubtedly realize that there is a price involved in reaching that specific level of environmental quality. As a result, even at the very basic stage of defining the desired environmental quality in a nation or a region,[6] it is necessary to ask this question: Can the benefits involved in reaching a particular – for example a high – level of environmental quality outweigh the costs? In practical terms, when the law determines the desired level of environmental quality, economic cost-benefit analysis will play a role.

Economic cost-benefit analysis can be relevant not only at the macro level. It can also involve the use of economics at a much more micro level. Consider two examples: when specific standards based on best available technology are formulated in environmental permits; and when, within the framework of liability rules, the level of efficient preventive measures to be implemented by a potential polluter is determined. Economics can undoubtedly play a role in support of environmental governance by assisting an administrative authority or a court in determining whether or not particular pollution prevention measures could be considered efficient.

THE STRUCTURE OF THIS ANALYSIS

It can reasonably be concluded that there is much scope for an economic approach to environmental governance generally and for an economic approach to environmental law more specifically. Notwithstanding this potential for collaboration, the starting points of analysis and the language used in environmental law often differ markedly from those relevant to the economic approach to environmental policy. It will be suggested that economics and law seem to be two worlds apart with much divergence – at least so far as the wordings and symbols are concerned. Notwithstanding this divergence, in some contexts a degree of convergence between economic and legal principles can be found. The use of economic notions will be addressed in three contexts:

- civil liability
- instrument choice generally and more particularly the choice between economic and regulatory instruments
- the area of law enforcement.

The central questions that will guide the analysis throughout this chapter are these:

- the normative question to what extent economics may have interesting lessons for environmental law in these particular areas
- the positive question to what extent there is in these specific areas – civil liability, instrument choice and enforcement – divergence between the economic and legal approaches
- whether some signs of convergence can be discovered as well.

This will allow an analysis of the comparative differences between economic and legal analysis and – especially important – the relationship between them. Moreover, the search for divergence versus convergence will be illustrated by some examples from contemporary legal systems.

LEGAL AND ECONOMIC ANALYSIS COMPARED

1. Introduction

The central purpose of the following paragraphs is to make clear how the legal and the economic approaches to environmental governance differ. This analysis will proceed in four stages:

- an explanation of the goals of environmental policy according to an economic approach
- a description of the instruments which are crucial to an economic approach
- a discussion of a few environmental principles specifically from an economic perspective
- an answer to the question to what extent there is convergence or divergence between the economic and legal approaches.

2. The Goals of Economic Policy

(a) Internalization of externalities

From an economic perspective the goal of environmental policy is to correct a market failure. This market failure results from the negative external effect – also referred to as an externality – created by environmental harm.[7] Since polluters will not feel the negative consequences of the harm they inflict outside of their enterprise, this is described as the external effect. It is, moreover, a negative external effect since it imposes costs rather than confers benefits on third parties. Such a negative external effect can create a market failure. The consequence is that, if polluters are not forced to pay for the external effects they create through their activities, they would lack any incentive for efficient cost abatement. The negative external effect would, in other words, not be incorporated into their decision-making process. This would encourage a firm that emits waste water into the surface waters not to install a water treatment plant. As a rational actor a firm would not incur costs to deal with externalities in the absence of legal rules forcing the firm to do so.

The negative externality is considered a market failure for the reason that the relative prices of products and services will be too low. Too low refers in this particular context to the fact that they do not reflect the true social costs of the activity. Since the externality is not taken into account and the polluter does not invest in pollution abatement, relative prices will be too low and consumers will demand too much of a product that creates high costs for society. Externalization, in other words, means that polluters are able to impose the costs of pollution on society. The costs are not 'gone' but borne by society at large.

(b) The Coase theorem

In the context of this economic approach, the main reason for introducing environmental regulation into the legal system would be to internalize the negative externalities resulting from pollution. This point of view needs to be nuanced in one important aspect. It has been the major achievement of Ronald Coase to show that, if transaction costs were sufficiently low, an optimal allocation of resources would always take place, irrespective of the contents of the governing legal rule.[8] The essence of the Coase theorem is that, even if polluters were not held liable and there would thus be a 'right to pollute', efficient preventive measures would nevertheless be taken but they would be paid for by the victims. An important element of the Coase theorem is that victims must have the resources to pay for abatement. In this way the Coase theorem considers only the efficiency aspect of pollution but not its distributional effects.[9]

There is a potential normative lesson to be learnt from the Coase theorem. Where an efficient allocation of resources – and hence an elimination of the market failure caused by externalities – is the goal to be achieved by the policy maker, a policy intervention would not be necessary where transaction costs are zero. Potential victims and polluters would then be free to negotiate. This emerges as a potential conflict with the legal approach. Lawyers, especially environmental lawyers, would in many cases consider the distributional effects. For the Coase theorem it is immaterial whether the prevention costs are paid by the polluter or by the potential victims. For an environmental lawyer it would probably be unacceptable that the potential victims – under a no liability regime – would have to pay for the installation of efficient abatement technology by the polluter. In these types of Coasean bargaining situations, from a purely legal perspective and according to a legal interpretation of the 'polluter pays' principle,[10] a legal rule should be put in place in order to force the polluter to pay the abatement costs. On the other hand, from an economic perspective that would not be necessary so long as transaction costs were zero. This would be so even if it implies that potential victims would – via Coasean bargaining – pay for efficient abatement.

(c) Cost-benefit analysis

The practical value of the Coase theorem for the formulation of environmental policy may not be overly important. This is because a zero or low transaction cost setting – whereby polluters and potential victims can bargain on efficient abatement – may often not be realized.[11] As a result, the most important next questions in formulating environmental policy are, first, how polluters can be forced to internalize – namely to take into account – the negative externality of pollution resulting from their activity and, second, to what level they should abate pollution. It will be recalled that, from an economic perspective, the goal of environmental policy is not to protect the environment at all costs – as it may be from some legal perspectives – but rather to correct the market failure resulting from the externality of environmental pollution. It will also be recalled that the level to which the externality should be abated is related to the fact that economic activities creating pollution very often have positive externalities – benefits to society – as well. This is why, from an economic perspective, a zero pollution level can never be required. Such an approach would imply the termination of any economic activity leading to pollution. It would accordingly stifle much economic activity and thus lead to large social losses.

The relevant question from an economic perspective becomes how to define efficient pollution levels and efficient abatement levels. The formulation of these levels depends upon the desired environmental quality. This in turn is to some extent dependent upon the preferences of the citizens concerning environmental quality and this is related to the level of economic development in a particular nation or region. The desired environmental quality will hence result in environmental quality standards which may depend upon the preferences of the citizens and upon the development level in a particular society. The discipline of economics can be used to determine the types of emissions according to which this particular environmental quality can be achieved. Cost-benefit analysis will indicate from an economic perspective whether the marginal costs of further pollution abatement outweigh the marginal benefits in terms of increased environmental quality. Where the costs of further marginal abatement are high, the further reduction in environmental harm would lead to higher costs than benefits and would make no sense.

3. Instruments

Assuming that the efficient pollution standard imposed upon polluters with the goal of internalizing environmental externalities has been determined, the next question is the range of instruments appropriate to achieve this efficient standard. These include direct regulation through command and control, liability rules, taxes and charges. Liability rules, as an instrument, force potential polluters to compensate victims for any environmental harm inflicted upon them.[12] The basic idea is that this flexible system can, under certain assumptions such as the solvency of the polluter, provide incentives for efficient pollution abatement. An element of choice is available to the polluter. Regulation, on the other hand, involves little or no choice. Are the legal and economic approaches different in this regard?

It is striking that the legal and economic approaches seem to diverge to an important extent in relation to the preferences afforded to the main instruments of environmental policy. According to the traditional approach of environmental economics, much of the analysis focuses on environmental taxation. There is considerable discussion on how the taxation mechanism, as developed by Arthur Pigou, could be used to provide incentives to environmental polluters for an optimal internalization of the externality. Economists discuss in detail how environmental taxes should be calculated efficiently. They strongly advocate the use of environmental taxes as efficient instruments that can, at relatively low cost, provide incentives to polluters for pollution abatement. Environmental taxes at the same time afford a degree of flexibility. The tax will not dictate how the polluter must internalize the externality. This will be determined by the polluter. This contrasts sharply with the instrumental approaches of environmental law. The types of instruments to which environmental lawyers pay most attention are these: government regulation, environmental permits, and standards – in other words regulation that in terms of environmental governance would be described as command and control regulation.

The question of instrument choice is dealt with in more detail later. At this point it is interesting to ask the question why, at least in this context, the prediction of economists – using environmental taxation – differs so strongly from reality. In many jurisdictions, especially in the United States (US), environmental taxes are rarely used. There are two explanations for this divergence. One is of a public interest nature. It relates to the fact that environmental economists may too readily assume that it is possible to calculate the costs created by the environmental externality. This may be extremely difficult in practice. A second is that environmental taxation will have beneficial incentive effects only on the condition that there are effective monitoring and enforcement systems in relation to environmental taxes.[13] Monitoring and enforcement are costly and seldom perfect. The effectiveness of environmental taxes reduces when polluters can escape paying the tax. In addition, especially in the US, taxes are seldom used because of the influence of private interests.

Rent-seeking behaviour may similarly explain why, more particularly in relation to environmental taxation, the 'economic prescriptions'[14] are not always followed. There is a further reason why in the US emission taxes are seldom used and policy still relies to a large extent on the command and control approach. This is because firms prefer emission standards to taxes. The reason is that standards serve as a barrier to entry by new firms, thus raising the profits of existing firms. Charges, on the other hand, do not preclude entry by new firms but they represent an additional cost to the existing firms in the market.[15] This basic point has been developed by those who have examined the implications of rent-seeking for pollution taxation.[16]

4. Principles

(a) The polluter pays principle

There are notable differences between the economic approach and the legal approach to the understanding and application of the principles and concepts of environmental law. First, there is the polluter pays principle. The simple way in which it is formulated in environmental policy is 'that the polluter should pay', which is, from an economic perspective, ambiguous to say the least.[17] On the one hand, one could argue that the fact that polluters have to pay for environmental harm equals the duty to internalize externalities. This is one of the starting points of environmental economics. It was on the basis of this polluter pays principle that Arthur Pigou advocated the use of environmental taxes as the main instrument to internalize externalities.[18] One of the problems with the Pigouvian approach is that the only solution thereby envisaged to environmental problems is the fact that the polluter should be exposed to the social costs created by the polluting activity.

It has been the major achievement of Ronald Coase to demonstrate that, by addressing externalities as a one-sided problem – namely the factory causing harm to the victims – this is a too one-sided approach. One could as easily argue that it is the presence of the neighbours – the potential victims – which in fact limits the rights of the operator of the factory. Harm from this perspective is not one-sided but reciprocal. According to the Coase theorem, the problem is rather the conflicting uses of property rights. The optimal solution is not necessarily that 'the polluter should pay'. As the Coase theorem illustrated, a victim pays model – in the sense that victims pay for preventive measures – could equally lead to the optimal solution. Accordingly, one problem with a one-sided presentation of the polluter pays principle is that it neglects the insights from the Coase theorem. To achieve optimal pollution abatement, it is not necessary that the polluter pays either the prevention costs or the damage costs.

There is a second problem with a one-sided presentation of the polluter pays principle. If it is transposed to environmental liability, the polluter pays principle would be interpreted as a duty imposed on polluters to pay not only the costs of prevention but also for any environmental damage that might occur. This would amount to a strict liability rule. Although there are strong arguments in favour of a strict liability rule – particularly when ultra-hazardous activities cause the pollution – in some cases a negligence rule could equally lead to an optimal internalization of the externality. A negligence rule requires polluters to pay for the costs of prevention. Since the polluters will be considered to have complied with the due care requirement, they will not have to pay compensation for the victim's damage. Thus the negligence rule illustrates that polluters can be given optimal incentives to take care, even though they do not pay the damage costs.

These examples show that the polluter pays principle is in these senses ambiguous. If a broad interpretation is applied and the polluter pays principle is considered only as the obligation of the injurer to internalize externalities, then the polluter pays principle is in line with economic analysis. However, internalizing the externality does not necessarily imply that polluters should in addition compensate victims for the environmental harm caused.

(b) The proximity principle

Conflicts between the legal and the economic approaches are apparent in yet another principle inherent in environmental policy: the proximity principle. This principle informs, especially in the area of waste, that waste should be both treated and, if possible, eliminated at its source. Such a principle has serious economic limitations. From an economic perspective, one could argue that a party with a comparative advantage should perform the production or service. An efficient alternative to waste treatment at its source is to trade the waste with other parties who can deal with it. It has been demonstrated that this issue often gives rise to conflicting views.[19] From an economic perspective, the law of comparative advantage should govern international trade and should apply to waste as a tradeable commodity. All participants would gain, if nations were allowed to ship waste to the country best equipped to deal with it. The waste exporting country would pay a lower price than if the waste had to be treated internally. The waste importing country would make a profit by providing a service at a lower cost.

Moral concerns expressed by environmentalists often oppose trade in waste. It is argued that dealing with waste remains the fundamental responsibility of the state where the waste originated from and that this responsibility cannot be delegated.[20] This demonstrates the conflicting views of economists and environmental lawyers. Indeed, from an economic perspective there would be no objection to shipping waste from Europe, for example to the Sahara desert, and to store it there at relatively low cost. Potential environmental harm may be low – assuming that the waste is not dangerous, toxic or treated illegally. However, these types of trade are usually prohibited or at least substantially restricted – for example by the Basle Convention on the Control of Transboundary Movements of Hazardous Wastes and their Disposal. These prohibitions are often put in place for ethical reasons. The proximity principle has a strong ethical appeal. The theory is that the community where the waste is generated should treat its own waste itself and not export it to its neighbours and especially not to developing countries.

(c) The precautionary principle

A third example of a potential divergence between the legal and economic approaches raises the question how to deal with uncertainty. The legal approach regulates the treatment of uncertain risks by the application of the precautionary principle.[21] Although there are many different interpretations of the precautionary principle,[22] the bottom line is that uncertainty about potential risks – for example the introduction of a new drug – should not be a reason to postpone taking measures. Principle 15 of the Rio Declaration provides that 'where there are threats of serious or irreversible damage, lack of full scientific certainty shall not be used as a reason for postponing cost-effective measures to prevent environmental degradation'.[23]

From an economic perspective the concern about the precautionary principle is that it could lead to overregulation and that costly precautions would be taken without evidence that this would lead to a reduction in environmental harm. In this sense economists would argue that a too narrow application of the precautionary principle may bring about a waste of scarce resources. The problem from the economic perspective is the asymmetry of information over time. This means that information on the costs of prevention and precaution are available and calculable today, whereas the benefits and costs to the environment in the future may be diffuse and hard to estimate.

An interesting example is the critical analysis by Ogus of the European Directive concerning screen equipment.[24] The Directive requires employers to meet standards relating to the design of the screen, the desk and the chair and to other environmental factors. The problem according to Ogus is that, although health problems may arise from the use of display screens, there is no hard evidence indicating serious effects.[25] The general concern is that a too strict application of the precautionary principle could lead, on the one hand, to high social costs today – in terms of positive externalities that are not generated since particular activities would be prohibited. On the other hand, the benefits of the strict regulation would be doubtful. There is hence a risk, in the words of Ogus, that the precautionary principle would lead 'to some loose reasoning about uncertain risks with, potentially at least, socially harmful results'.[26]

A too strict application of the precautionary principle may also lead to what is referred to as risk-risk trade-offs. For example, a particular substance – a drug – could be prohibited because of uncertain risks in the future, but this prohibition could in turn lead to greater risks – of diseases being spread.[27] These examples show that there is – at least potentially – some divergence between the way in which environmental principles are presented by environmental lawyers and the way in which they are interpreted from an economic perspective.[28]

5. Convergence or Divergence

(a) Introduction

It has been pointed out in preceding paragraphs that the starting points of environmental law and environmental economics may be different. Environmental lawyers stress the need to protect the environment using environmental legal instruments, whereas economists justify the need for environmental law via the theory of market failure by treating environmental pollution as an externality. When transaction costs are zero or low, then, according to economists, intervention of the legal system would not be necessary so long as the internalization of the externality is the goal to be achieved by the policy maker. A further important source of divergence can be identified: according to environmental lawyers distributional aspects may play an important role. Thus, even when the conditions of the Coase theorem – low transaction costs – are met, environmental lawyers would argue in favour of the imposition of a liability upon the polluter because it would be fair and equitable to let the polluter rather than the victims pay for the pollution abatement equipment. This would amount to a legal – here distributional – interpretation of the polluter pays principle.

(b) The use of environmental charges

It has already been emphasized in preceding paragraphs that environmental lawyers rely to a considerable extent on regulation via the command and control approach, whereas economists rely more on environmental taxes. Nevertheless, it must be acknowledged that environmental taxes are used increasingly by policy makers. This is true also for environmental charges. While each is a financial instrument, they are conceptually different. Charges have become relatively popular in Europe. In some cases charges are associated with standards. Here are some examples.

It has been pointed out[29] that in the Netherlands water pollution caused by the 14 industries responsible for 90 per cent of total water pollution decreased by 50 per cent between 1969 and 1975 and by another 20 per cent by 1980. Significantly, half of this reduction was due to the effluent charge. Similar success stories come from Germany,[30] where the imposition of water effluent charges led to significant increases in water treatment facilities. This in turn prompted most of the firms to comply with the existing emission standards. Germany – like most European countries – continues to have a combination of effluent charges and emission standards. It is hard to argue that the significant investments in water treatment facilities were due mainly to the charges system and not, for example, to the threat of administrative or criminal sanctions or both for a violation of emission standards. These findings indicating the success of effluent charges in Germany are consistent with independent findings that environmental taxes lead to a considerable reduction of emissions into the aqua system and into the air.[31] Then there is the study that compared water pollution charges in France, the Netherlands and the Federal Republic of Germany.[32] It came to the same conclusion that effluent charges provide a strong incentive to invest in water pollution abatement equipment. It remains impossible, however, to disentangle the separate effects of charges and emission standards. This is particularly so in Germany where the charges are halved for emitters who meet the effluent standards.

(c) The formulation of environmental standards

Environmental standards continue to be a significant instrument for the achievement of environmental goals. The use of cost-benefit analysis is being incorporated increasingly into the processes for setting standards and for developing environmental policy generally. An example is the European Directive on Integrated Pollution Prevention and Control (IPPC) of 1996.[33] More generally, however, legal analysis has been increasingly occupied with the question how a guideline for environmental standard setting can be provided. This question is important, first, to give a court some indication of what the balancing of interests means in practice in the environmental cases before the court. Second, guidelines are important to guide the standard setting behaviour of administrative agencies when no clear instructions from the legislator are at hand. Third, these general principles can guide the operator of a plant when there are no fixed environmental standards to inform what kind of process or abatement technology should be chosen. These issues have created an interest in providing general principles for the formulation of environmental standards.

The same philosophy underlies the concept that emerged later and known as the Best Available Technique (or technology) Not Entailing Excessive Costs (BATNEEC).[34] The required 'best available technique' (BAT) is in itself not much guidance to an agency or to the regulated industry. The vagueness is obvious. Guidelines like 'best practical means' (BPM) or BAT are imprecise in relation to the balancing of costs and benefits. It is, however, possible to find an implied reference to the economic cost-benefit test in the notion of BAT. In this case, in defining the term 'practical', the question of when costs are excessive needs to be answered. On the other hand, the reference to economic notions becomes more explicit in the BATNEEC principle. Indeed, the notion of 'not entailing excessive costs' seems to refer to cost-benefit analysis (CBA). A tentative conclusion is that the legal system seems to apply an economically relevant principle.

These concepts are to a large extent[35] reflected in the IPPC Directive discussed briefly above. Article 9(4) prescribes that the emission limit values and the equivalent parameters shall be based on BAT, without indicating the use of any technique or specific technology. The preparatory documents to the Directive had made clear that the emission limit values should take into account the quality standard to be achieved.[36] According to the IPPC Directive, therefore, emission limit values should be determined not only by BAT but also by the quality to be achieved. Article 2(11) of the IPPC Directive defines what BAT means, namely:

> the most effective and advanced stage in the development of activities and their methods of operation which indicates the practical suitability of particular techniques for providing in principle the basis for emission limit values designed to prevent and, where that is not practicable, generally to reduce emissions and the impact on the environment as a whole.

Reference to a cost-benefit test underlies the definition of 'available':

> available techniques shall mean those developments on a scale which allows implementation in the relevant industrial sector, and their economically and technically viable conditions, taking into consideration the costs and advantages, whether or not the techniques are used or produced inside the Member State in question, as long as they are reasonably acceptable to the operator.

This Directive thus makes reference to cost-benefit analysis and hence to economic reasoning.

(d) The use of the precautionary principle

The use of the precautionary principle reveals a similar tendency. Doctrinally the legal and economic approaches strongly diverge. It has already been noted that lawyers enthusiastically support the precautionary principle, while economists warn that it may be too costly and that it would stifle economic activity and innovation. It is noticeable at the policy level that policy makers on the one hand embrace the precautionary principle and on the other hand warn that a too far-reaching interpretation of the precautionary principle would simply become too costly. This emerges from a review of the European Commission's approach to the precautionary principle.

On 2 February 2000 the European Commission published a communication on the precautionary principle.[37] The purposes of this communication are, first, to establish guidelines for applying the principle and, second, to avoid unwarranted recourse to the precautionary principle as a disguised form of protectionism. The Commission accepts that recourse to the precautionary principle acknowledges that scientific evaluation does not allow the risk to be determined with sufficient certainty. The implementation of an approach based on the precautionary principle should accordingly start with a scientific evaluation that identifies the degree of scientific uncertainty. This is referred to as risk assessment. The precautionary principle continues to play a role at the second stage: namely that of risk management. Based on the scientific evaluation about the level of uncertainty, decision-makers then have to accept the political responsibility to determine the 'acceptable' level of risk for society. How this is done is important.

When measures are necessary to give effect to the precautionary principle, the Commission indicates that these measures should similarly be based on an examination of the potential benefits and costs of action or lack of action. The Commission stresses that this is not simply an economic cost-benefit analysis. The scope of this approach is much broader and includes non-economic considerations, such as the efficacy of possible options and their acceptability to the public. Measures taken to give effect to the precautionary principle should in addition be reviewed periodically in the light of scientific progress and amended as necessary.

The approach of the European Commission indicates that some of the fears of economists about a too-rigid interpretation of the precautionary principle seem to have been incorporated in this communication. An important point is that, when the precautionary principle is applied, the Commission explicitly states that account should be taken of the potential benefits and costs of action or lack of action. In other words, precisely as economists had proposed, cost-benefit analysis constitutes a part of the application of the precautionary principle.

ENVIRONMENTAL LIABILITY

1. Introduction

The different approaches of environmental lawyers and of environmental economists to policy instruments are helpfully revealed by discussing the ways in which environmental liability rules and liability rules in general are formulated and applied. This discussion is structured as follows:

- a description of the differing views about the goals of liability rules from a legal perspective and from an economic perspective
- an analysis of the economic approach to environmental liability as an instrument to provide incentives for efficient care levels
- a discussion of the classic dichotomy between the rules of strict liability and of negligence.

2. The Goals of Liability Rules

The economic analysis of law in general and of accident law in particular starts from the belief that a legal rule potentially leading to a finding of liability provides incentives for careful behaviour by those who may be involved in an accident setting.[38] In this way economists tend to stress the deterrent function of tort law. While lawyers acknowledge the deterrent function of tort law, they tend to attach more value to the compensation goal of accident law. This 'victim protection' argument is discussed in the literature of both law and economics.[39] In this respect, however, it is often stressed that the best form of victim protection is to avoid victimization in the first place. It is beyond argument, however, that the prevention of accidents is at the same time a way of victim protection.

The different goals of liability rules from these two perspectives are sometimes characterised as an ex ante versus an ex post vision. Lawyers tend to be more interested in the occurrence of an accident ex post. In this case there is an actual victim to be compensated. Economists look at the potential occurrence of an accident from an ex ante perspective by asking the question how an ex post finding of liability will influence ex ante the incentives for the taking of care in a potential accident setting.

The differences in the policy approaches of lawyers and economists are not particularly clear. There are lawyers who stress the deterrent function of tort law as well as its compensatory function.[40] There are some economists who pay attention to compensation issues by stressing that accident law should aim at an equitable spreading of loss.[41] At the same time lawyers argue that tort law should lead to the imposition of duties of care aimed at prevention.[42]

3. Minimization of Accident Costs through Efficient Care Levels

From an economic perspective the main goal of liability rules is the minimization of what Guido Calabresi called the primary accident costs:[43] namely, the costs of accident avoidance and of the expected damage. There are similarly two aspects from a social perspective. First, accidents involve costs from the moment an accident occurs and harm is suffered. Second, parties potentially involved in an accident, both injurers and victims, make investments in care to avoid the occurrence of an accident. Sometimes the costs of taking care are very clear and visible – for instance the costs undertaken by firms to reduce environmental pollution by investing in water cleaning equipment or to install safety controls to avoid product defects. Sometimes they are less clear. In the event of a traffic accident, both injurers and victims are limited in their freedom of movement because they have to drive or work carefully. This is considered a cost by economists.

There is a further difference to consider – between unilateral and bilateral accidents. A unilateral accident is one in which only the care taken by one of the parties – the injurer – can influence the accident risk. A bilateral accident is one in which the behaviour of both parties can influence the accident risk.[44] In a bilateral accident situation the goal of accident law should therefore be to provide incentives to minimize the total costs, first, of the taking of care both by the potential injurer and by the potential victim and, second, of the expected damage that will occur in the event of an accident.

Economists use classic cost-benefit analysis to determine what is the level of care that will lead to the minimization of the social costs of accidents. Not surprisingly, this can be found where the marginal costs of the taking of care equal the marginal benefits of accident reduction.[45] Indeed, because the taking of care also has its price, a legal rule should provide incentives to avoid not every possible accident that might occur but only accidents that could be avoided by investments in care where the marginal costs of avoidance are lower than or equal to the marginal benefits of accident reduction. It is possible that the taking of an extremely high level of care could in addition contribute to a reduction of the accident risk. But the marginal costs of the taking of care in such a case might well be much higher than the additional benefits of accident reduction. Investments in care would in this case be inefficient and scarce resources would be wasted.[46] The levels of care where marginal costs of the taking of care equal the marginal benefits of accident reduction are referred to in the literature as optimal or efficient care levels.[47]

4. Strict Liability and Negligence Compared

(a) Introduction

It has become clear that the starting points of the economic and the legal approaches to liability as well as the language used in the context of environmental liability are different. The differences seem to disappear, however, when the specific question is the design of environmental liability. For example, a fundamental question is whether a strict liability rule or a negligence rule should be applied. There is a difference in this respect between the situation where only the injurer – a polluting company – can influence the accident risk and the situation where both parties – victim and injurer – can influence the accident risk. The first is the unilateral accident situation, whereas the second is the bilateral accident situation. In relation to environmental pollution the focus is on the unilateral accident situation, usually because the contribution of the victim to the accident risk will be less important than that of the injurer.

(b) The economic approach

According to the economic literature, if a negligence rule is adopted in a unilateral accident situation, the injurer will take optimal care, provided the due care required by the legal system is equal to the optimal care as defined by the economic model.[48] This can be easily understood. If the judicial system sets the due care standard correctly, the injurer can avoid liability by taking due care. Thus the injurer will have to take the relevant standard of care to avoid the accident. If the injurer does so, the injurer can avoid paying the costs of the expected damage. It will be recalled that the optimal care standard has been defined as the level of care where the marginal costs of care equal the marginal benefits of accident reduction. Thus, if an individual injurer takes less than the due care standard, this will be of no benefit to the individual injurer, whose total expected costs will accordingly increase. Therefore, a negligence rule will lead to an efficient outcome provided the legal system defines the due care as equal to the optimal care of the economic model.

A strict liability rule will also lead to the optimum outcome in a case where only one party can influence the accident risk. The reason is simple. A strict liability rule basically states that the injurer has to compensate for all damage irrespective of the level of care taken. It is sometimes argued that this will encourage the injurer to take excessive precautions or to take no care at all, simply because the injurer is liable anyway. Neither of these statements seems true. By making the injurer strictly liable, the social decision is in fact shifted to the injurer. In a unilateral accident case, this simply means that the injurer has to bear all the social costs of an accident, namely not only the injurer's own costs of taking care but also those of the expected damage.[49] Accordingly, the injurer will reach exactly the same decision, namely to minimize the total expected accident costs. According to the economic model already discussed, this would amount to the optimal care level. In this way the injurer will take the optimal level of care since this is the way to minimize the total expected costs. Spending more on care would increase the costs of the taking of care inefficiently, while spending less on care would increase the costs of the expected damage inefficiently.

This analysis leads to the conclusion that, in a unilateral accident situation where only the influence of the injurer's level of care is considered, both negligence and strict liability provide incentives to take optimal care. There are nevertheless important nuances to discern. So far the discussion has been limited to the relevance of the levels of care. However, the number of times a particular injurer engages in an activity – referred to as the activity level – can also influence the accident risk. For example, the more a company produces, the higher is the risk of environmental harm. In this respect there is an important difference between strict liability and negligence. Strict liability places all the costs on the injurer and therefore provides incentives to adopt both efficient care as well as efficient activity levels. According to the standard of negligence, the injurer will be immune from liability as soon as the level of efficient care is achieved. The reason is that a court cannot incorporate optimal activity levels into the due care standard required by the legal system. Consequently, if activity levels have to be controlled, strict liability may be preferred to negligence.

(c) Ancillary issues

The administrative costs of applying these two rules differ. The strict liability rule has this disadvantage. Judicial proceedings will be instigated after the accident has occurred since the injurer is always bound to compensate. Court costs can therefore be expected to be high. On the other hand, the negligence rule has high information costs for the court since it will have to determine in a particular case what were the marginal costs and marginal benefits of the taking of care.[50] This has these further ramifications.

The application of the negligence rule requires the court to set the due care standard with the ancillary burden of obtaining the relevant information – probably at a high cost. The information necessary to weigh the costs and benefits and to fix the optimal care may not be readily available to the court. On the other hand, the strict liability rule shifts all costs to the injurer who will then have to define the optimal care level. It may well be that, in relation to environmental harm, the information on optimal precaution is more readily available from within the industry. If so, this reduces the burden on the court and thus constitutes an argument in support of the strict liability rule. In some cases an information advantage may lie with the regulator. This is, as will be discussed below, an argument in favour of regulation but not necessarily against strict liability. This information advantage may constitute an additional argument in favour of strict liability for environmental harm.

(d) The application of these rules to environmental liability

How does this analysis relate to environmental liability? Environmental pollution can in most cases be considered a unilateral accident – that is when only the injurer can influence the accident risk. In this case the economic model predicts that the advantage of the strict liability rule is that it will give to the injurer an incentive not only to adopt the optimum level of activity but also to take efficient care. Since the victim cannot influence the accident risk, strict liability seems to be the solution that provides the potential polluter with the optimal incentives for accident reduction in these cases.[51] To go one step further and apply the criteria proposed by Shavell[52] for determining the choice between negligence and strict liability in relation to environmental liability, there are strong arguments in favour of strict liability. In many cases environmental pollution will be truly unilateral in the sense that only the injurer's activity can influence the accident risk – a further argument in support of strict liability.[53]

So much for the economic approach. To what extent is this approach reflected in legal rules? There are strict liability rules in many international conventions: for example in the civil liability convention of 29 November 1969 with respect to oil pollution damage[54] and in the Paris and Brussels nuclear liability conventions which impose strict liability on the licensee of a nuclear power plant.[55] Strict liability has also been incorporated in the legislation of many states. Section 7 of the Environmental Act 1995 of the United Kingdom imposes strict liability for soil pollution.[56] Chapter 32 of the Swedish Environmental Code 1998 creates a strict joint and several liability regime and imposes a duty to compensate upon the party whose activity causes bodily injury, material damage and pecuniary losses. Chapter 10 of the Swedish Code creates a strict liability rule for soil contamination. The Environmental Liability Act 1990 of Germany creates a statutory regime of strict liability.[57] In some states the move towards strict liability has come about not from formal changes in legislation but from developments in case law. For instance in France a broad interpretation of article 1384 of the Civil Code has led effectively to a strict liability regime for polluted soils.[58]

This European-wide tendency towards strict liability is now reflected in the Environmental Liability Directive of the European Union.[59] Although the way in which strict liability is formulated in the Directive is complicated, it is essentially a system which imposes strict liability on the operator for the costs of preventive or remedial action if the damage is caused by a particular hazardous activity listed in the Annex to the Directive.[60] On the other hand, a fault or negligence regime applies to damage not caused by a listed – that is a hazardous – activity. It is the view of many commentators that the distinctive applications of strict liability and of negligence in the Directive make sense from an economic perspective. Ultra-hazardous activities can be considered as unilateral because the victim may have little influence on the accident risk. Hence the strict liability rule for these cases indeed makes sense. Circumstances which are not ultra-hazardous are bilateral in the sense that the victim as well as the injurer may exercise an influence on the accident risk. In these cases it may well make sense to apply a negligence rule. In this sense the differential application of strict liability rules and negligence rules from the legal perspective seems largely to be in line with economic theory.[61]

ECONOMIC INSTRUMENTS AND COMMAND AND CONTROL INSTRUMENTS COMPARED

1. Introduction

Lawyers would regard environmental regulation as the primary instrument to control environmental harm, while economists would rather stress economic instruments such as environmental taxation. There has been an impressive amount of commentary comparing the traditional command and control approach based upon regulation with the incentive-based mechanisms often referred to as economic or market-based instruments.[62] It is impossible to engage in a general comparison between regulation and market-based instruments. This is simply because the superiority of the one or the other is very much dependent upon specific context, type of pollutant regulated, and institutional design. There is evidence that a regulatory approach can lead not only to significant reductions of waste water emissions but can also encourage the implementation of less polluting production techniques in the long run.[63] Provided command and control instruments are designed with at least one eye on cost saving, incentive-based systems are not necessarily superior to command and control instruments.[64] Care has to be taken not to distinguish excessively between the two. After all, command and control approaches include a wide variety of measures. Some are quite crude; others produce results as efficient as economic incentives.[65]

On the face of it, the approach of lawyers differs sharply from the approach of economists. In theory economists would attach more weight to the flexibility of economic instruments that provide incentives to polluters to determine for themselves the optimal ways of abating pollution. Lawyers would rather rely upon the precision of regulation whereby government sets the standards ex ante. However, the commentary discussed in the foregoing paragraphs highlights the fact that command and control instruments are not necessarily any less effective environmentally provided they are designed with an eye on cost saving.

Increasingly, it has been noted, environmental taxation systems in a variety of forms have been incorporated in many legal systems and hence into environmental law. The same is true for emissions trading. It was Dales who pointed out in the 1960s that social welfare could be increased by trading in pollution rights.[66] Lawyers originally looked with a great deal of suspicion at the idea of 'selling pollution' and hence strongly opposed the creation of a market in pollution rights whereby polluters would be able to buy their right to pollute. However, the opposition faded away when an SO_2 trading program was introduced successfully in the US.

2. A Review of Trading Regimes

Evidence has emerged since the 1980s to show the effectiveness of trading in pollution rights. It has been demonstrated that the well known US emissions trading system for air pollutants has since 1986 made real headway in certain regions and that the system has been successful.[67] More particularly the trading programs involving the Clean Air Act of the US have led to considerable cost savings, albeit that the cost savings may have been less than anticipated.[68] One problem is that trading in some cases may have led to increased emissions. This is so where the pollution rights that were sold were not being fully utilized by the owner prior to the sale. Nevertheless, the SO_2 cap and trade program has been described as a 'living legend' of market effectiveness.[69] The total annual health benefits associated with the SO_2 emissions reductions under the program were estimated to have been more than \$50 million per year.[70] It has been estimated that the annual cost savings resulting from the trading program have been as much as $150 million.[71]

The enthusiasm about the trading system associated with the US Clean Air Act comes not only from its environmental effectiveness but also from its cost-saving benefit – at least in relation to the compliance costs for industry.[72] Additionally, it has been shown that the administrative costs of running the emissions trading system under the Clean Air Act are significantly less when compared to a traditional regulatory system.[73] A similar picture emerges from other American studies examining the trading programs under the Clean Air Act.[74]

Attention has recently shifted from the US to Europe because Europe has chosen emissions trading as the instrument to implement the Kyoto Protocol and the challenges posed by climate change. The effectiveness of the EU emissions trading scheme (ETS) has been extensively analyzed.[75] The ETS is interesting because it shows the difficulties in interpreting the results of empirical research. In accordance with Directive 2003/87 of 13 October 2003[76] the European Union decided to give emissions rights free to existing industry as a result of so-called grandfathering. The private interest theory of regulation explains why emissions trading with grandfathering was chosen instead of an environmental tax. This should not come as a surprise since the interests of industry are served better by grandfathering than by costly taxation measures.[77] Whatever the effectiveness of the EU ETS, it is clear that, while originally there may have been a large divergence between lawyers and economists about the use of market-based instruments – more particularly the use of emissions trading – that divergence has rapidly disintegrated – first in the US and then in Europe.[78]

3. The Continuing Need for Government Involvement

It is important to emphasize that it is sometimes believed that market-based or economic instruments reduce the need for government intervention by letting 'the market' decide on the optimal levels of pollution. The reality is totally different. Either an environmental taxation system or an emissions trading scheme is based on an elaborate set of arrangements designed by government: for example, setting the optimal tax rate, designing an effective taxation mechanism, and prescribing how emission rights are allocated. The effectiveness of these economic instruments will to an important extent be dependent upon the accuracy of the design – basically the responsibility of government. The only difference between an economic instrument and a regulatory or command and control instrument is that the methods selected to reduce the emissions or the pollution are not imposed by the government but are chosen by the polluters. That is precisely the positive incentive effect that should be gained through the use of these economic instruments.

There is one further example of the need for government involvement. All instruments must be supported by a detailed enforcement mechanism. No matter what type of instrument is chosen, either command and control or market-based, the effectiveness of the instrument will crucially depend upon an enforcement and sanctioning system. If emissions were to take place without emission permits or without paying the tax, the entire incentive effect would be lost.[79] There may be little difference in this respect between the economic instruments preferred by economists and the command and control or regulatory instruments favoured by lawyers. In the end, both need a detailed enforcement and sanctioning system – again the responsibility of government.

OPTIMAL ENFORCEMENT MECHANISMS

1. Introduction

What are the similarities and differences in relation to enforcement instruments between the legal and the economic approaches to environmental policy? This will be discussed from two perspectives:

- by asking the question whether administrative or criminal law should be used to enforce environmental law
- by discussing an optimal enforcement strategy.

2. Administrative or Criminal Law

In relation to the enforcement of environmental law, the economic and legal approaches seem to differ. This affects the instrument to be used as well as the enforcement strategy. Environmental law has traditionally been firmly based on a system whereby environmental regulations are enforced through the imposition of criminal sanctions. Violators of environmental regulations would be exposed to fines or imprisonment or both – on the assumption that this would lead to optimal deterrence of violators.[80]

Commentators from the disciplines of both law and economics have been relatively critical of this approach. It is based exclusively on criminalization. It is argued that the criminal law is not an appropriate tool to fight environmental violations. Some even argue that criminalization may be counter effective. The reason is that many of the few detected violations are not prosecuted – thus leading to low expectations of sanctions.[81] This has led law and economics scholars like Anthony Ogus to favour administrative fines.[82] The economic argument in favour of administrative fines is that they are less costly to impose since the threshold for a conviction under administrative law is often lower than under criminal law. The availability of administrative fines could deter some polluters in those cases where criminal proceedings were not available. Perhaps this is why Ogus questioned whether the United Kingdom had 'the right regime' since its enforcement mechanism was based only on criminalization.

At the same time a revolution has taken place in several European legal systems. In these jurisdictions the enforcement of environmental law is no longer based only on the criminal law. Significantly, administrative fines have been introduced to a realistic extent. In this respect again some convergence between the legal and economic approaches has taken place – at least in those legal systems where alternatives to the criminal law have been introduced.[83]

3. An Enforcement Strategy

(a) The range of strategies

Finally, what are the economic and legal approaches to enforcement strategies? Traditionally, it is suggested, economists might be expected to rely on a deterrence approach. The starting point of this approach is that a potential polluter will make a rational calculus of the costs and the benefits of complying with the environmental rule and will comply only when the expected costs of a violation are higher than the potential gains. It is well known that violating environmental rules – for example, not installing a water treatment plant or delaying such an investment – can generate substantial gains. In order to deter the violation of an environmental rule, there needs to be the expectation of a substantial penalty or sanction to convince the potential perpetrator to comply. The expected sanction consists, on the one hand, of the probability of being inspected, prosecuted and found guilty and, on the other hand, of the sanction being imposed.

Lawyers and criminologists as social scientists – but not economists – are more likely to favour a cooperation model. Thus an agency – probably a public agency – would try to convince the polluter to comply with the environmental rule through persuasion and the provision of relevant information.[84] The theoretical differences between the deterrence-based economic approach and the cooperation-based legal or criminological approach are in reality minimal. Each approach has attracted criticism.

(b) The effectiveness of these strategies

A cooperation strategy has the inherent risk that powerful and knowledgeable companies will de facto be able to control and 'capture' the agency. In a study of environmental law enforcement in Denmark, it has been demonstrated that cooperative enforcement was undermined by capture.[85] If an excessively strict deterrence approach is adopted, there is evidence that it may produce counter effects. For instance, where compliance is impossible because of practical difficulties, enforcement is regarded as unreasonable.[86] The evidence is not all negative. When administrative agencies are well informed but small and medium-sized enterprises are not, a cooperation strategy can lead to a situation where the controlling agency in fact assists the enterprise towards compliance with environmental regulation.[87]

The emerging approach to the selection of an enforcement strategy indicates that a distinction should be made between different types of violations and of violators. Accordingly, a cooperation compliance model would be used for first-time offenders who violated environmental law out of ignorance. A harsher but deterrence-based enforcement strategy would be followed in the case of repeat offenders who willfully violated environmental rules in order to obtain economic benefits. It has been concluded generally that neither a deterrence approach based on incentives nor a coordination or cooperation approach based on advice and persuasion can in isolation be an effective or efficient intervention strategy.[88] The most effective enforcement strategy thus depends to a large extent upon the type of violators and the type of violations in any particular set of circumstances.

CONCLUSION

This chapter has focused on the economic approach to environmental governance by analyzing the principles that constitute the basis for such an economic approach. It has complemented this by examining to what extent the economic approach differs from the legal approach. An analysis of environmental policy and legal doctrine with reference to environmental liability shows that the language used by each of the two approaches differs markedly. Economists talk about environmental pollution in terms of externalities and would consider the goal of environmental law to be the internalization of those externalities. Lawyers take a more rights-based approach and stress the importance of protecting the environment as such. To some extent this leads indeed to differing approaches. The legal perspective underpinning the polluter pays principle is different from the economic perspective. Lawyers may deduce from the polluter pays principle that polluters should pay not only for the costs of pollution abatement but also for the costs associated with environmental harm – essentially a strict liability rule. The economic perspective is more nuanced. The Coase theorem implies that, when transaction costs are zero, the optimal solution – pollution abatement – would be achieved if the victims pay for pollution abatement. The optimal incentives for the taking of care in the context of environmental liability could to some extent be secured by a negligence rule.

In relation to instrument choice, it is striking that economists tend to focus on the importance of environmental taxation, financial incentives and market-based instruments such as emissions trading. This contrasts sharply with the instruments not only advocated by lawyers but also applied in legal practice. In most legal systems the command and control approach based on permits and regulatory standards remains the most important mechanism for achieving environmental policy, while environmental taxation plays only a relatively modest role. Further, in relation to optimal enforcement policy, lawyers have traditionally had a tendency to focus on the criminal law as the only tool that would deter polluters from violating the rules of environmental law. Economists, on the other hand, stress that alternatives such as civil penalties and administrative fines would in appropriate circumstances not only constitute a deterrence incentive but also provide a proportionate sanction.

It is important to look beyond the differences in language between the economic and the legal approaches and to examine the extent of these differences in the context of specific policy outcomes. Although the approaches may have diverged in the past, economic insights are being incorporated increasingly into the development of environmental policy. This gives rise to a substantial convergence of approach. For instance, in relation to environmental liability lawyers would have stressed the importance of victim compensation, whereas economists would have seen liability rules as tools to deter polluters. However, if the outcome is an efficient liability rule, each of the two approaches leads to the conclusion that a strict liability rule may be appropriate for a particular group of ultra-hazardous activities. This outcome has emerged in a number of legal systems. This is because, at least to some extent, economic reasoning has been increasingly incorporated into the field of environmental policy. Because the goal of environmental liability is not only to provide compensation to victims but also to deter polluters, this argument has in some cases been explicitly mentioned at the stage of policy development.[89]

There are other examples of the increasing influence of the insights from economics on environmental policy. In some cases there is more divergence between the two approaches and in others more convergence. The documents preparatory to the IPPC Directive referred to the instruction that polluters should apply the best available technologies not entailing excessive costs.[90] This refers implicitly to the economic notion of cost-benefit weighing. In relation to enforcement policy there is increasingly a convergence between the potentially harsh economic deterrence-based approach and the softer criminological compliance or cooperation strategy directed at polluters. The identification of different polluter groups has recently led to the use of a range of different compliance strategies. On the one hand, a cooperation strategy is used for the polluters who have failed to comply with an environmental rule because of the absence of information: for example, small and medium-sized enterprises that have committed administrative violations because of ignorance. On the other hand, a deterrence-based approach is more appropriate for the more informed and rational but calculating offenders: for example, those repeat offenders who cause serious environmental harm with a profit-making objective – those engaged in wildlife crime.

What overall conclusions may be reached? Although the starting points and the language of the economic and the legal approaches may differ, the outcomes in practice may not be much different in the end. This is because, to an important extent, economic perspectives are increasingly being taken into account at the legislative level. One can even argue that there is undoubtedly more room for a further integration between the legal and the economic approaches, for example in the context of environmental liability. Nevertheless, many polluters continue to benefit from significant limitations on their liability – the so-called liability caps – which apply, for example, to the licensees of nuclear installations. Economic analysis suggests that these caps are undesirable because they lead to under-deterrence and constitute a de facto subsidy for the nuclear operator.[91] This is only one example to indicate that a further integration of the economic and the legal approaches may lead to fruitful results. These could in the end lead to an improvement in the quality of environmental law and hence to better protection of the environment.

NOTES

1. Barbier (1997).
2. Selden and Song (1995, p. 162).
3. Esty and Porter (2005, pp. 391–3).
4. Ibid. (pp. 424–5).
5. Barbier (1997, pp. 369–70).
6. In legal terms this would refer to setting ambient quality standards or defining environmental quality standards.
7. Faure and Betlem (2008, p. 129).
8. Coase (1960) and Coase (1990).
9. Faure and Weishaar (2012, pp. 400–401).
10. Discussed later in this chapter.
11. The Coase theorem remains relevant. For details, see Faure and Weishaar (2012, p. 401).
12. The use of civil liability is discussed later in this chapter.
13. See Peeters (2006b) for a discussion of the necessity to provide for the enforcement of market-based instruments.
14. Hahn (1989).
15. Buchanan and Tullock (1975). See also Coelho (1976, pp. 976–8) and Yohe (1976, pp. 981–2).
16. Lee (1985) and Brooks and Heijdra (1987).
17. The polluter pays principle is included in many legal instruments inter alia of the OECD and the European Union. For a detailed description, see Sands and Peel (2012, pp. 228–33).
18. See Pigou (1951).
19. Frey (1997).
20. Ibid.
21. This principle has been much discussed. See for example Fisher, Jones and Von Schomberg (2006) and Sands and Peel (2012, pp. 217–28).
22. See Zander (2009) and Haritz (2011).
23. De Sadeleer (2002).
24. Directive 90/270/EC, OJ 1990 L156/14.
25. Ogus (1995).
26. Ogus (2006, pp. 158–61).
27. Sunstein has discussed the costs associated with these risk-risk trade-offs in Sunstein (1996).
28. See further on this point Faure and Skogh (2003, pp. 19–39).
29. Dewees, Duff and Trebilcock (1996).
30. Brown and Johnson (1984, p. 929).
31. Frey (1992).
32. Bongaerts and Kraemer (1987).
33. OJ 1996 L257/27. This Directive has been replaced by the Directive 2010/75/EU on industrial emissions. It remains relevant to discuss the standard setting process in the earlier Directive because it is largely repeated in the later Directive. Both processes align with economic principles.
34. For a discussion of the legal meaning of some of these concepts, see Faure and Ruegg (1994) and Ogus (1984, p. 207).
35. With the exception that the IPPC Directive does not recognize the possibility of a differentiated approach to setting emission limit values for the purpose of reaching a similar target.
36. Faure (2010, p. 734).

37. Communication from the Commission on the precautionary principle (COM(200) 1 final of 2 February 2000).
38. For excellent overviews of the role of liability and insurability as 'engineering instruments', see Endres and Staiger (1996), Wagner (1999), Monti (2001) and Gimpel-Hinteregger (1994, pp. 19–58).
39. The rules of tort law may serve the aims both of deterrence and corrective justice. See Schwartz (1997).
40. Koziol (1997, pp. 8–13); Koziol (2015, pp. 746–50).
41. Veljanovski (1981).
42. For example Hein Kotz holds that it is not compensation as such, but rather prevention that is the goal of tort law: Kotz (2001, p. 17). For an overview of other opinions of lawyers, see Visscher (2015, pp. 14–16).
43. Calabresi (1961) and Calabresi (1970).
44. This distinction has been made by Shavell (1987, p. 7).
45. Ibid.
46. This is so only in a risk-neutral setting. In a case of risk aversion, higher investments in care may be efficient because a reduction of accident risk will in such a case also remove the disutility of risk from a risk-averse person.
47. Landes and Posner (1981, p. 870) and Polinsky (1983).
48. Shavell (1980).
49. Polinsky (1983, p. 39) and Shavell (1987, pp. 8 and 11).
50. Brown (1973, p. 343), Calabresi (1975, p. 666, fn 22) and Shavell (1987, p. 9).
51. See Faure (1995) for how it applies to nuclear liability.
52. Shavell (1987).
53. In some cases it is the victim's activity that caused the harm – if the victim knowingly came to the nuisance. This may lead to a denial of a claim for compensation. See Wittman (1980, pp. 557–68) for a discussion of the coming to the nuisance doctrine.
54. For details see Wang (2011, pp. 62–73).
55. Sands and Peel (2012, pp. 738–45).
56. For more details on the UK soil pollution regime, see McIntyre (1996). For an overview of environmental law in the UK, see Jones (1999). For an overview of the liability system for environmental damage in the UK, see the 1996 McKenna Report, *Study of Civil Liability Systems for Remedying Environmental Damage* [Report for the European Commission, by Cameron McKenna, Mistral House, 160 Aldersgate Street, London EC1A 4DD, UK] and the 2001 Chris Clarke Report for the European Commission, *Update Comparative Legal Study* [update on the Mckenna Report]; http://europa.eu.int/comm/environment/liability/legalstudy.htm.
57. For an overview of environmental law in Germany, see Pape and Schillhorn (1999). See also the 1996 McKenna Report, *Study of Civil Liability Systems for Remedying Environmental Damage* [Report for the European Commission, by Cameron McKenna, Mistral House, 160 Aldersgate Street, London EC1A 4DD, UK] and the 2001 Chris Clarke Report for the European Commission, *Update Comparative legal Study* [update on the McKenna Report]; http://europa.eu.int/comm/environment/liability/legalstudy.htm. See also Hager (1993, pp. 41–4).
58. See Faure (2001) for a critical discussion of French tort law from an economic perspective.
59. Directive 2004/35/CE of 21 April 2004, OJ L143/56.
60. Brans (2013, pp. 31–50) and Liu (2013, pp. 287–93).
61. For further details see Faure and De Smedt (2013) and De Smedt and Faure (2010).
62. See Revesz and Stavins (2007) and Freeman and Kolstad (2007).
63. Stephan (1998).
64. Oates, Portney and McGartland (1989).

65. Oates (1990) and Oates (1996).
66. Faure and Weishaar (2012, p. 406).
67. Oates (1986) and Oates and McGartland (1985).
68. Hahn and Hester (1989).
69. Burtraw and Palmer (2004).
70. See Burtraw and Palmer (2004, p. 47) and Ellerman (2007) who shows that the SO_2 emissions trading programme caused significant reductions in emissions.
71. Keohane (2007, p. 224).
72. Burtraw and Palmer (2004, p. 59).
73. Ellerman (2004) and Ellerman et al. (2000).
74. Nash and Revesz (2002) and Tietenberg and Johnston (2004).
75. See the discussion in Douma, Massai and Montini (2007).
76. OJ L275/32.
77. Rodi (2005).
78. For further details see Woerdman, Clò and Arcuri (2008) and Kuik and Oosterhuis (2008).
79. See Peeters (2006a) and Peeters (2006b) on the importance of ensuring compliance with market-based instruments and particularly with emissions-trading regimes.
80. The approach followed by environmental lawyers reflects the economic deterrence logic developed in the seminal work of Gary Becker. See Becker (1968). See Firestone (2003) for an application of Becker's crime theory to environmental crime.
81. See Faure and Svatikova (2012) for an assessment of expected sanctions in four European legal systems.
82. Ogus and Abbott (2002a), Ogus and Abbott (2002b) and Faure, Ogus and Philipsen (2009).
83. See Faure and Svatikova (2012) for an overview of these tendencies in some European countries.
84. Van Rooij (2006, pp. 228–33).
85. May and Winter (1999).
86. Hawkins (1984).
87. Johnston (2001, pp. 271–304).
88. Gunningham (2011, p. 66).
89. See the White Paper on Environmental Liability, COM(2000) 66 final of 9 February 2000, which explicitly refers to deterrence as one of the goals of an environmental liability regime. This White Paper constituted the basis for the later Environmental Liability Directive which was discussed above.
90. See COM(93) 423 final, p. 4.
91. Trebilcock and Winter (1997) and Faure and Fiore (2009).

REFERENCES

Barbier, B. (1997), 'Introduction to the Environmental Kuznets Curve. Special Issue', *Environmental and Development Economics*, 369–70.

Becker, G.S. (1968), 'Crime and Punishment: An Economic Approach', *Journal of Political Economy* **76**(2), 169–217.

Bongaerts, J.C. and R.A. Kraemer (1987), 'Water Pollution Charges in Three Countries. Control Through Incentives', *European Environment Review* **1**(4), 12–9.

Brans, E. (2013), 'Fundamentals of Liability for Environmental Harm under the ELD', in L. Bergkamp and B.J. Goldsmith (eds), *The EU Environmental Liability Directive. A Commentary* (Oxford, Oxford University Press), pp. 31–50.

Brooks, M.A. and B.J. Heijdra (1987), 'Rent-Seeking and Pollution Taxation: An Extension', *Southern Economic Journal* **54**(2), 335–42.
Brown, G. and R. Johnson (1984), 'Pollution Control by Effluent Charges: It Works in the Federal Republic of Germany, Why Not in the US?', *Natural Resources Journal* **24**, 929–66.
Brown, J.P. (1973), 'Toward an Economic Theory of Liability', *Journal of Legal Studies* **2**(2), 323–49.
Buchanan, J. and G. Tullock (1975), 'Polluters' Profits and Political Response: Direct Controls versus Taxes', *American Economic Review* **65**, 139–47.
Burtraw, D. and K. Palmer (2004), 'SO_2 Cap-and-trade Program in the United States. A "Living Legend" of Market Effectiveness', in W. Harrington, R.D. Morgenstern and Th. Sterner (eds), *Choosing Environmental Policy. Comparing Instruments and Outcomes in the United States and Europe* (Washington DC, Resources for the Future), pp. 41–66.
Calabresi, G. (1961), 'Some Thoughts on Risk Distribution and the Law of Torts', *Yale Law Journal* **70**, 499–553.
Calabresi, G. (1970), *The Costs of Accidents. A Legal and Economic Analysis* (New Haven, CT, Yale University Press).
Calabresi, G. (1975), 'Optimal Deterrence and Accidents', *Yale Law Journal* **84**, 656–71.
Coase, R.H. (1960), 'The Problem of Social Cost', *Journal of Law and Economics* **3**, 1–44.
Coase, R.H. (1990), *The Firm, the Market and the Law* (Chicago, University of Chicago Press).
Coelho, Ph.R.P. (1976), 'Polluters' Profits and Political Response: Direct Control versus Taxes: Comment', *American Economic Review* **66**(5), 976–78.
De Sadeleer, N. (2002), *Environmental Principles. From Political Slogans to Legal Rules* (Oxford, Oxford University Press).
De Smedt, K. and M.G. Faure (2010), 'The implementation of the Environmental Liability Directive', *Zeitschrift für Europäisches Privatrecht* **4**, 783–808.
Dewees, D., D. Duff and M. Trebilcock (1996), *Exploring the Domain of Accident Law; Taking the Facts Seriously* (Oxford, Oxford University Press).
Douma, W.Th., L. Massai and M. Montini (eds) (2007), *The Kyoto Protocol and Beyond. Legal and Policy Challenges of Climate Change* (The Hague, TMC Asser Press).
Ellerman, A.D. (2007), 'Are Cap-and-trade Programs more Environmentally Effective than Conventional Regulation?', in J. Freeman and C.D. Kolstad (eds), *Moving to Markets in Environmental Regulation. Lessons from 20 Years of Experience* (Oxford, Oxford University Press), pp. 48–62.
Ellerman, A.D., P.L. Joskow, R. Schmalensee, J-P. Montero and E.M. Bailey (2000), *Markets for Clean Air: the US Acid Rain Program* (Cambridge, Cambridge University Press).
Ellerman, D. (2004), *The US SO_2 Cap-and-trade Program* (Paris, OECD).
Endres, A. and B. Staiger (1996), 'Ökonomische Aspekte des Umwelthaftungsrecht', in M. Ahrens and J. Simon (eds), *Umwelthaftung, Risikosteuerung und Versicherung* (Berlin, Erich Schmidt Verlag GmbH & Co), pp. 79–93.
Esty, D.C. and M.E. Porter (2005), 'National Environmental Performance: An Empirical Analysis of Policy Results and Determinants', *Environment and Development Economics* **10**, 391–434.
Faure, M. (1995), 'Economic Models of Compensation for Damage Caused by Nuclear Accidents: Some Lessons for the Revision of the Paris and Vienna Conventions', *European Journal of Law and Economics*, 21–43.
Faure, M. (2001), 'Tort Liability in France: An Introductory Economic Analysis', in B. Deffains and Th. Kirat (eds), *Law and Economics in Civil Law Countries* (London, Routledge), pp. 169–81.

Faure, M. (2010), 'Optimal Specificity in Environmental Standard-Setting', in C. Dias Soares, J.E. Milne, H. Ashiabor, L. Kreiser and K. Deketelaere (eds), *Critical Issues in Environmental Taxation, International and Comparative Perspectives*, Vol. VIII (Oxford, Oxford University Press), pp. 730–45.

Faure, M. and G. Betlem (2008), 'Applying National Liability Law to Transboundary Pollution: Some Lessons from Europe and the United States', in M. Faure and Y. Song (eds), *China and International Environmental Liability, Legal Remedies for Transboundary Pollution* (Cheltenham, Edward Edgar), pp. 129–91.

Faure, M.G. and K. De Smedt (2013), 'The ELD's Effects in Practice', in L. Bergkamp and B.J. Goldsmith (eds), *The EU Environmental Liability Directive. A Commentary* (Oxford, Oxford University Press), pp. 299–314.

Faure, M.G. and K. Fiore (2009), 'An Economic Analysis of the Nuclear Liability Subsidy', *Pace Environmental Law Review* **26**(2), 419–47.

Faure, M. and M. Ruegg (1994), 'Environmental Standards Setting through General Principles of Environmental Law', in M. Faure, J. Vervaele and A. Weale (eds), *Environmental Standards in the European Union in an Interdisciplinary Framework* (Antwerp, Maklu), pp. 39–60.

Faure, M. and G. Skogh (2003), *The Economic Analysis of Environmental Policy and Law. An introduction* (Cheltenham, Edward Elgar).

Faure, M.G. and K. Svatikova (2012), 'Criminal or Administrative Law to Protect the Environment? Evidence from Western Europe', *Journal of Environmental Law* **24**(2), 253–86.

Faure, M. and S.E. Weishaar (2012), 'The Role of Environmental Taxation: Economics and the Law', in J.E. Milne and M.S. Andersen (eds), *Handbook of Research of Environmental Taxation* (Cheltenham, Edward Elgar), pp. 399–421.

Faure, M.G., A. Ogus and N. Philipsen (2009), 'Curbing Consumer Financial Losses: The Economics of Regulatory Enforcement', *Law & Policy* **31**(2), 161–91.

Firestone, J. (2003), 'Enforcement of Pollution Laws and Regulations: An Analysis of Forum Choice', *Harvard Environmental Law Review* **27**(105), 122–35.

Fisher, E., J. Jones and R. Von Schomberg (2006), *Implementing the Precautionary Principle. Perspectives and Prospects* (Cheltenham, Edward Elgar).

Freeman, J. and C.D. Kolstad (eds) (2007), *Moving to Markets in Environmental Regulation. Lessons from 20 Years of Experience* (Oxford, Oxford University Press).

Frey, B.S. (1992), *Umweltökonomie* (Göttingen, VandenHoeck & Ruprecht).

Frey, B.S. (1997), *Not Just for the Money. An Economic Theory of Personal Motivation* (Cheltenham, Edward Elgar).

Gimpel-Hinteregger, M. (1994), *Grundfragen des Umwelthaftung* (Vienna, Manz).

Gunningham, N. (2011), 'Enforcing Environmental Regulation', *Journal of Environmental Law* **23**(2), 169–201.

Hager, G. (1993), 'Umwelthaftungsgesetz: The New German Environmental Liability Law', *Environmental Liability*, 41–4.

Hahn, R.W. (1989), 'Economic Prescriptions for Environmental Problems: How the Patient Followed the Doctor's Orders', *Journal of Economics Perspectives* **3**(2), 95–114.

Hahn, R.W. and G.L. Hester (1989), 'Where Did all the Markets Go? An Analysis of EPA's Emissions Trading Program', *Yale Journal on Regulation* **6**, 109–53.

Haritz, M. (2011), *An Inconvenient Deliberation. The Precautionary Principle's Contribution to the Uncertainties Surrounding Climate Change Liability* (Deventer, Wolters Kluwer).

Hawkins, K. (1984), *Environment and Enforcement, Regulation and the Social Definition of Pollution* (Oxford, Clarendon Press).

Johnston, J.S. (2001), 'The Law and Economics of Environmental Contracts', in E.W. Orts and K. Deketelaere (eds), *Environmental Contracts: Comparative Approaches to a*

Regulatory Innovation in the United States and Europe (The Hague, Kluwer Law International), pp. 271–304.

Jones, B. (1999), 'Environmental Law in the United Kingdom', in N.S.J. Koeman (ed.), *Environmental Law in Europe* (The Hague, Kluwer Law International), pp. 561–628.

Keohane, N.O. (2007), 'Cost Savings from Allowance Trading in the 1990 Clean Air Act: Estimates from a Choice-based Model', in J. Freeman and C.D. Kolstad (eds), *Moving to Markets in Environmental Regulation. Lessons from 20 Years of Experience* (Oxford, Oxford University Press), pp. 194–229.

Kotz, H. (2001), *Deliktsrecht*, 9th edn (Neuwied, Luchterhand).

Koziol, H. (1997), *Österreichisches Haftpflichtrecht* (Vienna, Manz).

Koziol, H (2015), 'Comparative Conclusions', in H. Koziol (ed.), *Basic Questions of Tort Law from a Comparative Perspective* (Vienna, Jan Sramek Verlag), pp. 683–838.

Kuik, O. and F. Oosterhuis (2008), 'Economic Impacts of the EU ETS: Preliminary Evidence', in M. Faure and M. Peeters (eds), *Climate Change and European Emissions Trading. Lessons for Theory and Practice* (Cheltenham, Edward Elgar), pp. 208–22.

Landes, W. and R. Posner (1981), 'The Positive Economic Theory of Tort Law', *Georgia Law Review* **15**, 851–924.

Lee, D.R. (1985), 'Rent-Seeking and its Implications for Pollution Taxation', *Southern Economic Journal*, 731–44.

Liu, J. (2013), *Compensating Ecological Damage. Comparative and Economic Observations* (Antwerp, Intersentia).

May, P.J. and S. Winter (1999), 'Regulatory Enforcement and Compliance: Examining Danish Agro-Environmental Policy', *Journal of Policy Analysis and Management* **18**(4), 625–51.

McIntyre, O. (1996), 'The UK Environmental Act 1995: Section 57: A Contaminated Land Regime at Last!', *Environmental Liability* **4**, 67–74.

Monti, A. (2001), 'Environmental Risk: A Comparative Law and Economics Approach to Liability and Insurance', *European Review of Private Law* **9**(1), 51–79.

Nash, J.R. and R.L. Revesz (2002), 'The Design of Marketable Permit Schemes to Control Local and Regional Pollutants', in T. Swanson (ed.), *An Introduction to the Law and Economics of Environmental Policy: Issues in Institutional Design* (Amsterdam, Emerald Group Publishing Limited), pp. 331–77.

Oates, W. (1986), 'Market Incentives for Environmental Protection: A Survey of some Recent Developments', in M. Peston and R. Quandt (eds), *Prices, Competition and Equilibrium* (Lanham, Maryland, Rowman & Littlefield), pp. 251–67.

Oates, W.E. (1990), 'Economics, Economists and Environmental Policy', *Eastern Economic Journal* **16**(4), 292–303.

Oates, W.E. (1996), 'The Environment and the Economy: Environmental Policy at the Crossroads', in W.E. Oates (ed.), *The Economics of Environmental Regulation* (Cheltenham, Edward Elgar), pp. 311–45.

Oates, W. and A.M. McGartland (1985), 'Marketable Permits for the Prevention of Environmental Deterioration', *Journal of Environmental Economics and Management* **12**(3), 207–28.

Oates, W.E., P.R. Portney and A.M. McGartland (1989), 'The Net Benefits of Incentive-based Regulation: A Case Study of Environmental Standard Setting', *American Economic Review* **79**, 1233–42.

Ogus, A.I. (1994), *Regulation. Legal Form and Economic Theory* (Oxford, Clarendon Press).

Ogus, A.I. (1995), 'Quality Control for European Regulation', *Maastricht Journal of European and Comparative Law* **2**, 325–38.

Ogus, A.I. (2006), *Costs and Cautionary Tales. Economic Insights for the Law* (Oxford, Hart Publishing).

Ogus, A.I. and C. Abbott (2002a), 'Pollution and Externalities', in T. Swanson (ed.), *An Introduction to the Law and Economics of Environmental Policy: Issues in Institutional Design* (Boston, JAI Press), pp. 493–516.
Ogus, A.I. and C. Abbott (2002b), 'Sanctions for Pollution: Do We Have the Right Regime?', *Journal of Environmental Law* **14**(3), 283–98.
Pape, K.A. and K. Schillhorn (1999), 'Environmental Law in the Federal Republic of Germany', in N.S.J. Koeman (ed.), *Environmental Law in Europe* (The Hague, Kluwer Law International), pp. 273–92.
Peeters, M. (2006a), 'Inspection and Market-Based Regulation through Emissions Trading: The Striking Reliance on Self-Monitoring, Self-Reporting and Verification', *Utrecht Law Review* **2**(1), 177–95.
Peeters, M. (2006b), 'Enforcement of the EU Greenhouse Gas Emissions Trading Scheme', in M. Peeters and K. Deketelaere (eds), *EU Climate Change Policy. The Challenge of New Regulatory Initiatives* (Cheltenham, Edward Elgar), pp. 169–87.
Pigou, A.C. (1951), *A Study in Public Finance*, 3rd (revised) edn (London: MacMillan).
Polinsky, A.M. (1983), *Introduction to Law and Economics (*Boston and Toronto, Little, Brown & Co).
Revesz, R.L. and R.N. Stavins (2007), 'Environmental Law', in A.M. Polinsky and S. Shavell (eds), *Handbook of Law and Economics* (Amsterdam, Elsevier), pp. 499–589.
Rodi, M. (2005), 'Legal Aspects of the European Emission Trading Scheme', in B. Hansjürgens (ed.), *Emissions Trading for Climate Policy, US and European Perspectives* (Cambridge, Cambridge University Press), pp. 199–221.
Sands, Ph. and J. Peel (2012), *Principles of International Environmental Law*, 3rd edn (Cambridge: Cambridge University Press).
Schwartz, G. (1997), 'Mixed Theories of Tort Law: Affirming both Deterrence and Corrective Justice', *Texas Law Review* **75**, 1801–34.
Selden, Th.M. and D. Song (1995), 'Neoclassical Growth, the J-curve for Abatement and the Inverted U-curve for Pollution', *Journal of Environmental Economics and Management* **29**(2), 162–8.
Shavell, S. (1980), 'Strict Liability versus Negligence', *Journal of Legal Studies* **9**, 1–25.
Shavell, S. (1987), *Economic Analysis of Accident Law* (Cambridge Massachusetts, Harvard University Press).
Stephan, G. (1988), 'Economic Impact of Emission Standards: A Computational Approach to Waste Water Treatment in Western Europe', in D. Bös, M. Rose and Chr. Seidl (eds), *Welfare and Efficiency in Public Economics* (Berlin, Springer), pp. 401–22.
Sunstein, C.R. (1996), 'Health, Health Tradeoffs', *University of Chicago Law Review*, **63**(4), 1533–71.
Tietenberg, T. and M. Johnston (2004), 'Ex Post Evaluation of Marketable Permits: Methodological Issues and Literature Review', in OECD, *Tradable Permits. Policy Evaluation, Design and Reform* (Paris, OECD), pp. 9–44.
Tol, R.S.J. (2009), 'The Economic Effects of Climate Change', *Journal of Economic Perspectives* **23**(2), 29–51.
Trebilcock, M. and R. Winter (1997), 'The Economics of Nuclear Accident Law', *International Review of Law and Economics*, 215–43.
Van Rooij, B. (2006), *Regulating Land and Pollution in China, Law-making, Compliance and Enforcement: Theory and Cases* (Dissertation, Leiden University Press).
Veljanovski, C.G. (1981), 'The Economic Theory of Tort Liability – Toward a Corrective Justice Approach', in P. Burrows and C.G. Veljanovski (eds), *The Economic Approach to Law* (London, Butterworths), pp. 125–50.
Visscher, L. (2015), *Debated Damages* (The Hague, Eleven Publishing).
Wagner, G. (1999), 'Haftung und Versicherung als Instrumente der Techniksteuerung', *Versicherungsrecht*, 1441–80.

Wang, H. (2011), *Civil Liability for Marine Oil Pollution Damage. A Comparative and Economic Study of the International, US and Chinese Compensation Regime* (Alphen aan den Rijn, Kluwer Law International).
Wittman, D. (1980), 'First Come, First Served: An Economic Analysis of "Coming to Nuisance"', *Journal of Legal Studies*, 557–68.
Woerdman, E., S. Clò and A. Arcuri (2008), 'European Emissions Trading and the Polluter-Pays Principle: Assessing Grandfathering and Over-allocation', in M. Faure and M. Peeters (eds), *Climate Change and European Emissions Trading. Lessons for Theory and Practice* (Cheltenham, Edward Elgar), pp. 128–50.
Yohe, G. (1976), 'Polluters' Profits and Political Response: Direct Control versus Taxes: Comment', *American Economic Review* **66**, 981–2.
Zander, J. (2009), 'Different Kinds of Precaution. A Comparative Analysis of the Application of the Precautionary Principle in Five Different Legal Orders' (Dissertation, Maastricht University, 17 April).

6. Human rights and the environment: a tale of ambivalence and hope[1]

Anna Grear

INTRODUCTION

Deeply significant concerns lie behind contemporary efforts to bring human rights law and environmental law into productive and progressive alignment. The twenty-first century witnesses the Earth's living systems under relentless and destructive pressure from the adverse impacts of industrial capitalist and consumer lifestyles. Simultaneously—along with the multitudes of defenceless living species adversely affected by environmental degradation—millions of human beings are increasingly placed at profound environmental risk and forced to suffer brutally uneven impacts of economic globalization, deepening vulnerability and escalating violence.[2]

The convergence—or attempted convergence—between human rights and environmental obligations faces genuinely complex challenges. First, there is the frequently discussed risk of conflicts between, on the one hand, environmental policies, rules, rights and responsibilities and, on the other hand, the human rights to development, privacy and private property. Second, there is a related perception that the methodological individualism of mainstream human rights discourse impedes the collective action necessary to rescue 'the environment'[3] from human practices that degrade its quality. Third, there are ongoing issues concerning rights. These include questions of *whose* rights and *which* rights are to take priority in a conflict of legal paradigms. Such complexity extends, quite naturally, to the vexed question of whether the two institutionally separated international legal orders of human rights law and environmental law can be reconciled in a productive and progressive manner.[4]

This chapter will argue that international environmental law and international human rights law—despite the existence of very real separations and tensions between them—show hopeful signs of progress in their relationship. Notwithstanding such hopeful signs, however, both human rights law and environmental law share underlying subject-object relations inimical to their stated aims. This reality, once acknowledged, might, with sufficient imagination, become the departure point for their reconfigured engagement and transformation.

This chapter will begin by tracing the historical and institutional emergence of international human rights law and international environmental law before analyzing their shared subject-object relations. The chapter will then suggest how these fields of law might be re-imagined and placed on an alternative mutual foundation. Such a foundation could move them towards a more hopeful relationship with their own stated aims and thus enable them to respond more appropriately to the human and environmental crises of the twenty-first century and beyond.

THE ORIGINS OF HUMAN RIGHTS IN INTERNATIONAL LAW

The story of the genesis and evolution of human rights is thousands of years long. Human rights have antecedents in religious traditions emphasizing norms of human to human ethics; in well established philosophical traditions; in early national codes of antiquity; in early international interventions concerning the protection of religious liberty and the abolition of the slave trade; and in the emergence of international humanitarian law and rules concerning the protection of citizens abroad.[5]

However, despite this long antecedent story, traditional accounts of the history of international human rights law generally locate its emergence in a twentieth-century, post-Second World War fusion of natural law and positive law together with an unprecedented international 'consensus' 'on substantive norms with high moral voltage'.[6] It is generally agreed by historians of international human rights law that the 1945 United Nations Charter[7] brought human rights into the sphere of international law. In the process of doing so, the UN Charter achieved the simultaneous internationalization of human rights and the birth of the 'human individual' as a subject—rather than an object—of international law.[8] These developments authoritatively established the idea that ensuring respect for human rights should no longer be entrusted solely to the power of the nation state.[9] The international order of human rights created by the UN Charter was relatively limited in scope, but since then the United Nations has been instrumental in the production of an apparently ceaseless and expanding process of setting international human rights standards through an almost kaleidoscopic proliferation of instruments and treaties.

All international human rights treaties take their symbolic and juridical life from the Universal Declaration of Human Rights (UDHR).[10] Even in 2016 the UDHR is widely understood to be the symbolic fulcrum of the international human rights order. It possesses immense symbolic power and exerts a virtually irresistible degree of normative traction. The position of the UDHR at the apex of the system is amply supported by the fact that no state has ever denounced it since the moment of its adoption in 1948 right up until 2016. Indeed, the UDHR was affirmed by the 1993 Vienna Declaration and Programme of Action[11]—a reassertion of the UDHR's status entirely consistent with its self-enunciation as a 'common standard of achievement for all peoples and all nations'.[12] The UDHR also inspired an entire generation of post-colonial states. It provided the rights-centred template for a host of new national constitutional documents. It is also credited with being the normative source of over 200 international human rights instruments. As Donnelly puts it, 'for the purposes of international action, "human rights" means roughly "what is in the Universal Declaration of Human Rights"'.[13]

It is well recognized that international human rights law has developed in a series of phases or stages.[14] The initial vigour of human rights standard-setting activities by the United Nations chilled in the light of cold war politics. There was a marked lull in the production of human rights documents that remained unbroken until the adoption in 1965 of the International Convention on the Elimination of all Forms of Racial Discrimination (CERD).[15] This development primarily reflected the concerns of the newly decolonized nations swelling the ranks of UN membership and whose concerns were beginning to influence the preoccupations of the international community.[16] In 1966 there was a second phase of general or universal standard setting when the rights stated in the UDHR found further enunciation in two international legal documents. These are, in narrow chronological order, the International Covenant on Economic, Social and Cultural Rights (ICESCR)[17] and the International Covenant on Civil and Political Rights (ICCPR).[18] The dichotomy between these two 'categories' of rights is often traditionally explained as reflecting the cold war ideological fracture. However, for many the dichotomy simultaneously reflects perceived differences between the categories of rights in terms of their relative justiciability, their differing operation as primarily 'negative' or 'positive' rights, and their relative enforceability.[19]

Together the UDHR, the ICESCR and the ICCPR are referred to as the 'International Bill of Rights'. They are supplemented, further expressed or implicitly criticized—depending on one's viewpoint—by later standard-setting exercises. These tend to focus either upon specific rights, for example as does the United Nations Convention against Torture and Other Cruel, Inhuman or Degrading Treatment or Punishment (UNCAT)[20] or upon the holders of specific rights, for example as does the Convention on the Elimination of all Forms of Discrimination against Women (CEDAW).[21] Finally, the almost 'carnivalistic'[22] expansion of the number of international UN human rights treaties has been accompanied, at different times and rates, by the spread and maturation of a set of regional international human rights regimes.[23] Regional courts have been pivotal in such developments. Similarly, developments at the national level have deepened the juridical potency of human rights.

Human rights, despite their intensifying overlaps and interconnections, were traditionally—and often still are—viewed as having expanded through three generations: 'first generation' civil and political rights; 'second generation' social, economic and cultural rights; and 'third generation' solidarity rights. Environmental rights, which are sometimes linked to the 'greening' of human rights, are often placed in the third generation of such rights.[24]

THE ORIGINS OF ENVIRONMENTAL PROTECTION IN INTERNATIONAL LAW

Compared to human rights law, environmental law is a relatively recent legal innovation. There emerged before the middle of the twentieth century a few important and substantively environmentally responsive legal developments: for example, nineteenth-century private law rules relating to pollution damage; nineteenth-century statutory provisions about public health; and a few international conservation laws that emerged in the 1900s[25] and later.[26] However, environmental law did not exist as a recognized or a discrete category of law, either internationally or domestically, until the 1960s.[27]

There is evidence of environmental awareness and concern expressed in the writings of nineteenth-century thinkers such as John Muir, John Burroughs, Henry David Thoreau and George Perkins Marsh,[28] but it was not really until the 1960s that the complex and inter-systemic nature of ecology, the fragility of earth systems and their vulnerability to human activity were well understood. An important moment in the popularization of an emerging environmental consciousness was the publication of Rachel Carson's iconic *Silent Spring*.[29] This book evocatively expressed the growing concern that sparked the rapid proliferation of legal arrangements to protect soil, air and ecosystems such as forests and wetlands. These responses emerged initially in the United States, Europe, New Zealand and Australia. These largely statutory developments were significantly buttressed by grassroots energies and by the activities of non-governmental organizations. Accordingly, concern for the environment steadily became part of the mainstream political agenda. By the 1980s, environmental law was increasingly an important and widely discussed component of international law.[30]

The obvious intimacy between environmental law and environmentalism lends a certain degree of justification to scholars, such as Tarlock, who claim that environmental law is relatively discontinuous with earlier legal traditions because of its special focus upon environmental stewardship. Tarlock argues that the aim of environmental law is 'to change the system of resource use incentives from those that induce unsustainable development to those that induce environmentally sustainable development [and that] [e]nvironmental law is thus a fundamentally new concept with more discontinuity than continuity with past legal and intellectual traditions'.[31]

However, there are also different views of past legal and intellectual contributions. Coyle and Morrow, for example, argue that environmental law, in effect, revives stewardship ethics predating the industrial revolution. Further, that it is possible to discern in the English common law tradition a philosophical thread running through certain currents of legal thought concerning tort and property and a relationship between public and private law that can accurately be described, in contemporary terms, as being distinctively environmental.[32]

For Tarlock, however, environmentalism, as the wellspring of environmental law's concerns, places itself in an explicitly critical relationship to the philosophical and historical antecedents of western global capitalism and its colonial past. Thus environmental law, which he suggests exhibits a high degree of homogeneity across legal systems, for him signals a fundamental shift in values.[33]

It is clear, it is conceded, that there has been a shift, but the strength of Tarlock's claim is frayed not only by the work of scholars such as Coyle and Morrow but also by an examination of the dominant subject-object assumptions shared by human rights law and environmental law—discussed later in this chapter. Environmentalism may well place itself in a critical relationship to past commitments, but environmental law, as law, continues to reflect antecedent foundations that themselves reflect the complex and contradictory flows and eddies of legal thought and the philosophical suppositions that inform Eurocentric legal culture. This culture continues to a large extent to underwrite international law.[34] Indeed, it may well be that it is the framework of international law itself that produces the homogeneity of environmental law observed by Tarlock. The analysis of the foundations of international law undertaken later in this chapter indicate that Tarlock's claim concerning the 'value shift' represented by environmental law is somewhat more problematic than he implies.

Whatever its origins, there can be little room for doubt about the growing contemporary homogeneity of environmental law. Yang and Percival go so far as to identify the emergence of what they call 'global environmental law'. This is a development that signals what they describe as:

> a growing convergence around a few principal approaches to environmental regulation … [and a set of] growing international linkages … blurring the traditional divisions between private and public law and domestic and international law, promoting integration and harmonization. The result has been the emergence of 'global environmental law'—a field of law that is international, national, and transnational in character all at once.[35]

This development reflects a shared sense of the increasingly serious implications of environmental realities such as the climate crisis. Moreover, it reflects the combination of national efforts to improve national environmental law and regulation in the context of the ongoing efforts of nation states to coordinate global action through the integration and harmonization of environmental norms at the international level.[36]

HUMAN RIGHTS AND ENVIRONMENTAL PROTECTION—SIMULTANEOUS CONVERGENCE AND TENSION

1. The Normative Context

The relationship between human rights and environmental protection has become critically important. There has been, perhaps unsurprisingly given the growing sense of human and environmental crisis underpinning the global realities of the late twentieth and early twenty-first centuries, a notable convergence of energies between human rights law and environmental law. The two fields, however, still have a somewhat binary relationship and exhibit tensions that 'cannot be wished away'.[37] The links between the two fields were first explicitly formalized in the Stockholm Declaration at the culmination of the 1972 Stockholm Conference on the Human Environment.[38] Principle 1 of the Declaration, in particular, establishes an international normative foundation for the importance of linking human rights and environmental concerns: 'Man has the fundamental right to freedom, equality and adequate conditions of life, in an environment of a quality that permits a life of dignity and well-being.'[39]

According to this formulation, a healthy environment is understood to be a precondition for the fulfillment of human rights. This is an approach, perhaps unsurprisingly, echoed by 'many human rights tribunals and experts [for whom environmental protection is] a precondition to the enjoyment of several internationally guaranteed human rights, especially the rights to life and health'.[40] The relationship between human rights and the environment in this formulation reflects an axiomatic anthropocentrism often criticized by environmental activists. Additionally, in some respects the relationship between human rights law and the environment moves in two directions: for example, various international environmental agreements conceptualize human rights as key mechanisms for achieving environmental goals[41]—a position amounting, perhaps, to a certain degree of institutional instrumentalism.

Correspondingly, meanwhile, in international human rights law, substantive and procedural human rights entitlements involving environmental considerations and claims are also increasingly common. This evolution clearly does not yet fundamentally challenge the anthropocentric orientation either of international human rights law or of international environmental law. Nevertheless, despite this reality, which many regard as a key weakness of human rights-based approaches, the Stockholm Declaration is described by Morrow as a 'crucial institutional recognition of the escalating impact of human activity on the environment and a statement of intent to address it'.[42] And, also on the positive side, the Stockholm Declaration has at least moved responsibility for achieving its environmental goal beyond the involvement of the state towards a broader conception of human responsibility. It does this in two ways. First, it invokes the responsibility of 'citizens and … enterprises and institutions at every level, all sharing equitably in common efforts'. Second, it notes that 'individuals in all walks of life as well as organizations in many fields, by their values and the sum of their actions will shape the world environment of the future'.[43]

2. Emerging Convergences

The human rights approach to environmental protection has taken three predominant forms: the greening of existing human rights; the pursuit of procedural guarantees through which concerned citizens can make clear their environmental concerns; and arguments centering upon the provision of substantive rights to environmental quality, and this includes a 'global environmental right'.[44] Procedural guarantees aiming at participatory justice in the solving of environmental dilemmas have proved particularly powerful as mechanisms for the pursuit of environmental democracy. Prominent examples are the participatory rights underlined by principle 10 of the Rio Declaration on Environment and Development[45] and by the Aarhus Convention.[46]

The impressive international evolution of environmental rights as constitutional rights has likewise pointed the way to convergence between human rights and environmental concerns.[47] This is, moreover, a development decisively influenced by civil society initiatives and the energies of human rights and democratic impulses.[48] Human rights rhetoric and law have thus been highly influential in the search for environmental protection and accountability. It may be that the prime position given to human rights-based justifications and normative strategies in this field reflects, among other things, the relative histories of human rights law and environmental law. Human rights law, after all, significantly pre-dates environmental law. Shelton, for example, points out that the paucity of references to the environment in human rights instruments is 'because most human rights treaties were drafted and adopted before environmental protection became a matter of international concern'.[49] In addition, enforcement mechanisms for international human rights law are more developed than those embedded in international environmental law. Accordingly, 'the availability of individual complaints procedures has given rise to extensive jurisprudence from which the specific obligations of states to protect and preserve the environment are detailed'.[50]

Despite the paucity of references to environmental protection in human rights treaties, the juridical links between human rights and the environment have increasingly emerged over time in a range of normative instruments and two of the regional human rights treaties even contain specific provisions on the 'right to environment'.[51] The increasingly forceful normative energies driving such convergence are also richly evident in the 'environmental rights revolution' analysed by Boyd and by Gellers.[52] More than 90 national constitutions have now codified environmental rights for human beings. Arguments are also increasingly made for a freestanding 'right to environment or a global environmental right'[53] as a way of addressing the shortcomings of environmental law. There is also a nascent case for arguing that something like a right to environmental quality is emerging as a norm of customary international law.[54]

3. Continuing Tensions

Despite all this progress, important tensions persist. Even the mutual distrust between environmentalists and human rights activists is still palpable. Both sides uneasily eye the other's priorities, even though, as Gearty reminds us, 'the need to bring the environmental and human rights movements together has been rendered both urgent and vital by the impending climate change catastrophe'.[55] All things considered, and despite evidence of a growing normative convergence, it would be, on balance, deeply premature to assert the untroubled interdependence of human rights and environmental protection. Indeed, their interdependence is often asserted precisely by ignoring the depth of the tensions between them. These tensions do not vitiate interdependence per se but they do render it uneasy in certain respects and point to very profound challenges. And, as just intimated, some of these tensions ultimately reflect underlying concerns over past, present and future injustices particularly well reflected in activist suspicions.

This ultimate concern is captured rather well by Gearty, who reminds us that:

> … just as the human rights protagonist has often given the impression that he or she does not care about the natural world, so too have some environmentalists seemed at times to despise people. There is in such activists a potential casualness about humankind which may be understandable emotionally (it is our reckless species which has brought us to the verge of collapse) but which when worked through into policies and positions will—if left unchallenged—invariably involve the poor and the vulnerable (whose personal responsibility for environmental change is nonexistent) paying a heavy price for the polluting and destructive recklessness of others.[56]

Themes reflected in Gearty's comment bring to mind, again, Tarlock's argument that environmental law, unlike human rights law, fundamentally reflects *environmentalism.* Tarlock, as noted above, suggests that contestation within environment law has increasingly moved to the sidelines as international environmental law has matured and gained greater normative consistency. However, there is good reason to suggest that despite Tarlock's optimism, environmental law overwhelmingly still facilitates 'business as usual',[57] and that greater consistency in environmental law might be predicated on something less progressive than an innocent form of environmentalism. This possibility takes this analysis to a review of ambivalence and contradiction in environmental law: a challenge ultimately shared by human rights law. This challenge, in turn, indicates the depth of the need for radically new foundations for human rights law and environmental law alike.

HUMAN RIGHTS AND ENVIRONMENTAL PROTECTION—POWER IMBALANCES, DEEP ASSUMPTIONS, AMBIVALENCE AND CONTRADICTION

1. Central Structural Challenges

In his 2013 review of environmental law and governance, Turner argues that 'the very design of the law itself is fundamentally predisposed to environmental degradation and forms part of a dysfunctional global legal architecture which cannot achieve environmental sustainability'.[58] This is a challenging proposition. Turner's conclusion might come as something of a surprise to many, including, perhaps, some environmentalists. But to anyone well versed in critical accounts of law's ideological structures, including those of international human rights law, Turner's conclusion would be unsurprising, if not entirely predictable.

Turner relates his conclusion to the historical development of 'the global legal architecture' of environmental law as part of international law. This architecture, he points out, was not ad hoc, 'but was developed through careful and deliberate design'.[59] Turner is unequivocal that the existing foundational commitments of international law make international environmental law very unlikely to succeed. These foundations, he argues, make it extremely challenging to hold some of the most egregious offenders against environmental standards to account. In particular, the centrality of the corporate form and its interests are of decisive significance for his argument. In his words, 'even during [their] formative years, certain features were being built into [corporations'] design that would eventually have huge impacts on the environment in the modern era'.[60] Turner concludes that separate legal personality, limited liability, the separation between ownership and control of corporations, and the legal duty placed upon company directors to pursue the company's best interests as a profit-making entity are all key structural reasons that explain why environmental legal responses fail to meet important accountability targets for modes of environmental degradation.[61]

Support for Turner's analysis, amongst other sources, comes from the work of Dangerman and Schellnhuber concerning the unsustainability of what they call the 'contemporary industrial metabolism'.[62] Dangerman and Schellnhuber argue that the unsustainable fossil-nuclear energy system is, in effect, *locked in* by structural conditions. Significantly, their extensive assessment of the various factors involved in this lock-in identifies 'modern corporate law as a crucial system element that has thus far been largely ignored'.[63] They point to fundamental design features of the juridical corporate form, which are central to the structural features at the heart of Turner's analysis. These features include the intensification of shareholder control, a development that produces an asymmetry operating as a key block to feedback loops capable of liberating energy structures from fossil fuel dependency paths. It should be noted, moreover, that the structural components of the corporate form are increasingly globalized. Critiques of the modern corporate entity are now as relevant for China and Japan as they are for France and Germany, and continue to be particularly salient for the Anglo-American corporate form now so dominant in the international order.[64]

2. Contemporary Structural Trajectories

Turner anticipates the response that there are new forms of 'environmentally-facing corporations'. He counters this by arguing that 'even in a corporation that has certain environmental standards, there is still a bottom line as [the corporation] is a business venture that is designed for the creation of profit and therefore such standards can only go so far'.[65] Structural factors, moreover, are pivotal. Sinden, for example, points out that it is too easy:

> to lose sight of the vast power imbalance that still forms the backdrop for the political debate on climate change. Increasingly, … stories of corporations going green are being spun into a larger cultural narrative of the corporation as redeemed sinner. Like the Grinch stopping at the top of the mountain to hear the joyful voices of the carolers below, the new green corporation has heard the environmental gospel and its heart has grown five sizes. But it would be a mistake to think that the recent concessions of many in the fossil fuel industry with respect to global warming mean that corporations have suddenly come around to represent the best interests of the general public. Corporations are still structured by law to put the short-term profits of shareholders first. Even as they abandon their oppositionist stance and come to the table acknowledging the existence of climate change and the need for regulation to curb it, they will come to the bargaining table with the primary purpose and duty of protecting short-term share price.[66]

Sinden's point highlights the radical power imbalance and market dominance structurally embedded by contemporary neoliberal globalization and ideology. These factors are associated with deepening human vulnerability[67] and with the climate crisis.[68] Business corporations have exerted and continue to exert considerable global influence, with the complex complicity of neoliberal states. This influence affects, moreover, not only states themselves but also the specialist legal architectures, including the key international institutions, set up to respond to centrally important law and governance challenges, including climate change.[69] Indeed, the global dominance exercised by the business corporation is the most widely accepted characteristic of the global age for theorists of globalization—whatever else they disagree upon.[70] The degree of systemic closure is stifling. Transnational corporations (TNCs)[71] exert almost unimaginable power. They are supported in their dominance by powerful economic institutions, which are themselves 'both a symptom of and a stimulus for globalization'.[72] These include the International Monetary Fund (IMF), the World Trade Organization (WTO) and the European Central Bank (ECB).

It is not unreasonable to see such current trajectories as continuances of earlier patterns notable in nineteenth-century industrialization[73] and colonialism.[74] These, and the foundations of the international legal order itself, were deeply entangled in the search by imperial colonial powers for raw materials to fuel progress 'at home'. Both international human rights law and international environmental law are core components of an international legal order built upon distinctively colonial foundations.[75] As such, they are implicated in highly problematic and questionable modes of privileging and come freighted with the self-same subject-object assumptions that drove European rationalistic expansionism and underpinned colonial orders of hierarchy: human-human and human-nature hierarchies.[76] Despite the fact that more recently, in both international human rights law and in international environmental law, changing world perspectives have emerged clearly in relation to ecological concerns, the underlying tensions remain relatively intractable. These tensions directly relate to a history and a lingering contemporaneity of European epistemic mastery. Eurocentric epistemic bias still dominates, notwithstanding counter-hegemonic narratives and participatory mechanisms.[77]

3. Going Deeper

The subject-object relations between humans and 'their environment' assumed and enacted by colonialism and industrialization are those that Merchant famously implicates in the phrase 'death of nature'.[78] Her analysis centres upon the Cartesian rendering of 'nature' as dead *res extensa*—mere inert matter—and upon the Baconian inauguration of a distinctively masculinist mode of scientific dominance. This convergence produced a system of values at the top of which a prurient and masterful 'man' was dominant: the subject constructed as epistemic overlord acting on the world as 'object'. In the process, an entire hierarchy of human beings considered to be less than fully rational was folded into an imposed order of masculinist European mastery. The less than fully rational included women, children, the indigenous and the nomadic. The Eurocentric ordering of humanity was accompanied by the elevation of private property and market rationality as 'givens' of civilizational progress. These essentially hierarchizing dynamics are deeply familiar themes to anyone versed in critical accounts of international human rights law which, in line with these patterns, still produces entirely predictable marginalized subjectivities.[79]

These ideological trajectories and formations have produced a situation in which international human rights law has been widely colonized by formations of global corporate capital.[80] At the same time, as noted above, the very foundations of environmental law work against its commitments from 'within'.[81] It is therefore important to face the eco-destructive and inhumane implications of the historically powerful ideological imperatives that haunt the law as subterranean archetypes expressed in tropes of legal subjectivity and sovereignty. These ideological imperatives are emerging with deepening force in the era of neoliberal globalization and of an industrialization-driven Anthropocene crisis. In short, for all the tensions between them that reflect differing fundamental moral impulses and institutional distinctions, international human rights law and international environmental law share the same set of fundamental subject-object relations and the ideologies that feed off them. Both international human rights law and international environmental law exhibit ambivalence and haunting ambiguities that fracture the very hopes they each purport to offer.

What, then, is to be done? What future foundations might bring a renewal of the hope thus far betrayed? New philosophical foundations need to be considered before reflecting on conduits for their values in the form of epistemic access to the juridical order. In short, what might be the future sites of legal 'hearing', whether formal or informal, in which grassroots energies can bring different future histories to bear?

FUTURE FOUNDATIONS AND HOPE RENEWED

1. The Changing Contexts of Human Rights Law and Environmental Law

The commitments resting upon Cartesian subject-object relations and so central to the underlying ideological tilt of the international legal order have been thoroughly exposed and critiqued by critical legal scholarship. However, as the twenty-first century complexity deepens, it seems especially urgent and potentially hopeful to emphasize that the implications of new scientific insights increasingly render Cartesian subject-object relations impossible to maintain with any degree of intellectual plausibility. Such scientific insights and developments, together with the new materialist philosophy that responds to them, push thinking beyond the broadly anti-Cartesian critique offered by critical scholarship towards an essentially post-Cartesian account of reality. This development has significant implications for the entire range of assumptions upon which human rights law and environmental law alike are based.

Coole and Frost argue that what is at stake in the scientific and technological developments informing new materialism is 'nothing less than a challenge to some of the most basic assumptions that have underpinned the modern world, including its normative sense of the human and its beliefs about human agency, [and] … its material practices such as the ways we labor on, exploit and interact with nature'.[82] Such a challenge problematizes the very foundations of human rights law and environmental law and of their relationship. In particular, the collapse of their supposed foundations necessitates a radical questioning of the entire range of assumptions upon which human rights law and environmental law are based—including the human subject at their axis.

The distinctively twenty-first century complexities in relation to which human rights law and environmental law must be situated include climate change, instantaneous algorithm-driven global capital flows, population movements, genetically modified organisms (GMOs), bio-engineering, artificial intelligence, robotic systems and the sheer saturation of contemporary life in biotechnologies, digitalization and virtual technologies. These and other such complexities necessarily 'disturb the conventional sense that agents are exclusively humans who possess cognitive abilities, intentionality and freedom to make autonomous decisions and the corollary presumption that humans have the right or ability to master nature'.[83]

2. Philosophical Responses to the Challenges of Twenty-first Century Complexities

What might emerge from a newly de-centred vision of the world in which matter itself has lively agencies and none of the assumed stability or inertia presumed by traditional subject-object relations? Perhaps the first step is to acknowledge the evaporation of the human agent at 'the centre' and to appreciate that humans are, as Philippopoulos-Mihalopoulos has put it, 'thrown' into 'the middle' of a radically open ontology.[84] New materialism and the sciences with which it engages conclusively demonstrate that there is simply *no centre there* for the 'human' to occupy. What is revealed is instead an affectable and open entanglement of multiple bodies at multiple scales—from the global to the microscopic. These bodies are both human and non-human and, as Haraway puts it, the world unfolds as a 'spatial and temporal web of interspecies dependencies'.[85] There is no 'autonomous'—in the Kantian sense—subject of human rights. There are no stable subject-object categorizations: 'species of all kinds, living and not, are consequent on a subject- and object-shaping dance of encounters'.[86]

Accordingly, it makes more sense, as Barad has argued, to eschew any notion of a stable subject-object division at all. But this does not mean abandoning the meaning-making function of boundary-drawing. There may be, as Barad suggests, no 'natural, pure and innocent separations [but this is not to reach] for the rapid dissolution of boundaries'.[87] Subject and object *emerge* through intra-actions in an entangled ontology. Distinctiveness emerges from *divergence*—otherwise 'diffraction patterns'.[88] It is still meaningful to speak of the 'human' even as there is recognition of the fractures, frays and contingencies accompanying that term. The hermeneutical suspicion of critical legal scholarship retains its relevance. And critique can embrace a more process-based ontology according to which the world is made up *not* by the interaction of separate entities but by differential patterns of matter*ing*.

This might seem hopelessly philosophical. Yet science now urges such a view of matter and life. Moreover, the shift is deeply practical. It radically resituates the human of human rights law and of environmental law. Humans are resituated by such accounts as being embedded in intelligent and sensitive or sensing engagements of 'world-making entanglements' and the 'material-semiotic nodes or knots in which diverse bodies and meanings coshape one another'.[89] The call invoked by the shift is a highly intelligent one. It invites a response to the *factity* of 'our' ontological co-constitution with multiple collaborators, including microscopic collaborators, in the co-production of 'the world'. What does this mean for law?

3. Re-imagining Law through a New Materialist Lens

First, the 'human' itself, while remaining a meaningful referent, now stands in its full contingency and productivity. The 'human', instead of being a fixed, autonomous agent or subject radically separated from 'nature' by an ontology of disembodiment, stands revealed as continuously emergent and evolutive. The 'human' is always an 'I'/'we' 'in-the-making' and becomes radically folded into the rest of a living open field of liveliness. This forces human beings to have to renegotiate their sense of the possible.

In this light, human rights law and environmental law alike become sites for the generation of response-ability; in other words, for the responsibilization of ways and modes of co-situated and differentially situated living.[90] Law can no longer hinge upon or revolve around the entitlements of abstractly dignified, rationalistic and exceptionalist human creatures. Human rights—including human rights law—would, in this light, be better understood as a mode of special political and juridical attentiveness to the patterns of privilege and marginalization endured by human 'critters'. Human 'critters' themselves are understood—to evoke Haraway—as being entangled with multiple non-human 'critters' of all kinds. Environmental law likewise becomes a field radically open to a new ontology of the middle.[91] Environmental law is drawn away from abstractionist tendencies and the production of reified categories, such as 'global water', to respond to the material and radically situated complexities revealed by ecological science in intimate conversation with law.[92] The central task facing human rights law and environmental law alike becomes that of the legal reimagination of the 'situation of the human in a more than human world'.[93]

At a practical level, this will mean that law will require a conscious sense of epistemic humility. This involves appreciating the unsustainability of 'the centre' while embracing the energies of 'the in-the-midst-of' new modes of hearing and engagement. In environmental matters, for example, it will require a rejection of law's linear concept of causation and of law's unhelpful focus on a reductive view of 'harm', and a fresh appreciation of law's need to develop the conceptual resources to enable it to respond to the immense systemic complexities of climate crisis and lively ecological energies.[94] New, possibly as yet unimagined, constituencies of concern will need to be factored into legal decision-making.

These include the perspectives of indigenous peoples; animal movements; ecological patterns and flows; and other material and semiotic sources of insight. In this way a whole range of additional perspectives beyond the idea of the central human agent of Cartesian and Kantian legal foundations must be welcomed into the heart of law's responsiveness to the materialities of the world.

There are already signs of practical developments moving in this direction. These include commons-based environmental governance strategies; new modes of advocacy and hearing; the increasing attempt to include indigenous and other marginalized perspectives in environmental justice questions; the emergence of biocultural rights discourse; the converging energies of social movement activisms; the extension of legal personhood or status to a river in New Zealand; and the enshrining of rights of nature in, for example, the Ecuadorian constitution. Judicially inspired incrementalism, affected by participation rights, is also starting to show shifts in a direction more progressive for the relationship between human rights law and environmental law. However, unless the currently assumed foundations of human rights law and environmental law are replaced, progress will remain impeded. The necessary adjustments might take place in various ways: for example, by the spread of new scholarship; by the wildfire of urgent memes; by imaginative litigation and adjudication strategies; by enlightened legal and political norm formulation; and by the trickle-up effect of ground-level ambiguities arising from multiple situated communities of concern that confront law in its entirety with its own ideological and structural limitations. In the final analysis, though, without a significant shift in the fundamental *taken for granted* of human rights law and environmental law, howsoever achieved, the progressiveness of both will remain inhibited by shared and outmoded foundations inimical to their aims.

NOTES

1. This chapter builds on earlier work, particularly A. Grear, 'Framing the Project of International Human Rights law: Reflections on the Dysfunctional "Family" of the Universal Declaration' in C. Gearty and C. Douzinas (eds), *Cambridge Handbook of Human Rights* (Cambridge, Cambridge University Press, 2012), pp. 17–35; A. Grear, 'Human Rights and New Horizons? Thoughts Towards a New Juridical Ontology' (2015/6) *Science, Technology and Human Values*, Special Issue (forthcoming). The author would like to thank Professor Louis J. Kotze and Professor Karen Morrow for their invaluable comments and reflections. Any errors remain the author's alone.
2. Kirby (2006).

3. A revealing term exposing the sense in which 'the environment' is that which surrounds a centre—the human subject. For a fuller discussion, see Philippopoulos-Mihalopoulos (2011a) and (2011b).
4. Some of these tensions are explored in Dias (2008).
5. Shelton (2007, pp. 1–9).
6. De Sousa Santos (2002, p. 260).
7. Charter of the UN, 1 UNTS XVI, 24 October 1945.
8. See Buergenthal (1997).
9. For an argument drawing on the quasi-constitutional character of the UN Charter as the basis of a constitutionalized international order, see Fassbender (2009).
10. GA Res 217 (111) of 10 December 1948, UN Doc A/810 at 71 (1948).
11. UN Doc A/CONF.157/23 (1993), 25 June 1993, endorsed by GA Res 48/121 of 14 February 1994, [2].
12. UDHR, Preamble.
13. Donnelly (2003, p. 22).
14. Buergenthal (1997).
15. Opened for signature 7 March 1966, 660 UNTS 195 (entered into force 4 January 1969).
16. Joseph and McBeth (2010, editorial introduction).
17. Opened for signature 16 December 1966, 993 UNTS 3 (entered into force 3 January 1976).
18. Opened for signature 16 December 1966, 999 UNTS 171 (entered into force 23 March 1976).
19. Turner (2008).
20. Opened for signature 10 December 1984, 1465 UNTC 85 (entered into force 26 June 1987).
21. Opened for signature 18 December 1979, 1249 UNTS 13 (entered into force 3 September 1981).
22. Baxi (2006, p. 46).
23. The European Convention for the Protection of Human Rights and Fundamental Freedoms, 213 UNTS 222 (entered into force 3 September 1953), as amended by Protocols Nos 3, 5, 8 and 11 (entered into force on 21 September 1970, 20 December 1971, 1 January 1990 and 1 November 1998, respectively); American Convention on Human Rights OAS Treaty Series No.36, 1144 UNTS 123 (entered into force 18 July 1978); African Charter on Human and Peoples' Rights (adopted 27 June 1981, entered into force 21 October 1986) (1982) 21 ILM 58 ('African Charter'); League of Arab States, Arab Charter on Human Rights, 22 May 2004, reprinted in (2005) 12 *International Human Rights Reports* 893 (entered into force 15 March 2008).
24. Handl (1992, p. 117).
25. All primarily designed to protect commercially valuable species: see Brown Weiss (1992–93, p. 676). Brown Weiss lists the 1902 Convention for the Protection of Birds Useful to Agriculture, the 1916 Convention for the Protection of Migratory Birds in the United States and Canada and the Treaty for the Preservation and Protection of Fur Seals signed in 1911. She notes that '[o]nly one convention focused on wildlife more generally: the 1900 London Convention for the Protection of Wild Animals, Birds and Fish in Africa' (p. 676).
26. Brown Weiss lists conservation laws of the 1930s and 1940s.
27. Tarlock (2009).
28. Johnson and Powell (2014, p. 13).
29. Carson (1962/3).
30. Tarlock (2009).
31. Ibid. (p. 2).

32. Coyle and Morrow (2004).
33. Tarlock (2009, pp. 2–4).
34. Anghie (2005).
35. Yang and Percival (2009, p. 616).
36. Ibid. (p. 617).
37. Anderson (1996, p. 3).
38. Stockholm Declaration of the United Nations Conference on the Human Environment, 16 June 1972, UN Doc A/CONF48/14/Rev.1 (1973).
39. A formulation whose gendered anthropocentrism is difficult to ignore.
40. Shelton (2011, p. ix).
41. Ibid. (p. x).
42. Morrow (2015).
43. Stockholm Declaration (n.38) (preamble, para.7).
44. Turner (2013).
45. UN Doc A/CONF.151/26 (vol.I); 31 ILM 874 (1992).
46. Convention on Access to Information, Public Participation in Decision-Making and Access to Justice in Environmental Matters: 2161 UNTS 447; 38 ILM 517 (1999).
47. Boyd (2012).
48. Gellers (2015).
49. Shelton (2011, p. x).
50. Ibid.
51. Article 16 of the African Charter on Human and Peoples' Rights: OAU Doc. CAB/LEG/67/3 rev. 5; 1520 UNTS 217; 21 ILM 58 (1982); Additional Protocol to the American Convention on Human Rights in the Area of Economic, Social and Cultural Rights (San Salvador, 17 November 1988), OAS T.S. 69.
52. Boyd (2012); Gellers (2015).
53. Turner (2013).
54. Boyd (2012, pp. 111–13).
55. Gearty (2010, p. 21).
56. Ibid.
57. Turner (2013).
58. Turner (2014, p. 32).
59. Ibid.
60. Ibid. (p. 38).
61. Ibid.
62. Dangerman and Schellnhuber (2012).
63. Ibid. (p. 1).
64. Turner (2013, pp. 42–4).
65. Ibid. (p. 42).
66. Sinden (2007, p. 268).
67. Kirby (2006).
68. Koch (2012).
69. De Sousa Santos argues emphatically that TNCs are the 'key agents of the new world economy': De Sousa Santos (2002, p. 167).
70. See Shamir (2005, p. 92).
71. Paragraph 20 of the UN Document, 'Norms on the Responsibilities of Transnational Corporations and other Business Enterprises with regard to Human Rights' (2003) UN Doc E/CN/.4/Sub.2/2003/12/Rev.2, defines a TNC as 'an economic entity operating in more than one country or a cluster of economic entities operating in two or more countries—whatever their legal form, whether in their home country or country of activity, and whether taken individually or collectively'.
72. McCorquodale and Fairbrother (1999, p. 737).
73. Malm and Hornborg (2014).

74. McLean (2004).
75. Anghie (2005).
76. See Huggan and Tiffin (2007) for intimations of these hierarchical patterns.
77. Adelman (2015).
78. Merchant (1990).
79. Otto (2005; 2006); Kapur (2006).
80. Evans and Ayers (2006).
81. Turner (2013).
82. Coole and Frost (2010, Kindle Location 137).
83. Ibid. (Kindle Location 250).
84. Philippopoulos-Mihalopoulos (2011a; 2011b).
85. Haraway, (2008, p. 11).
86. Ibid. (p. 4).
87. Barad (2007, p. 187).
88. Ibid. (Kindle Location 2810), emphasis added.
89. Haraway (2008, p. 4).
90. See Code (2006) for an extended discussion of situated knowledge and the responsibilization of knowing.
91. Philippopoulos-Mihalopoulos (2011b).
92. Pallonitty (2015).
93. Neimanis (2014, p. 14).
94. For a theoretical foundation for a new environmental law, see Philippopoulos-Mihalopoulos (2011b).

REFERENCES

Adelman, S. (2015), 'Epistemologies of Mastery' in A. Grear and L.J. Kotze (eds), *Research Handbook on Human Rights and the Environment* (Cheltenham, Edward Elgar), pp. 9–27.

Anderson, M.R. (1996), 'Human Rights Approaches to Environmental Protection: An Overview' in A. Boyle and M. Anderson (eds), *Human Rights Approaches to Environmental Protection* (Oxford, Oxford University Press), pp. 1–24.

Anghie, A. (2005), *Imperialism, Sovereignty and the Making of International Law* (Cambridge University Press, Cambridge).

Barad, K. (2007), *Meeting the Universe Halfway: Quantum Physics and the Entanglement of Matter and Meaning* (Durham NC, Duke University Press: Kindle DX Version, retrieved from Amazon.co.uk).

Baxi, U. (2006), *The Future of Human Rights* (Oxford, Oxford University Press).

Boyd, D.R. (2012), *The Environmental Rights Revolution: A Global Study of Constitutions, Human Rights, and the Environment* (Berkeley, University Berkeley Press).

Brown Weiss, E. (1992–3), 'International Environmental Law: Contemporary Issues and the Emergence of a New World Order', *Georgetown Law Journal* 81, 675–710.

Buergenthal, T. (1997), 'The Normative and Institutional Evolution of International Human Rights', *Human Rights Quarterly* 19(4), 703–23.

Carson, R. (1962/3), *Silent Spring* (London, Hamish Hamilton).

Code, L. (2006), *Ecological Thinking: The Politics of Epistemic Location* (Oxford, Oxford University Press).

Coole, D. and S. Frost (2010), *New Materialisms: Ontology, Agency and Politics* (Durham NC, Duke University Press: Kindle DX Version, retrieved from Amazon.co.uk).

Coyle, C. and K. Morrow (2004), *The Philosophical Foundations of Environmental Law* (Oxford, Hart).

Dangerman, J. and H.J. Schellnhuber (2012), 'Energy Systems Transformation' 110/7 *Proceedings of the National Academy of Sciences of the United States of America*, PNAS Early Edition; http://www.pnas.org/cgi/doi/10.1073/pnas.1219791110.

De Sousa Santos, B. (2002), *Towards a New Legal Common Sense: Law, Globalization and Emancipation* (London, Butterworths).

Dias, A. (2008), 'Human Rights, Environment and Development with Special Emphasis on Corporate Accountability' Human Development Report 2008 Background Paper; http://www.core.ac.uk/download/pdf/6248783.pdf.

Donnelly, J. (2003), *Universal Human Rights in Theory and Practice* (Ithaca, NY, Cornell University Press).

Evans, T. and A.J. Ayers (2006), 'In the Service of Power: The Global Political Economy of Citizenship and Human Rights', *Citizenship Studies* 10, 239–308.

Fassbender, B. (2009), *The United Nations Charter as the Constitution of the International Community* (Leiden and Boston, Brill/Nijhoff).

Gearty, C. (2010), 'Do Human Rights Help or Hinder Environmental Protection?', *Journal of Human Rights and the Environment* 1(1), 7–22.

Gellers, J.C. (2015), 'Explaining the emergence of global constitutional rights: a quantitative analysis', *Journal of Human Rights and the Environment* 6(1), 75–97.

Handl, G. (1992), 'Human Rights and Protection of the Environment: A Mildly "Revisionist" View' in A.A. Cançado Trindade (ed.), *Human Rights, Sustainable Development and the Environment* (San Jose de Costa Rica/Brasilia, Instituto Interamericano de Derechos Humanas/Banco Interamericano de Desarolo), pp. 117–42.

Haraway, D. (2008), *When Species Meet* (Minnesota, University of Minnesota Press).

Huggan, G. and H. Tiffin (2007), 'Green Postcolonialism', *Interventions: International Journal of Postcolonial Studies* 9(1), 1–11.

Johnson, L. and F. Powell (2014), *Environmental Law* (Boston, Cengage).

Joseph, S. and A. McBeth (2010), *Research Handbook on International Human Rights Law* (Cheltenham, Edward Elgar).

Kapur, R. (2006), 'Human Rights in the 21st Century: Take a Walk on the Dark Side', *Sydney Law Review* 28, 664–87.

Kirby, P. (2006), *Vulnerability and Violence: The Impact of Globalisation* (London, Ann Arbor, Pluto Press).

Koch, M. (2012), *Capitalism and Climate Change: Theoretical Discussion, Historical Development and Policy Responses* (Basingstoke, Palgrave Macmillan).

Malm, A. and A. Hornborg (2014), 'The Geology of Mankind? A Critique of the Anthropocene Narrative', *The Anthropocene Review* 1(1), 62–9.

McCorquodale, R. and R. Fairbrother (1999), 'Globalization and Human Rights', *Human Rights Quarterly* 21, 735–66.

McLean, J. (2004), 'The Transnational Corporation in History: Lessons for Today?', *Indiana Law Journal* 79, 363–77.

Merchant, C. (1990), *The Death of Nature: Women, Ecology and the Scientific Revolution* (London, Harper Collins).

Morrow, K. (2015), 'Sustainability, Environmental Citizenship Rights and the Ongoing Challenges of Shaping Supra-National Environmental Governance' in A. Grear and L.J. Kotze, *Research Handbook on Human Rights and the Environment* (Cheltenham, Edward Elgar), pp. 200–218.

Neimanis, A. (2014), 'Alongside the right to water, a posthumanist feminist imaginary', *Journal of Human Rights and the Environment* 5(1), 5–24.

Otto, D. (2005), 'Disconcerting "Masculinities": Reinventing the Gendered Subject(s) of International Human Rights Law' in D. Buss and A. Manji (eds), *International Law: Modern Feminist Approaches* (Oxford, Hart Publishing), pp. 105–29.

Otto, D. (2006), 'Lost in Translation: Rescripting the Sexed Subjects of International Human Rights Law' in A. Orford (ed.), *International Law and its Others* (Cambridge, Cambridge University Press), pp. 318–56.

Pallonitty, T. (2015), 'Taking aims seriously—how legal ecology affects judicial decision-making', *Journal of Human Rights and the Environment* 6(1), 55–74.

Philippopoulos-Mihalopoulos, A. (2011a), '... the sound of a breaking string': critical environmental law and ontological vulnerability', *Journal of Human Rights and the Environment* 2(1), 5–22.

Philippopoulos-Mihalopoulos, A. (2011b), 'Towards Critical Environmental Law' in A. Philippopoulos-Mihalopoulos (ed.), *Law and Ecology: New Environmental Foundations* (Abingdon, Routledge/Glasshouse), pp. 18–38.

Shamir, R. (2005), 'Corporate Social Responsibility: A Case of Hegemony and Counter-Hegemony' in B. De Sousa Santos and C.A. Rodrigues-Garavito (eds), *Law and Globalisation from Below: Towards a Cosmopolitan Legality* (Cambridge, Cambridge University Press), pp. 92–117.

Shelton, D. (2007), 'An Introduction to the History of Human Rights Law', *The George Washington University Law School Public Law and Legal Theory Working Paper* No.346; *Legal Studies Research Paper* No.346, 1–30.

Shelton, D.L (2011), *Human Rights and the Environment Volume* 1 (Cheltenham, Edward Elgar).

Sinden, A. (2007), 'Climate Change and Human Rights', *Journal of Land Resources and Environmental Law* 27, 255–71.

Tarlock, D. (2009), *Environmental Laws and their Enforcement* Volume 1: 'History of Environmental Law' in *Encyclopedia of Life Support Systems* (EOLSS).

Turner, B. (2008), 'Human Vulnerabilities: On Individual and Social Rights'; http://web.gs.emory.edu/vulnerability/zpdfs/turnerpub.pdf.

Turner, S. (2014), *A Global Environmental Right* (London, Routledge).

Yang, T. and R.V. Percival (2009), 'The Emergence of Global Environmental Law', *Ecology Law Quarterly* 36, 615–64.

7. A constitutional human right to a healthy environment

Nicholas Bryner

INTRODUCTION: A HUMAN RIGHT TO A HEALTHY ENVIRONMENT

In the face of modern environmental crises—for example, climate change, air and water quality, water scarcity, and biodiversity loss—human societies have an acute need to develop and employ principles of environmental governance to ensure that human activities do not threaten ecological sustainability. One critical challenge in this process is determining how to incorporate environmental principles into an effective legal framework that leads to needed changes in behavior and appropriately balances short-term needs and interests with long-term social and environmental concerns.

There is some tension in law, policy, and legal doctrine regarding the appropriate frame of reference for law related to environmental protection. Scholars have articulated different schools of thought on environmental ethics. Although it is an oversimplification, systems of environmental ethics can be described in two categories: *anthropocentric*—that is, focused on the welfare of human beings as the guiding principle, to the exclusion of or paramount over that of the rest of the Earth system; and *ecocentric*—that is, nature-based, encompassing an ecosystem or the Earth as a whole.[1]

As the field of environmental law developed in the second half of the twentieth century, a growing number of countries began to weave together environmental law and elements of human rights law. The concept of a human right evokes notions of dignity, freedom, and equality. It is designed to protect humans and to respond to the potential for harm or interference with those values. In 1972, the Declaration of the United Nations Conference on the Human Environment—the Stockholm Declaration—articulated a principle that humans have 'the fundamental right to freedom, equality and adequate conditions of life, in an environment of a quality that permits a life of dignity and well-being, and

[bear] a solemn responsibility to protect and improve the environment for present and future generations'.[2]

Nonetheless, the relationship between human rights and environmental law is not always clear. As many scholars have argued, environmental law and human rights can overlap in several different but complementary ways.[3] Professor Shelton describes four areas of interaction between human rights law and environmental protection: first, employing, from an environmental perspective, human rights guarantees that serve environmental protection ends; second, application of existing human rights law, such as rights, among others, to life and water, in the context of environmental degradation that threatens enjoyment of those rights; third, the articulation of a new human right defined in terms of ecological balance and sustainability; and fourth, reference to human responsibilities with regard to the environment as a counterbalance to rights.[4]

Around the time of the Stockholm Declaration in 1972, and particularly in the decades since, countries built on environmental law principles and began including environmental provisions in national constitutions.[5] These included provisions with rights-based language such as a right to an 'ecologically balanced environment'[6] or a 'right to live in a healthy and balanced environment'.[7] Placing *humans* as the subjects and holders of such a right is an expressly anthropocentric endeavor. However, inasmuch as the content of the right is defined in reference to an ecological balance or a 'healthy environment', it diverges from an exclusively anthropocentric view, by recognizing ecological integrity as valuable to human dignity, irrespective of the degree to which the natural environment is instrumental to meeting or supporting human needs and development.[8]

This chapter is centered on exploring the issues associated with constitutional rights for humans to enjoy a healthy environment.[9] The thesis is that a constitutional human right to a healthy environment should lead to better outcomes than would occur in the absence of the right. By 'better outcomes', the concept is a higher quality of human life. This is measurable in three ways: first, by substantive environmental quality—better long-term ecological prospects for all life on Earth, together with its preservation for human health, aesthetic, cultural, and spiritual reasons; second, by opportunities for socio-economic development—subject to constraints of sustainability; and third, by the opportunities for public participation, access to information, and access to justice that guarantee the enjoyment of these outcomes in legal systems and administrative decision-making.

David Boyd succinctly described these elements. He argued that the 'paramount objectives' of including such a right in a constitution are to 'reduce the level of harm being inflicted on humans and the Earth and to redistribute inequitable allocations of environmental harms'.[10] Boyd further suggests that a constitutional human right to a healthy environment can support a 'broad range of legal and extra-legal outcomes that will advance environmental protection'. These range from encouraging stronger environmental laws and enforcement of those laws; to filling gaps in environmental legislation; to fostering appropriate balancing between environmental and other concerns; and to strengthening accountability and opportunities for public participation.[11]

According to the Toronto Initiative for Economic and Social Rights (TIESR) database,[12] which includes analysis of 195 constitutions, a right to a safe or healthy environment is mentioned in 92 constitutions. Of these 92, 63 are 'justiciable', while the other 29 are 'aspirational' or take the form of 'directive principles' for the state.[13] With regard to state duties, 107 of the 195 constitutions include some form of state responsibility to protect the environment. Among these, 54 were considered justiciable, with the other 53 aspirational or as directive principles.[14]

It may be difficult to show a causal relationship between human rights to a healthy environment in these constitutions and improved environmental quality. But it is possible to articulate a theory regarding the mechanisms for positive influence, based on a consideration of the purpose and weight of constitutional rights. A constitution as a 'social compact' lays out a statement of government structure, organization, and authority. But it is also a reflection of shared values. Placing a human right to environmental protection in a constitution emphasizes either that that society recognizes environmental protection as a core value or that it is taking steps to encourage such recognition.

Environmental rights in constitutions serve an important function as rights vis-à-vis the state to assure the 'safe' or 'healthful' enjoyment of an individual's common interactions and interdependence with the environment. This includes a right to enjoy and interact with the elements of the natural environment necessary to support human life—clean air, water, and soil, and a healthy ecosystem with the requisite biodiversity and capacity to provide ecosystem services. Does a human right to a healthy environment effectively protect only humans or the biotic community as a whole? Can it do both? However, part of the exploration here is to assess the strengths and limitations of a 'human' rights approach. The reader is encouraged to compare these two different but related constitutional environmental rights.

This chapter divides the topic into three main frames of analysis. First, there is a discussion of the definitional challenges in determining the content of a constitutional human right to a healthy environment.

Constitutions differ as to who holds the right and to the extent that the right includes both procedural and substantive elements. Second, there is an analysis of the function of constitutional rights and of how environmental rights fit into this structure. Location within a constitution, parallel phrasing, and other characteristics may affect how this fit works in practice. Third, there is an analysis of specific examples to highlight both successes and implementation challenges, including discussion of judicial reasoning with regard to environmental rights. In what ways have constitutional environmental rights been applied? Who may enforce them? While dozens of countries and subnational jurisdictions include a specific constitutional human right to a healthy environment and numerous others contain relevant environmental provisions, this chapter does not provide a comprehensive case-by-case examination. The goal here is to look for common themes and challenges that shed light on the meaning and value of these rights. Ultimately, a successful right is one that is effectively implemented and one that values the integrity of the planetary system that supports human and all other forms of life.

DEFINING THE RIGHT

1. The Issue

The first critical question in examining the concept of a human right to enjoy a healthy environment is how to define the content of the right. What would be included in the definition of a 'healthy environment' if it were to be included in a constitution and how would it be construed? There is a range of other issues spanning the spectrum of environmental rights: for example, whether a healthy environment extends beyond the anthropocentric perspectives of the environment and the degree to which the right includes substantive environmental guarantees—those that are outcome-specific—as well as procedural rights.

2. What is a Healthy Environment?

When a constitutional provision grants humans the right to enjoy a healthy environment, how should the definition of a 'healthy environment' be construed? One interpretation is that a right to enjoy a healthy environment, if held by humans, refers specifically and exclusively to the integrity of the environment's ability to support healthy humans. In other words, this vision would define a 'healthy environment' with direct reference to what is healthful for humans, including clean air, clean water, clean soil, and other ecosystem services directly beneficial to humans. Michael R. Anderson describes this type of environmental right as 'a means to the end of fulfilling human rights standards'.[15] A second and broader understanding of this right, which Anderson favors, is a right held by humans to co-exist with or enjoy a 'healthy environment'. In this case environmental health is defined in terms of an ecosystem as a whole, regardless of whether a particular function or aspect of the environment is tied closely to human health.

This dichotomy helps to address the question of what environmental rights mean, what they add to the discourse, and the intent behind the inclusion of such rights in a constitution. On the one hand, the first interpretation does not appear to call for a new right, but rather a more robust recognition of the right to human life and health by taking environmental considerations into account. On the other hand, a definition of 'healthy environment' without reference to humans may not be possible or coherent. All ecosystems and ecosystem functions affect human activity and vice versa. The differences are a matter of degree. Measurements on human time scales do not necessarily capture environmental variation. Dynamism and change are more often associated with the environment than equilibrium or balance.[16]

With this in mind, what makes an environment 'healthy' is the absence of substantial human interference or pollution that would compromise ecological integrity as it is understood or would threaten irreversible environmental harm. At a minimum, a healthy environment must include clean air, clean water, and clean soil sufficient to support human life, including food production, and to maintain the ecosystem services and biological diversity that are familiar to humans and that have been common at least in this contemporary period of Earth's history.

Constitutions with environmental rights frequently provide some sense of how to define the terms of what they protect. For example, Angola's constitution calls on the state to 'adopt the measures necessary for protection of the environment and of the species of flora and fauna' in the country and to 'maintain ecological equilibrium'.[17] Brazil's provision establishes the state's mandate to 'preserve and restore essential ecological processes' and refers to the 'right to an ecologically balanced environment' as both a public good for use in common by the people and as 'essential to healthy quality of life'.[18]

Defining the content of the right more broadly to extend it to an ecocentric notion of a healthy environment as a human-centered right is more abstract and challenging. This approach places humans as the subject, the holders of the rights, but defines the content of the right in terms of the environment as a whole—for example its health and ecological balance. By doing so, it more effectively carries the message of incorporating environmental values into a constitution. It forces more express balancing and consideration of environmental issues and concerns vis-à-vis other rights, even when those environmental concerns are not directly tied to impacts on humans. For example, even if a country's judicial system is limited to vindicating human rights and interests as opposed to rights held by nature, the inclusion of a broadly defined human right to a healthy or balanced environment means that there is an articulated human interest in the overall well-being of the ecosystems around humans. That interest must be considered. Actions that interfere with or impair the environment must be reasonably justified.

3. Substantive and Procedural Rights

In addition to the question of defining a 'healthy environment' is the key challenge of determining how the right can be enjoyed and the ways in which a legal system is operationalized to protect that right. Some constitutions simply guarantee a right to a healthy environment.[19] Other constitutions describe a right *to live in* a healthy environment.[20] In either case, what is it that the right holder has a right to enjoy or to demand from the state?

Scholars have broken down environmental rights into the categories of procedural and substantive rights. Procedural rights do not mandate a specific outcome or measure of environmental quality. They require certain steps in decision-making and policy design in order to safeguard vulnerable interests and to promote transparency, accountability, and representative participation. Substantive rights add to environmental protection by placing 'limits on the outcome of the process'.[21] This is to guard against situations in which, even when made in keeping with procedural guarantees, policy decisions are insufficient to ensure human or environmental health. The formulation of a right to a healthy environment is, on its face, a substantive requirement. Constitutional frameworks may also include specific substantive aspects, such as a right to clean air, clean water, or clean soil, in addition to broader statements of rights to environmental protection.[22] A substantive right would create some minimum enforceable guarantee of environmental quality or outcome.

Categorizing substantive versus procedural rights may not always be a clear distinction. The most comprehensive systems clearly define and protect both. Principle 10 of the Rio Declaration on Environment and Development sets an international standard in terms of participation in environmental decision-making as a crucial element of procedural rights. Principle 10 calls for the protection of three 'access rights' related to the environment: access to information on environmental matters; access to public participation processes; and effective access to justice to remedy environmental harms or violations.[23] An additional procedural right critical to the enjoyment of a right to a healthy environment is the requirement for a prior environmental impact assessment in the case of activities that may have adverse environmental consequences.[24]

The *process*-based requirements are, in many ways, the point of constitutionalizing environmental values. This is because environmental rights do not exist in a vacuum. Rather they shape and are shaped by other rights. The recognition of substantive environmental rights does not mean that environmental concerns would always trump other concerns. On the contrary, the key question for the enjoyment of substantive environmental rights is defining the extent to which and under what circumstances those rights may be infringed in the face of additional competing interests. In other words, if there is a right to a healthy environment, *how healthy* must it be? If rights are not absolute, how should environmental concerns be addressed when conflicts with other rights are alleged: such as rights to development, private property, food, shelter, or self-determination? Procedural rights are then the method for guaranteeing the principle and for proper balancing.

Applied properly, the procedural right to effective participation, information, and access to justice creates a mechanism for reasoned and deliberative balancing of a right to the environment with complementary or competing concerns. However, on the other hand, without some measure of substantive environmental rights, the legal system, including the institutions performing judicial functions, is limited in its capacity to review decision-making or laws to an evaluation of whether proper process has been followed, regardless of the actual outcome.[25]

ENVIRONMENTAL RIGHTS AND CONSTITUTIONS

1. Introduction

Broadly speaking, constitutions serve as foundational documents that lay out the structure, power, and authority of governments. In terms of social contract theory, a constitution forms a framework in which individuals agree to subject themselves to a government, conceding some of their liberty, in exchange for protection of life and other fundamental rights.[26] Rights in this sense can include, first, those which a government is obligated to protect via its police power: for example, the ability to enjoy personal rights, free from private interference, such as the use and enjoyment of property and the enforcement of contracts. Rights can include, second, those with which a government is prohibited from interfering: for example, rights defined through restrictions on government authority, such as freedom of expression or free exercise of religion. These categories may also be characterized as 'negative' rights—liberty or freedom from state interference—or 'positive' rights—welfare rights that articulate some form of state duty to fulfill them.[27]

In the United States (US), the Constitution establishes a federal government of limited, enumerated powers. The US Constitution does not specifically charge the government with duties to uphold rights,[28] but it is heavily influenced by natural law theory that holds the purpose of government to be 'to secure' fundamental rights.[29] The first ten amendments to the Constitution, known as the Bill of Rights, list constitutional 'rights' in terms of restrictions on government action.[30] While states within the US retain plenary authority to legislate, state action is also constrained by 'rights' in state constitutions and in the federal Constitution.[31] At the time of the establishment of the US Constitution in the 1780s, Alexander Hamilton argued against including a constitutional bill of rights. He understood rights to be held fully by the people in the absence of specific provisions to the contrary—a reservation of diffuse power not granted to government rather than an exercise of a government granting a set of privileges to people—and he believed that any express listing or definition of rights would inevitably limit their scope.[32] Nonetheless, the Bill of Rights was ratified. The concept of listing rights is commonplace today in written constitutions.

Different constitutions have different structures for laying out the authority and organization of government as well as for organizing the rights guaranteed to individuals and the public. As such, for constitutions containing a human right to enjoy a healthy environment, the location or description of the right can indicate how it is to be construed and how it may potentially apply in that legal system. A constitutional right to enjoy a healthy environment may specifically be described as 'aspirational' or as justiciable and enforceable. It can take the form of an individual guarantee or a right enjoyed by society in common[33] and, at the same time, as either a restraint on government or as a duty for state action to take some positive action.

2. Constitutionalizing Environmental Values

Incorporating a value into a constitution signifies both that there is a deep commitment and consensus with regard to that value, as well as some fear or apprehension that individual and public policy choices are likely to place that value at risk.[34] In a democratic constitutional system, while the government's power lies in the people, the people place constitutional restrictions on governmental authority to ensure that short-term interests or majorities do not trample long-term commitments and values and the concerns of minorities—much as Odysseus had his crew tie his hands and feet to avoid the persuasion of the sirens' song.[35]

Enshrining environmental principles in a constitution sets up the environment as a concern and value that can guide a society in its policies and relations with future generations in mind. Environmental rights are closely related to each other and frequently include specific mention of intergenerational equity as a principle. For these reasons the rights are most apt for a constitution, which can ideally consider long-term interests that a society envisions beyond short-term political decision-making processes.[36]

3. Fundamental Rights

One issue is whether the structure of a constitution purports to delineate 'fundamental' rights or other categorization of rights, and how environmental human rights fit into that structure. This is critical to the message that an environmental human right can convey about the values upon which a legal system purports to be based.

Take, for example, Bolivia's Constitution of 2009. Title II includes 'fundamental rights and guarantees'. These are broken down into several chapters or categories, including civil and political rights, rights of indigenous nations and peoples, social and economic rights, education and cultural rights, and social communication rights, such as those related to freedom of expression and freedom of information.[37] Within the chapter on social and economic rights, article 33 states that 'all persons have a right to healthy, protected, and balanced environment. The exercise of this right shall allow individuals and societies in present and future generations, as well as other living beings, to develop in a usual and permanent manner'.[38] The Constitution of Turkey contains, under the chapter on 'social and economic rights and duties', article 56: 'Everyone has the right to live in a healthy and balanced environment'.[39] Angola's Constitution of 2010 includes in its chapter on 'fundamental rights, liberties, and guarantees' the provision that 'all have the right to live in a healthy and unpolluted environment, as well as the duty to defend and preserve it'.[40]

By contrast, Brazil's constitutional environmental right is placed in a separate chapter, article 225, which specifically addresses the environment, apart from the list of fundamental guarantees in article 5.[41] This type of formulation can potentially lead to an interpretation that the environmental rights do not need to be regarded on the same plane or with the same importance as other rights. However, in the specific case of Brazil, other provisions related to the environment and embedded throughout the constitution weigh against any such implication. For example, Brazil's constitution places limits on property rights based on 'adequate use of available natural resources and preservation of the environment'[42] and lists 'protection of the environment' as one of the key principles on which the country's economic order must be based in order to 'ensure for all a life with dignity'.[43]

Similarly, the Constitution of the Philippines, in article II, section 16, provides that 'the State shall protect and advance the right of the people to a balanced and healthful ecology in accord with the rhythm and harmony of nature'.[44] This section is found in the 'declaration of principles and state policies', rather than in the Constitution's Bill of Rights stated in article III. Nonetheless, in 1993, in the seminal *Minors Oposa* case the Supreme Court of the Philippines determined that this separate placement of the right did not matter and had no bearing on the importance of the right.[45]

4. Implementation Challenges for Integrating Environmental Rights in a Constitution

(a) Self-execution

One of the key questions in understanding the role of a constitutional environmental right is whether the right is self-executing: whether it can be enforced on its own without further legislative action. This goes in part to the question of how specifically a right to a healthy environment must be defined in a constitution. A right that is listed as aspirational or as a goal of the state will likely not be interpreted as self-executing. On the other hand, specific substantive provisions with clearer standards for evaluation would be more likely to be directly enforceable.

In the *Minors Oposa* case, the petitioners, on behalf of present and future generations, had challenged the government's issuance of timber licensing permits as a violation of the constitutional right to a balanced and healthful ecology.[46] The trial court had dismissed the claim based on a failure to state a claim of a sufficiently specific legal right. In other words, the constitutional right could not be enforced without some greater specificity or standard to define it. The Supreme Court reversed the decision of the trial court, allowing the petitioners to bring the case.[47]

(b) Justiciability

A related issue that can create a barrier to effective implementation are the questions of justiciability and standing. Due to concerns about separation of powers, judicial institutions may be reluctant to decide environmental questions or to nullify actions of the legislative or executive branches that threaten environmental rights. This is the concern of justiciability. Standing goes to the question of precisely who may bring a legal action to enforce the constitutional provision—whether it be individuals or associations that represent environmental interests and whether they must show specific or individualized harm. Explicit constitutional language on the issues of justiciability and standing make it easier for legal systems to recognize and to implement effectively strong environmental rights. As noted above, in the TIESR's comparative analysis of national constitutions, while 92 include a human right to a healthy environment in some form, only 63 of these were considered 'justiciable' by the researchers who reviewed them.[48]

Consider some examples of justiciability. First is a case from Hong Kong interpreting the right to life and right to health in Hong Kong's Basic Law. Although it does not specifically address a right to environment, it illustrates the potential unwillingness of courts to order specific action to further environmental protection. In the *Clean Air Foundation* case environmental advocates sought a judgment of the court to compel the government to strengthen the environmental regulation of air pollution.[49] The court refused to allow the action. It framed the action as a challenge to the merits of government policy rather than as an issue of whether the government had acted within the scope of its authority. In other words, it was not a justiciable question because the government had wide discretion to 'make difficult decisions in respect of competing social and economic priorities'.[50]

Consider, on the other hand, the decision of a state court, which, interpreting the state of Pennsylvania's constitution, turned this line of thinking on its head. The court struck down a state law pre-empting local regulation of hydraulic fracturing. A plurality of the state Supreme Court noted that the state 'should be aware of and attempt to compensate for the inevitable bias toward present consumption of public resources by the current generation, reinforced by a political process characterized by limited terms of office'.[51] In other words, environmental issues with potential long-term impacts are well suited for judicial resolution and should not be simply entrusted to political branches with incentives to maximize short-term interests.[52]

(c) Standing

Next there are the rules about standing. Specific examples of constitutional provisions illustrate this aspect of the implementation and enforceability of environmental rights. Angola's constitution states that 'each citizen, individually or through associations representing specific interests, has the right to bring a judicial action … seeking to annul acts injurious … to the environment and quality of life'.[53] Argentina's constitution—and many others in Latin America—give 'any person' the ability to file an *amparo* action 'against any act or omission of the public authorities or individuals which currently or imminently may damage, limit, modify or threaten rights and guarantees recognized by this Constitution'.[54] Cape Verde's constitution guarantees to all 'personally or through associations organized for the defense of shared interests' the right to bring an action seeking cessation of violations against health, the environment, quality of life or cultural patrimony.[55] In addition, some countries specifically mention environmental threats in standing-related provisions. In Bolivia 'any person, as an individual or in representation of a group, has standing to bring a legal action in defense of the right to environment, without prejudice to the obligation of public institutions to respond to threats to the environment'.[56]

These broad rights of standing exist in contrast to systems that do not guarantee constitutional environmental rights, such as the US. Although jurisprudence has developed to allow for causes of action based on aesthetic injuries related to the environment and not limited to economic injuries, the US Supreme Court has interpreted the constitution to require that individuals show a concrete and particularized injury—'injury in fact'—that is causally connected to the action challenged and that the judicial decision sought could provide redress for that injury.[57]

APPLICATIONS: EXAMPLES AND ANALYSIS

1. Introduction

In light of the foregoing discussion of the issues associated with defining the content of a right to a healthy environment and integrating the right into a constitutional structure and system, this section is devoted to examining a few select case examples from different regions of the world. Analysis of these examples provides not only a survey for understanding the range of approaches to addressing the issues noted above but also as an opportunity to compare judicial decisions and the legal reasoning that has been used to support the application of environmental rights. This section, like the rest of the chapter, focuses on national level constitutions, with some references to subnational constitutions and the relationship between constitutional environmental rights and relevant international instruments.

2. The Influence of Constitutional Provisions on the Interpretation of National Legislation

The inclusion of an environmental right in a constitution can shape the understanding of other levels of laws and norms in a legal system. In this way, environmental rights lead to more innovative judicial guarantees of environmental protection, even indirectly. As with other fundamental rights, a right to a healthy environment implies the need for principles throughout a legal system—even as applied to 'non-environmental' laws—that promote and give preference to enjoyment of that right. In this respect many countries have adopted the emerging principle *in dubio pro natura*—resolving ambiguity in favor of nature—in applications such as statutory interpretation and shifting or reallocating legal burdens of proof in environmental matters.[58]

In South Africa, the post-Apartheid constitution adopted in 1996 includes the right to 'an environment that is not harmful to … health or well-being' within its Bill of Rights.[59] Eric Christiansen recently explored the history of this constitutional provision and its implementation. He argued that, although judicial enforcement has been 'meek' to this point, the country has significant opportunities to continue to develop the right and shape how constitutional environmental rights are seen elsewhere in the world.[60]

In 2007, the South African Constitutional Court's decision in the *Fuel Retailers* case[61] is an important example of how the inclusion of constitutional environmental rights can indirectly impact on other legislation and administrative action. The *Fuel Retailers* case involved a challenge to a permit authorization that had been granted for construction of a fuel station.[62] The decision involved an environmental issue regarding the presence of a groundwater aquifer below the proposed site.[63] At issue in the case was whether the relevant permitting authorities had followed the requirements of the National Environmental Management Act (NEMA). However, the court found a constitutional issue in the case because NEMA gives effect to the environmental protections in the constitution.[64]

The court, while not addressing specifically the right to a healthy environment, highlighted ways in which the constitutional provision could influence the rest of the country's legal system. From the constitution—and specifically the responsibilities of the government in protecting the right—the court read in to NEMA a set of constitutionally grounded and strengthened principles of sustainable development and a requirement for the administrative agency to balance development with environmental concerns.[65] As the court put it, 'promotion of development requires the protection of the environment'.[66] This was linked to additional rights guarantees: protection of the environment 'is vital to the enjoyment of the other rights contained in the Bill of Rights; indeed, it is vital to life itself'.[67]

In Brazil, the courts have been reluctant to apply constitutional environmental rights directly as a substantive standard for challenging legislation or government action. However, federal courts have referred to the constitutional guarantee in reviewing and interpreting other laws, with the intent of ensuring that they give full effect to the right to an ecologically balanced environment—even when those laws pre-date the current constitution.[68]

3. Constitutional Environmental Rights and Intergenerational Equity

As discussed earlier, the inclusion of environmental rights in a constitution is strongly tied to notions of intergenerational equity. As Hiskes suggests, the inclusion of both substantive and procedural environmental rights in constitutions allows for a balancing of interests so as to protect the rights, needs, and preferences of current generations as well as the needs of future generations.[69] Substantive guarantees are required to create a minimum standard needed to protect future generations and fulfill current generations' obligations, although such guarantees do necessarily limit present choices.[70] Complementarily, procedural rights ensure the participation of current generations in decisions with intragenerational distributional impacts, even in cases in which substantive rights concerns are not implicated.

In the Philippines, the *Minors Oposa* case addressed the concept in granting standing to the petitioners to challenge timber licenses. Significantly, the petitioners brought the action on behalf of both current and future generations.[71] The case presents an important example of judicial willingness to consider intergenerational issues. However, it is not clear that the court's opinion in the case would have been different if it had limited its consideration to the class of children in the current generation who brought the action.

The decision in the *Robinson Township* case in 2013 in Pennsylvania is a recent example of how courts examine intergenerational values in constitutional environmental rights. Article I, section 27 of Pennsylvania's constitution states:

> The people have a right to clean air, pure water, and to the preservation of the natural, scenic, historic and esthetic values of the environment. Pennsylvania's public natural resources are the common property of all the people, including generations yet to come. As trustee of these resources, the Commonwealth shall conserve and maintain them for the benefit of all the people.[72]

The Supreme Court of Pennsylvania undertook considerable analysis of intergenerational concerns. Because the right includes 'generations yet to come' and places responsibility on the government as trustee of resources related to the right, judicial review extends to issues with present as well as long-term impacts. The court noted that the constitutional right 'offers protection equally against actions with immediate severe impact on public natural resources and against actions with minimal or insignificant present consequences that are actually [sic] or likely to have significant or irreversible effects in the short or long term'.[73] This is a critical point inasmuch as it allows courts to reach beyond doctrinal constraints of imminent harm and causation to enable a more precautionary approach in safeguarding environmental rights.

4. Environmental Rights and Property

A further way in which constitutional rights to a healthy environment are implemented is by reference to other fundamental rights when conflicts arise. Constitutionalizing an environmental right is important within a hierarchical system of norms and law because it places the right on the same level as the right to the use and enjoyment of private property. This allows for more rational balancing of risks and interests among private concerns and individual rights and collective environmental rights.

In Brazil, the right to an ecologically balanced environment is read together with other provisions on the environment and on property rights to define an *ecological function of property*.[74] The constitutional human right to a healthy environment works in tandem with other provisions to shape limits on private property rights. Courts have relied on this concept to uphold various regulations as reasonable limitations on the exercise of property rights, such as a prohibition of clearing of Atlantic rainforest vegetation.[75]

CONCLUSIONS

The concept of constitutionalizing a human right to a healthy environment has been tremendously successful. In only four decades, nearly half of all countries have included specific substantive provisions in their basic document, while dozens of others have included state duties regarding environmental protection.[76] However, pollution, biodiversity loss, and other local and global environmental challenges make it clear that contemporary societies need significant changes to allow the full realization of this right. Enforcement of the right has not been as widespread as the inclusion of the right in a constitution.[77] Environmental rights do not exist in a vacuum. They are subjected to resistance and invite a necessary balancing with other concerns. But, because these rights have been embodied in so many countries' constitutions, much more effort to promote these rights is critically needed.

Boyd's study of constitutional environmental rights shows that countries with such rights tend to rank higher by measures of environmental performance and tend to have smaller per capita ecological footprints.[78] As Boyd notes, this correlation does not necessarily imply that constitutionalizing environmental rights has produced better environmental outcomes.[79] Nevertheless, it does show that environmental values complement those in other areas of the legal and political systems as a consequence of their recognition and definition in a constitution as a foundational document.

As the human right to a healthy environment grows in importance at national levels, it will increasingly interface with notions of environmental rights in international law. In particular, regional instruments in Africa, Latin America, and Europe have been devised to strengthen these concepts. The African Charter on Human and Peoples' Rights, adopted in 1981 and in force since 1986, guarantees to 'all peoples' 'the right to a general satisfactory environment favorable to their development'.[80] In the Inter-American system, the San Salvador Protocol to the American Convention on Human Rights states that 'everyone shall have the right to live in a healthy environment' and places obligations on states to 'promote the protection, preservation, and improvement of the environment'.[81]

The European Convention on Human Rights does not include a specific environmental provision but it has been applied in cases of connection between environmental issues and other human rights.[82] Further, the Aarhus Convention in Europe establishes environmental 'access rights'—access to information, public participation, and access to justice—as international human rights.[83] Countries in Latin America have begun negotiating a potential international instrument to develop these principles with reference to principle 10 of the Rio Declaration.[84] As this intersection with international human rights law grows, there is greater potential for additional countries to recognize obligations with regard to a human right to a healthy environment and the potential for development of new jurisprudence and legal thinking on how to strengthen implementation of the right where it has already been adopted.

While comparisons among constitutions come with certain limitations—general differences between the style and application of constitutions in civil law versus common law traditions, as well as other key differences among legal systems—scholars have identified 'good practices' moving forward to safeguard the enjoyment of environmental rights. James May and Erin Daly list ten such practices. These include clear and positive articulation of the right; ensuring that the right is self-executing and aligned with substantive rights tied to environmental protection; the formulation of principles of open access to justice to vindicate the right; and the recognition that the underlying constitutional and governance framework should be 'amenable to environmental constitutionalism'.[85]

John Knox, UN Special Rapporteur on Human Rights and the Environment, has highlighted the importance of constitutional environmental law in a 2014 report.[86] In providing a rationale for constitutional environmental rights, Knox suggested that such rights can provide a safety net to 'protect against gaps in statutory environmental laws' and can help to 'raise the profile and importance of environmental protection as compared to competing interests'.[87]

All of these factors and practices demonstrate the importance of a constitutional human right to a healthy environment as a basic principle of environmental governance and as a key method for expressing shared societal values about the relationship between humans and the environment. It has already been noted that fulfillment of the right raises challenges in defining the content of the right, in establishing complementary substantive and procedural environmental guarantees, and in creating arrangements that can lead to effective changes in environmental outcomes. This may be via judicial supervision of the right or through less tangible impacts.

Given the fundamental interdependence of humans and the rest of the Earth around them, especially the human need to breathe air, drink water, and eat food—all of which are supported by environmental processes—there will need to be greater creativity, greater commitment, and greater effort to safeguard the right to a healthy environment and to ensure a sustainable future.

NOTES

1. See generally Rasband et al. (2009, pp. 11–28).
2. Stockholm Declaration (1972, principle 1).
3. See, eg, Shelton (2001).
4. Ibid. (pp. 187–9).
5. See generally Anton and Shelton (2011, p. 118) who trace the development of international human rights law and environmental law leading up to and following the Stockholm Conference.
6. Constitution of Brazil, art.225.
7. Constitution of Turkey, art.56.
8. See Anderson (1996).
9. This chapter focuses specifically on national and subnational constitutional rights. However, the definition and implementation of national-level rights is influenced by international human rights law, and international sources (in treaties and in declarations) of rights-based environmental norms are highly relevant.
10. Boyd (2012, p. 28).
11. Ibid.
12. The database was most recently updated in April 2014. Toronto Initiative for Economic and Social Rights; http://www.tiesr.org/data.html.
13. Ibid. The database distinguishes between constitutional provisions that provide for a right to a safe or healthy environment from provisions that give the state responsibility to protect the environment. As of 2014, 107 out of the 195 constitutions studied contain such provisions regarding state responsibility, with a total of 127 including at least one of the two types of environmental provisions.
14. Ibid.
15. See Anderson (1996).
16. Cf. Denevan (1992).
17. Constitution of Angola, art.39, para.2 (author trans.).
18. Constitution of Brazil, art.225 (author trans.).
19. Eg, Constitution of Argentina, art.41 ('All inhabitants are entitled to the right to a healthy and balanced environment …') (author trans.); Constitution of Belgium, art.23.4 (including the 'right to the protection of a healthy environment' among economic, social, and cultural rights) (Belgian House of Representatives trans.); Constitution of Bolivia, art.33 ('All persons have the right to an environment that is healthy, protected, and balanced') (author trans.)
20. Eg, Constitution of Armenia, art.33.2 ('Everyone shall have the right to live in an environment favorable to his/her health and well-being …') (Armenian Parliament trans.); Constitution of Azerbaijan, art.39.I ('Everyone has the right to live in a healthy environment') (Government of Azerbaijan trans.).
21. Anton and Shelton (2011, p. 436).
22. Eg, Constitution of Bolivia, arts 16, 20 (guaranteeing the right to water and to food as well as to basic services, including drinking water and sanitation; these provisions are separate from environmental human rights in arts 33 and 34).
23. Rio Declaration (1992, principle 10). Procedural environmental rights were further articulated in the Draft Principles on Human Rights and the Environment, Part III,

included as an Annex to the final report of UN Special Rapporteur Fatma Zohra Ksentini in 1994. See also Hiskes (2009, p. 134).

24. Eg, Constitution of Brazil, art.225, para.1, cl.4.
25. For example, although the US does not have a national right to a healthy environment, government action is constrained by the National Environmental Policy Act (NEPA)—a statute with procedural guarantees that requires an environmental impact assessment for major action with the potential to significantly impact the environment. See NEPA § 102(2)(C) [42 USC § 4332(2)(C)]. However, because NEPA guarantees only the procedure, and not any substantive outcome, a government agency is free to ignore the findings and environmental recommendations in a properly undertaken environmental impact assessment.
26. See generally Locke (1980); Rousseau (1968). Robert Alexy notes that constitutional norms include two categories: organizing norms that 'empower' government, on the one hand, and norms that 'constrain and direct public power', on the other. Alexy (2003, p. 131).
27. See Boyd (2012, p. 23).
28. Under the 'state action' doctrine, the Constitution protects individual rights from state action but not from the action of private parties; in other words, it does not itself obligate the government to ensure the enjoyment of rights, although this is accomplished through police power at the state level. See Maggs and Smith (2009, pp. 1351–89) (on the state action doctrine).
29. US Declaration of Independence, 4 July 1776 ('We hold these truths to be self-evident, that all men are created equal, that they are endowed by their Creator with certain unalienable Rights, that among these are Life, Liberty and the pursuit of Happiness. That to secure these rights, Governments are instituted among Men, deriving their just powers from the consent of the governed …').
30. See, eg, US Constitution, amend. I ('Congress shall make no law respecting an establishment of religion, or prohibiting the free exercise thereof; or abridging the freedom of speech, or of the press; or the right of the people peaceably to assemble, and to petition the Government for a redress of grievances'); amend. V ('No person shall be… deprived of life, liberty or property, without due process of law …').
31. See US Constitution, amend. XIV (applies to states). Note that under the doctrine of incorporation, most of the rights in the federal Bill of Rights also operate to restrict state governments. See generally Maggs and Smith (2009, pp. 546–54).
32. Hamilton (1788).
33. Compare, for example, Argentina's provision that 'all inhabitants' (*todos los habitantes*) hold the right (art.41) and Rwanda's provision that 'every person' has the right (art.49), with Angola and Brazil, which use the less specific term 'all' (*todos*), and the Philippines, in which the constitution refers to 'the right of the people' (art.II, § 16).
34. Hiskes (2009, p. 130).
35. Homer (2014, pp. 142–3).
36. See Hiskes (2009, p. 130). Although Thomas Jefferson famously encouraged each new generation to create a new constitution so as to prevent the undue exercise of control over future generations, the oldest constitutions in the world have become entrenched cultural symbols that stretch across decades and even centuries.
37. Constitution of Bolivia, Title II, ch 3–7.
38. Ibid. art.33.
39. Constitution of Turkey, art.56.
40. Constitution of Angola, art.39 (author trans.).
41. Constitution of Brazil, arts 5, 225.
42. Ibid. art.186, II.
43. Ibid. art.170, VI.

44. Constitution of the Philippines, art.II, § 16.
45. *Oposa v Secretary of the Department of Environment and Natural Resources* [Supreme Court of the Philippines, 1993] PHSC 577 (en banc), 33 ILM 168 (1994).
46. Ibid.
47. Ibid. Concurring in the judgment, Justice Feliciano expressed some caution with regard to this decision and indicated that the implications of making a broad provision self-executing would be 'large and far-reaching in nature': ibid. (Feliciano J, concurring). However, the case itself was only decided with regard to standing, and the case did not ever reach a decision on the merits. See Boyd (2012, p. 281).
48. See n.12 above and accompanying text.
49. *Clean Air Foundation Limited & Gordon David Oldham v Government of the Hong Kong Special Administrative Region*, HCAL 35/2007, Court of First Instance, Constitutional and Administrative Law List, No.35 of 2007, Judgment of 26 July 2007; reprinted in Anton and Shelton (2011, pp. 457–60).
50. Ibid.
51. *Robinson Twp v Commonwealth*, 83 A.3d 901, 959 n.46 (Pa. 2013).
52. See Daly and May (2015).
53. Constitution of Angola, art.74 (author trans.).
54. Constitution of Argentina, art.43 (Georgetown Political Database of the Americas trans.).
55. Constitution of Cape Verde, art.22 (author trans.).
56. Constitution of Bolivia, art.34.
57. See *Lujan v Defenders of Wildlife*, 504 US 555 (1992). Note that this is for federal courts in the US. Some states, such as Minnesota, have expanded standing for environmental cases. See Minn. Stat. 116B.03 (Minnesota Environmental Rights Act) ('Any person residing within the state … may maintain a civil action in the district court for declaratory or equitable relief in the name of the state of Minnesota against any person, for the protection of the air, water, land, or other natural resources located within the state … .').
58. See Bryner (2015).
59. Constitution of South Africa, art.24. A thorough exploration of the history of South Africa's constitutional environmental provisions can be found in Christiansen (2013).
60. Christiansen (2013, p. 217).
61. *Fuel Retailers Ass'n of Southern Africa v Director-General Envtl. Mgmt., Dep't of Agriculture, Conservation and Envt., Mpumalanga Province*, 2007 (10) BCLR 1059 (CC) (S. Afr.).
62. Ibid. (paras 8–19).
63. Ibid. (para.21).
64. Ibid. (para.40).
65. Ibid. (paras 44, 59); see also Christiansen (2013, p. 258) ('The Court essentially "constitutionalizes" sustainable development').
66. *Fuel Retailers Ass'n of Southern Africa v Director-General Envtl. Mgmt., Dep't of Agriculture, Conservation and Envt., Mpumalanga Province*, 2007 (10) BCLR 1059 (CC) (S. Afr.) at para.44.
67. Ibid. (para.102).
68. See Bryner (2012, pp. 486–96) (discussing interpretation of Brazil's Forest Code).
69. Hiskes (2009, p. 140).
70. Ibid.
71. *Oposa v Secretary of the Department of Environment and Natural Resources* [Supreme Court of the Philippines, [1993] PHSC 577 (en banc), 33 ILM 168 (1994).
72. Pennsylvania Constitution, art.I, § 27.
73. *Robinson Twp. v Commonwealth*, 83 A.3d 901, 959 (Pa. 2013).

74. Eg, STJ, REsp No.1.240.122/PR (2d Panel), Relator: Min. Antonio Herman Benjamin, Decision of 28 June 2009, DJe 11 September 2012 (Braz.); see also Bryner (2016).
75. STJ, REsp No.1.109.778/SC (2d Panel), Relator: Min. Antonio Herman Benjamin, Decision of 10 November 2009 (Braz.).
76. See nn.12–14 above and accompanying text.
77. As noted by Eric Christiansen, '[e]ven in this era of triumphant constitutionalism and pending and present environmental crisis, we have only infrequently seen robust enforcement of constitutional environmental rights': Christiansen (2013, pp. 216–17).
78. Boyd (2012, p. 276).
79. Ibid. (pp. 276–7).
80. African (Banjul) Charter on Human and Peoples' Rights (1982), art.24.
81. Protocol of San Salvador to the American Convention on Human Rights (1988), art.11.
82. See generally Council of Europe (2010).
83. Aarhus Convention (1998).
84. See Declaration on the application of Principle 10 of the Rio Declaration on Environment and Development (2012).
85. May and Daly (2014).
86. Knox (2014).
87. Ibid. (paras 21–2).

REFERENCES

Alexy, R. (2003), 'Constitutional Rights, Balancing, and Rationality', *Ratio Juris* 16(2), 131.

Anderson, M. (1996), 'Human Rights Approaches to Environmental Protection: An Overview', in A. Boyle and M. Anderson (eds), *Human Rights Approaches to Environmental Protection* (Oxford, Clarendon Press).

Anton, D. and D. Shelton (2011), *Environmental Protection and Human Rights* (Cambridge, Cambridge University Press).

Boyd, D. (2012), *The Environmental Rights Revolution: A Global Study of Constitutions, Human Rights, and the Environment* (Vancouver, UBC Press).

Bryner, N. (2012), 'Brazil's Green Court: Environmental Law in the *Superior Tribunal de Justiça* (High Court of Brazil)', *Pace Environmental Law Review* 29, 470.

Bryner, N. (2015), 'In dubio pro natura: A Principle for Strengthening Environmental Rule of Law', *Revista de Direito Ambiental* 78, 245 (Braz.).

Bryner, N. (2016), 'Public Interests and Private Land: The Ecological Function of Property in Brazil', *Virginia Environmental Law Journal* 34, 122.

Christiansen, E. (2013), 'Empowerment Fairness, Integration: South African Answers to the Question of Constitutional Environmental Rights', *Stanford Environmental Law Journal* 32, 215.

Council of Europe (2010), *Manual on Human Rights and the Environment* (2nd edn); http://www.echr.coe.int/LibraryDocs/DH_DEV_Manual_Environment_Eng.pdf.

Daly, E. and J. May (2015), '*Robinson Township v Pennsylvania*: A Model for Environmental Constitutionalism', *Widener Law Review* 21, 151.

Denevan, W. (1992), 'The Pristine Myth: the Landscape of the Americas in 1492', *Annals of the Association of American Geographers* 82, 369.

Hamilton, A. (1788), *The Federalist*, No.84, Paul Negri (ed.) (2011) (New York, Dover Publications).

Hiskes, R. (2009), *The Human Right to a Green Future: Environmental Rights and Intergenerational Justice* (Cambridge, Cambridge University Press).
Homer (2014), *The Odyssey*, Book XII (T.E. Lawrence trans.) (London, Sovereign Classic).
Knox, J. (2014), Human Rights and the Environment: Regional Consultation on the Relationship between Human Rights Obligations and Environmental Protection, with a Focus on Constitutional Environmental Rights, John Knox, UN Independent Expert on Human Rights and the Environment, Johannesburg, South Africa (23–24 January 2014); http://srenvironment.org/wp-content/uploads/2014/11/Johannesburg-consultation-report-final1.pdf.
Locke, J. (1980), *Second Treatise of Government*, C.B. Macpherson (ed.) (Indianapolis, Hackett Publishing).
Maggs, G. and P. Smith (2009), *Constitutional Law: A Contemporary Approach* (Washington, West).
May, J. and E. Daly (2014), 'Ten Good Practices in Environmental Constitutionalism: Structure, Text, and Justiciability', *Widener Law School Legal Studies Research Paper Series*, No.14–39.
Rasband, J., J. Salzman and M. Squillace (eds) (2009), *Natural Resources Law and Policy* (2nd edn) (St. Paul, Foundation Press).
Rousseau, J. (1968), *The Social Contract* (Maurice Cranston, trans.) (London, Penguin Books).
Shelton, D. (2001), 'Environmental Rights', in P. Alston (ed.), *Peoples' Rights* (Oxford, Oxford University Press), pp. 185–258.
Toronto Initiative for Economic and Social Rights; http://www.tiesr.org/data.html.

CASES

Clean Air Foundation case: *Clean Air Foundation Limited & Gordon David Oldham v Government of the Hong Kong Special Administrative Region*, HCAL 35/2007, Court of First Instance, Constitutional and Administrative Law List, No.35 of 2007, Judgment of 26 July 2007, reprinted in Anton and Shelton (2011), pp. 457–60
Fuel Retailers case: *Fuel Retailers Ass'n of Southern Africa v Director-General Envtl. Mgmt., Dep't of Agriculture, Conservation and Envt., Mpumalanga Province*, 2007 (10) BCLR 1059 (CC) (S. Afr.).
Lujan v Defenders of Wildlife, 504 US 555 (1992).
Minors Oposa case: *Oposa v Secretary of the Department of Environment and Natural Resources* [Supreme Court of the Philippines, [1993] PHSC 577 (en banc)], 33 ILM 168 (1994).
Robinson Township case: *Robinson Township v Commonwealth*, 83 A.3d 901 (Pa. 2013).
First Brazil case: STJ, REsp No.1.240.122/PR (2d Panel), Relator: Min. Antonio Herman Benjamin, Decision of 28 June 2009, DJe 11 September 2012 (Braz.).
Second Brazil case: STJ REsp No.1.109.778/SC (2d Panel), Relator: Min. Antonio Herman Benjamin, Decision of 10 November 2009 (Braz.).

CONSTITUTIONS

Belgian Constitution (Belgian House of Representatives trans.); http://www.const-court.be/en/basic_text/belgian_constitution.pdf.
Constitución Nacional [Const. Nac.] (Arg.); http://www.senado.gov.ar/deInteres.

Constitución Política del Estado Plurinacional de Bolivia.
Constituição da República de Angola; http://www.governo.gov.ao/Arquivos/Constituicao_da_Republica_de_Angola.pdf.
Constituição da República de Cabo Verde [Cape Verde]; http://www.wipo.int/edocs/lexdocs/laws/pt/cv/cv008pt.pdf.
Constituição da República Federativa do Brasil de 1988 [Brazil]; http://www.planalto.gov.br/ccivil_03/constituicao/constituicaocompilado.htm.
Constitution of the Republic of Armenia (National Assembly of the Republic of Armenia trans.); http://www.parliament.am/parliament.php?id=constitution&lang=eng#2.
Constitution of the Republic of Azerbaijan (Government of Azerbaijan trans.); http://azerbaijan.az/portal/General/Constitution/doc/constitution_e.pdf.
Constitution of the Republic of the Philippines (1987); http://www.gov.ph/constitutions/the-1987-constitution-of-the-republic-of-the-philippines/.
Constitution of the Republic of Rwanda; http://www.parliament.gov.rw/fileadmin/Images2013/Rwandan_Constitution.pdf.
Constitution of the Republic of South Africa.
Constitution of the Republic of Turkey (Grand National Assembly of Turkey trans.); https://global.tbmm.gov.tr/docs/constitution_en.pdf.
Pennsylvania Constitution, art.I, § 27.

INSTRUMENTS

Aarhus Convention 1999: Convention on Access to Information, Public Participation in Decision-Making and Access to Justice in Environmental Matters, 28 June 1998, 2161 UNTS 447, 38 ILM 517 (1999).
Additional Protocol to the American Convention on Human Rights in the Area of Economic, Social and Cultural Rights 1988: Protocol of San Salvador, art.11, OAS Treaty Series no.69 (1988).
African (Banjul) Charter on Human and People's Rights 1982: art.24, OAU Doc. CAB/LEG/67/3 rev. 5, 21 ILM 58 (1982).
Declaration on the application of Principle 10 of the Rio Declaration on Environment and Development, UN Doc. A/Conf. 216/13, 25 July 2012; http://www.cepal.org/rio20/noticias/paginas/3/54423/Declaracion-eng-N1244043.pdf.
Draft Declaration of Principles on Human Rights and the Environment (1994), Fatma Zohra Ksentini, Special Rapporteur, UN Doc. E/CN.4/Sub.2/1994/9, Annex I.
Minn. Stat. 116B.03 (Minnesota Environmental Rights Act).
National Environmental Policy Act of 1969 (NEPA) § 102(2)(C) [42 USC § 4332(2)(C)].
Rio Declaration 1992: Declaration on Environment and Development, Report of the UN Conference on Environment and Development, UN Doc. A/CONF.151/26/Rev.1 (Vol.1), Annex I.
Stockholm Declaration 1972: Declaration of the United Nations Conference on the Human Environment, Principle 1, Report of the United Nations Conference on the Human Environment, UN Doc. A/CONF.48/14 (1972).

APPENDIX

Table 7A.1 Selected examples of national constitutional provisions

Country	Year of adoption	Text	Notes
Angola	2010	Article 39 1. All have the right to live in a healthy and unpolluted environment, as well as the duty to defend and preserve [it]. 2. The State [shall] adopt the measures necessary for the protection of the environment and of the species of flora and fauna throughout the national territory, for maintaining ecological equilibrium, for the appropriate siting of economic activity and for the exploration and rational use of all natural resources, in a framework of sustainable development and of respect for the rights of future generations and the preservation of different species. Article 74 1. Each citizen, individually or through associations representing specific interests, has the right to bring a judicial action, in the cases and under the terms established by law, seeking to annul acts injurious to … the environment … and other collective interests. (Author translation) Online source (in Portuguese): http://www.tribunalconstitucional.ao/uploads/%7B9555c635-8d7c-4ea1-b7f9-0cd33d08ea40%7D.pdf	Included in title on fundamental rights and duties Duty to defend and preserve environment, in addition to state responsibility for environmental protection
Argentina	1994	Article 41. All inhabitants are entitled to the right to a healthy and balanced environment fit for human development in order that productive activities shall meet present needs without endangering those of future generations; and shall have the duty to preserve it. … The authorities shall provide for the protection of this right, the rational use of natural resources, the preservation of the natural and cultural heritage and of the biological diversity, and shall also provide for environmental information and education.	

Country	Year of adoption	Text	Notes
		Article 43. Any person shall file a prompt and summary proceeding regarding constitutional guarantees (*amparo*), provided there is no other legal remedy, against any act or omission of the public authorities or individuals which currently or imminently may damage, limit, modify or threaten rights and guarantees recognized by this Constitution, treaties or laws, with open arbitrariness or illegality. Online source (Georgetown Political Database of the Americas, English translation): http://pdba.georgetown.edu/Constitutions/Argentina/argen94_e.html	Right defined with reference to sustainable development *Amparo* action provides universal standing to challenge actions that threaten constitutional rights
Belgium	1994	Article 23. Everyone has the right to lead a life in keeping with human dignity. To this end, the laws… guarantee economic, social and cultural rights, taking into account corresponding obligations, and determine the conditions for exercising them. These rights include among others: . . . 4. The right to the protection of a healthy environment . . . Online source (English translation): http://www.const-court.be/en/basic_text/belgian_constitution.pdf	Ties environmental rights to the concept of human dignity
Bhutan	2008	Article 5. Environment 1. Every Bhutanese is a trustee of the Kingdom's natural resources and environment for the benefit of the present and future generations and it is the fundamental duty of every citizen to contribute to the protection of the natural environment, conservation of the rich biodiversity of Bhutan and prevention of all forms of ecological degradation including noise, visual and physical pollution through the adoption and support of environment friendly practices and policies. 2. The Royal Government shall: (a) Protect, conserve and improve the pristine environment and safeguard the biodiversity of the country; (b) Prevent pollution and ecological degradation; (c) Secure ecologically balanced sustainable development while promoting justifiable economic and social development; and (d) Ensure a safe and healthy environment.	Does not specifically grant a right to individuals, but lists obligations of the government. Individual duties are tied to intergenerational concerns

		3. The Government shall ensure that, in order to conserve the country's natural resources and to prevent degradation of the ecosystem, a minimum of sixty percent of Bhutan's total land shall be maintained under forest cover for all time. 4. Parliament may enact environmental legislation to ensure sustainable use of natural resources and maintain intergenerational equity and reaffirm the sovereign rights of the State over its own biological resources. 5. Parliament may, by law, declare any part of the country to be a National Park, Wildlife Reserve, Nature Reserve, Protected Forest, Biosphere Reserve, Critical Watershed and such other categories meriting protection. Online source (English translation): http://www.bhutanaudit.gov.bt/About%20Us/Mandates/Constitution%20of%20Bhutan%202008.pdf	
Bolivia	2009	Article 33 Everyone has the right to a healthy, protected, and balanced environment. The exercise of this right must be granted to individuals and collectives of present and future generations, as well as to other living things, so they may develop in a normal and permanent way. Article 34 Any person, in his or her own right or on behalf of a collective, is authorized to take legal action in defense of environmental rights, without prejudice to the obligation of public institutions to act on their own in the face of attacks on the environment. Article 109, I (Applicability and jurisdiction) All the rights recognized in the Constitution are directly applicable and enjoy equal guarantees of their protection. Online source (Constitute Project, Max Planck Institute English translation): https://www.constituteproject.org/constitution/Bolivia_2009.pdf	Includes intergenerational equity; right tied to development of humans and other species Universal standing, with recognition of state responsibility to respond to environmental threats Direct applicability (self-execution) of environmental rights

Country	Year of adoption	Text	Notes
Brazil	1988	Article 225. All have the right to an ecologically balanced environment, which is an asset of common use and essential to a healthy quality of life, and both the Government and the community shall have the duty to defend and preserve it for present and future generations. Paragraph 1—In order to ensure the effectiveness of this right, it is incumbent upon the Government to: 1. Preserve and restore the essential ecological processes and provide for the ecological treatment of species and ecosystems . . . 4. Demand, in the manner prescribed by law, for the installation of works and activities which may potentially cause significant degradation of the environment, a prior environmental impact study, which shall be made public . . . 7. Protect the fauna and the flora, with prohibition, in the manner prescribed by law, of all practices which represent a risk to their ecological function, cause the extinction of species or subject animals to cruelty. Online source (Georgetown Political Database of the Americas, English translation): http://pdba.georgetown.edu/Constitutions/Brazil/english96.html	Written as a stand-alone chapter in the constitution Includes constitutional mandate for environmental impact study as a means for ensuring the effectiveness of the right Interaction with several additional constitutional provisions related to the environment (e.g., on property law and on principles of the country's economic order
Cabo Verde (Cape Verde)	2010	Article 22 . . . 1. To all is conferred, personally or through associations organized for the defense of shared interests, the right to bring an action seeking the prevention, cessation, or judicial prosecution of violations against health, the environment, quality of life or cultural patrimony. Article 73 1. All have the right to a healthy and ecologically balanced environment and the duty to defend and value it. 2. In order to guarantee the right to the environment, the government shall: a. Enact and execute appropriate policies for land use, preservation and defense of the environment, and ensure rational exploration of all natural resources, safeguarding their capacity for renewal and ecological stability	

		b. Promote environmental education, respect for environmental values, the fight against desertification and the effects of drought. (Author translation) Online source (World Intellectual Property Organization database, in Portuguese): http://www.wipo.int/edocs/lexdocs/laws/pt/cv/cv008pt.pdf	
Philippines	1987	Article II, Section 16 The State shall protect and advance the right of the people to a balanced and healthful ecology in accord with the rhythm and harmony of nature. Online source: http://www.gov.ph/constitutions/the-1987-constitution-of-the-republic-of-the-philippines/	Located within the 'Declaration of Principles and State Policies' (Article II), rather than the Bill of Rights (Article III)
South Africa	1996	Article 24. Environment Everyone has the right: 1. to an environment that is not harmful to their health or well-being; and 2. to have the environment protected, for the benefit of present and future generations, through reasonable legislative and other measures that a. prevent pollution and ecological degradation; b. promote conservation; and c. secure ecologically sustainable development and use of natural resources while promoting justifiable economic and social development. Online source (Government of South Africa): http://www.gov.za/documents/constitution/chapter-2-bill-rights#24	Part of the Bill of Rights (Chapter 2)
Turkey	1982	Article 56 Everyone has the right to live in a healthy and balanced environment. It is the duty of the State and citizens to improve the natural environment, to protect the environmental health and to prevent environmental pollution. . . . Online source (Grand National Assembly of Turkey, English translation): https://global.tbmm.gov.tr/docs/constitution_en.pdf	Located in the chapter on social and economic rights and duties Expresses concept of human interdependence with and interest in ensuring health of environment

8. Rights of nature: a constructive analysis

Peter Burdon and Claire Williams

INTRODUCTION

In 1972 Professor Christopher Stone of the University of Southern California was approaching the final minutes of an introductory lecture on property law. He noted that, like human culture, property law is an evolving social institution and has progressed through different stages of growth and development.[1] Throughout history, there has been a continual evolution in the type of things that can be owned, who was considered capable of ownership and the meaning of ownership itself.[2] Stone commented to his class that 'it was easy to see how each change shifted the focus and quality of power … each advance in the law-legitimated concept of "ownership", fuelling a change in consciousness, in the range and depth of feelings'.[3] Stone was awakened from this historical narrative by the shuffling and voices of his students who had begun to 'pack away their enthusiasm for the next venture'.[4] In an effort to maintain their attention, he wondered aloud:

> So, what would a radically different law-driven consciousness look like? … One in which Nature had rights … Yes, rivers, lakes … trees … animals … How would such a posture in law affect a community's view of itself?[5]

According to Stone, his thought experiment created uproar. He emerged from the lecture theatre dazed and asked 'What did you just say in there? How could trees have rights?'[6] Fuelled by intellectual curiosity, Stone penned his now classic article 'Should Trees Have Standing' (hereafter 'Trees') for a special edition of the *Southern California Law Review*.[7] Had this been the end of the story, Stone's article may have faded into obscurity. However, the ecologically minded Justice William O. Douglas[8] of the Supreme Court of the United States was editing the special edition to which Stone had submitted his article. Stone knew this and hoped that his article would influence the opinion of Justice Douglas in the *Sierra Club* case before the Supreme Court.

In the *Sierra Club* case the United States Forest Service had permitted development of Mineral King near Sequoia National Park in California. The central legal question before the court was whether the Sierra Club had sufficient injury to give them standing to sue for an injunction to halt the development. In response, the majority of the Supreme Court affirmed the existing test for standing that required the party seeking review to have suffered actual damage. However, in a dissenting judgement, Justice Douglas held:

> The critical question of standing would be simplified and also put neatly in focus if we ... allowed environmental issues to be litigated ... in the name of the inanimate object about to be despoiled, defaced, or invaded ... Contemporary public concern for protecting nature's ecological equilibrium should lead to the conferral of standing upon environmental objects to sue for their own preservation ... this suit would therefore be more properly labelled as 'Mineral King v. Morton' (See Should Trees Have Standing?).[9]

Justices Blackmun and Brennan favoured the conventional interpretation of standing but noted in passing that they would have permitted the 'imaginative expansion' endorsed by Justice Douglas. These comments gave Stone's thesis a credibility and an exposure that it may not otherwise have enjoyed. It also cemented 'Trees' as a foundation for the burgeoning field of environmental law.[10]

For three decades Stone's thesis lay dormant. As environmental law developed into a professional discipline[11] it focused on regulating human conduct by prescribing the various duties and responsibilities of human beings in relation to the environment. Legal standing continued to depend on human injury and nature was not accorded independent legal rights.[12] This began to change in 2006 when a community in Blaine in Pennsylvania drafted a local ordinance that granted to wetlands, rivers and streams 'inalienable and fundamental rights to exist and flourish within the Township of Blaine'.[13] Since then, 27 communities in the United States have approved similar ordinances.[14] In 2008 the Republic of Ecuador became the first country in the world to grant rights to nature in its national constitution.[15] More recently, in 2012, the New Zealand Government signed an agreement that recognised the Whanganui River as a legal entity with a legal voice.

As a result of these developments, the time is ripe for an analysis and a critique of the emerging rights of nature discourse and practice. Importantly, the critique here offered is in the spirit of critical loyalty to our colleagues working toward environmental protection.[16] This analysis does not deny the potential function of rights of nature, nor does it suggest that the project is without merit or that it should be abandoned. Rather, it constitutes a perspective and a method that try to reveal the underlying assumptions and preconditions upon which a discussion of rights of nature rests. It also shines a light on these assumptions and considers whether they aid or inhibit the goal of environmental protection.

This chapter begins by surveying the most recent legal developments that recognise the rights of nature. Then it engages with the philosophical and political objections to implementing rights of nature legislation. The critical question guiding this analysis is whether attempts to safeguard the environment through the existence of legal rights advance ecological goals in a sustained and transformative way. It also considers whether discussion should be directed towards a more egalitarian approach to justice that tackles the underlying causes of environmental harm, such as failings in governance and an economic system that supports infinite economic growth. Nevertheless, it is concluded that, while granting legal rights to nature may offer limited environmental protection, it is a radically insufficient response to the current environmental emergency.

RIGHTS OF NATURE: FROM THEORY TO PRACTICE

1. The Context

Western law treats the environment and non-human animals as property that can be bought, sold and used by humans. Law does not reflect contemporary scientific understanding of the planet. There is a vast knowledge as to how planetary scale systems and the biosphere work. All life is dependent on the health of the earth as a whole. The least sophisticated forms of life support the more complex forms. Yet in practice the law places humans above all else. Environmental law does not provide sufficient protection of the environment. It rarely defines nature as having value separate from human use.

One of the main arguments in support of granting rights to nature is that nature should be valued for itself and not just for human enjoyment or profit. According to this view, assigning legal rights to nature could shift the way humans relate to the world around them. This would be similar to recognising the rights of other groups, such as women or people of colour. Following this history, several jurisdictions around the world have enacted laws that recognise nature as a rights holder.[17] A few key examples are discussed below. Importantly, each instrument gives to nature or to aspects of nature standing in a court of law and the right to seek a legal remedy.

2. United States

In 2006 the Community Environmental Legal Defence Fund (CELDF) assisted the citizens of Blaine, a rural town in the state of Washington, to draft an ordinance to protect the health, safety and general welfare of its citizens and the natural environment by acknowledging the rights of local communities and ecosystems. The ordinance sought to ban corporations from conducting the destructive practice of longwall coal mining in the Blaine area. The ordinance also allowed the community to defend the rights of nature without the need to prove legal standing.

CELDF has now assisted almost 200 communities across the United States and countries such as Bolivia, Turkey and Nepal to establish community rights ordinances which protect citizens and the environment from environmentally damaging practices. These include longwall coal mining, shale gas drilling and fracking, corporate water withdrawals, factory farming, the land application of sewage sludge and uranium mining.

However, these local ordinances may still be overridden by state or constitutional law. In 2008 two mining corporations filed a federal lawsuit against the township of Blaine asserting that the community rights ordinance violated the supremacy clause of the US Constitution. The District Court for the Western District of Pennsylvania ultimately decided in favour of the mining companies. Judge Ambrose held that the Blaine community did not have the authority to ban longwall mining and other industrial practices which state law allowed. The court made clear that corporations enjoy the same constitutional rights as other 'persons' and that the Supreme Court alone had jurisdiction to overturn this doctrine.[18]

Following this case, in November 2014 an ecosystem in the township of Grant in Indiana County in Pennsylvania filed a motion to intervene in the *General Energy* case[19] to defend its rights 'to water and a healthy environment'.[20] Little Mahoning Watershed was granted rights by a Community Bill of Rights ordinance drafted in conjunction with CELDF. This ordinance banned frack wastewater injection wells. Pennsylvania General Energy was suing the township of Grant to overturn the Bill of Rights on the ground that the ordinance violated its constitutional right to inject frack wastewater into the ecosystem.

The case has now been decided.[21] However, it is interesting to note different reactions from the legal community. In response to the intervener motion, lawyers for Pennsylvania General Energy stated that 'a watershed lacks consciousness, intelligence, cognition, communicability, or agency … [t]he Watershed cannot decide to intervene, cannot accept representation or engage with counsel as a client, and cannot appear in court or testify'. Oil and gas legal expert Bruce Kramer added that 'people who propose this and say that these are valid ordinances are coming close to engaging in legal malpractice'.[22]

Alternatively, Lindsey Schromen-Wawrin, who represents CELDF, does not see it that way: '[F]or the ecosystem's rights to be defended, the ecosystem must be present in this litigation'. CELDF executive director Thomas Linzey also views the rights of nature argument as a much needed revolutionary approach to environmental protection as a result of the fast emerging and widespread practice of hydraulic fracturing: 'When an injection well comes in or a frack site, the adverse impacts caused by that project are not only to the community of humans but also to the natural environment … [f]or the last 1,000 years, nature has been treated as property rather than something with rights'.[23]

No matter how the case is decided, the enactment of ordinances which mobilise a community's right to self-government and assert nature's rights against the power of corporations may be viewed as an important step in this direction. This approach may transform the organizational framework of a legal system that has long been set up to protect the 'unholy alliance between government and the corporations'.[24]

3. Ecuador

After years of being used as a dumping ground by western corporations for their huge amounts of toxic waste, in 2008 Ecuador became the first country in the world to grant constitutional rights to the natural environment. The new 'Rights of Nature' chapter of the Ecuadorian Constitution reads:

> Nature or Pacha Mama, where life is reproduced and exists, has the right to exist, persist, maintain and regenerate its vital cycles, structure, functions and its processes in evolution. Every person, people, community or nationality, will be able to demand the recognitions of rights for nature before the public bodies.[25]

The rights of nature provision has been applied in several cases. It has also been considered in government development initiatives.[26] In November 2010 a case was filed by nine plaintiffs from five countries in the Constitutional Court of Ecuador under this chapter against British Petroleum (BP). The plaintiffs alleged that the rights of nature were violated when BP's deepwater horizon rig exploded in the Gulf of Mexico in April 2010 and caused extraordinary environmental damage. No monetary sum was sought: only an order that BP released its data surrounding the environmental destruction the oil spill caused and that BP refrained from mining as much oil underground as it spilled.[27] On 26 July 2012 the suit was admitted as No.0523-2012 under the Juzgado Segundo de Pichincha (Second Labour Court of Pichincha).[28] The case now appears to have been decided.[29]

In March 2011, the Provincial Court in the *Vilcabamba* case became the first to uphold the rights of nature chapter by granting an injunction in favour of the Vilcabamba River against the government of Loja.[30] The government had undertaken work to widen the Vilcabamba-Quinara road and, as a result, rocks, sand, trees and other rubble from the excavation were left to accumulate along the banks of the river. Large quantities of debris fell into the river. The river's channel narrowed. Its flow increased and caused substantial erosion and flooding as well as destruction of adjoining properties. For three years the project had been in progress without any impact assessment or consultation. The plaintiffs sued under the rights of nature provision rather than in their own capacity as landowners. The court upheld the claim stating that 'we cannot forget that injuries to Nature are "generational damages" which are such that, in their magnitude have repercussions not only in the present generation but whose effects will also impact future generations'.[31]

A number of important legal principles are revealed by this case. First, the court held that in rights of nature cases where environmental damage is based on possible or probable harm and not on certainty, the precautionary principle should be applied. In the court's words, 'until it can be shown that there is no probability of danger to the environment of the kind of work that is being done in a specific place, it is the duty of constitutional judges to immediately guard and to give effect to the constitutional right of nature, doing what is necessary to avoid contamination or to remedy it'.[32] Second, in rights of nature cases the burden of proof lies with the defendant to show that they have not caused damage to the relevant aspect of nature.[33] Third, the court held that where a conflict arises between nature's rights and other constitutional rights, the rights of nature would prevail simply because a healthy environmental is vital to all beings.[34]

In addition, the court issued remedial orders. These included a public apology, a plan for remediation and rehabilitation for the river and proprietors, a clean-up order and instructions to find suitable sites for any future dumping of debris. The court also ordered the government of Loja to acquire environmental permits before undertaking any more construction.[35] The court finally concluded that, while the constitutional provision was unprecedented in legal history, protective action was the 'only suitable and effective way to end and remedy in an immediate way a specific harm to the environment'.[36]

The Ecuadorian rights of nature provision has been commended as a revolutionary step towards environmental protection. It transforms the relationship between humans and nature. In addition, it indicates a move beyond an unsustainable extractive economy.[37] However, there are grave concerns about enforcement mechanisms and the power of the state to relax environmental regulations if it is believed to be in the national interest to do so.[38] Although in the *Vilcabamba* case the court ruled in favour of the river, the decision has proved difficult to enforce as the local government has not properly complied with the mandated clean-up order.

Not long after the decision in the *Vilcabamba* case, the government of Ecuador in the *Ecuador Rivers Pollution* case filed a suit complaining about gold mining activities which were polluting the Santiago, Bogota, Onzole and Cayapas Rivers and violating the constitutional rights of nature provision. The Second Court of Criminal Guarantees of Pichincha ordered the mining to cease 'for the protection of the rights of nature and of the people'.[39] This case was different from the *Vilcabamba* case in two respects. First, the government brought the matter to the court. Second, the court ordered the armed forces of Ecuador to enforce the decision. The success of the new provision in protecting the environment thus largely remains dependent on the will of the government. Indigenous and local communities have also expressed concern that the provision does not allow citizens to reject development projects that may damage their land and thus undermine their ability to defend the rights of nature.[40]

4. Bolivia

In April 2010 over 35,000 people gathered in Bolivia for the first Peoples' World Conference on Climate Change and Mother Earth Rights. An instrument entitled the Universal Declaration of the Rights of Mother Earth was drafted. It has been submitted to the United Nations for consideration. Consistent with similar 'soft law' instruments like the Earth Charter, the preamble recognises that 'we are all part of Mother Earth, an indivisible, living community of interrelated and independent beings with a common destiny'.[41] Article 2 considers that Mother Earth and all life have rights. These include the right to exist,[42] the right to continue their vital life cycles and processes free from human disruptions,[43] the right to integral health[44] and the right to full and prompt restoration for the violation of the rights recognised in the declaration caused by human activity.[45] The provisions in article 3 'recognise and promote the full implementation and enforcement of rights' and 'empower human beings and institutions to defend the rights of Mother Earth'.[46] The Universal Declaration of the Rights of Mother Earth was presented at the headquarters of the United Nations at the Third Interactive Dialogue of the General Assembly on Harmony with Nature. This dialogue sought to look at 'ways to promote a holistic approach to a sustainable development in harmony with nature'.[47]

Bolivia has conferred legal rights on nature by enacting 'la Ley de Derechos de la Madre Tierra' (the Law of Mother Earth). Bolivia, already one of the world's poorest countries, is now experiencing the devastating effects of climate change. Glaciers, which communities rely on for fresh water supply, are disappearing and crops are failing as a result of floods and drought. This pre-eminent law grants legal status to nature and classifies the preservation of earth as 'a collective subject of public interest'.[48] The law aims to diminish exploitation of the country's resources by focusing on conservation and acknowledging the inherent rights of Mother Nature.

5. New Zealand

In August 2012, in a landmark agreement between the New Zealand government and the Whanganui iwi (a local indigenous community), the Whanganui River became a legal entity 'in the same way a company is, which will provide the river with legal rights and interests'.[49] The agreement is the result of over a hundred years of advocacy by the Whanganui iwi who have a long history of reliance on the river and its abundant natural resources. The river, which now has legal status under the name Te Awa Tupua, will be protected by two guardians: the Whanganui River iwi and the Crown. Each guardian is under a duty to safeguard the river's interests and care for its long-term future.

The agreement is the first of its kind in New Zealand. The Minister for Treaty for Waitangi Negotiations, Christopher Finlayson, notes that an 'agreement which recognises the status of the river as Te Awa Tupua (an integrated, living whole) and the inextricable relationship of iwi with the river is a major step towards the resolution of the historical grievances of Whanganui iwi and is important nationally'.[50]

A CONSTRUCTIVE CRITIQUE

1. Introduction

When Christopher Stone first published 'Trees', the immediate response from the legal profession was scorn, derision and criticism. For example, John Naff wrote a poem in response to the judgment of Justice Douglas in the *Sierra Club* case. An extract from his poem reads:

> If Justice Douglas has his way
> O Come not that dreadful day
> We'll be sued by lakes and hills
> Seeking a redress of ills
> Great Mountain peaks of name prestigious
> Will suddenly become litigious.[51]

Naff's refusal to engage seriously with Stone's thesis is instructive. While American law had recently affirmed rights for women and African Americans, it could not countenance a further extension to the environment. Stone anticipated this resistance: 'Throughout legal history, each successive extension of rights to some new entity has been, thereto, a bit unthinkable … each time there is a movement to confer rights onto some new 'entity', the proposal is bound to sound odd or frightening or laughable'.[52] Stone explains it in this way. Until the entity in question is recognised as having rights, 'we cannot see it as anything but a thing for the use of "us" – those who are holding rights at the time' – in other words an object not a subject of rights.

Stone's argument is powerful and unsettles a perceived bias against recognising nature as a holder of rights. This is partly because Stone is working within the broad parameters of liberal political theory.[53] According to this view, legal rights confer more than protection by the state. Rights make an entity visible and cause other holders of rights to view it with increased respect. Many of Stone's readers would have lived through the civil rights or feminist movements and have read the liberatory aspects of his argument through that lens. Whether or not either of these movements fully realised their substantive aims is doubtful.[54]

Over time, intellectual engagement with Stone's thesis shifted from criticism to critique.[55] While these terms are often conflated, there is no necessary relationship between the two.[56] Bell Hooks explains: 'There is a useful distinction to be made between critique that seeks to expand consciousness and harsh criticism that attacks or trashes'.[57] The analysis of rights of nature in this chapter seeks to revive the creative aspects of critique and distinguish them from rejection or abolition. Properly understood, critique is an attempt to evaluate critically the premises, the preconditions and the implications of something that may not be obvious or reveal itself in everyday self-description. It is a method that can be directed toward understanding what a problem symptomatises or represents that is larger than itself.

It is similarly important to distinguish the analysis in this chapter from that conventionally undertaken under the name 'critical legal studies' (CLS). The proponents of CLS, while providing instructive analysis, have advocated the abandonment of liberal rights discourse.[58] The analysis in this chapter does not abandon a liberal rights discourse. As Patricia Williams has pointed out, such an approach from a position of relative privilege is both strategically naïve and a disavowal of cultural prerogatives.[59] Indeed, in the context of the impending environmental crisis it is maintained that individuals and communities should have the liberty to deploy whatever discursive strategy or law is appropriate to attain even modest or perhaps temporary protection. However, it is argued here that the instrumental or political deployment of rights of nature will be more easily justified by having understood its limits.

2. Rights: A Troublesome Concept – A Jurisprudential Dimension

The first significant objection to recognising the rights of nature is that legal rights are a uniquely human construct and prove 'troublesome when used to protect the biological world'.[60] There were no rights for the billions of years prior to human beings and outside of the human community. There are no rights today.[61] Trees, rivers, mountains and soil do not have rights and they are unable to recognise the rights of others.[62] Thus, a mountain slide that uproots a small pine forest does not violate the rights of the tree community. Even if the mountain slide kills human beings, it does not violate human rights. The mountain is not guilty of reprehensible behaviour and one cannot bring it to be shamed in a court of law.

Legal rights necessarily correspond with legitimate claims and entitlements. Thus, a person has a legal right to protection from a police officer because of the existence of a duty of care between the two parties. If a police officer stood by and watched a person being robbed or beaten, the police officer would be both legally and morally responsible. Reflecting on this point, Rolston notes that 'Using the language of rights for rocks, rivers, plants and animals is comical, because the concept of rights is an inappropriate category for nature'.[63]

An intellectually sound discourse about rights must acknowledge this critique. It is plainly nonsense to speak of nature owing duties to human beings or to suppose that rights exist between one and another part of nature. On the other hand, a proponent of the rights of nature may retort that the concept simply establishes human duties toward parts of the environment. From the perspective of implementing legal rules, this is possible. But it does not explain why the argument is framed in terms of rights rather than human duties. As Wesley Newcomb Hohfeld revealed,[64] duties are the corollary of rights and focusing on human duties would be politically easier for law makers.

A further problem with formulating a human legal construct like rights in relation to the environment is that the content of the right is unclear. It is a complex and politically difficult task to give substance to a human right across cultures and time.[65] However, the specificity required to make rights meaningful decreases when the focus goes beyond humans – for example, to children who cannot legally represent their interests; to corporate persons; or finally, to natural objects or ecosystems.

Stone confronted this objection in 'Trees' where he argued that nature would not have every right imaginable or even necessarily the same body of rights as human beings.[66] The theologian Thomas Berry picked up on Stone's point and argued that, rather than simply conferring the full range of human rights on nature, one could implement the concept in a limited and relative fashion. According to Berry, the recognition of legal rights is not an all-or-nothing conferral. Rather, he proposes that 'rights in the nonliving form are role-specific; rights in the living form are species specific and limited'.[67] Thus, according to Berry, rivers have river rights; trees have tree rights; birds have bird rights; and humans have human rights. The difference is qualitative not quantitative. The rights of one part of nature would be of no value to another part.

Berry's approach is interesting. But it does not add substance or specificity. It is one thing to say that a tree has distinct rights from a river. It is quite another to say what those rights are and how a court could judge whether that right had been infringed.[68] Arguably, some scientific standard like ecological integrity might be applied. But it is difficult to imagine how that would operate in conjunction with any of the legislation detailed above. Legal rights have traditionally been applied to discrete individuals rather than to interconnected ecosystems or nature more generally.

The philosopher Mark Sagoff was the first to raise this objection. In 1974 Sagoff mocked Stone's thesis and the idea that 'all of nature marches forward in legal equality, with rights for all, without regard to race, creed, color, sex, leaf structure, or atomic number'.[69] How, he wondered, did Stone or the environment movement purport to know the interests of a voiceless object? Turning to the facts under examination in the *Sierra Club* case Sagoff asked this question: 'Why wouldn't Mineral King [mountain] want to host a ski resort, after doing nothing for a billion years?'[70] Sometimes much can be learnt from the detractors of an idea. The power of Sagoff's combative approach comes from his ability to flip the issue on its head and highlight the inherent difficult of determining what is in nature's interest. If a presumption is in favour of conservation or an individual case is decided in favour of conservation, this will need to be justified and considered with reference to the needs of other parts of nature, including human beings.[71]

Further to this, even if parts of the environment, like a river or forest, were granted legal rights, human beings would still want to use and enjoy that part of the environment For example, while the Whanganui River has legal status, human beings still want to take water from the river, fish in its waters, and use it for recreation. Granting rights to nature does not have the same emancipatory consequence as it does, or at least could, for human beings. Despite arguments to the contrary,[72] granting rights to nature does not free it from its designation as human property. It is qualitatively different from granting rights to a human being. Indeed, while it may be possible to accept Kant's dictum never to treat human beings as a 'mere means to our ends',[73] it is difficult to see how this is compatible with the ongoing biological need of humans to access and use the environment.

Fundamentally granting rights to nature is motivated by the desperate need to halt ecological destruction. That is a noble aim, but what good will it serve if it is not possible meaningfully to define the nature of the right? While it might temporarily stop a specific project, could the right be appropriately redefined to satisfy the extractive industry? In the end, legal rights are empty signifiers – everything depends on how the right comes into existence.[74] This in turn relates to who is able to fill the right with meaning and enforce its particular application. The more general the right, the more room there is for manipulation and green washing.[75] One need only look at the way the term 'sustainability' has been appropriated by big business to understand the risk.[76]

3. The Final Conquest of Nature – A Moral Dimension

Consistently with this critique, some commentators have described the advocacy of rights of nature as 'a zero-order orthodoxy of the absolute human right over Nature'.[77] This critique contests the liberatory potential of rights and highlights the risks of domesticating the environment by bringing all of nature inside the human legal system.

The most vocal proponent of this critique is the Canadian environmental philosopher John Livingston. He seeks to protect relationships of intimacy and genuine compassion from intervention by the state. He begins by describing common relationships where reciprocal expectations have evolved to become rituals over time. For example, he argues that 'my wife and I observe "natural" fairness and justice in dealing with our dogs, and we expect "natural" decency and propriety from them'.[78] In reciprocal relationships like this, one need not invoke the legal language of rights and duties. Livingston contends:

> It is pointless, indeed wrongheaded, to attempt to apply any fabricated structure of rights and duties, or claims and obligations, to an interspecies relationship … it has nothing to do with politics … To suggest that the dogs have the right to demand our company, and we have the duty to provide it, is to perceive our relationship as a political one based on power and dominance, submission and subservience, tempered by an abstract system of moral canons.[79]

For Livingston, legal rights arise out of 'perceived inequalities' and are inexorably linked to contests regarding the distribution of power and privilege.[80] Advocates for rights of nature understand this political and intellectual context and point to the incredible influence human beings have over the environment as a contemporary iteration of exploitative power. In support of this position, it must be noted that not every relationship is based on the same level of sympathy and care that Livingston enjoys with his wife or dog. Indeed, the argument for recognising human rights becomes much stronger in abusive households. Similarly, if a dog owner was cruel or neglectful, few would deny the obligation of organisations such as the Royal Society for the Prevention of Cruelty to Animals to intervene to protect the animal. Liberal legal theorist, Jeremy Waldron, captures this point with respect to human relationships:

> There is a need for an array of formal and legalistic rights and duties, not to constitute the affective bond, but to provide each person with secure knowledge of what she can count on in the unhappy event that there turns out to be no basis for her dealings with her erstwhile partner in the relationship.[81]

Extending this logic, advocates for rights of nature would claim that in some circumstances it is appropriate to engage with the environment to the extent of recognition of its rights and the corresponding duties owed by humans to nature. This is most obvious in extractive economic relationships where natural love and affection cannot be relied on to prevail. In these circumstances rights may occupy a fall back position to regulate human behaviour and to intervene when necessary to protect the environment. As Waldron notes, there is value in being realistic enough to notice the tragedy of a broken bond and ask: What happens next?[82]

This retort is powerful. But it does not clarify the conceptual objection noted above. Moreover, Livingston is surely right to contextualise rights arguments and draw attention to their development in western history. As Richard Routley and Val Routley contend, 'western ethics are … human-chauvinist in that they characteristically take humans … to be the only items worthy of proper moral consideration, and sanction or even enjoin substantially inferior treatment' for the rest of the natural world.[83] In practice, ethical constructs are the foundation for rights of nature arguments. Ethics are not static. But when ethical constructs are adopted, there is a risk that this argument may be confined within the 'domesticated metaphysical dome of zero-order humanism'.[84]

This argument has particular implications for wilderness and ecosystems relatively untouched by human intervention. Reflecting a romantic perspective,[85] Livingston argues that 'wilderness requires no organisational intervention, even of the purest and highest democratic sort … wilderness is whole'.[86] However, if general laws, such as those recognised in the Ecuadorian Constitution, were taken seriously, then the 'right' conferred must extend beyond the human environment to embrace 'the entire ecosphere' and everything in it.[87] In response, Livingston notes:

> This may be an attractive notion at first blush, but even a modicum of thought reveals the most crashing irony. *It plays directly into the hands of zero-order humanism.* It represents the dedication of the entire planet to the human organization, the final conquest of Nature.[88]

Advocates for rights of nature consistently neglect to articulate this implication of their argument. Further, given the lack of specificity in rights of nature discourse and the interconnected nature of ecosystems, it is difficult to see how the right could be limited to a discrete part of the environment. For example, could the rights of a river to exist, persist and flourish be meaningfully realised without granting the same rights to the riverbank and trees that surround the water? If not, what about the grass, soil and microbes on the surrounding land? Can a line be drawn that defines the 'nature' that holds the legal right without absorbing 'nature' as a whole in the process? Such demarcations are difficult enough with human beings and lead to quite absurd implications when applied to the environment.

4. Monopolising Space – A Political Dimension

This final critique of rights of nature is historical and political. It concerns the potential for legal rights to 'organise political space' with the view to monopolise it and displace more radical political projects.[89] This potential has previously been highlighted with respect to identity based rights[90] and environmental human rights.[91]

To appreciate this critique, there is, first, Samuel Moyn's recent history of human rights in his book *The Last Utopia*.[92] According to Moyn, the linearity of rights has been grossly overestimated and the political values protected today 'bear no essential relationship' to earlier rights arguments.[93] In his book, Moyn demonstrates that it was not until the mid-1970s that rights talk spread and human rights emerged as a viable discourse to pursue justice claims.[94] Prior to this, justice projects were animated by a moral radical vision, evidenced in anticolonial struggle and the 1960s' student movement.[95] It was only after these more radical alternatives were defeated – or assimilated – that the language of rights gained ascendency.[96] In fact, Moyn argues that it was precisely because human rights did not require a commitment to political and social upheaval that they emerged as the safest strategy for the ideologically disenchanted.[97]

Arguments for extending legal rights to nature are marked by this history and the important extension of rights talk more generally. Legal rights are a liberal democratic construction that is predicated upon the abandonment of alternative political formations and more radical visions for the future. For example, in countries where rights of nature have been legislated, advocates have not sought to challenge fundamentally the prevailing economic system. This presents a significant problem because it is difficult to see how to protect the environment or combat climate change from within the confines of capitalist economics.[98] This tension has erupted in countries like Ecuador which, despite its constitutional provision, continues to extract oil from the Amazon and Yasuni National Park.[99] Similarly, Bolivia has struggled to reconcile proposed legislation for rights of nature with its desire to exploit the 5.4 million tonnes of lithium that sits below the Salar de Uyuni salt flat.[100]

Examples like this demonstrate that rights of nature arguments are not a substantive or transformative alternative. They are not about displacing growth economics or democratising power in a way that empowers communities or builds resilience. Rather, a right of nature represents a minimalist alternative and seeks to mitigate environmental damage from firmly within the co-ordinates of the current system.[101] This protection is important if that is all that is available. However, protection should not be confused with justice or with a resolution of the underlying problem.

What happens when demands are framed in the particular and putatively post-political paradigm of rights of nature? What other possibilities for social and environmental justice are silenced and displaced? What is concerning about rights of nature advocacy is that larger proposals relating to post-growth economics, justice, equality, power sharing, self-governance and the collectivisation of power will be set aside. Granting rights to nature is no substitute for these more radical proposals and the reinstatement of existing normative concepts such as rights. Rights derived from liberalism are 'inadequate to the task of grasping both new subject formations and new forms of social and political antagonism'.[102]

CONCLUSION: SHOULD WE BE SPEAKING OF RIGHTS?

This chapter has explored whether granting legal protection to nature in the form of 'rights' would substantially transform the way western legal systems protect the environment. Advocates for environmental conservation share many of the same objectives as advocates for rights of nature. However, it is critically important that advocates for rights of nature understand the presuppositions upon which their advocacy rests. It is concluded that, while the notion that nature could possess basic rights which humans should respect is attractive, there are a number of practical and theoretical difficulties in granting standing to trees.

There is no doubt that the current legal system needs to reflect contemporary scientific understanding of how the earth functions and how it is being impacted by human beings. Governance systems should acknowledge that humans are not separate from nature and that all life is connected. Nonetheless, granting legal rights to nature without drastic overhaul of current economic and political structures is unlikely to have the desired outcome.

Environmental lawyers must have the imagination to think outside the limits of the current system and of contemporary power structures. This was recognised by feminist scholar Audre Lorde who argued that 'the master's tools will never dismantle the master's house'. These tools may 'allow us temporarily to beat him at his own game' but they 'will never enable us to bring about genuine change'.[103] Following Lorde, it is contended that granting rights to nature is, on its own, an insufficient response to the environmental crisis. Indeed, whether it is politically useful to insist that the capitalist political class lives up to liberal principles is one thing, but to imagine that a politics grounded in rights of nature can displace extractive economics is a serious error.

NOTES

1. See generally Schlatter (1951).
2. Stone (2010, p. vii).
3. Ibid.
4. Ibid.
5. Ibid. Christopher Stone was not the first to propose granting nature rights. For a comprehensive historical survey, see Nash (1989).
6. Ibid.
7. Stone (1972).
8. Justice Douglas is unique amongst justices of the Supreme Court for his public advocacy of environmental ethics. See, in particular, Douglas (1965); Douglas (2011); Douglas (1972). See also O'Fallon (2009).
9. *Sierra Club* case. See also Schrepfer (1989).
10. Bosselmann (1999, p. 14)
11. On the foundations of environmental law as a discrete discipline, see Coyle and Morrow (2004).
12. Many statutes have described nature as having intrinsic moral value. At the federal level in Australia the Antarctic Treaty Environment Protection Act 1980 (Cth) states: 'the intrinsic value of Antarctica … shall be [a] fundamental consideration … in the planning and conduct of all activities in the Antarctic Treaty area'. The Convention on Biological Diversity [1993] ATS 32 provides that contracting parties 'must be conscious of the intrinsic value of biological diversity'. In South Australia, the Natural Resources Management Act 2004 (SA) commits in s.71a to 'recognise and protect the intrinsic value of natural resources'. Similarly, s.82 of the Nature Conservation Act 1992 (Qld) defines nature to include 'intrinsic scientific value'.
13. Margil (2011, p. 251).
14. For information, see http://celdf.org/-1-98.
15. Shuttleworth (2012).
16. Engel (2014, p. xv).
17. See in particular the work of the the Community Environmental Legal Defense Fund (CELDF) at http://www.celdf.org/ and the Global Alliance for the Rights of Nature at http://therightsofnature.org/.
18. See *Penn Ridge* case (2010).
19. *General Energy* case (2014).
20. Linzey (2014).
21. The Federal District Court decided that the township exceeded its legislative authority when it enacted the ordinance which prohibited the disposal of waste from oil and gas extraction. An appeal was dismissed: *Pennsylvania General Energy Co. v Grant Township* No.14-cv-209 (WD Pa., 15 October 2015).
22. Gilmer (2015).
23. Ibid.

24. See CELDF, 'The Opening Salvo: Blaine Township, Washington County Picks a Fight With Coal Corporations in Western Pennsylvania'; http://www.celdf.org/the-opening-salvo-blaine-township-washington-county-picks-a-fight-with-coal-corporations-in-western-pennsylvania-.
25. Constitution of Ecuador 2008, art.71.
26. In particular the the Yasuni-Ishpingo, Tambococha, and Tiputini (ITT) (now abandoned) Initiatives.
27. Shiva (2010).
28. See the Environmental Justice Organisations, Liabilities and Trade (EJOLT), 'BP Summoned to Answer for Assault on Mother Earth for Gulf of Mexico Spill' (2 August 2012); http://www.ejolt.org/2012/08/bp-summoned-to-answer-for-assault-on-mother-earth-for-gulf-of-mexico-spill.
29. The *BP* case appears to have been decided in favour of BP and an appeal refused. The reason appears to be that the court lacked jurisdiction because the events took place outside Ecuador.
30. *Vilcabamba* case (2011).
31. Daly (2011).
32. Ibid.
33. In the third edition of 'Trees' Christopher Stone also contends that the burden of proof should reflect our experience that environmental harm often has greater long-term effects than what can first be anticipated: see Stone (2010, p. 16).
34. Daly (2011).
35. Ibid.
36. Ibid.
37. Arsel (2012).
38. Becker (2011).
39. See *Ecuador Rivers Pollution* case (2011).
40. Ibid. See also Whittemore (2011, p. 659).
41. Universal Declaration (2010), preamble.
42. Ibid. art.2(1)(a).
43. Ibid. art.2(1)(c).
44. Ibid. art.2(1)(g).
45. Ibid. art.2(1)(j).
46. Ibid. art.3(2)(b) and (h).
47. See United Nations Harmony with Nature, 'Interactive Dialogue of the General Assembly on Harmony with Nature' (22 April 2014); http://www.harmonywithnatureun.org/index.php?page=view&type=12&nr=40.
48. Ley (Corta) 2010, art.5.
49. Shuttleworth (2012).
50. Ibid.
51. Naff (1972).
52. Stone (2010, pp. 2–3).
53. See generally Waldron (1993).
54. See for example Mckinnon (2007) and Alexander (2012).
55. For an in-depth discussion, see Burdon (2014).
56. Heath (2012).
57. Hooks (2010).
58. Significant articles on this subject include Tushnet (1984) and Hutchinson and Monahan (1984).
59. Williams (1987).
60. Rolston (1993).
61. Ibid.

62. This reasoning is influenced by Joel Feinberg's development of the interest principle. See Feinberg (1974). Feinberg considered that an entity could possess rights if it had the ability to be harmed or benefited and was conscious of such treatment. He notes: 'without awareness, expectation of belief, desire, aim and purpose, a being can have no interest; without interests, he cannot be benefited; without the capacity to be benefited, he can have no rights'.
63. Ibid. (p. 257).
64. This was made clear by Hohfeld (1913) and Hohfeld (1917).
65. It is increasingly common for scholars to critique human rights advocates on the basis that they seek to impose western, 'universal' standards on the rest of the world. See, for example, Douzinas (2007).
66. Stone (2010, p. 4).
67. Berry (2006, p. 111).
68. See further Code (2012).
69. Sagoff (1974, p. 221).
70. Ibid. (p. 222).
71. See also Sagoff (2005).
72. See Linzey (2005): 'Nature, under our current structure of law, is property, which means that mountains have no rights, ecosystems have no rights, streams have no rights, forests have no rights. They are property under the law. There was a time when people were property too. That's what the abolitionist movement addressed.'
73. Kant (1993, p. viii). The key to Kant's argument is the term 'mere'. Clearly we need other people to pursue our goals. What Kant rules out is using human beings in a pervasive way and not recognising their humanity.
74. Harvey (2013 p. xv).
75. Rogers (2013).
76. Parr (2009).
77. Livingston (1994, p. 159). See also Jensen (2004, pp. 53–66) and Livingston (1984).
78. Livingston (1994, p. 161).
79. Ibid. (p. 162).
80. Ibid. (p. 163).
81. Waldron (1988).
82. Ibid. (p. 647).
83. Routley and Routley (1980, p. 109).
84. Livingston (1994, p. 171).
85. It was common for early environmental thinkers to uphold 'wildness' as having supreme value. For critiques of this perspective, see, for example, Cronon (1995) and Crane (2012).
86. Livingston (1994, p. 172).
87. Ibid. (p. 173).
88. Ibid (emphasis in original).
89. Brown (2004)
90. Brown (2002, pp. 420–34).
91. Burdon (2014).
92. Moyn (2012).
93. Ibid. (p. 19).
94. Ibid. (p. 3). Moyn highlights the events of 1977 as being pivotal – in this year US President Carter stated in his inauguration speech 'Our commitment to human rights must be absolute' and Amnesty International won the Nobel Peace Prize.
95. Ibid. (pp. 2, 45–7 and 195–203). For analysis of two influential revolutionary movements in America and Germany, see Varon (2004).
96. Moyn (2012, p. 2).

97. Ibid. This sentiment was recognised by the founder of Amnesty International, Peter Benenson: 'The underlying purpose of this campaign … is to find a common base upon which the idealists of the world can co-operate [and to] absorb the latent enthusiasm of great numbers of such idealists who have, since the eclipse of socialism, become increasingly frustrated; similarly it is geared to appeal to the young in search of an ideal': (ibid. p. 130. Further to this, see Jessica Whyte's work mapping the links between the early human rights movement and anti-communism in Whyte (2012).
98. See Klein (2014).
99. Vaughan (2014). In a similar vein, foundational documents for environmental human rights, such as the UN Universal Declaration of Human Right 1948, have also been used to promote an egoistic form of market-based individualism. This has been explored in detail by Cheah (2007).
100. Carroll and Schipani (2009).
101. Ibid. (p. 121).
102. Butler (2009, p. 146).
103. Lorde (1984, p. 112).

REFERENCES

Alexander, Michelle (2012), *The New Jim Crow: Mass Incarceration in the Age of Colorblindness* (New York, The New Press).

Arsel, Murat (2012), 'Between "Marx and Markets"? The State, The "Left Turn" and Nature in Ecuador', *Tijdschrift Voor Economische En Sociale Geografie (Journal of Economic & Social Geography)* 103(2), 150.

Becker, Marc (2011), 'Correa, Indigenous Movements, and the Writing of a New Constitution in Ecuador', *Latin American Perspectives* 38(1), 47.

Berry, Thomas (2006), *Evening Thoughts: Reflecting on Earth as Sacred Community* (San Francisco, Sierra Club Books).

Bosselmann, Klaus (1999), *When Two Worlds Collide: Society and Ecology* (Auckland, RSVP Publishing).

Brown, Wendy (2002), 'Suffering the Paradoxes of Rights', in Wendy Brown and Janet Halley' (eds), *Left Legalism/Left Critique* (Durham, Duke University Press).

Brown, Wendy (2004), 'The Most We Can Hope For: Human Rights and the Politics of Fatalism', *The South Atlantic Quarterly* 103(2/3), 451.

Burdon, Peter (2014), 'Environmental Human Rights: A Constructive Critique', in Anna Grear and Louis Kotze (eds), *Research Handbook on Human Rights and the Environment* (Cheltenham, Edward Elgar).

Butler, Judith (2009), *Frames of War: When is Life Grievable?* (New York, Verso).

Carroll, Rory and Andres Schipani (2009), 'Multinationals Eye Up Lithium Reserves Beneath Bolivia's Salt Flats', *The Guardian*, 18 June; http://www.theguardian.com/world/2009/jun/17/bolivia-lithium-reserves-electric-cars.

Cheah, Pheng (2007), *Inhuman Conditions: On Cosmopolitanism and Human Rights* (Cambridge, Harvard University Press).

Code, Lorraine (2012), 'Ecological Responsibility: Which Trees? Where? Why?', *Journal of Human Rights and the Environment* 3, 84.

Coyle, Sean and Karen Morrow (2004), *The Philosophical Foundations of Environmental Law: Property, Rights and Nature* (Oxford, Hart Publishing).

Crane, Kylie (2012), *Myths of Wilderness in Contemporary Narratives: Environmental Postcolonialism in Australia and Canada* (New York, Palgrave Macmillan).

Cronon, William (1995), 'The Trouble with Wilderness; or, Getting Back to the Wrong Nature', in William Cronon (ed.), *Uncommon Ground: Rethinking the Human Place in Nature* (New York, W.W. Norton & Co).

Daly, Erin (2011), 'Ecuadorian Court Recognizes Constitutional Right to Nature, Widener Environmental Law Centre'; http://blogs.law.widener.edu/envirolawblog/2011/07/12/ecuadorian-court-recognizes-constitutional-right-to-nature.

Douglas, William O. (1965), *A Wilderness Bill of Rights* (Boston, Little Brown and Co).

Douglas, William O. (1972), *The Three Hundred Year War: A Chronicle of Ecological Disaster* (New York, Random House).

Douglas, William O. (2011), *Of Men and Mountains* (New York, Pierides Press).

Douzinas, Costas (2007), *Human Rights and Empire: The Political Philosophy of Cosmopolitanism* (London, Routledge-Cavendish).

Engel, Ron (2014), 'Summons to a New Axial Age: The Promise, Limits and Future of the Earth Charter', in Laura Westra and Mirian Vilela (eds), *The Earth Charter, Ecological Integrity, and Social Movements* (New York, Earthscan).

Feinberg, Joel (1974), 'The Rights of Animals and Unborn Generations', in William Blackstone (ed.), *Philosophy and Environmental Crisis* (Athens, University of Georgia Press).

Gilmer, Ellen (2015), 'Speaking for the Trees, Lawyer Pushes Unconventional Doctrine' (7 January), EnergyWire; http://www.eenews.net/stories/1060011209.

Harvey, David (2013), *Rebel Cities: From the Right to the City to the Urban Revolution* (New York, Verso).

Heath, Mary (2012), 'On Critical Thinking', *International Journal of Narrative Therapy and Community Work* 4, 11.

Hohfeld, Wesley Newcomb (1913), 'Some Fundamental Legal Conceptions as Applied to Judicial Reasoning', *Yale Law Journal* 23, 16.

Hohfeld, Wesley Newcomb (1917), 'Fundamental Legal Conceptions as Applied in Judicial Reasoning', *Yale Law Journal* 26, 710.

Hooks, Bell (2010), *Teaching Critical Thinking: Practical Wisdom* (New York, Routledge).

Hutchinson, Allan and Patrick Monahan (1984), 'The Rights' Stuff: Roberto Unger and Beyond', *Texas Law Review* 62, 1477.

Jensen, Derrick (2004), *Listening to the Land: Conversations about Nature, Culture and Eros* (White River Junction, Chelsea Green).

Kant, Immanuel (1993), *The Groundwork of the Metaphysics of Morals* (New York, Hackett Classics).

Klein, Naomi (2014), *This Changes Everything: Capitalism vs. The Climate* (New York, Simon & Schuster).

Linzey, Thomas (2005), 'Of Corporations, Law, and Democracy: Claiming the Rights of Communities and Nature', Schumacher Center for a New Economics; http://www.centerforneweconomics.org/publications/lectures/of-corporations-law-and-democracy.

Linzey, Thomas (2014), 'First-in-Nation: Ecosystem Files to Defend Legal Rights to Exist & Flourish' (18 November), Community Environmental Legal Defence Fund; http://www.celdf.org/press-release-first-in-nation-ecosystem-files-to-defend-legal-rights-to-exist–flourish.

Livingston, John (1984), 'Rightness or Rights?', *Osgoode Hall Law Journal* 22(2), 309.

Livingston, John (1994), *Rogue Primate: Exploration of Human Domestication* (Bolton, Key Porter Books).

Lorde, Audre (1984), *Sister Outsider: Essays and Speeches by Audre Lorde* (Berkeley, The Crossing Press).

Margil, Mari (2011), 'Stories from the Environmental Frontier', in Peter Burdon (ed.), *Wild Law: A Reader in Earth Jurisprudence* (Adelaide, Wakefield Press).

Mckinnon, Catherine (2007), *Are Women Human?: And Other International Dialogues* (Cambridge, Belknap Press).

Moyn, Samuel (2012), *The Last Utopia: Human Rights in History* (Cambridge, Belknap Press).
Naff, John (1972), 'Rejoinder', *American Bar Association Journal* 58, 727.
Nash, Roderick (1989), *The Rights of Nature: A History of Environmental Ethics* (Madison, University of Wisconsin Press).
O'Fallon, James (2009), *Nature's Justice: Writings of William O. Douglas* (Corvallis, Oregon State University Press).
Parr, Adrian (2009), *Hijacking Sustainability* (Cambridge, The MIT Press).
Rogers, Heather (2013), *Green Gone Wrong: Dispatches from the Front Lines of Eco-Capitalism* (New York, Verso).
Rolston, Holmes II (1993), 'Rights and Responsibilities on the Home Planet', *Yale Journal of International Law* 18, 251.
Routley, Richard and Val Routley (1980), 'Human Chauvinism and Environmental Ethics', in D.S. Mannison, M.A. McRobbie and R. Routley (eds), *Environmental Philosophy* (Canberra, ANU Press).
Sagoff, Mark (1974), 'On Preserving the Natural Environment', *Yale Law Journal* 84, 221.
Sagoff, Mark (2005), 'Do Non-Native Species Threaten the Natural Environment?', *Journal of Agricultural and Environmental Ethics* 18, 215.
Schlatter, Richard (1951), *Private Property: The History of an Idea* (Crows Nest, Allen & Unwin).
Schrepfer, Susan (1989), 'Establishing Administrative "Standing": The Sierra Club and the Forest Service, 1897–1956', *The Pacific Historical Review* 58(1), 55.
Shiva, Vandana (2010), *Historic Movement in the Defence of the Rights of Nature* (26 November); http://www.navdanya.org/news/142-historic-moment-in-the-defence-of-the-rights-of-nature.
Shuttleworth, Kate (2012), 'Agreement Entitles Whanganui River to Legal Identity', *New Zealand Herald*, 30 August; http://www.nzherald.co.nz/nz/news/article.cfm?c_id=1&objectid=10830586.
Stone, Christopher (1972), 'Should Trees Have Standing', *Southern California Law Review* 45, 450.
Stone, Christopher (2010), *Should Trees Have Standing: And Other Essays on Law, Morals and the Environment* (Oxford, Oxford University Press).
Tushnet, Mark (1984), 'An Essay on Rights', *Texas Law Review* 62, 1363.
Varon, Jeremy (2004), *Bringing the War Home: The Weather Underground, the Red Army Faction, and Revolutionary Violence in the Sixties and Seventies* (Berkeley, University of California Press).
Vaughan, Adam (2014), 'Ecuador Signs Permits for Oil Drilling in Amazon's Yasuni National Park', *The Guardian*, 23 May; http://www.theguardian.com/environment/2014/may/23/ecuador-amazon-yasuni-national-park-oil-drill.
Waldron, Jeremy (1988), 'When Justice Replaces Affection: The Need for Rights', *Harvard Journal of Law and Public Policy* 11, 625.
Waldron, Jeremy (1993), *Liberal Rights* (Oxford, Oxford University Press).
Whittemore, Mary (2011), 'The Problem of Enforcing Nature's Rights under Ecuador's Constitution: Why the 2008 Environmental Amendments have no Bite', *Pacific Rim Law & Policy Journal* 20(3), 659.
Williams, Patricia (1987), 'Alchemical Notes: Reconstructing Ideals from Deconstructed Rights', *Harvard Civil Rights – Civil Liberties Law Review* 22, 401.
Whyte, Jessica (2012), 'Intervene, I said', *Overland*; http://overland.org.au/previous-issues/issue-207/feature-jessica-whyte/.

INSTRUMENTS

Antarctic Treaty Environment Protection Act 1980 (Cth).
Convention on Biological Diversity 1992: *International Legal Materials* 31, 818.
Ley (Corta) de Derechos de Madre Tierra 2010.
Natural Resources Management Act 2004 (SA).
Nature Conservation Act 1992 (Qld).
Universal Declaration of the Rights of Mother Earth 2010: Peoples Conference on Climate Change and Mother Earth Rights, Universal Declaration of the Rights of Mother Earth (Mother Earth Rights); http://motherearthrights.org/2010/04/27/world-peoples-conference-on-climate-change-and-the-rights-of-mother-earth/viewed.

CASES

Ecuador Rivers Pollution case: República del Ecuador Asamblea Nacional, Comisión de la Biodiversidad y Recursos Naturales, Acta de Sesión No.66 (15 June 2011) ('República del Ecuador Asamblea Nacional'); http://asambleanacional.gov.ec/blogs/comision6/files/2011/07/acta-66.pdf.
General Energy case: Pennsylvania General Energy case No.14-cv-209 (WD Pa., filed 8 August 2014).
Penn Ridge case: *Penn Ridge LLC and Range Resources-Appalachia v Blaine Township*, US District Court for the Western District of Pennsylvania (2010) Civil Action No.08-1452; http://docs.justia.com/cases/federal/district-courts/pennsylvania/pawdce/2:2008cv01452/88840/45/0.pdf?1270165584.
Sierra Club case: *Sierra Club v Morton* 405 US 727 (1972); https://supreme.justia.com/cases/federal/us/405/727/case.html.
Vilcabamba case: *Wheeler c. Director de la Procuraduria General Del Estadode Loja, Juicio* No.11121-2011-0010; http://blogs.law.widener.edu/envirolawblog/2011/07/12/ecuadorian-court-recognizes-constitutional-right-to-nature/.

PART 2

THE DEVELOPING INTERNATIONAL ENVIRONMENTAL LAW REGIME

9. The development of international environmental law by the International Court of Justice

Tim Stephens

INTRODUCTION[1]

The International Court of Justice (ICJ, and hereafter 'the court') is performing an increasingly important role in the development of the fundamental rules, principles and processes of international environmental law. Until relatively recently the court occupied a position on the margins of international environmental law-making and dispute-settlement. It had decided only a relatively small number of disputes with environmental dimensions, and in these cases environmental concerns were often set to one side. The court tended to refrain from offering definitive views on them. The narrative in the literature describing the court's foray into environmental matters was therefore one of a conservative judicial institution that had neither grasped nor wished to grasp the significance of environmental law rules and concepts. According to this narrative the court has been labelled a follower rather than a leader in the advancement of environmental law principles by responding slowly and cautiously to external developments. This chapter contends that there are strong indications, revealed in several recent decisions, that the court has both the willingness and the capacity to address environmental matters more directly and substantively.

PROCEEDINGS BEFORE THE INTERNATIONAL COURT OF JUSTICE

1. Introduction

It is useful to begin with a brief review of the history and jurisdiction of the court. The Permanent Court of International Justice (PCIJ) and its successor court, the ICJ, remain the only two international courts to have been created with a general jurisdiction in terms of both subject matter and geographical reach. Any state may conceivably bring any type of international legal dispute before the court and this clearly includes those involving environmental issues.

The PCIJ operated from 1920 until the Second World War. In this period it decided one case relating to natural resources and access to them: namely the *River Oder* case, which concerned access to an international river. The court set out the 'community of interest' approach to international rivers. According to this approach all riparian states are to have shared access to such watercourses. This dictum has influenced the development of international water law generally. In recent decades it has acquired a strong environmental protection emphasis.

After the Second World War, the League of Nations and the PCIJ were replaced by the United Nations and the ICJ. The ICJ has a more central role in the United Nations system than the PCIJ had in the League of Nations system. It was established as the principal judical organ of the United Nations. As with all international courts, the ICJ's jurisdiction derives from the consent of states. There are several ways in which states may consent to having their disputes – environmental or otherwise – brought before the ICJ.

2. The Jurisdiction of the Court

States may consent in advance by depositing a declaration under article 36(2) of the Statute of the International Court of Justice. This allows states to accept the jurisdiction of the court in advance of a dispute arising. Such 'optional clause' declarations may be cast in general terms or subject to exceptions and limitations. As of 17 November 2015, 72 states have made optional clause declarations. A number of these have included reservations excluding either environmental disputes or certain types of environmental dispute. An example is Japan's revised article 36(2) declaration submitted in the aftermath of the *Whaling in the Antarctic* case. It provides that Japan no longer accepts the jurisdiction of the court with respect to 'any dispute arising out of, concerning, or relating to research on, or conservation, management or exploitation of, living resources of the sea'.[2]

Cases may also be brought before the court on an ad hoc basis, when states involved in a particular dispute agree to refer the dispute to the court. This normally occurs via the mechanism of a 'compromis'. This is a special agreement that confers jurisdiction on the court in relation to a specific dispute. It is also possible for cases to be referred to the court via compromissory clauses in environmental treaties. However, unlike some areas of international law, multilateral environmental treaties tend not to confer jurisdiction on the court. These treaties instead usually refer disputes to their own internal mechanisms of dispute-settlement.[3] In addition to the court's 'contentious' jurisdiction to decide controversies between states, the court also has an advisory jurisdiction which enables authorised United Nations bodies to request the opinion of the court on legal questions.

Notwithstanding the limitations found in some article 36(2) declarations, there are ample opportunities for environmental disputes to come before the court. After a slow start, there has been a quickening tempo of environmental litigation in the court. Moreover, the court's advisory jurisdiction provides a very broad opportunity for the court to address environmental issues. Given the tendency of major questions of international concern – such as the legality of the use of nuclear weapons – to come before the court in this way, it may only be a matter of time before the court's advisory jurisdiction is utilised to examine climate change and similar topics of global environmental significance and urgency.

3. Cases on Environmental Matters before the Court between 1949 and 2015

Table 9.1 lists the cases which were before the court between 1949 and 2014 and which involved, to a greater or lesser extent, environmental elements. In the list the use of '/' rather than 'v' indicates that the matter was brought before the court jointly by consent rather than unilaterally through the use of the article 36(2) procedure.

Included in the list are not only several cases that were discontinued before being heard on their merits but also some pending cases in which environmental issues have been raised in the applications that commenced the proceedings. Excluded from the list are those cases that may relate to natural resources in some way – such as maritime boundary delimitation cases – but which do not concern directly or indirectly conservation of resources, damage to the environment or protection of the environment. It should be noted that a number of the court's decisions have major significance for international environmental law even if they do not touch directly on environmental matters. For instance, in the *Corfu Channel* case – its very first decision – the court laid down some general principles underpinning the responsibility of states to prevent damage to other states. These form the basis of the obligation imposed upon states to prevent transboundary harm as set out in principle 21 of the 1972 Stockholm Declaration and principle 2 of the 1992 Rio Declaration.

Table 9.1 Cases involving environmental issues in the International Court of Justice

Year	Case name	Parties	Reported
1973	*Fisheries Jurisdiction*	*Germany v Iceland*	[1973] ICJ Rep 49
1973	*Fisheries Jurisdiction*	*United Kingdom v Iceland*	[1973] ICJ Rep 3
1974	*Nuclear Tests*	*Australia v France*	[1974] ICJ Rep 253
1974	*Nuclear Tests*	*New Zealand v France*	[1974] ICJ Rep 457
1993	*Certain Phosphate Lands in Nauru* (*Nauru* case)	*Nauru v Australia*	[1992] ICJ Rep 240 Discontinued
1995	*Nuclear Tests (Request for an Examination of Situation)*	*New Zealand v France*	[1995] ICJ Rep 288
1996	*Legality of the Threat or Use of Nuclear Weapons (Nuclear Weapons Advisory Opinion)*	*Advisory Opinion*	[1996] ICJ Rep 226
1997	*Gabčíkovo-Nagymaros Project* (*Danube Dam* case)	*Hungary/Slovakia*	[1997] ICJ Rep 7
1998	*Fisheries Jurisdiction* (*Estai* case)	*Spain v Canada*	[1998] ICJ Rep 431
2008	*Aerial Herbicide Spraying*	*Ecuador v Colombia*	Discontinued
2010	*Pulp Mills on the River Uruguay*	*Argentina v Uruguay*	[2010] ICJ Rep 14
2011	*Certain Activities Carried out by Nicaragua in the Border Area* (*Nicaragua Border Area* case) *Construction of a Road in Costa Rica along the San Juan River* (*San Juan River* case)	*Nicaragua v Costa Rica* *Costa Rica v Nicaragua*	Pending Pending

Year	Case name	Parties	Reported
2014	*Whaling in the Antarctic*	*Australia v Japan (New Zealand intervening)*	[2014] ICJ Rep 226
2014	*Nuclear Arms Race and Nuclear Disarmament*	*Marshall Islands v India; Marshall Islands v Pakistan; Marshall Islands v United Kingdom*	Pending

4. Some Organisational and Contextual Matters

Before turning to examine the court's emerging jurisprudence on environmental issues, it is necessary to discuss the organisation of the court and the legal status of its decisions. The court normally sits in plenary session with all 15 judges deciding disputes. However, the court has the capacity to establish chambers comprising a smaller number of judges to decide certain categories of dispute. Significantly, in 1993 the court created a Chamber for Environmental Matters. This Chamber continued to exist until 2006 when the court decided to hold no further elections for the Chamber for the reason that, in its 13-year existence, no state had ever brought a case before the Chamber. This is a very strong indication that states prefer to have their disputes, including those with environmental dimensions, decided by the court in full. Moreover, it tends to cast doubt on the merits of proposals for the creation of a dedicated environmental dispute institution. In reality it is impossible to separate environmental disputes from general international law disputes. Thus it is generally preferable for environmental matters to be integrated and 'mainstreamed' into international dispute-settlement generally.[4]

The decisions of the court in contentious cases must be made according to international law and by applying the sources of international law as set out in article 38(1) of the Statute of the International Court of Justice. These sources are treaties, custom, general principles of law, and judicial decisions and academic writings as subsidiary sources. The court's decisions are binding only upon the parties to the dispute. They have no legal force for other states.[5] Decisions of the court do not bind other international courts and tribunals. So there is no strict rule of precedent in international law that gives to the court's decisions any formal legal effect for the international community at large. However, in practice, the decisions of the court have been enormously influential, including in the environmental field.

Where the court has pronounced on major questions – such as the customary status of the precautionary principle or of environmental impact assessment – other international courts and states have tended to follow.[6] The court has had a major influence on the jurisprudence of the multiplicity of international courts and tribunals established in the United Nations era. Many of these have competence over environmental cases – such as the International Tribunal for the Law of the Sea with respect to the environmental protection provisions of the 1982 United Nations Convention on the Law of the Sea. As Shany notes, the court's 'seniority, primacy and pedigree combine to imbue the ICJ with a unique character and a considerable degree of influence over the goals and design of other subsequent courts and tribunals'.[7]

5. The Classification of the Cases before the Court

There has been extensive analysis of the contribution that the court has made to the development of international environmental law.[8] Fitzmaurice has argued that this contribution may be divided into five groupings:[9]

- Cases that have not raised environmental questions but have discussed fundamental concepts of relevance to international environmental law – for example the *Corfu Channel* case.
- Cases in which the court has shown a high degree of reluctance in addressing environmental disputes – for example the 1974 *Nuclear Tests* cases.
- Cases where there have been tentative steps towards recognising environmental problems – for example the 1995 *Nuclear Tests* case.
- Cases in which the court has placed environmental concepts within mainstream international law – for example the *Danube Dam* case.
- Cases that have examined and elaborated upon the relevant procedural requirements of international environmental law – for example the *Pulp Mills* case.

It is clear that Fitzmaurice's categorisation is as much historical as it is conceptual. It illustrates that over time there has been a significant enrichment of the court's environmental jurisprudence.

Another approach to the categorisation of the court's environmental cases is to divide them according to subject matter. The following discussion proceeds on this basis by examining, in turn, the cases concerning:

- Transboundary environmental harm and hazardous activities.
- Freshwater resources and ecosystems.
- Marine living resources and ecosystems.

It should be noted, however, that not all of the cases fit neatly into these categories. An obvious example is the *Nauru* case which was concerned with environmental damage to Nauru's natural environment while the nation was being managed through the United Nations trusteeship system. In this case Nauru argued that, while it was under the administration of Australia, New Zealand and the United Kingdom, the island state was stripped of its phosphate mineral resources and its environment seriously harmed. Although Nauru did not rely upon international environmental norms in its application, the factual basis of the case was fundamentally environmental.[10] After the court ruled that the case could proceed, notwithstanding the absence of New Zealand and the United Kingdom from the proceedings, Australia and Nauru reached a settlement.[11] As a consequence the court did not determine the merits of the case. This analysis proceeds now to consider the cases in accordance with the threefold classification based on subject matter.

TRANSBOUNDARY ENVIRONMENTAL HARM

1. Introduction

It has already been observed that the *Corfu Channel* case was important in the development of the general principles of international law concerning state responsibility for transboundary harm. Although it was as early as 1938 in the *Trail Smelter* case that an international dispute over transboundary environmental harm was litigated before an arbitral tribunal, it was not until 1973 that such cases were brought before the ICJ. These were the 1974 *Nuclear Tests* cases.

2. The 1974 *Nuclear Tests* Cases

In the 1974 *Nuclear Tests* cases Australia and New Zealand challenged the legality of French nuclear weapons testing in the Pacific. The Australian and New Zealand applications raised a number of legal objections to France's testing programme. In particular Australia's application made implicit reference to the prohibition of transboundary harm. Australia argued that France had committed a type of international trespass by carrying out tests resulting in nuclear fallout – albeit at very low levels – on Australian territory. However the balance of the arguments related to issues of high seas freedom of navigation and of environmental protection. Hence the litigation crossed subject matter categories, by addressing not only the issue of transboundary harm but also aspects of marine environmental law.

France did not participate in the case. This placed the court under significant pressure to find a solution to the dispute that would not undermine its legitimacy if, as expected, France would have rejected any adverse finding. The court therefore focused upon a statement by the French government following the hearings that it was to cease atmospheric testing. The court characterised the statement as a legally binding unilateral undertaking that had the effect of rendering the dispute moot. The court therefore determined that the dispute had been resolved and did not need judicial determination. There was a logical basis for this conclusion to support the non-utility of any remedy sought to injunct future atmospheric testing. But the French government's announcement did not cure any previous wrongdoing (assuming that its actions had in fact contravened international law). There was considerable uncertainty about this assumption given the then nascent character of international environmental law. Nevertheless the arguments presented by Australia and New Zealand were creative in a very real sense as they were seeking to fashion new propositions of law.

The court's judgment confronted neither the evidence relating to environmental harm arising from France's tests nor the possible rules of international law infringed as a result. However, in a number of the separate and dissenting opinions, individual judges did consider these matters, at least to some extent. Judge de Castro was the only judge to refer expressly to the transboundary harm principle.[12] In their joint dissenting opinion, Judges Onyeama, Dillard, Jimenez de Arechaga and Waldock explored the important question of standing on the part of Australia and New Zealand to complain of damage to the high seas. In an important anticipation of arguments that now appear to be accepted without controversy, these judges found that Australia and New Zealand enjoyed standing to bring the claim in respect of their collective interests. It will be noted in the context of the discussion below of the *Whaling in the Antarctic* case that the potential for states to bring claims before the court to vindicate obligations of a collective or community character now appears firmly settled.

3. The 1995 *Nuclear Tests* Case

There was a reprise of the nuclear tests litigation in 1995 following France's announcement that it would resume nuclear testing after a fairly short moratorium and that it would do so only underground. New Zealand sought to reactivate the earlier proceedings through the provision of the court's judgment in 1974 which stated that, if France were to rescind its undertaking, then the applicants could request an examination of the situation. To the consternation of New Zealand – and of Australia, which in these proceedings participated as an intervener – the court again found an inventive way to avoid deciding the substance of the dispute. It concluded that the 1974 decision related exclusively to atmospheric testing and that, as France's testing was now wholly underground, there was no basis for scrutinising the new programme.

As with the 1974 decision, the 1995 conclusion attracted considerable criticism. However, it is noteworthy that, in the formulation and consideration of the New Zealand application, there was considerably more pith and substance to the environmental law dimensions of the dispute. New Zealand expressly raised the transboundary harm principle in its argument. The court in its ruling reminded the parties that its decision was 'without prejudice to the obligations … to protect the natural environment'.[13] This was at least an acknowledgment that such obligations existed, even if the court did not wish to pronounce upon them. Notwithstanding this reluctance, in their individual dissenting opinions Judges Weeramantry and Koroma and Judge ad hoc Palmer did discuss in considerable length the rules and principles of international environmental law that had developed since 1974.

The two decades following the original nuclear tests litigation had seen a flourishing of the formulation of international environmental legal norms. This included not only the adoption of the 1972 Stockholm Declaration and the 1992 Rio Declaration but also the creation of a constellation of multilateral environmental agreements addressing all major topics of global environmental significance from biodiversity, to marine environmental protection and to climate change. It is equally significant that the 1995 proceedings drew the attention of the court both to substantive rules of environmental protection and also to procedural norms such as environmental impact assessment.

4. The *Nuclear Weapons Advisory Opinion*

Before concluding a discussion of the court's consideration of nuclear weapons technologies and their accompanying environmental impact, mention must be made of the court's advisory opinion in the *Nuclear Weapons Advisory Opinion.* Highlighting once again the enormous political sensitivity surrounding nuclear weapons issues, the court avoided answering the question put to it. This was whether 'the threat or use of nuclear weapons [is] in any circumstances permitted under international law'. Nevertheless there were a number of highly significant elements of the decision of relevance to international environmental law. The court acknowledged the catastrophic environmental harm caused by nuclear weapons; characterised the environment not as 'an abstraction' but rather as 'the living space, the quality of life and the very health of human beings, including generations unborn'; and found that 'the general obligation of States to ensure that activities within their jurisdiction and control respect the environment of other States or of areas beyond national control is now part of the corpus of international law relating to the environment'.[14]

5. Ancillary Transboundary Environmental Harm Cases

Subsequent to the nuclear tests litigation, several other cases involving transboundary damage have been brought before the court. In the now-discontinued *Aerial Herbicide Spraying* case, Ecuador argued that Colombia had damaged the environment within Ecuador through the use of powerful herbicides sprayed on cocoa and poppy plantations. In two proceedings that have now been joined, the *Nicaragua Border Area* case and the *San Juan River* case, the court is being asked to consider the environmental impacts of road construction and other activities taking place on the border between Costa Rica and Nicaragua. A number of environmental law questions arise, including those relating to the protection of wetlands and biodiversity.[15] Then there are the cases recently commenced before the court by the Marshall Islands against India, Pakistan and the United Kingdom in relation to the alleged failure of these three states to comply with their nuclear non-proliferation obligations under treaty and customary law. They also raise, as a factual matter, the risk of global transboundary harm resulting from the use of nuclear weapons.

Transboundary harm issues were considered by the court to some extent in its judgment in the *Pulp Mills* case discussed in more detail later in this chapter. The court strongly reaffirmed what it had stated in the *Nuclear Weapons Advisory Opinion* but it went further in finding that 'the principle of prevention, as a customary rule, has its origins in the due diligence that is required of a State in its territory'.[16] The court observed that in accordance with this principle a 'State is thus obliged to use all the means at its disposal in order to avoid activities which take place in its territory, or in any area under its jurisdiction, causing significant damage to the environment of another State'.[17]

FRESHWATER RESOURCES AND ECOSYSTEMS

1. Introduction

International water law is the body of international law concerned with regulating access to shared freshwater systems such as international rivers, lakes and aquifers, and their use and protection. Although it has a lengthy history, it has only relatively recently acquired strong environmental protection elements. The key global instrument is the 1997 United Nations Convention on the Law of Non-Navigational Uses of International Watercourses, which entered into force in 2014 after a long period in abeyance.

2. The *Danube Dam* Case

(a) The context

Even before the 1997 Watercourses Convention had entered into force, it was referred to approvingly by the court in its best known and most important case on environmental questions: the *Danube Dam* case. It arose from a dispute between Hungary and Slovakia in relation to a joint project between the two countries to construct locks and dams along a shared stretch of the Danube. The details for the project were contained in the treaty between Hungary and Slovakia's parent state, Czechoslovakia, concluded in 1977.[18] In 1989 Hungary suspended work on the project. It cited concerns that the project would result in serious impacts on river and floodplain ecology and would impair water quality in the Danube. Slovakia insisted that the project be continued and commenced work on a unilateral alternative – labelled 'Variant C' – whose purpose was to divert up to 90 per cent of the river flow to a side channel to feed hydroelectric turbines. Hungary and Slovakia agreed to submit their dispute over the project to the court. Three questions were presented for determination:

- Whether Hungary could suspend and abandon the project.
- Whether Slovakia could proceed with Variant C.
- What legal effects flowed from Hungary's purported termination of the 1977 treaty.

On all three questions Hungary advanced arguments that drew upon international environmental law.

(b) Ecological necessity

On the first question, Hungary contended that the project could be suspended for reasons of 'ecological necessity'. The court accepted that, in principle, ecological damage could be a defence raised by states in respect of a breach of a treaty obligation. The court observed that the environment could be regarded as an 'essential interest' for the purposes of the necessity defence in international law.[19] However it was concluded that the defence was not supported by the facts for three reasons: Hungary had not sufficiently established the environmental perils of which it complained; there was no imminent risk of harm; and such harm could be avoided through mitigation measures.[20]

In relation to the second question, the legality of Variant C, the court drew on recognised principles of international water law and found that Slovakia's plans violated Hungary's 'right to an equitable and reasonable sharing of the resources of an international watercourse'.[21] The court expressly approved the community of interest theory, namely that all states along an international river share a common legal right in relation to the resources and use of the watercourse. It also noted that Slovakia's plans entailed continuing impacts on the ecology of riparian areas in Hungary.[22]

The court then addressed the third question on termination. In support of its position, Hungary had formulated a number of creative arguments as to why the 1977 treaty had been rendered out of date and ineffective as a result of major developments in international environmental law. The court in several passages acknowledged the importance of the environment and the evolution of international environmental law. However it found that these developments could be accommodated within the 1977 treaty because it included provisions allowing for the project to be adjusted in the light of new knowledge. The court therefore rejected Hungary's argument that the expansion of international environmental law, during the period between the conclusion of the 1977 treaty and the bringing of this case, amounted to a 'fundamental change of circumstances' for the purposes of the law of treaties[23] thereby allowing Hungary to terminate the treaty.

(c) Prevention and sustainable development

The court then turned to consider the future conduct of the parties. In this context it made express reference to several principles of international environmental law including prevention and sustainable development:

> The Court is mindful that, in the field of environmental protection, vigilance and prevention are required on account of the often irreversible character of damage to the environment and of the limitations inherent in the very mechanism of reparation of this type of damage.
>
> Throughout the ages, mankind has, for economic and other reasons, constantly interfered with nature. In the past, this was often done without consideration of the effects upon the environment. Owing to new scientific insights and to a growing awareness of the risks for mankind – for present and future generations – of pursuit of such interventions at an unconsidered and unabated pace, new norms and standards have been developed, set forth in a great number of instruments during the last two decades. Such new norms have to be taken into consideration, and such new standards given proper weight, not only when States contemplate new activities but also when continuing with activities begun in the past. This need to reconcile economic development with protection of the environment is aptly expressed in the concept of sustainable development. For the purposes of the present case, this means that the Parties together should look afresh at the effects on the environment of the Gabčíkovo power plant. In particular they must find a satisfactory solution for the volume of water to be released into the old bed of the Danube and into the side-arms on both sides of the river.[24]

This clear recognition of sustainable development as an organising principle of international environmental law was an enormously significant moment in the history of environmental litigation before the court. It signalled that the court had finally come to grasp the importance of environmental concerns after several 'false start' cases. Although the court did not recognise sustainable development as a binding rule of international law of customary law status, it did use the concept in a meaningful way throughout its judgment in order to arrive at an outcome that balanced the two competing interests at the heart of the concept – economic development and environmental protection.[25]

(d) Environmental impact assessment

One of the significant features of the *Danube Dam* case from the perspective of international environmental law is the way in which the court emphasised the importance of following robust procedures when planning and implementing activities that have environmental impacts with transboundary dimensions. In this respect the decision may be seen as an endorsement of the then developing idea of transboundary environmental impact assessment (EIA). Although the court did not refer to EIA expressly, it was clearly adverting to the concept when it observed that 'environmental risks have to be assessed on a continuous basis'[26] and when it encouraged the parties 'to look afresh' at the effects that the Danube dams project would have upon the environment.

3. The *Pulp Mills* Case

Much more important than the *Danube Dam* case from the perspective of the court's contribution to the development of procedural dimensions of international environmental law was the *Pulp Mills* case. In this litigation Argentina contended that Uruguay had violated the terms of a river treaty, the 1975 Statute of the River Uruguay ('1975 Statute'), when it authorised the construction of pulp mills that could discharge pollution and damage the River Uruguay. The dispute was concerned mainly with the 1975 Statute. For this reason there were only limited opportunities for the court to address the general principles of international environmental law. However, the court did reiterate the transboundary harm principle[27] and it made several references to sustainable development as the overriding objective in reconciling the interests of the riparian states.[28] The court also referred to the precautionary principle, when it indicated that 'while a precautionary approach may be relevant in the interpretation and application of the provisions of the Statute, it does not follow that it operates as a reversal of the burden of proof'.[29]

The court determined that Uruguay had breached several procedural obligations contained in the 1975 Statute. These included the requirement to notify Argentina of the EIA that had been carried out before going ahead and authorising the mills.[30] Importantly in this context the court did not simply confine its observations to the effect of the 1975 Statute. It also concluded that EIA was a requirement under general international law:

> [I]t may now be considered a requirement under general international law to undertake an environmental impact assessment where there is a risk the proposed industrial activity may have a significant adverse impact in a transboundary context, in particular, on a shared resource.[31]

The court concluded that Argentina had not established that Uruguay had failed to comply with its duties under the 1975 Statute, including its duty to prevent pollution and preserve aquatic life. Significantly, the court's reasoning indicated that EIA should be treated as a bridge between procedural and substantive obligations. While the court found that the duty to notify the existence of the EIA was a procedural obligation, EIA itself was part of the substantive obligation to act with due diligence in seeking to prevent pollution.[32] Nonetheless, on the evidence before it, the court was not satisfied that Uruguay's EIA was insufficient. Accordingly it found that Uruguay had complied with all of its substantive obligations under the 1975 Statute. The consequence was that the only remedy awarded by the court was a declaration that the procedural obligations had been violated.

The decision in the *Pulp Mills* case signifies a growing sophistication in the way in which the court has addressed environmental disputes. It indicates a capacity on the part of the court to provide a degree of judicial supervision and review of the compliance by states with their procedural obligations when planning and implementing projects that carry risks of transboundary environmental harm. This is likely to be a fruitful avenue for further jurisprudential development. It allows the court to avoid highly contested questions regarding the status and legal effect of overarching principles such as sustainable development and the precautionary principle in favour of a close assessment and adjudication of the procedural or administrative dimensions of environmental decision-making.[33]

MARINE LIVING RESOURCES

1. Introduction

The court has been called upon to examine a large number of disputes with maritime dimensions. Most of these have related to maritime boundary delimitation. In these cases environmental concerns have generally been considered to be irrelevant. But environmental issues have arisen more centrally in a number of cases relating to fisheries, beginning with the *Fisheries Jurisdiction* cases between Germany and the United Kingdom, on the one hand, and Iceland, on the other hand.

2. The *Fisheries Jurisdiction* Cases

The *Fisheries Jurisdiction* cases were the culmination of the so-called 'Cod Wars' over access to cod fisheries around Iceland. Iceland had progressively extended its exclusive fisheries zone designed to conserve fisheries and protect its fishing industries. It culminated in a claim in 1971 to a 50-nautical-mile fishing zone. This was, at the time, a broader zone than one permitted under customary international law. The United Kingdom and Germany objected. After some efforts to negotiate with Iceland, they brought the dispute before the court. Iceland declined to participate in any stage of the proceedings.

These cases raised important questions relating to the sustainable management of fisheries resources so as to avoid the 'tragedy of the commons' that open access fishing practices may facilitate. In its decision on the merits, the court avoided answering directly the question posed – whether Iceland's 50-nautical-mile fishing zone was lawful. Rather the court confined itself to less controversial issues. It concluded that Iceland had a right to a fishing zone of at least 12 nautical miles. Beyond that, Iceland enjoyed 'preferential rights'.[34] But these rights were not exclusive, in the sense that coastal states and other states with an interest in the fishery were required to negotiate an accommodation of their competing claims.

The court's judgment evidences very little attentiveness to the differences between fisheries management questions and the challenges of resource management in general. Hence there was no awareness of the biological and ecosystem characteristics of fisheries management. Indeed the preferential rights doctrine created a perverse incentive for coastal states to overexploit their fisheries so as to have the upper hand in any negotiations with other interested states. In the event the court's judgment proved to have little lasting impact. It was handed down as negotiations leading to the United Nations Convention on the Law of the Sea (UNCLOS) were getting under way. UNCLOS decisively superseded the preferential fisheries concept with the 200-nautical-mile exclusive economic zone. At the same time it included extensive provisions relating to the conservation and sustainable management of fisheries in all maritime zones.

Even after UNCLOS had been adopted and had entered into force, there were some unresolved questions over fisheries management, particularly as regards fish stocks that straddled exclusive economic zone and high seas areas. This was made apparent in the *Estai* case between Spain and Canada in 1998. In this case Spain commenced proceedings after Canada had arrested on the high seas a Spanish fishing vessel that was fishing for endangered turbot stocks. The court did not rule on the merits. It decided that it had to give effect to Canada's article 36(2) declaration, which excluded North Atlantic fisheries disputes from its acceptance of the court's jurisdiction. Nonetheless the litigation served to illustrate some deficiencies in UNCLOS. It provided further impetus for international negotiations to supplement UNCLOS through a new implementing agreement, the 1995 Fish Stocks Agreement,[35] to deal specifically with management issues surrounding straddling and migratory fish stocks.

3. The *Whaling in the Antarctic* Case

(a) Introduction

The most recent and most anticipated case before the court concerning marine living resources has been the *Whaling in the Antarctic* case.[36] In this case Australia successfully challenged the legality of Japan's research whaling programme in the Southern Ocean near Antarctica. As it was originally pleaded by Australia, the case was imbued with very strong environmental elements. Australia's application advanced five legal arguments and invoked three international environmental agreements.

(b) The three international conventions

The primary contention was that Japan was violating the 1946 International Convention for the Regulation of Whaling (ICRW) by engaging in whaling that was not undertaken 'for the purposes of scientific research' as required by article VIII of the ICRW.[37] Australia's application also referred to the 1973 Convention on the International Trade in Endangered Species of Wild Fauna and Flora (CITES). CITES prohibits trade in endangered species including whales listed in Appendix I to the Convention. Japan's whaling programme may be said to be 'trade' within the meaning of CITES because it involves the 'introduction from the sea' of a listed specimen other than in 'exceptional circumstances'.[38] The argument relating to CITES could apply only to humpback whales, as Japan has entered reservations for minke and fin whales. The obvious difficulty that Australia would have faced in making its CITES argument is that Japan has not yet taken any humpback whales under the programme.

The third environmental instrument relied upon by Australia was the 1992 Convention on Biological Diversity (CBD). It was argued on a threefold basis that Japan had violated the obligation in article 3 to ensure that activities within its jurisdiction or control did not cause damage to the environment of other states or of areas beyond the limits of national jurisdiction; that Japan had not cooperated, as required by article 5, with other parties directly or through a competent international organisation; and that Japan had not adopted measures as demanded by article 10(b) to avoid or minimise adverse impacts on biological diversity.

The scene therefore appeared to be set for a truly environmental dispute to be considered by the court. But when the case was brought on for hearing, Australia withdrew its arguments relating to CITES and CBD. Consequently the argument was focused on various asserted breaches of the ICRW. It is not surprising therefore that the court's judgment does not have a strong environmental flavour. Rather it revolves around treaty interpretation questions concerning the meaning and application of the ICRW.

(c) Japan's research programmes

The court found by 12 votes to 4 that Japan's whaling programme in the Southern Ocean (known as 'JARPA II'[39]) was not undertaken 'for purposes of scientific research' as required by article VIII of the ICRW. By the same margin the court held that Japan's program violated the moratorium on whaling for commercial purposes.[40] It must be noted that the court did not rule that the lethal whaling research activity was necessarily unlawful. The court emphasised that article VIII of the ICRW expressly allows for the conduct of 'lethal scientific whaling programmes'.[41] However, while article VIII 'gives discretion to a State party to the ICRW' to issue special permits to take whales, the decision to issue such a permit 'for purposes of scientific research cannot depend simply on that State's perception'.[42] Rather, in echoes of the *Pulp Mills* case and its focus on procedural requirements for environmentally sound decision-making, the court set out an objective standard of review comprising two steps. The first involves an assessment as to whether Japan's programme 'involves scientific research'. The second is whether 'the killing, taking and treating of whales is 'for purposes of scientific research' having regard to 'whether, in the use of lethal methods, the programme's design and implementation are reasonable in relation to achieving its stated objectives'.[43]

In scrutinising Japan's research programme, the court concluded, in relation to the first step, that it did in fact involve activities that 'can broadly be characterized' as 'scientific research' thus relieving the court of the need to consider generally the meaning of 'scientific research'.[44] But, in relation to the second step, the court found against Japan, by concluding that JARPA II was not conducted 'for purposes of scientific research'. There is accordingly an important distinction between general characterisation and actual purpose.

The court provided a number of reasons to support this finding. First, Japan did not consider the feasibility of using non-lethal methods.[45] Second, there were failings in the manner by which Japan set sample sizes for the three whale species targeted: minke whales, fin whales and humpback whales. These sample sizes 'were not driven by strictly scientific considerations' as Japan's 'priority was to maintain whaling operations without any pause'.[46] Moreover there was a lack of information and transparency in relation to the selection of particular sample sizes.[47] There was also a major discrepancy between the target sample sizes and the actual number of whales taken. In addition to these reasons, the court identified further deficiencies in the implementation of JARPA II: first, the limited scientific output – only two peer-reviewed papers to date;[48] and, second, limited evidence of cooperation with other research institutions.[49]

The court's concluding remarks brought all of these issues together in these terms:

> It considers that JARPA II involves activities that can broadly be characterized as scientific research (see paragraph 127 above), but that the evidence does not establish that the programme's design and implementation are reasonable in relation to achieving its stated objectives. The Court concludes that the special permits granted by Japan for the killing, taking and treating of whales in connection with JARPA II are not 'for purposes of scientific research' pursuant to Article VIII, paragraph 1, of the Convention.[50]

Following the court's decision, Japan developed a revised research plan for the Southern Ocean known as the Proposed Research Plan for New Scientific Whale Research Program in the Antarctic Ocean (NEWREP-A) in an effort to meet the criteria set out in the court's judgment. It involves a significantly reduced quota as regards both the species to be caught (only minkes) and the sample size (333 per annum).[51] In June 2015 the Scientific Committee of the International Whaling Commission (IWC) released the report of its annual meeting. The report concluded that the committee could not reach a consensus view on NEWREP-A. Moreover a majority of scientists on the committee subscribed to an annex to the report which stated that 'the need for lethal sampling has not been demonstrated'.[52]

This indicates potential grounds for another challenge to Japan's planned Southern Ocean whaling activities. This is because one of the key reasons for the decision that JARPA II was not 'for purposes' of scientific research was Japan's failure to provide a compelling justification for the use of lethal sampling methods. While such a challenge may not be brought before the ICJ given Japan's revised article 36(2) declaration, it could conceivably be made through UNCLOS and its dispute-settlement provisions on the ground that Japan has not co-operated through the IWC in planning and implementing NEWREP-A.

(d) Assessment

The court's judgment focused on the ICRW. It did not venture generally into a discussion of international environmental law. The evidence enabled some important environmental issues to be raised and to some extent considered by the court. For instance the court considered whether Japan's whaling programme was in fact meeting the stated objective of researching and understanding the Southern Ocean marine ecosystem.[53] But there was no general discussion of cetacean conservation issues or of marine environmental protection challenges. However, the decision does have broader significance and enduring value for the way in which the court subjected Japan's whaling programs to scrutiny. It was not assumed that any permits purportedly issued in compliance with article VIII of the ICRW must be in order. Rather the court devised an objective standard of review which allowed it to determine whether Japan's research methods were reasonable having regard to the stated objectives for its research programme.

(e) Separate opinions

Several judges in their separate opinions did take the opportunity to connect the issues raised in the litigation with general questions of international environmental law. According to Judge Cançado Trindade, 'when deciding whether a programme is "for purposes of scientific research" so as to issue a special permit under Article VIII (1), the State Party concerned has, in my understanding, a duty to abide by the principle of prevention and the precautionary principle'.[54] Judge Cançado Trindade also made express reference to the principle of intergenerational equity and reasoned that it was at the centre of the ICRW, which was designed to safeguard whale stocks for future generations.[55]

In her separate opinion, Judge ad hoc Charlesworth addressed the relevance of the precautionary principle in more detail. She reasoned that the precautionary principle was relevant to the interpretation of article VIII, and devoted a significant part of her opinion to explaining the history and contemporary relevance of precaution. These important passages merit full quotation:

> 6. The precautionary approach to environmental regulation also reinforces this analysis of the conditions in which lethal research methods may be undertaken. The approach was formulated in Principle 15 of the Rio Declaration on Environment and Development in 1992 as '[w]here there are threats of serious or irreversible damage, lack of full scientific certainty shall not be used as a reason for postponing cost-effective measures to prevent environmental degradation'. The precautionary approach entails the avoidance of activities that may threaten the environment even in the face of scientific uncertainty about the direct or indirect effects of such activities. It gives priority to the prevention of harm to the environment in its broadest sense, including biological diversity, resource conservation and management and human health. The essence of the precautionary approach has informed the development of international environmental law and is recognized implicitly or explicitly in instruments dealing with a wide range of subject-matter, from the regulation of the oceans and international watercourses to the conservation and management of fish stocks, the conservation of endangered species and biosafety.

> 7. This Court has referred to the precautionary approach in *Gabčíkovo Nagymaros Project (Hungary/Slovakia)* (although not using this term) and *Pulp Mills on the River Uruguay (Argentina v. Uruguay).* In both these cases, the Court contemplated the interpretation of treaty obligations in light of new approaches to environmental protection.
>
> 8. In the *Pulp Mills* case, the Court considered that 'a precautionary approach may be relevant in the interpretation and application of the provisions of [the 1975 Statute of the River Uruguay]' [at para.164].
>
> 9. These observations suggest that treaties dealing with the environment should be interpreted wherever possible in light of the precautionary approach, regardless of the date of their adoption
>
> 10. Both Parties to this dispute endorsed the precautionary approach at a theoretical level, although they disagreed about its application to the facts. In my view, the precautionary approach requires that non-lethal methods of research be used wherever possible. In relation to Article VIII, which contemplates the killing of the subject of research by the research activity, an implication of the precautionary approach is that lethal methods must be shown to be indispensable to the purposes of scientific research on whales.

Judge ad hoc Charlesworth's separate opinion illustrates, among other things, the capacity for the court's previous decisions to be reviewed and interpreted in later decisions to lend support to the consolidation of environmental norms. As seen in the *Danube Dam* case, although the conclusions of the court were ambiguous on the meaning and legal force of the sustainable development principle, the value of the concept was clearly acknowledged and it was used to provide structure for the court's assessment of the parties' conduct and for the court's prescriptions for their future behaviour.

(f) The issue of standing

Before concluding a discussion of the *Whaling in the Antarctic* case, it should be noted that one of the decision's most important aspects is found in its silence on the issue of standing. While Japan unsuccessfully challenged the jurisdiction of the court (on the unconvincing basis that Australia's article 36(2) declaration excluded maritime boundary disputes) it did not question Australia's standing. This was an important acceptance of the court's capacity to uphold collective regimes, by allowing any state party to complain of another's breach of the ICRW.[56] This passed without mention in the judgment. This indicates that the court is now willing to entertain claims pursued in the common interest, even where a litigant state does not have a 'special interest'.

CONCLUSION

It cannot be said that the ICJ has been a driving force in the development of international environmental law, at least not to date. But in fairness nor could that be said about many, if any, domestic courts. The evolution of environmental law, both national and international, has been driven by extra-curial processes: primarily, in the case of national law, by legislation and, in the case of international environmental law, by treaties, especially the major multilateral agreements.[57] It is this legislation and these agreements that contain the conceptual articulation and practical operationalisation of environmental principles. Of especial importance for both national and international environmental law have been the declarations of the 1972 Stockholm and the 1992 Rio conferences and their progeny including, most recently, the 2030 Agenda for Sustainable Development adopted by the United Nations General Assembly in September 2015. These are complemented by other mechanisms for normative development in international environmental law such as the International Law Commission. The Commission has undertaken important work on the topic of transboundary harm and is now working on a reference on the 'Protection of the Atmosphere', albeit within exceptionally confined subject matter limitations.[58]

Given the importance of law making through multilateral treaties, it is unlikely that the ICJ will ever be at the forefront of normative development in international environmental law. However, the court can be entrusted with greater responsibility by holding states to account for their environmental obligations and, in particular, by being called upon to scrutinise the processes by which states make and implement decisions that impact upon the natural environment. International environmental law has tended to be parochial in selecting its dispute-settlement mechanisms. There is a preference for the use of internal or 'endogenous' bodies – such as compliance committees – over the outsourcing of dispute-settlement tasks.[59] Perhaps this approach was appropriate several decades ago but the ICJ has since demonstrated that it can perform an important function in international environmental dispute-settlement. In relation to issues of standing, the processes of environmental decision-making and the several substantive environmental principles, the court now appears disposed to assume an active and central role when called upon to do so.

This is entirely appropriate and indeed necessary for two reasons: the rapid decline in environmental conditions at a global scale and a corresponding rise in disputes over environmental matters and over access to natural resources. These constitute the most serious challenges to the international order this century and beyond. The court, as the principal judicial organ of the United Nations, enjoys a unique position to render legitimate and authoritative decisions that address not only bilateral environmental disputes between states but also the collective interest of all states and peoples in a habitable and healthy global environment.

NOTES

1. The law as stated in this chapter is correct as of 24 November 2015. The chapter was completed before the ICJ handed down its judgment in Certain Activities carried out by Nicaragua in the Border Area (*Costa Rica v Nicaragua*) and Construction of a Road in Costa Rica along the San Juan River (*Nicaragua v Costa Rica*). The author thanks Jialu Xu for his very able research assistance.
2. Declaration of Japan Recognising as Compulsory the Jurisdiction of the ICJ (2015); http://www.icj-cij.org.
3. See Stephens (2009, pp. 22–7).
4. Boyle and Harrison (2013). See also Stephens (2009, pp. 56–61).
5. Statute of the ICJ, art.60.
6. See for instance the advisory opinion of the Seabed Disputes Chamber of the International Tribunal for the Law of the Sea in the case concerning 'Responsibilities and Obligations of States Sponsoring Persons and Entities with Respect to Activities in the Area' (2011). In its opinion the Chamber cited the ICJ in *Pulp Mills* (2010) and its conclusion, at para. 204, that 'it may now be considered a requirement under general international law to undertake an environmental impact assessment where there is a risk that the proposed industrial activity may have a significant adverse impact in a transboundary context, in particular, on a shared resource'.
7. Shany (2014, pp. 161–2).
8. See in particular Fitzmaurice (2013, p. 351); Viñuales (2008). For the author's own assessment of the ICJ's contribution, and of the jurisprudence of other international courts and tribunals on environmental matters, see Stephens (2009).
9. Fitzmaurice (2013).
10. 'Application by Nauru' (1989, p. 14), *Nauru* case.
11. 1993 Settlement of the Case in the ICJ Concerning Certain Phosphate Lands in Nauru.
12. *Nuclear Tests* case (1974, para.390, per Judge de Castro dissenting).
13. *Nuclear Tests* case (1995, para.64).
14. Ibid. (para.29).
15. Fitzmaurice (2013).
16. *Pulp Mills* case (2010, para.101).
17. Ibid.
18. 1977 Treaty Concerning the Construction and Operation of the Gabčíkovo-Nagymaros System of Locks.
19. *Danube Dam* case (1997, para.53).
20. Ibid. (para.57).
21. Ibid. (para.78).
22. Ibid. (para.85).
23. Vienna Convention on the Law of Treaties 1969, art.62.

24. *Danube Dam* case (1997, para.140).
25. See Vaughan Lowe (1999).
26. *Danube Dam* case (1997, para.112).
27. *Pulp Mills* case (2010, para.101).
28. Ibid. (paras 75 and177).
29. Ibid. (para.164).
30. Ibid. (para.121).
31. Ibid. (para.204).
32. Ibid. (para.67).
33. See Ong (2011, pp. 137, 138). See also Stephens (2014).
34. *Fisheries Jurisdiction* case (1973, para.27).
35. 1995 Agreement for the Implementation of the Provisions of the United Nations Convention on the Law of the Sea of 10 December 1982 Relating to the Conservation and Management of Straddling Fish Stocks and Highly Migratory Fish Stocks.
36. Some of the discussion that follows is developed from Rothwell and Stephens (2016, pp. 335–6) and Stephens (2012, p. 243).
37. Article VIII allows states parties to issue special permits to their nationals to take whales for scientific purposes.
38. CITES, arts II(1) and III(5).
39. JARPA II stands for 'The Second Phase of Japan's Whale Research Program under Special Permit in the Antarctic'.
40. *Whaling in the Antarctic* case (2014, para.247).
41. Ibid. (para.58).
42. Ibid. (para.61).
43. Ibid. (para.67).
44. Ibid. (para.127).
45. Ibid. (para.144).
46. Ibid. (para.156).
47. Ibid. (paras 181 and 188).
48. Ibid. (para.219).
49. Ibid. (para.222).
50. Ibid. (para.227).
51. Proposed Research Plan for New Scientific Whale Research Program in the Antarctic Ocean (NEWREP-A).
52. Normville (2015).
53. *Whaling in the Antarctic* case (2014, para.196).
54. Ibid. (para.23).
55. Ibid. (para.41).
56. See also the case concerning 'Questions relating to the Obligation to Prosecute or Extradite' (*Belgium v Senegal*) (para.69).
57. See generally de Sadeleer (2002).
58. See legal.un.org/ilc/guide/8_8.shtml. The Commission's consideration of the topic is subject to several limitations, including that it 'not interfere with relevant political negotiations, including on climate change, ozone depletion, and long-range transboundary air pollution'. And 'The topic will not deal with, but is also without prejudice to, questions such as: liability of States and their nationals, the polluter-pays principle, the precautionary principle, common but differentiated responsibilities, and the transfer of funds and technology to developing countries, including intellectual property rights'.
59. See Romano (2007, p. 1036).

REFERENCES

Boyle, Alan and James Harrison (2013), 'Judicial Settlement of International Environmental Disputes: Current Problems', *Journal of International Dispute Settlement* 4, 245.

de Sadeleer, Nicholas (2002), *Environmental Principles: From Political Slogans to Legal Rules* (Cambridge, Cambridge University Press).

Fitzmaurice, Malgosia (2013), 'The International Court of Justice and International Environmental Law', in Christian J Tams and James Sloan (eds), *The Development of International Law by the International Court of Justice* (Oxford, Oxford University Press).

Normville, Dennis (2015), 'Scientists Renew Objections to Japan's Whaling Program', *ScienceInsider*, 19 June.

Ong, David M. (2011), 'Procedural International Environmental Justice? The Evolution of Procedural Means for Environmental Protection: From Inter-State Obligations to Individual State Rights', in Duncan French (ed.), *Global Justice and Sustainable Development* (Leiden, Martinus Nijhoff).

Proposed Research Plan for New Scientific Whale Research Program in the Antarctic Ocean (NEWREP-A); http://www.jfa.maff.go.jp/j/whale/pdf/newrep–a.pdf.

Romano, Cesare P.R. (2007), 'International Dispute Settlement', in Daniel Bodansky, Jutta Brunnée and Ellen Hey (eds), *The Oxford Handbook of International Environmental Law* (Oxford, Oxford University Press).

Rothwell, Donald R. and Tim Stephens (2016), *The International Law of the Sea* (2nd edn, Oxford, Hart Publishing).

Shany, Yuvay (2014), *Assessing the Effectiveness of International Courts* (Oxford, Oxford University Press).

Stephens, Tim (2009), *International Courts and Environmental Protection* (Cambridge, Cambridge University Press).

Stephens, Tim (2012), 'A Model Litigant? Australia's Record in Transboundary Environmental Litigation', in Robin Warner and Simon Marsden (eds), *Transboundary Environmental Governance: Inland, Costal and Marine Perspectives* (Farnham, Ashgate).

Stephens, Tim (2014), 'Litigating International Environmental Disputes: To Sue or Not to Sue?', in Natalie Klein (ed.), *Litigating International Disputes: Weighing the Options* (Cambridge, Cambridge University Press).

Vaughan Lowe, Alan (1999), 'Sustainable Development and Unsustainable Arguments', in Alan E. Boyle and David Freestone (eds), *International Law and Sustainable Development: Past Achievements and Future Challenges* (Oxford, Oxford University Press).

Viñuales, Jorge E. (2008), 'The Contribution of the International Court of Justice to the Development of International Law', *Fordham International Law Journal* 32, 232.

Viñuales, Jorge E. (ed.) (2014), *The Rio Declaration on Environment and Development: A Commentary* (Oxford, Oxford University Press).

INSTRUMENTS

Agreement for the Implementation of the Provisions of the United Nations Convention on the Law of the Sea of 10 December 1982 Relating to the Conservation and Management of Straddling Fish Stocks and Highly Migratory Fish Stocks 1995: opened for signature 4 December 1995, (1995) 24 ILM 1542 (entered into force 11 December 2001).

Convention on Biological Diversity 1992: opened for signature 5 June 1992, [1993] ATS 32 (entered into force 29 December 1993).

Convention on the International Trade in Endangered Species of Wild Fauna and Flora 1973: opened for signature 3 March 1973, [1976] ATS 29 (entered into force 1 July 1975).
Declaration of Japan Recognising as Compulsory the Jurisdiction of the ICJ.
International Convention for the Regulation of Whaling 1948: opened for signature 2 December 1946, 161 UNTS 72 (entered into force 10 November 1948).
Rio Declaration 1992: Declaration of the United Nations Conference on Environment and Development 1992, UN Doc A/CONF.48/14/Rev.1 (1973).
Settlement of the Case in the ICJ Concerning Certain Phosphate Lands in Nauru (1993) 32 ILM 1471.
Statute of the International Court of Justice 1945.
Statute of the River Uruguay 1975: opened for signature 26 February 1975, 1295 UNTS 340 (entered into force 18 September 1976).
Stockholm Declaration 1972: Declaration of the United Nations Conference on the Human Environment 1972, UN Doc A/CONF.151/5/Rev.1 (1992).
Transforming Our World: the 2030 Agenda for Sustainable Development 2015: GA Res A/70/L.1, UN GAOR, 70th sess, 4th plen mtg, Agenda Items 15 and 116, UN Doc A/RES/70/1 (25 September 2015).
Treaty Concerning the Construction and Operation of the Gabčíkovo-Nagymaros System of Locks 1997: opened for signature 16 September 1977, (1993) 32 ILM 1247 (entered into force 30 June 1978).
United Nations Convention on the Law of Non-Navigational Uses of International Watercourses 1997: opened for signature 21 May 1997, (1997) 36 ILM 700 (entered into force 17 August 2014).
United Nations Convention on the Law of the Sea 1982: opened for signature 10 December 1982, 1833 UTS 397 (entered into force 16 November 1994).
Vienna Convention on the Law of Treaties 1969: opened for signature 23 May 1969, 1155 UNTS 332 (entered into force 27 January 1980).

CASES

Corfu Channel case: *United Kingdom v Albania* [1949] ICJ Rep 4.
Danube Dam case (Gabčíkovo-Nagymaros Project: *Hungary/Slovakia*) [1997] ICJ Rep 7.
Estai case (*Fisheries Jurisdiction* case): *Spain v Canada* [1998] ICJ Rep 431.
Fisheries Jurisdiction case: *Germany v Iceland* [1973] ICJ Rep 49.
Fisheries Jurisdiction case: *United Kingdom v Iceland* [1973] ICJ Rep 3.
Nauru case (Certain Phosphate Lands in Nauru: *Nauru v Australia*) [1992] ICJ Rep 240.
Nuclear Tests case 1974: *Australia v France*; *New Zealand v France* [1974] ICJ Rep 253; [1974] ICJ Rep 457.
Nuclear Tests case 1995: *Request for an Examination of the Situation in Accordance with Paragraph 63 of the Court's Judgment of 20 December 1974 in the Nuclear Tests (New Zealand v France) case* [1995] ICJ Rep 288.
Nuclear Weapons Advisory Opinion: Legality of the Threat or Use of Nuclear Weapons [1996] ICJ Rep 226.
Pulp Mills case (Pulp Mills on the River Uruguay: *Argentina v Uruguay*) [2010] ICJ Rep 14.
Questions relating to the Obligation to Prosecute or Extradite (Belgium v Senegal) [2012] ICJ Rep 422.
'Responsibilities and Obligations of States Sponsoring Persons and Entities with Respect to Activities in the Area' (2011) 50 ILM 458.

River Oder case (Territorial Jurisdiction of the International Commission of the River Oder: *Czechoslovakia, Denmark, France, Germany, Great Britain, Sweden/Poland*) [1929] PCIJ (ser. A) no.23.
Trail Smelter case: *Canada/United States of America* (1938 and 1941) 3 RIAA 1911.
Whaling in the Antarctic case: *Australia v Japan; New Zealand intervening* [2014] ICJ Rep 226.

10. The structure, form and language of international environmental norms – from absolute to relative normativity

Niko Soininen

INTRODUCTION

International law has a dual nature.[1] On the one hand it is based on formalist premises of law creation and interpretation. According to the formalist conception, law is created and changed by treaties portraying state will[2] and interpreted prima facie in the light of linguistic formulations of norms contained in legal sources created in this way. Endorsing formalism, article 38 of the Statute of the International Court of Justice states that international conventions, custom recognised by the civilized nations and international legal principles shall be applied as sources of law by the International Court of Justice.[3] Formalism as an interpretative paradigm gains support from article 31(1) of the Vienna Convention on the Law of Treaties (VCLT), which states that a treaty shall be interpreted in good faith and in accordance with the ordinary meaning to be given to the terms of the treaty.

On the other hand international law is instrumental. According to the instrumental conception, legal validity is based – in addition to formal validity – on legitimacy and effectiveness. Law is purposive and uses form as a vehicle for advancing certain objectives. Consistently with this, the discussions about new instruments of governance, soft law, *jus cogens* and obligations *erga omnes* are reflections of legal instrumentalism. In ways similar to formalism, instrumentalism as an interpretative paradigm gains support from article 31(1) of the VCLT, which states that a treaty has to be interpreted – in addition to its wording – in light of its object and purpose. The difficulties associated with the construction of object and purpose objectively in legal interpretation make them susceptible to considerations of equity and justice.[4]

Environmental law is one of those areas of law which troubles formalists.[5] Much of the recent discussion within the field has revolved around governance and the function of soft law. From a formalist perspective this means that political discussions have taken over some of law's domain.[6] As a consequence, 'we find ourselves adrift in ever-widening circles of increasing uncertainty'.[7] From an instrumental perspective one could argue that we also find ourselves in ever-widening circles of wicked environmental problems such as climate change and declining biodiversity which have to be addressed internationally. Legal certainty is of no avail if there is no earth to inhabit.[8] Questions of *lex lata* and *lex ferenda* – law and non-law – become blurred in the context of environmental law. This is because the protection of the quality of the environment aimed at in formal legal instruments may, in the face of scientific uncertainty and new insights, require measures beyond those originally agreed upon by the contracting states. Instrumentalism is deeply embedded in environmental law as a legal discipline. Nevertheless formalism remains an important safeguard for reaching environmental objectives.[9] Environmental law is both formal and instrumental.

The purpose of this chapter is to study the doctrinal importance of how legal norms are structured in formally binding instruments – hard law – and in non-binding instruments – soft law. The main argument is that not only the problems of natural language but also the diversity of rules of interpretation corrode the normativity of formal law. The interpretatively constructed indeterminacy of formally binding legal norms causes unbearable softness of hard law.[10] In contrast, soft law can gain legal significance as a result of either wide acceptance – legitimacy – or of effectiveness in actual state practice, even if it lacks formal validity.[11] This is here described as the unbearable hardness of soft law. The weakening of formal validity and the strengthening of legitimacy and effectiveness as the criteria of normative validity lead to the conclusion that the normativity of international environmental norms is somewhat relative. The structure, form and language of international environmental law create a space in which the normativity of international environmental norms oscillates.[12]

THE UNBEARABLE SOFTNESS OF HARD LAW

1. The Softness of Language

Law is embedded in natural language in which it is created, changed and debated. Language is open textured to the extent that it usually does not convey completely unequivocal meanings from the law maker to the interpreter.[13] As Hart states, 'there is a limit, inherent in the nature of language, to the guidance which general language can provide'.[14] This fundamental feature of law makes all aspects of law more or less relative and thus a matter of interpretation. As a consequence, legal disputes are often about the meaning of the text of a treaty. This is why the text can function only as the starting point of legal reasoning.[15]

The open texture of language is a well-known feature of international environmental law.[16] For example, the framework conventions relating to ozone, biodiversity and climate are formally binding instruments but they contain few clear legal rules.[17] According to article 2(1) of the Vienna Convention on the Protection of the Ozone Layer, parties to the Convention shall take appropriate measures in accordance with the Convention to protect human health and the environment against the adverse effects resulting or likely to result from human activities which modify or are likely to modify the ozone layer. Despite the precautionary approach embedded in the provision and the obligatory form of the words 'shall take measures', the particular measures to be taken are left mainly to the discretion of the member state. This is because no specific measures have been identified.[18] The Convention mainly includes only procedural obligations to cooperate and to adopt appropriate legislation in mitigating the depletion of the ozone layer.

A second case in point is the Convention on Biological Diversity. According to article 1 the overarching aim of the Convention is to pursue conservation of biological diversity, sustainable use of its components and fair and equitable sharing of the benefits arising from the utilisation of genetic resources. Vague and seemingly conflicting objectives are facilitated into the substantive provisions of the Convention. Under article 6(1), the contracting parties are obliged to develop national strategies, plans and programmes for the conservation and sustainable use of biological diversity in accordance with their particular conditions and capabilities. This obligation is, however, subject to the test of possibility and appropriateness. Similarly, according to articles 8(1) and 9(1), the parties are obliged – as far as possible and appropriate – to establish a system of protected areas and adopt measures for *in situ* and, to a lesser extent, *ex situ* conservation. Here, despite the binding formulation 'shall', the normativity of obligations is weakened by the reference to criteria that are contextual and state specific. The implementation of the obligation is thus left to the discretion of the contracting state.[19]

The same is true of the United Nations Framework Convention on Climate Change (UNFCCC). Under article 2, the overall objective of the UNFCCC is the stabilisation of greenhouse gas concentration in the atmosphere at a level that would prevent dangerous anthropogenic interference with the climate system. This should be done facilitating economic development simultaneously. Article 4 imposes these commitments and transforms them into normative commitments:

- to develop, update and make available to the Conference of the parties inventories of anthropogenic emissions
- to implement national programmes to mitigate climate change
- to cooperate in the development and diffusion of technology.

These commitments are weakened normatively by state-specific criteria that are left largely unspecified. This is because the relevant practices and processes are subject to the national and regional development priorities, objectives and circumstances of each state.[20]

Based on the above examples, international treaties often specify only the 'least common denominators' when they seek to clarify the minimum obligations of the negotiating states. Effectively this approach requires the states to clarify, elaborate and implement unclear concepts at some time in the future.[21] This manifests, first, as the willingness of states to tackle environmental problems coupled with a reluctance to adopt measures that would infringe substantially on their sovereignty and their legal competence to use natural resources to produce economic and social welfare.[22] From this perspective the use of open-textured language can be seen as deliberate and functional by allowing legal institutions to develop dynamically and to address problems as they arise in the future.[23] From an interpretative perspective, however, the soft formulation of legal norms weakens the legal obligations contained in formally binding treaty law. Open-textured language is the first mechanism through which hard law is softened.[24] The second, and more severe mechanism for the softening of hard law is structural. The interpretative dance of formalism and instrumentalism makes the softening of hard law a necessary characteristic of law even in cases where language would not seem to leave any leeway for interpretation. The attention turns next to this softness of structure.

2. The Softness of Structure

Koskenniemi has argued that, while language as a medium creates certain problems, there is a much deeper and more severe reason for the indeterminacy of international law. Law unites 'an *instrumentalist logic*, one that looks for the realization of the objectives through law, with a *formalist logic*, one that establishes standards of behaviour'.[25] These two overarching paradigms of legal validity and of interpretation create a 'constant push and pull' in international law.[26] As a consequence the structure or the fabric of law is open textured:[27]

> The dilemma of rules and standards undermines the ability of the mode of control to establish behavioural hierarchies by reference to the 'lawful'/ 'illegal' scheme. It pits 'law' against 'justice' in a fashion that reverses the hierarchy between the two. We have recourse to law in the control of social behaviour precisely to avoid reference to principles of justice, undemonstrable and open to misuse by those in power. If now we are required to know justice before we can know the law, then we must either give up the ideal of control or assume that justice is not so subjective and undemonstrable after all.[28]

The ontological plurality of law – that is the relationship between formalism and instrumentalism – leads to two conclusions. First, there cannot be clear and unambiguous criteria for recognising valid legal norms from invalid legal norms. Second, even when everyone would agree on the validity or the hard normativity of the norm, the question of what the rule requires – what is the content of rights and obligations emanating from it – remains open. Positive law can be interpreted through plain meaning, contextual or systemic meaning, historical meaning or teleological meaning. Doctrinal methods cannot be reduced to a single rule of interpretation.[29] This, however, immediately causes a problem. If interpretative methods cannot be reduced to one or be placed in a strict hierarchy, there is always a choice to be made in interpreting the law. In other words, it is always possible to interpret formal law from an instrumentalist perspective. Formalism becomes injected with instrumentalism through one or other mode of interpretation.

Law is a thoroughly interpretative phenomenon and the rules of interpretation in international law facilitate a pluralist definition of normativity. As Koskenniemi states, 'there are no rules on when to apply a literal and when dynamic interpretation, when to give recourse to party will and when to the instrument's object and purpose'.[30] A metaphorical example may be helpful. According to Russell, when we look at a table – a law – it is possible to view it as both smooth *and* rough – precise and imprecise in legal parlance – at the same time. But this depends on whether we look at it with our bare eyes or through a microscope: that is formalism or instrumentalism. According to Russell, it is arbitrary to claim that one or the other is the essential or the real characteristic of the table – the law.[31] Remove instrumentalism through the front door – the question of validity – and it will come back through the back door – with rules of interpretation. This results in the structural indeterminacy of law.

The struggle between form and substance can be constructed as one of the structural dichotomies of legal interpretation.[32] It is no surprise that, according to Koskenniemi, 'the modern programme is one of reconciliation'.[33] This approach includes both the acceptance and the denial of formalism and instrumentalism. Both are impossible to accept as single theories of law. As Peczenik notes, 'a study of classical theories of valid law leaves the reader in despair. One gets an impression the theories destroyed each other'.[34] In international law the dilemma manifests itself as a conflict between, on the one hand, law as the product of the actions and the will of the state and the state being bound by those actions through *pacta sunt servanda* and, on the other hand, the need to create a distance between the will of the state and the law – the possibility to evaluate the actions of the state critically. As Koskenniemi explains in the context of sovereignty:

> But a choice between the two positions cannot be made. The former [a fact-based view of sovereignty] ultimately ends up in apologism, affirming the State's self definition of the extent of its sovereignty. The dispute [about sovereignty] will remain unsettled. The latter [a rule-based view] will lead into utopianism, fixing the extent of sovereignty by reference to a natural, non-State related morality. Neither solution seems acceptable. Rather, both seem needed because they limit each other's negative consequences.[35]

The argument from structural indeterminacy becomes attractive once it is realised that formalism and instrumentalism can endlessly be pitted against each other. It becomes even more so when formalism and instrumentalism are seen to occupy both sides of a legal dispute. A formalistic argument from a treaty provision rests on the idea of treaty provisions as the highest source of information about the positive intent of the state and this intent in turn is based on the sovereignty of the state and upon *pacta sunt servanda*. A formalistic argument based on state sovereignty and intent can also be used against itself negatively when a state denies that the text of the treaty describes or described its actual intent. Intent visible from the text of the treaty and the 'real' intent of the state are on the opposing sides of the argument: on the one hand, the exercise of the right of sovereignty to conclude a treaty and, on the other hand, the exercise of the right of sovereignty not to be bound by a treaty that is not in line with state intent. Furthermore, a treaty may contain conflicting formal obligations which can be invoked against each other. Similarly, an instrumentalist argument from equity may be inconclusive. Formalism evokes the justice of *pacta sunt servanda* against the instrumentalist justice of changed circumstances.[36] In these ways each side to the interpretative conflict often invokes both formalism and instrumentalism. This interplay between formal and instrumental arguments will be demonstrated in more detail in the following.

THE OPEN TEXTURE OF LANGUAGE AND LAW IN PRACTICE IN THE *DANUBE DAM* CASE

1. Introduction

The *Danube Dam* case is a good illustration of the softness of hard law. Hungary and Czechoslovakia had entered into a formally binding agreement in 1977 concerning the construction and operation of the Gabcikovo-Nagymaros system of locks. According to article 1, this was a joint investment for the utilisation of the natural resources of the River Danube: mainly the production of hydroelectricity, the improvement of navigation and the protection of the quality of the water. Article 4 of the bilateral treaty stipulated that the joint project was to be concluded during the period between 1986 and 1990. Under article 5, the costs of the project were to be borne equally by the contracting states and article 8 specified that the series of locks would be jointly owned. Article 15 stipulated that the parties had to ensure that the quality of water in the Danube was not impaired as a result of the project. Under article 16, both states had to ensure uninterrupted and safe navigation in the international fairway. Article 19 specified that both parties were obliged to ensure compliance with the agreement. Following intense criticism in Hungary, the Hungarian government decided in 1989 to suspend the project due to scientific uncertainty about the environmental risks of the project. In 1991, the Slovak government decided to initiate a modified Gabcikovo project for the production of hydropower – the so-called Variant C. Hungary unilaterally terminated the treaty in 1992.[37]

2. The First Issue for the International Court of Justice

The International Court of Justice was first asked whether Hungary was entitled to abandon the project despite its treaty obligations. Hungary justified its action by relying on a circumstance of ecological necessity and accused Czechoslovakia of violation of articles 15 and 19 of the treaty concerning environmental protection.[38] It further argued that the precautionary principle was a part of customary international law.[39] Slovakia argued that a state of necessity was not a permissible legal ground for failing to fulfil treaty obligations and denied that it had breached its environmental obligations under the treaty.[40] Hungary was advocating an instrumental approach – justice of changed circumstances – coupled with a formal argument that abandoning the project was justified under articles 15 and 19 of the treaty. Slovakia was presenting a formal argument that Hungary's action was inter alia contrary to articles 4, 5 and 8 of the treaty coupled with an instrumental argument – justice of *pacta sunt servanda*.

In view of these arguments the court had to choose between the two sets of formal and instrumental arguments presented by each of the two litigants. Relying on article 33 of the International Law Commission's Draft Articles on the International Responsibility of States regarding a state of necessity, the court first concluded that a state of necessity in the form of changed circumstances was not a defence to justify withdrawing from a treaty because the environmental threat was not grave and imminent.[41] This was so because the environmental damage had already occurred due to the deepening of the river prior to the treaty and Hungary had decided to engage in a formally binding treaty after this event.[42] The court further stressed that, even if there had been a state of necessity, it would not have justified the unilateral abandonment of the treaty.[43] The final decision could be based only on evaluative criteria without the possibility of resorting to a universal and clear legal rule. One set of formal and instrumental arguments was chosen at the expense of another set without a possibility to objectively justify this choice.

3. The Second Issue for the Court

The court was next asked whether the then separated Czech and Slovak federal republic was entitled to proceed with Variant C unilaterally. Hungary claimed that such unilateral actions were contrary to the treaty and other international obligations.[44] In reply, Slovakia argued that its measures were in conformity with the treaty and that, even if they were not, Variant C could be justified as a countermeasure to Hungary's decision not to fulfil the obligations of the treaty.[45] A familiar pattern of reasoning is emerging. Hungary was invoking a formalist argument based on the text of the treaty and an instrumentalist argument that treaty law should be upheld – justice of *pacta sunt servanda*. Slovakia was similarly invoking formal and instrumental arguments in support of its just counter measures in response to Hungary's breach of its formal obligations. Compared to the first question, the set of arguments used are reversed. This time Hungary resorted to formal arguments to uphold the treaty and justice of *pacta sunt servanda* while Slovakia resorted to changed circumstances and formal treaty provisions as justification for moving forward unilaterally.

The court stressed that Hungary had, in accordance with the treaty, agreed only to the joint but not to a unilateral fulfilment of the project. The court concluded that Czechoslovakia was in violation of the treaty when it engaged in Variant C unilaterally.[46] The treaty did not justify unilateral action.[47] The court went on to state that unilateral actions involving Variant C were disproportionate to the damage caused by Hungary depriving it of the right to an equitable and reasonable share of the natural resources of the River Danube.[48] Formal and instrumental arguments once again underpinned the decision of the court. The breach of the treaty did justify some counter measures but the development of Variant C was disproportionate. The court adopted a subtle line of reasoning for not having to choose conclusively between either set of arguments put forward by the parties. The justification was in this way both formal and instrumental.

4. The Third Issue for the Court

The court was then asked what were the legal effects of the notification with which Hungary unilaterally terminated the treaty.[49] Hungary presented five arguments – some already familiar – in support of the lawfulness and effectiveness of the notification and of the termination of the treaty:

- state of necessity
- impossibility of performance of the treaty
- fundamental change of circumstances
- material breach of the treaty by Czechoslovakia
- the development of new norms of environmental law – for example an obligation owed *erga omnes* for precaution.[50]

The second, third and fourth claims amounted to a formalist argument based on treaty law and an instrumentalist argument from *pacta sunt servanda*. The first and fifth claims were based on an instrumentalist argument based on changed circumstances and on scientific uncertainty but supported by formalist arguments from treaty and customary law.

The court concluded that the first argument was not a ground for the termination of a treaty even if a state of necessity did exist.[51] The second argument was not compelling as the treaty did contain provisions for readjusting the project if performance in line with the treaty proved impossible.[52] Similarly, the court dismissed the third argument because the political and ecological circumstances at hand were not completely unforeseen. Furthermore, articles 15, 19 and 20 of the treaty would have facilitated changing the treaty.[53] The fourth argument was rejected because the unilateral termination of the 1977 treaty took place prior to Czechoslovakia's illegal actions – the declaration to terminate the treaty in May and the diversion of waters in October 1992. The court noted that the construction of Variant C itself was not contrary to the treaty.[54] The court concluded that both parties had agreed to take environmental concerns seriously but they could not deviate from the principle of *pacta sunt servanda*. Environmental obligations had to be fulfilled within the confinements of the treaty. The notification of termination made by Hungary did not have legal effect.[55]

5. The Final Issue for the Court

Finally, the court was asked what legal consequences would follow from its response to these three questions. In deciding this question the court took into account that the treaty was in force but that interpretation of the treaty was evolving through time with the changing of factual circumstances. The court gave weight to a series of events that had already taken place when the court reached its decision:

- the hydropower plant built by Czechoslovakia had been operational for almost five years
- it received water from a significantly smaller reservoir which was relocated to cause less harm than the original reservoir planned by the parties
- the plant was operating in a 'run-of-the-river mode' and not in peak hour mode.[56]

The court stated that the objectives of the treaty had been at least partially achieved as a result of the existing structures built by Czechoslovakia.[57] Instrumentalism abounds within the very flexible boundaries of form. In other words, consequentialist and teleological reasoning allows the court to adjust formal requirements and to justify this from within the formal instrument itself.

According to the court, the treaty had always been a dynamic instrument because it had been amended frequently before the escalation of the conflict.[58] The conclusion of the court was that the treaty obliged the parties to negotiate only for the purpose of attaining the treaty's multiple objectives – economic use and environmental protection.[59] It was not for the court to decide what the outcome of these negotiations should be.[60] *Pacta sunt servanda* obliged the parties to ongoing negotiations without setting substantive requirements other than the objective of reconciling the different uses of the river by the two states.[61] With regard to damages, the court stated that both states had committed unlawful acts under international law. This justified the decision of the court to encourage the parties to renounce all financial claims.[62] The principle of cooperation was established as the main instrument for repairing the damage caused to both parties.[63]

6. The Importance of the Case

The *Danube Dam* case is an example that illustrates the dance between formalism and instrumentalism in legal reasoning.[64] It is also a good example of the structural inconsistencies of treaty law when treaty obligations come into conflict with each other. Instrumentalist arguments were carefully utilised when each of the parties argued for a certain normative content of treaty obligations. Hungary's refusal to fulfil its obligations under the treaty and Czechoslovakia's unilateral actions to proceed were both unlawful. Hungary's unilateral termination of the treaty was not valid as the dispute, in light of *pacta sunt servanda* and environmental considerations, was decided within the framework of the treaty. Both states had equally strong formal and instrumental grounds for their claims. For this reason the court could not bring itself to order the demolition of the unlawful hydropower plant or to decide the question of damages as both litigants had acted wrongfully. The procedural obligation to cooperate formed a nice halfway house which allowed the court to escape the impossibility of having to choose between formal and instrumental interpretation.

Overall, the *Danube Dam* case portrays two types of structural indeterminacy. First, structural indeterminacy can be a question of inconsistent rules within a treaty – formal indeterminacy. The inconsistency arises from the relationship between the right to use the environment and the obligation to protect it.[65] Second, structural indeterminacy can be a question of incoherent objectives between the use and the protection of the environment – instrumental indeterminacy.[66] These two mechanisms create structural softness in environmental treaty law and this softness in turn weakens the normativity of obligations contained therein. The formal validity of an international treaty cannot enshrine its norms with hard normativity if the formal and instrumental structure of norms fails to uphold this normativity.

The conclusion that softness of hard law causes it to be less normative is a controversial claim. Weil has argued that a 'rule of treaty or customary law may be vague, "soft"; but, as the above examples show, it does not thereby cease to be a legal norm'.[67] The argument presented here is not, however, that norms in formally binding instruments lose their validity due to their indeterminacy. The argument here is epistemological. It is not that unclear hard law would not be law but that it is impossible to know what the law requires. Decreased effectiveness robs formally valid law of some of its normativity.[68]

THE UNBEARABLE HARDNESS OF SOFT LAW

1. The Normativity of Soft Law

Formalists typically hold that there is a more or less clear line of demarcation between law and non-law – *lex lata* and *lex ferenda* – which facilitates the distinction between binding and non-binding norms. Norms that do not bind their addressees create neither legal rights nor legal obligations. From this perspective, relative normativity in the form of soft law is a mirage. Legal rights and obligations can be based only on legal sources of formal pedigree. Legal validity and normativity are not matters of degree.[69] As Weil puts it, 'without this positivistic approach, the neutrality so essential to international law *qua* coordinator between equal, but disparate, entities would remain in continual jeopardy'.[70] From a formalist perspective soft law and hard law are separated only by their potentially binding effect.[71]

The formalist challenge of separating law from other normative systems and the development of governance systems towards the penumbra of traditional conceptions of international law has forced scholars to invent new concepts which would do justice to the ever more complex normative universe of environmental law.[72] Soft law, situated normatively in the twilight zone between law and politics, is one attempt to address the normative complexity of law.[73] Traditionally, the concept of soft law has been an element of the open textured treaty provisions already analysed.[74] Currently, the concept is used for the most part to describe legal instruments that lack formal validity but contain nonetheless normative requirements that are complied with.[75]

In terms of formalism and instrumentalism, soft law is something of a hybrid. It is often based on the absence of formal state consent. At the same time soft law instruments often contain normative requirements whose normative validity is based on legitimacy and effectiveness.[76] Applying these two criteria, 'the *hardness of soft law* lies in its capacity for openness, flexibility and simplicity, which is expected to foster the coherence, unification, stability and diversity of rules of conduct, as well as speed of regulation, empirical legitimacy and low negotiation costs'.[77] According to Shelton, 'if states expect compliance and in fact comply with rules and principles contained in soft law instruments as well as they do with norms contained in treaties and custom, then perhaps the concept of international law, or the list of sources of international law, requires expansion'.[78] The increasing acknowledgment and development of soft law seem to imply that the functions of hard and soft law do not necessarily differ. The aim of each is to steer state actions.[79]

Although soft law cannot by definition be formally binding, formalism as the singular theory of normativity is being increasingly challenged. Instead of a binary category of binding and non-binding norms, legal validity becomes a question of degree. The test for separating legal norms from other norms is not as straightforward as formalism requires.

2. Towards Relative Normativity

According to Shelton the expansion of normativity is based on three trends in international environmental policy and law. First, there is the relationship between treaty law and customary international law. One major governance challenge for many environmental problems is that treaty law is prima facie binding only on states parties to the treaty, unless norms embedded in the treaty can be seen to form a part of customary international law. This creates an incentive for some states to withdraw from formally binding environmental agreements if this would advance their economic goals at the expense of other states willing to comply with legal restraints. This raises the question whether these states operating as free riders can be subjected to other than formal legal requirements. Second, the expanded scope of international law, the recognition of the interests of non-state actors as well as those of state actors, and the increasing use of codes of conduct and other soft law instruments challenge the traditionally clear boundaries between law and non-law. Third, peremptory norms and general international obligations in the field of international criminal law challenge the formal idea of normativity based on state consent.[80]

It has already been noted that soft law norms lack formal validity. This means that whatever normativity they may have relies on the norm's legitimacy and effectiveness. Soft law does not merit any legal status if these criteria are not fulfilled. For this reason there remains a considerable area of environmental governance occupied by politics even if the concept of law is expanded to include non-formal criteria. The 1972 Stockholm Declaration, the 1982 World Charter for Nature and the 1992 Rio Declaration are good examples of normative instruments which do not form law properly so-called. This is so even if they were and are influential in the development of international environmental law. Lack of formal validity, vagueness of instrumental language and lack of effectiveness suggest policy goals rather than legal norms.

3. Soft Law in Practice

(a) Introduction

The softness of the Stockholm Declaration, the World Charter for Nature and the Rio Declaration can be contrasted to instruments which – regardless of their lack of formal validity – can be seen to create legal obligations based on their legitimacy and effectiveness.[81] From a formal perspective this unbearable hardness of soft law manifests itself, inter alia, in these examples:

- the status of United Nations General Assembly resolutions regarding driftnet fishing
- the status of the World Bank Nile Basin Initiative
- the status of the Clean Development Mechanism
- the status of non-binding guidance documents in the European chemical governance framework (REACH).

(b) Driftnet fishing

After rising international concern over unsustainable fishing in the high seas and in the exclusive economic zones, the UN General Assembly adopted several resolutions purporting to ban driftnet fishing globally.[82] In article 4(a) of the 1989 Resolution, the UN General Assembly stated that a moratorium on all large scale pelagic driftnet fishing should be imposed by the end of June 1992.[83] In 1990 the General Assembly further expressed concern over the unsustainability of driftnet fishing leading to the adoption of Resolution 46/215 in 1992 with substantive requirements for national implementation and enforcement for the banning of driftnet fishing:[84]

> Recognizing that a moratorium on large-scale pelagic drift-net fishing is required, notwithstanding that it will have adverse socio-economic effects on the communities involved in high seas pelagic drift-net fishing operations … Calls upon all members of the international community to implement resolutions 44/225 and 45/197 by … [ensuring] that a global moratorium on all large-scale pelagic drift-net fishing is fully implemented on the high seas of the world's oceans and seas, including enclosed seas and semi-enclosed seas, by 31 December 1992.[85]

Because the resolutions were adopted by consensus, imposed clear normative requirements on all members of the international community and were adopted by a large number of states, some commentators have concluded that the ban on using drift nets may reflect a rule of customary international law.[86] The effectiveness of these UNGA resolutions has been well documented.[87] One major factor in securing compliance with the resolutions was that the United States was strongly driving a moratorium on driftnet fishing. This was supported by a threat that a failure to comply with the resolution could have resulted in trade sanctions imposed by the US on any state which failed to comply.[88] The legitimacy of international concern over the well-being of fisheries coupled with effective political consequences for non-compliance and supported by the clear language and structure of the resolution led to the acknowledgment of specific legal obligations regardless of the lack of formal validity.

(c) The Nile Basin Initiative

A second example of hard soft law is the World Bank sponsored Nile Basin Initiative (NBI) – a regional and inter-governmental partnership formed by ten riparian states adjacent to the River Nile. The initiative provides, inter alia, for the joint management and planning of Nile Basin water resources.[89] The NBI is an overarching strategic action plan which is divided into seven Shared Vision Programmes and Subsidiary Action Programmes. It aims at developing the Nile's water resources in an equitable and sustainable way: by ensuring efficient water management and cooperation; by targeting poverty eradication; and by ensuring effective implementation of mutually agreed objectives. The NBI has been largely responsible for changing a culture of competition over scarce water resources into a culture of mutual benefit and cooperation.[90] This was originally managed under a non-legally binding instrument – the NBI – which enjoyed considerable legitimacy among the Nile riparian states.[91] Following the informal NBI, the Nile riparian states are in the process of adopting a formally binding agreement – the Co-operative Framework Agreement[92] – for the governance of the Nile river basin.[93] From this perspective the NBI can be seen to have had an important catalytic effect in moving towards a binding and more permanent framework.[94]

(d) International carbon markets and the clean development mechanism

A third example can be taken from international climate law. The clean development mechanism (CDM) is one of the tools designed to mitigate climate change under the UNFCCC framework. The basic idea of the mechanism is to allow countries with carbon emission reduction targets under the Kyoto Protocol – that is Annex I countries – to implement projects resulting in reduced emissions in developing countries.[95] Although the CDM is formally based on article 12 of the Kyoto Protocol, it is normatively shaped at the international level by the Marrakesh Accords[96] as well as the decisions of the CDM Executive Board. This governance framework is further complemented by host and purchasing country regulations as well as voluntary standards such as the CDM Gold Standard.[97] Hard law and soft law instruments form a concerted effort to regulate global carbon markets. Here, soft law plays an important function in the interpretation and implementation of article 12 of the Kyoto Protocol. As Kulovesi summarises:

> All this goes to show that what was originally a provision in an international treaty has become a dynamic regulatory process that involves not only sovereign states that are Parties to the Kyoto Protocol, but also the CDM Executive Board, the UNFCCC Secretariat, national CDM authorities, private sector and civil society actors, local stakeholders as well as donor countries and organizations.[98]

Interestingly, and opposite to the NBI discussed above, the governance framework around CDM displays a regulatory development moving from formally binding requirement towards softer normative instruments fleshing out the commitments originally set out in a formally binding instrument. Soft law has a strong role to play in understanding the normative requirements forming the CDM.

(e) The EU chemical governance framework

Examples of hard soft law abound outside of international law as well. This is clearly visible, inter alia, in the EU chemical governance framework. Under a legally binding regulation concerning registration, evaluation, authorisation and restriction of chemicals (REACH), manufacturers and importers of chemicals have a legal obligation to register substances introduced into the EU to protect human health and the environment from the adverse effects of chemicals.[99] Due to the highly technical and complex nature of REACH, the European Chemicals Agency has produced a set of guidance documents which aim to clarify the legal obligations imposed by the legally binding REACH for the benefit of the public. These documents are paradigmatic soft law materials with a disclaimer that the information and guidance contained in them do not constitute legal advice.[100] Despite this, it is often noted that the REACH Guidance Documents have tangible legal effects in fleshing out the obligations contained in the legally binding regulation.[101] In this case, formally non-binding guidance documents perform de facto an important interpretative function. Their validity is based on legitimacy and effectiveness and clearly not on formal validity.

(f) Conclusion

These examples illustrate three distinctive normative routes which constitute and construct the heightened normativity of soft law. The UN General Assembly driftnet resolutions demonstrate how soft law becomes illustrative of customary law.[102] The NBI illustrates the dynamic effect of soft law. Legitimate and effective soft law instruments, such as the NBI, can have an important catalytic effect in paving the way for formally binding instruments.[103] On the other hand – and as the CDM illustrates – hard law obligations can also be a starting point for further normative developments using hard and soft law in a concerted effort to address environmental problems such as climate change. Furthermore, the CDM on the international level and the REACH Guidance Documents on the European level illustrate the important interpretative effect of soft law in a situation where legally binding obligations are indeterminate, complicated or conflicting. Here soft law functions in conjunction with hard law.[104] This, however, need not be the case as soft law can perform an independent steering function, as in the case of driftnet fishing and the NBI. Acting as a normative source of law, a catalyst of normative change and an interpretative aid, soft law can be seen to have the potential to create hard normative effects even if it lacks formal validity.[105]

SUMMARY

The foregoing paragraphs have analysed how a strictly doctrinal distinction between formality and informality, between binding and non-binding norms and between law and politics can often become blurred in international environmental law. There are simultaneously two trends which blur these linear distinctions. The first trend is the softening of hard law which follows from the open texture of language and structure of the law. The second is the hardening of soft law. Each is now summarised in turn.

The first trend, the softening of hard law, is a reflection of the language and of the structure of the relevant instruments. In framework conventions such as the Convention for the Protection of the Ozone Layer, the Biodiversity Convention and the Climate Change Convention, the use of vague language is often intentional in order to facilitate the recognition of the diverse environmental interests of the negotiating states. Softening of hard law, however, goes beyond language. It is partially constructed by the variety of secondary – interpretative – rules or canons which facilitate the existence of two competing interpretative paradigms – formalism and instrumentalism. The interplay between the two paradigms causes international environmental law to be structurally indeterminate. This has the potential effect of weakening even the clearest linguistic formulation of a norm. Lack of clarity erodes the foundations of the normativity of hard law through decreased effectiveness.

The second trend behind the blurring of normativity in international environmental law is the hardening of soft law.[106] The examples from the UN General Assembly reactions to driftnet fishing, the development of a governance framework for the waters of the Nile, the governance framework surrounding the CDM and the role of guidance documents in the interpretation of the European chemicals regulation lead to the conclusion that soft law can have a direct effect on the actions of states independently of hard law.[107] In addition, the existence of soft law can be an important step towards the recognition of hard law – which may be described as the catalytic effect – and it has a considerable interpretative effect when fleshing out the normative requirements of hard law. In this way soft law can have a considerable normative effect on the actions of states. As a consequence, a focus on formally binding hard law can often give only a partial and limited view of the de facto legal rights and obligations of states. Soft – non-treaty – agreements and arrangements are of legal relevance even if they lack formal validity. This is simply because 'their political function resembles that of treaties' and this provides the 'parties to international arrangements with the power to "justify and persuade"'.[108]

This conclusion may, from a formal perspective, sound more dramatic than it actually is. Formal validity still plays an important role in ascertaining normativity. This analysis has sought to demonstrate that the formal source of normativity is not the only one. Legitimacy and effectiveness should be factored in as supplementary criteria. This means that the test for evaluating what international environmental law requires is an evaluation of multiple *traces of normativity*. These traces include formal criteria such as the formal validity of the instrument in which the norms in question are embedded, the clarity of the rights and obligations emanating from the instrument and the degree of delegation of the implementation and enforcement of the norm to a third party.[109] In addition, traces of normativity include instrumental criteria based on legitimacy and effectiveness linked to the evaluation of contextual criteria in terms of aims, equity and consequences.[110]

The softness of hard law and the hardness of soft law challenge traditional ideas of normativity.[111] The monopoly of form for the purpose of defining validity – despite its theoretical beauty and rigour – does not portray international environmental law in an accurate light. Normativity becomes relativised through the complementary criteria of validity. Validity is a more subtle phenomenon than the simple dichotomy between formally binding and non-binding norms – normative and non-normative – suggests. Instead of strict hierarchies, international environmental norms should be seen to inhabit a relative scale of interlinked norms which often comes much closer to a heterarchy than to a hierarchy.[112] In other words, the normative structure of international environmental law is as much horizontal as it is vertical.

NOTES

1. Here applying loosely Alexy's (2010) dual nature thesis. According to Koskenniemi, international law is simultaneously concerned with facilitating state interests and their critique: see Koskenniemi (2014, p. 48).
2. This is based on the binding nature of international agreements – *pacta sunt servanda* – which has been endorsed in international case law at least since the *Lotus* case (1927, p. 18). See also Thirlway (2014, p. 93).
3. Of the formal sources, treaty law is the most significant one: see Beyerlin and Marauhn (2011, p. 265); Redgwell (2014, p. 695). To be exact, principles are not a purely formal source as they always contain an element of justice: see Dworkin (1978, p. 40). Despite this, Verschuuren (2003, p. 128) views legal principles as hard law (setting legally binding obligations).
4. See, on the problems of ascertaining purpose in interpretation in general, Weinberger (1979, pp. 142–3); Summers (1982); Peczenik (1989, pp. 353–4); Petman (2012, p. 285). Koskenniemi (2014, p. 37): 'The difficulty with the instrumentalist mindset is that there never are simple, well-identified objectives behind formal rules. Rules are legislative compromises, open-ended and bound in clusters expressing conflicting considerations'.
5. Weil (1983, p. 417): 'It is inadmissible within, say, "development law" or "environmental law", to give equal status to conventional or customary rules, on the one hand, and non-normative resolutions, on the other'.
6. See, on the discussion, Kotzé (2012), and the formalist criticism, Klabbers (1996, pp. 167–70, 181).
7. Weil (1983, p. 428).
8. This is why ecological sustainability is often seen as a Grundnorm of environmental law: see Bosselmann (2013, pp. 83–4); Fisher (2013, p. 433). Ecological sustainability is a means of transforming the law: see Kotzé (2013, p. 136).
9. Bugge (2013, p. 7); Voigt (2013, p. 147).
10. In one sense, soft law can be used to describe indeterminate and weak obligations adopted in formally binding law: see Weil (1983, pp. 414–15, fn.7); Shelton (2014, p. 159). In this chapter I retain the term for formally non-binding norms. The concept of hard law is reserved for formally binding norms. Despite soft law's formally non-binding character, the concept has been criticised as unclear as some view law referring only to formally binding obligations. See, for a concise criticism on the concept of soft law, Friedrich (2013, p. 12).
11. See also Toope (2007, p. 114).
12. Fisher (2013 p. 224): 'It is the structure, form and language of the instruments that comprise this normative framework that constitutes the architectural jurisprudence of the system'.

13. Aarnio, Alexy and Peczenik (1992, p. 20): '[U]nambiguity is actually rare in law texts. The normal case is for instance *ambiguous, vague, evaluatively open, incomplete* text of law or the case where the law text contains an internal *incompatibility* (or inconsistency)'.
14. Hart (1994, p. 126). See also Leiter (2001, p. 295).
15. Fisher (2013, pp. 73, 201).
16. A good example of this is the *North Sea Continental Shelf* case (1969) in which the ICJ stated that the equidistance principle enshrined in art.6 of the 1958 Continental Shelf Convention was not of norm creating character due to vagueness of the 'special circumstances' requirement in the provision.
17. Vihma (2013, p. 155): 'Framework conventions in international environmental law are formal, ratifiable and legally binding treaties. However, framework conventions typically do not contain clear, detailed, or specific rules that could be implemented in domestic legislation in a straightforward manner'.
18. See also Birnie, Boyle and Redgwell (2009, p. 350). The 1985 Vienna Convention was an empty framework and the ozone regime only received proper legal mechanisms with the introduction of the 1987 Montreal Protocol and following amendments to it: see ibid. (pp. 351–5).
19. Ibid. (p. 617). They do, however, highlight the importance of interpreting the treaty in light of its preambular provisions and state that the success of the treaty can only be evaluated in light of national implementation measures, and not so much based on the vague formulations of the provisions. It must also be noted that the overall obligations emanating from a legal framework can rarely be evaluated based on the treaty text alone. For instance, protective measures have been fleshed out by the Conference of the Parties (CoP) of the Convention on Biological Diversity (CBD) in later decisions: see the Work Programme on Protected Areas; https://www.cbd.int/protected/pow/learnmore/intro/. In this context hard law sets only soft obligations which get more specific in soft law. This is actually the case in both the CBD and the ozone frameworks: see Friedrich (2013, pp. 47–9, 49–51).
20. Birnie, Boyle and Redgwell (2009, pp. 359–60). See, on the early criticism of the legal weakness of the framework, Bodansky (1993, p. 454).
21. Balekjian (2015, p. 360).
22. Beyerlin (2007, p. 427).
23. Balekjian (2015, p. 358). See, on the necessarily dynamic aspects of law functioning through the 'relative indeterminacy of aim' and 'relative ignorance of fact', Hart (1994, p. 128). See also Koskenniemi (1997, p. 574); Shelton (2003, p. 7). Law is always an exercise in finding a balance between legal certainty and legitimacy (past and future): see Singer (1984, p. 11).
24. Hillgenberg (1999, pp. 500–501) argues that weak language of a formal treaty can bring it closer to formally non-binding instruments.
25. Koskenniemi (2014, p. 42).
26. Ibid. (p. 41).
27. Koskenniemi (2005, p. 590): 'But the claim of indeterminacy is not at all that international legal words are semantically ambivalent. It is much stronger (and in a philosophical sense, more "fundamental") and states that even where there is no semantic ambivalence whatsoever, international law remains indeterminate because it is based on contradictory premises and seeks to regulate the future in regard to which even single actors' preferences remain unsettled'. See also on a more general level Kress 2003, p. 253: 'Critical legal scholars, building on the work of legal realists, have developed an extensive array of arguments concluding that law is radically indeterminate, incoherent, and contradictory. Law is indeterminate to the extent that legal questions lack single answers. In adjudication, law is indeterminate

to the extent that authoritative legal materials and methods permit multiple outcomes to lawsuits'.
28. Koskenniemi (1997, p. 575).
29. Many categorisations have been suggested but most of them have been unsatisfied with a single interpretative method: see MacCormick and Summers (1991, pp. 512–15).
30. Koskenniemi (1997, p. 575).
31. Russel (1998, ch.1).
32. Peczenik (1989, p. 34).
33. Koskenniemi (2005, p. 164).
34. Peczenik (1989, p. 237). See also Aarnio, Alexy and Peczenik (1992, p. 233).
35. Koskenniemi (2005, p. 239).
36. This illustration of structural indeterminacy is from Koskenniemi (1997, p. 576).
37. *Danube Dam* case (1997, paras 1–26).
38. Ibid. (paras 40–41).
39. Ibid. (para. 42).
40. Ibid. (paras 44–5).
41. Ibid. (paras 50–51, 54, 57).
42. Ibid. (paras 55–7).
43. Ibid. (paras 57–8).
44. Ibid. (para. 70).
45. Ibid. (para. 69).
46. Ibid. (para. 78).
47. Ibid. (para. 86).
48. Ibid. (paras 85, 87).
49. Ibid. (para. 89).
50. Ibid. (para. 92).
51. Ibid. (para. 101).
52. Ibid. (para. 103).
53. Ibid. (para. 104).
54. Ibid. (para. 108).
55. Ibid. (paras 113–15).
56. Ibid. (para. 134).
57. Ibid. (para. 136).
58. Ibid. (para. 138).
59. Ibid. (para. 139).
60. Ibid. (para. 141).
61. Ibid. (para. 142).
62. Ibid. (para. 153).
63. Ibid. (para. 150). It is no surprise that the court resorted in the end to procedural criteria as '[t]he law is for stability but equally for change, and which of its contradictory aspects is stressed cannot be determined from within the law itself': Koskenniemi (1997, p. 577).
64. Koskenniemi (1997, p. 579): 'Law continues to set up hierarchies and provide the resources for reversing them. … never fully determined by the context (or the text) but never completely free from it either'.
65. Shelton (2014, p. 152) has argued that '[t]here are potentially numerous problems of hierarchy posed by the need to apply or balance different rights and obligations contained within a single treaty, reconcile norms and procedures in multiple treaties governing the same topic, or resolve conflicts across regimes'.
66. Taking a broader view, instrumental indeterminacy is not rare in international treaties. This is especially visible in the CBD and in the Convention on Climate Change but it is not restricted to framework conventions. The United Nations

Convention on the Law of the Non-navigational Uses of International Watercourses contains this feature as well in the form of the principle of equitable utilisation and the 'no harm' rule. Under art. 5 of the UN Watercourses Convention, the principle of equitable utilisation is premised on the use of water resources. The starting point of the provision is utilisation, which is limited to a sustainable level. Sustainability from an environmental perspective means in this context that environmental protection measures are adequate. This requirement lessens the importance of protection measures and tips the scales toward use. Under art. 6, when assessing the substantive criteria for equitable utilisation, environmental protection and conservation are only one element to be taken into account in legal evaluation. At the same time, the 'no harm' rule protects only other watercourse states, not the environment per se. In addition, harm can be caused to the environment and to other states if it is not significant. Toope (2007, pp. 118–19) has argued that the effectiveness of the 'no harm' rule and the principle of equitable utilisation can be characterised as formally binding treaty law, which includes 'formal adjudicative procedures that were never employed'.

67. Weil (1983, p. 414). More recently, d'Aspremont (2008, pp. 1084–5) has argued in a similar vein: 'Accepting that there may be legal acts with a soft *negotium* means that the normative character of an act is not the prerequisite of its legal character'.
68. See also Baxter (1980, pp. 550–7).
69. Weil (1983, pp. 421, 423). Klabbers (1996, p. 181): 'Our binary law is well capable of handling all kinds of subtleties and sensitivities; within the binary mode, law can be more or less specific, more or less exact, more or less determinate, more or less wide in scope, more or less pressing, more or less serious, more or less far-reaching; the only thing it cannot be is more or less binding'.
70. Weil (1983, p. 421). According to Weil (p. 420), international law cannot carry out its function of peaceful cooperation between countries in a value-pluralistic world without being neutral.
71. Beyerlin and Marauhn (2011, p. 290).
72. Hey (2007, p. 767) observes that 'within global environmental governance formal state consent, which is pivotal to the traditional doctrine of international law, plays only a limited role'.
73. Shelton (2014, p. 138): 'It is not always clear where law ends and non-law begins, or, to use the common terminology, where "soft" law should be placed'.
74. Ibid. (p. 160): 'Treaty mechanisms are including more "soft" obligations, such as undertakings to endeavour to strive to cooperate. Non-binding instruments in turn are incorporating supervisory mechanisms traditionally found in hard law texts'.
75. Ibid. (p. 159): 'There is no accepted definition of "soft law" but it usually refers to any international instrument other than a treaty containing principles, norms, standards, or other statements of expected behaviour'. See Friedrich (2013, pp. 3–8) for a concise description of the discussion in international law regarding soft law.
76. See Weil (1983, pp. 414–15, fn.7) arguing that some norms are not even meant to be binding in the formal sense.
77. Dorbeck-Jung and van Amerom (2008, p. 134) (emphasis in original).
78. Shelton (2014, p. 160).
79. Beyerlin and Marauhn (2011, p. 290). Shelton (2003, p. 8): 'In the international arena, law is not the only form of social control or normative claim. Other basic requirements of behaviour emerge from morality, courtesy, and social custom. They form part of the expectations of social discourse. Compliance with such norms may be expected and violations sanctioned'.
80. Shelton (2014, pp. 139–41). It is the nature of environmental problems that their polycentricity requires 'a rich variety of normative strategies, both formal and

informal': see Toope (2007, pp. 115–16). See, on the variety of motivators behind opting for a soft law instrument instead of a hard law instrument, Shelton (2003, pp. 12–13).

81. Shelton (2003, p. 4): 'Some soft law instruments may have a specific normative content that is "harder" than the soft commitments in treaties'. Effectiveness is closely linked to compliance, which is subject to the institutional setting cultural differences and regional diversity, type of obligations (requiring positive actions or abstention) and specificity of the obligation: see Shelton (2003, pp. 3–4, 13–17).
82. Driftnet fishing is a particularly harmful means of fishing as it relies on up to 50-km-long nets, which typically lead to the catching of a wide variety of marine wildlife of which up to 40 per cent is discarded. Furthermore, driftnet fishing causes harm to navigation: see Rothwell (2003, pp. 122–3).
83. UNGA Res. 44/225 (1989).
84. UNGA Res. 45/197 (1990) and UNGA Res. 46/215 (1991).
85. UNGA Res. 46/215 (1991). Since then the sustainability of driftnet fishing has been an annual concern for the General Assembly resulting in a series of resolutions elaborating the ban: see http://www.un.org/depts/los/general_assembly/general_assembly_resolutions.htm.
86. Sands et al. (2012, p. 431).
87. Rothwell (2003, pp. 131–44).
88. Rothwell (2003, p. 135).
89. See http://www.nilebasin.org/index.php/about-us/nile-basin-initiative. For a brief description of the history of water (non)cooperation, see Brunnée and Toope (2002, pp. 105–108, 132–7).
90. Ibid. (p. 137). Mekonnen (2010, pp. 425–6) has argued that this change had begun already before the NBI and so the success it has had cannot be fully attributed to it alone.
91. Brunnée and Toope (2002, p. 158): '[A]n assessment of the various informal processes in the Nile Basin illustrates that norms can generate adherence even if they are not formally binding'. See also Toope (2007, p. 119).
92. Agreement on the Nile River Basin Cooperative Framework; http://www.nilebasin.org/images/docs/CFA%20-%20English%20%20FrenchVersion.pdf.
93. See http://www.nilebasin.org/index.php/spotlight/99-cfa-overview.
94. The Cooperative Framework Agreement has been ratified by three countries (Ethiopia, Rwanda and Tanzania). Under art. 43 of the Agreement, the framework enters into force on the sixtieth day following the date of deposit of the sixth instrument of ratification or accession with the African Union.
95. See http://unfccc.int/kyoto_protocol/mechanisms/clean_development_mechanism/items/2718.php.
96. UN Doc. FCCC/KP/CMP/2005/8/add.1, 30 March 2006.
97. For a brief description, see Kulovesi (2013, p. 36).
98. Ibid.
99. For an overview, see http://echa.europa.eu/web/guest/regulations/reach/understanding-reach.
100. See European Chemical Agency Guidance on Data Sharing, Version 2.0, April 2012, p. 3.
101. Korkea-Aho (2013, p. 367): 'Guidance documents are primarily technical notes on different aspects of REACH, but this says little about how they are applied in normative and practical contexts. The main text of REACH makes no reference to guidance documents; they are classic soft law material. They shirk binding commitments: the cover page of each REACH guidance document reads "the information in this document does not constitute legal advice". Nonetheless, they rule in practice'.

102. See Grnchalla-Wesierski (1984, pp. 52–7); Shelton (2003, p. 1).
103. See on the catalytic effect of soft law, Shelton (2003, p. 4).
104. See on a general level, Shelton (2003, p. 10). See on the interpretative effect of soft law, Fastenrath (1993, p. 339). Soft law can either strengthen the normative basis of hard law or delegitimise it. See on the delegitimising effect of soft law, Grnchalla-Wesierski (1984, pp. 52–7).
105. As Toope (2007, p. 114) observes: '[f]ormal and informal approaches to shaping behaviour are therefore inextricably intertwined. Nowhere is this more apparent than in the range of issue areas brought together under international environmental law'. See also ibid (p. 124): 'Formal and informal norms operate side by side. Each can be influential and each can fail to influence'.
106. Soft law can be used for evoking mutual understanding, good faith and voluntary compliance but without the formal legal obligation as a mechanism of compliance: see Boyle (2014, p. 120).
107. Despite this, the independence of soft law from hard law is a matter of degree. In the case of UN General Assembly (UNGA) driftnet resolutions, there is a hard mandate for the UNGA to establish normative guidelines. Similarly with regards to the NBI, governance of the Nile river basin was covered to a certain extent by hard law even before the initiative making the NBI partially linked to hard law. The CDM also has art. 12 of the Kyoto Protocol as its normative basis. Finally, with regard to REACH, the European chemicals legislation is based on hard law but is being complemented by soft law interpretatively. These linkages between formal and non-formal instruments suggest a close relationship between law and non-law rather than independence.
108. Hillgenberg (1999, p. 515).
109. Abbott et al. (2000, p. 401).
110. This is clearly visible in Sands et al.'s (2012, pp. 187–8) description of evaluating the normativity of legal principles. Application of a principle depends on 'the source of the principle; its textual content and language; the particular activity at issue; the environmental and other consequences of the activity; and the circumstances in which it occurs (including the actors and the geographical region)'.
111. Separating material and formal sources of law similarly to Thirlway (2014, pp. 92–3), one can argue that formally binding sources need not embrace material rights and obligations. The same is true in reverse: informal sources can sometimes function as sources of material rights and obligations. Applying d'Aspremont (2008, pp. 1081–7) in separating between *instrumentum* (source of normative obligation) and *negotium* (content of the obligation), hard law is hard in *instrumentum* but can be soft in *negotium.* In contrast, soft law is soft *instrumentum* but can be hard in *negotium.*
112. Brunnée and Toope (2002, p. 115): '[T]here are certain internal characteristics that distinguish law from other forms of social ordering. They may be summarized as requiring that rules be compatible with one another, that they ask reasonable things, that they are transparent and relatively predictable, and that known rules actually guide the discretion of officials. It is these internal characteristics that account for the "bindingness" of law, rather than hierarchical authority or pedigree'. Softening this message somewhat leads to normativity being based on tripartite criteria: form, legitimacy and effectiveness. Shaffer and Pollack (2010, p. 716) and Vihma (2013, p. 162) have talked about the legislation continuum meaning the partial blurring of the criterion for normativity.

REFERENCES

Aarnio, Aulis, Robert Alexy and Aleksander Peczenik (1992), 'The Foundation of Legal Reasoning' in Aulis Aarnio and Neil MacCormick (eds), *Legal Reasoning Volume 1* (Aldershot, Dartmouth), pp. 15–40, 233–81.

Abbott, Kenneth W., Robert O. Keohane, Andrew Moravcsik, Anne-Marie Slaughter and Duncan Snidal (2000), 'The Concept of Legalization', *International Organisation* 54(3), pp. 401–19.

Alexy, Robert (1989), *A Theory of Legal Argumentation. The Theory of Rational Discourse as Theory of Legal Justification* (Oxford, Clarendon Press).

Alexy, Robert (2010), 'The Dual Nature of Law', *Ratio Juris* 23(2), pp. 167–82.

Balekjian, W.H. (2015), 'The Language of International Law. Linguistic Considerations Involved in the Drafting and Interpretation of International Legal Instruments'; http://biblio.juridicas.unam.mx/libros/1/468/35.pdf.

Baxter, R.R. (1980), 'International Law "in Her Infinite Variety"', *International & Comparative Law Quarterly* 29, pp. 549–66.

Beyerlin, Ulrich (2007), 'Different Types of Norms in International Environmental Law. Policies, Principles and Rules' in Daniel Bodansky, Jutta Brunnée and Ellen Hey (eds), *The Oxford Handbook of International Environmental Law* (Oxford, Oxford University Press), pp. 423–48.

Beyerlin, Ulrich and Thilo Marauhn (2011), *International Environmental Law* (Oxford, Hart Publishing).

Birnie, Patricia, Alan Boyle and Catherine Redgwell (2009), *International Law and the Environment* (3rd edn, Oxford, Oxford University Press).

Bodansky, Daniel (1993), 'The United Nations Framework Convention on Climate Change: A Commentary', *Yale Journal of International Law* 18, pp. 451–558.

Bosselmann, Klaus (2013), 'Grounding the Rule of Law' in Christina Voigt (ed.), *Rule of Law for Nature. New Dimensions and Ideas in Environmental Law* (Cambridge, Cambridge University Press), pp. 75–93.

Boyle, Alan (2014), 'Soft Law in International Law-making' in Malcom D. Evans (ed.), *International Law* (4th edn, Oxford, Oxford University Press), pp. 118–36.

Brunnée, Jutta and Stephen J. Toope (2002), 'The Changing Nile Basin Regime: Does Law Matter?', *Harvard International Law Journal* 43(1), pp. 105–59.

Bugge, Hans Christian (2013), 'Twelve fundamental challenges in environmental law. An Introduction to the concept of rule of law for nature' in Christina Voigt (ed.), *Rule of Law for Nature. New Dimensions and Ideas in Environmental Law* (Cambridge, Cambridge University Press), pp. 3–26.

d'Aspremont, Jean (2008), 'Softness in International Law: A Self-Serving Quest for New Legal Materials', *European Journal of International Law* 19(5), pp. 1075–93.

Dorbeck-Jung, Bärbel and Marloes van Amerom (2008), 'The Hardness of Soft Law in the United Kingdom: State and Non-State Regulatory Activities Related to Nanotechnological Development' in Hanneke van Schooten and Jonathan Verschuuren, *International Governance and Law. State Regulation and Non-state Law* (Cheltenham, Edward Elgar Publishing), pp. 129–50.

Dworkin, Ronald (1978), *Taking Rights Seriously* (Cambridge, MA, Harvard University Press).

Fastenrath, Ulrich (1993), 'Relative Normativity in International Law', *European Journal of International Law* 4, pp. 305–40.

Fisher, Douglas (2013), *Legal Reasoning in Environmental Law. A Study of Structure, Form and Language* (Cheltenham, Edward Elgar Publishing).

Friedrich, Jürgen (2013), *International Environmental 'Soft Law'. The Functions and Limits of Nonbinding Instruments in International Environmental Governance and Law* (Heidelberg, New York, Springer).
Grnchalla-Wesierski, Tadensz (1984), 'A Framework for Understanding "Soft Law"', *McGill Law Journal* 30, pp. 37–88.
Hart, H.L.A. (1994), *The Concept of Law* (2nd edn, Oxford, Oxford University Press).
Hey, Ellen (2007), 'International Institutions' in Daniel Bodansky, Jutta Brunnée and Ellen Hey (eds), *The Oxford Handbook of International Environmental Law* (Oxford, Oxford University Press), pp. 749–69.
Hillgenberg, Hartmut (1999), 'A Fresh Look at Soft Law', *European Journal of International Law* 10, pp. 499–515.
Klabbers, Jan (1996), 'The Redundancy of Soft Law', *Nordic Journal of International Law* 65, pp. 167–82.
Korkea-Aho, Emilia (2013), 'Laws in Progress? Reconceptualizing Accountability Strategies in the Era of Framework Norms', *Transnational Environmental Law* 2(2), pp. 363–85.
Koskenniemi, Martti (1997), 'Hierarchy in International Law: A Sketch', *European Journal of International Law* 8, pp. 566–82.
Koskenniemi, Martti (2005), *From Apology to Utopia. The Structure of International Legal Argument* (Cambridge, Cambridge University Press).
Koskenniemi, Martti (2014), 'What is International Law For?' in Malcom D. Evans (ed.), *International Law* (4th edn, Oxford, Oxford University Press), pp. 29–52.
Kotzé, Louis (2012), *Global Environmental Governance. Law and Regulation for the 21st Century* (Cheltenham, Edward Elgar Publishing).
Kotzé, Louis (2013), 'Sustainable development and rule of law for nature' in Christina Voigt (ed.), *Rule of Law for Nature. New Dimensions and Ideas in Environmental Law* (Cambridge, Cambridge University Press), pp. 130–45.
Kress, Ken (2003), 'Legal Indeterminacy' in Dennis Patterson (ed.), *An Anthology of Philosophy of Law and Legal Theory* (Malden, MA, Oxford, Melbourne, Berlin, Blackwell Publishing), pp. 253–91.
Kulovesi, Kati (2013), 'Exploring the Landscape of Climate Law and Scholarship: Two Emerging Trends' in Erkki J. Hollo, Kati Kulovesi and Michael Mehling (eds), *Climate Change and the Law* (Dordrecht, Heidelberg, New York, London, Springer), pp. 31–62.
Leiter, Brian (2001), 'Legal Realism and Legal Positivism Reconsidered', *Ethics* 111(2), pp. 278–301.
MacCormick, Neil and Robert S. Summers (1991), 'Interpretation and Justification' in Neil MacCormick and Robert S. Summers (eds), *Interpreting Statutes. A Comparative Study* (Dartmouth, Ashgate Publishing), pp. 511–44.
Mekonnen, Dereje Zeleke (2010), 'The Nile Basin Cooperative Framework Agreement Negotiations and the Adoption of a "Water Security" Paradigm: Flight into Obscurity or a Logical Cul-de-sac?', *European Journal of International Law* 21(2), pp. 421–40.
Peczenik, Aleksander (1989), *On Law and Reason* (Dordrecht, Kluwer Academic Publishers).
Petman, Jarna (2012), *Human Rights and Violence. The Hope and the Fear of the Liberal World* (Helsinki, University of Helsinki).
Redgwell, Catherine (2014), 'International Environmental Law' in Malcom D. Evans (ed.), *International Law* (4th edn, Oxford, Oxford University Press), pp. 688–726.
Rothwell, Donald R. (2003), 'The General Assembly Ban on Driftnet Fishing' in Dinah Shelton (ed.), *The Role of Non-binding Norms in the International Legal System* (Oxford, Oxford University Press), pp. 121–46.
Russel, Bertrand (1998), *The Problems of Philosophy*. Introduction by John Skorupski (2nd edn, Oxford, Oxford University Press).

Sands, Philippe, Jacqueline Peel, Adriana Fabra and Ruth Mackenzie (2012), *Principles of International Environmental Law* (3rd edn, Cambridge, Cambridge University Press).
Shaffer, Gregory C. and Pollack, Mark A. (2010), 'Hard vs. Soft Law: Alternatives, Complements, and Antagonists in International Governance', *Minnesota Law Review* 94, pp. 706–99.
Shelton, Dinah (2003), 'Introduction: Law, Non-Law and the Problem of "Soft Law"' in Dinah Shelton (ed.), *The Role of Non-binding Norms in the International Legal System* (Oxford, Oxford University Press), pp. 1–20.
Shelton, Dinah (2014), 'International Law and "Relative Normativity"' in Malcom D. Evans (ed.), *International Law* (4th edn, Oxford, Oxford University Press), pp. 137–65.
Singer, Joseph (1984), 'The Player and the Cards: Nihilism and Legal Theory', *Yale Law Journal* 94(1), pp. 1–70.
Summers, Robert S. (1982), *Instrumentalism and American Legal Theory* (Ithaca, London, Cornell University Press).
Thirlway, Hugh (2014), 'The Sources of International Law' in Malcom D. Evans (ed.), *International Law* (4th edn, Oxford, Oxford University Press), pp. 91–136.
Toope, Stephen J. (2007), 'Formality and Informality' in Daniel Bodansky, Jutta Brunnée and Ellen Hey (eds), *The Oxford Handbook of International Environmental Law* (Oxford, Oxford University Press), pp. 107–24.
Verschuuren, Jonathan (2003), *Principles of Environmental Law. The Ideal of Sustainable Development and the Role of Principles of International, European and National Environmental Law* (Baden-Baden, Nomos Verlagsgesellschaft).
Vihma, Antto (2013), 'Analyzing Soft Law and Hard Law in Climate Change' in Erkki J. Hollo, Kati Kulovesi and Michael Mehling (eds), *Climate Change and the Law* (Dordrecht, Heidelberg, New York, London, Springer), pp. 143–64.
Voigt, Christina (2013), 'The Principle of Sustainable Development. Integration and Ecological Integrity' in Christina Voigt (ed.), *Rule of Law for Nature. New Dimensions and Ideas in Environmental Law* (Cambridge, Cambridge University Press), pp. 146–57.
Weil, Prosper (1983), 'Towards Relative Normativity in International Law?', *American Journal of International Law* 77, pp. 413–42.
Weinberger, Ota and Christiane Weinberger (1979), *Logik, Semantik, Hermeneutik* (München, C.H. Beck'sche Verlagsbuchhandlung).

INSTRUMENTS

Continental Shelf Convention: Geneva, 29 April 1958, in force 10 June 1964, 499 *United Nations Treaty Series*, p. 311.
Convention on Biological Diversity: Rio de Janeiro, 5 June 1992, in force 29 December 1993, 31 *International Legal Materials* (1992), p. 818.
Convention on the Law of the Non-navigational Uses of International Watercourses: New York, 21 May 1997, in force 17 August 2014, 36 *International Legal Materials* (1998), p. 700.
Framework Convention on Climate Change: Rio de Janeiro, 9 May 1992, in force 21 March 1993, 31 *International Legal Materials* (1992), p. 849.
Kyoto Protocol to the United Nations Framework Convention on Climate Change: Kyoto, 10 December 1997, in force 16 February 2005, 37 *International Legal Materials* (1998), p. 22.
Regulation No 1907/2006 of the European Parliament and of the Council of 18 December 2006 concerning the Registration, Evaluation, Authorisation and Restriction of Chemicals (REACH), establishing a European Chemicals Agency, amending Directive

1999/45/EC and repealing Council Regulation (EEC) No 793/93 and Commission Regulation (EC) No 1488/94 as well as Council Directive 76/769/EEC and Commission Directives 91/155/EEC, 93/67/EEC, 93/105/EC and 2000/21/EC, OJ L 396/1.
Vienna Convention on the Law of Treaties: Vienna, 23 May 1969, in force 27 January 1980, 1155 *United Nations Treaty Series*, p. 331.
Vienna Convention for the Protection of the Ozone Layer: Vienna, 22 March 1985, in force 22 September 1988, 26 *International Legal Materials* (1986), p. 1529.

CASES

Danube Dam case: 25 September 1997 (Hungary v. Slovakia) ICJ Rep., 37 *International Legal Materials* (1998).
Lotus case: 7 September 1927 (France v. Turkey) Publications of the Permanent Court of International Justice, Series A – No. 10.
North Sea Continental Shelf case: 20 February 1969 (Germany v. Denmark and the Netherlands) ICJ Rep.

11. The growing significance of the principle of sustainable development as a legal norm

Jonathan Verschuuren

INTRODUCTION

This chapter seeks to determine the current legal status of the principle of sustainable development in international law. There has been considerable debate about the legal nature of the principle of sustainable development as well as its meaning. Is it really a legal principle? These debates are related because the rather vague and ambiguous terminology makes a straightforward legal implementation or application of the principle of sustainable development in legal practice difficult. Legal scholars have labelled 'sustainable development' a concept,[1] a goal,[2] a policy objective,[3] a guideline,[4] an ideal,[5] a meta-principle,[6] a weak norm of international law,[7] a concept or principle of customary law,[8] or a legal principle.[9] Much depends on the respective author's view of the normative power of the principle and the practical consequences for day-to-day legal decision-making.

Since its rise in international environmental law in 1992, sustainable development has been increasingly referred to by drafters of environmental and other treaties as well as by international and domestic courts. Has this increasing reference led to a stronger normative power and a stronger legal status of the principle and, if so, what does this imply for environmental decision-making at the international level? This question will be addressed through traditional legal desk study methodology as follows:

- a description of the emergence of sustainable development in soft law instruments
- a description of the references to sustainable development in legally binding international instruments as in multilateral conventions
- a description of the references to sustainable development in decisions by courts and tribunals

- an analysis of these instruments and decisions whose aim is to determine the status of sustainable development as a legal norm.

THE EMERGENCE OF THE PRINCIPLE OF SUSTAINABLE DEVELOPMENT IN SOFT LAW: THE STOCKHOLM DECLARATION AND BEYOND

1. Introduction

The number of publications in the field of law that deal with sustainable development or sustainability has reached staggering proportions![10] Most of these publications start by searching for the roots of the principle. Some go back for centuries,[11] but most start in the year 1972. That year saw the publication of the influential report *Limits to Growth* by the Club of Rome in which it was argued that current economic and population growth trends harm the environment in such a way that it will constrain further economic growth. The report searched for a 'sustainable world system',[12] and concluded that 'it is possible to alter these growth trends and to establish a condition of ecological and economic stability that is sustainable far into the future'.[13] In their famous article in *The Ecologist* in that same year, Goldsmith and colleagues wrote:

> Our task is to create a society which is sustainable and which will give the fullest possible satisfaction to its members. Such a society by definition would depend not on expansion but on stability. This does not mean to say that it would be stagnant – indeed it could well afford more variety than does the state of uniformity at present being imposed by the pursuit of technological efficiency. We believe that the stable society … , as well as removing the sword of Damocles which hangs over the heads of future generations, is much more likely than the present one to bring peace and fulfilment which hitherto have been regarded, sadly, as utopian.[14]

2. From 1972 to 1982

In 1972 the Stockholm Declaration on the Human Environment was adopted during the first United Nations (UN) conference on the environment.[15] This early international environmental law instrument does not mention the words 'sustainable development' as such but it does, in its preamble, acknowledge that 'in our time, man's capability to transform his surroundings, if used wisely, can bring to all peoples the benefits of development and the opportunity to enhance the quality of life'. The Declaration argues that 'to defend and improve the human environment for present and future generations has become an imperative goal for mankind – a goal to be pursued together with, and in harmony with, the established and fundamental goals of peace and of worldwide economic and social development'.[16] Principle 1 then puts this in legal terms. Man bears the responsibility 'to protect and improve the environment for present and future generations'. Principle 2 adds that 'the natural resources of the earth, including the air, water, land, flora and fauna and especially representative samples of natural ecosystems, must be safeguarded for the benefit of present and future generations through careful planning or management, as appropriate'.

For the first time, three years later in 1975, a United Nations Environment Programme (UNEP) decision explicitly used the term 'sustainable development'. In these words: 'environmental management implies sustainable development of all countries, aimed at meeting basic human needs without transgressing the outer limits set to man's endeavours by the biosphere'.[17] In 1980, the International Union for the Conservation of Nature (IUCN), with the support of several UN organisations, drafted the World Conservation Strategy. This had as a subtitle: 'Living Resource Conservation for Sustainable Development'. This led to the adoption of the World Charter for Nature in 1982. The term 'sustainable development' does not appear prominently in the latter document.

3. The Brundtland Report 1987

Although the term does not remain unmentioned in international documents throughout the first half of the 1980s,[18] the explicit acknowledgement of 'sustainable development' as the central objective of future environmental policies came in 1987, with the publication of the report of the World Commission on Environment and Development (WCED) entitled *Our Common Future* (also known as 'the Bundtland Report'). In this report, sustainable development was described as a 'concept'[19] and as 'a process of change in which the exploitation of resources, the direction of investments, the orientation of technological development and institutional change are all in harmony and enhance both current and future potential to meet human needs and aspirations'.[20] The work of the WCED was inspired by an urgent call of the General Assembly of the United Nations to 'help define shared perceptions of long-term environmental issues and the appropriate efforts needed to deal successfully with the problems of protecting and enhancing the environment, a long-term agenda for action during the coming decades and aspirational goals for the future'.[21] The WCED clearly came up with such an aspiration by holding man responsible for the future of the earth and by stating that today's generation may not fulfil its needs while endangering the possibility for future generations to fulfil their needs.[22] Sustainable development at the same time focuses on present generations. Accordingly economic growth should be achieved in nations in which the majority is poor and these poor should get their fair share of the resources required to sustain their economic growth.[23]

4. The Rio Declaration 1992

Given the influence of the WCED's report, especially in UN circles, it is not remarkable that 'sustainable development' emerged as the key underlying concept during the 1992 UN Conference on Environment and Development (UNCED) in Rio de Janeiro.[24] The Rio Declaration on Environment and Development mentions the words 'sustainable development' explicitly 12 times. According to principle 1, 'human beings are at the centre of concerns for sustainable development. They are entitled to a healthy and productive life in harmony with nature'. Principle 4 codifies the integration principle in these words: 'In order to achieve sustainable development, environmental protection shall constitute an integral part of the development process and cannot be considered in isolation from it'. Sustainable development is here presented as the goal of the integration principle.

5. Rio+20: 2012

Up until 1992, the principle of sustainable development appeared mostly in soft law documents. This has continued to be true. The 2002 Johannesburg Declaration on Sustainable Development is, as its name suggests, all about sustainable development.[25] The major difference compared with its predecessor of 1992 is that this declaration has softer legal language. For instance it does not refer to 'principles'. The 2012 UN Conference on Sustainable Development, again in Rio de Janeiro and often referred to as Rio+20, produced an even softer legal 'outcome document' entitled *The Future We Want*.[26] This document reaffirms the Rio Principles and refers to these principles several times but without explicitly mentioning the principle of sustainable development.

6. Conclusion

The foregoing paragraphs are based solely on these international soft law documents. Accordingly it cannot be argued that the principle of sustainable development has been recognized as a legally binding principle of law. The most clear and authoritative reference to the principle was contained in the Rio Declaration. In its statement of 'principles', it regularly refers to sustainable development as a goal to be attained by the implementation of more concrete principles. These include the integration principle mentioned above, as well as – for example – the precautionary principle stated in principle 15, the polluter pays principle stated in principle 16, and the environmental impact assessment principle stated in principle 17.

THE ADOPTION OF THE PRINCIPLE OF SUSTAINABLE DEVELOPMENT IN LEGALLY BINDING CONVENTIONS

1. Introduction

Since 1992 the principle of sustainable development started to emerge in binding international law instruments and in international and domestic case law as well. The following paragraphs describe the emergence of the principle in binding legal instruments with the aim of determining the legal status of the principle. Accordingly they will review binding international law instruments to see whether the concept of sustainable development is accepted as a legally binding principle. The discussion incorporates a review of environmental law conventions followed by a review of other international law instruments, especially trade law agreements and regional treaties.

2. Environmental Law Conventions

(a) Biological diversity and climate change

The two legally binding conventions adopted in 1992 at the Rio Conference are the Convention on Biological Diversity (CBD)[27] and the UN Framework Convention on Climate Change (UNFCCC)[28] and their associated protocols. These instruments regularly refer to sustainable development. In the CBD, 'sustainable use' is defined as 'the use of components of biological diversity in a way and at a rate that does not lead to the long-term decline of biological diversity, thereby maintaining its potential to meet the needs and aspirations of present and future generations'.[29] Almost all of the provisions of the CBD show that policies and measures have to be aimed at achieving a sustainable use. Article 6, for example, lists the 'general measures for conservation and sustainable use', whereas article 10 lays down the duties of the parties on the sustainable use of components of biological diversity.

The Cartagena Protocol to the CBD has multiple references to 'the conservation and sustainable use of biological diversity' in several of its specific and legally binding rules, such as the rule that the state of import may review its decision regarding a transboundary movement of a living genetically modified organism at any time, 'in light of new scientific information on potential adverse effects on the conservation and sustainable use of biological diversity'.[30] The same is true of the Nagoya Protocol, which, for instance, provides that 'the Parties shall encourage users and providers to direct benefits arising from the utilization of genetic resources towards the conservation of biological diversity and the sustainable use of its components'.[31]

Turning to the UNFCCC, article 2 states the objective of the convention: stabilization of greenhouse gas concentrations with the aim to 'enable development to proceed in a sustainable manner'. Article 3 is entitled 'Principles'. It primarily codifies the principle of common-but-differentiated responsibilities by referring to both elements of the definition of sustainable development by the WCED: it includes in paragraphs 1 and 2 the principles of intergenerational and intragenerational equity. Paragraph 4 states that 'parties have a right to, and should, promote sustainable development'. From a legal point of view, the latter is a somewhat peculiar provision, entailing both a right and a duty for state parties, albeit in the article on 'principles'. It thus mixes up no less than three different types of legal norms in one short sentence. The fifth and last paragraph of article 3 codifies the cooperation principle, again with the aim to achieve sustainable economic development.[32] Article 4 lists the specific obligations: amongst others, the duty of all states to 'promote sustainable management … of sinks and reservoirs of all greenhouse gases … , including biomass, forests and oceans as well as other terrestrial, coastal and marine ecosystems'.[33] National mitigation policies in developed countries have to aim at maintaining strong and sustainable economic growth.[34]

The Kyoto Protocol, the instrument that set binding reduction targets for the countries listed in Annex I to the UNFCCC, refers extensively to sustainable development.[35] The reference to sustainable development in the provision on the clean development mechanism (CDM) is especially significant. This instrument allows Annex I states to achieve part of their emission reduction target through projects in developing countries, so long as these projects, besides achieving a reduction of greenhouse gas emissions, achieve sustainable development in the developing country hosting the CDM project.[36] There is an extensive approval process, part of which focuses on the requirement that sustainable development must be achieved. This includes that the project developer must obtain confirmation from the competent authority in the developing country that the project activity assists in achieving sustainable development.[37] This requirement met with much criticism once it was established that clearly unsustainable projects, for instance leading to human rights violations, had been carried out.[38] In an effort to ensure that the project would lead to a sustainable development, the CDM Executive Board in 2014 launched a voluntary online tool for highlighting the sustainable development benefits of the CDM in a 'structured, consistent, comparable and robust manner', primarily by asking the project developers to respond to a checklist of predefined sustainability indicators – the 'SD Tool'.[39]

(b) Fisheries and the marine environment

In the area of the marine environment, the term 'sustainable yield' is used extensively in relation to fisheries and preserving fish stocks. The UN Convention on the Law of the Sea, for example, requires states to take measures within their exclusive economic zone (EEZ) 'to maintain or restore populations of harvested species at levels which can produce the maximum sustainable yield'.[40] Maximum sustainable yield is a theoretical concept and has been used extensively in fisheries science and management since the 1930s.[41] The use of the word 'sustainable' in maximum sustainable yield, therefore, pre-dates the emergence of the principle of sustainable development and has a very specific meaning. In fisheries, maximum sustainable yield indicates the maximum catch that can be removed from a population over an indefinite period without depleting the population.[42]

Since 1992, however, the broader concept of sustainable development has been infiltrating fisheries-related conventions. Probably the best example is the 1995 Agreement on the Conservation and Management of Straddling Fish Stocks and Highly Migratory Fish Stocks.[43] Sustainable development is the overarching objective of the Agreement and is the basis for more specific obligations imposed on the parties, such as: to adopt measures to ensure long-term sustainability of fish stocks; to ensure that measures are based on the best scientific evidence available and are designed to maintain or restore stocks at levels capable of producing maximum sustainable yield, as qualified by relevant environmental and economic factors, including the special requirements of developing states; to apply the precautionary approach; to minimize pollution, waste, discards, catch by lost or abandoned gear; and to take into account the interests of artisanal and subsistence fishers.[44]

Another example is the 1992 Convention for the Protection of the Marine Environment of the North-East Atlantic (OSPAR). It mentions sustainable development: albeit only in Annex V about the protection and conservation of the ecosystems and biological diversity of the maritime area. This Convention was adopted in 1998.[45] In December 2014, the UN General Assembly adopted a resolution on sustainable fisheries that calls on states to take actions to address unsustainable fishing practices, climate change and ocean acidification.[46]

(c) Post-1992 developments

A number of environmental conventions concluded since 1992 refer to the principle of sustainable development in several ways. The Stockholm Convention on Persistent Organic Pollutants, for example, allows developing country parties to give precedence to sustainable economic and social development over full and effective implementation of their commitments under the Convention.[47] The UN Convention on the Law of the Non-navigational Uses of International Watercourses recognizes sustainable utilization as the main objective.[48] The Protocol on Strategic Environmental Assessment to the Espoo Convention on Environmental Impact Assessment in a Transboundary Context has as its objective to integrate – by means of strategic environmental assessment – environmental and health concerns into measures and instruments designed to further sustainable development.[49]

It should be noted, however, that there are important post-1992 international environmental instruments that do not refer to sustainable development: for example the Convention on Civil Liability for Damage Resulting from Activities Dangerous to the Environment.[50] Some instruments refer to sustainable development only in their preamble: for example the London Protocol on the Prevention of Marine Pollution by Dumping of Wastes and Other Matter[51] and the Aarhus Convention on Access to Information, Public Participation and Decision-Making and Access to Justice in Environmental Matters.[52]

3. Other International Treaties: the WTO

Since sustainable development is all about integrating environmental and developmental concerns, it is appropriate to consider non-environmental instruments to assess whether the principle of sustainable development has had an impact on treaties with primarily an economic purpose. Probably the most significant instruments in this regard are the World Trade Organization (WTO) instruments. The 1994 Agreement Establishing the WTO refers to sustainable development only in the preamble. The

Agreement starts by recognizing that trade and economic endeavour should allow 'for the optimal use of the world's resources in accordance with the objective of sustainable development, seeking both to protect and preserve the environment'.[53] Although these are very clear intentions, integrating environmental concerns into international trade law, as currently discussed in the Doha Round of negotiations on trade and the environment, is a cumbersome process.[54] Nevertheless, the WTO Appellate Body did expand the potential for environmental measures to restrict trade.[55] These developments are discussed below in relation to how the principle of sustainable development has influenced international case law.

4. Regional Environmental Law

(a) Africa, America and Asia

Most regional organizations have adopted sustainable development as one of their core aims. One of the objectives of the African Union (AU), laid down in the Constitutive Act of the African Union, is to 'promote sustainable development at the economic, social and cultural levels as well as the integration of African economies'.[56] There are only a few concrete principles or binding rules that are explicitly aimed at sustainable development within the AU legal system. The African Charter on Human and Peoples' Rights of 1981 has two separate rights: a right to a satisfactory environment in article 24 and a right to development in article 22. Some commentators suggest that one approach is to implement and achieve these two rights in an integrated way by using sustainable development as the linking pin.[57]

The Organisation of American States has soft law instruments aimed at achieving sustainable development.[58] The most important are the Inter-American Program on Sustainable Development (PIDS)[59] and the Declaration of Santo Domingo for the Sustainable Development of the Americas.[60] In similar fashion within the ASEAN (the organization of southeast Asian states), sustainable development is for the most part addressed by soft law instruments, especially by the Declaration on Environmental Sustainability.[61] Sustainable development in these instruments, however, 'cannot yet be said to have acquired a normative content in the region, either at the level of legislative development or in judicial decisions'.[62]

(b) The European Union

The approach in the European Union (EU) has been remarkably different. In 1997 sustainable development[63] received a firm place in legally binding instruments. Currently, sustainable development is embedded in the EU's constitutive treaties: the Treaty on the European Union (TEU), the Treaty on the Functioning of the European Union (TFEU) and the Charter of Fundamental Rights. These are considered in turn.

The preamble to the TEU refers to the 'principle of sustainable development'.[64] Article 3 then mentions sustainable development as the main goal of the EU's internal market: the EU 'shall work for the sustainable development of Europe'.[65] A similar goal has to be achieved with the EU's external relations policies.[66] Finally, article 21 states that the EU's foreign policy must foster the sustainable economic, social and environmental development of developing countries and help develop international measures to preserve and improve the quality of the environment and the sustainable management of global natural resources, in order to ensure sustainable development.[67]

Consider some of the more detailed provisions in the TEU. Given the very broad and general wording of these provisions in the TEU, it is generally thought that the concept of sustainable development in these provisions cannot be regarded as a normative-legal concept,[68] nor can precise obligations be deduced from article 3.[69] The provision rather serves as a guideline to policy. In the EU's sustainable development strategies of 2001[70] and 2006,[71] as well as the 2009 review by the European Commission of these strategies, sustainable development is characterized as 'the overarching long-term goal' of the EU.[72] The 2009 review shows that, despite the relatively weak legal character of article 3, the adoption of sustainable development as an overarching policy goal has been successful.

In recent years, the EU has demonstrated its clear commitment to sustainable development. The European Commission has found that the EU:

> has successfully mainstreamed this sustainability dimension into many policy fields. The EU's climate change and energy policies are evidence of the impact that sustainable development strategy has had on the political agenda. The EU has started to integrate the sustainability dimension in many other policy fields also.[73]

The current general strategy indicated for the EU in the instrument entitled 'Europe 2020' has sustainable development as a central theme together with a strong emphasis on resource efficiency and a low carbon economy.[74]

The TFEU contains more specific provisions on the various policy areas of the EU and this includes environmental policy. It codified a series of legal principles that play an important role in EU environmental law and policy. The integration principle was codified in article 11 TFEU. This provision makes it clear that the achievement of sustainable development is the ultimate aim of integrating environmental considerations in all EU policies:[75] 'environmental protection requirements must be integrated into the definition and implementation of the Union's policies and activities, in particular with a view to promoting sustainable development'. In the provision that lists the principles of EU environmental law, sustainable development is not mentioned. Here there is reference only to the principle of a 'high level of protection', the precautionary principle, the prevention principle, the principle that environmental damage should be rectified at source, and the polluter pays principle.[76] Interestingly, the Sustainable Development Strategy of 2006 mentioned above not only lists some of these principles but also describes them as 'policy guiding principles'. These include the precautionary principle and the polluter pays principle.[77] This shows that these legal principles are considered to be important by giving substance – flesh and blood – to the concept of sustainable development.

The third constitutive document of the EU, the Charter of Fundamental Rights, refers to sustainable development in the preamble and in article 37.[78] The preamble states that the EU 'seeks to promote balanced and sustainable development and ensures free movement of persons, services, goods and capital, and the freedom of establishment'. Article 37 codifies the right to an adequate environment by imposing a duty on the organs of the EU: 'A high level of environmental protection and the improvement of the quality of the environment must be integrated into the policies of the Union and ensured in accordance with the principle of sustainable development'. The wording of this provision shows that the various constitutive documents of the EU do not use consistent terminology. The Charter and the preamble to the TEU refer to the 'principle' of sustainable development, whereas the TFEU, which lists all the 'principles' of environmental law, does not mention that principle but rather refers to sustainable development as an overarching policy goal. This is similar to article 3 TEU and the various policy documents on sustainable development.

The last issue is the way a range of the legal instruments of the EU refer to sustainable development. Many of these instruments refer to the principles mentioned in the treaties, including the principle of sustainable development. These references appear both in the recitals and in the substantive provisions. The Environmental Liability Directive, for example, states in recital 2 that 'the prevention and remedying of environmental damage should be implemented through the furtherance of the "polluter pays" principle, as indicated in the Treaty and in line with the principle of sustainable development'.[79] Article 1 of the Strategic Environmental Assessment Directive states that its objective is 'to provide for a high level of protection of the environment and to contribute to the integration of environmental considerations into the preparation and adoption of plans and programmes with a view to promoting sustainable development, by ensuring that, in accordance with this Directive, an environmental assessment is carried out of certain plans and programmes which are likely to have significant effects on the environment'.[80]

JUDICIAL ANALYSIS OF THE PRINCIPLE OF SUSTAINABLE DEVELOPMENT

1. Introduction

Given the widespread use of the concept of sustainable development in international law since 1992, it can be expected that courts and tribunals have started to refer to sustainable development in their judicial reasoning. This could shed more light on the legal status of the concept. Do courts consider sustainable development as a legal principle? This chapter does not give a complete overview of all relevant cases decided by international and domestic courts. Instead, it provides important examples that show how judicial institutions have integrated the principle of sustainable development into their judgments. The main focus is on international courts and tribunals – particularly the International Court of Justice, the Permanent Court of Arbitration, the International Tribunal on the Law of the Sea and the WTO Appellate Body. There then follow some references to the approach adopted by regional and domestic courts.

2. International Courts and Tribunals

(a) International Court of Justice (ICJ)

In its most important judgment in an environmental case so far, the ICJ relied heavily on 'the objective of sustainable development'.[81] In the *Pulp Mills* case between Argentina and Uruguay, decided in 2010, the court had to interpret the meaning of article 27 of the 1975 Statute of the River Uruguay. This stipulates that the 'right of each party to use the waters of the river, within its jurisdiction, for domestic, sanitary, industrial and agricultural purposes shall be exercised without prejudice to the application of the procedure laid down in Articles 7 to 12 when the use is liable to affect the regime of the river or the quality of its waters'.[82] Argentina argued that the range of legal principles to be applied to interpret the 1975 Statute included 'the principles of sustainable development, prevention, precaution and the need to carry out an environmental impact assessment'.[83]

The ICJ referred, first, to its previous order in this case in which it argued that use of the river 'should allow for sustainable development which takes account of "the need to safeguard the continued conservation of the river environment and the rights of economic development of the riparian State"'.[84] In this respect the court followed its 1997 decision in the *Danube Dam* case in which the court had stated that there is a need to reconcile economic development with protection of the environment – a need 'aptly expressed in the concept of sustainable development'.[85]

Based on these earlier references to sustainable development, the court found in the *Pulp Mills* case that the formulation of article 27 of the Statute reflected not only:

> the need to reconcile the varied interests of riparian States in a transboundary context and in particular in the use of a shared natural resource, but also the need to strike a balance between the use of the waters and the protection of the river consistent with the objective of sustainable development … Consequently, it is the opinion of the Court that Article 27 embodies this interconnectedness between equitable and reasonable utilization of a shared resource and the balance between economic development and environmental protection that is the essence of sustainable development.[86]

This is a remarkable and far-reaching interpretation by the court. It basically inserts the 'objective' of sustainable development into the text of the 1975 Statute.[87]

(b) Permanent Court of Arbitration

The most relevant decision of the Permanent Court of Arbitration (PCA) on the principle of sustainable development is the *Iron Rhine* arbitration between Belgium and the Netherlands. This case was about the reactivation of an abandoned railway line from Antwerp to Germany across Dutch territory. Belgium wanted to reactivate the railway line for economic purposes and relied upon the 1839 Treaty of Separation between the two states. The Treaty guaranteed continued use of the railway line, despite the separation. The Netherlands, on the other hand, had ecological objections because the track crossed several protected areas.[88]

In its award, the tribunal explicitly dealt with the principle of sustainable development – not only its content but also its legal status. The tribunal stated:[89]

> There is considerable debate as to what, within the field of environmental law, constitutes 'rules' or 'principles'; what is 'soft law'; and which environmental treaty law or principles have contributed to the development of customary international law. Without entering further into those controversies, the Tribunal notes that in all of these categories 'environment' is broadly referred to as including air, water, land, flora and fauna, natural ecosystems and sites, human health and safety, and climate. The emerging principles, whatever their current status, make reference to conservation, management, notions of prevention and of sustainable development, and protection for future generations.

Referring to the ICJ's use of the concept of sustainable development in the *Danube Dam* case, the tribunal then noted that 'environmental law and the law on development stand not as alternatives but as mutually reinforcing, integral concepts, which require that where development may cause significant harm to the environment there is a duty to prevent, or at least mitigate, such harm'. According to the tribunal, this duty had become a principle of general international law.[90]

This conclusion had far-reaching consequences for the final decision in this case because the tribunal, later in the award, referred back to the duty to prevent environmental damage in decisions on economic development: 'Today, in international environmental law, a growing emphasis is being put on the duty of prevention'.[91] As it was obvious that the proposed new use of the old railway would have a negative impact on the environment, the tribunal concluded that the 'reactivation of the Iron Rhine railway cannot be viewed in isolation from the environmental protection measures necessitated by the intended use of the railway line. These measures are to be fully integrated into the project and its costs'.[92]

(c) International Tribunal on the Law of the Sea

It has already been noted in relation to international fisheries instruments that the terms 'sustainable yield' and 'sustainable use' in the context of fisheries pre-date the rise of the concept of sustainable development and that a specific meaning has been attributed to them. It is no surprise that the principle of sustainable yield plays an important role in the various decisions by the International Tribunal on the Law of the Sea (ITLOS) on fisheries disputes.[93]

In a recent advisory opinion, the ITLOS expressed its view on the meaning of the term 'sustainable management' as laid down in the

Convention on the Determination of the Minimal Conditions for Access and Exploitation of Marine Resources within the Maritime Areas under Jurisdiction of the Member States of the Sub-Regional Fisheries Commission ('the MCA Convention'). The tribunal observed that the ultimate goal of sustainable management of fish stocks is to conserve and develop them as a viable and sustainable resource.[94] This means, first, that parties to the Convention have to assure the maintenance of shared stocks, through conservation and management measures; second, that they must take conservation and management measures based on the best scientific evidence available; and, third, that, when such evidence is insufficient, they must apply the precautionary approach.[95] In addition, 'conservation and management measures are to be designed to maintain or restore stocks at levels which can produce the maximum sustainable yield, as qualified by relevant environmental and economic factors, including the economic needs of coastal fishing communities'.[96]

On the one hand, the tribunal suggested that the states involved should develop a sustainable fisheries management regime and that this might include the development of responsible fisheries, aimed at ensuring the long-term sustainability of exploited stocks and stock restoration.[97] On the other hand, it is remarkable that no reference was made to sustainable development in non-fisheries cases in which environmental issues played a major role: such as the *MOX Plant* case, the *Singapore Land Reclamation* case and the *Arctic Sunrise* case.[98]

(d) WTO Appellate Body

Although, as noted earlier in this chapter, the debate about the integration of environmental objectives into trade law has been ongoing for many years without much progress, the WTO Appellate Body has made a landmark decision in relation to the principle of sustainable development. In the famous *US Shrimp Turtle* case, the Appellate Body used the reference to the objective of sustainable development in the preamble to justify an interpretation of all relevant WTO law in the light of the principle.

In this case the United States, as well as the European Community – now the European Union – asked the Appellate Body to take the principle into consideration in deciding the case, despite the use of different wording. The United States argued that an 'environmental purpose is fundamental to the application of Article XX, and such a purpose cannot be ignored, especially since the preamble to the Marrakesh Agreement Establishing the World Trade Organization acknowledges that the rules of trade should be "in accordance with the objective of sustainable development" and should seek to "protect and preserve the environment"'.[99]

Interestingly, the United States avoided using the term 'principle' but instead used the word 'objective' – an approach more consistent with the text of the preamble.

The European Community specifically referred to sustainable development as a principle: an approach – more or less – in line with EU law. As the Appellate Body itself said, 'the principle of sustainable development, also laid down in the first paragraph of the preamble to the WTO Agreement, as well as the precautionary principle, play an important role in the implementation of all EC policies'.[100] The Appellate Body followed these arguments and gave great weight to the paragraph of the preamble which refers to the objective of sustainable development.[101] In its words, 'as this preambular language reflects the intentions of negotiators of the WTO Agreement, we believe it must add colour, texture and shading to our interpretation of the agreements annexed to the WTO Agreement, in this case, the GATT 1994'.[102]

Colour, texture and shading! These may prove to be prescient for the future. What interpretative approach does the Appellate Body suggest? It is clear that the Appellate Body, at least in theory, allows for far-reaching interpretation of the WTO rules in the light of the objective of sustainable development. What this means becomes clear, for instance, when the Appellate Body discussed the interpretation of the term 'conservation of exhaustible natural resources' in article XX(g) of the GATT 1994. It did so in these words:

> Given the recent acknowledgement by the international community of the importance of concerted bilateral or multilateral action to protect living natural resources, and recalling the explicit recognition by WTO Members of the objective of sustainable development in the preamble of the WTO Agreement, we believe it is too late in the day to suppose that Article XX(g) of the GATT 1994 may be read as referring only to the conservation of exhaustible mineral or other non-living natural resources … We hold that, in line with the principle of effectiveness in treaty interpretation, measures to conserve exhaustible natural resources, whether living or non-living, may fall within Article XX.[103]

It is equally interesting to note that the Appellate Body, albeit in two footnotes, explained that the 'objective of sustainable development' basically means that economic and social development and environmental protection have to be integrated.[104] Despite this potentially far-reaching use of the principle or objective of sustainable development, judicial interpretation of the WTO rules makes it clear that in practice it is extremely difficult to integrate environmental protection measures into trade policies while at the same time complying with WTO rules on free trade.[105]

3. Regional and Domestic Courts

(a) Court of Justice of the European Union

Probably the most developed case law on the principles of environmental law at the regional level is that of the Court of Justice of the European Union (CJEU). This will not come as a surprise given that environmental principles have been firmly embedded in the various EU treaties. A review of the case law on these principles, however, shows that practically all cases have been decided by relying on more specific principles, such as the prevention principle and the precautionary principle.[106] The CJEU refers often to the principle of sustainable development – a search in the database shows 52 hits[107] – but these are almost always references to texts in treaties, directives or regulations that refer to the principle. There has been no further substantive discussion about the meaning of the principle or about the impact the principle has in the specific case.[108]

The CJEU has sometimes referred to the principle of sustainable development as laid down either in the treaties or in more specific legal instruments to underpin its interpretation of specific obligations. Consider this judicial comment in the *Green Network* case decided in 2014:

> Nevertheless, it is also important to consider that, as Article 1 of Directive 2001/77 makes clear, that directive seeks to promote an increase in the contribution of renewable energy sources to electricity production in the internal market for electricity. Recital 1 in the preamble to that directive emphasises that the potential for the exploitation of renewable energy sources is presently underused in the Community and it recognises the need to promote renewable energy sources as a priority measure, given that their exploitation contributes to environmental protection and sustainable development and can, in addition, also create local employment, have a positive impact on social cohesion, contribute to security of supply and make it possible to meet Kyoto targets more quickly.[109]

A case in which the 'objective' of sustainable development did play a major role was the relatively old *First Corporate Shipping* case decided in 2000. At that time, sustainable development was listed in article 2 of the EC Treaty as a goal of the European Community but clearly not as a principle. In this case, the court had to give a preliminary ruling on the question whether member states had to take into account economic and social interests when drafting a list of protected areas under the EU Habitats Directive.

In his opinion, the Advocate General of the court referred, first, to one of the recitals in the preamble to the Habitats Directive, which expressly states that the Directive, the aim of which is to 'promote the maintenance of biodiversity, taking account of economic, social, cultural and regional requirements', makes 'a contribution to the general objective of sustainable development'.[110] The Advocate General then explained what the concept of sustainable development means:

> The concept sustainable development does not mean that the interests of the environment must necessarily and systematically prevail over the interests defended in the context of the other policies pursued by the Community in accordance with Article 3 of the EC Treaty … On the contrary, it emphasises the necessary balance between various interests which sometimes clash, but which must be reconciled.[111]

The next question was how to reconcile these interests. After having referred to environmental policy documents and the Brundtland Report, the Advocate General referred to the integration principle, which offered a means of actual reconciliation:

> To reconcile these diverse interests in the context of sustainable development the Treaty on European Union introduced the principle of integration in article 130R(2) – now article 11 TFEU. That principle requires the Community legislature to conform with environmental protection requirements in the definition and implementation of other policies and actions. Integration of the environmental dimension is thus the basis of the strategy of sustainable development enshrined in both the Treaty on European Union and the Fifth Environment Programme.[112]

The Advocate General directed his attention to the second stage of the designation process, which takes place at the level of the EU agencies. In doing so, he identified the necessary steps in designating a protected area. Two obligations were imposed on the European Commission and its member states. The first was to observe 'the objective of sustainable development and the principle of integration' and the second was to ascertain 'whether or not the maintenance of human activities in the area concerned may be reconciled with the objective of conservation or restoration of natural habitats and wild fauna and flora, and drawing the necessary consequences'. Significantly, the references were to sustainable development and integration.

(b) Regional human rights courts

The principle of sustainable development does not in itself seem to play a major role in the case law that emerges from the various regional human rights instruments. This is particularly true of the European Court of Human Rights. This court does not explicitly refer to sustainable development in its extensive and impressive environmental case law.[113] It is somewhat different in the African region. In the *SERAC* case, which concerned the environmental impacts associated with oil production in Ogoniland in Nigeria, the African Commission on Human and Peoples' Rights explained the meaning and role of the right to a satisfactory environment laid down in article 24 of the African Charter on Human and Peoples' Rights. The Commission stated that article 24 requires states 'to take reasonable and other measures to prevent pollution and ecological degradation, to promote conservation, and to secure an ecologically sustainable development and use of natural resources'.

This interpretation suggests that the principle of sustainable development may be used as a means to reconcile the right to development and the right to a satisfactory environment. Significantly both of these rights have been directly incorporated in the African Charter.[114] Rather differently, cases emerging from the Inter-American Human Rights system do not seem to have paid a great deal of attention to the principle of sustainable development. However, a recent study concludes that the procedural rights that have been acknowledged in environmental cases enable local communities to direct major development projects in a more sustainable direction.[115]

(c) Domestic courts

It is not the purpose of this chapter to review systematically any relevant domestic case law. There are many countries in which courts have relied on the principle, notion or objective of sustainable development: for instance Brazil,[116] Argentina,[117] New Zealand[118] and Pakistan.[119] There is particular merit in discussing briefly the recent judgment by a Dutch court in the *Urgenda* case. This case shows how the principle of sustainable development can influence judicial reasoning on the issue of standing in a case where international environmental law – the UNFCCC, in this case – applies.

Urgenda is a citizen's platform. In legal terms it is a foundation with the aim 'to stimulate and accelerate the transition processes to a more sustainable society, beginning in the Netherlands'. In a public interest suit, the foundation sued the State of the Netherlands and asked the court to rule that current Dutch policies to reduce greenhouse gases are not strict enough and to order the state to achieve a larger reduction by 2020.

Because of the occurrence of the word 'sustainable society' in the foundation's bylaws and because the claim was partly brought on behalf of future generations, the court, when deciding on the foundation's standing, dealt with the principle of sustainable development but without calling it a principle.

In its analysis the court relied on two authoritative sources. The first was the focus on sustainable development in articles 2 and 3(4) of the United Nations Convention on Climate Change.[120] The second was the definition of 'sustainability' in the Brundtland Report.[121] The court accepted Urgenda's standing in this case in these words:

> In defending the right of not just the current but also the future generations to availability of natural resources and a safe and healthy living environment, it also strives for the interest of a sustainable society. This interest of a sustainable society is also formulated in the legal standard invoked by Urgenda for the protection against activities which, in its view, are not 'sustainable' and threaten to lead to serious threats to ecosystems and human societies.[122]

This example shows how references to sustainable development in international conventions – such as the UNFCCC – and even in non-binding documents – such as the Brundtland Report – can have an impact on judicial decisions in a domestic context.

ANALYSIS: CURRENT LEGAL STATUS AND THE POTENTIAL FUTURE ROLE OF THE PRINCIPLE OF SUSTAINABLE DEVELOPMENT

As predicted in the introduction to this chapter, the foregoing analysis, first, of internationally binding and non-legally binding instruments and, second, of judgments by international and domestic courts and tribunals discloses an increasing number of references to sustainable development. These references are not necessarily to the principle of sustainable development. Sustainable development is also regularly referred to as a concept, an objective or otherwise. Have these increasing references led to a stronger normative power and a stronger legal status of the principle? And, if so, what does this imply for environmental decision-making at the international level?

There is a relative consensus among legal scholars that the principle of sustainable development in and of itself cannot be used to solve complex environmental disputes. Sands and his colleagues, for example when discussing references to sustainable development in biodiversity related instruments, reached this conclusion: 'The fact that so many species and natural resources are in fact not sustainably managed illustrates the difficulty in translating the concept of sustainable development into a practical conservation tool'.[123] Interestingly, this statement of 'fact' suggests that the many references to sustainable development in the relevant instruments are difficult to implement rather than ignored. That the principle does not give sufficient guidance is also shown by Baetens in her analysis of the *Iron Rhine* arbitration. Both sides relied on the principle of sustainable development to support the legality of the state's conduct. Belgium argued that its request for reactivation of the railway line was motivated by a desire to protect the environment, for example because transportation across railroads is cleaner than air and road transport. The Netherlands equally invoked its pursuit of sustainable development as a legitimate ground for its decision to block the reactivation of the railway line for nature conservation purposes.[124]

Some commentators, it has already been noted, have argued that the concept of sustainable development should not be regarded as a legal principle. The author of this chapter in earlier commentary adopted this view by arguing that sustainable development should be seen as an ideal – or a value – that needs to be made more concrete through legal principles and legal rules.[125] Environmental principles such as the prevention principle, the precautionary principle and the polluter pays principle are principles that could play such an 'implementing' role.

The foregoing overview of the use of sustainable development in legal texts and in judicial interpretations indicates that such 'translation' of the concept into more concrete legal principles has emerged as a common practice. The role of the integration principle seems to have been especially important because this principle forces authorities actively to integrate environmental objectives into economic and developmental policies and decisions. Courts and drafters of treaties and of other legal instruments at the various levels of governance seem to regard sustainable development as the ultimate goal that can only be achieved when a number of more concrete principles and rules are applied. These include a precautionary approach or the precautionary principle; the requirement to carry out an environmental impact assessment; and the prevention principle.

The explanations given by many commentators of the meaning of the concept of sustainable development refer in addition to a series of principles or elements all of which are aimed at making the concept of sustainable development more concrete and more easily applicable in particular sets of circumstances. Consider three examples. Sands and his colleagues have distinguished four recurring 'legal elements of the concept of sustainable development'. These are the principle of intergenerational equity, the principle of sustainable or wise use, the principle of intragenerational equity and the principle of integration.[126] Birnie and her colleagues have listed the following elements of sustainable development: the integration principle, the right to development, the principle of sustainable utilization and intergenerational equity.[127] Schrijver, even more ambitiously, has come up with 'seven main elements of the concept of sustainable development'. These are the sustainable use of natural resources; sound macro-economic development; environmental protection; the time dimension – that is temporality, longevity and promptness; public participation and human rights; good governance; and integration and interrelatedness.[128]

There is much commonality among these principles and elements. In addition these lists link up nicely with the way drafters of legal texts and judicial institutions have dealt with the concept of sustainable development over recent years. On the one hand, it shows that sustainable development is not so vague that it has no legal meaning in decision-making processes. On the other hand, it shows that sustainable development becomes useful only when it is linked to more specific principles and rules. In practice, it has even become possible to develop detailed sets of indicators to measure sustainability.[129]

CONCLUSION

The question that forms the basis of this chapter – the status of the principle of sustainable development – has to be answered in the affirmative. Increased reference to sustainable development – sometimes as a principle but more often as an objective or a concept – has indeed led to its stronger normative power and its stronger legal status. The integration of environmental concerns into decision-making processes has been broadly accepted and it can authoritatively be seen as a firm legal duty. Although many commentators probably think that this process has not gone fast enough, it is the view of the author of this chapter that an extrapolation of the use of the principle of sustainable development will see a further increase of its impact upon judicial reasoning and upon how legal texts will be drafted in the near future.

NOTES

1. Fitzmaurice (2009, p. 67); Dupuy and Viñuales (2015, p. 79).
2. Bell and McGillivray (2006, p. 63).
3. Birnie, Boyle and Redgwell (2009, p. 127); Ellis (2008).
4. Epiney (2006, p. 27).
5. Verschuuren (2003, p. 37).
6. Lowe (1999, p. 31); Marceau and Morosini (2013, p. 60).
7. Schrijver (2008, p. 220).
8. Sands et al. (2012, pp. 208, 217).
9. Bosselmann (2013, p. 43);
10. There is no attempt to provide a full list here but instead to refer to some selected sources that deal with the principle of sustainable development in a comprehensive way with specific and detailed attention to its legal status: Bosselmann (2013); Cordonier Segger and Khalfan (2004); Handl (1995); Malanczuk (1995); Matsui (1995); Sands et al. (2012); Schrijver (2008); Verschuuren (2003); Voigt (2009).
11. Authors often refer to a German book on forestry by Von Carlowitz (1713) as the first publication in which sustainable production is advocated. When focusing on legal sources, late nineteenth-century international agreements in the sphere of hunting are often mentioned as early appearances of the idea of sustainability: see, for instance, Sands et al. (2012, p. 206).
12. Meadows et al. (1972, p. 157).
13. Ibid. (p. 22).
14. Goldsmith et al. (1972, para.166).
15. Declaration of the United Nations Conference on the Human Environment, Stockholm, 16 June 1972, UN Doc. A/CONF. 48/14/REV. 1 (1972).
16. Ibid., preambular paras 3 and 6 respectively.
17. UNEP Governing Council Decision 20(III) of 2 May 1975.
18. The terms 'sustainable utilisation' and 'sustainable development' were explicitly mentioned in the 1983 International Tropical Timber Agreement and the 1985 ASEAN Agreement respectively; Sands et al. (2012, p. 211).
19. World Commission on Environment and Development (1987, p. 8).
20. Ibid. (p. 46).
21. Ibid. (p. ix).
22. Ibid. (p. 8).
23. Ibid. (p. 8).
24. Distr. Gen. A/Conf. 151/5/Rev. 1, Rio de Janeiro, 13 June 1992.
25. Distr. Gen. A/CONF. 199/20.
26. This outcome document was endorsed by the UN General Assembly in Resolution 66/288 of 27 July 2012, Distr. Gen. A/RES/66/288.
27. Convention on Biological Diversity (CBD) (Rio de Janeiro, 5 June 1992), (1992) 31 ILM 818, entered into force 29 December 1993.
28. United Nations Framework Convention on Climate Change (UNFCCC) (New York, 9 May 1992), (1992) 31 ILM 849, entered into force 21 March 1994.
29. CBD, art.2. This definition was later copied in other conventions, such as the Agreement for the Conservation of African-Eurasian Migratory Waterbirds (The Hague, 16 June 1995), (1995) 6 YIEL 504, entered into force 16 June 1995.
30. Cartagena Protocol on Biosafety to the Convention on Biological Diversity (Cartagena, 29 January 2000), (2000) 39 ILM 1027, entered into force 11 September 2003, art.12.
31. Nagoya Protocol on Access to Genetic Resources and the Fair and Equitable Sharing of Benefits Arising from their Utilization to the Convention on Biological

Diversity (Nagoya, 29 October 2010), UNEP/CBD/COP/DEC/X/1, entered into force 12 October 2014, art.9.

32. Article 3(5) reads: 'The Parties should cooperate to promote a supportive and open international economic system that would lead to sustainable economic growth and development in all Parties'.
33. UNFCCC, art.4(1)(d).
34. UNFCCC, art.4(2)(a).
35. Kyoto Protocol to the United Nations Convention on Climate Change, UN Doc. FCCC/CP/1997/7/Add. 1 (Kyoto, 10 December 1997), (1998) 37 ILM 22, entered into force 16 February 2005.
36. Kyoto Protocol, art.12(2): 'The purpose of the clean development mechanism shall be to assist Parties not included in Annex I in achieving sustainable development and in contributing to the ultimate objective of the Convention'.
37. Distr. Gen. FCCC/KP/CMP/2005/8/Add.1, 30 March 2006, Decision 3/CMP.1, Modalities and procedures for a clean development mechanism as defined in Article 12 of the Kyoto Protocol, Annex at 15.
38. There has been much research into this issue. By way of example, reference is made to Sutter and Parreño (2007, pp. 75–90) who concluded: 'While a large part (72%) of the total portfolio's expected Certified Emission Reductions (CERs) are likely to represent real and measurable emission reductions, less than 1% are likely to contribute significantly to sustainable development in the host country'. Authors used three sustainability criteria for their assessment: employment generation, distribution of CER returns and improvement in local air quality.
39. See UNFCCC's website at http://climate-l.iisd.org/news/unfccc-publishes-tool-for-elaborating-cdms-sustainable-development-benefits/.
40. United Nations Convention on the Law of the Sea (UNCLOS) (Montego Bay, 10 December 1982), (1982) 21 ILM 1261, entered into force 16 November 1994, art.61. The same applies to the high seas: art.119.
41. Maunder (2008, pp. 2292–6).
42. Ibid.
43. Agreement for the Implementation of the Provisions of the United Nations Convention on the Law of the Sea of 10 December 1982 relating to the Conservation and Management of Straddling Fish Stocks and Highly Migratory Fish Stocks (New York, 4 August 1995), (2003) 2167 UNTS 3, entered into force 11 December 2001.
44. Ibid., art.2.
45. The Convention for the Protection of the Marine Environment of the North-East Atlantic (Paris, 22 September 1992), (1993) 32 ILM 1072, entered into force 25 March 1998. Annex V entered into force 30 August 2000. In its arts 2 and 3(1)(b)(iii), the Annex takes over CBD terminology including the phrase 'conservation and sustainable use of biological diversity'.
46. Resolution 69/109, Distr. Gen. A/RES/69/109, 6 February 2015.
47. Convention on Persistent Organic Pollutants (Stockholm, 22 May 2001), (2001) 40 ILM 532, entered into force 17 May 2004, art.13(4).
48. UN Convention on the Law of the Non-navigational Uses of International Watercourses (New York, 21 May 1997), (1997) 36 ILM 700, entered into force 17 August 2014, art.5.
49. Protocol on Strategic Environmental Assessment to the Espoo Convention on Environmental Impact Assessment in a Transboundary Context (Kiev, 21 May 2003), (2003) UN Doc. ECE/MP.EIA/2003/2, 85, entered into force 11 July 2010, art.1.

50. Convention on Civil Liability for Damage Resulting from Activities Dangerous to the Environment (Lugano, 21 June 1993), (1993) 32 ILM 1228, not yet entered into force.
51. Protocol to the Convention on the Prevention of Marine Pollution by Dumping of Wastes and Other Matter (London, 7 November 1996), (1997) 36 ILM 1, entered into force 24 March 2006.
52. Convention on Access to Information, Public Participation and Decision-Making and Access to Justice in Environmental Matters (Aarhus, 25 June 1998), (1999) 38 ILM 517, entered into force 30 October 2001.
53. Agreement Establishing the World Trade Organization (WTO) (Marrakesh, 15 April 1994), (1994) 33 ILM 1125, entered into force 1 January 1995.
54. de Sadeleer (2002, p. 343). For the latest developments in the Doha Round negotiations, see the WTO website https://www.wto.org/english/tratop_e/envir_e/envir_negotiations_e.htm.
55. Sands et al. (2012, p. 867).
56. Constitutive Act of the African Union, adopted by the 36th ordinary session of the assembly of heads of state, Lomé (Togo), 11 July 2000, art.3(j).
57. See in more detail Scholtz and Verschuuren (2015, pp. 102, 116).
58. For a full overview see de Windt and Orellana (2015, p. 131).
59. Inter-American Program for Sustainable Development, adopted 11 May 2007, OEA/XLIII.1.
60. Declaration of Santo Domingo for the Sustainable Development of the Americas, adopted 19 November 2010, OEA/Ser.K/XVIII.2.
61. ASEAN Declaration on Environmental Sustainability, adopted 20 November 2007; http://www.asean.org/news/item/asean-declaration-on-environmental-sustainability.
62. Boer (2015, p. 215).
63. Sustainable development was first acknowledged as an overarching objective of EU policies in the Treaty of Amsterdam amending the Treaty establishing the European Community, (1997) OJ C 340/173, introducing this objective in art.2 of the EC Treaty.
64. Consolidated version of the Treaty on European Union, (2012) OJ C 326/13: 'Determined to promote economic and social progress for their peoples, taking into account the principle of sustainable development and within the context of the accomplishment of the internal market and of reinforced cohesion and environmental protection, and to implement policies ensuring that advances in economic integration are accompanied by parallel progress in other fields'.
65. TEU, art.3(3): 'The Union shall establish an internal market. It shall work for the sustainable development of Europe based on balanced economic growth and price stability, a highly competitive social market economy, aiming at full employment and social progress, and a high level of protection and improvement of the quality of the environment. It shall promote scientific and technological advance …'.
66. TEU, art.3(5): 'In its relations with the wider world, the Union shall uphold and promote its values and interests and contribute to the protection of its citizens. It shall contribute to peace, security, the sustainable development of the Earth, solidarity and mutual respect among peoples, free and fair trade, eradication of poverty and the protection of human rights, in particular the rights of the child, as well as to the strict observance and the development of international law, including respect for the principles of the United Nations Charter'.
67. TEU, art.21(2)(d) and (f), respectively.
68. Jans and Vedder (2012, p. 8).
69. Epiney (2006, p. 27).
70. European Commission, *A Sustainable Europe for a Better World: A European Union Strategy for Sustainable Development*, COM(2001)264 final.

71. European Council, DOC 10917/06.
72. European Commission, *Mainstreaming sustainable development into EU policies: 2009 Review of the European Union Strategy for Sustainable Development*, COM(2009) 400 final. For an overview and links to all relevant EU documents on the sustainable development strategy, see http://ec.europa.eu/environment/eussd/.
73. Ibid (p. 3).
74. European Commission, *Europe 2020. A strategy for smart, sustainable and inclusive growth*, COM(2010) 2020. One of the policy objectives, for instance, is to create a resource-efficient Europe 'to help decouple economic growth from the use of resources, support the shift towards a low carbon economy, increase the use of renewable energy sources, modernise our transport sector and promote energy efficiency'.
75. Consolidated version of the Treaty on the Functioning of the European Union, (2012) OJ C 326/47.
76. TFEU, art.191(2). See extensively, Verschuuren (2003) and de Sadeleer (2002).
77. European Council, DOC 10917/06, at 5. These principles were copied from the European Commission's *Draft Declaration on Guiding Principles for Sustainable Development*, COM(2005) 218 final.
78. Charter of Fundamental Rights of the European Union, (2012) OJ C 326/391.
79. Directive 2004/35/EC of 21 April 2004 on environmental liability with regard to the prevention and remedying of environmental damage, OJ L 143/56.
80. Directive 2001/42/EC of 27 June 2001 on the assessment of the effects of certain plans and programmes on the environment, OJ L 197/30.
81. For a much broader overview of the ICJ's case law, see Schrijver (2015).
82. *Pulp Mills* case (para.103).
83. Ibid. (para.55).
84. Ibid. (para.75).
85. *Danube Dam* case (paras 140–1).
86. *Pulp Mills* case (para.177).
87. See in more detail, Tladi (2015).
88. See in more detail, Baetens (2015).
89. *Iron Rhine* arbitration (para.58).
90. Ibid. (para.59).
91. Ibid. (para.222).
92. Ibid. (para.223).
93. E.g. *Southern Bluefin Tuna* cases (*New Zealand v Japan; Australia v Japan*), Order of 27 August 1999, cases no.3 and 4.
94. SRFC Advisory Opinion (2015, para.190).
95. Ibid. (para.208).
96. Ibid.
97. Ibid. (para.198).
98. *MOX Plant* case (*Ireland v United Kingdom*), Order of 3 December 2001, case no.10; Case concerning land reclamation by Singapore in and around the Straits of Johor (*Malaysia v Singapore*), Order of 8 October 2003, case no.12; *'Arctic Sunrise'* case (*Kingdom of The Netherlands v Russian Federation*), Order of 22 November 2013, case no.22. For a detailed overview of all cases, see Stephens and Jaeckel (2015).
99. *US Shrimp Turtle* case (para.12).
100. Ibid. (para.67).
101. Ibid. (para.129).
102. Ibid. (para.153).
103. Ibid. (para.131).

104. Ibid. (para.129) where the Appellate Body referred to principle 4 of the Rio Declaration. On the principle of integration and the WTO, see more extensively Grosse Ruse-Khan (2015).
105. Gehring (2015).
106. Avilés (2012, pp. 32–3). Although he sets out to discuss case law on the 'principle of sustainable development', Avilés discusses case law only on other principles,
107. Text search on 'sustainable development' in all judgments by the CJEU (excluding opinions of the Advocate General), 31 July 2015 through the CJEU case law search form, http://curia.europa.eu/juris. Note that not all judgments are available in English, so the search does not cover all judgments.
108. Recent examples are: Case C-369/14 *Sommer Antriebs- und Funktechnik v Rademacher Geräte-Elektronik*, 16 July 2015; Case C-461/13 *Bund für Umwelt und Naturschutz Deutschland v Bundesrepublik Deutschland*, 1 July 2015.
109. *Green Network* case (para.109).
110. *First Corporate Shipping* case (Advocate General, para.53).
111. Ibid. (para.54).
112. Ibid. (para.57).
113. Verschuuren (2015, pp. 363, 385).
114. Scholtz and Verschuuren (2015, p. 116).
115. Meijknecht (2015, p. 219).
116. Sarlet and Fensterseifer (2009, p. 257).
117. Carballo (2009, p. 283).
118. Bosselmann (2009, p. 368).
119. Hassan and Hassan (2009, p. 396).
120. *Urgenda* case (para.2.38).
121. Ibid. (para.4.8).
122. Ibid.
123. Sands et al. (2012, p. 211).
124. Baetens (2015).
125. Verschuuren (2005).
126. Sands et al. (2012, p. 207).
127. Birnie et al. (2009, p. 116.)
128. Schrijver (2008, p. 208).
129. Many different instruments to measure sustainability have been developed and are applied in practice. See the overview provided through http://www.measuring sustainability.org.

REFERENCES

Ambrus, M. (2012), 'The Precautionary Principle and a Fair Allocation of the Burden of Proof in International Environmental Law', *Review of European, Comparative and International Environmental Law* 21, 259–270.

Avilés, L.A. (2012), 'Sustainable development and the legal protection of the environment in Europe', *Sustainable Development Law and Policy* 12(3), 29.

Baetens, F. (2015), 'The Iron Rhine case: on the right track to sustainable development?' in M.C. Cordonier Segger, Y. Saito and C.G. Weeramantry (eds), *Sustainable Development Principles in the Decisions of International Courts and Tribunals 1992–2012* (New York, Routledge).

Bell, S. and D. McGillivray (2006), *Environmental Law* (6th edn, Oxford, Oxford University Press).

Bergkamp, Lucas and Lawerence Koga (2013), 'Trade, the Precautionary Principle, and Modern Regulatory Process: Regulatory Convergence in the Transatlantic Trade and Investment Partnership', *European Journal of Risk* 4, 493–507.

Beyerlin, U. (1996), 'The Concept of Sustainable Development', in R. Wolfrum (ed.), *Enforcing Environmental Standards: Economic Mechanisms as Viable Means?* (New York, Springer).

Birnie, P., A. Boyle and C.I. Redgwell (2009), *International Law and the Environment* (3rd edn, Oxford, Oxford University Press).

Boer, B. (2015), 'Introduction to ASEAN regional environmental law' in W. Scholtz and J. Verschuuren (eds), *Regional Environmental Law* (Cheltenham: Edward Elgar).

Bosselmann, K. (2009), 'New Zealand', in L.J. Kotzé and A.R. Paterson (eds), *The Role of the Judiciary in Environmental Governance. Comparative Perspectives* (Deventer, Wolters Kluwer).

Bosselmann, K. (2013), *The Principle of Sustainability. Transforming Law and Governance* (Farnham, Ashgate).

Carballo, J. (2009), 'Argentina', in L.J. Kotzé and A.R. Paterson, *The Role of the Judiciary in Environmental Governance. Comparative Perspectives* (Deventer, Wolters Kluwer).

Cordonier Segger, M.C. and A. Khalfan (2004), *Sustainable Development Law: Principles, Practices and Prospects* (Oxford, Oxford University Press).

Cordonier Segger, M.C., Y. Saito and C.G. Weeramantry (eds), (2015), *Sustainable Development Principles in the Decisions of International Courts and Tribunals 1992–2012* (New York, Routledge).

de Sadeleer, N. (2002), *Environmental Principles. From Political Slogans to Legal Rules* (Oxford, Oxford University Press).

de Waart, P.J.I.M. (ed.), *Sustainable Development and Good Governance* (Leiden, Martinus Nijhoff).

de Windt, C.S. and M.A. Orellana (2015), 'Introduction to environmental law in the Americas', in W. Scholtz and J. Verschuuren (eds), *Regional Environmental Law* (Cheltenham, Edward Elgar).

Dupuy, P-M. and J.E. Viñuales (2015), *International Environmental Law* (Cambridge, Cambridge University Press).

Ellis, J. (2008), 'Sustainable development as a legal principle: a rhetorical analysis' (SSRN-paper 2008; http://ssrn.com/abstract=1319360; also published in H.R. Fabri, R. Wolfrum and J. Goglin (eds), (2008), *Select Proceedings of the European Society of International Law*, vol.2 (Oxford, Hart Publishing).

Epiney, A. (2006), 'Environmental Principles' in R. Macrory (ed.), *Reflections on 30 Years of EU Environmental Law* (Europa Law Publishing).

Fitzmaurice, M. (2009), *Contemporary Issues in International Environmental Law* (Cheltenham, Edward Elgar).

Gehring, M. (2015), 'The WTO regime and disputes', in M.C. Cordonier Segger, Y. Saito and C.G. Weeramantry (eds), *Sustainable Development Principles in the Decisions of International Courts and Tribunals 1992–2012* (New York, Routledge).

Goldsmith, E., R. Allen, M. Allaby, J. Davoll and S. Lawrence (1972), 'A Blueprint for Survival', 2 *The Ecologist* 1.

Grosse Ruse-Khan, (2015), 'The principle of integration in WTO/TRIPS jurisprudence', in M.C. Cordonier Segger, Y. Saito and C.G. Weeramantry (eds), *Sustainable Development Principles in the Decisions of International Courts and Tribunals 1992–2012* (New York, Routledge).

Handl, G. (1995), 'Sustainable Development: General Rules versus Specific Obligations', in W. Lang (ed.), *Sustainable Development and International Law* (London, Graham & Trotman).

Hassan, P. and J. Hassan (2009), 'Pakistan', in L.J. Kotzé and A.R. Paterson, *The Role of the Judiciary in Environmental Governance. Comparative Perspectives* (Deventer, Wolters Kluwer).
Jans, J.H. and H.H.B. Vedder (2012), *European Environmental Law after Lisbon* (4th edn, New York, Europa Law Publishing).
Kotzé, L.J. and A.R. Paterson (2009), *The Role of the Judiciary in Environmental Governance. Comparative Perspectives* (Deventer, Wolters Kluwer).
Lowe, V. (1999), 'Sustainable Development and Unsustainable Arguments', in A. Boyle and D. Freestone (eds), *International Law and Sustainable Development: Past Achievements and Future Challenges* (Oxford, Oxford University Press).
Malanczuk, P. (1995), 'Sustainable Development: Some Critical Thoughts in the Light of the Rio Conference', in K. Ginther, E. Denters and P.J.I.M. de Waart (eds), *Sustainable Development and Good Governance* (Leiden, Martinus Nijhoff).
Marceau, G. and F. Morosini (2013), 'The Status of Sustainable Development in the Law of the World Trade Organization', in U. Celli Jr, M. Basso and A. do Amaral Jr (eds), *Arbitragem E Comércio Internacional. Estudos em Homenagem a Luiz Olavo Baptista* (Montreal, Quartier Latin).
Matsui, Y. (1995), 'The Road to Sustainable Development: Evolution of the Concept of Sustainable Development in the UN', in K. Ginther, E. Denters and P.J.I.M. de Waart (eds), *Sustainable Development and Good Governance* (Leiden, Martinus Nijhoff).
Maunder, M.N. (2008), 'Maximum Sustainable Yield', 5 *Encyclopedia of Ecology* 2292–6.
Meadows, D.H., D.L. Meadows, J. Randers and W.W. Behrens III (1972), *The Limits to Growth* (Milford, Connecticut, Universe Books).
Meijknecht, A. (2015), 'The contribution of the Inter-American human rights system to sustainable development', in W. Scholtz and J. Verschuuren (eds), *Regional Environmental Law* (Cheltenham, Edward Elgar).
Sands, Ph., J. Peel, A. Fabra and R. MacKenzie (2012), *Principles of International Environmental Law* (3rd edn, Cambridge, Cambridge University Press).
Sarlet, I. and T. Fensterseifer (2009), 'Brazil', in L.J. Kotzé and A.R. Paterson, *The Role of the Judiciary in Environmental Governance. Comparative Perspectives* (Deventer, Wolters Kluwer).
Scholtz, W. and J. Verschuuren (2015) (eds), *Regional Environmental Law* (Cheltenham, Edward Elgar).
Schrijver, N. (2008), *The Evolution of Sustainable Development in International Law: Inception, Meaning and Status* (Hague, Hague Academy of International Law).
Schrijver, N. (2015), 'An overview of the jurisprudence of the International Court of Justice', in M.C. Cordonier Segger, Y. Saito and C.G. Weeramantry (eds), *Sustainable Development Principles in the Decisions of International Courts and Tribunals 1992–2012* (New York, Routledge).
Stephens, T. and A. Jaeckel (2015), 'The interpretation of sustainable development principles in ITLOS', in M.C. Cordonier Segger, Y. Saito and C.G. Weeramantry (eds), *Sustainable Development Principles in the Decisions of International Courts and Tribunals 1992–2012* (New York, Routledge).
Sutter, Ch. and J.C. Parreño (2007), 'Does the current Clean Development Mechanism (CDM) deliver its sustainable development claim? An analysis of officially registered CDM projects', 84 *Climatic Change* 75–90.
Tladi, D. (2015), 'The principles of sustainable development in the Case Concerning Pulp Mills on the River Uruguay', in M.C. Cordonier Segger, Y. Saito and C.G. Weeramantry (eds), *Sustainable Development Principles in the Decisions of International Courts and Tribunals 1992–2012* (New York, Routledge).
Verschuuren, J. (2003), *Principles of Environmental Law. The Ideal of Sustainable Development and the Role of Principles of International, European, and National Environmental Law* (Baden-Baden, Nomos).

Verschuuren, J. (2015), 'Contribution of the case law of the European Court of Human Rights to sustainable development in Europe', in W. Scholtz and J. Verschuuren (eds), *Regional Environmental Law* (Cheltenham, Edward Elgar).

Voigt, Ch. (2009), *Sustainable Development as a Principle of International Law. Resolving Conflicts between Climate Measures and WTO Law* (Leiden, Martinus Nijhoff).

Von Carlowitz (1713), *Sylvicultura oeconomica, oder haußwirthliche Nachricht und Naturmäßige Anweisung zur wilden Baum-Zucht.*

World Commission on Environment and Development (1987), *Our Common Future* (Oxford, Oxford University Press).

CASES

Danube Dam case: International Court of Justice, Gabčíkovo-Nagymaros Project (Hungary/Slovakia), Judgment, ICJ Reports 1997, 78.

First Corporate Shipping case: Case C-371/98 *First Corporate Shipping*, Court of Justice of the EU, 7 March 2000.

Green Network case: Case C-66/13 *Green Network*, Court of Justice of the EU, 26 November 2014.

Iron Rhine arbitration: Permanent Court of Arbitration, Belgium/Netherlands ('Iron Rhine Arbitration'), Award of the arbitral tribunal, 24 May 2005.

Pulp Mills case: Pulp Mills on the River Uruguay (Argentina/Uruguay), International Court of Justice, ICJ Reports 2010, 14.

SERAC case: *African Commission on Human and Peoples' Rights, Social and Economic Rights Action Centre (SERAC) and another v Nigeria* (2001) AHRLR 60 (ACHPR, 2001).

SRFC Advisory Opinion: International Tribunal for the Law of the Sea, Request for an advisory opinion submitted by the Sub-Regional Fisheries Commission (SRFC), Advisory opinion of 2 April 2015, case no.21.

Urgenda case: District Court The Hague, *Urgenda Foundation v The State the Netherlands*, 24 June 2015, ECLI:NL:RBDHA:2015:7196.

US Shrimp Turtle case: WTO Appellate body, United States – Import prohibition of certain shrimp and shrimp products, WT/DS58/AB/R, 12 October 1998, Rep. AB-1998-4.

12. The concept of the common heritage of mankind

Prue Taylor

INTRODUCTION

The 'common heritage of mankind' (CHM) is a controversial legal concept.[1] The controversial issues include its scope, content and status, together with its relationship with other legal concepts. Despite this controversy and a lack of clear state practice, CHM remains a pivotal concept. It attempts to change traditional international law radically. Its original purpose was to move the law from a competitive system that reflected the national interests of powerful states to one that requires global cooperation for the benefit of all humanity. At the same time it attempts to overcome the territorial obsession[2] that remains at the core of international environmental law. Ecological systems are an integrated but complex whole that transcend legal and political jurisdictions. Accordingly, ecological protection, social equity and peace are central to the concept of CHM. In practice the concept represents a limitation on the exercise by states of their rights of sovereignty – a radical change. Notwithstanding its critics, escalating global ecological degradation, ongoing inability to arrest the tragedy of the commons[3] and creeping sovereignty all ensure the continued relevance of CHM. This is reflected in continual efforts to apply CHM to natural and cultural heritage, marine living resources, global ecological systems – such as the atmosphere – and, at the highest level of integration, the entire Earth System.

This chapter proceeds on the basis that, although uncertainty exists regarding CHM's exact legal status outside specific treaty regimes, it can be considered an emerging concept of international environmental law.[4] The chapter follows this structure:

- A brief overview of some of the core principles of international environmental law
- A discussion of the origins of CHM as a legal concept
- A summary of how CHM is incorporated into key treaty regimes
- An analysis of the specific elements of CHM

- An assessment of the normative foundations of CHM
- A review of how CHM is and can be applied in practice.

The terms 'common heritage of mankind' and CHM are used in this chapter although the gender-neutral words 'humankind' and 'humanity' are sometimes used elsewhere instead of mankind. While gender-neutral terms are preferable, 'mankind' is used here to avoid any confusion between this chapter and other references. Equally, it is not inherently an anthropocentric concept, despite its terminology.[5]

THE RELEVANT PRINCIPLES OF INTERNATIONAL ENVIRONMENTAL LAW

1. The Development of the Concept of State Sovereignty

State sovereignty is one of the cornerstones of international law. The traditional interpretation is that states have the absolute and independent right to regulate their own internal affairs and external relations without interference. In the specific context of the environment, state sovereignty is expressed as the principle of 'permanent sovereignty over natural resources'. Thus states have the sovereign right to exploit the resources under their jurisdiction according to their own policies. The 1972 Stockholm Declaration on the Human Environment was the first international document to balance 'permanent sovereignty over natural resources' with an expression of legal responsibility for the environment. Principle 21 provides:

> States have … the sovereign right to exploit their own resources pursuant to their own policies, and the responsibility to ensure that activities within their jurisdiction and control do not cause damage to the environment of other States or of areas beyond the limits of natural jurisdiction.

This formulation of the principle of state responsibility for transboundary environmental harm has been repeated many times in a variety of conventions and declarations.[6] It has generally been accepted as a rule of customary international environmental law and is often referred to as the 'do no harm' or the 'responsibility to not cause environmental damage' principle.[7]

International environmental law has developed rapidly since the 1972 Stockholm Declaration. The 1992 Rio Declaration on Environment and Development sets out a number of core principles for environmental governance of varying legal status.[8] The following general rules or principles complement the responsibility not to cause transboundary harm. However, their legal status, interpretation and impact in particular circumstances remain open to debate:[9]

- the principle of preventive action
- the principle of cooperation
- the principle of sustainable development
- the precautionary principle
- the polluter pays principle
- common but differentiated responsibility.

2. Towards Recognition of Common Interests

As the scale of ecological degradation increases, nation states and international agencies are increasingly developing legal frameworks to coordinate common global, regional and national responses. Given the complexities of dealing with global and transboundary ecological harm, multi-lateral environmental agreements (MEAs) have become the most prominent legal instrument. In this context, state sovereignty means that MEAs are only binding with the consent of individual states. States are, therefore, free to give or withhold their consent, or to withdraw consent, in accordance with their own evaluation of their national interest. The role of non-state actors in the 'international community of states' remains restricted. There are limited exceptions to the requirement for consent – the doctrine of consent. For example, obligations either formulated in an MEA or evident in state practice may become legally binding if one of two conditions is satisfied. The first is where there is sufficient consensus among states to create a rule of customary international law. The second is when obligations express a universally accepted ethical concept of normative value and have attained social legitimacy as a legal norm from which states cannot derogate – *jus cogens*. These are the principles and rules from which the concept of CHM has emerged.

What are some of the practical consequences of this framework? Fundamentally this view of international environmental law reflects the hallmarks of the *inter-state* Westphalian system that aims to balance or mediate the competing claims of sovereign states. As law makers, states are free to develop whatever law reflects their individual values or interests or their definition of collective state interests. Moreover, states are the law enforcers and are therefore free to choose whether or not to enforce. In the absence of clear treaty-based obligations and enforcement mechanisms, states must rely on a violation of *their* sovereign rights. In the case of the 'do no harm' principle, there are serious limitations with this system. A state's rights to use its territory and natural systems are limited only when serious transboundary harm is inflicted on a neighbouring state. The international community of states must tolerate harm below the legal threshold. As a consequence, harm to shared global ecological systems – often referred to as the 'global commons' – and harm to ecological systems beyond national jurisdiction – often referred to as 'common areas' or the 'international commons' – do not fit within this legal framework.

3. Towards the Management of Common Areas and Global Ecological Systems

The foregoing analysis does not lead to the conclusion that there is no international environmental legal framework of rights and obligations applicable to common areas beyond national jurisdiction – for example, the high seas, Antarctica and outer space – or to global ecological systems – for example, the oceans, the global atmosphere and biodiversity. However, it will be demonstrated later that these frameworks not only reflect the limitations of the concepts just discussed but also prioritize the need to reconcile competing sovereign rights. In a contemporary context, these are often presented as the competing imperatives of economic development through resource use, on the one hand, and environmental protection, on the other hand.

The current climate change arrangements are illustrative of these problems in the context of global ecological systems. The ultimate objective of the United Nations Framework Convention on Climate Change (UNFCCC) is 'stabilization of greenhouse gas concentrations in the atmosphere at a level that would prevent dangerous anthropogenic interference with the climate system'.[10] Its achievement is now totally dependent upon the implementation of nationally determined mitigation contributions of states within a treaty framework of uncertain legal force. 'Nationally determined contributions' (NDCs) form the basis of a legal regime to replace the Kyoto Protocol.[11] The NDCs that states 'offer' are based largely on their evaluation of their own national economic interests. States are not currently required to demonstrate how their NDCs are a fair contribution to the level of carbon dioxide reductions needed to prevent the rise in global atmospheric temperatures from exceeding 1.5 to 2 degrees Celsius. It is commonly accepted that the NDCs will not collectively add up to sufficient reductions. As a consequence, one of the most fundamental ecological challenges – protection of the global atmosphere and its climate stability function – is being treated as a pollution control problem. States are acting collectively through cooperation in a very 'weak' or 'thin' sense. This is because it is impossible to address climate change functionally in the absence of a stated level of collective action. Additionally it is difficult legally – if not impossible – for states to use the 'no harm' principle to protect their territories and citizens.[12]

International law regimes for common areas and their resources and for shared natural systems such as international watercourses demonstrate a similar form of weak cooperation. Common areas and resources lie beyond the jurisdiction of individual states. All states have access to them and equal rights to use them while they remain international common areas. Furthermore, a state cannot impose a particular regime for its use or protection. As a consequence, the obligations consensually undertaken by states represent *their* individual and collective goals or interests. While this approach – cooperation in pursuit of the common interests of states – may historically have been sufficient to deliver some level of environmental protection, it is now clearly inadequate. As Judge Weeramantry remarked in the dispute between two states about the use and protection of the Danube river (the *Danube Dam* case):

> International environmental law will need to proceed beyond weighing … rights and obligations … within a closed compartment of individual State self-interest, unrelated to the global concerns of humanity as a whole.[13]

4. Towards CHM

These examples point to a key issue confronting international law: when and to what extent can states be required to act beyond either their self-interest or beyond what they have accepted as their collective interests, so as to prioritize and act consistently with the common interests of all humanity and all life on Earth? As Brunnée notes, this constitutes a very different conception of common interests. To take this articulation of common interests beyond a rhetorical or aspirational statement, states must become:

> facilitators of solutions and their actions will be measured not simply against their individual and collective goals but also against 'the greater interests of humanity and planetary welfare'.[14]

This is the fundamental question that CHM seeks to answer. It will be argued later in this chapter that CHM has emerged as one of most developed ethical and legal 'manifestations' of the common interest of humanity. It is a contribution to the creation of a new international legal order. At the centre of this new international legal order is:

> a benefit for all mankind that can be obtained only by international cooperation and obligations by all governments, even if they receive no immediate return.[15]

When a CHM regime is in place, states become charged with a new legal responsibility. This is to 'act on behalf of all mankind and in its interest'.[16] It is for this reason that CHM is considered the most developed form of international environmental trust.[17]

THE ORIGINS OF CHM AS A LEGAL CONCEPT

Legal discussion of CHM usually begins with the 1967 speech of Maltese ambassador Arvid Pardo to the United Nations. In this speech he proposed that the seabed and ocean floor, beyond national jurisdiction, be declared the common heritage of mankind. This was an important event that triggered the negotiation of the 1982 Law of the Sea Convention (UNCLOS III) and other legal developments that subsequently earned UNCLOS III the status of the 'constitution for the oceans' and Arvid Pardo the title 'father of the law of the sea'.[18] As Tuerk notes: 'this proposal was the basis for the idea of the [CHM] being enshrined in international legal instruments and becoming a principle of international law'.[19] But CHM has a much longer history upon which Pardo drew in developing CHM as a legal concept for the oceans.

This history is important in elucidating the ethical core of CHM: a topic considered later in this chapter. But it is also important in understanding its potential scope beyond the narrow context of UNCLOS III and contemporary treaty regimes. In 1946, concern about the use of nuclear technology and resources, for military and peaceful purposes, led to an early proposal that nuclear resources be collectively owned and managed and not owned by any one state.[20] Traces of CHM are also found in the 1962 United Nations General Assembly Resolution comprising its Declaration on the Use of Outer Space. This instrument refers to the exploration and use of outer space being 'carried out for the benefit and in the interests of mankind'.[21] The subsequent 1967 Treaty on Principles Governing the Activities of States in the Exploration and Use of Outer Space, which governs state exploration and use of outer space, the moon and other celestial bodies, refers to exploration and use of outer space as being the 'common province of all mankind'.[22]

Prior to its use in the outer space context, a 1945 proposal that the UN Charter should recognize culture as the common heritage of mankind was attributed to Brazil.[23] This proposal was rejected. But the establishment of the United Nations Educational, Scientific and Cultural Organization (UNESCO) and of the international legal regime on protection of cultural and natural heritage is an indirect acknowledgement of the validity of this proposal.[24] However, CHM has achieved most prominence in the context of the law of the sea. The 1967 World Peace through Law Conference referred to the high seas as 'the common heritage of mankind' and stated that the seabed should be subject to UN jurisdiction and control.[25]

When he introduced the concept of CHM, Pardo was concerned that the ongoing unmanaged use of the world's oceans would become a serious threat to international peace and security from the environmental impact of new technologies, from the militarization of the seafloor and from expanding state claims to jurisdiction over large parts of the oceans – creeping sovereignty. He was also deeply concerned about the connection between growing economic and social disparity. Developed states had a clear economic and technological advantage in claiming and exploiting the ocean's resources, adding to existing inequalities and further threatening peace and security. In short, Pardo was arguing for an international management regime for the equitable use and long-term environmental protection of the seabed and ocean floor, with CHM as its guiding legal principle.

More specifically, the CHM concept was intended to overcome the problems associated with other legal regimes applying to the oceans: claims to extend state sovereignty; common property; and freedom of the high seas. Sovereignty and common property both imply legal rights of use and abuse – *jus utendi et abutendi*; whereas freedom of the high seas implies an open access regime – first in, first served – according to which all are free to degrade and exploit.[26] These legal regimes were seen to serve the rights and interests of only a few members of the international community in a manner that was inconsistent with 'the ever more urgent need for cooperation in addressing world problems, and for environmental sensitivity and sustainable cooperative development of world resources'.[27]

THE INCORPORATION OF CHM INTO INTERNATIONAL ENVIRONMENTAL AGREEMENTS

1. Law of the Sea

Arvid Pardo, it has been noted, introduced the innovative proposal that the seabed and ocean floor, beyond the limits of national jurisdiction, should be considered the common heritage of mankind and managed accordingly. This proposal led to the adoption of the 1970 Declaration of Principles Governing the Sea-Bed and the Ocean Floor, and the Subsoil Thereof, beyond the Limits of National Jurisdiction. This set out the legal principles needed to implement the CHM regime and created the momentum for the negotiation of UNCLOS III.

Part XI of UNCLOS is key to the legal implementation of CHM. It defines the 'Area' as the 'sea-bed and ocean floor, and the subsoil thereof, beyond the limits of national jurisdiction'. According to article 136, the Area and its resources, including minerals, are declared the 'common heritage of mankind': thus leaving other parts of the ocean system to be governed by other legal principles. Article 137 states that neither a claim nor the exercise of sovereignty or sovereign rights over any part of the Area or its resources nor appropriation by any state, natural or juridical person shall be recognized. Article 141 reserves the Area exclusively for peaceful purposes. All rights to the Area's resources are vested in 'mankind' in accordance with article 140, and the International Seabed Authority (ISA) is established to act on behalf of, and for the benefit of, mankind. The ISA must ensure the equitable sharing of benefits arising from activities conducted in the Area: these include the economic and technological benefits from mining. In addition, the ISA must take into particular account the needs and interests of developing and other states. The key tasks specified in articles 143 to 145 include promoting marine scientific research, transferring technology to developing states, and protecting the marine environment from harm – the latter task being one of the ISA's main functions. All states parties to the Convention are members of the ISA. It is implicit that they are to act through it. Articles 158, 166 and 170 indicate that the Enterprise was created to carry out operational activities in the Area.

The combined effect of these articles was to create a unique international commons management regime. However, this regime applied only to a very small part of the whole ocean environment: namely the 'Area' – that is, the deep seabed beyond the limits of national jurisdiction and its mineral resources. Despite its limited scope, the CHM regime described in Part XI proved so controversial that the United States initially refused to sign UNCLOS III because of a difference of opinion about the use of the Area and its resources in relation to benefiting mankind as a whole.[28] On the one hand, many developing states argued that the only way to ensure equitable benefit sharing, taking into account their needs, was via a global entity with exclusive mineral exploitation rights. On the other hand, developed states viewed this as a form of distributive justice that was hostile to commercial investment and contrary to market-orientated approaches.[29] UNCLOS III eventually came into force 12 years later, following the 1994 Implementation Agreement that substantially reduced the distributive justice elements of the mining regime in favour of greater protection of commercial exploitation interests.[30]

By the end of negotiations in 1982, Pardo expressed grave disappointment about what had been achieved.[31] A combination of political and economic factors had greatly restricted the scope of CHM as set out in Part XI to mineral resources on the deep seabed and ocean floor but only in areas outside national jurisdiction. As a result, it had effect in isolation from the sea column and space above; it excluded marine living resources; and it did not apply to the ocean space and resources *within* national jurisdiction. Thus the concept of CHM did not apply to the entire ocean environment as a complex and interconnected ecological whole.[32] This created an ecological nonsense that has left much of the oceans vulnerable to traditional notions of state sovereignty, common property and freedom of the high seas. This application of CHM, it will be suggested, was contrary to Pardo's original intention.

2. Laws Relating to Outer Space and the Moon

It has already been noted that aspects of CHM appeared in the 1967 Outer Space Treaty. But it was not until 1979 that a clear statement appeared in the Agreement Governing the Activities of States on the Moon and Other Celestial Bodies 1979 ('the Moon Treaty') which was designed to govern exploration and exploitation of the Moon's resources. Article 11(1) declares that the Moon and its natural resources are the common heritage of mankind. Article 4(1) requires the cooperation of states in all their undertakings concerning the Moon and other celestial bodies. Article 11(3) declares that the Moon and its resources shall not become the property of any state, organization, entity or person. Disputes over the details of an international system for resource exploitation, including provision for equitable benefit sharing, were resolved by deferring the details of a management regime for future agreement. The Moon Treaty has been ratified by only a few states. Nevertheless, it has been used to reject claims to property rights on the basis that it creates a general principle of law which applies to the whole of the international community and not only to states that ratified the treaty.[33]

3. Laws for the Protection of Natural and Cultural Heritage

The 1972 UNESCO Convention for the Protection of the World's Cultural and Natural Heritage provides that features of natural and cultural heritage of universal value to mankind should be subject to a legal regime. Under the Convention it is the duty of individual states to protect, conserve and transmit identified natural and cultural heritage for future generations. It is also the duty of the international community as a whole to cooperate to ensure protection of world heritage for the benefit of present and future generations. The term 'common heritage of mankind' is not used explicitly. Nevertheless, many elements of the concept are considered to be present.[34] UNESCO has been a champion of the CHM concept for many years, as it has to some extent acknowledged the centrality of CHM to the protection of the world's natural and cultural heritage.[35]

4. Laws about Antarctica

The treaty regime for Antarctica has referred to CHM less explicitly. The preamble to the 1959 Antarctic Treaty proclaims that:

> It is in the interest of all mankind that Antarctica shall continue forever to be used exclusively for peaceful purposes and shall not become the scene or object of international discord.

In subsequent years, additional measures were agreed for the purposes of environmental protection, preservation of wildlife, scientific research and international scientific cooperation. For example, the Protocol on Environmental Protection to the Antarctic Treaty states in the preamble:

> That the development of a comprehensive regime for the protection of the Antarctic environment and dependent and associated ecosystems is in the interest of mankind as a whole.

Although the term 'common heritage of mankind' has not been used, some of the specific elements of the treaty regime are considered to reflect elements of CHM.[36] These include those relating to environmental protection and the surrounding ocean.

5. Laws about Climate Change and Biodiversity

In the 1990s states rejected CHM as a concept to guide UN treaty regimes on climate change and biodiversity conservation. Consider first climate change. The UNFCCC refers to the *problem* of climate change as being the 'common concern of humankind'. The original intention of Malta – reflecting Pardo's legacy – was a treaty based on CHM for the conservation and protection of the Earth's climate system. Malta argued that the vital nature of the climate system required an international approach that would transcend state sovereignty and protect the interests of present and future generations. However, when it became clear that states would reject this, the less ambitious option of a treaty on the specific problem of climate change emerged.[37] The 'common concern' concept was intended to be a compromise solution.

During the UNCLOS III negotiations, developing states were major supporters of CHM as a means of establishing a new international economic order and of winning access to resources otherwise inaccessible to them. However, by 1992 the suggestion that the Earth's biological diversity should be declared the CHM – or a part of it – was rejected. Developing states perceived it as a threat to their sovereignty over biological resources *within* their jurisdiction. From their perspective, CHM was being interpreted by developed states as a form of common property regime. Such an interpretation would facilitate acquisition of intellectual property rights in genetic resources and potentially interfere with economic and social development – under the guise of environmental protection. As a result, the Convention on Biological Diversity (CBD) states that the conservation of biological diversity is the 'common concern' of humankind.[38] Nevertheless, its treaty provisions impliedly acknowledge some attributes of CHM and these include references to future generational equity, peace and the exercise of property rights consistent with conservation objectives.[39]

The UNFCCC and CBD are referred to as 'common concern' regimes and apply to environmental concerns arising not only beyond but also within the jurisdictions of states. These regimes are considered to be an alternative to a narrow understanding of CHM's scope as applying *only* to areas beyond national jurisdiction. Commentary suggests that the legal ramifications of 'common concern' are imprecise. Brunnée notes that it may entitle or require all states to cooperate internationally to address the concern. If and how this would limit sovereign rights is unclear.[40]

THE CORE ELEMENTS OF CHM

1. Introduction

The foregoing discussion indicates that there is no concise and fully agreed definition of CHM. However, the following core elements can be identified from the treaty regimes and the literature. The later discussion about CHM as a normative concept clarifies that not all elements are essential and their application depends upon the object to which CHM is applied.

2. Non-appropriation

No state can claim or exercise sovereignty or sovereign rights and no person, either natural or juridical, can appropriate the object of a CHM regime. Appropriation may take a variety of forms – from occupation of property to acquisition of property. This element – non-appropriation – is important in the context of objects in two ways: objects that can freely become the property of those that use and exploit them (*res nullius*); and objects that may not be appropriated because they are recognized as belonging to everyone and therefore should not be appropriated (*res communes omnium*). In both instances, this element ensures that the object cannot be owned, enclosed or disposed of. But it must remain or become a part of the international common heritage or patrimony *belonging to all humanity* but not to states. In this sense, CHM creates or preserves the legal status of an 'international commons'.

3. Obligation to Cooperate

States are obligated to cooperate in the management and use of CHM for the benefit of all humanity. As will be discussed below, this has been interpreted as creating obligations to cooperate that go beyond those required by general international law and have more in common with the concept of a 'trust'. The immediate reciprocal benefit of states is not the point of reference for this new kind of cooperation. Rather, states are acting in respect of the object as trustees for the benefit of all humanity.[41]

4. Intergenerational and Intragenerational Equity

Use of the word 'heritage' or 'patrimony' in combination with 'mankind' or 'humankind' is generally taken to indicate that the interests of future generations have to be respected alongside the interests of present generations. This is often achieved through explicit reference to obligations to protect the environment and to conserve resources, thereby ensuring the transmission of the valued heritage from one generation to another.

Because management and use of the CHM object is for the benefit of *all* humanity, this implies an element of intragenerational equity or fairness, with particular regard to the needs of the poor. This has been described as requiring the elimination of situations that endanger life or are contrary to basic human values and the creation of conditions for a *better life for everyone*.[42]

Taken together, these elements of CHM have much in common with the concept of sustainable development.[43] The notion of benefit should be understood broadly to include a wide range of intangible and tangible values. But, when a markedly different capacity to benefit arises – due to wealth or technological capacity – and resource use is an element, the intragenerational equity aspect of CHM may require elements of distributive justice. As one jurist has noted:

> What belongs to the international community and is 'the common heritage of mankind' should be shared among all States in accordance with the maxim 'to each according to his needs'.[44]

5. Resource Use

Resource use can be a component of CHM regimes, for example the resources of the Area of the seabed and ocean floor and those of the Moon and celestial bodies. In the former instance, this resulted in the creation of complex institutional arrangements designed to regulate use and ensure that the interests of humanity are protected. This replaces a freedom-based approach, which would have applied using the freedom of the high seas principle. But, when resources of economic value are present, a CHM regime may require elements of distributive justice. UNCLOS III, for example, requires activities to be carried out for the benefit of mankind as a whole, taking into particular consideration the interests and needs of developing countries. This is implemented via a range of specific obligations.

6. Peaceful Use

Peaceful use is an important element of CHM. It is explicitly mentioned in a number of treaty regimes. It stems from concern that spaces such as the deep seabed, Moon and celestial bodies might become places of militarization with detrimental effects on the environment and for humanity. But it should also be understood more broadly as encompassing the interdependence between peace, human development and environmental protection.[45]

CHM AS A NORMATIVE CONCEPT

1. Ethical Foundations

The concept of CHM is much more than a legal principle. It is also an ancient moral or ethical concept. Pardo focused on its legal articulation and implementation, while others traced and developed its ethical foundations. The historical origins and equivalents of the concept can be traced to Christian theology, Islamic law, African customary law, Asian non-theist traditions and pre-Christian Roman law.[46]

In essence CHM embraces a moral force that unifies humanity and is capable of generating an integrated 'view of ourselves in our environment that is both new and old and that departs from uniquely Eurocentric, Western tradition and attempts to blend Western scientific values with Eastern philosophical values'.[47] At its core is the notion of sustaining the basis or foundations of life, as a precious gift of inheritance or patrimony, for the benefit of all. It expresses concern and responsibility for the 'other' that encompasses not only human interactions between present and future generations but also the human-nature relationship. This includes elements of social equity in recognition of the interdependence between ecological degradation and social inequity. However, ultimately it is about *collective human responsibility* for the ecological commons rather than the 'rights' of some to its resources.

An understanding of the moral foundations of CHM is critical to its legal development for a number of reasons. First, it is important for its acceptance by the international community,[48] central to which is its capacity to create moral solidarity through its articulation of global values. Second, international legal principles can be vague because of the legal processes by which they develop and which leave their content and interpretation vulnerable to intentional and unintentional distortion. A clearer understanding of the ethical foundations of legal principles can mitigate this. There is a growing acceptance that this is a legitimate part of legal process that may be necessary to counter the rigidity of legal positivism.[49] A third, and related, reason is that a deeper appreciation of CHM is helpful to understanding the potential scope of its application, beyond the narrow context of its historical use in UNCLOS III and in other treaties. In this regard, in 1993 Pardo noted the development of the concept since the 1970s, and commented that some scholars consider CHM should 'form the basis of international law on [other] matters concerning humanity as a whole, such as the environment, climate, technology and food resources'.[50]

2. The Concept of a Common Interest

In a seminal article, jurist Alexandre Kiss sought to clarify the essential legal criteria of CHM. He traced the emergence of a new conception of 'common interest' in international law: one that goes beyond the immediate interests of a state or states. In this context, the aim of cooperation and the imposition of obligations on states are 'to eliminate situations which may endanger future life or which are contrary to elementary human values and to create the conditions for a better life for everyone, including future generations'.[51] Human rights regimes are used as an example. However, he argued that common interest can extend beyond the maintenance of peace to the management of resources to protect them for future use. In his view:

> The common heritage is the complete territorial expression, the materialization of the common interest of mankind. This means that states suspend or do not assert rights or claims, or in some cases exercise such jurisdiction only within set limits, for the benefit of the whole human community, without any immediate return, and conserve and if necessary manage areas in conformity with the common interest for the benefit of all mankind.[52]

After reviewing the use of CHM in treaty regimes, Kiss concludes that the most essential criteria are peaceful use and good management in the interest of all mankind – 'in essence, a trust'.[53] This is supported by Wolfrum who notes, in the UNCLOS III context, that states 'act as a kind of trustee on behalf of mankind as a whole'.[54]

This analysis of the core of CHM helps overcome some fundamental misunderstandings that have limited its use and acceptance by both states and academics.[55] It raises the questions whether non-appropriation, an international management regime and the sharing of economic profits are indispensible elements of CHM. These are discussed in the context of the emergence of a form of trust.

3. Emergence of a Form of Trust

(a) Non-appropriation

If CHM creates a form of trust, then Kiss argues that non-appropriation is not an indispensible element of CHM. As a result, this reasoning enables CHM to be applied not only to common areas and resources beyond national jurisdiction but also to areas, ecological systems and resources *within* state territory and *within* areas of national jurisdiction. A precedent for this application of CHM is the 1972 Convention for the Protection of the World's Cultural and Natural Heritage. It imposes duties to protect and a duty imposed on the international community as a whole to cooperate, irrespective of whether specific areas or resources are within areas of national jurisdiction or are private property.

The potential of CHM to apply not only externally beyond states but also internally within states is highly controversial because it challenges the territorial obsession of states and rejects unfettered state sovereignty. Applied to shared ecological systems, this would require states to protect and restore ecological systems and manage their use for the benefit of all. Thus CHM attempts to redefine or transform state sovereignty rather than conflict with it. However, for this aspect of CHM to be truly transformative, it must be implemented in a way that requires and enforces coordinated international standards.

While non-appropriation is not an essential element of CHM in all contexts, it is fundamental in relation to resources subject to an existing commons regime – *res communes omnium* – or to resources that can be freely appropriated – *res nullius*. This is because non-appropriation prevents forms of dispossession or enclosure and ensures that they continue to belong to all and remain available to all for certain uses.

The non-essential aspect of non-appropriation is also consistent with Pardo's original intention for CHM in the oceans context. In 1971 he drafted an Ocean Space Treaty in an attempt 'to show how the common heritage concept could be implemented in the marine environment as [an integrated] whole'.[56] CHM would have applied without regard to the pre-existing jurisdictional status of any particular area. However, it would be applied in a different way to areas *within* national jurisdiction. States would retain the legal power to control and regulate. But this sovereign authority would be subject to limitations specifically designed to protect the interests of all humanity. As Pardo put it, 'a new legal order had to be created in the oceans based on a new principle which constrained both sovereignty and freedom in the common interest'.[57] While this was not achieved, Pardo saw Part XI of UNCLOS III as opening a small crack in the 'wall of opposition' to CHM as a basic principle of international law.[58]

(b) An international management regime

Many commentators argue that an institutional management regime similar to the one created by UNCLOS III is a necessary feature of CHM.[59] However, if trusteeship obligations are at the core of CHM, then the question of *who* can act as trustee becomes easier. Thus:

> Whether the trustee is the international community through the intermediary of an international organ, or whether it is the concerned state that has agreed to act on the community's behalf, is a matter of policy.[60]

The key is that those charged with responsibility for the CHM 'act on behalf of all mankind and in its interest'.[61]

(c) Sharing of economic profits

It has been suggested that the equitable benefit sharing of economic profits from resource exploitation is critical to the distributive justice elements of the Area regime under UNCLOS III. Its inclusion caused considerable controversy and required complex machinery. However, this precedent does not mean that CHM is a concept only for resource utilization or for internationalization of resources that involve equitable benefit sharing. This interpretation of the concept is too narrow. Depending on the situation to which CHM is applied, 'benefit sharing' can be interpreted 'in a more generous way to include aesthetic, cultural, and scientific benefits as well as economic revenues'.[62]

Precedents for alternative forms of 'benefit' sharing of CHM exist. UNCLOS III refers to the sharing of scientific knowledge as a benefit for all. Article 149 provides that archaeological and historic objects found in the Area must be preserved or disposed of for 'the benefit of mankind as a whole'. These uses of a public character – research and exhibition – are given priority over uses for private interest – trade and personal gain – which 'are given little weight, if any'.[63] Robust environmental protection measures in the context of mining in the Area were recently acknowledged as being for the benefit of all humanity.[64] Indeed, environmental protection, as a benefit for humanity and an objective of a CHM regime, is one of the least contentious elements of CHM.[65]

(d) Conclusion

While aspects of CHM are controversial, Pardo sought to clarify that CHM does not imply disregard for the interests of states. He summed up the essence of CHM in these words:

> Traditionally, international law has been essentially concerned with the regulation of relations between states. In ocean space, however, the time has come to recognize as a basic principle of international law the overriding common interest of mankind in the preservation of the quality of the marine environment and in the rational and equitable development of resources lying beyond national jurisdiction. *This does not imply disregard of the interest of individual states, but rather the recognition of the fact that in the long term*

> *these interests can be protected only within the framework of a stable international regime of close co-operation between states.*[66]

If properly implemented, CHM as a 'form of trust' has the potential to ensure the 'original promise of the environmental movement as a "public good" to be administered in the interest of all and of the generations to come'.[67] While there may be cogent reasons for applying CHM regimes, it cannot be overlooked that international law is currently confronted by an ongoing dilemma. In the absence of an international law maker, humanity must rely on states to agree to restrict their own sovereignty and to act in the interest of humanity.

TOWARDS THE APPLICATION OF CHM

1. Introduction

Some commentators consider that CHM has gone out of fashion.[68] This is largely due to a lack of state acceptance. The 'politicization' of CHM in the context of UNCLOS III continues to be an impediment. In addition, the non-appropriation and benefit sharing principles are not well understood or are seen as a direct challenge to state sovereignty and as an undesirable precedent.[69] On the basis of treaty practice, it is accurate to conclude that its use has been restricted to resources that are difficult to access in areas beyond national jurisdiction. Two additional legal issues inhibit CHM's acceptance and further application: recognition of humanity as a subject of international law; and enforcement. However, it should be noted that both of these issues are generally problematic for international environmental law.

There are differing views on whether CHM amounts to legal recognition of humanity as a subject of international law.[70] Some commentators see this aspect of CHM as an important opportunity to put the *demos* into international law, thereby rectifying a significant democratic deficit created by state sovereignty.[71] However, to operationalize this element fully, robust institutional structures and mechanisms for participation and legal representation would be needed to give a direct and powerful voice on behalf of the interests of present and future generations.

In relation to enforcement in the environmental context, states tend to avoid binding legal obligations that can be enforced via liability and compliance regimes. Enforcement remains locked within the paradigm of reciprocity according to which a state or states may or may not elect to enforce. As a consequence, little, if any, consideration will be given to protection of the collective interests beyond those of states.[72] The development of *erga omnes* obligations – namely those owed by one state to all other states and to the international community as a whole – together with the necessary legal standing to enforce these obligations – in other words an *actio popularis* – has been very limited. These developments are needed to codify the commitment 'of every state actively to engage in the promotion and protection of environmental quality as an essential public good'.[73]

A less 'positivist' view acknowledges that, beyond the doctrine of consent, international law is not the sole domain of states. From this perspective, there are a number of inter-related legal developments which have the potential to keep CHM on the agenda.

It has been suggested that CHM is considered by many to be a legal articulation of fundamental ethical values. As a consequence, it is closely associated with renewed interest in cosmopolitanism, global environmental constitutionalism and global ecological citizenship. Central to these trends are efforts to articulate global values of care and respect for Earth and its communities.[74] More specifically, CHM is part of a broader discussion about states as environmental trustees, owing fiduciary obligations to present and future generations. This discussion ranges from the macro 'global governance' level to reinvigoration of the public trust doctrine both within and beyond national jurisdictions.[75] In the view of Sand, sovereignty 'bounded' by the responsibility to provide for human wellbeing has the potential to enhance the democratic legitimacy of the nation state rather than to undermine it.[76] CHM is also closely related to the modern commons discourse because it is an effort to create a commons-based governance regime that challenges states and private entities as the sole source of authority and as sole beneficiaries.[77]

Some states and legal commentators continue to support CHM and argue for new and extended applications. These reflect an effort to address fundamental contemporary challenges by requiring states to hold certain things – the environment and its resources vital to all humanity – on trust and to act cooperatively for the benefit of all. They also reflect the linkages between CHM, sustainable development and peace. Arvid Pardo certainly intended and understood that CHM was widely applicable and beyond UNCLOS III. In 1968 he said that CHM was a new legal principle that his country wished to introduce into international law. Noting the growing complexity of problems that will confront humanity, he stated:

> We cannot deal effectively with the accumulating and increasingly serious problems of the total environment in which we live … on the narrow,

outdated basis of traditional international law; new concepts must be introduced, new solutions sought to enable us all, from the greatest powers to the smallest society, to cope intelligently with new problems.[78]

2. Marine Living Resources

Since 2004, states have been attempting to negotiate a legal regime on governance of marine living resources, including genetic resources, in the high seas and on the deep seabed – together referred to as occurring in areas beyond national jurisdiction (ABNJ).[79] From an ecological perspective, the current incremental, fragmented and simplistic approach to oceans governance is an ecological nonsense.[80] The negotiations on marine living resources are ongoing, with the use of the CHM concept proving to be controversial. Current indications are that many states will not agree to the use of CHM, either by extending the scope of the Area and its resources under UNCLOS III or by declaring marine living resources (including genetic resources) the CHM.[81] This contrasts with the view of other states that marine living resources in ABNJ are the CHM and that a specific legal regime is needed to implement this concept.[82]

A possible way forward could be negotiation of an Implementation Agreement to UNCLOS III that sets out common understandings for the protection and sustainable use of marine diversity in ABNJ. The possibility of benefit sharing, in relation to the exploitation of marine genetic resources, will make it difficult to apply CHM. However, there may be more willingness to use the CHM concept for a network of marine protected areas where the concept of benefit does not extend to economic returns. This would ensure a governance regime requiring states to cooperate for the benefit of all humanity.[83]

3. Human Genome

Article 1 of the 1997 Universal Declaration on the Human Genome and Human Rights states that the human genome underlies the fundamental unity of all humanity and 'in a symbolic sense, [it] is the heritage of humanity'. It further provides that the human genome, in its natural state, shall not give rise to financial gains[84] and that an international framework for cooperation be established to make the benefits of research available to all.[85] While this formulation stops short of declaring the human genome the CHM, academic commentary both supports and opposes this possible future development. At the core is disagreement about the management of international cooperation and justification for the 'propertization' of genetic heritage. On the latter point Francioni, for example, regards this as a form of enclosure that cannot be justified. He states:

> This race to the enclosure of the most intimate essence of the natural world, our genetic patrimony, reduces life itself to merchandise to produce profit. It makes us lose the sense of what is the common good.[86]

The practical outcome of a CHM regime for the human genome would be to allow for the equitable use of the human genome but to prevent it from being appropriated in any form.

This is consistent with Pardo's intent that CHM was a non-property concept. He explained that, in relation to CHM, the word 'property' was deliberately avoided because it implies the legal rights of use and misuse – *jus utendi et abutendi* – and 'gives excessive emphasis to just one aspect [of CHM]: resource exploitation and benefit therefrom'.[87] As a non-property concept, CHM is capable of articulating an important distinction. It embraces a positive vision of CHM belonging to *everyone*, giving rise to collective responsibilities as well as use rights. This contrasts with a potentially negative vision of belonging to *no one* and therefore left vulnerable to the tragedy of the commons or hidden agendas to enclose or propertize.

4. Global Atmosphere

It will be recalled that a treaty for the conservation of the Earth's global climate system as an integral part of the CHM was rejected by states. However, in 2014, 'protection of the atmosphere' became a topic for the International Law Commission. This created the opportunity for states to readdress and develop legal principles for the protection of the global atmosphere as a whole. Again, CHM was favoured by some states. Others preferred the less defined concept of 'common concern of humankind'.[88] As a component of the Earth's ecological systems, vital to all life on Earth and vulnerable to human perturbations, the atmosphere is an obvious candidate for a CHM regime.[89] An international approach, which transcends state sovereignty involving the *unilateral* decisions of states and is in the interests of present and future generations, is required. A possible practical outcome of this approach would be to require states to demonstrate, to an independent authority, how their mitigation and other relevant commitments are a fair contribution to keeping global temperature increases below 2 degrees.

5. From Global Environment to the Earth System

Recent scientific developments have helped to articulate and advance understanding of a shared global environment. Earth System science has identified nine planetary boundaries, four of which have been transgressed and have created varying degrees of risk. Of these four, two – climate change and biosphere integrity – are 'core planetary boundaries' because of their importance and interrelationship.[90] The combined impact of these four transgressions is to push the Earth System, a complex integrated system, into a condition in which life is imperiled. This important work demonstrates, in scientific terms, that the Earth is an interconnected living system upon which all humanity and all other life depends. It also reveals that humanity is destabilizing the Earth System and 'beginning to undermine our own life support system'.[91] Therefore there is a need for a coherent Earth System-focused governance system which respects this biophysical reality and manages human behaviour.

Earth System science enables us to conceptualize the Earth System as a true global commons, according to which the whole is bigger than the sum of the parts. Used in this context, CHM identifies the Earth System as a legal object and requires a management regime that is an alternative to the current tragedy of the open access commons, supplemented by a piecemeal system of international treaties and agencies. It challenges states as the sole source of authority to determine a legal framework necessary to ensure management of human activities for the benefit of all. Crucially, it requires states to act as environmental trustees, with moral and legal responsibility to act in the interests of all humanity, including their own citizens and future generations, both within and outside state jurisdiction, and according to globally coordinated standards that prioritize ecological protection and restoration.[92]

6. Transformation of the UN Trusteeship Council

In concert with new applications of CHM, it is common to find reference to the idea of a transformed or reconstituted UN Trusteeship Council. This stems from an early proposal by Malta that the Council be given a new mandate as a means to institutionalize broader application of CHM within the UN. The proposal was to reconstitute the Council 'as the forum through which Member States exercise their collective trusteeship for the integrity of the global environment and common areas such as the oceans, atmosphere and outer space'.[93] Advancement of this idea has been controversial, with little action taken. The Commission on Global Governance made a similar proposal in 1994, although it did not explicitly use CHM. The Commission argued that the need had emerged for international trusteeship to be exercised over the global commons in the collective interest of humanity, including future generations. Management of the global commons, including articulation of rights and responsibilities of states and other entities for the use of resources, should be subject to trusteeship exercised by a principal organ of the UN, acting on behalf of all nations.[94] One of the objectives of this approach was to create a central coordinating governance authority.

Thus far, both proposals have proved to be too radical for states. However, they represent an important conceptual development – acknowledgement that the health of Earth is a shared responsibility requiring new legal and institutional responses that transcend conventional international law and empower the UN to take some kind of leadership role. Given the growing urgency and scale of global ecological threats, the search for new governance approaches for the global commons is accelerating.

CONCLUSION

There is a sense of growing alarm among senior jurists about the inability of state-centred international law to deal with urgent global commons problems.[95] The law is in need of conceptual development to provide for the protection of the vital common interests of all. CHM was intended to revolutionize the law by creating a duty to protect and to share for the benefit of all. Both the triumph and the tragedy of CHM reside in its revolutionary intent. Thus far, the dominant agendas of sovereign states have impeded its use. Notwithstanding this legal reality, CHM continues to attract considerable academic support and interest.[96] CHM may be a concept whose time is yet to come.

NOTES

1. This chapter is partially based on previously published work: Taylor (2012) and (2014).
2. This term is attributable to Georges Scelle.
3. Hardin (1968).
4. Wolfrum (2008), Tuerk (2010) and Taylor and Stroud (2013).
5. Taylor (1998).
6. Rio Declaration 1992, art.3.
7. Sands and Peel (2012, p. 195).
8. Kiss and Shelton (2000, p. 71).
9. Sands and Peel (2012, p. 185).

10. Climate Change Convention 1992, art.2.
11. Paris Agreement 2015.
12. Brunnée (2008, p. 553).
13. *Danube Dam* case (1997, Separate Opinion at para.C(c)).
14. Brunnée (2008, p. 554).
15. Kiss (1985, p. 427).
16. Ibid. (p. 440).
17. Birnie, Boyle and Redgwell (2009, p. 198).
18. Commemoration of the thirtieth anniversary of UNCLOS (2012).
19. Tuerk (2010, p. 159).
20. Mann Borgese and Vanderbilt (undated, p. 7).
21. Article 1.
22. Ibid.
23. Wolfrum (2008, para.10).
24. Ibid.
25. Tuerk (2010, p. 158).
26. Ibid. (p. 159).
27. Pardo (1993, p. 69).
28. Beesley (2004).
29. Tuerk (2010, p. 165).
30. Ibid. (pp. 166–70); Anand (1997).
31. Mann Borgese (2000).
32. But see art. 192, creating a general obligation to preserve and protect the marine environment.
33. Tuerk (2010, p. 172).
34. Kiss (1985).
35. Ibid. (pp. 433–4) and UNESCO Universal Declaration on Cultural Diversity (2001).
36. Kiss (1985, pp. 428–9) and Wolfrum (2008, p. 8).
37. Borg (2009).
38. Preamble.
39. Mann Borgese (2002, pp. 1328–31).
40. Brunnée (2008, p. 565).
41. Wolfrum (2008, para.15).
42. Kiss (1985, p. 427).
43. Wolfrum (2008, para.22) and Mann Borgese (2002, p. 1332).
44. Bedjaoui (1991, p. 1192).
45. Mann Borgese (2002, p. 1332).
46. Ibid.
47. Mann Borgese (1986, p. 131).
48. Noyes (2012).
49. Peters (2013, p. 548).
50. Pardo (1993, p. 68).
51. Kiss (1985, p. 427).
52. Ibid. (p. 428).
53. Ibid. (p. 433).
54. Wolfrum (2008, para.15) and Tuerk (2010, p. 164).
55. Kiss (1985).
56. Pardo (1993, p. 67).
57. Pardo (1992).
58. Pardo (1993, p. 69).
59. Wolfrum (2008, para.15).
60. Kiss (1985, p. 435).
61. Ibid. (p. 440).

62. Ibid. (p. 438) and Wolfrum (2008, para.18).
63. Scovazzi (2014, p. 217).
64. ITLOS, Advisory Opinion, 2011.
65. Wolfrum (2008).
66. Pardo (1975, p. 176 – emphasis added).
67. Francioni (2012, p. 455).
68. Wolfrum (2008, para.28).
69. Pardo (1993).
70. Mann Borgese (2002, p. 1325), Tuerk (2010, p. 159) and Wolfrum (2008, para.2).
71. Peters (2012, p. 131).
72. Francioni (2012, p. 455).
73. Ibid. (p. 456).
74. See, for example, the Earth Charter.
75. See, for example, Bosselmann (2015a), Turnipseed et al. (2010) and Taylor (2013).
76. Sand (2004, pp. 58–9).
77. Bollier (2014).
78. Mann Borgese (2002, p. 1318).
79. The United Nations working group (Ad Hoc Open-ended Informal Working Group to study issues relating to the conservation and sustainable use of marine biological diversity beyond areas of national jurisdiction) has been considering this issue since 2004. See: A/69/780 (13 February 2015); http://www.un.org/ga/search/view_doc.asp?symbol=A/69/780.
80. IPSO, *State of the Oceans Report* (2013).
81. UN Working Group Report to the UN, 23 September 2013.
82. UN Working Group Report to the UN, 13 February 2015; A/69/780 (13 February 2015, paras 16–18 and 25).
83. Scovazzi (2013).
84. Human Genome Declaration (1997, art.4).
85. Ibid. (arts 17–19).
86. Francioni (2012, p. 457).
87. Mann Borgese (2000, p. xxvii).
88. Murase (2015, para.29) and Sand and Wiener (2015).
89. Taylor (1998) and Westing (1989).
90. Steffen (2016).
91. Ibid.
92. Magalhaes (2016).
93. UN General Assembly Document A/52/795, 18 February 1998, para.15.
94. Commission on Global Governance.
95. Hafner (2011) and Treves (2011).
96. Taylor and Stroud (2013) and Baslar (1998).

REFERENCES

Anand, R.P. (1997) 'The Common Heritage of Mankind: Mutilation of an Ideal', *Indian Journal of International Law* 37(1), 1–18.

Baslar, K. (1998) *The Concept of the Common Heritage of Mankind in International Law* (The Hague, Kluwer Law International).

Bedjaoui, Mohammed (1991) 'The Right to Development' in Mohammed Bedjaoui (ed.), *International Law: Achievements and Prospects* (London, Martinus Nijhoff Publishers), pp. 1177–204.

Beesley, Allan (2004) 'Grotius and the new law', *Ocean Yearbook* 18, 98–116.

Birnie, Patricia, Alan Boyle and Catherine Redgwell (2009) *International Law and the Environment* (3rd edn) (Oxford, Oxford University Press).

Bollier, David (2014) *Thinking Like a Commoner: A Short Introduction to the Life of the Commons* (British Columbia, New Society Publishers).

Borg, Simone (ed.) (2009) *Malta's Initiative on Climate Change* (Ministry of Foreign Affairs, Malta).

Bosselmann, Klaus (2015a) *Earth Governance: Trusteeship of the Global Commons* (Cheltenham, Edward Elgar).

Bosselmann, Klaus (2015b) 'Global Environmental Constitutionalism: Mapping the Terrain', *Widener Law Review* XXI(2), 171–85.

Brunnée, Jutta (2008) 'Common Areas, Common Heritage, and Common Concern' in Daniel Bodansky, Jutta Brunnée and Ellen Hey (eds), *The Oxford Handbook of International Environmental Law* (Oxford, Oxford University Press), pp. 551–73.

Commission on Global Governance (1995) *Our Global Neighbourhood* (Oxford, Oxford University Press).

Francioni, Francesco (2012) 'Realism, Utopia and the Future of International Environmental Law' in Antonio Cassese (ed.), *Realizing Utopia: The Future of International Law* (Oxford, Oxford University Press), pp. 442–60.

Francioni, Francesco (2014) 'International Common Goods: An Epilogue' in Federico Lenzerini and Ana Filipa Vrdoljak (eds), *International Law for Common Goods: Normative Perspectives on Human Rights, Culture and Nature* (Oxford, Hart Publishing), pp. 443–8.

Hafner, Gerhard (2011) 'The Division of the Commons?: The Myth of the Commons: Divide or Perish' in H. Hestermeyer, N. Matz-Lück, A. Seibert-Fohr and S. Vöneky (eds), *Law of the Sea in Dialogue* (Berlin, Springer), pp. 91–111.

Hardin, Garrett (1968) 'The Tragedy of the Commons', *Science* 162, 1243–8.

Kiss, Alexandre (1985) 'The common heritage of mankind: utopia or reality?, *Law in the International Community* (Summer) 40(3), 423–41.

Kiss, Alexandre and Dinah Shelton (2000) *International Environmental Law* (2nd edn) (New York, Transnational Publishers).

Magalhaes, Paulo (2016) 'Safe Operating Space for Humankind Treaty – A Proposal', in Paulo Magalhaes, Will Steffen, Klaus Bosselmann, Alexandra Aragao and Viriato Soromenho-Marques (eds), *The Safe Operating Space Treaty: a new approach to managing the Earth's system use* (Newcastle on Tyne, Cambridge Scholars Publishing), ch.14.

Mann Borgese, Elisabeth (1986) *The Future of the Oceans: A Report to the Club of Rome* (Montreal, Harvest House).

Mann Borgese, Elisabeth (2000) 'Arvid Pardo (1914–1999): In Memoriam', *Ocean Yearbook* 14, xix–xxxviii.

Mann Borgese, Elisabeth (2002) 'The Common Heritage of Mankind: From Non-living to Living Resources and Beyond' in Nisuke Ando, Edward McWhinney and Rüdger Wolfrum (eds), *Liber Amicorum Judge Shigeru Oda* (Netherlands, Kluwer International Law), pp. 1313–34.

Mann Borgese, Elisabeth and Caroline Vanderbilt, 'The Beginnings' in Elisabeth Mann Borgese, Krishan Saigal and Gunnar Kullenberg (undated), *The IOI Story: International Ocean Institute* (Dreiviertelverlag Verlag, Hamburg), pp. 6–31.

Murase, Shinya, *Second Report on the Protection of the Atmosphere*, UN Doc A/CN.4/681, 2 March (2015).

Noyes, John E. (2012) 'The Common Heritage of Mankind: Past, Present, and Future', *Denver Journal of International Law and Policy* 447–71.

Pardo, Arvid (1975) *The Common Heritage; Selected Papers on Oceans and World Order, 1967–1974* (Valetta, Malta University Press).

Pardo, Arvid (1992) 'From Mare Liberum to the Common Heritage of Mankind', speech delivered to the Maritime Museum, Malta, November (unpublished).
Pardo, Arvid (1993) 'The Origins of the 1967 Malta Initiative', *International Insights* 9(2), 65–9.
Peters, Anne (2012) 'Are we Moving Towards Constitutionalization of the World Community?' in Antonio Cassese (ed.), *Realizing Utopia: The Future of International Law* (Oxford, Oxford University Press), pp. 118–35.
Peters, Anne (2013) 'Realizing Utopia as a Scholarly Endeavour', *European Journal of International Law* 24(2), 533–52.
Sand, Peter H. (2004) 'Sovereignty Bounded: Public Trusteeship for Common Pool Resources?', *Global Environmental Politics* 4, 47–71.
Sand, Peter H. and Jonathan B. Wiener (2015) 'Towards a New International Law of the Atmosphere?', *Goettingen Journal of International Law* 7(2), 1–25 (pre-published version).
Sands, Philippe and Jacqueline Peel (2012), *Principles of International Environmental Law* (3rd edn) (Cambridge, Cambridge University Press).
Scelle, Georges (1958) 'Obsession du territoire' in Frederik Mari van Asbeck and William Jan Henrik (eds), *Symbolae Verzijl* (The Hague, Nijhoff).
Scovazzi, Tullio (2013) 'The exploitation of genetic resources in areas beyond national jurisdiction' in Laura Westra, Prue Taylor and Agnés Michelot (eds), *Confronting Ecological and Economic Collapse: Ecological integrity for law, policy and human rights* (London, Routledge), pp. 47–64.
Scovazzi, Tullio (2014) 'Underwater Cultural Heritage as an International Common Good' in Federico Lenzerini and Ana Filipa Vrdoljak (eds), *International Law for Common Goods: Normative Perspectives on Human Rights, Culture and Nature* (Oxford, Hart Publishing), pp. 175–230.
Steffen, Will (2016) 'The Planetary Boundaries Framework: Defining a safe operating space for humanity' in Paulo Magalhaes, Will Steffen, Klaus Bosselmann, Alexandra Aragao and Viriato Soromenho-Marques (eds), *The Safe Operating Space Treaty: a new approach to managing the Earth's system use* (Newcastle on Tyne, Cambridge Scholars Publishing), ch.2.
Taylor, Prue (1998) *An Ecological Approach to International Law: Responding to challenges of climate change* (London, Routledge).
Taylor, Prue (2012) 'The Common Heritage Principle and Public Health: Honouring Our Legacy' in Laura Westra, Colin Solskolne and Donald Spady (eds), *Human Health and Ecological Integrity: Ethics, Law and Human Rights* (London, Earthscan), pp. 43–55.
Taylor, Prue (2013) 'The future of the common heritage of mankind: Intersections with the public trust doctrine' in Laura Westra, Prue Taylor and Agnés Michelot (eds), *Confronting Ecological and Economic Collapse: Ecological integrity for law, policy and human rights* (London, Routledge), pp. 32–46.
Taylor, Prue (2014) 'The Earth Charter, the commons and the common heritage of mankind principle' in Laura Westra and Mirian Vilela, *The Earth Charter, Ecological Integrity and Social Movements* (London, Routledge), pp. 12–23.
Taylor, Prue and Lucy Stroud (2013) *Common Heritage of Mankind: A Bibliography of Legal Writing* (Fondation de Malte, Malta).
Treves, Tullio (2011) 'Judicial Action for the Common Heritage' in H. Hestermeyer, N. Matz-Lück, A. Seibert-Fohr and S. Vöneky (eds), *Law of the Sea in Dialogue* (Berlin, Springer) pp. 113–33.
Tuerk, Helmut (2010) 'The Idea of Common Heritage of Mankind' in M.A. Gutiérrez Martinez (ed.), *Serving the Rule of International Maritime Law* (Oxfordshire, Routledge), pp. 156–75.
Turnipseed, Mary, Raphael Sagarin, Peter Barnes, Michael C. Blumm, Patrick Parenteau and Peter H. Sand (2010) 'Reinvigorating the public trust doctrine: expert opinion on

the potential of the public trust mandate in US and international environmental law', *Environment: Science and Policy for Sustainable Development* 52(5), 6–14.
Westing, Arthur (1989) 'The Atmosphere as a Common Heritage of Humankind', *Peace and the Sciences* 2(3), 78–82.
Wolfrum, Rüdiger (2008) 'Common Heritage of Mankind'; http://www.mpepil.com.

INSTRUMENTS

Agreement Governing the Activities of States on the Moon and Other Celestial Bodies (adopted 5 December 1979, entered into force 11 July 1984): 1363 UNTS 3.
Agreement relating to the Implementation of Part XI of the United Nations Convention on the Law of the Sea of 10 December 1982: 1836 UNTS 41.
Antarctic Treaty: 402 UNTS 71.
Commemoration of the thirtieth anniversary of the opening for signature of the United Nations Convention on the Law of the Sea (2012): UNGA, A/67/PV.49 (2012).
Commission on Global Governance (1994): *Our Global Neighbourhood* (Oxford, Oxford University Press).
Convention on Biological Diversity 1992: (1992) *International Legal Materials* 31, 818.
Earth Charter 2000; http://www.earthcharterinaction.org/content/pages/Read-the-Charter.html.
Human Genome Declaration (1997): Universal Declaration on the Human Genome and Human Rights 1997; http://www.unesco.org/new/en/social-and-human-sciences/themes/bioethics/human-genome-and-human-rights/.
International Programme on the State of the Ocean (2013): *State of the Oceans Report* (2013); http://coastal-futures.net/archives/220.
Kyoto Protocol to the Framework Convention on Climate Change 1997: (1997) *International Legal Materials* 37, 22.
Paris Agreement 2015: Adopted under the Framework Convention on Climate Change, contained as annex to a decision of the Conference of the Parties: http://unfccc.int/resource/docs/2015/cop21/eng/l09r01.pdf.
Protocol on Environmental Protection to the Antarctic Treaty: (1991) *International Legal Materials* 30, 1455.
Rio Declaration 1992: Declaration of the United Nations Conference on Environment and Development (1992) *International Legal Materials* 31, 874.
Second Report on Protection of the Atmosphere (2015) (Shinya Murase) UN Doc A/CN.4/681, 2 March 2015.
Stockholm Declaration 1972: Declaration of the United Nations Conference on the Human Environment (1972) *International Legal Materials* 11, 1416.
Treaty on Principles Governing the Activities of States in the Exploration and Use of Outer Space, including the Moon and other Celestial Bodies (signed 27 January 1967, entered into force 10 October 1967): 610 UNTS 205.
United Nations Ad Hoc Open-ended Informal Working Group report to the UN (23 September 2013); http://www.un.org/ga/search/view_doc.asp?symbol=A/68/399&referer=http://www.un.org/Depts/los/biodiversityworkinggroup/biodiversityworkinggroup.htm&Lang=E.
United Nations Ad Hoc Open-ended Informal Working Group report to the UN (13 February 2015); http://www.un.org/ga/search/view_doc.asp?symbol=A/69/780.
United Nations Convention on the Law of the Sea 1982: 1833 UNTS 397.
United Nations Educational, Scientific and Cultural Organisation (2002): Universal Declaration on Cultural Diversity (2002) *International Legal Materials* 41, 57.

United Nations Framework Convention on Climate Change 1992: (1992) *International Legal Materials* 31, 849.
United Nations General Assembly Res. 1962 (XVIII): Declaration of Legal Principles Governing the Activities of States in the Exploration and Use of Outer Space (13 December 1963) – GAOR 18th Session Supp. No.15, 15.
United Nations General Assembly (2012): Sixty-seventh session, 49th plenary meeting, Monday, 10 December 2012 (A/67/PV.49).

CASES

Danube Dam case (1997): Judgment in the Case Concerning the Gabcikovo-Nagymaros Project (Hungary and Slovakia) (1997) *International Legal Materials* 37, 162.
ITLOS Advisory Opinion (2011): Seabed Disputes Chamber of the International Tribunal for the Law of the Sea – Responsibilities and Obligations of States Sponsoring Persons and Entities with Respect to Activities in the Area: Advisory Opinion of 1 February 2011.

PART 3

CONCEPTUAL APPROACHES TO THE ACHIEVEMENT OF ENVIRONMENTAL GOALS

13. Environmental policy integration: the importance of balance and trade-offs

Jørgen K. Knudsen and William M. Lafferty

INTRODUCTION[1]

Since the publication in 1987 by the World Commission on Environment and Development of *Our Common Future* there has been both an academic and a political focus on the issue of governance for sustainable development (SD). This report, known as the Brundtland Report, pointed to the need to amend the political-administrative systems within which sectoral policies – such as energy – are formulated and implemented.[2] A core assumption here is that the integration of environmental concerns into decision-making at the outset would enable policy decisions to contribute substantially to a transition towards SD. This political-institutional thinking has been associated with the concept of 'environmental policy integration' (EPI). EPI has been perceived as a particular challenge to public governance and it has constituted a core focus in several related studies.[3] Various processes and governance mechanisms related to EPI have been introduced at international, national and sub-national levels. Building on previous conceptual and empirical work, this chapter elaborates on EPI as a normative-procedural governing mechanism for SD. Emphasis is placed on EPI as an instrument of 'principled priority' for resolving trade-offs between economic, social and environmental concerns.

The particular focus of this chapter is to clarify the meaning of EPI as an approach with respect to three major bodies of research in the area: the comprehensive work on the political-strategic nature of EPI; the more academic work on EPI as policy analysis; and the research conducted on the nature and practice of EPI within the European Union. In particular it is here contended that an approach stressing the normative-procedural aspect of EPI is completely in line with the normative position adopted by the Brundtland Report. The chapter then briefly indicates three governing mechanisms for strenghtening EPI as 'procedure' and 'policy output'. First, it develops a 'canon for practical judgement' for resolving EPI-related trade-offs. Second, it strengthens the canon through a more focused integration of science, strategic assessments and the precautionary principle. Third, it anchors the mandate for EPI in a more robust institutionalization of 'political will' for SD.

The concept of EPI can be viewed as an integral aspect of two major discourses on SD:[4] the political discourse and the academic discourse. The political discourse takes its point of departure from the report of the World Commission on Environment and Development (WCED)[5] – the Brundtland Report. This line of analysis focuses on the promotion of SD as a principal goal of the United Nations (UN) and its member states. In this context, EPI has been identified as a key instrument for promoting SD in all the major documents, strategies and action plans adopted by the UN. This perspective has in turn been taken up by other international and regional organizations such as the European Union (EU), the Nordic Council, the Organisation for Economic Cooperation and Development (OECD) and, most specifically for EPI, the European Environment Agency (EEA). This discourse has established SD as an overarching normative goal in Europe, with EPI as a highly consensual instrument for achieving this goal.

Within the academic discourse EPI has been treated as an aspect mainly of political science studies of policy implementation. The present chapter aims to contribute to an improved scientific understanding of EPI both as a part of the general policy-making process and as a steering mechanism for environmental and SD governance. What does EPI entail as a concept and how does it actually work to achieve the implied goals? Major issues here are clarity and consistency of definition; exploration of relevant theoretical approaches from policy analysis; definitions of testable criteria for measurement – how will we know it when we see it; and the generalization of empirical findings for policy theory and practical implementation.

While the crucial role of EPI with respect to SD goals and programs is relatively non-controversial, questions relating to what EPI actually involves as an instrument of governance and to the development of criteria for assessing its success or failure definitely are controversial. Furthermore, a great deal of the controversy seems to revolve around alternative understandings of the interdependency between the normative aspect of the 'political' discourse and the practical and applied aspect of the 'academic' approach. Viewing EPI as a question of 'what works, where, when and how' tends to convert into three debates: first, what EPI 'really' entails as a normative goal; second, how it should be operationalized to achieve the goal; and third, how it can be assessed for determining success and revision. A clarification of the normative interpretation of EPI is thus a decisive point of departure and an ongoing reference point for not only defining the concept as a pragmatic instrument of governance but also for assessing the effects of the instrument in practice.

It can be contended that EPI has evolved recursively over several decades at the interface between policy, politics and science at national, at regional – for present purposes the European Union – and at international or global levels – the UN, the World Bank and the Intergovernmental Panel on Climate Change.[6] A large body of research literature has gradually appeared, particularly on the European stage.[7] At the same time, a growing number of studies have assessed the preconditions and factors which could also impinge on EPI in non-European settings.[8] Furthermore, the relatively stronger focus on climate change mitigation, as compared to the broader issue of SD, has set its mark upon the thematic approach of recent EPI studies.[9] This has even been associated with a sub-field of 'climate policy integration'.[10] As extensively illustrated by other contributors to this book, there have also been substantial contributions from legal scholars. Of these, several focus on the linkage between SD as a principle, on its legal codification and on related legal aspects of natural resource governance.[11] No consensus, however, has yet emerged about the definition and implications of EPI as a governing principle. Given the coincident lack of consensus on the concept itself in the academic community, the result has been a lack of systematic comparative research documenting 'what works, where, when and how'.[12]

A major challenge thus remains to communicate clearly, to clarify and to expand on the conceptual understanding of EPI as a way of identifying viable governance mechanisms that can actually strengthen the environmental dimension. Towards this end – in the service of promoting synthesis and a broader consensus on the issues – the approach of this chapter will be profiled in relation to three major bodies of EPI analysis:

- first, work directed at the political-strategic aspects of EPI by the OECD and by the EEA and the Institute for European Environmental Policy (IEEP)[13]
- second, work directed at the more academic and policy-analytic aspects of EPI[14]
- third, work on EPI in an EU context and on a multi-level governance system with different strategies for implementation within different national and regional jurisdictions.[15]

These works are by no means exhaustive of former and current research on EPI. However, they represent leading-edge contributions in the EPI research field,[16] most particularly with respect to the two 'critical issues' selected here.

The analysis presented here opens with an outline of major points for further reference from each of the three approaches selected and then goes on to elaborate on the two critical issues of balance and trade-offs. The concluding section then discusses possible strategies for governance which would provide more effective assurance that EPI as a steering principle becomes manifest in actual sectoral policy decisions and outcomes.

MAJOR EPI ORIENTATIONS: KEY IDEAS AND SELECTED MODELS

1. The Three Pillars and Decoupling

The task of relating EPI to SD comes down to a choice of which SD principles and ideas are most relevant for the EPI concept. Earlier work by the authors of this chapter has come to the conclusion that the most relevant ideas for associating EPI with strategies for SD are: first, the widely recognized central SD goal of 'balancing' the 'interests', 'concerns' and 'priorities' of the so-called 'three pillars' – namely the economic, social and environmental dimensions of societal development; and, second, the crucial OECD notion of 'decoupling' the drivers of 'business as usual' from negative environmental impacts.[17]

With respect to the first point, it can be contended that the conventional 'three-pillar' language is either too vague by balancing 'interests', 'pillars' and 'dimensions' or too narrow by focusing on sectoral priorities. Therefore, the use of either 'objectives' or 'concerns' in this context has been suggested.[18] The notion of economic, social or environmental 'objectives' captures the goal-oriented nature of what is to be 'balanced'. The notion of 'concerns' indicates that the policies or initiatives in question are inherently normative. The second of the notions is particularly important since claims on behalf of the 'environment' are usually put forth by organizations that express 'interests' that are different from the concept of 'interests' normally employed by mainstream economists and social scientists. Whereas the latter are related to either specific market actors or identifiable 'interest groups' within the means of production, the former are most often put forth by 'idealistic organizations' that speak on behalf of the environment.

In relation to the concept of 'decoupling', OECD and EEA reports have contributed key insights into this idea.[19] In a very fundamental and direct way, the idea proclaims, first, that the dominant economic practices of existing western societies – or at least pre-Brundtland western societies – can be shown to be negative for the environment and, second, that efforts should be made to 'decouple' these practices from their negative environmental impacts. The idea has been developed in direct conjunction with the OECD's work on the Drivers Pressures States Impacts Responses (DPSIR) model: where the logic is that the existing *drivers* create *pressures* on environmental *states*, resulting in demonstrable *impacts*, which must then be addressed by appropriate decoupling *responses* (policies, initiatives). The model and its inherent logic have been widely applied in OECD countries. Accordingly, they provide a vital common reference point for analysing and applying EPI principles and instruments.

2. EPI as a Governing Principle in the EU

Over the last two-and-a-half decades extensive research has been conducted on EPI practice within the context of the EU.[20] A major effort in this regard was the research project called EPI and Multi-Level Governance (EPIGOV). This was an EU-sponsored 'concerted action' that involved 19 research institutions from ten European countries.[21] This project was conducted in the aftermath of the establishment of major governance mechanisms within the EU – both at the EU and national level – which could be associated with EPI.

Moreover, it could be claimed that the EU has had a long historical record in addressing issues pertaining to both SD and EPI.[22] For example the Treaty of Rome 1957 spoke of the need for 'harmonious development'; the Single European Act 1986 spoke of the need for 'prudent and rational utilisation of resources'; and the Treaty on European Union 1991 spoke of 'sustainable and non-inflationary growth'. A deeper awareness of SD issues was, however, signalled for the first time in the EU's Fifth Environmental Action Programme (EAP) launched in 1992. Substantially inspired by the WCED report of 1987, the Fifth EAP defined 'sustainable development' as 'continued economic and social development without detriment to the environment and natural resources'.[23] Nevertheless, the acknowledgement of SD as a policy challenge for the EU remained unclear. It was not until the negotiation of the Amsterdam Treaty in 1997 that the EU commitment to SD was formulated.

The EU recognition of the SD challenge was given formal treaty status in article 6 of the 1997 Amsterdam Treaty which stipulates that 'environmental protection requirements must be integrated into the definition and implementation of Community policies ... in particular with a view to promoting sustainable development'.[24] This principle is currently covered by article 11 of the EU Treaty.[25] Article 6 can also be considered to be the most explicit and principal endorsement of EPI as a steering principle for the EU.

As underlined by the UN work on promoting SD and reflected in the Agenda 21 from 1992, the EU also emphasized the importance of promoting and strengthening EPI as part of the SD promotional efforts. This became an even more central concern at the European Council meeting in Cardiff in 1998. Building on an earlier Swedish proposal, European leaders at Cardiff launched what became known as the 'Cardiff process', which required the Council of Ministers in all its formations to integrate environmental and SD objectives into its respective policy areas.[26]

Despite the relatively 'soft law' nature of article 11 of the Treaty for the Functioning of the European Union (TFEU) – formerly article 6 – this constitutional principle implies a substantial responsibility for the governing procedures of the different policy sectors. There remains, however, considerable disagreement as to how EPI in general and article 11 in particular are to be interpreted.[27] It is therefore important to provide further assessments of what EPI entails in practice in specific EU settings, such as the energy policy sector.[28]

Prior to the EPIGOV project major contributions to the development of studies on EU practice were provided by the German researcher Andrea Lenschow. Given that EPI has struggled under different interpretations as to what the concept 'really' implies, Lenschow's work continues to offer a possible common reference point for the EPI discourse. Space only allows for the briefest of references, but they contain essential perspectives for the analyses that follow.

First, there is Lenschow's fundamental differentiation between what she sees as three 'dimensions worth investigating in order to explain patterns of EPI in policy sectors and in [EU] Member States': *ideas, institutions and actors*.[29] Lenschow's 'actors dimension' can be seen as a more contingent aspect of the EPI discourse. Thus which actors, individual and collective, exert what kind of influence on EPI processes and what does this tell us more inductively about the possibility of trans-contextual generalizations?

The differentiation thus progresses from a relatively abstract discussion of meaning and norms; through a more focused discussion of the possible institutions and procedures deemed necessary or advantageous to pursuing norms; down to a very focused discussion of empirical analyses of actors, influence and outcomes.

Here it is important to stress the acceptance of a fundamental meta-feature of social science: that the choice of ideational-normative content structures the perceived purpose of institutions and procedures, as well as the interpretation of empirical analyses. While this observation may for some appear both obvious and trite, it fails to acknowledge the perspective that underlies a great deal of the dissensus within the field.

In the present analysis the focus is upon ideational-normative and institutional-procedural dimensions. The goal is to structure each of these dimensions in a manner conducive to a better integration of national assessments and empirical analyses of the role and effects of given actors. If successful, the exercises should contribute to a more fruitful research dialogue within the scope of studies already conducted and continually being conducted along the lines laid out by Lenschow and her colleagues.

Second, a number of further points are worth specific attention in relation to the basic ideational position staked out by Lenschow. She cites, in the introduction to her widely cited collection of EPI studies,[30] the following statement by Angela Liberatore:[31]

> The relevance of integration for moving towards sustainable development is straightforward: if environmental factors are not taken into consideration in the formulation and implementation of the policies that regulate economic activities and other forms of social organization, a new model of development that can be environmentally and socially sustainable in the long term cannot be achieved.

This is immediately followed up by Lenschow as follows:

> Put differently, EPI represents a first-order operational principle to implement and institutionalize the idea of sustainable development. However, its legitimacy was based not only on this conceptual linkage, but equally on the evolution of the EU treaties. By the early 1980s, the concept of sustainable development had entered the policy programmes of most European governments and the EU; the legal obligation to policy integration was established with the Single European Act in 1987; and a commitment to 'sustainable development' was made in the Amsterdam Treaty (1999).[32]

One can consider that the clear gist of these two statements is to establish EPI as a 'first-order operational principle' – both normatively and 'legally' – for the achievement of SD within the EU. Two problems immediately arise with this interpretation. First, Lenschow fails to state clearly what are the implications of EPI as a 'first-order principle'. She does not discuss in detail what the operationalization of EPI should and would mean, if it is indeed an integral first principle of SD. Second,

Lenschow offers other perspectives in her introduction which clearly place the 'first-order' nature of EPI-for-SD in doubt. The immediate follow-up discussion of her definitional treatment of EPI gives evidence of a two-pronged ambivalence as to the normative status of the concept. On the one hand, she engages in a discussion of why and how the normative-legal intent of EPI has been undermined by conflicting interpretations of how it should be implemented in practice. In other words she here shifts the discourse from a normative-conceptual perspective to a descriptive perspective without adequately differentiating between the two.

More importantly, she reveals a fundamental ambivalence as to the first-order nature of the concept. At one point – after citing the work of the EEA as a driving force for moving beyond 'end-of-pipe' initiatives towards the decoupling sectoral driving forces – she states that:

> In the absence of clearly defined policy goals, indicators and timetables, however, there remains ample room for sectoral policy-makers to evade such substantive environmental responsibilities. *The integration process currently faces the challenge of ensuring that substance follows from procedure*.[33]

This very forceful endorsement of the 'substantive' intent of EPI is immediately followed by these words:

> The impact of EPI may be reduced not only due to conceptual and hence operational ambiguities, its impact may suffer even more due to conceptual inconsistencies in connection with its 'mother concept'. The compatibility assumptions inherent in sustainable development apply to a highly aggregated (possibly global) level, while EPI applies to sector or even sub-sector policies where there may be real winners and losers as a consequence of policy integration. EPI is likely to encounter conflict which sustainable development causes us to forget. Therefore the legitimating power of sustainable development may collapse on the operational level of EPI.[34]

Neverthless, nothing is more critical for an understanding of the conceptual-normative nature of EPI than the issues here raised. In relation to the first point, Lenschow provides a clear and concise endorsement of EPI as a normative and legal 'first principle' vis-à-vis economic and social dispositions. In relation to the second point, she places this interpretation in serious doubt by laying the blame on a purported conceptual-operational incompatability between EPI and SD.

This ambivalence has been shared by a great number of EPI commentators. In her more recent writing Lenschow has clearly acknowledged the need for greater conceptual clarity regarding EPI and the importance of moving beyond 'win-win solutions' in order to ensure that EPI amounts to a deliberate attempt to prioritize the protection of the environment.[35] The issue of 'what is trump in environmental governance' remains a crucial principle to be clarified in both the academic and political discourses. Towards this end, the focus in the following section is on the key normative issue of 'trade-offs' and on how the issue can be institutionalized by governments for more effective EPI 'policy outputs'.[36] Reference is made throughout to the concepts and approaches here outlined.

3. The EEA-OECD 'Evaluation Framework'

In 2005 the EEA coordinated, in cooperation with the IEEP, a comprehensive review of EPI concepts and approaches. The two major reports resulting from this effort[37] still constitute the best single overview of the political-strategic approach to EPI. Given that the reports also incorporate significant aspects of the more academic discourse on EPI, this body of work can be considered as the 'definitive' reference point for concrete and operational specifications of EPI approaches.

The executive summary of the first report concludes by outlining 'Key challenges and opportunities' and 'Next steps' for promoting and improving EPI as a vital governing mechanism for SD. These aspects of the report will be treated in more detail below. A third feature of the summary may usefully be noted at this stage – namely 'a proposed framework for evaluating EPI'. The framework proposed builds on the DPSIR orientation of the OECD and serves to express in a very succinct form many of the most crucial aspects of the EPI discourse. The EEA refers to the framework as a 'checklist' designed to promote comparative assessments of EPI in practice.[38] In particular, the checklist expressed by the framework is specifically directed towards 'sectoral and cross-sectoral' criteria; that these criteria are viewed in the context of sectoral 'drivers, pressures, states and impacts'; and that the framework identifies 'eco-efficiency' through 'decoupling' as a principal goal of EPI.

With respect to 'key challenges and opportunities', the executive summary makes the following concise statement:

> Clear internal mission statements, new structures and better coordination mechanisms within organisations, greater resources and capacity, and improved information, decision-support and public participation mechanisms can help to overcome existing 'compartmentalisation'. An overarching independent authority to push forward integration can also be valuable. The need for integration to be reflected across multiple levels of governance is also increasingly important.[39]

This framework clearly reflects and complements the OECD 'checklist' of measures for 'improving policy coherence and integration for sustainable development'.[40] It can be viewed as a short list of crucial governing mechanisms for promoting EPI.

Finally, one should note that in terms of 'next steps' the EEA maintains that, despite positive developments along certain dimensions, 'progress is not sufficiently visible across the board'. The executive summary then concludes by pointing out that:

> additional analysis appears to be warranted, in order to deepen our understanding of whether and under what circumstances certain EPI mechanisms can be effective. Work should help with the identification of concrete examples of good practice covering both general and sector-specific activities, as well as supporting refinements of the EPI evaluation framework.[41]

The mechanisms outlined in the following sections of this chapter should be considered as directly related to the two crucial issues raised by the EEA.

4. EPI as Policy Analysis and Learning

Turning to the more 'academic' discourse on EPI, one can highlight the focus of research-based policy analysis. This is related to the effect of different institutional settings as well as to the question of policy learning. The Stockholm Environment Institute (SEI) has addressed these questions over several years – not least in the research project called 'Policy Integration for Sustainability' (PINTS).[42] This research has focused, first, on the question of explanation – how EPI is achieved in practice – and, second, empirically – on how EPI is realized and implemented within different sectors. Two features are of particular interest: the differentiation by Persson[43] of the 'analytical variables and underlying factors' that have been used to explain EPI; and how the analytic framework developed by Nilsson and Persson has been the foundation for further analyis.

Persson has conducted a thorough review of the EPI literature within a policy-analysis perspective and summarized her results in terms of three categories of explanatory factors: normative factors, organizational factors and procedural factors.These appear in Table 13.1.

The approaches are divided, first, into the toolbox approach, 'which involves identifying concrete measures that can be implemented in the short to medium-term' and, second, into the longer-term policy reform approach, 'which involves trying to change fundamental structures in

Table 13.1 Categories of explanatory factors in EPI research

Normative factors: • High-level political commitment • Societal backing • Definition of a policy framework for EPI or sustainable development • Fundamental change in policy paradigm and tradition • Time perspective • Use of knowledge and science
Organisational factors: • Changes in governmental architecture to overcome sector compartmentalisation, e.g. integrated departments, new institutions, new mandates • Accountability mechanisms • Coordination and communcation mechanisms, e.g. environmental correspondents, networks among bureaucrats • Restructuring of the government budgetary process • Training and awareness programmes • Interaction with external actors
Procedural factors: • Implementation of an EPI system: sector report, consultation forum, sector strategy, action plan, monitoring • Change of routine procedures: impact assessment of policy proposals, consultation and participation, rules of decision-making

Source: Persson (2004: p. 36).

policy-making'. Persson then points out, first, that the relative effectiveness of measures to achieve EPI 'is likely to be dependent on context' and, second, that most commentators suggest 'a comprehensive approach comprising a mix of measures'.[44]

These perspectives constitute a summary baseline of explanatory variables and conditions that clearly underlie the more descriptive 'checklists' of assessment criteria provided by the OECD and EEA. They provide a conceptual bridge to the field of policy analysis within political science which aims to develop more comprehensive and robust theories of how change is achieved through policy-making and implementaton.[45] In many ways, the challenge here is to determine either the degree to which the factors identified are general enough to warrant broad recommendation in action plans or whether the contextual effect is, in fact, so strong as to warrant a much more ideographic approach.

Nilsson and Persson build further on these perspectives by formulating the selected factors into an analytic framework for understanding the nature of 'policy outcomes' from EPI. The framework depicts a relatively standard social-science approach by distinguishing between 'background', 'independent' and 'dependent variables'. There are three features of the framework worth emphasizing in the present context. The first is the 'contextualization' of EPI with respect to (a) the nature of the 'the relevant problem' – that is, the type of sectoral activity – and (b) the 'international policy context' – that is, for Europe, international policy as channelled and sanctioned through the EU. The second is an emphasis on three key conditioning variables in specific national contexts – 'political will', 'assessment processes' and 'policy-making rules'.[46] The third is a residual 'black box' for EPI which presumably contains parameters for the organizational and procedural factors listed in Table 13.1 but which are not brought directly into the framework. In relation to the latter, one can also note that – given the designation of the dependent variable as 'policy outcomes' – the EPI box warrants further discussion as to what is actually prescribed or expected as an indication of EPI in practice.

RESOLVING SECTORAL POLICY TRADE-OFFS

1. EPI as a 'First-order Principle'

Given the uncontestable 'mission' nature of EPI, there is no more crucial question than the issue of normative intent in relation to communicating, implementing or assessing the idea of EPI: whether the EPI 'glass' is happily half full or sadly half empty; whether a specific instrument for filling the glass is really appropriate to the task; or whether it is indeed EPI that is in the glass. These are all questions directly related to what it is believed EPI should be. The fact that there are very obvious and very pointed differences of opinion on this question gives testimony to how complex mission-oriented policy analysis can be. It is important to recall in this context, therefore, that a 'clear and consistent goal' is the first of the well-known set of 'critical factors' identified by Sabatier and Mazmanian[47] when judging whether an 'authoritative decision to change an existing state of affairs' is likely to achieve its goal.[48] As documented in the previous section, there can be no doubt that implementing EPI for decoupling for SD is a strongly sanctioned 'authoritative decision to change an existing state of affairs'. Yet there is considerable doubt as to how the decision should be realized in practice.

Differences of opinion on this issue can best be focused on the question of assessing the final result – the status of the EPI 'glass'. The conflict considered to be of central importance here is the question of 'balance' or 'cohesion'. In short, is it the intent of EPI to produce policies, programmes or initiatives that are somehow balanced with respect to the three dimensions or pillars of SD? Or is it rather the intent to produce decisions, outputs or outcomes that, in one way or another, reflect the semantic essence of the concept: the integration of environmental concerns? Clearly, it must be the latter. The discussion is not about strategic goals, guidelines or treaty provisions for policy integration per se but for 'environmental policy integration'. Whatever other disagreements may arise, there can be no doubt that the issue in question is related to a specific normative goal: the integration of environmental concerns *into* 'the definition and implementation' of other policies and activities – for example the goals of the Treaty of the European Union. This is not disputed by any of the approaches outlined above. It is most clearly stated by Lenschow in her characterization of EPI as a 'first-order operational principle to implement and institutionalize sustainable development'.[49] While some choose automatically to equate the EPI acronym with 'balance' and 'coherence', this seriously begs the question of what EPI implies as a pre-ordained standard for what 'balance' and 'coherence' should look like.

In this context it is again Lenschow who provides at the outset a clear signal. Citing Nollkaemper's excellent analysis of EPI in 2002[50] as a 'principle in international law' in her own analysis, Lenschow endorses EPI as 'a procedural principle' and goes on to say that 'it implies that policy-makers in non-environmental sectors recognize the environmental repercussions of their decisions and adjust them when they undermine sustainable development'.[51] It is in this context that she associates EPI with the goal of achieving 'substantive environmental responsibilities': a 'challenge' she identifies as 'ensuring that substance follows from procedure'.[52]

It was this same line of reasoning that led to the following definition of EPI:

> the incorporation of environmental objectives into all stages of policymaking in non-environmental policy sectors, with a specific recognition of this goal as a guiding principle for the planning and execution of policy.[53]

To clarify what is meant by 'balance' and 'coherence', it was consdiered to be necessary to go further. The definition continues, therefore, by stating that the application of the 'guiding principle':

> should be accompanied by: an attempt to aggregate presumed environmental consequences into an overall evaluation of policy, and a commitment to minimize contradictions between environmental and sectoral policies by giving priority to the former over the latter.[54]

This latter part of the definition can be seen as directly addressing: the 'key challenge' raised by the OECD and the EEA – more effective EPI governing mechanisms; the specific nature of both the 'EPI black box' and EPI 'policy outcomes' in the Nilsson-Persson analytic model; and, most specifically, the issue of 'procedure vs. substance' raised by Lenschow.

2. Clarifying the Nature of 'Principled Priority'

In his work, Lafferty[55] has pursued further the implications of the definition along three lines: first, by addressing the question of aggregating 'presumed environmental consequences into an overall evaluation of policy' by further developing a checklist of 'benchmarks' for vertical (sectoral) and horizontal (cross-sectoral) governing mechanisms; second, by stressing that 'environmental objectives' and 'environmental consequences' signify consequences that undermine the natural life-support capacity of ecosystems; and, third, by elaborating on the very difficult issue of what is termed 'principled priority': namely, the 'why' and 'how' of resolving contradictions among sectoral and environmental objectives. The first of these issues is taken up in the following section. The second and third warrant further clarification here. They both go to the heart of Lenschow's perceived 'dilemma' in the relationship between EPI and SD.

The question of what is or should be meant by 'environmental objectives' or 'concerns' is a fundamental condition for a more effective application of EPI. It is here suggested that this issue can be directly resolved within the discourse about the meaning of 'sustainable development'.[56] The 'mother text' of SD is the Brundtland Report, which makes two highly relevant distinctions with respect to 'the environment'. The first distinction is a warning at the very outset of the Brundtland Report to guard against a 'naive' understanding of the environment as something 'separate from human actions, ambitions and needs': 'the "environment" is where we all live; and "development" is what we all do in attempting to improve our lot within that abode. The two are inseparable'.[57]

This 'warning' is particularly relevant for reserving the normative applicability of EPI for policy trade-offs that involve a reasonable presumption of conflict between sectoral drivers and the natural life-support capacity of ecosystems. The Brundtland Report is very specific in its neglect of any concern for ecosystems that are *not* specifically related to economic drivers. This sets up a normative 'filter' against trade-offs related not only to 'aesthetic environmentalism' – for example Tidy Town Awards – but also to 'traditional nature conservation' – namely the protection of nature for nature's own sake.

But the report goes even farther. In a second crucial distinction, the report stresses a need to move away from looking at negative environmental effects *in* isolation. The environmental aspect of SD is, in other words, to be viewed solely in relation to 'policy sources'. This principle is expressed throughout the report. It is given the most explicit treatment in the opening section of the concluding chapter on 'The Challenge for Institutional and Legal Change'. The section is entitled 'Shifting the Focus to Policy Sources'. Of the numerous relevant propositions, the following two stand out as particularly succinct:

> Approaches to environment policy can be broadly characterized in two ways. One, characterized as the 'standard agenda', reflects an approach to environmental policy, laws, and institutions that focuses on environmental effects. The second reflects an approach concentrating on the policies that are the sources of those effects. These two approaches represent distinctively different ways of looking both at the issues and at the institutions to manage them.
>
> Environmental protection and sustainable development must be an integral part of the mandates of all agencies of governments, of international organizations, and of major private-sector institutions. These must be made responsible and accountable for ensuring that their policies, programmes, and budgets encourage and support activities that are economically and ecologically sustainable both in the short and longer terms. They must be given a mandate to pursue their traditional goals in such a way that those goals are reinforced by a steady enhancement of the environmental resource base of their own national community and of the small planet we all share.[58]

Our Common Future – the Brundtland Report – is cited at length on these issues. This is because there is a strong tendency – as evident in Lenschow's 'dilemma' – to use SD as an excuse for not applying EPI as a 'first-order principle'. Practitioners and academics alike sometimes choose to interpret SD to the effect that an abstract balance among the economic, social and environmental pillars is more important for an assessment of EPI results than a clear judgment as to environmental consequences. Such a perspective, it is suggested, is simply not defensible. A close reading of *Our Common Future* is unequivocal in this regard and is the only extensive textual source for delineating the essential political meaning of 'sustainable development'. Neither the Rio Declaration nor the extensive Rio action plan – *Agenda 21* – provides further explicit textual assistance about the meaning of the concept.

Hence, the lynchpin of the present approach is a contention that the Brundtland Report is the seminal key text for interpreting the relationship between EPI and SD. To summarise:

- The SD concept assigns *no* principled priority to economic activities per se. Economic activities are only treated in the Brundtland Report as a problematic 'pressure' on the sustainability of ecosystems. The 'economic dimension' is explicitly associated with 'traditional' policy goals: business as usual.
- The 'social dimension' of SD is most specifically and most consistently related to the goal of satisfying the 'essential needs of the world's poor'. The dimension thus clearly indicates an emphasis on 'poverty' and an assumption that 'essential needs' can – and, with respect to consumption, should – be distingushed from needs that are not essential.
- The 'environmental dimension' is clearly profiled as a limiting condition for the pursuit of both economic and social objectives. The 'environment' is viewed as the necessary natural resource base for maintaining life on earth.
- The need for integrating environmental concerns into all policy areas is the distinct defining 'variable' in the SD equation. It is worth pointing out in this regard that one of the major reasons for establishing the WCED in the first place was to address the man-made degradation of ecosystem capacity as a consequence of extreme poverty.

The language of article 11 in Part 1 of the EU Treaty is explicit: 'Environmental protection requirements must be integrated into the definition and implementation of Community policies and activivites … in particular with a view to promoting sustainable development'. The explicit nature of this language 'can be seen to be in line with this understanding'.[59] Importantly, EPI is here given a separate article under the introductory section on 'Principles'. Moreover, it is the only article where the term 'must' is used to prescribe a given action. Note also that the integration of 'protection requirements' is to be manifest in both the 'definition' and 'implementation' of policies. This clearly implies both a stipulated procedure and a specific goal-oriented enactment. Policies that do not include provisions for environmental protection are, in principle, to be avoided by this prescription.

It is primarily as a logical consequence of all of these perspectives that EPI can be formulated as a question of principled priority in favour of the Brundtland understanding of 'environmental objectives'. In addition to this normative position, however, one can also understand the notion of 'principled priority' as a necessary pragmatic response to the very obvious and well-documented fact that existing attempts to promote SD through a 'balanced' understanding of EPI clearly are not working. This is particularly obvious with respect to the most significant threat to SD – climate change. It is also apparent with respect to a much broader range of ecosystem-threatening factors. On the basis of evaluations of SD implementation in Norway demonstrating that environmental concerns were being consistently overrun by other policy objectives, the ProSus research team focused its EPI research on the issue of intra-governmental trade-offs.[60] The burden of proof for EPI initiatives that aim only at 'balanced win-win policies objectives' is becoming increasingly precarious.

It is in light of these considerations that the EPI problematic is here formulated as a question of designating environmental concerns as 'trump' in relation to critical trade-offs among competing policy objectives. Having the status of 'trump' in card games implies that certain cards or suits of card have an extraordinary status in relation to the normal rules for resolving the basic competitions of the game. The status of trump is determined prior to the dealing of the cards; it is most often applied under special conditions and decision-making rules; and it is game-specific. The relevance of trump in the context of EPI is that implied by the Brundtland Report. Achieving SD means introducing a new legal and institutional structure for transcending the 'existing' or 'traditional' set of value priorities in the trade-off between economic, social and environmental activities. The existing 'trumps' in highly developed societies are invaribly to the advantage of either economic or social welfare priorities. All such priorities imply burdens on natural resources and life-support systems. The essence of EPI is to decouple this situation by assigning principled priority to ecosystem requirements.

Does this mean that policy concerns other than the environment must invariably give way before environmental concerns? Clearly not. Just as the rules of trump are always stipulated within, and made conditional on, the broader rules of the game, so it is with EPI. At the same time, the resolution of policy trade-offs must be made within a more fundamental set of democratic decision-making rules. The nature of these rules can, however, vary considerably from democratic system to democratic system. It is a normal feature of democracies to designate certain values as more fundamental than others. Whether determined by constitutions, statutes or administrative rules, all democracies have certain values that are assigned exceptional rights within the fundamental rules of decision-making. It is to address this most fundamental aspect of EPI that the EEA identifies simultaneously a high-level requirement for EPI as a key aspect of political commitment and strategic vision together with a mission statement that reflects environmental values as a basis for administrative culture and practices.[61] It is also to explore the nature of the aspect that Nilsson and Persson designate 'policy making rules' as one of two crucial 'independent variables' in explaining EPI outcomes. Given, first, that the EEA framework is specifically directed towards sectoral – vertical – integration and does not address cross-sectoral trade-offs and, second, that the Nilsson-Persson approach focuses mainly on policy learning with little attention actually devoted to decision-making rules, a major task has emerged: namely to stipulate just how EPI as 'principled priority' might be applied.

It is towards this end that a number of possible governing mechanisms for enhancing the substantive output of EPI by strengthening the procedural 'trump' status of environmental and ecosystem protection have been suggested. Three of these mechanisms will be elaborated upon here: the general form of a 'canon for practical judgment' for EPI; the application of science, assessments and the 'precautionary principle'; and the challenge of finding means to secure the 'political will' that is necessary to support EPI in practice.

GOVERNING MECHANISMS FOR ENHANCING EPI AS POLICY OUTPUT

1. Introduction

Given the prospect of increased consensus as to the normative status of EPI, the implementation discussion can then turn to the question of differentiated assessment. EPI can be analyzed and evaluated as procedure, policy and outcome. EPI systems can be imagined that vary on all three dimensions – and not necessarily in a cumulative manner. Only aspects of decision-making that enhance the status of environmental concerns in policy output are examined here. How the policy itself is implemented by governments and what the ultimate outcome of the policy is are not covered.[62]

2. A 'Canon for Practical Judgment'

The notion of developing a 'canon for practical judgment' as a basic guideline for EPI-related decision-making is inspired by Kant's 'analytic of principles'.[63] A 'canon' in this context is 'a general rule, fundamental principle, aphorism, or axiom governing the systematic or scientific treatment of a subject'.[64] The process for applying the 'rule' here is governmental decision-making and the 'subject' is EPI. In the context of the present discussion, the following is proposed as a core statement of the canon for any given political domain:

1. Applying EPI as a first-order principle for decision-making for SD involves the resolution of trade-offs between sectoral policy objectives and environmental objectives.
2. The designated types of policy in question are:
   a. economic policies designed to promote sustainable livelihoods for current and future generations
   b. social policies designed to satisfy essential needs and eliminate poverty – nationally and globally
   c. environmental policies designed to protect and enhance the long-term life-support capacity of ecosystems.
3. The principles and criteria necessary to achieve (c) constitute a priority 'proviso' for regulating the policy objectives of (a) and (b).

The logic of this statement can be considered to correspond roughly with the normative intent attributed to EPI by the three research approaches outlined above. This statement can also be considered to lay an initial foundation for further developing the canon as a practical set of standards and guidelines for making necessary judicious decisions on policy trade-offs under an EPI mandate. The judicious nature of the process is here stressed in order to avoid any further misunderstanding as to the nature of EPI as 'trump'. To be 'judicious' in this context means to apply an EPI canon in a reflective, prudent and transparent manner. Once more it does not mean that environmental concerns will override economic and social objectives in every incidence of decision-making. The balance among the environmental and ecosystem concerns and other policy objectives will have to be decided on a case-by-case basis. The only requirements of EPI as 'first principle' are, first, to guarantee that every effort is made to assess the impacts of the policies – short, medium and long term – on the life-sustaining capacities of the affected ecosystems and, second, to limit clearly or otherwise qualify in advance those impacts that represent unacceptable risks of degradation.

3. Science, Assessments and the Precautionary Principle

If the general notion of 'principled priority' is attached to a clearly expressed EPI mandate, much would be accomplished. The diffuse notion of EPI as 'balanced policy' together with the dominant but very limited view of EPI as primarily a search for win-win solutions would be superseded. Environmental concerns could not, however, be expected to trump all trade-offs. But transparent arguments and political-administrative accountability should be expected if environmental concerns are judged to be unaffected by sectoral policies.

This does not resolve the very difficult issue of determining risk in the application of the canon. Here the challenge clearly lies with the posited status of the ecosystem in question; with the quality of the assessed 'impacts' from sectoral 'drivers'; and with the ability to formulate and communicate risk factors directly into the decision-making process. The first issue is a challenge to the integration of scientific knowledge into the policy-making process; the second is a challenge to the quality, scope and weight of environmental and SD assessments; and the third is a challenge to find practical mechanisms for applying the precautionary principle.

The introduction of scientific knowledge on the 'limits of nature' is a question of both determining and communicating consensual estimates as to the long-term sustainability of whichever resource or ecosystem service is most affected by the policy initiative in question. While there are several excellent initiatives in place for promoting the 'science of sustainability' on a more general level, there are relatively few examples of scientific advisory councils with a mandate similar to that implied here. There is the relatively high-profile Science Advisory Council (SAC) that is part of the Department for Environment, Food and Rural Affairs in the United Kingdom and the similar National Council for Science and the Environment (NCSE) in the United States. Their tasks, however, are very broad and largely informative. Two more appropriate examples would be, first, the Advisory Council for Research on Spatial Planning, Nature and the Environment (RMNO) in the Netherlands which operated until 2009 and contributed directly to outlining alternative paths and possible general consequences of policy and, second, perhaps most relevant, the Scientific Support Plan for a Sustainable Development in Belgium.[65]

In relation to the role of environmental assessments, there is extensive documentation on the usage and consequences of both 'environmental' and 'strategic' impact assessments (EIAs and SEAs). There are separate

EU directives for both. This is clearly a crucial subfield of both the political and academic approaches to EPI.[66]

Finally, there is the much-discussed role of the 'precautionary principle'. This principle – added to the normative-conceptual core of SD at the Bergen Conference on Sustainable Development in 1990 and included as principle 15 of the Rio Declaration – can be considered to represent a true bottom-line for EPI implementation. Without going into detail here on all of the numerous controversial issues surrounding the principle which are covered in other chapters, it is worth referring to a significant collection of studies in 2006 by Fisher and her colleagues.[67] This work brings together both conceptual and empirical analyses of a number of different application areas in Europe, Australia and the United States. Three aspects of the study are particularly relevant for the EPI discourse.

First, there is a proposal for a consensual definition of the concept by René von Schomberg, an expert on science, uncertainty and policy implementation within the European Commission. After a thorough analysis of recent legal and conceptual work on the principle, von Schomberg presents the following definition:

> Where, following an assessment of available scientific information, there are reasonable grounds for concern for the possibility of adverse effects but scientific uncertainty persists, provisional risk management measures based on a broad cost-benefit analysis whereby priority will be given to human health and environment, necessary to ensure the chosen high level of protection in the Community and proportionate to this level of protection, may be adopted, pending further scientific information for a more comprehensive risk assessment, without having to wait until the reality and seriousness of those adverse effects become fully apparent.[68]

One interpretation of this definition is that it can serve as a normative point of departure for institutionalizing procedures and for governing bodies to give principled priority to the advantage of environmental concerns put forth on the basis of scientific grounds but without a consensus on scientific certainty. Such an interpretation would anchor EPI's 'trump' status within a general principle that is specifically designed to bridge the normative and the practical. It would nonetheless be subject to specific forms of argument and evidence. The major challenge here is to continue working on the specifics of developing legal-administrative institutional procedures.

Second, it is important to stress that such a legal-administrative institutionalization of the precautionary principle would not only allow a more forceful and effective implementation of EPI – the major goal of the OECD and EEA assessments; it would also allow for a much more transparent and accountable politics of SD. If major decisions on policy trade-offs for SD are carried out within structured procedures that reflect the values of joining the first-order EPI principle with the bottom-line precautionary principle, it would be clear for both media and public-stakeholder scrutiny *why* such decisions have the policy-output profile they do. It is in the 'spotlight' of such trade-off deliberation that the judicial application of EPI as 'trump' will be decided. If the level of risk of environmental degradation is below a given threshold,[69] then a decision to compromise potential environmental damage will have been made in an open forum and the political-administrative actors will have to stand responsible for the result.

This points to a third suggestion that can be made on the basis of the work by Fisher and Harding.[70] A key distinction is here made between two competing frameworks for the 'administrative constitutional' anchoring of the precautionary principle. These commentators here differentiate between a 'deliberative-constitutive' framework and a 'rational-instrumental' framework. Whereas the former is primarily an academic normative model, applying the standards of deliberative democratic theory,[71] the latter is a reconstructed model of implementation as derived from a report on impact assessment from the European Commission.[72] Space does not allow for further elaboration here of the very rich analysis undertaken by Fisher and Harding. However, it can be concluded that the work lays a solid theoretical basis for a more widespread and consequent institutionalization of the precautionary principle as a crucial feature of EPI governance. The authors' concluding admonition offers a perfect bridge to the view of the principle expressed in this chapter: a view that stresses a need for 'principled priority' rather than 'balance' through institutional deliberation and accomodation:

> there is a need for scholars and policy makers to take a far more sophisticated approach to thinking about the [precautionary] principle's application because that process of application is not about writing a checklist or carrying out an algorithm but rather about developing the institutional capacity for effective and legitimate decision making in circumstances where there is considerable polarization over what these terms mean.[73]

4. EPI and 'Political Will'

No variable has received stronger support as a *sine qua non* for improved SD implementation than 'political will'. It has also been profiled – usually as a predominant factor – in all of the major overviews of EPI problematics in each of the 'political' and 'academic' discourses. As initially stated by the OECD:

> A strong political commitment is crucial to achieve the policy integration needed to underpin sustainable development. This must come from the highest levels of government, and be embraced by prime ministers, as well as ministers of economy/finance, social welfare, and the environment. …
>
> Collective responsibility within government for implementation of decisions which support a sustainable development strategy needs to be clearly established, and include explicit procedures and an assessment of training needs. Coherence across government departments and among different levels of government is vital.[74]

This statement clearly expresses one of the most decisive administrative requirements for improving EPI. Securing 'first-principle' status for environmental policy integration – preferably connected to a judicious application of the precautionary principle – means that the principles in question must be 'blessed' by the political-administrative system in a specific constitutional way. Essential to this process is that the principles must be not only strongly endorsed by the democratically elected heads of government but also firmly anchored in and through the ongoing political-administrative processes that govern for society. As stated earlier, 'governance is the responsibility of governments'.[75] It is important to acknowledge a need for greater interaction among governments at all levels, citizens and stakeholders as well as a need for greater deliberation and dialogue among competing discourses as an essential mode of interaction. It is also crucial to acknowledge that both 'sovereignty' and 'subsidiarity' imply political responsibility for public mandates.

According to Fisher and Harding, the 'deliberative-constitutive' and 'rational-instrumental' models of 'administrative constitutionalism' can be viewed as potentially complementary in achieving substantive EPI-SD results.They can also be viewed as essentially inimical to such results. Pluralist access to the business of making EPI trade-offs together with the institutionalization of serious deliberative-discursive processes can increase the total democratic input into the process and thereby increase transparency. The same process can, however, also increase both conflict and disagreement – leading at best to minimalist 'log-rolling' and at worst to deadlock and inaction. Either way, the issue of political accountability for the achievement of long-term, holistic and consequential goals – that is the goals of SD – can be seriously compromised. The issue is a 'dilemma' in the truest sense of the word. What is needed is inclusive decision-making and deliberation to improve not only effectiveness in implementation but also general norms of democratic legitimacy. Also needed is more robust, cumulative and expert administrative steering to achieve the transformative changes necessary for SD. The strong consensus about a need for increased political will seems to grasp this dilemma by the proverbial 'horns'. Few are the analysts who choose to confront this particular bull head on.

Here is a list of several of the OECD's key questions on the issue of political leadership and EPI implementation:[76]

- Is there a clear commitment at the highest level to the formulation and implementation of SD objectives and strategies?
- Is this commitment effectively communicated to the various sectors of government machinery and across levels of government?
- When gaps exist between the administrative and political agendas, are specific efforts made to bridge or fill them?
- Is leadership expressed through a sequence of priorities over time?
- Is government maintaining a sense of urgency, despite the longer-term nature of the issues related to SD?
- Is there an institutional 'catalyst' – a ministry or a select committee – in charge of enforcing SD strategies?
- Is this 'catalyst' located strategically within the government machinery perhaps at the level of the Prime Minister's office?
- Are there specific reviews of laws and regulations to check whether they conflict with SD, and are SD objectives embedded in new legislation and regulations?
- Are organizations moving from narrow sectoral perspectives – agriculture, industry and transport – to a more 'issues-oriented' agenda – air quality, mobility or poverty reduction?
- Is SD integrated into regular government exercises – for example the budget process?

If the answer to all of these questions is 'yes', the 'bull' of unsustainable governance would be turned more surely in the direction of effective EPI for SD. With such governing benchmarks in place, the cumulative effect of a 'rational-instrumental constitutional administration' would, in principle, be biased towards Brundtlandesque outcomes. At that point – but hardly before – one could move safely on to the added value of strengthening the 'deliberative constitutive' mode of governance.

CONCLUSION

This book appears in a situation where – in Europe at least – there is a growing acknowledgment of a pressing need to be more consequential with governance for SD. In this context, attention has increasingly turned toward the challenges of consensually defining and implementing environmental policy integration.[77] This is viewed as crucial if the goal is to enable and coordinate clear governance strategies designed to fulfil the declared policy objectives of national and international political authorities over the last two-and-a-half decades. A concerted effort by all responsible and affected actors is required if the environmental dimension of 'sustainable development' is to be more than a common talking point.

Towards this end, the major argument presented here can be summarized as follows. First, EPI has been identified as a crucial instrument for achieving decoupling, which in turn is a crucial goal of SD. Second, the normative intent of EPI is to function as a 'first-order principle' for resolving trade-offs between sectoral policy goals and environmental and ecological concerns. Third, existing attempts to achieve EPI through governance are widely acknowledged as relatively weak and relatively non-consequential. Fourth, the previous three conclusions are in fact common for leading-edge EPI research efforts today. Fifth, the major challenge confronted by EU member states is to develop governing mechansims that strengthen the 'principled-priority' status of EPI in both vertical – sectoral – and horizontal – governmental – decision making.

More systematic research is clearly still needed in relation to governing mechanisms. Recent comprehensive overviews of EPI research have stressed the need for more systematic evaluations and for an overall research framework for the analysis of governing mechanisms pertaining to EPI with particular emphasis on comparative analysis.[78]

Another important aspect to stress is that applying EPI as 'principled priority' in no way compromises a creative and innovative search for 'win-win' solutions or for other 'cohesive' policies for SD. There can be no doubt that the Brundtland Report views this possibility as an important means for changing the quality of economic growth in a more sustainable direction. Problems arise, however, when the very difficult prospect of achieving a win-win balance – as massively documented by negative progress on crucial ecological indicators – becomes the dominant approach to environmental integration.

Finally, a concluding caveat. The focus here is principally on the normative premises for institutionalizing EPI as a mechanism for governmental decision-making. It is *not* contended that such an institutionalization will, or even should, guarantee EPI policy 'output' in favour of natural life-support systems in *every* decision-making instance. Nor is it contended that even the strongest pro-environmental policies will guarantee effective implementation or that governmental decision-making is enough to achieve change. What has been established, it is suggested, is a normative 'bottom line', in principle and procedurally, for a more effective realization of environmental goals.

Without such a mandate at the inception of EPI application, without greater consensus as to the normative intent of EPI within the SD political discourse, and without more effective governing mechanisms for resolving crucial trade-offs in policy formulation, the chances of realizing EPI for SD are slim indeed. Institutionalizing EPI as 'principled priority' clearly does not solve all the challenges hindering more substantive EPI results. However, it should, at least, provide not only clearer signals as to what is expected but also clearer standards for transparency and accountability. Ultimately, the nature and effectiveness of EPI must be viewed within a broader discussion as to the overall functionality of current western models of democratic governance for achieving SD.[79] EPI is not, in short, a 'silver bullet' for achieving global sustainability. It is, however, a crucial aspect of an open acknowledgement that new and more difficult targets require new modes of gunnery.

NOTES

1. This chapter builds upon a research paper originally prepared for the EU-sponsored 'Concerted Action' on Environmental Policy Integration and Multi-Level Governance (EPIGOV) – a consortium of 19 research institutions from ten European countries (Lafferty and Knudsen (2007); European Research Area (2009)).
2. WCED (1987, p. 313).
3. The present chapter builds and expands upon research undertaken by the authors within the Programme for Research and Documentation for a Sustainable Society (ProSus), at the University of Oslo, Norway (1995–2008). A main activity of the programme was to document and evaluate Norway's follow-up of the Rio accords and the guidelines of the United Nations Commission for Sustainable Development (CSD) through ongoing evaluations of Norway's progress with respect to the stated goals and action plans. This activity was conducted in cooperation with other national and international research institutions, applying the standards of comparative methodology and systematic political evaluation. The programme was designed to provide alternative strategies of governance, identifying effective steering instruments at regional, national and local levels of governance. There gradually emerged within the programme a concerted effort to clarify the conceptual character and implications of EPI, with a special emphasis on the goal of assigning 'principled

priority' to environmental concerns when confronted by difficult policy trade-offs (Lafferty and Hovden (2002); Lafferty (2004b)).

4. Cf. Lafferty (2004c).
5. WCED (1987).
6. Mullaly and Dunphy (2014).
7. European Research Area (2009); Jordan and Lenschow (2008b, 2010); Runhaar (2014).
8. Mullaly and Dunphy (2014); Knudsen (2010).
9. Adelle and Russell (2013).
10. Ibid.
11. Cf. Fisher (2009).
12. Runhaar, Driessen and Uittenbroek (2014).
13. OECD (2001a, 2001b, 2002a, 2002b); EEA (2005a, 2005b, 2005c).
14. Nilsson and Eckerberg (2007); Persson (2004, 2007); Nilsson and Persson (2003).
15. Lenschow (2002a); European Research Area (2009); Jordan and Lenschow (2008b, 2010).
16. Cf. Mullaly and Dunphy (2014).
17. Lafferty and Hovden (2002); Lafferty and Knudsen (2007).
18. Lafferty and Hovden (2003); Lafferty (2004a).
19. OECD (2001a, 2001b); EEA (2005a).
20. Wilkinson (1997); Lenschow (2002a); Jordan, Schout and Unfried (2008); European Research Area (2009).
21. European Research Area (2009).
22. Jordan, Schout and Unfried (2008).
23. Bomberg (2004).
24. European Commission (2002).
25. European Union (2009).
26. Jordan, Schout and Unfried (2008, p. 163).
27. Pallemaerts (2006); Williams (2007); Jordan, Schout and Unfried (2008, pp. 159–60).
28. See, e.g. Knudsen (2012).
29. Lenschow (2002a, pp. 16–18).
30. Ibid. (p. 6).
31. Liberatore (1997, p. 107).
32. Lenschow (2002a, pp. 6–7).
33. Ibid. (p. 7, emphasis added).
34. Ibid. (pp. 7–8).
35. Jordan and Lenschow (2008a, p. 8).
36. The differentiation between 'policy process' (procedure), 'policy output' (document and/or programme) and 'policy outcome' (the actual results of policies and programmes) is common to policy analysis in political science. Vedung (1997) provides an excellent overview with respect to policy evaluation.
37. EEA (2005a, 2005b).
38. In both form and substance, the EEA framework reflects the somewhat broader 'checklist' of the OECD (2002b) with criteria for 'Improving policy coherence and integration for sustainable development'.
39. EEA (2005a, p. 9).
40. OECD (2002b).
41. EEA (2005a, p. 9).
42. The PINTS Project – 'Policy Integration for Sustainability' – funded by the Swedish Research Council for Environment, Agricultural Sciences and Spatial Planning

(FORMAS), and carried out principally at the Stockholm Environment Institute (SEI). The final report of the project was published in 2007 (Nilsson and Eckerberg 2007).
43. Persson (2004, pp. 26–36); Persson (2007).
44. Persson (2004, p. 36).
45. See, e.g. Parsons (1995); Sabatier (1999); and the critical discussion in the concluding chapter of Lafferty (2004a).
46. Nilsson and Persson (2003) designate 'political will' as a 'background variable', but this is open for discussion. The 'will' in question is, in our view, so directly related to both the national context and the EPI process that it can just as well be categorized as an 'independent' variable.
47. Sabatier and Mazmanian (1979).
48. See Lafferty (2004a, p. 10) for the other factors, and for a broader discussion of the factors in relation to governance for sustainable development.
49. Lenschow (2002a, pp. 6–7).
50. Nollkaemper (2002).
51. Lenschow (2002a, p. 7).
52. Ibid.
53. Lafferty and Hovden (2003, p. 9).
54. Lafferty (2001, p. 9); Lafferty and Hovden (2003, p. 12).
55. Lafferty (2004a, 2004b).
56. Lafferty and Langhelle (1999).
57. WCED (1987, p. xi).
58. WCED (1987, pp. 310 and 312).
59. European Commission (2009).
60. Lafferty et al. (1997); Lafferty, Nordskag and Aakree (2002); Lafferty, Knudsen and Larsen (2007).
61. EEA (2005b).
62. See, however, Lafferty (2004b); Lafferty, Larsen and Ruud (2008); and Larsen (2005) for approaches to the question of governmental implementation.
63. See, e.g. Caygill (1994); and Kemp (1968).
64. OED (1987, p. 207).
65. See BSP (2005, 2006).
66. See, in particular, Sadler (2005); Dalal-Clayton and Sadler (2005); Hertin, Jacob and Volkery (2008); Bina (2008).
67. Fisher and Harding (2006).
68. von Schomberg (2006, p. 37).
69. Fisher and Harding (2006) present several mechanisms for risk assessment in relation to specific policy issues.
70. Fisher and Harding (2006).
71. Deville and Hardin (1997).
72. CEC (2002).
73. Fisher and Harding (2006, p. 132).
74. OECD (2001b, p. 120).
75. Lafferty (2004a).
76. OECD (2002b, pp. 8–9).
77. Cf. Mullally and Dunphy (2014); Runhaar, Driessen and Uittenbroek (2014).
78. Ibid.
79. Lafferty (2012).

REFERENCES

Adelle, C. and D. Russel (2013), 'Climate Policy Integration: a Case of Déjà Vu?', *Environmental Policy and Governance* 23, 1–12.

Bina, O. (2008), 'Strategic Environmental Assessment', in A. Jordan and A. Lenschow (eds), *Innovation in Environmental Policy? Integrating the Environment for Sustainability* (Cheltenham, Edward Elgar), pp. 134–58.

Bomberg, E. (2004), 'Adapting form to function? From economic to sustainable development governance in the European Union', in W.M. Lafferty (ed.), *Governance for Sustainable Development: The Challenge of Adapting Form to Function* (Cheltenhem, Edward Elgar), pp. 61–94.

BSP (Brussels Science Policy) (2005), *Science and Precaution: An Interactive Risk Assessment – SPIRE*, D/2005/1191/25 (Brussels, Belgium Science Policy).

BSP (2006), The Role of Public Authorities in Integrated Product Policy: Regulators or Coordinators, D/2006/2201/12 (Brussels, Belgium Science Policy).

Caygill, H. (1994), *A Kant Dictionary* (Oxford, Blackwell Publishers).

CEC (Commission of the European Communities) (2002), *Communication from the Commission on Impact Assessment*, COM(2002) 276 final (Brussels, Commission of the European Communities).

Dalal-Clayton, B. and B. Sadler (2005), *Strategic Environmental Assessment: A Sourcebook and Reference Guide to International Experience* (London, Earthscan).

Deville, A. and R. Harding (1997), *Applying the Precautionary Principle* (Sydney, Federation Press).

EEA (2005a), *Environmental Policy Integration in Europe: State of Play and an Evaluation Framework*, EEA Technical Report No.2/2005 (Copenhagen, EEA).

EEA (2005b), *Environmental Policy Integration in Europe: Administrative Culture and Practices*, EEA Technical Report No.5/2005 (Copenhagen, EEA).

EEA (2005c), *The European Environment: State and Outlook 2005* (Copenhagen, EEA).

European Commission (2002), Consolidated Version of the Treaty Establishing the European Community, Official Journal C 325, 24 December 2002; http://europa.eu.int/eur-lex/en/treaties/dat/C_2002325EN.003301.html.

European Research Area (2009), 'Environmental Policy Integration and Multi-Level Governance (EPIGOV). Finalised Project', *European Policy Brief* (Brussels, European Research Area).

EU (2009), Consolidated Version on the Treaty of the Functioning of the European Union [2009] OJ C115/47, 9 May 2009 (Brussels, The European Communities).

Fisher, D. (2009), *The Law and Governance of Water Resources. The Challenge of Sustainability* (Cheltenham and Northampton MA, Edward Elgar).

Fisher, E. and R. Harding (2006), 'The precautionary principle and administrative constitutionalism: The development of frameworks for applying the precautionary principle', in E. Fisher, J. Jones and R. von Schomberg (eds), *Implementing the Precautionary Principle: Perspectives and Prospects* (Cheltenham and Northampton MA, Edward Elgar), pp. 113–36.

Fisher, E., J. Jones and R. von Schomberg (eds) (2006), *Implementing the Precautionary Principle: Perspectives and Prospects* (Cheltenham and Northampton MA, Edward Elgar).

Hertin, J., K. Jacob and A. Volkery (2008), 'Policy appraisal' in A. Jordan and A. Lenschow (eds), *Innovation in Environmental Policy? Integrating the Environment for Sustainability* (Cheltenham, Edward Elgar), pp. 114–33.

Jordan, A. and A. Lenschow (2010), 'Environmental policy integration: a state of the art review', *Environmental Policy and Governance* 20, 147–58.

Jordan, A.J. and A. Lenschow (2008a), 'Environmental policy integration: an innovation in environmental policy?', in A.J. Jordan amd A. Lenschow (eds), *Innovation in Environmental Policy? Integrating the Environment for Sustainability* (Cheltenham, Edward Elgar), pp. 3–23.

Jordan, A.J. and A. Lenschow (eds) (2008b), *Innovation in Environmental Policy? Integrating the Environment for Sustainability* (Cheltenham, Edward Elgar).

Jordan, A. and D. Liefferink (eds) (2004), *Environmental Policy in Europe: The Europeanization of National Environmental Policy* (London and New York, Routledge).

Jordan, A. and A. Schout (2006), *The Coordination of the European Union: Exploring the Capacities of Networked Governance* (Oxford, Oxford University Press).

Jordan, A., A. Schout and M. Unfried (2008), 'The European Union', in A. Jordan and A. Lenschow (eds), *Innovation in Environmental Policy? Integrating the Environment for Sustainability* (Cheltenham, Edward Elgar), pp. 159–79.

Kemp, J. (1968), *The Philosophy of Kant* (Oxford, Oxford University Press).

Knudsen, J.K. (2010), 'Integrating environmental concerns in a trans-Atlantic perspective: The case of renewable electricity', *Review of Policy Research* 27(2), 127–46.

Knudsen, J.K. (2012), 'Renewable energy and environmental policy integration: Renewable fuel for the European energy policy?', in F. Morata and I.S. Sandoval (eds), *European Energy Policy. An Environmental Approach* (Cheltenham, Edward Elgar), pp. 48–65.

Lafferty, W.M. (2001), 'Adapting government practice to the goals of sustainable development'. Paper prepared for the OECD/PUMA, Seminar on 'Improving governance for sustainable development', Paris, OECD, 22–23 November 2001.

Lafferty, W.M. (2004a), 'Introduction' and 'Lessons and implications', in W.M. Lafferty (ed.), *Governance for Sustainable Development: The Challenge of Adapting Form to Function* (Cheltenham UK, Edward Elgar), pp. 1–31 and 319–60.

Lafferty, W.M. (2004b), 'From environmental protection to sustainable development: The challenge of decoupling through sectoral integration', in W.M. Lafferty (ed.), *Governance for Sustainable Development: The Challenge of Adapting Form to Function* (Cheltenhem, Edward Elgar), pp. 191–220.

Lafferty, W.M. (2004c), 'Governmental initiatives for environmental policy integration: A further specification of benchmarks and normative standards'. Plenary address to the 2004 Berlin Conference on the Human Dimensions of Global Environmental Change, The Free University of Berlin, 3–4 December 2004.

Lafferty, W.M. (2012), 'Governance for sustainable development: The impasse of dysfunctional democracy' in J. Meadowcroft, O. Langhelle and A. Ruud (eds), *Governance, Democracy and Sustainable Development: Moving Beyond the Impasse* (Cheltenham and Northampton MA, Edward Elgar), pp. 297–337.

Lafferty, W.M. and E. Hovden (2002), 'Environmental Policy Integration: Towards an analytical framework', *ProSus Report* No.7/02 (Oslo, ProSus, University of Oslo).

Lafferty, W.M. and E. Hovden (2003), 'Environmental Policy Integration: Towards an Analytical Framework', *Environmental Politics* 12(3), 1–22.

Lafferty W.M. and J. Knudsen (2007), 'The issue of "balance" and trade-offs in environmental policy integration: How will we know EPI when we see it?', *EPIGOV Paper* No.11 (Berlin, Ecologic).

Lafferty, W.M. and O. Langhelle (1999), *Towards Sustainable Development: On the Goals of Development – and the Conditions of Sustainability* (London, Macmillan Publishers).

Lafferty, W.M. and A. Ruud (2006), 'Standards for Green Innovation: Applying a Proposed Framework to Governmental Initiatives in Norway', *Evaluation* 12(4), 453–72.

Lafferty, W.M., J. Knudsen and O.M. Larsen (2007), 'Pursuing sustainable development in Norway: The challenge of living up to Brundtland at home', *European Environment* 17, 177–88.

Lafferty, W.M., O. Langhelle, P. Mugaas and M.R. Holmboe Ruge (eds) (1997), *Rio +5: Norges Oppfølging av FN-konferansen om miljø og utvikling* (Oslo, Tano Aschehoug).
Lafferty, W.M., O.M. Larsen and A. Ruud (2008), 'Norway' in Andrew Jordan and Andrea Lenschow (eds), *Integrating the Environment for Sustainable Development* (Cheltenham, Edward Elgar), pp. 202–23.
Lafferty, W.M., M. Nordskag and H.A. Aakree (eds) (2002), *Realizing Rio in Norway: Evaluative Studies of Sustainable Development* (Oslo, ProSus).
Lafferty, W.M., A. Ruud and O.M. Larsen (2005), 'Environmental Policy Integration: How Will We Recognize It When We See It? The Case of Green Innovation Policy in Norway' in *Governance of Innovation Systems: Case Studies in Cross-Sectoral Policy* (Paris, OECD), pp. 221–44.
Larsen, O.M. (2005), 'Governing Innovation for Sustainable Development: Integration of Environmental and Innovation Policies in Norway', Report No.4/2005 (Oslo, ProSus).
Lenschow, A. (2002a), *Environmental Policy Integration. Greening Sectoral Policies in Europe* (London, Earthscan).
Lenschow, A. (2002b), 'New regulatory approaches in "greening" EU policies', in A. Jordan (ed.), *Environmental Policy in the European Union* (London, Earthscan), pp. 295–316.
Liberatore, A. (1997), 'The integration of sustainable development objectives into EU policy-making: Barriers and prospects', in S. Baker, M. Kousis, D. Richardson and S. Young (eds), *The Politics of Sustainable Development: Theory, Policy and Practice within the European Union* (London, Routledge), pp. 107–26.
Mullally, G. and N. Dunphy (2014), 'State of Play Review of Environmental Policy Integration Literature. A report for the National Economic and Social Council (NESC), prepared by the Cleaner Production Promotion Unit, University College Cork, December 2014.
Nilsson, M. and K. Eckerberg (eds) (2007), *Environmental Policy Integration in Practice: Shaping Institutions by Learning* (London, Earthscan).
Nilsson, M. and Å Persson (2003), 'Framework for Analysing Environmental Policy Integration', *Journal of Environmental Policy and Planning* 5(4), 333–59.
Nollkaemper (2002), 'Three conceptions of the integration principle in international law' in A. Lenschow (ed.), *Environmental Policy Integration: Greening Sectoral Policies in Europe* (London, Earthscan), pp. 22–32.
OECD (2001a), *Policies to Enhance Sustainable Development* (Paris, OECD).
OECD (2001b), *Sustainable Development: Critical Issues* (Paris, OECD).
OECD (2002a), *Governance for Sustainable Development: Five OECD Case Studies* (Paris, OECD).
OECD (2002b), 'Improving policy coherence and integration for sustainable development: A checklist', OECD Policy Brief, PUMA, October, Paris.
OED (1987), *The Compact Oxford English Dictionary* (2nd edn) (Oxford, Oxford University Press).
Pallemaerts, M. (2006), 'The EU and Sustainable Development: An Ambiguous Relationship' in M. Pallemaerts and A. Azmanova (eds), *The European Union and Sustainable Development* (Brussels, VUB Press), pp. 19–52.
Parsons, W. (1995), *Public Policy: An Introduction to the Theory and Practice of Policy Analysis* (Aldershot, UK and Brookfield, US, Edward Elgar).
Persson, Å. (2004), 'Environmental Policy Integration: An Introduction'. Background Paper: Project on Policy Integration for Sustainability (PINTS) (Stockholm, Stockholm Environment Institute (SEI)).
Persson, Å. (2007), 'Different Perspective on EPI' in M. Nilsson and K. Eckerberg (eds), *Environmental Policy Integration in Practice: Shaping Institutions by Learning* (London, Earthscan), pp. 25–48.

Runhaar, H., P. Driessen and C. Uittenbroek (2014), 'Towards a Systematic Framework for the Analysis of Environmental Policy Integration', *Environmental Policy and Governance* 24, 233–46.

Sabatier, P.A. (1999), *Theories of the Policy Process* (Boulder, Westview Press).

Sabatier, P.A. and D. Mazmanian (1979), 'The conditions of effective implementation: A guide to accomplishing policy objectives', *Policy Analysis* 5, 481–504.

Sadler, B. (ed.) (2005), *Strategic Environmental Assessment at the Policy Level: Recent Progress, Current Status and Future Prospects* (Prague, Ministry of the Environment, Czech Republic).

Vedung, E. (1997), *Public Policy and Programme Evaluation* (New Brunswick, Transaction Publications).

von Schomberg, R. (2006), 'The precautionary principle and its normative challenges', in E. Fisher, J. Jones and R. von Schomberg (eds), *Implementing the Precautionary Principle: Perspectives and Prospects* (Cheltenham UK and Northampton MA, Edward Elgar), pp. 19–41.

WCED (1987), *Our Common Future* (Oxford, Oxford University Press).

Wilkinson, D. (1997), 'Towards Sustainability in the European Union? Steps Within the European Commission to Integrate Environment into Other European Union Policy Sectors', *Environmental Politics* 6(1), pp. 153–73.

Williams, R. (2007), 'The integration of environmental protection requirements into EC development cooperation policy', *EPIGOV Research Papers* (Berlin, Ecologic – Institute for International and European Environmental Policy).

14. The role played by policy objectives in environmental law

Chris McGrath

INTRODUCTION

Environmental governance is as much a matter of policy as it is a matter of law. Over recent years the achievement of objectives prescribed by the law has emerged as one of the core elements of modern environmental governance and of the environmental legal system. Accordingly, the relationship between law and policy in the management of the environment and of its resources has become critical. It is the purpose of this chapter to analyse this relationship from a number of perspectives. It does so by:

- reviewing the nature and meaning of objectives in environmental governance
- analysing sustainable development and climate change as two examples of objectives in practice
- discussing the role of objectives in the system of environmental governance as a whole
- assessing how objectives are created and measured.

OBJECTIVES IN ENVIRONMENTAL GOVERNANCE

1. How and Why they Emerged

Identifying what is intended to be achieved is a central component of any successful action, program, plan or review. In the absence of objectives, these activities are undirected and uncoordinated. Their success cannot be judged because there is no criterion against which they can be assessed. In governance and public policy, both internationally and nationally, what is intended to be achieved is normally communicated through identified goals, objectives, purposes, outcomes or targets. These terms are defined in different ways and their usage is not uniform. Whatever they are called, in this context their common feature is that they identify *what is to be achieved* in some way at a strategic and overall level rather than state prescriptive rules or standards for conduct – such as regulatory rules.[1]

Objects clauses in legislation, for example stating that the purpose of an Act is to 'protect the environment', are strategic statements of intent rather than detailed statements about how to make decisions, about standards of conduct or about administrative processes.[2] The Environmental Protection Law of the People's Republic of China provides an example of this. It states in the context of the strategic rules in article 1:

> This law is formulated for the purpose of protecting and improving people's environment and the ecological environment, preventing and controlling pollution and other public hazards, safeguarding human health.[3]

Although the expression 'purpose' is used in this example, the terminology used at large is variable. In this chapter the expression 'objectives' is used to describe the variety of terms used in this sense, including visions, aims, goals, objectives, purposes, outcomes and targets.

Objectives, whether expressly stated or implied, are often important in legal reasoning, such as statutory interpretation, and are a core component of modern environmental legal systems.[4] More broadly, they are also core components for implementing and reviewing government policies.[5] Objectives manifest themselves in a variety of ways. Commonly they are thought of as an end-point to be achieved specifically at a particular point in time, for example to conserve at least 10 per cent of coastal and marine areas by 2020. Alternatively, they may be something that occurs occasionally or continuously in a process without a specific end-point, for example to maintain a healthy environment.

There are four broad, and often overlapping, objectives against which governance and public policy are typically judged:

- effectiveness: whether the intended outcome is achieved, such as unacceptable harm being avoided
- efficiency: whether the intended outcome is achieved at minimal cost and as simply as is reasonably possible
- equity: whether there is fairness in the burden-sharing within the community, including intergenerational equity across generations
- political acceptability: whether the outcome and the means of achieving it are acceptable to political leaders, the community generally and key stakeholders, including such factors as budgetary expenditure, liberty, transparency and accountability.[6]

Objectives that are expressly stated in treaties or in legislation generally focus on the outcome intended to be achieved in terms of protecting the aspect of the environment that is the focus of the treaty or the legislation – for example, the protection of the marine environment. Equity issues are commonly formulated as an objective, for instance to respect the rights of indigenous peoples and of future generations. Political acceptability is an objective that is rarely stated expressly other than in relation to issues such as transparency and accountability.

Objectives may be stated broadly and qualitatively: such as the purpose stated in article 1 of the Charter of the United Nations (UN) – namely 'to maintain international peace and security'. They may be stated specifically and quantitatively, as in article 2 of the Paris Agreement: 'Holding the increase in the global average temperature to well below 2 °C above pre-industrial levels and to pursue efforts to limit the temperature increase to 1.5 °C above pre-industrial levels'. Qualitative and quantitative objectives such as these are commonplace in many forms in environmental governance and public policy at all levels and all areas.

2. Lack of Support for an Objective Approach

It is important to recognise that not everyone supports or agrees with clearly stating the outcomes or objectives to be achieved in environmental laws and policies. Judges who prefer pure textual analysis rather than a purposive or teleological approach to statutory interpretation tend to place little value on objects clauses even where, ironically, these are expressly included in the text. More fundamentally, there remains considerable opposition to regulation and government programs for environmental protection generally.

The anti-regulation philosophy of neoliberalism, in particular, has had a strong influence in countries such as the United States (US) in opposing UN and government programs and regulation that are perceived to infringe on market approaches and individual freedoms.[7] Reducing the involvement of government and promoting markets and individual freedoms are themselves strategic objectives but they are not objectives that are found in legislation. Rather, they are policy objectives that are realised by the *lack or reduction* of the regulation of business activity, of the exercise of private property rights, and of individual freedoms. Conservative politics in the US, in particular, have become characterised in recent decades by a steadfast commitment to the ideal of laissez-faire. This amounts to minimal government interference with the marketplace, along with hostility to taxation, regulation, organised labour and state ownership.[8] This hostility to business and individual regulation needs to be borne in mind by those interested in designing governance regimes for environmental protection, particularly within the US and at an international level when the US is involved.

Bearing in mind that considerable hostility to business and individual regulation exists in some countries, policy-makers should always recognise that, while regulation is an important means for maintaining a healthy environment, it is not the only means and it should be used sparingly and equitably. The broad policy objectives should always be to create effective, efficient, equitable and politically acceptable environmental regulation.[9] Smart regulation in designing environmental policy prefers less interventionist measures and avoids regulation where this is possible as part of a policy mix that incorporates a broad range of complementary instruments and institutions.[10]

THE USE OF OBJECTIVES IN PRACTICE

1. Introduction

Leaving aside criticism of environmental regulation in general, the best way to understand the importance of objectives is to examine the role they play in practice. Two important areas of environmental law and policy are examined here. The first examines sustainable development and the recent UN Sustainable Development Goals. The second examines the objective of avoiding dangerous climate change under the United Nations Framework Convention on Climate Change 1992 (UNFCCC).

2. Sustainable Development

The emergence and ubiquity of outcomes and objectives in environmental governance are well illustrated by the norm of sustainability. It emerged 30 years ago following the seminal Brundtland Report as the overarching objective of international environmental governance.[11] It defined sustainable development and stated its minimum criteria as follows:

> Development which meets the needs of present generations while not compromising the ability of future generations to also meet their needs. … in the end, sustainable development is not a fixed state of harmony, but rather a process of change … At a minimum, sustainable development must not endanger the natural systems that support life on Earth; the atmosphere, the waters, the soils and the living resources.[12]

Some commentators argue that sustainable development is not the over-arching objective of environmental law and environmental legal systems but merely one of multiple objectives. For instance, Patricia Birnie and Alan Boyle suggested that:

> not all environmental questions necessarily involve sustainable development, or vice versa. We may wish to preserve Antarctica, or endangered species such as the great whales or the giant panda, for reasons that have little or nothing to do with sustainable development, or put another way, we may wish to preserve them from sustainable development.[13]

To suggest that sustainable development is but one of a multiple set of objectives of an environmental legal system is a fundamental misconception of the concept. Gerry Bates and Zada Lipman have rejected such an interpretation. In particular they have criticised the approach in domestic Australian legislation which listed ecologically sustainable development (ESD) – the Australian version of sustainable development – as only one of a number of objectives to be achieved:

> it is difficult to resist the criticism of the legislation that, by including ESD as one of a number of features to which regard should be had, it has missed the point that ESD is not a factor to be balanced against other considerations; ESD *is* the balance.[14]

Sustainable development, it is suggested, is the over-arching objective and paradigm of the international and national environmental legal systems rather than merely a factor to be balanced against other considerations such as environmental protection and conservation. To use the example given by Birnie and Boyle, preservation of protected areas such as the Antarctic and of endangered species such as the great whales or the giant panda has everything to do with, and is an integral part of, sustainable development. Planning processes – the principal practical mechanism through which sustainable development is achieved – have everything to do with balancing competing uses such as exploitation and conservation.

The latest and most detailed iteration of sustainability is now found in the 17 Sustainable Development Goals and 169 targets resolved by the UN General Assembly on 25 September 2015 to stimulate action over the next 15 years in areas of critical importance for humanity and the planet. The resolution begins with a vision statement illustrated by the following extract:

> In these Goals and targets, we are setting out a supremely ambitious and transformational vision. We envisage a world free of poverty, hunger, disease

> and want, where all life can thrive. We envisage a world free of fear and violence. A world with universal literacy. A world with equitable and universal access to quality education at all levels, to health care and social protection, where physical, mental and social well-being are assured. A world where we reaffirm our commitments regarding the human right to safe drinking water and sanitation and where there is improved hygiene; and where food is sufficient, safe, affordable and nutritious. A world where human habitats are safe, resilient and sustainable and where there is universal access to affordable, reliable and sustainable energy. …

The subsequent 17 goals and 169 targets are lengthy and detailed. Two extracts are sufficient to illustrate their nature:

> **Goal 6. Ensure availability and sustainable management of water and sanitation for all**
>
> 6.1 By 2030, achieve universal and equitable access to safe and affordable drinking water for all
>
> 6.2 By 2030, achieve access to adequate and equitable sanitation and hygiene for all and end open defecation, paying special attention to the needs of women and girls and those in vulnerable situations
>
> 6.3 By 2030, improve water quality by reducing pollution, eliminating dumping and minimizing release of hazardous chemicals and materials, halving the proportion of untreated wastewater and substantially increasing recycling and safe reuse globally …
>
> …
>
> **Goal 14. Conserve and sustainably use the oceans, seas and marine resources for sustainable development**
>
> 14.1 By 2025, prevent and significantly reduce marine pollution of all kinds, in particular from land-based activities, including marine debris and nutrient pollution
>
> 14.2 By 2020, sustainably manage and protect marine and coastal ecosystems to avoid significant adverse impacts, including by strengthening their resilience, and take action for their restoration in order to achieve healthy and productive oceans
>
> …
>
> 14.5 By 2020, conserve at least 10 per cent of coastal and marine areas, consistent with national and international law and based on the best available scientific information

These goals and targets illustrate the use of qualitative and quantitative objectives at multiple levels and with differing degrees of specificity. Notably, all of the targets begin with a timeframe for their achievement but most are qualitative. These are good illustrations of typical practice in stating objectives in international governance and public policy.

3. Avoiding Dangerous Climate Change

The objective of avoiding dangerous climate change provides another good example of the role of objectives in environmental governance and policy. The evolution of this objective from the broad and qualitative criterion in article 2 of the UNFCCC to specific and quantitative criteria in the Copenhagen Accord and the Paris Agreement is very useful in understanding the nature and development of objectives generally in environmental law.

Article 2 of the UNFCCC states:

> The ultimate objective of this Convention and any related legal instruments that the Conference of the Parties may adopt is to achieve, in accordance with the relevant provisions of the Convention, stabilization of greenhouse gas concentrations in the atmosphere at a level that would prevent dangerous anthropogenic interference with the climate system. Such a level should be achieved within a time frame sufficient to allow ecosystems to adapt naturally to climate change, to ensure that food production is not threatened and to enable economic development to proceed in a sustainable manner.

This objective is commonly summarised as avoiding dangerous climate change. It states three qualitative criteria to explain what this means. To prevent dangerous climate change, greenhouse gas concentrations in the atmosphere must be stabilised at a level sufficient to:

- allow ecosystems to adapt naturally to climate change
- ensure that food production is not threatened
- enable economic development to proceed in a sustainable manner.

While objectives are commonly stated only in qualitative terms such as these, the nature of these criteria reflects, in part, the state of climate science and policy at the time the UNFCCC was signed in 1992. Over the subsequent decade, scientists and policy-makers suggested a variety of quantitative limits representing dangerous climate change as defined in article 2. These limits were based on further research and on the emerging evidence of the occurrence of rapid climate change. These ranged from limiting mean global temperature rises from 1 to 4°C above pre-industrial levels, to limiting the net concentrations of greenhouse gases and other climate forcings ranging from 450 to 700 parts per million (ppm) of carbon dioxide (CO_2) equivalents.[15] In one of the most cited and influential papers suggesting quantitative limits to avoid dangerous climate change, James Hansen and his colleagues argued that:

> If humanity wishes to preserve a planet similar to that on which civilization developed and to which life on Earth is adapted, paleoclimate evidence and ongoing climate change suggest that CO_2 will need to be reduced from its current 385 ppm to at most 350 ppm, but likely less than that.[16]

In 1996 the European Union proposed limiting mean global temperature rises to below 2°C above pre-industrial levels.[17] Despite ongoing scientific debates, the 2°C target became a political anchor for mitigation policy.[18]

The impacts on coral reefs are a relatively simple indicator to assess whether stabilising mean global temperature rises at 2°C above pre-industrial levels meets the objective of article 2 of the UNFCCC. Most of the globe's coral reefs are expected to be severely degraded or lost if global temperatures are stabilised at or near to 2°C above pre-industrial levels.[19] These ecosystems support enormous amounts of biodiversity and sustain millions of people through associated fisheries and tourism. Widespread loss or degradation of the world's coral reefs clearly conflicts with the criteria stated in article 2 of the UNFCCC. Consequently, on this basis the 2°C target is too high to achieve the objective stated in article 2 of the UNFCCC.

In 2009 many parties to the UNFCCC agreed to the Copenhagen Accord, which adopted the 2°C target in the following terms:

> To achieve the ultimate objective of the Convention to stabilize greenhouse gas concentration in the atmosphere at a level that would prevent dangerous anthropogenic interference with the climate system, we shall, recognizing the scientific view that the increase in global temperature should be below 2 degrees Celsius, on the basis of equity and in the context of sustainable development, enhance our long-term cooperative action to combat climate change.

The statement made in the Copenhagen Accord that 'the scientific view' was that the increase in mean global temperatures should be below 2°C to avoid dangerous climate change as defined in article 2 of the UNFCCC glosses over strong scientific debate as well as value judgments on the level of impacts that meet the qualitative criteria stated in article 2. These warrant analysis.

Scientists such as Reto Knutti and his colleagues have pointed out that the statement is simply incorrect:

> The world's governments agreed to limit global mean temperature change to below 2°C compared with pre-industrial levels in the years following the 2009 climate conference in Copenhagen. This 2°C warming target is perceived by the public as a universally accepted goal, identified by scientists as a safe limit that avoids dangerous climate change. This perception is incorrect: no scientific assessment has clearly justified or defended the 2°C target as a safe level of warming, and indeed, this is not a problem that science alone can address. We argue that global temperature is the best climate target quantity, but it is unclear what level can be considered safe. The 2°C target is useful for anchoring discussions, but has been ineffective in triggering the required emission reductions; debates on considering a lower target are strongly at odds with the current real-world level of action. These debates are moot, however, as the decisions that need to be taken now to limit warming to 1.5 or 2°C are very similar. We need to agree how to start, not where to end mitigation.[20]

Knutti and his colleagues have pointed out that:

> Defining a climate target, and deciding who needs to do how much to achieve it, are normative problems that depend on values and world views, on arguments about fairness and on ethics. But science can and should contribute to this discussion and point out the consequences of different proposals.[21]

Some commentators have gone so far as to suggest that the 2°C target should be abandoned entirely. For instance, David Victor and Charles Kennel argued:

> Politically and scientifically, the 2°C goal is wrong-headed. Politically, it has allowed some governments to pretend that they are taking serious action to mitigate global warming, when in reality they have achieved almost nothing. Scientifically, there are better ways to measure the stress that humans are placing on the climate system than the growth of average global surface temperature ...[22]

Part of their argument was that the 2°C target:

> is impractical. It is related only probabilistically to emissions and policies, so it does not tell particular governments and people what to do. In other areas of international politics, goals have had a big effect when they have been translated into concrete, achievable actions. For example, the eight Millennium Development Goals (MDGs) adopted by the United Nations in 2000 were effective when turned into 21 targets and 60 detailed indicators – measurable, practical and connected to what governments, non-governmental and aid organizations and others could do.[23]

In the context of these criticisms and the lack of scientific justification for the 2°C target, the Paris Agreement 2015 marks a significant strengthening of the parties' intent. Article 2 of the Paris Agreement states:

> This Agreement, in enhancing the implementation of the Convention, including its objective, aims to strengthen the global response to the threat of climate change, in the context of sustainable development and efforts to eradicate poverty, including by:
>
> (a) Holding the increase in the global average temperature to well below 2°C above pre-industrial levels and to pursue efforts to limit the temperature increase to 1.5°C above pre-industrial levels, recognizing that this would significantly reduce the risks and impacts of climate change; …

The language of article 2 of the Paris Agreement is significantly more ambitious than the Copenhagen Accord.

The Paris Agreement was built upon voluntary pledges given by each country and contained in intended nationally determined contributions (INDCs).[24] The United Nations Development Program (UNDP) and the World Resources Institute (WRI) provided guidance on the preparation of INDCs in the lead-up to Paris.[25] Based on their recommendations, most INDCs included matters such as:

- a reference point (e.g. the base year of 2005 for emissions reduction targets)
- timeframes and/or periods of implementation
- scope and coverage in terms of sectors (e.g. agriculture) and greenhouse gases covered, geographical coverage and percentage of national emissions covered
- planning processes for preparation and implementation of the INDC, such as stakeholder engagement and public consultation
- assumptions and methodological approaches (e.g. estimating and accounting for greenhouse gas emissions)
- how the Party considers that its INDC is fair and ambitious, in light of its national circumstances, and how it contributes towards achieving the objective of the UNFCCC as set out in article 2.[26]

The guidance provided by the UNDP and WRI for the preparation of INDCs is an excellent and detailed example of good practice in designing policy objectives and actions in a contentious multinational setting.

The evolution of the objective of the UNFCCC and the subsequent decisions of the parties implementing it illustrate the role and importance of objectives. These developments in the governance of climate change similarly illustrate many of the challenges in defining the objectives in ways that are scientifically accurate yet still comprehensible by the broad public. This lays a good foundation for a discussion of the functions of such objectives.

A REVIEW OF THE FUNCTIONS OF OBJECTIVES

1. Introduction

It is evident from the discussion of sustainable development and dangerous climate change that the inclusion of objectives in international and national laws and policies performs multiple functions. Three of the main functions can be summarised as providing:

- communication and public relations tools
- aids to interpreting treaties and statutes
- criteria for success in program review as part of the policy cycle.

2. Objectives as Communication and Public Relations Tools

Statements of objectives play an obvious role in communicating government intentions to the public and are as a consequence important public relations tools. Building and maintaining public support is a crucial part of successful governance and public policy. A simple, clear and positive objective that ordinary people in the community understand, support and see as relevant directly to them is invaluable in building and maintaining support for laws and programs.

An example is the US Clean Air Act 1970. The title of the Act states its basic objective in simple terms that are meaningful and directly relevant to all people: clean air. Every person has an interest in this. Who does not want to breathe clean air? The link to everyone's welfare and benefit is also made clear in the Act's objectives. For example, the first objective of Title I – Air Pollution Prevention and Control – stated in §101(b)(1) of the Act is:

> to protect and enhance the quality of the Nation's air resources so as to promote the public health and welfare and the productive capacity of its population.

By linking clean air and public health directly and simply, the legislature has created a powerful public relations weapon to build support for the

Act. This is the first important function of a well-written objective in any legislation: namely to communicate what it aims to achieve in simple and clear terms for ordinary members of the community.

3. Objectives as Aids to Interpreting Treaties and Statutes

In addition to communicating clearly the aim of a treaty or of legislation to members of the community, objectives can play an important function in interpretation. However, this role rarely displaces clear words in the text of the treaty or the legislation and should not be overstated.

The role that objectives perform as an aid to interpreting international treaties is stated in the general rule of interpretation found in article 31 of the Vienna Convention on the Law of Treaties:

> A treaty shall be interpreted in good faith in accordance with the ordinary meaning to be given to the terms of the treaty in their context and in the light of its object and purpose.

While this article does not apply to the interpretation of national legislation, the requirements to apply 'the ordinary meaning to be given to the terms … in their context and in the light of [the] object and purpose' reflect important principles for statutory interpretation in most countries – including both common law and civil law jurisdictions.

In some countries, legislation itself prescribes that an interpretation that best achieves the purpose or object of legislation should be adopted. For instance, in Australia, the Acts Interpretation Act 1901 (Cth) provides:

> **15AA Interpretation best achieving Act's purpose or object**
>
> In interpreting a provision of an Act, the interpretation that would best achieve the purpose or object of the Act (whether or not that purpose or object is expressly stated in the Act) is to be preferred to each other interpretation.

Statements of objectives rarely prevail over clear and unambiguous language in the statute itself. Moreover it is the exception rather than the norm for courts to refer to such objects. An interesting example is the majority judgment of the US Supreme Court in the *Massachusetts* case in 2007. It illustrates the normal emphasis on the plain language of the text of the statute without reference to stated objectives. This case involved a challenge to the refusal by the US Environmental Protection Agency to regulate vehicle emissions of carbon dioxide under §202(a)(1) of the Clean Air Act 1970. The majority's reasons focused on the text of the statute without any direct reference to any of the objectives of the Act. They stated first:

> On the merits, the first question is whether §202(a)(1) of the Clean Air Act authorizes EPA to regulate greenhouse gas emissions from new motor vehicles in the event that it forms a 'judgment' that such emissions contribute to climate change. We have little trouble concluding that it does. In relevant part, §202(a)(1) provides that EPA 'shall by regulation prescribe … standards applicable to the emission of any air pollutant from any class or classes of new motor vehicles or new motor vehicle engines, which in [the Administrator's] judgment cause, or contribute to, air pollution which may reasonably be anticipated to endanger public health or welfare.' 42 U.S.C. §7521(a)(1). Because EPA believes that Congress did not intend it to regulate substances that contribute to climate change, the agency maintains that carbon dioxide is not an 'air pollutant' within the meaning of the provision.
>
> The statutory text forecloses EPA's reading. The Clean Air Act's sweeping definition of 'air pollutant' includes '*any* air pollution agent or combination of such agents, including *any* physical, chemical … substance or matter which is emitted into or otherwise enters the ambient air …' §7602(g) (emphasis added). On its face, the definition embraces all airborne compounds of whatever stripe, and underscores that intent through the repeated use of the word 'any.'[27]

Then finally:

> Because greenhouse gases fit well within the Clean Air Act's capacious definition of 'air pollutant,' we hold that EPA has the statutory authority to regulate the emission of such gases from new motor vehicles.[28]

Purposes and objectives stated in legislation need to be seen in the context that the normal emphasis remains on the plain and ordinary meaning of the text of a statute. The emphasis given to a strict adherence to the text over consideration of broader objectives of the legislation reflects differing approaches to statutory interpretation that have long histories. Writing from a US perspective, Frank Cross noted:

> Historically, the dispute over the goal of statutory interpretation has largely been drawn between those who believe that judges should hew closely to their assessment of what the legislature intended, based upon all available evidence of that intent, and those who think the purpose is simply to give effect to the statutory language adopted by the legislature and eschew consideration of extrinsic evidence about the legislature's intent. … Those who believe that the purpose of the process is to discern intent commonly argue for consideration of legislative history, while those who would limit interpretation to language are of the textualist school. … The debate over the proper purpose of statutory interpretation has lasted for many decades. … While one approach or another

> has gained ascendancy for a time, it has eventually lost its position. None of the theories have knocked out competing theories. …[29]

Similar debates have taken place around the world in common law, civil law and other legal systems. For instance, Claire Germain noted that in France:

> The major methods of [statutory] interpretation under different classifications are exegetic and teleological, according to French scholarship. The exegetic method makes use of legislative history [and literal interpretation of the text of the statute]. The teleological method, which looks at the social objective of the statute, has several different variations.[30]

While judges who prefer pure textual analysis to a purposive or teleological approach to statutory interpretation tend to place little value on objects clauses even when these are expressly stated in the text of a statute, there is still value in stating clearly the objectives of the legislation. At the very least, a statement of objectives in legislation constitutes an aid to the interpretation of its provisions in most jurisdictions even though it rarely prevails over clear words in the text of the legislation.

4. Objectives as Criteria for Success in Program Reviews

A third important function of stating objectives is that they provide criteria for evaluating success in reviews of government policies and programs, including the implementation of laws to protect the environment. Evaluation and review are a normal part of the policy cycle when government policy is created, implemented, monitored and reviewed.[31]

A law or policy will be 'effective' if it has solved or contributed to solving the problem it was designed to address.[32] However, in the real world, the question of the effectiveness of laws and policies rarely receives a clear and unambiguous answer. The complexity of the real world – associated with multiple and confounding sources of pressures on the environment and often with multi-layered regulatory systems comprised of overlapping laws and policies – means that attributing a positive effect to any one law or policy is typically difficult or impossible to achieve.[33]

Robert Bartlett colourfully described such issues as 'patently tangled, wicked environmental policy problems'.[34] His 1994 comments about the need for improving environmental policy evaluation remain apt:

> Programs, policies, processes, and institutions, particularly environmental ones, are messy things, and environmental policy evaluation must develop richer theories, concepts, and methodologies to provide useful information for further policymaking in spite of that messiness.[35]

Accordingly, Bartlett cautioned of the need to be very careful about the questions to be asked in seeking to evaluate environmental policies:

> Both success and failure [of environmental policy] are variably defined, often implicitly. Claims are often consciously crafted to be consistent with some ideological standpoint and perspective or to support or attack some *a priori* political position. Such claims, forcefully advanced, may be persuasive in environmental policy debates if definitions of failure are not questioned, criteria for success are not articulated, and the process of evaluation is conceived as a narrow technical one reserved for experts of one particular type.[36]

While the task of determining policy success or failure is a complex one and rarely yields clear-cut answers, it is still an important one to undertake as part of the ongoing process of evaluation and review of government policy. By defining what the law or policy is designed to achieve, well-written objectives lay the foundation for implementation, evaluation and review.

CREATING AND MEASURING OBJECTIVES

1. Introduction

Given the multiple and important functions of stating objectives, the question becomes not whether but how they should be stated. There is no simple answer to this question. To a large extent how objectives should be formulated depends on the nature of the instrument in which they are included and on the problem to be addressed. For example, objectives related to fisheries management differ logically from objectives for protecting the cultural heritage values of a city. While they necessarily depend for their relevancy on their context, two broad considerations for formulating objects are:

- how to balance specific and quantifiable objectives with ambiguous and qualitative objectives
- whether and how best to link the objectives to indicators to evaluate policy success or failure in the complexity of real world environmental problems.

2. Balancing Specific and Quantifiable Objectives with Ambiguous and Qualitative Objectives

The foregoing analysis of the UN Sustainable Development Goals and of objectives for avoiding dangerous climate change demonstrates that a balance is often required between making objectives specific and quantifiable and making them ambiguous and qualitative. Relevantly, Dovers and Hussey have noted:

> Policy goals stated in vague terms may be highly problematic when the policy intervention is evaluated, as there will be uncertainty as to the extent to which it has succeeded. … Quantitative goals are easier to measure progress against, and as long as the goals are well-formulated and meaningful may be less open to contest and disagreement. But in many situations quantitative goals may not be able to be expressed, either because of uncertainty or missing information of the nature of the intended outcome. … a policy program will generally utilise both quantitative and qualitative goals.[37]

The foregoing analysis similarly noted that a layered arrangement of objectives is often used, which is usually the best approach to meet the multiple functions of objectives. Higher-level objectives that are qualitative, simpler and easier to communicate to the general public are supported by more detailed but quantitative objectives and targets at lower levels and in individual programs. The higher level objectives can be used for communicating with the public and the more detailed and quantitative objectives and targets can be used for program evaluation.

An interesting example is the formulation of four layers in the UN Sustainable Development Goals. Namely:

- a top and overarching objective of 'sustainable development'
- a broad vision, comprised of aspirational statements such as 'a world free of poverty, hunger, disease and want, where all life can thrive'
- 17 goals, such as goal 14 – 'Conserve and sustainably use the oceans, seas and marine resources for sustainable development'
- 169 targets within the 17 goals, each of which has a stated timeframe to be achieved, such as target 14.5 – 'By 2020, conserve at least 10 per cent of coastal and marine areas, consistent with national and international law and based on the best available scientific information'.

Layering objectives from higher level objectives – broad and qualitative – to lower level objectives – more detailed and quantitative – provides flexibility to meet the multiple functions of objectives. Additionally, a common approach for measuring the success of objectives, whether qualitative or quantitative, is to use indicators.

3. The Use of Indicators

Environmental indicators are widely used to provide simple and measurable criteria for evaluating environmental health and the effectiveness of environmental policies. The use of indicators can amalgamate raw environmental data into a small set of numbers that can be used to monitor change and the effectiveness of response strategies. The essential rationales for the use of environmental indicators are, first, pragmatism in the face of complexity and, second, large gaps in information about the environment. While the overarching objective against which the effectiveness of environmental policy – and any environmental legal system – must be assessed is sustainable development, this objective is too general and difficult to measure to provide a criterion for assessment in its own right. Because of the scale, complexity and uncertainty of the environment, the objective of sustainability needs to be broken down into more measurable indicators. Despite the presence of the 17 goals and 169 targets in the UN Sustainable Development Goals, indicators provide measures of the success in achieving the goals and qualitative targets.

The Organisation for Economic Cooperation and Development (OECD) has played a leading role in the development of a common conceptual framework for environmental indicators over the past 40 years. The OECD defines an 'indicator' as a parameter, or a value derived from parameters, which points to, provides information about, and describes the state of a phenomenon/environment/area, with a significance extending beyond that directly associated with a parameter value.[38] A 'parameter' is a property that is measured or observed.[39] The two principal functions of indicators are:

- to reduce the number of measurements and parameters that would normally be required to give an *exact* presentation of a situation
- to simplify the communication process by which the results of measurement are provided to the user.[40]

The OECD uses a core set of 40 to 50 environmental indicators covering a broad range of environmental issues as a commonly agreed-upon minimum set of indicators for OECD countries and for international use. These are published regularly[41] and commonly disaggregated at sectoral and territorial levels, provided the data is available.[42] OECD indicators are classified using the pressure-state-response model of state of the environment reporting: indicators of environmental pressures, both direct and indirect; indicators of environmental conditions; and indicators of society's responses. For example, atmospheric concentrations of greenhouse gases and global mean temperature are indicators of the condition of climate change.

The OECD warns that indicators are only one tool and that care needs to be taken in their use in evaluating environmental policies:

> Indicators are not designed to provide a full picture of environmental issues, but rather to help reveal trends and draw attention to phenomena or changes that require further analyses and possible action. Indicators are thus *only one tool* for evaluation; scientific and policy-oriented interpretation is required for them to acquire their full meaning. … indicators are not a mechanical measure of environmental performance. They need to be complemented with background information, data, analysis and interpretation. One should also note that some issues or topics do not lend themselves to evaluation by quantitative measures or indicators.[43]

Indicators are often used to assess success in achieving broad and qualitative objectives. In addition, quantitative objectives often incorporate an indicator directly. For instance, the broad and qualitative target of avoiding dangerous climate change in article 2 of the UNFCCC is now supplemented by the quantitative goals of the Paris Agreement to hold:

> the increase in the global average temperature to well below 2°C above pre-industrial levels and to pursue efforts to limit the temperature increase to 1.5°C above pre-industrial levels.

The quantitative objectives in the Paris Agreement are themselves indicators of the condition of climate change simplified as a single parameter of the rise in global average temperature above pre-industrial levels.

CONCLUSION AND SUMMARY

The use of statements of objectives is widespread in international treaties and national legislation and they perform multiple roles. Simple and qualitative objectives such as 'sustainable development' play an important role in communicating to the general public the broad outcome that is intended to be achieved. For this reason alone, broad and qualitative objectives have an important role to play in most, perhaps all environmental policies and laws. If the public cannot understand the value of a policy or law immediately, in simple terms and without needing to understand the technical details of it, then it is unlikely to obtain strong public or political support.

Statements of objectives are also important as aids to interpreting treaties and legislation in many jurisdictions. However, their importance should not be overstated. They rarely prevail over clear and unambiguous language in a treaty or the statute itself and many courts rarely refer to such objects with more than a passing note.

Statements of objectives are also important as criteria for evaluating success in program review as part of the normal policy cycle. By defining what a law or policy is intended to achieve, clearly stated objectives lay the foundation for ongoing implementation, monitoring and review.

How objectives should be formulated depends to a large extent on the nature of the instrument in which they are included and the problem it is addressing. There is a need to balance specific and quantifiable objectives with ambiguous and qualitative objectives. A common approach is to layer the range of objectives: broad and high-level objectives providing simple messages for the public complemented by more detailed objectives at lower levels for the technical aspects of implementation and policy review. Objectives, particularly qualitative ones, are often also linked to environmental indicators to evaluate policy success or failure in the complexity of real world environmental problems.

NOTES

1. See Fisher (2013, chs 1 and 14–17).
2. Ibid. (ch.16).
3. Ibid. (p. 333).
4. Ibid. (chs 1 and 14–17).
5. Dovers and Hussey (2013).
6. Gunningham, Grabosky and Sinclair (1998, p. 26).
7. Harvey (2005).
8. Frank (2008, p. 30).
9. Gunningham, Grabosky and Sinclair (1998, p. 26).
10. Ibid. (pp. 387–95).
11. World Commission on Environment and Development (1987); Cordonier Segger and Khalfan (2004); Bosselmann (2008).
12. World Commission on Environment and Development (1987, p. 9).
13. Birnie and Boyle (2002, p. 3).
14. Bates and Lipman (1998, p. 47).
15. Oppenheimer and Petsonk (2005).
16. Hansen et al. (2008).
17. Randalls (2010).
18. Ibid. (p. 602).
19. Hoegh-Guldberg et al. (2007); Vernon et al. (2009); Frieler et al. (2012).
20. Knutti et al. (2016, p. 13).

21. Ibid. (p. 16).
22. Victor and Kennel (2014, p. 30).
23. Ibid. (p. 31).
24. See Savaresi (2016).
25. UNDP and WRI (2015).
26. Ibid. (pp. 39–41).
27. *Massachussetts* case (2007, pp. 528–9).
28. Ibid. (p. 532).
29. Cross (2009, p. 2).
30. Germain (2003, p. 197).
31. Dovers and Hussey (2013, p. 71).
32. Zaelke, Kaniaru and Kružíková (2005, p. 22); McGrath (2010, pp. 12 and 45–54).
33. McGrath (2010, pp. 45–54).
34. Bartlett (1994, p. 183).
35. Ibid.
36. Ibid.
37. Dovers and Hussey (2013, pp. 122–3).
38. OECD (2003, p. 5).
39. Ibid.
40. Ibid.
41. E.g. OECD (2015).
42. OECD (2003, pp. 8–9).
43. Ibid. (pp. 14–6) (emphasis in original).

REFERENCES

Bartlett, R. (1994), 'Evaluating Environmental Policy Success and Failure' in N. Vig and M. Kraft (eds), *Environmental Policy in the 1990s – Towards a New Agenda* (2nd edn, Washington, CQ Press).

Bates, G. and Z. Lipman (1998), *Corporate Liability for Pollution* (Sydney, Lawbook Co).

Birnie, P. and A. Boyle (2002), *International Law & the Environment* (2nd edn, Oxford, Oxford University Press).

Bosselmann, K. (2008), *The Principle of Sustainability: Transforming Law and Governance* (Aldershot, Ashgate Publishing Ltd).

Cordonier Segger, M.C. and A. Khalfan (2004), *Sustainable Development Law: Principles, Practices and Prospects* (Oxford, Oxford University Press).

Cross, F.B. (2009), *The Theory and Practice of Statutory Interpretation* (Redwood City, Stanford Law Books).

Dovers, S. and K. Hussey (2013), *Environment and Sustainability: A Policy Handbook* (2nd edn, Sydney, The Federation Press).

Fisher, D. (2013), *Legal Reasoning in Environmental Law: A Study of Structure, Form and Language* (Northampton, Edward Elgar Publishing).

Frank, T. (2008), *The Wrecking Crew: How Conservatives Rule* (New York, Metropolitan Books).

Frieler, K.M., M. Meinshausen, A. Golly, M. Mengel, K. Lebek, S.D. Donner and O. Hoegh-Guldberg (2012), 'Limiting global warming to 2°C is unlikely to save most coral reefs', *Nature Climate Change* 3, 165–70.

Germain, C.M. (2003), 'Approaches to statutory interpretation and legislative history in France', *Duke Journal of Comparative and International Law* 13, 195–206.

Gunningham, N., P. Grabosky and D. Sinclair (1998), *Smart Regulation: Designing Environmental Policy* (Oxford, Oxford University Press).

Hansen, J. et al. (2008), 'Target Atmospheric CO2: Where Should Humanity Aim?', *The Open Atmospheric Science Journal* 2, 217–31.
Harvey, D. (2005), *A Brief History of Neoliberalism* (Oxford, Oxford University Press).
Hoegh-Guldberg, O., P.J. Mumby, A.J. Hooten, R.S. Steneck, P. Greenfield, E. Gomez, C.D. Harvell, P.F. Sale, A.J. Edwards, K. Caldeira, N. Knowlton, C.M. Eakin, R. Iglesias-Prieto, N. Muthiga, R.H. Bradbury, A. Dubi and M.E. Hatziolos (2007), 'Coral Reefs under Rapid Climate Change and Ocean Acidification', *Science* 318, 1737–42.
Knutti, R., J. Rogelj, J. Sedláček and E.M. Fisher (2016), 'A scientific critique of the two-degree climate change target', *Nature Geoscience* 9, 13–18.
McGrath, C. (2010), *Does Environmental Law Work? How to Evaluate the Effectiveness of an Environmental Legal System* (Saarbrücken, Lambert Academic Publishing).
Oppenheimer, M. and A. Petsonk (2005), 'Article 2 of the UNFCCC: Historic origins, recent interpretations', *Climatic Change* 73, 195–226.
Organisation for Economic Co-operation and Development (OECD) (2003), *OECD Environmental Indicators: Development, Measurement and Use – Reference Paper* (Paris, OECD).
Organisation for Economic Co-operation and Development (OECD) (2015), *Environment at a Glance 2015: OECD Indicators* (Paris, OECD).
Randalls, S. (2010), 'History of the 2°C climate target', *WIREs Climate Change* 1, 598–605.
Savaresi, A. (2016), 'The Paris Agreement: a new beginning?', *Journal of Energy & Natural Resources Law* 34(1), 16–26.
United Nations Development Program (UNDP) and World Resources Institute (WRI) (2015), *Designing and Preparing Intended Nationally Determined Contributions (INDCs)* (Washington, WRI).
Veron, C., O. Hoegh-Guldberg, T.M. Lenton, J.M. Lough, D.O. Obura, P. Pearce-Kelly, C.R.C. Sheppard, M. Spalding, M.G. Stafford-Smith and A.D. Rogers (2009), 'The coral reef crisis: The critical importance of <350 ppm CO_2', *Marine Pollution Bulletin* 58, 1428–36.
Victor, D.G. and C.F. Kennel (2014), 'Ditch the 2°C warming goal', *Nature* 514, 30–31.
World Commission on Environment and Development (1987), *Our Common Future* (Oxford, Oxford University Press) ('the Brundtland Report').
Zaelke, D., D. Kaniaru and E. Kružíková (eds) (2005), *Making Law Work – Environmental Compliance & Sustainable Development* (London, Cameron May Ltd International Law Publishers).

INSTRUMENTS

Acts Interpretation Act 1901 (Cth), s.15AA.
Charter of the United Nations (1945) 1 UNTS XVI.
Clean Air Act 42 USC §7401 et seq. (1970).
Convention Concerning the Protection of the World Cultural and Natural Heritage: (1972) *International Legal Materials* 11, 1358.
Copenhagen Accord: Decision 2/CP.15 at COP15 to the UNFCCC, done in Copenhagen on 18 December 2009.
Environmental Protection Law of the People's Republic of China: Law Press China.
Paris Agreement: Resolution FCCC/CP/2015/L.9/Rev.1 to COP21 to the UNFCCC, done at Paris on 12 December 2015.
Sustainable Development Goals: United Nations General Assembly resolution 70/1 Transforming our world: the 2030 Agenda for Sustainable Development, A/RES/70/1 N, adopted 25 September 2015.

United Nations Framework Convention on Climate Change: (1992) *International Legal Materials* 31, 849.
Vienna Convention on the Law of Treaties: (1969) *International Legal Materials* 8, 679.

CASES

Massachussets case: *Massachusetts v Environmental Protection Agency*, 549 US 497 (2007).

15. The functions of rights of property in environmental law

David Grinlinton

INTRODUCTION

Property rights can play both a positive and a negative role in environmental governance. Some scholars argue that the strong protection provided by the law for property rights can militate against the imposition of measures that limit the exercise of those rights in the interests of environmental protection and ecological sustainability.[1] Those of a neo-liberal economics persuasion consider that the exercise of strong property rights with minimal interference from government produces the best long-term environmental outcomes. They argue that well-defined and enforced private property rights encourage sustainable use of land and natural resources as it is in the landowner's best interest to maintain and enhance the value of the underlying resource – thus avoiding the 'tragedy of the commons'.[2] Accordingly, property rights can be both an asset and, in some contexts, a liability in the protection of the environment and the furtherance of sustainability principles.

Environmental governance and the holding and exercise of individual property rights are intimately connected and inherently in tension. Yet the interrelationships between these areas of the law are not as well explored as might seem appropriate. Seldom are the subjects dealt with together in regulation, in textbooks, in academic teaching and research, or in legal practice areas. There are a number of reasons for this. Traditionally there is little conceptual overlap between property law, which is classified primarily as a private law discipline, and environmental law and policy, considered to be primarily a public law discipline. Further, the two legal subject areas have developed in response to different social, economic and political considerations. Moreover they rest on differing jural foundations. Generally they are directed towards different objectives. Property law is concerned primarily with the legal rights of ownership, occupation, use and dealings with land, including structures and natural resources that are part of land.[3] Environmental law, on the other hand, is generally concerned with the effects of the exercise of such rights, including the effects on neighbouring landowners, communities and the public interest. It is also concerned with the cumulative effects of land and natural resource development; with the use of publicly held land and resources; and, at a higher level of abstraction, with the effects of such development on the public domain and the global biosphere.

There are difficulties in defining property rights. There are also difficulties in defining the values that environmental law may aim to protect. While the costs of extraction, processing and marketing of natural resources such as minerals, forestry and agricultural products – including the effects of those activities on the immediate environment – can generally be expressed through conventional financial analysis, the same cannot be said of many environmental values such as aesthetics, amenity and wilderness. There are no true markets for such values. Few entities – private or public – are prepared to pay for protecting them. In the context of intergenerational equity, there are significant challenges in predicting the needs and value premises of future generations, and the appropriate horizon for such considerations.

Another dimension is the disjunction between international and domestic law and policy. Many of the foundational principles of environmental protection, such as sustainability and the precautionary approach, are recognized and implemented in the international arena through various agreements and instruments.[4] Notwithstanding their normative value, such measures are seldom implemented in the domestic constitutional, legal, and policy landscape in a way in which the exercise of private property rights in land and resources is significantly constrained.

Notwithstanding these challenges, there is a growing body of writing that explores the interrelationships between property rights, environmental law and natural resources.[5] This chapter will briefly discuss the nature of property rights before examining property rights from political, economic and legal perspectives. It will then explore the function of property rights in environmental governance and the impact of environmental law and policy upon the exercise of those rights. Next it will discuss new uses and applications of property law in the protection of environmental quality and in natural resource management. Finally it will make some suggestions for the future. Reference will be made throughout to developments and innovations in the laws and regulations of a number of jurisdictions.

THE NATURE OF 'PROPERTY'

Just as the concept of sustainability is difficult to define and implement in an enforceable way, so too the concept of property defies concise definition.[6] Property is an abstract construct that contributes to managing social and economic relations in the interests of cohesiveness and the economic advancement of society. The concept is inherently dynamic. It will change and adapt as the demands and circumstances of society change and develop.[7] While there is no unitary theory that covers all existing and potential manifestations of the so-called 'bundle of rights'[8] that constitute property, it is one of the foundational elements not only of legal relations but also of economic productivity and of the creation of wealth.

Individually held property rights have never been absolute under the law. Such rights have always been subject to the rights of neighbouring property owners not to have their property and natural resource interests adversely affected or damaged by others. This is reflected in the common law torts of trespass to land and of nuisance. Private property rights have always been subject to limitations in the public interest often expressed through planning, environmental and natural resource regulatory regimes. Arguably, the holding of property rights carries correlative obligations of good stewardship and respect for ecological processes. This is because the ecological community at large, including humanity, depends upon the health and sustainability of these ecological processes.

Natural resources found on land – such as minerals, trees, structures and other fixed objects – are normally considered to be part of the land. Migratory resources – such as natural water percolating under or flowing through land, geothermal steam, fish, wild animals, and oil and gas – are generally not within the surface landowner's bundle of rights. The common law has struggled to assign clear rules of ownership and management to such resources, often falling back on the ancient 'rule of capture'.[9] The uncertainty of this regime and its inappropriateness for high-value strategic resources such as oil, gas and geothermal energy have together led to intervention in many jurisdictions, with the state nationalizing ownership and control over such resources.[10]

Today many new types of rights are being created that go far beyond traditional property rights. These include water and land use permissions and management regimes,[11] fisheries quota,[12] mining and energy permits and access rights,[13] forestry harvesting rights,[14] rights of indigenous peoples to traditional resources and food sources,[15] and rights to emit greenhouse gases (GHGs) under climate change measures.[16] The variety and novelty of many of these rights illustrate the nature of property as both a dynamic and abstract concept that eludes precise definition. In the context of this chapter, but at the risk of being too simplistic, property rights are treated as encompassing the collection of enforceable rights and correlative obligations relating to land and associated natural resources.[17] Whether the land or the resource is private or public, the substance of these rights relates inter alia to exclusive or non-exclusive possession of, access to, ability to deal with, and ability to use land and natural resources.

POLITICAL, ECONOMIC AND LEGAL PERSPECTIVES ON PROPERTY RIGHTS

1. Political Perspectives

At the political level, the creation, acquisition, protection and transferability of property rights are the foundational elements of capitalism. Early political philosophers, such as Thomas Hobbes and John Locke, expounded social contract theory both as an explanation of why individuals group together to form civil society, and as a justification for the authority of the state over individuals. Under this theory, government acquires legitimacy through individuals surrendering some of their freedoms in nature to the authority of the state in return for political order, government and protection of their rights.[18] Such rights include the right to acquire and hold property. Locke considered that property was a natural right and derived from the application of labour. He considered that protection of property was one of the core purposes of the state.[19] In the eighteenth century Adam Smith built on these concepts in formulating his theory of capitalism. In his *Wealth of Nations* Smith argued that individuals will, in their own rational self-interest, direct their labour and efforts to maximize the value of their production.[20] Such specialization maximizes the efficiency of capital accumulation which is tradeable in a competitive market. This leads to economic prosperity. This theory forms the basis of modern capitalism. It relies upon maximizing the efficient use of capital – property – to generate maximum value.[21] Most capitalist societies therefore provide strong protections for property ownership in their constitutions[22] and in their legal systems.[23] As one judge has observed, 'next to constitutional rights, property rights are the strongest interests recognized by our law'.[24]

2. Economic Perspectives[25]

In a capitalist society, economic structures flow from, and are designed to support, the prevailing political ideology. The early views of political and economic theorists such as Locke and Smith have endured in the neo-liberal view that better-defined and appropriately allocated property rights will counteract market failures that cause negative environmental externalities. In the early 1960s Ronald Coase argued that as long as property rights are well defined, divisible and defendable, and that transaction costs and externalities are low, parties will negotiate to achieve the most efficient use of land and resources and to reduce the impact of pollution.[26] The 'Coase theorem' is often relied upon to justify deregulation and privatization of traditional government functions. Some property rights, however, are not always well defined, easily tradeable or legally enforceable, while the externalities and transaction costs of their exercise are often poorly defined and unquantifiable.

The view that clearly defined and strongly enforced property rights will avoid the 'tragedy of the commons' effect[27] relies on the presumption that the owner of the resource operates within a regulatory and economic system that rewards the resource's continued existence and productivity. Examples might include farming and agricultural activities, forestry (with some reservations), fisheries quota management systems,[28] and emissions trading schemes (ETSs).[29] On the other side of the debate is the view that conventional economic theory rewards the maximization of short-term exploitation of the utility value of resources for profit or speculation, with little long-term consideration for ensuring sustainable productive capacity.[30] This is particularly the case with mineral and energy resources where there is no possibility of sustainably managing the depletion of those resources and consequently little long-term incentive to protect the host environment. The short-term profit made by the full exploitation of the resource will often outweigh any long-term reduction in its productive capacity for other uses and, depending upon what economic theory and valuation criteria are applied, the ecological value of the land. This is so in either case, unless the costs of such externalities can be calculated with some precision and imposed on the user through regulatory measures or penalties.

Adherence to an unrestricted 'absolute rights' concept of property can result in a failure to consider neighbouring owners' rights, the wider environment and the public interest. Furthermore, mainstream economics cannot easily accommodate unquantifiable values. Many environmental and ecological features that people value are not easily susceptible to individual ownership or conventional economic valuation, let alone their value to future generations. Many wilderness areas are still vested in the state. Unless they are recognized as having environmental value through reservation as a national park or conservation area under the control of an agency charged with protecting those values, they are often unprotected and largely unprotectable by private individuals or public interest groups.

Since the mid-1980s many governments have pursued economic reform including corporatization and privatization of government activities. Many of these activities are concerned with the supply of infrastructural services – such as transportation, production and reticulation of energy; the utilization of resources such as minerals and hydrocarbons; and the harvesting of forest resources.[31] The management of significant natural resources and infrastructure networks by government agencies is often argued to be less economically efficient. The counter-argument is that government agencies have an inherent obligation and capacity to act in the public interest, can accommodate non-economic environmental values, and can demonstrate a sense of social responsibility – obligations neither characteristically exhibited by, nor in fairness to be expected of, private corporations.

3. Legal Perspectives[32]

Legal rights play a major supporting role in achieving economic and political objectives.[33] Legal rights in property have been a cornerstone of modern industrial and economic development. This is reflected in an extensive range of legal principles and of specific legislation designed to ensure their recognition and protection. Property rights are also at the heart of many environmental conflicts. Property owners often seek remedies for interference with their property rights by others or resist restrictions on their rights to use their land as they see fit. The 'absolute rights' view of private property rights 'produced intolerable evils' including destructive exploitation of minerals, wastage of forest, reduction of soil fertility, water pollution and social costs.[34]

In the early development of the common law, as noted above, property rights were not, in fact, regarded as absolute. They were subject to 'the law of the land' and, where necessary, to 'public convenience'.[35] The early feudal system of land tenure recognized the inherent obligations of the tenant owed to the grantor of the feudal estate: for example, maintaining the land and avoiding wastage or permanent damage.[36] Many of these constraints and obligations relating to land were progressively neglected in the interests of rapid commercial and industrial development from the industrial revolution onwards.

By the mid-twentieth century, it had become apparent that the unrestrained use of natural resources and the use of air and water as waste sinks were causing long-term ecological damage and were imposing increasing economic costs on societies that were in turn dependent upon sustainable resource bases.[37] Improved protections for town planning, health and safety, and the environment were progressively introduced. Greater government control was exercised over strategic natural resources such as petroleum, uranium, coal, and iron and steel.[38] Access to common property resources became increasingly controlled by the state.[39] As the High Court of Australia noted, 'to fail to protect [limited public natural resources] may destroy, and to preserve the right of everyone to take what he or she will, may eventually deprive that right of all content'.[40]

Despite its dynamic and constantly changing attributes, private property underpins western economic and social organization. It is likely to continue to do so for the foreseeable future. Nevertheless, the arguments for the primacy of private property rights continue to be challenged as the protection of those rights is often in direct conflict with ecological health and environmental values.

PROPERTY RIGHTS IN ENVIRONMENTAL GOVERNANCE

1. Introduction

The following paragraphs examine, first, property rights mechanisms for the allocation of land and natural resources and, second, the common law limitations on their use and exploitation. They will then discuss the various forms of public regulatory intervention that are commonly imposed to manage the environmental externalities of land and natural resource exploitation.

2. Property Rights in Land and in Natural Resources in General

Land ownership includes certain rights to use the land and the natural resources associated with it. Such rights extend to flora and most fauna, minerals and certain riparian rights.[41] Ownership also carries obligations such as support for neighbouring land[42] and the obligation not to commit a nuisance[43] or waste.[44] Private property rights are often overridden by the state in respect of minerals, town planning, environmental protection and land takings for public works and infrastructure.[45]

In contrast to land, water is regarded by the common law as incapable of ownership in its natural state. But once contained, it can become the property of the landowner.[46] Historically, it was a 'free resource' that could be dammed, diverted, used for domestic purposes or have waste discharged into it. Again such rights have been subject to limitations located mainly in the law of torts – for example, nuisance, trespass and the doctrine of *Rylands v Fletcher*.[47] They have also been progressively restricted by legislation.[48] Air has historically been regarded in a similar way to water as a free resource and 'free sink' for waste products. It has also been protected to a limited extent through the law of torts and through clean air legislation.

Standing timber in forests is traditionally the property of the surface landowner, although it has, from very early times, been subject to some control by the state.[49] Subsequently, forestry activity on both public and private land has increasingly been subject to limitations through planning and resource management legislation and a range of specific statutory measures.

Fisheries were traditionally considered a common property resource to which the 'rule of capture' applied. Offshore, fish caught lawfully would become the fisher's property upon being hooked, netted or harpooned.[50] In inland waters where the bed of the water body was privately owned, access to the resource would be limited by the law of trespass. If the fisher had legal access to the water body, he or she could take as property any fish caught in this way.

In more recent times, extensive limitations on fishing have been imposed by states through the application of international agreements such as the United Nations Convention on the Law of the Sea. This recognizes that a state has jurisdiction to limit access to fisheries within the 200-nautical-mile exclusive economic zone (EEZ).[51] Aquaculture and freshwater fisheries activities are also closely regulated today.

In many post-colonial states, including the United States, Canada, Australia and New Zealand, indigenous rights can also limit the exercise of private property rights.

3. Common Law Constraints on the Exercise of Property Rights[52]

(a) Introduction

The common law provides a number of options to constrain the exercise of property rights to prevent environmental harm to neighbouring property owners or to the public interest. Apart from the general rules of property law and contract, the main sources of such constraints are the tortious remedies of trespass to land, private nuisance, the principle of

Rylands v Fletcher, negligence, and the doctrine of waste. The general criminal law also provides some protection against environmental damage to land or resources.

(b) Trespass to land

Trespass to land has been defined as a 'direct and intentional interference, by a defendant, with a plaintiff's exclusive possession of land'.[53] Examples of trespass relevant to environmental harm include projectiles,[54] rock from blasting operations,[55] noise and vibration,[56] discharge of water and debris,[57] and the emission of pollutants that subsequently end up on another's property.[58] Trespass may be available where airborne particulate or other toxic matter is carried across neighbouring land, whether or not it settles on the land itself.[59] The courts in some jurisdictions, however, have been reluctant to allow trespass claims in the latter types of cases.[60]

The range of interests protected under an action for trespass to land can include trespass into airspace to a limited extent above land[61] and intrusions through the substrata underlying land.[62] The latter has clear application to oil and gas activities, including fracking. Remedies for trespass to land include injunctive relief, the recovery of land, and mesne profits with or without damages. Liability is normally strict, allowing a claim for all reasonable and natural consequences of a trespass regardless of foreseeability.[63]

(c) Nuisance

Nuisance is traditionally regarded as the primary environmental tort, although today much of its ambit is the subject of specific regulation.[64] Nevertheless it does have a continuing role as an independent remedy. It supplements and assists in the interpretation of statutory measures that are based on the concept of nuisance.[65]

Private nuisance refers to 'invasions of an occupier's interest in the beneficial use and enjoyment of land'.[66] Today, it extends beyond direct physical intrusions of persons or things. It may include noise, smell, vibration, and other intangible and consequential interferences emanating from a neighbour's land.[67] The tort is particularly well suited as a remedy for the negative effects of industrial and agricultural activities and of the activities of extractive industries. An actionable nuisance requires an injury or wrongful act causing substantial and unreasonable interference.[68] The prerequisites for liability are 'reasonable foreseeability' of the risk and a failure to prevent it.[69]

Of particular relevance to environmental conflict are situations where industrially caused harm or injury has occurred or where pollution has been an issue. Examples include emission of noise or vibration,[70] offensive activities,[71] threats to health, comfort or safety,[72] air or water pollution,[73] spread of noxious weeds,[74] and even blockage of solar access[75] or solar reflection.[76] The remedy may also have application to the introduction of genetically modified organisms into the environment.[77]

There are several defences to a claim of private nuisance. These include statutory authority,[78] consent and contributory negligence. Remedies available for private nuisance include damages, injunctive relief, or a combination of both, and in some circumstances the old privilege of abatement.[79]

Public nuisance is an interference 'which materially affects the reasonable comfort and convenience of life of a class of Her Majesty's subjects'.[80] It rests primarily upon collective personal or public injury or loss and so may assist, directly or indirectly, an individual who experiences environmental harm – including to property interests – within the parameters of the tort.

The distinction between public nuisance and private nuisance is that 'in cases of private nuisance the injury is to individual property, and in cases of public nuisance the injury is to the property of mankind'.[81] Thus a claim of public nuisance may be presented in situations similar to those that may give rise to a private nuisance claim – but on a much wider scale affecting a large number of people or a community.[82] Public nuisance may also lie for the interference with a public right or the use of a public place.[83]

A private claimant in public nuisance must be able to show a particular or special loss over and above that sustained by the public at large or that the interference also involves a violation of a private right.[84] Liability is not strict and will depend upon the causation and the reasonable foreseeability of the damage from the activity causing it,[85] and often upon considerations of public interest.[86] Remedies include injunctive relief or, less commonly, damages on a basis similar to that for private nuisance.

(d) *Rylands v Fletcher*

The rule of *Rylands v Fletcher* is that a person who 'brings on his land, and collects and keeps there anything likely to do mischief if it escapes' is liable for any damage or injury caused if it does escape.[87] There must be a non-natural user of land: namely 'some special use bringing with it increased danger to others'.[88] The object that escapes must be dangerous in itself and must in fact escape. It would seem that the more hazardous the activity, the more flexible the courts have been in applying the requirement of escape.[89]

The principle has been applied in situations where there has been damage caused by fire,[90] explosive or combustible materials,[91] sewage and effluent,[92] water,[93] noise and vibration,[94] industrial or mechanical failure,[95] pesticides, herbicides and chemicals,[96] and the supply of services such as gas and electricity.[97] Hence, the principle has considerable application to actions involving environmental harm.

The rule of *Rylands v Fletcher* is now regarded as a special form of private nuisance liability in the United Kingdom[98] and in New Zealand.[99] In Australia it has been abolished and subsumed into the law of negligence.[100] Where it is considered a sub-set of nuisance, similar remedies will apply.

(e) Negligence

Negligence actions have been successful where fire has spread to a neighbour's land,[101] for water usage,[102] and for dangerous articles or matter that have caused property damage,[103] including herbicide spray drift.[104] The remedy therefore has considerable applicability to environmental harm as a result of implementing development projects and of the activities of the agriculture and extractive industries.

Notwithstanding the dominance of environmental protection legislation in recent decades, negligence may still provide a powerful remedy for individuals, corporates and public interest groups seeking redress for environmental injury or damage that may not be recoverable through other legal avenues.

(f) The doctrine of waste

The doctrine of waste usually arises in the context of a lease. It comprises 'any act or omission on the part of the tenant which causes a lasting alteration to the nature of the land … to the prejudice of the person who has the remainder or reversion of the land'.[105] Causes of action in waste are not co-extensive with negligence. However, 'acts giving rise to liability in negligence are always likely to attract the doctrine of waste'. The difference is that waste applies to '*any* act or omission (other than those constituting reasonable use of the land), whereas negligence self-evidently applies only to acts or omissions which are in breach of a duty of care'.[106] Waste therefore has significant potential as a tool of environmental law enforcement in relation to leases of land, including long-term leases of state-owned industrial and agricultural land and private commercial leases.

(g) The role of the criminal law

In most jurisdictions common law crimes have been abolished and replaced with criminal codes.[107] Some offences under such codes are applicable to property damage with associated environmental consequences. There are also specific offences under most environmental, natural resources, planning and resource management regulatory regimes.

Damaging property through fire or explosives or attempting to do so is often an offence, particularly if the perpetrator knows that damage to property is likely to result, or if the act was done with reckless disregard for the safety of other property.[108] This has some relevance to hazardous activities – particularly in the mining and energy sectors and in relation to agricultural activities such as burning off scrubland.[109] Another common offence is causing disease or sickness in animals.[110] This has application to animal welfare and biosecurity issues. Another possible application is where the reckless conduct of mining, or oil and gas exploration and production activities, causes illness in animals or marine species.

The offence of contamination of food, crops, water or other products is often found in the laws of states heavily reliant on agriculture.[111] One possible application of this offence is the import and distribution of pathogens or genetically modified organisms, or the use of biological pest control where these circumstances cause environmental and property damage. A further possible application is the reckless conduct of mining and petroleum activities that causes contamination of food, crops, water or other products for human consumption. Fracking would appear to be within the range of possible offences here.

(h) Complementary property mechanisms relevant to environmental governance

In addition to the tortious and criminal law restrictions on the use of property rights discussed above, traditional property law principles prescribe qualifications on the exercise of such rights and the mechanisms that may be used to actively protect environmental values.

The obligation of support is a property law principle whereby the owner of land has a right of support for the land in its natural state. The right has been described as 'a natural right of property or incident of ownership'.[112] It protects landowners from the removal of support – both laterally and vertically – through non-natural means. The right and its correlative obligation have application to mining activities[113] and to other uses and developments of land where support to adjacent or superjacent land is compromised.

Easements, restrictive covenants and even leases can be used to protect access, views and amenity. But such protection depends upon the willingness of property owners to restrict the use of their property and upon the willingness of the person or entity seeking the restriction to pay the price or accept a correlational obligation. While these are generally matters of contract and private law, there are some interesting examples of institutional protection through the use of 'conservation covenants' to protect amenity and ecological values. These usually operate through a legislative regime that provides financial incentives or some other encouragement for landowners to set aside part of their land in perpetuity to be protected from development or clearance of vegetation. The mechanism can be a statutory 'open space covenant' that may be registered or noted against a land title – in which case it binds the future owners of the land.[114]

4. Statutory Measures Affecting Property Rights

(a) Town planning and resource management governance

As already noted, general town planning and natural resource management legislation restricting property rights is a common feature of most common law and civil law jurisdictions. Such regulatory regimes generally provide for central or local government policy and planning instruments specifying what activities may, or may not, be undertaken on land and include a discretionary permitting system for obtaining planning or 'resource' consent. Water use and discharges into water or the atmosphere are usually controlled under specific regulation. It is beyond the scope of this chapter to examine the multiplicity of such regimes. Instead, the New Zealand 'resource management' regime will be discussed as a case study of a modern planning system for managing land, air and water use.

The Resource Management Act 1991 of New Zealand (RMA) was an attempt to bring the management of land, air and water under a single integrated regime guided by the principle of sustainability.[115] While the management of a number of natural resources remains outside the RMA,[116] the Act is the core environmental and resource management statute with application to the environmental externalities of most activities affecting land, air, water and the coastal marine area. The RMA regime has been described as 'float[ing], rather like oil on water, across the top of ownership rights without affecting the underlying substance'.[117] It generally prevails over common law property rights where there is a conflict.[118]

The exercise of private property rights in land is closely controlled through rules in planning instruments.[119] Riparian rights to the foreshore, the bed of the sea, and the beds of lakes and rivers are significantly curtailed.[120] So are the traditional rights of landowners that exist *cujus est solum ejus est usque ad coelum et ad inferos*.[121] Discharges into water are strictly controlled.[122] Access to minerals is closely regulated by government.[123]

Landowners normally need to obtain resource consents to undertake activities on the land. Other RMA restrictions on the traditional rights of surface landowners include:

- restricting discharges of contaminants on to land[124]
- compulsory takings of land for provision of public services by public and private 'network utility operators'[125]
- potential liability of a present landowner for historic pollution[126]
- extensive rights of entry on to land for collecting and seizing evidence for prosecutions.[127]

Control of water is for the most part the responsibility of regional councils acting through regional planning instruments and the resource consent procedure. In terms of usage rights, the reverse approach to land use applies: namely that no one can take or use water[128] or discharge contaminants into water[129] unless expressly allowed by a rule in a plan or permitted by a resource consent issued by the local authority. The traditional principle that air is a free 'sink' for waste emissions is also curtailed.[130]

Most activities affecting land, air and water will require resource consents under the RMA. Such consents create rights to undertake activities using land, air or water. They are transferable, have economic value, may be used as security, and may devolve upon death in certain circumstances. Curiously, however, section 122(1) of the RMA states that 'a resource consent is neither real nor personal property'. The effect of this provision has caused considerable judicial uncertainty and academic debate.[131]

The nature of rights such as these has been the subject of comment by the High Court of Australia in the context of abalone harvesting consents. They have been described as 'an entitlement of a new kind created as part of a system for preserving a limited public natural resource'.[132] One possibility, therefore, is to characterize resource consents as a new form of 'statutory property' governed by the rules contained in the statutes that create them[133] but not subject to the general rules and statutes dealing with real or personal property. They may, however, be subject to other generic principles of law that do not require a traditional 'real' or 'personal' property interest such as derogation from the grant, legitimate expectation and administrative law remedies.

To summarize, under the RMA – and similar planning regimes – the traditional presumption of the right to use private land remains largely intact. But the right is usually subject to limitations for the community or public benefit. Conversely, water and air are considered no longer as free resources or sinks for waste but rather as public property. In this case, for most purposes, a private landowner cannot use or discharge contaminants into such 'property' without express authorization. In many jurisdictions land use planning is dealt with in separate regulatory regimes that do not apply to water use management and atmospheric protection.[134]

(b) Complementary statutory measures modifying property rights in natural resources

In addition to town planning, water and clean air regulation, the major economic resources of minerals, fisheries and forestry are often heavily regulated by the state. Further limitations on such activities have been imposed to address matters of global concern – such as climate change and atmospheric pollution. The following paragraphs describe examples relating to resource management in New Zealand, including mining, fisheries, forestry, indigenous rights and climate change.

Landowners today have few rights to minerals under their land. Often the primary strategic minerals – such as gold, silver, petroleum and uranium – are state owned. To similar effect, minerals have been progressively reserved to the state when it grants land rights, or by automatic reservation provisions in land and minerals legislation. Thus landowners seldom own the minerals under their land. Miners generally need a permit from the state for mining activities.[135] Access rights may need to be negotiated with the surface landowner.[136] Compliance with planning and environmental regulations will often be required even where minerals are privately owned.[137]

In regard to fisheries resources most states are signatories to the United Nations Convention on the Law of the Sea (UNCLOS), which recognizes the power of states to exercise sovereign rights over fisheries within their 200-mile exclusive economic zone (EEZ). This is usually effected through a licensing system. In some jurisdictions such as Iceland,[138] Australia[139] and New Zealand,[140] these regimes are aimed at ensuring the sustainability of commercial fisheries.[141]

In Iceland all exploitable marine species within the 200-mile EEZ are deemed the 'common property' of the Icelandic nation.[142] Commercial fisheries are managed under a system of individual transferrable quotas (ITQs). A holder of a quota has a specific share of whatever is the annual total allowable catch (TAC) set by the Ministry of Fisheries for a particular species. While the legislation explicitly states that quota shares convey neither ownership of, nor irrevocable control over, harvesting rights, such rights are regarded as a valuable property right. They are devisable and transferrable, attract property taxes when transferred, are property for the purposes of divorce settlements, and attract inheritance tax.[143]

The Fisheries Act 1996 in New Zealand is similar to the Icelandic regime. It has as its central purpose the 'sustainable utilization'[144] of fisheries resources. It contains a quota management scheme (QMS) continued from prior legislation. The QMS allocates ITQ rights in certain species to fishers. As in Iceland, the ITQ entitles the holder to a certain proportion of a fish stock from the total allowable commercial catch (TACC) set by the Minister of Fisheries every year at a level that ensures that a particular species is fished sustainably. Because the quota is transferable and may be used as security, it has many characteristics of a property right. Individual transferable quotas are a hybrid form of property right disclosing elements of a land title and of company shares. They are similar to a non-exclusive *profit à prendre* in relation to the fish stock in respect of which they are granted. But they are expressed as a share – out of a total 1 million shares[145] – of the TACC for that stock. As such, it is not a right to an absolute tonnage of fish stock. Rather it is a right to a proportion of the TACC for any particular year.[146] ITQs can be sold, transferred or mortgaged.

Fisheries quota management systems as applied in Iceland and New Zealand provide a very effective means of managing common property resources in an economically efficient and environmentally sustainable way. Such schemes may also have utility in the management of other common property resources including water, geothermal energy and even clean air.

In most jurisdictions commercial forestry, whether on public or private land, is generally treated in the same way as any other agricultural land use and therefore subject to the relevant planning system. Consents will often be required for forestry activities. In some jurisdictions harvesting is subject to sustainability requirements. For example, harvesting indigenous species on private land in New Zealand is subject to a planning regime that requires the preparation of a sustainable forest management plan or the acquisition of a sustainable forest management permit.[147] Such measures are a major restriction on a landowner's use of his or her land, and a breach of the rules attracts heavy financial penalties.

Recognition and protection of indigenous claims to land and natural resources has, in recent years, experienced a renaissance in many post-colonial jurisdictions. This adds a further layer of qualification and restriction on private property rights. Often objections to land and resource developments by indigenous people are based on interference with cultural, spiritual and environmental values. There are many examples where court decisions have restricted private property rights in favour of those elements.[148]

Legislation has created new types of usufructuary and similar property rights for indigenous people These rights recognize traditional and customary uses that have historically been overlooked or held to be incompatible with the common law.[149] For example, in New Zealand Māori groups can apply for 'protected customary rights' or 'customary marine title' if certain criteria – including proof of historic and continuing use of the area and natural resources therein – are met.[150]

Addressing greenhouse gas (GHG) emissions through the use of economic instruments is a relatively recent and innovative use of property rights to achieve sustainable outcomes. Signatories to the 1997 Kyoto Protocol to the UN Framework Convention on Climate Change (UNFCCC) of 1992 agreed to reduce levels of GHGs – variable depending upon the country – by 2012. Many countries did not achieve their targets, and in 2015 the twenty-first Conference of the Parties to the UNFCCC (COP 21) agreed to a new approach to combatting climate change based on 'nationally determined obligations' (the 'Paris Agreement').[151]

Some countries and regions have introduced emissions trading schemes as an economics or market-based approach to reduce GHG emissions.[152] These schemes essentially create transferrable quasi-property rights to emit GHGs. Emissions trading units (ETUs) are usually issued free by governments to existing industrial, forestry, fisheries and agricultural emitters. They are intended to be tradeable domestically and internationally. Emitters must surrender units in proportion to specified levels of emissions. Over time, the level of emissions can be managed through the government setting caps on levels of GHGs in much the same way as a fisheries quota may be adjusted under quota management schemes. Again, this represents a new form of property right in the nature of a reverse, non-exclusive *profit à prendre* comprising the right to emit GHGs into the atmosphere.

THE CHANGING NATURE OF PROPERTY RIGHTS IN ENVIRONMENTAL GOVERNANCE[153]

Conventional policy in most developed states is to maintain strong private property rights in order to encourage investment and economic growth. Limitations have historically been imposed on the exercise of these rights through planning, building and health regulation and more recently through environmental and resource management regulation. But even with sophisticated modern environmental legislation there is usually a conceptual and legal separation between, on the one hand, the individualized 'ownership' or property right itself and, on the other hand, the public interest focused layer of environmental protective regulation. Property rights are regarded as legally complete and enforceable in themselves, qualified only by whatever limitations may be applied externally through the operation of applicable environmental and resource management laws. If there are no such laws, or if the laws are incomplete or technically inapplicable to particular situations, then the owner can generally exercise his or her property rights to their fullest extent.

An emerging approach requires the modification of the concept of property to incorporate sustainability as an 'inherent' or fundamental responsibility of holding rights of possession or of ownership in land and natural resources. While this approach may be harder to achieve and requires a major paradigm shift in perceptions of property rights in most developed legal systems, it is not so novel in the history of human development.[154]

Some commentators have noted the need to internalize environmental values in human interaction with the natural environment. Aldo Leopold called for a new land ethic recognizing that humans are a part of the biotic community – not apart from it.[155] More recently, Kevin Gray observed that it 'no longer seems strange to speak of the responsibilities of "ecological citizenship"'.[156] Gray also notes that there are sound economic arguments to recognize the vital interrelationship between environmental values and human well-being.[157]

Principles of sustainable development and management of natural resources are now widely accepted at the global level and at local levels in many jurisdictions. In some jurisdictions sustainability is at the core of policy, planning and decision-making about the use of land, air and water.[158] Where this is the case, to the extent that consents and planning permissions for the use of land, air and water are property rights, it can be said that sustainability considerations have been integrated into both the creation and the exercise of these rights. Rights to fell and mill indigenous trees[159] and the allocation of commercial fisheries quota[160] are also governed by the sustainability principle in some jurisdictions. Emissions trading units created by climate change measures are a new form of property in carbon.[161] Designed to reduce greenhouse gas emissions through economic and market forces, sustainability underlies their very raison d'être. It is therefore possible to integrate sustainability into the process of creating and managing property rights in natural resources through regulation. But even this falls short of an inherent obligation of sustainability *embedded* in property rights in land and natural resources.

It can be argued that the law needs to articulate sustainability as a non-derogable norm designed not only to establish baseline community expectations but also to protect 'sustainability' from political agendas. However, establishing the principle of sustainability as an 'inherent' internalized incident of property ownership will require more than legislative intervention. It will also require judicial support. As the principle of sustainability is now an internationally accepted normative principle – and may even be approaching the status of customary international law – it may also inform and guide the decisions of domestic courts. It is now widely accepted that courts may be guided by international law and normative principles where there is some ambiguity in domestic regulation; where there is some dispute over the exercise of a statutory discretion; or where a balancing of private rights and community interests is required in any particular case.[162]

CONCLUSION

This chapter has reviewed property rights and their role in environmental governance. This has included an analysis of traditional property rights; a discussion about their adaptation and evolution to accommodate environmental challenges; and an assessment of the creation of new forms of property and trading systems to address environmental conflict and to promote more sustainable use of land and natural resources.

Property rights can provide versatile and creative solutions to some of the resource scarcity and environmental degradation problems the planet faces. Further developments of tradeable rights in resources – such as QMS schemes for fisheries, and emissions trading schemes for carbon – may be expected, particularly in water, geothermal and similar renewable energy contexts. The management of indigenous claims to land and resources is another area where innovative quasi-property rights are being developed. Further, with the information technology now available, it is possible to develop much more sophisticated property and resource data and registration systems. These allow immediate access to current data and offer effective solutions for reducing conflict and disputes over access to land and use of natural resources.

Property rights-based systems must, however, become more sensitive and responsive to the impacts of the exercise of land and resource rights. Such rights must not only accommodate but also advance the principle of sustainability. While environmental and planning regulatory regimes are beginning to incorporate sustainability to a greater or lesser extent, systems of allocation and management must accommodate a broader range of values beyond those that can be reduced to a conventional economic utility value. Many critical elements of the biosphere and ecological health are not amenable to quantifiable and market-based economic accounting. Such values will continue to require ongoing government oversight and intervention to ensure that ecological sustainability and intergenerational equity are incorporated in the exercise of property rights. Finally, the principle of sustainability must be accepted as an inherent and universal obligation of property ownership and incorporated into law, policy and judicial decision-making to mitigate the impact on ecological values of the exercise of property rights.

NOTES

1. Sax (2008, pp. 9–25); Guth (2008, p. 511); Freyfogle (2006); Circo (2009, p. 91).
2. Adler (2012); Adler (2001, p. 653); Adler (2005, p. 987). For recent commentary on 'free-market environmentalism', see Anderson and Leal (2015); Rose (2004); Schlager and Ostrom (1992, p. 249).
3. Land ownership normally carries with it ownership of structures attached to the land, trees and other flora, minerals (where these have not been expropriated by the state) and certain other natural features.
4. Grinlinton (2015a, pp. 60–65).
5. See, for example, Schlager and Ostrom (1992); Sax (1993); Rose (1994); Frazier (1995); Coyle and Morrow (2004, pp. 1–7); Rose (2004); Barnes (2009); McHarg et al. (2010); Gray (2010); and the collection of writings in Grinlinton and Taylor (2011).
6. For discussion of the theoretical bases of property rights and obligations, see Honoré (1961, pp. 107–148); Waldron (1996, pp. 560–73); Penner (1996).
7. See, for example, Lippman (1955, p. 108); Murphy (1977, p. 186). See also Cribbet (1986, p. 40); Guth (2008, pp. 511–52).
8. See, for example, Penner (1996).
9. The 'rule of capture' provides that the first person to 'capture' a migratory resource such as groundwater, oil, gas or wild animals acquires ownership: see, for example, *Acton v Blundell* [1843] 152 ER 1223; *Ballard v Tomlinson* (1885) 29 Ch D 115 at 121; *Ohio Oil Co v Indiana* (1900) 177 US 190 at 203.
10. For example, the nationalization of oil by many common law jurisdictions leading up to World War II as the strategic importance of petroleum was realized: Petroleum (Production) Act 1934 (UK); Mines (Petroleum) Act 1935 (Vic); Petroleum Act 1936 (WA); Petroleum Act 1937 (NZ), s 3 (now Crown Minerals Act 1991 (NZ), s 10). Rights to control access to water have been asserted by many governments: see, e.g., Water Sustainability Act 2014 (BC), s 5; Water Management Act 2000 (NSW), s 392; Water and Soil Conservation Act 1967 (NZ), s 21(1) (now see Resource Management Act 1991 (NZ), s 354(1)(b)).

11. For example, Town and Country Planning Act 1990 (UK); Resource Management Act 1991 (NZ); Ontario Planning and Development Act 1994 (Ont.); Sustainable Planning Act 2009 (Qld).
12. For example, the fisheries 'Quota Management Systems' in Iceland under the Fisheries Management Act 2006 (Iceland), and in New Zealand under the Fisheries Act 1996 (NZ).
13. For example, Mineral Resources Act 1989 (Qld); Mines and Minerals Act 2000 (Alta.); Crown Minerals Act 1991 (NZ).
14. For example, Crown forest licences under the Crown Forest Assets Act 1989 (NZ); sustainable forest management permits under the Forests Act 1949 (NZ). See also Forests Act 1958 (Vic.); Forest Act 1996 (BC).
15. In New Zealand formalized 'protected customary rights' or 'customary marine title' were created under the Marine and Coastal Area (Takutai Moana) Act 2011, Pt 3.
16. Forms of property rights in carbon dioxide and other greenhouse gas emissions have been developed with emissions trading schemes such as the European Union's Emissions Trading Scheme (EU Directive 2003/87/EC of the European Parliament and of the Council of 13 October 2003 (OJ 2003 L275/32)). See also Climate Change Response (Emissions Trading) Amendment Act 2008 (NZ).
17. Grinlinton (2011, p. 281). In this context 'land' normally includes the surface, subsurface and airspace above except for property rights alienated to another, expropriated by the state (e.g. subsurface minerals), or constrained by other legitimate activities (e.g. civil aviation regulations). 'Associated natural resource' includes air, water, minerals, geothermal energy, other forms of energy, flora, fauna, marine resources and fisheries, amenity and wilderness areas.
18. For a full account of social contract theory, see Riley (2006, pp. 347–75). See also Gough (1936).
19. Locke (1689, ch.V). See also Vaughn (1978, pp. 311–26).
20. Smith (1776).
21. For an excellent, and brief, explanation of capital and the importance of property, see de Soto (2001). For a fuller version see de Soto (2000, ch.3).
22. See, for example, the US Constitution Amendments V and XIV; compare Commonwealth of Australia Constitution Act 1900, cl 51 (xxxi), and comments of Deane J on the acquisition of property on 'just terms' in *Commonwealth v Tasmania* (1983) 4 ALR 625 at 824–833, especially at 832. In civil law jurisdictions, see the Constitution of the Kingdom of the Netherlands, June 2002, art 4(1) and the Basic Law of the Federal Republic of Germany, 23 May 1949, arts 1–2 (life, liberty) and 14–15 (property).
23. The guarantees in Magna Carta 1215 inter alia that 'No freeman shall be … disseised of his Freehold' became binding law in England in Confirmatio Cartarum 1297 (UK) 25 Edw I c 9, and is reflected in the Bill of Rights 1688 (UK) 1 Will & Mar Sess 2 c 2 and the Act of Settlement 1701 (UK) 12 & 13 W III c 2. In *Munn v People of State of Illinois* (1876) 94 US 113, the US Supreme Court noted that the principle that no property should be taken without due process dated back to Magna Carta, and was an expression of fundamental rights that underlay the US Constitution, Amendments V and IV. The concept of eminent domain and provisions for compensation for statutory takings of land found in most states implements the protection of property rights in legal systems: e.g. Land Clauses Consolidation Act 1845 (UK), Public Works Act 1981 (NZ) (and predecessors) and Land Acquisition (Just Terms Compensation) Act 1991 (NSW).
24. *White v Chandler* [2001] 1 NZLR 28 at [67], per Hammond J.
25. This section draws from Grinlinton (2015a, pp. 56–8).
26. See Coase (1960). See also Posner (1998); Demsetz (1967).

27. Proponents of this approach suggest that environmental problems are not caused by the exercise of property rights, but because there are not enough property rights and the selective use of different types of property rights will provide efficient solutions; see, for example, Rose (1997, p. 49); Ostrom (1990).
28. An example is the fisheries Quota Management Scheme in New Zealand: Lock and Leslie (2007).
29. Again, the Emissions Trading Scheme in New Zealand provides a useful example: see the Ministry for the Environment's website at http://www.climatechange.govt.nz/emissions-trading-scheme/. The European Union's Emissions Trading Scheme (Directive 2003/87/EC of the European Parliament and of the Council of 13 October 2003 (OJ 2003 L275/32)): see the EC Climate Action website at http://ec.europa.eu/clima/policies/ets/pre2013/index_en.htm.
30. O'Riordan (1981, p. 265). See also Rose (2004, pp. 279–81 and 288–92).
31. One example is the privatization of the New Zealand government-owned Petrocorp Exploration Ltd, which is described in *Petrocorp Exploration Ltd v Minister of Energy* [1991] 1 NZLR 1 at 4–5 (HC).
32. This section draws from Grinlinton (2015a, pp. 37–42).
33. Barzel (1989, p. 3).
34. Lippman (1955, p. 109); compare Schlatter (1973, chs 8–10). See also Leopold and Meine (2013, p. 171) (the 'Land Ethic'); and Leopold (1991).
35. Blackstone (1765, p. 135). See Blackstone's elaboration at p. 125 that 'The rights themselves… [are] either that residuum of natural liberty, which is not required by the laws of society to be sacrificed to public convenience, or else those civil privileges which society hath engaged to provide, in lieu of the natural liberties so given up by individuals'. See also Code Civil des Français (French Civil Code), arts 537–46 (especially arts 544–46).
36. See Plucknett (1956, pp. 506–20) for a description of feudalism in relation to personal property. See also Bergin and Haskell (1984, ch.1).
37. See Murphy (1977, p. 177); compare Turley (1994, p. 407) where the author states: 'Environmentalism, therefore, is not only compatible, it is essential to private property rights'.
38. For example, the expropriation of petroleum by the state as it became indispensible for heavy industry, transport and military purposes: Petroleum (Production) Act 1934 (UK) 24 & 25 Geo 5 c 36, s 1 (as originally enacted); Petroleum Act 1915 (Qld); Mines (Petroleum) Act 1935 (Vic.); Petroleum Act 1936 (WA); and Petroleum Act 1937 (NZ).
39. For example, in New Zealand, allocation and management of water and geothermal energy resources was brought under government control under the Water and Soil Conservation Act 1967 and the Geothermal Energy Act 1953, both now incorporated in the RMA. Fisheries allocation and management has been regulated under successive fisheries Acts since 1908.
40. *Harper v Minister for Sea Fisheries* [1989] HCA 47, (1989) 168 CLR 314 at 325.
41. An owner (or occupier) of land abutting a water body has a common law natural right to access to and regress from the water. For more detail on 'riparian rights', see Burn and Cartwright (2011, pp. 163–5); Butt (2010, pp. 24–5); Brookfield (2010, paras 46–55).
42. Butt (2010, pp. 19–23).
43. As represented in the ancient maxim, *sic utere tuo ut alienum non laedas*: '[u]se your property so as not to damage another's'. Garner (2009, Appendix B, 1872).
44. Burn and Cartwright (2011, pp. 609–11); Butt (2010, pp. 154–6).
45. See the discussion on 'Town planning and resource management governance' at 4(a), p. 403 below.

46. Burn and Cartwright (2011, pp. 163–5); Brookfield (2010, para.39); *Embrey v Owen* (1851) 6 Exch 353 at 369.
47. *Rylands v Fletcher* [1868] LR 3 HL 330.
48. Burn and Cartwright (2011, pp. 165–7); Butt (2010, pp. 25–6); Brookfield (2010, para.40).
49. See Bosselmann (2015). The importance of forests for soil, water and atmospheric health has long been recognized in some jurisdictions: see the preamble to the Forests Act 1874 (NZ), which states: '[w]hereas it is expedient to make provision for preserving the soil and climate by tree planting …'.
50. For an illuminating account of the rule of capture in relation to nineteenth-century whaling, see Melville (1851, ch.89).
51. The United Nations Convention on the Law of the Sea 1833 UNTS 3; 21 ILM 1261 (1982) (hereinafter 'UNCLOS') was signed in 1982 and came into force in 1994 after the sixtieth nation (Guyana) signed it.
52. For a fuller account of the role of the common law in environmental law, from which material in this part is drawn, see Grinlinton (2015b, pp. 175–202).
53. Barker et al. (2012, p. 155).
54. For example, *Rigby v Chief Constable* [1985] 1 WLR 1242 (QB).
55. Early examples from the US include *Wheeler v Norton* (1904) 86 NYS 1095 and *Watson v Mississipi River Power Co* (1916) 156 NW 188.
56. *Jacobson v Crown Zellerbach Corp* (1975) 539 P 2d 641 (SC) (logging trucks); *Lone Star Producing Co v Jury* (1968) 445 P 2d 284 (SC) (vibration).
57. For example, *McMillan v The Great Extended Sluicing Co (Reg)* (1886) 4 NZLR 377 (SC) (water and debris).
58. For example *Pride of Derby and Derbyshire Angling Association Ltd v British Celanese Ltd* [1952] 1 All ER 1326 (Ch); and discussion in *Southport Corp v Esso Petroleum Co Ltd* [1954] 2 QB 182 at 204, per Morris LJ (CA).
59. US examples include *Borland v Sanders Lead Co Inc* (1979) 369 So 2d 523 (lead smelter); *Roberts v Permanente Corp* (1961) 10 Cal Rptr 519 (quarry dust); *Reynolds Metals Co v Yturbide* (1958) 258 F 2d 321 (fluoride deposits); and *Renken v Harvey Aluminium (Inc)* (1963) 226 F Supp 169 (emissions from an aluminum factory). See also Centner (2014).
60. In *Geothermal Produce New Zealand Ltd v Goldie Applicators Ltd* HC Rotorua A26/81, 17 February 1983, a claim in trespass for spray drift damage from the herbicide 245T was dismissed.
61. *Break Fast Investments Pty Ltd v PCH Melbourne Pty Ltd* (2007) 20 VR 311 (CA).
62. *Bocardo SA v Star Energy UK Onshore Ltd* [2011] 1 AC 380, [2010] 3 All ER 975 at [26]–[27], per Lord Hope.
63. See Grinlinton (2015b, pp. 179–80).
64. See comments of Lord Goff in *Cambridge Water Co Ltd v Eastern Counties Leather Plc* [1994] 2 AC 264 at 305 (HL).
65. Murphy and Witting (2012, pp. 440–1).
66. Sappideen and Vines (2011, p. 487). See also *Hunter v Canary Wharf Ltd* [1997] AC 655 (HL) (plaintiff must possess interest in land).
67. See examples in Todd (2013, paras 10.2.02(1) and 10.2.03(1)).
68. *Harrison v Southwark and Vauxhall Water Co* [1891] 2 Ch 409 (substantial/unreasonable interference).
69. *The Wagon Mound (No 2)* [1966] 2 All ER 709 at 716–17 (PC); *Cambridge Water Co Ltd v Eastern Counties Leather Plc* [1994] 2 AC 264 (HL). In New Zealand, see *Hamilton v Papakura District Council* [2000] 1 NZLR 265 (CA), affirmed [2002] NZLR 308 (PC).
70. *Halsey v Esso Petroleum* [1961] 1 WLR 683 (QB); *Bloodworth v Cormack* [1949] NZLR 1058 (SC).

71. *St Helens Smelting Co v Tipping* [1861–73] All ER Rep Ext 1389 at 1395–6, per Lord Westbury LC (HL); *Halsey v Esso Petroleum* [1961] 2 All ER 145; *Wheeler v JJ Sanders Ltd* [1996] Ch 19 (CA); *Hunter v Canary Wharf Ltd* [1997] AC 655 (HL).
72. *Copeland v Stanthorpe Shire Council* [1941] St R Qd 86.
73. *Munro v Southern Dairies Ltd* [1955] VLR 332 (VSC) (air pollution); *Nicholls v Ely Beet Sugar Factory* [1931] 2 Ch 84; *Connery v Manitoba* (1971) 21 DLR (3d) 234 (MBCA) (water pollution).
74. *French v Auckland City Corporation* [1974] 1 NZLR 340 (wind-blown thistle seeds).
75. *Prah v Maretti* 321 NW 2d 182 (Wis 1982).
76. *Bank of New Zealand v Greenwood* [1984] 1 NZLR 525 (HC).
77. Rodgers (2003).
78. *Allen v Gulf Oil Refining Ltd* [1981] AC 1001 (HL).
79. See generally Sappideen and Vines (2011, pp. 520–5).
80. *Attorney-General v PYA Quarries Ltd* [1957] 2 QB 169 at 184 (CA).
81. *Attorney-General v Sheffield Gas Consumers Co* (1853) 43 ER 119 at 125, per Turner LJ (QB).
82. *Cartwright v McLaine & Long Pty Ltd* (1979) 143 CLR 549 at 553–4, per Gibb ACJ (HCA).
83. See Sappideen and Vines (2011, pp. 488–96).
84. *Halsbury's Laws of England* (2008, vol 78, p. 187).
85. *Wagon Mound (No 2)* [1967] 1 AC 617 (PC). Note, the relator to such an action may still have to bear the costs.
86. *Attorney-General v Abraham and Williams Ltd* [1949] NZLR 461 (SC).
87. *Rylands v Fletcher* (1866) LR 1 Exch 265 at 279–80, approved by the House of Lords in *Rylands v Fletcher* [1868] UKHL 1, (1868) LR 3 HL 330 at 339–40, per Lord Cairns.
88. *Rickards v Lothian* [1913] 16 CLR 387 at 401, per Lord Moulton for the Board (PC).
89. See Sappideen and Vines (2011, pp. 391–3).
90. For example, *McCarty v Leeming* [1937] SASR 432; *Balfour v Barty-King* [1956] 1 WLR 779; *New Zealand Forest Products Ltd v O'Sullivan* [1974] 2 NZLR 80 (SC).
91. For example, *LMS International Ltd v Styrene Packaging and Insulation Ltd* [2005] EWHC 2065 (TCC), [2006] TCLR T105; *Harooni v Rustins Ltd* [2011] EWHC 1632 (TCC).
92. For example, *Smeaton v Ilford Corp* [1954] Ch 450.
93. For example, *Greenock Corp v Caledonian Railway* [1917] AC 556 (HL); *Autex Industries Ltd v Auckland City Council* [2000] NZAR 324 (CA).
94. For example, *Hoare & Co v McAlpine & Co* [1923] 1 Ch 167; *Barette v Franki Compressed Pile Co of Canada Ltd* [1955] 2 DLR 665.
95. For example, *Hale v Jennings Bros* [1938] 1 All ER 579; *Pett v Sims Paving & Road Construction Co Pty Ltd* [1928] VLR 247.
96. *Cruise v Niessen* (1977) 76 DLR (3d) 343; *Attorney-General v Geothermal Produce New Zealand Ltd* [1987] 2 NZLR 348 at 363, per Somers J (CA).
97. *Hillier v Air Ministry* [1962] CLY 2084 (electricity); *North Western Utilities Ltd v London Guarantee & Accident Co* [1936] AC 108 (HL) (gas). Bulk storage or conveyance of water, gas or electricity for network utilities may today no longer be regarded as 'non-natural': Todd (2013, pp. 581–3).
98. *Cambridge Water Co Ltd v Eastern Counties Leather Plc* [1994] 2 AC 264 (HL); *Transco Plc v Stockport Metropolitan Borough Council* [2003] UKHL 61, [2004] 2 AC 1.
99. *Hamilton v Papakura District Council* [2000] 1 NZLR 265 (CA).

100. *Burnie Port Authority v General Jones Pty Ltd* [1994] HCA 13, (1994) 179 CLR 520.
101. *Goldman v Hargrave* [1967] 1 AC 645 (PC); *Wilson & Horton Ltd v Attorney-General* [1997] 2 NZLR 513 at 519–24, per Hammond J (CA) (for the majority: Richardson P, Blanchard and Hammond JJ).
102. *Dunn v Birmingham Canal Co* (1872) LR 8 QB 42; and *Torette House Pty Ltd v Berkman* (1940) 62 CLR 637 (HCA).
103. *Streets Ice Cream Pty Ltd v Australian Asbestos Installations Pty Ltd* [1967] 1 NSWR 50; *Hunter v Canary Wharf Ltd* [1997] AC 655 (CA) (dust damage); *Blue Circle Industries Plc v Ministry of Defence* [1998] EWCA Civ 945, [1999] 2 WLR 295 (radioactive contamination of soil).
104. *Attorney-General v Geothermal Produce NZ Ltd* [1987] 2 NZLR 348 (CA).
105. *Halsbury's Laws of England* (2012, vol 62, para.577).
106. *BP Oil New Zealand Ltd v Ports of Auckland Ltd* [2004] 2 NZLR 208 at [78] (HC).
107. In Australia, for example, some states have fully codified their criminal laws, whereas others rely on a mixture of partial codification and the common law: *Halsbury's Laws of Australia* (vol 9, para.130–5); Bagaric and Arenson (2004, p. 17).
108. Criminal Code Act 1995 (Qld), s 191 (explosives); Criminal Code Act Compilation Act 1913 (WA), ss 444 (fire), 454 (explosives); Crimes Act 1961 (NZ), ss 267–8.
109. See, for example, *Canterbury Regional Council v Newman* [2002] 1 NZLR 289 (NZCA), although the prosecution was brought under the Resource Management Act 1991 (NZ) rather than the general criminal law.
110. See, for example, Crimes Act 1961 (NZ), s 298A (inserted by the Crimes Amendment Act (No 2) 2003, s 5).
111. In New Zealand see Crimes Act 1961 (NZ), s 298B.
112. *Howley Park Coal and Cannel Co v London and North Western Railway Co* [1913] AC 11 at 25, per Viscount Haldane LC (HL); and see discussion of the rule in *Holbeck Hall Hotel Ltd v Scarborough Borough Council* [2000] QB 836, [2000] 2 All ER 705 at [27]–[38], per Stuart-Smith LJ.
113. See *Humphries v Brogden* (1850) 12 QB 739 at 744, per Lord Campbell CJ.
114. For example, the Queen Elizabeth the Second National Trust Act 1977 (NZ) which established the QEII National Trust which facilitates open space covenants with landowners; http://www.openspace.org.nz.
115. The statutory purpose of the RMA is to 'promote the sustainable management of natural and physical resources': RMA, s 5(1). On the history and theoretical underpinnings of the RMA reform process, see Grinlinton (1995). For general reference on the RMA, see Salmon and Grinlinton (2015, esp. chs 11–14).
116. For example, allocation of mining permits under the Crown Minerals Act 1991 (NZ); allocation of fisheries rights under the Fisheries Act 1991 (NZ); and to some extent, management of the forestry estate and indigenous forests under the Forests Act 1949 (NZ) and the Conservation Act 1987 (NZ).
117. *Coleman v Kingston* (unreported), High Court, Auckland (AP 103-SW00) (3 April 2001) at [28], per Hammond J; noted in Grinlinton (2001).
118. *Falkner v Gisborne District Council* [1995] 3 NZLR 622 at 632 (NZHCt).
119. RMA, ss 9(1) and (3).
120. Ibid., ss 9(6), (7), 12 and 13.
121. Ibid., s 15 controls discharges of contaminants into the atmosphere.
122. Ibid., s 15.
123. Crown Minerals Act 1991, ss 8–11.
124. RMA, s 15(1)(d), (2).
125. Ibid., ss 166–86.
126. Ibid., ss 314(1)(da), 322(1)(b)(ii), 338(1)(b) and (c).

127. Ibid., ss 332–5.
128. Ibid., s 14.
129. Ibid., s 15. There is an extensive definition of 'contaminant' in s 2(1).
130. Ibid., s 15.
131. For example, *Aoraki Water Trust v Meridian Energy Ltd* [2005] 2 NZLR 268 (HC); *Cavell v Thornton* [2008] NZCA 191 at [43]; *Hume v Auckland Regional Council* [2002] NZRMA 49 at [39]; *Hampton v Hampton* [2010] NZEnvC 9; *Marlborough District Council v Valuer-General* [2008] 1 NZLR 690. Academic writing includes: Fraser (2008); Barton (2009); Grinlinton (2011, pp. 291–7).
132. *Harper v Minister for Sea Fisheries* (1989) 168 CLR 314 at 325, per Chief Justice Sir Anthony Mason, and Justices William Deane and Mary Gaudron. The court in *Aoraki Water Trust v Meridian Energy Ltd* [2005] NZRMA 251, quoted this extract with approval (at para.29).
133. See *Bienke v Minister for Primary Industries* [1996] FCA 1220 at [54].
134. For example, in Western Australia, the Planning and Development Act 2005 (land use), Water Agencies (Powers) Act 1984 and Rights in Water and Irrigation Act 1914 (water), and Clean Air (Determination of Air Impurities in Gases Discharged to the Atmosphere) Regulations 1983 (air – deemed to be made pursuant to the Environmental Protection Act 1986, s 123 (see s 127)).
135. For example, Crown Minerals Act 1991 (NZ), ss 8(1)(a), 22–9.
136. Ibid., ss 8(1)(b), 49–54.
137. *Gebbie v Banks Peninsula District Council* [2000] NZRMA 553.
138. Fisheries Management Act 2006 (Iceland), art 1 (to promote conservation and efficient utilization of fisheries).
139. Fisheries Management Act 1991 (Cth), ss 3(1) and 3A, and Environment Protection and Biodiversity Conservation Act 1991 (Cth). In a number of states, individually transferrable quota (ITQ) systems have been introduced: see Barnes (2009, pp. 335–40).
140. Fisheries Act 1996 (NZ), ss 8–10 ('sustainable utilization' purpose, environmental principles and the precautionary approach).
141. For full discussion, see Barnes (2009, pp. 333–44 (Australia), pp. 345–57 (Canada), and pp. 365–78 (US)).
142. Fisheries Management Act 2006 (Iceland), art 1.
143. Barnes (2009, pp. 352–5).
144. Fisheries Act 1996 (NZ), s 9 (Environmental Principles).
145. Fisheries Act 1996 (NZ), s 42. On the nature of ITQs under the New Zealand fisheries regime, see also *Lim v McLean* [1997] 1 NZLR 641 (PC).
146. See *NZ Fishing Industry Association (Inc) v Minister of Fisheries* (unreported), Court of Appeal, CA 82–97, 83–97, and 96–97, 22 July 1997, at 15–16.
147. Pursuant to the Forests Act 1949 (NZ), Pt 3A, added by the Forests (Amendment) Act 1993 (NZ). For a discussion of the history and implementation indigenous forestry policy on government land, see *Westco Lagan v Attorney-General* [2001] 1 NZLR 40 (HCt), and the article by Palmer (2001).
148. In Australia, see *Mabo v State of Queensland (No 2)* [1992] HCA 23, (1992) 175 CLR 1 at 57; *Wik Peoples v Queensland* (1996) 187 CLR 1; and *Members of the Yorta Yorta Aboriginal Community v Victoria* [2002] HCA 58, (2002) 214 CLR 422. Aboriginal customary rights in resources can exist independently of rights in land: *Yarmirr v Northern Territory of Australia* (1997) 74 FCR 99 (FCA); *Mason v Tritton* (1994) 34 NSWLR 572 (NSWCA); in Canada, *Guerin v R* [1984] 2 SCR 335 (SCC); *Hamlet of Baker Lake v Minister of Indian Affairs and Northern Development* [1980] 1 FC 518 (FC); in New Zealand, *Attorney-General v Ngati Apa* [2003] 3 NZLR 643 (CA), and the early cases of *R v Symonds* (1847) NZPCC 387 at 390 and *Re the Lundon and Whitaker Claims Act 1871* (1892) 2 NZCA 41 at

49. See also early developments in the United States in *Worcestor v Georgia* 31 US 515 at 544 and 559 (1832) and *US v Santa Fe Pacific Railway Co* 314 US 339 at 345 (1941).

149. For a full discussion of the intersection of common law 'property rights' and 'native title rights and interests' in the Australian context, see *Yanner v Eaton* [1999] HCA 53, (1999) 201 CLR 351 at [17]–[56]. See also the Native Title Act 1993 (Cth), s 233(1) (definition of 'native title' or 'native title rights and interests'). In the New Zealand context, see *Attorney-General v Ngati Apa* [2003] 3 NZLR 643 (CA), especially at [29]–[34], [99]–[101], [143]–[149], [183]–[186] and [208].
150. Marine and Coastal Area (Takutai Moana) Act 2011 (NZ), Pt 3. See especially s 51 (meaning of 'protected customary rights') and s 58 (meaning of 'customary marine title').
151. For a full account of COP 21 and the Paris Agreement of 2015, see the UNFCCC website at unfccc.int/paris_agreement/items/9485.php.
152. For example, the European Union's Emissions Trading Scheme (EU Directive 2003/87/EC of the European Parliament and of the Council of 13 October 2003 (OJ 2003 L275/32)); see EC Climate Action website at http://ec.europa.eu/clima/policies/ets/pre2013/index_en.htm. See also the New Zealand scheme introduced under the Climate Change Response (Emissions Trading) Amendment Act 2008; https://www.climatechange.govt.nz/emissions-trading-scheme/.
153. See Grinlinton (2011, pp. 300–303) from which this section draws.
154. Weeramantry (2011, pp. xvi–ii).
155. Leopold and Meine (2013, p. 173). This collection of Leopold's writings includes his classic *A Sand County Almanac* (Leopold (1949)).
156. Gray (2010, p. 63). See also Smith (1989, p. 99).
157. Gray (2010, p. 55).
158. For example, the Resource Management Act 1991 (NZ), s 5.
159. Forests Act 1949 (NZ), s 67B and s 2(1) (definition of 'sustainable forest management'), as inserted by the Forests Amendment Act 1993 (NZ).
160. Fisheries Act 1996 (NZ), s 8 (Purpose).
161. Climate Change Response Act 2002 (NZ), as amended by the Climate Change Response (Emissions Trading) Amendment Act 2008 (NZ).
162. For example, *Minister of Immigration v Teoh* (1995) 183 CLR 273 (HCA); *Mabo v Queensland (No 2)* (1992) 175 CLR 1 at 42, per Brennan J (HCA); *Derbyshire County Council v Times Newspapers Limited* [1992] 1 QB 770 (UKCA); *Tavita v Minister of Immigration* [1994] 2 NZLR 257 (NZCA); and *Sellers v Maritime Safety Inspector* [1999] 2 NZLR 44. See also The 'Bangalore Principles' that were initially developed in the Judicial Colloquium in Bangalore, 24–26 February 1988: Commonwealth Secretariat (1991); and Kirby (1998).

REFERENCES

Adler, J. H. (2001), 'Free and Green: A New Approach to Environmental Protection' *Harvard Journal of Law and Public Policy* **24(2)**, 653.

Adler, J. H. (2005), 'Back To The Future Of Conservation: Changing Perceptions Of Property Rights & Environmental Protection' *NYU J.L. & Liberty* **1**, 987.

Adler, J. H. (2012), 'How Property Rights Could Help Save the Environment', *The Atlantic*, 29 May 2012.

Anderson, T. L. and D. R. Leal (2015), *Free Market Environmentalism for the Next Generation* (New York, Palgrave Macmillan).

Bagaric, M. and K. J. Arenson (2004), *Criminal Laws in Australia* (Melbourne, Oxford University Press).
Barker, K., P. Cane, M. Lunney and F. Trindade (2012), *The Law of Torts in Australia* (5th edn, Melbourne, Oxford University Press).
Barnes, R. (2009), *Property Rights and Natural Resources* (Portland, Hart Publishing).
Barton, B. (2009), 'The Nature of Resource Consents: Statutory Permits or Property Rights' (paper presented to New Zealand Law Society Seminar, New Zealand Law School, Wellington).
Barzel, Yoram (1989), *Economic Analysis of Property Rights* (Cambridge, Cambridge University Press).
Bergin, T. F. and P. G. Haskell (1984), *Preface to Estates in Land and Future Interests* (2nd edn, Mineola, NY, Foundation Press).
Blackstone, Wm. (1765), *Commentaries on the Laws of England* (19th edn, London, Sweet, Pheney, Maxwell, Stevens & Sons, 1829) Book I.
Bosselmann, K. (2015), 'Sustainability and the Law', in Peter Salmon and David Grinlinton (eds), *Environmental Law in New Zealand* (Wellington, Thomson Reuters), Ch.3.
Brookfield, F. M. (2010), 'Water: Riparian Rights', in *Laws of New Zealand*, edited by Hon. Justice McGrath (Wellington, LexisNexis), pp. 1–279.
Burn, E. H. and J. Cartwright (2011), *Cheshire and Burn's Modern Law of Real Property* (18th edn, Oxford, Oxford University Press).
Butt, P. (2010), *Land Law* (6th edn, Sydney, Thomson Reuters).
Centner, T. J. (2014), 'Damages from Pesticide Spray Drift under Trespass Law' *Ecology Law Currents* **41(1)**, 1.
Circo, C. J. (2009), 'Does Sustainability Require a New Theory of Property Rights?' *Kansas Law Review* **58**, 91.
Coase, R. H. (1960), 'The Problem of Social Cost' *Journal of Law & Economics* **3**, 1.
Commonwealth Secretariat (1991), *Developing Human Rights Jurisprudence* (London, Commonwealth Secretariat) (the 'Bangalore Principles').
Coyle, S. and K. Morrow (2004), *The Philosophical Foundations of Environmental Law: Property, Rights and Nature* (London, Hart Publishing).
Cribbet, J. E. (1986), 'Concepts in Transition: The Search for a New Definition of Property' *University of Illinois Law Review* **1**, 1.
Demsetz, H. (1967), 'Towards a Theory of Property Rights' *American Economic Review* **57(2)**, 347.
de Soto, H. (2001), 'The Mystery of Capital' *Finance & Development* **38(1)**, 1.
de Soto, H. (2000), *The Mystery of Capital: Why Capitalism Triumphs in the West and Fails Everywhere Else* (New York, Basic Books).
Fraser, L. (2008), 'Property Rights in Environmental Management: The Nature of Resource Consents in the Resource Management Act 1991' *New Zealand Journal of Environmental Law* **12**, 145.
Frazier, T. (1995), 'The Green Alternative to Classical Liberal Property Theory' *Vermont Law Review* **20**, 299.
Freyfogle, E. (2006), *Why Conservation is Failing and How it Can Regain Ground* (New Haven, CT, Yale University Press).
Garner, B. A. (ed.) (2009), *Black's Law Dictionary* (9th edn, St. Paul, MN, Thomson Reuters), Appendix B, 1872.
Gray, K. (2010), 'Pedestrian Democracy and the Geography of Hope' *Journal of Human Rights and the Environment* **1**, 45.
Grinlinton, D. (1995), 'Natural Resources Law Reform in New Zealand – Integrating Law, Policy and Sustainability' *Australasian Journal of Natural Resources Law & Policy* **2**, 1.
Grinlinton, D. (2001), *Butterworths Resource Management Bulletin* **4**, 59.

Grinlinton, D. (2011), 'Evolution, Adaptation, and Invention: Property Rights in Natural Resources in a Changing World', in David Grinlinton and Prue Taylor (eds), *Property Rights and Sustainability: The Evolution of Property Rights to Meet Ecological Challenges* (Leiden, NL, Martinus Nijhoff), Ch.12.

Grinlinton, D. (2015a), 'The Context of Environmental Law', in Peter Salmon and David Grinlinton (eds), *Environmental Law in New Zealand* (Wellington, Thomson Reuters), Ch.2.

Grinlinton, D. (2015b), 'The Role of the Common Law', in Peter Salmon and David Grinlinton (eds), *Environmental Law in New Zealand* (Wellington, Thomson Reuters), Ch.5.

Grinlinton, D. and P. Taylor (eds) (2011), *Property Rights and Sustainability: The Evolution of Property Rights to Meet Ecological Challenges* (Leiden, NL, Martinus Nijhoff).

Gough, J. W. (1936), *The Social Contract* (Oxford, Clarendon Press).

Guth, J. H. (2008), 'Law for the Ecological Age' *Vermont Journal of Environmental Law* **9**, 431.

Halsbury's Laws of Australia (LexisNexis Butterworths, Sydney), Vol.9.

Halsbury's Laws of England (2012) (5th edn, Butterworths Lexis, London), Vol.62.

Honoré, A. (1961), 'Ownership', in A. G. Guest (ed.), *Oxford Essays in Jurisprudence* (London, Oxford University Press), p. 107.

Jeffery, M. I., J. Firestone and K. Bubna-Litic (eds) (2008), *IUCN Academy of Environmental Law Research Studies: Biodiversity, Conservation, Law and Livelihoods. Bridging the North South Divide* (New York, Cambridge University Press).

Kirby, Hon. M. (1998), 'The Road From Bangalore, The First Ten Years of the Bangalore Principles on the Domestic Application of International Human Rights Norms', Speech to Conference on the 10th Anniversary of the Bangalore Principles, Taj West End Hotel (Bangalore, India, 28 December); http://www.hcourt.gov.au/assets/publications/speeches/former-justices/kirbyj/kirbyj_bang11.htm.

Leopold, A. (1949), *A Sand County Almanac and Sketches Here and There* (New York, Oxford University Press).

Leopold, A. (1991), *The River of the Mother of God and Other Essays* (Madison, WI, University of Wisconsin Press).

Leopold, A. and C. Meine (ed.) (2013), *A Sand County Almanac and Other Writings on Ecology and Conservation* (New York, Literary Classics of the United States).

Lippman, W. (1955), *Essays on the Public Philosophy* (London, Hamish Hamilton).

Lock, K. and S. Leslie (2007), *New Zealand's Quota Management System: A History of the First 20 Years* (Motu Economic and Public Policy Research Working Paper 07–02, April 2007).

Locke, John. (1689), *Two Treatises on Government* (London, Printed for R. Butler, etc., 1821); Bartleby.com, 2010; http://www.bartleby.com/169/.

McHarg, A.. B. Barton, A. Bradbrook and L. Godden (eds) (2010), *Property and the Law in Energy and Natural Resources* (London, Oxford University Press).

Melville, H. (1851), *Moby Dick* (New York, Harper and Brothers).

Murphy, E. F. (1977), *Nature, Bureaucracy, and the Rules of Property – Regulating the Renewing Environment* (New York, North-Holland).

Murphy, J. and C. Witting (2012), *Street on Torts* (13th edn, Oxford, Oxford University Press).

O'Riordan, T. (1981), *Environmentalism* (2nd edn, Pion, London).

Ostrom, E. (1990), *Governing the Commons: the Evolution of Institutions for Collective Action* (Cambridge, Cambridge University Press).

Palmer, G. (2001), '*Westco Lagan v A-G*' *New Zealand Law Journal* 163.

Penner, J. E. (1996), 'The "Bundle of Rights" Picture of Property' *UCLA Law Review* **43**, 711.

Plucknett, T. F. T. (1956), *A Concise History of the Common Law* (5th edn, London, Butterworth).
Posner, R. A. (1998), *Economic Analysis of Law* (5th edn, New York, Aspen Law & Business).
Riley, P. (2006), 'The Social Contract and Its Critics' in Mark Goldie and Robert Wokler (eds), *The Cambridge History of Eighteenth-Century Political Thought* (Cambridge, Cambridge University Press), p. 347.
Rodgers, C. (2003), 'Liability for the Release of GMOS into the Environment: Exploring the Boundaries of Nuisance' *Cambridge LJ* **62(2)**, 371.
Rose, C. M. (1994), 'Given-ness and Gift: Property and the Quest for Environmental Ethics' *Environmental Law* **24**, 1.
Rose, C. (1997), 'Property Rights and Responsibilities' in Marian Chertow and Daniel Esty (eds), *Thinking Ecologically: The Next Generation of Environmental Policy* (New Haven, CT, Yale University Press), p. 49.
Rose, C. M. (2004), 'Economic Claims and the Challenges of New Property' in Katherine Verdery (ed.), *Property in Question: Value Transformation in the Global Economy* (Oxford, Berg Publishers), p. 275.
Salmon, P. and D. Grinlinton (eds) (2015), *Environmental Law in New Zealand* (Wellington, Thomson Reuters).
Sappideen, C. and P. Vines (eds) (2011), *Fleming's The Law of Torts* (10th edn, Sydney, Thomson Reuters).
Sax, J. L. (1993), 'Property Rights and the Economy of Nature: Understanding *Lucas v. South Carolina Coastal Council*' *Stanford Law Review* **45**, 1433.
Sax, J. L. (2008), 'Environmental Law Forty Years Later: Looking Back and Looking Ahead' in Michael I. Jeffery, Jeremy Firestone and Karen Bubna-Litic (eds), *IUCN Academy of Environmental Law Research Studies: Biodiversity, Conservation, Law and Livelihoods. Bridging the North South Divide* (New York, Cambridge University Press), p. 9.
Schlager E. and E. Ostrom (1992), 'Property-Rights Regimes and Natural Resources: A Conceptual Analysis' *Land Economics* **68(3)**, 249.
Schlatter, R. (1973), *Private Property – The History of an Idea* (New York, NY, Russell and Russell).
Smith, A. (1776), *Wealth of Nations,* edited by C. J. Bullock, Vol. X, The Harvard Classics (New York, P.F. Collier & Son, 1909–14), Bartleby.com, 2001; http://www.bartleby.com/10/.
Smith, M. J. (1989), *Ecologism: Towards Ecological Citizenship* (Buckingham, Open University Press).
Todd, S. (ed.) (2013), *The Law of Torts in New Zealand* (6th edn, Wellington, Brookers).
Turley, J. (1994), 'Panel I: Liberty, Property, and Environmental Ethics' *Ecology LQ* **21**, 403.
Vaughn, K. (1978), 'John Locke and the Labor Theory of Value' *Journal of Libertarian Studies* **2(4)**, 311.
Waldron, J. (1996), 'Property Law' in D. Paterson (ed.), *A Companion to Philosophy of Law and Legal Theory* (London, Blackwell Publishers), p. 560.
Weeramantry, C. (2011), 'Foreword: Rights, Responsibilities, and Wisdom from Global Cultural Traditions' in David Grinlinton and Prue Taylor (eds), *Property Rights and Sustainability: The Evolution of Property Rights to Meet Ecological Challenges* (Leiden, NL, Martinus Nijhoff), pp. xv–xx.

INSTRUMENTS

Act of Settlement 1701 (UK).
Basic Law of the Federal Republic of Germany, 23 May 1949.
Bill of Rights 1688 (UK).
Code civil des Français (French Civil Code) 1804.
Commonwealth of Australia Constitution Act [Australia], 9 July 1900.
Confirmatio Cartarum 1297 (UK) 25 Edw I c 9.
Constitution of the Kingdom of the Netherlands, June 2002.
European Union's Emissions Trading Scheme (EU Directive 2003/87/EC of the European Parliament and of the Council of 13 October 2003 (OJ 2003 L275/32).
Magna Carta 1215.
United Nations Convention on the Law of the Sea (1982) 1833 UNTS 3; 21 ILM 1261.

16. Environmental impact assessment: 'setting the law ablaze'

*Elizabeth Fisher**

INTRODUCTION

Environmental impact assessment (EIA) is often understood as a defining feature of 'modern' environmental law. Rodgers has described the National Environmental Policy Act 1969 (NEPA) which introduced EIA into US Federal law as the 'Magna Carta' of US environmental law,[1] and O'Riordan has stated that EIA is a 'sensitive barometer of environmental values in a complex environmental society'.[2] More recently, Yang and Percival have identified EIA as a defining feature of 'global environmental law'[3] and 'arguably the most widely adopted management tool across the world'.[4]

This chapter provides an overview of EIA and the type of legal frameworks and obligations its implementation creates.[5] Judge Leventhal of the District of Columbia Circuit of the US Federal Court of Appeals noted that NEPA was one of a number of statutes that 'set the law ablaze'[6] and this is an apt description of the legal consequences of EIA. By creating a new legal frame that cuts across the existing legal order, EIA gives rise to difficult legal questions in most jurisdictions.

The chapter is structured as follows. First, there is a brief discussion of what EIA is, and its three major legal features are examined. These are its procedural nature; the way it acts as a classificatory process; and the fact that it is primarily an administrative procedure. In the second section, it is shown that EIA is a form of 'hot' law that is dealing with 'hot' situations.[7] 'Hot' situations are polycentric, scientifically uncertain and normatively conflicted. 'Hot' law thus often needs to cut across existing legal frames to deal with such situations. In the third section, examples are drawn from a range of cases in different jurisdictions to show how EIA 'sets the law ablaze'. These examples are grouped into two categories: the challenges involved in giving legal meaning to EIA obligations and the difficulties courts have had in reviewing administrative discretion in relation to EIA decision-making.

It is useful to make three caveats before starting. First, there is both a rich regulatory theory and social science literature on environmental impact assessment that this chapter does not touch on.[8] Likewise, this chapter does not explore the different normative assumptions behind EIA.[9] This is because this analysis is focused on the type of legal obligations EIA creates. Second, in discussing the type of legal obligations to which EIA gives rise and the ways in which it sets the law 'ablaze' there is constant moving between legal systems. This is problematic from the perspective of comparative law methodology,[10] but this approach is taken to illustrate that the 'hot' nature of EIA can be seen in a range of different legal cultures. Third, there is an analytical tension in this chapter. On the one hand, this piece is about taking law seriously. On the other, due to space and comprehensibility, legal detail has been kept to a minimum, which results in an over-simplified discussion of the law. The best way to make sense of this tension is to see this chapter as doing no more than initiating a conversation.

ENVIRONMENTAL IMPACT ASSESSMENT: THREE KEY LEGAL FEATURES

1. Introduction

EIA is a systematic and formalized legal process that obligates a decision-maker to make a decision about whether a project or activity should proceed – and on what basis – after considering, first, information about the potential environmental impacts of a project and, second, wider public consultation in light of that information.[11] Since 1969 EIA has become an entrenched feature of most national, supranational and international regimes around the world.[12] Very quickly after the passing of NEPA, other jurisdictions introduced EIA into their environmental law including Canada (1973); Australia (1974); West Germany (1975); and France (1976).[13] EIA was introduced into what was then the European Economic Community – now the European Union (EU) – in 1985.[14] By the 1990s, EIA was also being promoted at the international level. In 1991 the UN Economic Commission for Europe's Espoo Convention on Environmental Impact Assessment in a Transboundary Context was signed.[15] Principle 17 of the Rio Declaration on Environment and Development in 1992 stated that:

> Environmental impact assessment, as a national instrument, shall be undertaken for proposed activities that are likely to have a significant adverse impact on the environment and are subject to the decision of a competent authority.[16]

Major international lending organizations now require those states borrowing funds to carry out EIA.[17]

In this process of transplantation and translation the concept of EIA has not remained static. What is included in the EIA process varies from jurisdiction to jurisdiction. EIA can take many different forms, involve different obligations, and apply to a range of different types of activities and projects. Thus, for example, in the US, NEPA applies to 'proposals for legislation and other major Federal actions significantly affecting the quality of the human environment'.[18] In contrast, the EU EIA regime applies to both public and private projects that are 'projects likely to have significant effects on the environment by virtue, inter alia, of their nature, size or location'.[19] Thus, while in this chapter there are references to EIA applying to certain 'activities', what is included under that term can vary significantly.

Furthermore, the introduction of EIA has led to the development of other forms of environmental assessment including strategic environmental assessment, species impact assessment and sustainability assessment.[20] Despite this rich variation in EIA regimes, three common legal features can be identified – the procedural nature of EIA, the classificatory significance of screening, and the way in which EIA is an administrative process.

2. EIA as Procedure

The first and most obvious feature of EIA is that it legally manifests itself primarily as a procedure. Thus, EIA sets out a series of procedural steps that a decision-maker must take in applying EIA. Regimes vary in where and how these steps are set out. They may be included in a mixture of legislation, delegated legislation and guidance. While regimes vary, five main legal steps can be identified.[21] The first is screening, which involves making a decision about which activities should be subject to an EIA. As will emerge, this step is particularly important and has given rise to the most litigation. The second step is scoping: that is, making a decision about what impacts of a project should be assessed. The details of scoping processes were historically primarily set out in administrative documentation or not given legal significance at all. That has changed in recent decades. Thus in the EU, there are now scoping obligations in the EU Directive.[22] Scoping has become a focus of litigation, particularly in regards to whether climate change should be taken into account.[23]

The third step is preparing an environmental impact statement (EIS). This involves the collection, collation and analysis of information, a process which involves experts from a range of different disciplines. In many regimes the obligation of preparing an EIS is placed on the private actor wishing to carry out a development or activity. Alongside the third step is the fourth step of public participation where members of the public have the right to see the EIS and comment on it. This has always been a significant feature of the EIA process. As Lord Hoffmann has noted in relation to the EU EIA regime:

> The Directive requires not merely that the planning authority should have the necessary information, but that it should have been obtained by means of a particular procedure, namely that of an EIA. And an essential element in this procedure is that what the Regulations call the 'environmental statement' by the developer should have been 'made available to the public' and that the public should have been 'given the opportunity to express an opinion' in accordance with article 6.2 of the Directive.[24]

Public participation is thus not just an add-on to EIA procedure, but is integral to it.[25]

The fifth and final step in EIA is making a decision about whether a project should go ahead and, if so, on what basis. EIA needs to be taken into account at this stage but an EIA does not usually formally dictate what the final decision is to be. With that said, if an EIA identifies serious concerns about an activity, then it is less likely that that activity will be given permission to proceed. Likewise, decision-makers will decide to impose conditions on an activity in light of the EIA procedure. The fact that EIA does not dictate a final outcome has led some commentators to doubt its efficacy. In a 1973 article, the American environmental lawyer Joseph Sax stated that the 'redemptive quality of procedural reform is about nine parts myth and one part coconut oil' in expressing his frustration with the wishful thinking that underlay the US EIA regime.[26]

The fact that EIA is a legal procedure makes it both legally familiar and legally alien. It is familiar because lawyers, particularly administrative lawyers, are well acquainted with procedural obligations in the form of natural justice and procedural fairness.[27] It is alien, because most such procedural obligations are focused on protecting individual rights while EIA is a procedure in the public interest. Thus the explicit aims set out in NEPA talk in aspirational terms of a better society and a better environment. NEPA is thus requiring the US Federal government to 'use all practicable means, consistent with other essential considerations of national policy' to pursue a range of normative aims including to 'fulfill the responsibilities of each generation as trustee of the environment for succeeding generations'.[28] The Australian Environment Protection and Biodiversity Conservation Act 1999 has as one of its objects 'to promote ecologically sustainable development through the conservation and ecologically sustainable use of natural resources'.[29]

3. EIA as a Classification System

The second fundamental feature of EIA is that it acts as a classification system. Under most regimes, EIA only applies to a subset of activities. These activities are usually described as projects 'likely to have a significant effect on the environment' or some variation of this wording. The process of screening classification varies from regime to regime and usually involves a mixture of identifying a list of activities that are prima facie understood to have likely significant environmental effects – nuclear reactors and hydro-electric dams – as well as vesting a public decision-maker with the discretion to assess whether a particular activity falls into this category.[30]

The classificatory process at the screening stage is a pivotal one with practical implications. If it is decided that an EIA is required, then environmental impacts must be studied in detail and consulted upon. This process is often the only way in which third parties can influence a particular activity. On the other hand, the decision to carry out an EIA will usually impose extra costs on the proponent of an activity and slow down the decision-making process. The practical importance of screening has led it to be the most litigated aspect of EIA regimes across all jurisdictions. There is also no doubt that the decision that an EIA is required has a symbolic aspect – it is a signal that the state has decided that this particular activity requires extra scrutiny. This is the 'Magna Carta' nature of EIA and, just like that document, it is an official statement of the principles of governance, and accordingly it is an articulation of a good society.[31]

From a more institutional perspective, while EIA hinges on a legally constructed classification system, for it to work it requires a diverse group of actors to be involved including scientists, engineers, administrative decision-makers, developers and members of the wider public. This is particularly so in regards to the preparation of an EIA and the consultation process, but it also relates to the process of screening. The

EIA process is thus acting as a boundary object.[32] Susan Leigh Star has described a boundary object as a:

> sort of arrangement that allows different groups to work together without consensus. However, the forms this may take are not arbitrary. They are essentially organic infrastructures that have arisen due to … 'information needs' … I would now add 'information and work requirements', as perceived locally and by groups who wish to cooperate.[33]

The EIA process acts as a framework for bringing together different diverse groups who are drawing on the same information but have distinctive agendas and priorities. Within the legal framework of EIA many different practices and industries have developed. All this means that EIA is a classification system that has practical, symbolic and institutional dimensions. While the focus of this chapter is on the legal nature of EIA, these other aspects cannot be ignored, and manifest themselves in EIA case law.

4. EIA as an Administrative Process

The final thing to note about EIA is that it is primarily a legal procedure embedded in administrative decision-making: namely that public decision-making about EIA will be mostly made in the administrative context. Thus NEPA applies to Federal administrative agencies and, in the United Kingdom, the EU EIA Directive applies mostly to planning decision-makers.[34] The administrative nature of EIA is significant because public administration occupies a difficult and constantly awkward role in public life.[35] While public administration is a necessary feature of advanced liberal democracies committed to constitutionalism, it is also at odds with these regimes due to its fundamentally undemocratic nature.[36] Discussion and debate about EIA are thus often intertwined with discussion and debate about the legitimacy of administrative institutions.[37] Moreover, the legal application of EIA is nearly always embedded in administrative law doctrine and on the basis of public law principles.[38]

This is important to note because EIA cannot be thought about in a legal vacuum. Wrestling with the legal nature of EIA is about wrestling with public law doctrine. This is particularly so when, as already touched upon, EIA does not sit easily with that doctrine. This is not only because of its lack of a private rights focus, but also because its legal obligations cut across the settled constitutional order. This will be explored later in this chapter. Moreover, EIA is requiring an administrative process that incorporates both scientific analysis and public participation. How to think legally about these processes and in particular how courts should scrutinize these processes has created new and difficult legal questions. These will be explored in the paragraphs dealing with EIA in the courts.

EIA AS 'HOT LAW'

What the analysis above makes clear is that EIA is not just a simple 'tool' of decision-making. It is creating a legal procedure requiring administrative decision-makers to classify activities on the basis of their future likely effects. That process of classification has practical, symbolic and institutional implications. It also requires lawyers to think, and think hard, about the relationship between EIA and existing legal doctrines, particularly administrative law doctrine.

It is therefore not surprising that Judge Leventhal described EIA as 'setting the law ablaze'.[39] Indeed, EIA can be thought of as a type of 'hot' law. The 'heat' of EIA is due to the fact that EIA is explicitly identifying 'hot situations' and requiring a specific legal response to them.[40] Much of law is about working with what the economic sociologist Michel Callon has described as 'cold' situations – that is situations where 'actors are identified, interests are stabilized, preferences can be expressed, responsibilities are acknowledged and expressed'.[41] This means that actors can calculate the costs and benefits of various actions and negotiate and then act or not act on that basis.[42] Law is creating the coldness of these situations through creating frames for agreement – contract law; frames for the consequences of actions – tort law and criminal law; or creating networks of responsibility – company law and public law. Any legal frame will be imperfect and creates what Callon calls 'overflows' as no frame controls and contains everything. But the assumption is that those overflows can be recognized and managed.[43]

In contrast, the classification system of EIA is specifically concerned with 'hot' situations:

> everything becomes controversial: the identification of intermediaries and overflows, the distribution of source and target agents, the way effects are measured. These controversies which indicate the absence of a stabilised knowledge base, usually involve a wide variety of actors. The actual list of actors, as well as their identities will fluctuate in the course of a controversy itself and they put forward mutually incompatible descriptions of future world states.[44]

Activities that 'are likely to have a significant effect on the environment' are 'hot' because: they are shrouded in scientific uncertainty due to the fact that they are dealing with future effects;[45] they are dealing with polycentric situations involving complex interrelationships between a wide range of parties;[46] and decisions about environmental impact cannot be disentangled from assumptions about how communities want to live.[47] Hot situations are not just 'controversial'; they also have structural and foundational aspects.

First, and most significantly, there have historically been no agreed legal frames for dealing with such situations. EIA is thus novel – it is a law dealing with 'hot situations' – and thus can be thought about as 'hot' law. As 'hot law' it has two key features. First, unlike areas of law such as contract law, it does not have well-honed grooves of legal reasoning that have been hollowed out over centuries. Administrators and courts, in applying EIA and dealing with disputes in relation to it, must craft a new body of administrative practice and legal doctrine. As noted above, this will build on existing law, but it must also be developed in light of the 'hot' nature of the type of issues EIA is addressing.

Second, 'hot' situations and 'hot' law often cut across traditional legal structures – across ideas of property ownership,[48] across jurisdictions,[49] and across ideas of public power.[50] The 'overflows' from environmental problems cannot be simply managed. Rather, there needs to be a rethinking of legal frames, the end result being often a challenging of pre-existing legal ideas.[51] The creation of novel legal frames is why the substance of so much EIA is so 'technical' – it is about creating complex legal schemes in which law is constituting and limiting in different ways.[52]

EIA IN THE COURTS: 'HOT LAW' IN ACTION

1. Introduction

At this stage of the analysis the reader may be thinking that the idea of EIA as 'hot law' is a great sound bite but not necessarily illuminating. The purpose of this section is to show that thinking about the legal nature of EIA in these terms is helpful because it helps identify the tensions and complexities in EIA law. The focus here is upon case law concerning legal disputes over the application of EIA and related forms of assessment. What is common in all of these cases is how a procedural framework embedded in administrative process that integrates analysis and deliberation in the interests of environmental protection gives rise to legal issues that challenge the existing legal order.

Most of these cases are judicial review challenges, or some variation on such review – for example merits review. These cases are rarely discretely EIA cases and in these cases a range of different legal arguments is being made. At the same time EIA is embedded deeply within the thickness of environmental law in any particular legal culture. This analysis draws on examples from a range of different jurisdictions and considers them in two categories: cases concerning the type of legal obligation to which EIA gives rise and cases concerning how the courts review EIA decision-making. It should be stressed that this analysis is lightly illustrative, not exhaustive. In many jurisdictions there is a very large body of EIA case law – a state of affairs that highlights the contested nature of EIA and its 'hot nature'.

2. The Legal Nature of EIA Obligations

(a) Introduction

From a legal perspective, EIA is primarily envisaged as a set of procedural obligations but, as noted above, it does not create individual rights in those procedural obligations. This means that EIA is at odds with much of administrative law doctrine, which has developed out of a rights-based paradigm.[53] As Mashaw has noted about the developments of which NEPA was a part:

> an activist state – a state that emphasizes the administration of social and economic life in pursuit of collective ends – will tend to redefine rights in ways that de-emphasize individual legal remedies. In such a state, the judiciary will ultimately adopt what I shall term here a 'statist' conception of legal rights and legal personality, that is, a conception crucially dependent for its content on legislative definitions of public welfare and on the organizational imperatives of the state's administrative-governmental apparatus.[54]

This has meant that the introduction of EIA into any legal system has required an adjustment to conventional public law doctrine to accommodate these distinctive types of legal obligations. That process of accommodation often requires adjustment to basic public law principles and this leads to EIA taking on a 'constitutional hue'.[55] The following are a few examples of how EIA forces a reflection about the nature of legal obligations.

(b) Standing

In most legal systems, some form of standing is required to bring a public law action. This may be set out in the common law or in a legislative or constitutional provision. While the criteria to be met to establish standing vary from legal culture to legal culture, two things are of note. First, historically, in most legal cultures, standing was understood primarily in private rights terms, but over the last 40 years doctrine has evolved to encompass those seeking to protect or represent the public interest or both.[56] Second, a major catalyst for this process of evolution has been environmental law and, more importantly, EIA. The catalytic nature of EIA has three aspects.

First, in a jurisdiction such as Australia where standing doctrine is narrow and individual rights-based, the granting of no standing in cases where an environmental group was seeking to challenge EIA decision-making is of note. In the *Australian Conservation Foundation* case,[57] a case concerning the Commonwealth EIA scheme, the High Court of Australia interpreted standing narrowly. Gibbs J noted:

> For the reasons I have given, the action was not brought by the Foundation to assert a private right. It is brought to prevent what is alleged to be a public wrong. The wrong is not one that causes, or threatens to cause, damage to the Foundation, or that affects, or threatens to affect, the interests of the Foundation in any material way. The Foundation seeks to enforce the public law as a matter of principle, as part of an endeavour to achieve its objects and to uphold the values which it was formed to promote. The question is whether, in these circumstances, it has standing to sue.
>
> … It is quite clear that an ordinary member of the public, who has no interest other than that which any member of the public has in upholding the law, has no standing to sue to prevent the violation of a public right or to enforce the performance of a public duty.[58]

This approach was followed in later cases, albeit with some exceptions coming into play.[59] This line of cases has led not only to criticisms that this approach creates serious barriers to the enforcement of legal accountability in environmental cases[60] but also to a more general debate about the purpose of judicial review.[61]

Second, some EIA regimes provide for standing for members of the public or non-governmental organizations in recognition of the importance of allowing members of the public to enforce EIA procedures through judicial review procedures.[62] Article 11 of the EU EIA Directive is an example.[63] It was included in a 2003 amendment to the Directive that implemented the second and third pillars of the Aarhus Convention on Access to Information, Public Participation in Decision-Making and Access to Justice in Environmental Matters.[64] In the preamble to the Directive it was stated that 'effective judicial mechanisms should be accessible to the public, including organizations, so that its legitimate interests are protected and the law is enforced'. To this end, article 11 now includes a broad standing provision that also includes non-governmental organizations. Not only does this formally grant broad standing rights, it has also resulted in judicial consideration of what such rights entail. Thus Advocate General Sharpston, commenting on a preliminary reference before the Court of Justice of the EU (CJEU) about how to interpret article 11 noted:

> The provisions on access to justice in environmental matters here at issue start from the premise that the natural environment belongs to us all. Preventing environmental damage is society's responsibility, not just the responsibility of individuals or isolated interests. Viewed in that light, the provisions of the Aarhus Convention and Directive 85/337 [now 2014/92/EU], as amended, give legal form to the logic of collective action. The individual is protected by acting in a group and the group is collectively strengthened by its individual members. Both the individual and the general interest are thus better protected; and the benefits for all concerned outweigh the disadvantages. This is why both measures accord an important role to non-governmental organisations promoting environmental protection.[65]

In other words, courts are forced to engage with the question of what exactly the law protects and why.

Third, and related to this, courts have broadened the standing doctrine in EIA cases to ensure that members of the public have standing. Thus in the US, the non-NEPA *Sierra Club* case broadened standing to include those within the 'zone of interests' that a statute was designed to protect.[66] That broadening was consolidated in NEPA cases.[67] Likewise in the United Kingdom, the UK Supreme Court elaborated on the importance of a broader test of standing in the *Walton* case.[68] This case involved the application of the Strategic Environmental Assessment Directive.[69] The standing requirement in that case was a 'person aggrieved' as set out in Scottish roads legislation. Lord Reed, in concluding that the applicant fell into that category, noted that he did so because he had participated in the process, lived in the area of part of the road development, was 'an active member of local organisations concerned with the environment' and had 'demonstrated a genuine concern about what he contends is an illegality in the grant of consent for a development which is bound to have a significant impact on the natural environment'.[70] Lord Hope, responding to an argument for a narrow standing test, noted that:

> I think, with respect, that this is to take too narrow a view of the situations in which it is permissible for an individual to challenge a scheme or order on grounds relating to the protection of the environment. An individual may be personally affected in his private interests by the environmental issues to

> which an application for planning permission may give rise. Noise and disturbance to the visual amenity of his property are some obvious examples. But some environmental issues that can properly be raised by an individual are not of that character. Take, for example, the risk that a route used by an osprey as it moves to and from a favourite fishing loch will be impeded by the proposed erection across it of a cluster of wind turbines. Does the fact that this proposal cannot reasonably be said to affect any individual's property rights or interests mean that it is not open to an individual to challenge the proposed development on this ground? That would seem to be contrary to the purpose of environmental law, which proceeds on the basis that the quality of the natural environment is of legitimate concern to everyone. The osprey has no means of taking that step on its own behalf, any more than any other wild creature. If its interests are to be protected someone has to be allowed to speak up on its behalf.[71]

This reference to the osprey is reminiscent of Christopher Stone's argument that trees should have standing.[72] Again, what is important to appreciate is that EIA, as a legal framework designed to promote environmental protection, forces courts to readjust their understanding of who is entitled to bring a legal action.

It should be stressed that these processes of adjustment and reflection are not straightforward and that all these developments have led to a debate about the nature of standing and the reasons for and against its expansion.[73] EIA, with its non-individual rights focus, has been a catalyst for this and the debate has broadened out to encompass issues such as the relationship between law and politics,[74] the role of public law in a democracy[75] and the role of civil society.[76]

(c) Tensions between procedure and outcome

Even if standing is established, EIA gives rise to further questions about the nature of the legal obligations it creates. Thus, while its procedural nature is relatively legally straightforward to enforce, there are questions about how a court should review procedure – discussed in later paragraphs – and whether there should be remedies in cases where procedural flaws made no difference to the outcome of the decision.[77]

One of the best examples of the way in which EIA forces a reflection on the nature of legal obligations is in regards to the question of the 'direct effect' of the EU EIA Directive in the national courts of member states. The concept that EU legal norms have 'direct effect' is a fundamental feature of EU law.[78] But historically there was a presumption that for a provision to have direct effect it must normally give rise to an individual right.[79] Thus in the mid-1990s when the CJEU ruled that the EIA Directive had direct effect,[80] a number of lawyers and academics saw the reasoning as problematic.[81] Some saw it as a variation on direct effect[82] and others thought it was 'not direct effect in the traditional sense and it would perhaps be as well to find another formula to avoid confusion'.[83] This discussion about direct effect was overlapping with other developments in direct effect doctrine more generally. The end result was that the EIA case law led to a richer and more nuanced understanding of the doctrine.[84]

The 'hot' nature of the EU EIA Directive does not stop there. The recent *HS2* case in the UK Supreme Court raised the question of whether the EU EIA Directive required a court to scrutinize parliamentary process to ensure compliance with the Directive – a form of scrutiny that potentially infringed the constitutional principle of parliamentary privilege.[85] The question arose because of the interrelationship between EU and UK law.[86] It was resolved relatively easily and has been overtaken by further amendments to the EIA Directive.[87] But even though this is the case, the novelty of the question is of note. It is another example of EIA cutting across the existing legal order.

From this smattering of cases, what can be seen is that the types of legal obligations that EIA creates do not fit easily into the pre-existing frames of the legal order and legal reasoning. To say this is not to criticize or praise EIA. Rather it is to point out its 'hot' nature and that EIA cannot be thought of as legally straightforward. As a form of environmental governance it is legally disruptive, but that legal disruption has been mandated by the state and is an inevitable consequence of dealing with 'hot situations'.

3. Reviewing EIA Decision-making

(a) Introduction

The last paragraphs focused on the nature of the legal obligations that EIA creates. A related issue is how a court reviews EIA decision-making. This question arises because of the institutional and constitutional competence issues confronted by a court,[88] usually of a generalist nature, when the court is reviewing the type of 'analytic-deliberative' decision-making[89] that is involved in EIA decision-making. From a constitutional perspective, courts are limited to reviewing legal validity, and from an institutional perspective courts find it difficult to review specialist decision-making. The nature of review not only relates to these questions, it also has a practical aspect. As Edgar has noted, 'why extend access to an accountability institution that cannot review the decision?'[90] In other words, these issues about the scope of review of EIA decision-making directly relate to the ability of judicial review to act as an accountability mechanism.

Most of the litigation concerning EIA is in the form of judicial review challenges to screening decisions. These are brought primarily by third parties arguing that a particular activity should be subject to an EIA. In most systems, the nature of the court's task will be determined by existing doctrinal approaches to questions of legal validity that exist in that legal culture's administrative law. Those approaches tend to rest on a categorization of administrative decision-making into law, discretion and fact. If so, the courts understand that their primary role is to review decision-makers' assessment of the law rather than their assessment of fact. Discretionary decision-making also tends to be subject to deferential review.

Accordingly, in the United Kingdom, the assessment of whether a development falls into a particular development category under Annex I of the Directive is reviewed as a question of law.[91] The assessment of whether something is 'likely to have a significant effect on the environment' is assessed under the deferential standard of *Wednesbury* unreasonableness for the exercise of discretion.[92] The problem is that EIA decision-making, even at the screening stage, is a mixture of analysis and deliberation and not easily definable in a simple fact-law-discretion taxonomy.[93]

(b) The emerging 'jurisdictional fact' approach in Australia

A good example of these difficulties can be seen in relation to how New South Wales (NSW) courts, and in particular the NSW Land and Environment Court, have developed case law in relation to reviewing screening in regards to EIA and related endangered species legislation that requires a species impact assessment (SIS). The problems of judicially reviewing this type of decision-making were recognized from very early on[94] and were complicated by the legally formalistic nature of Australian judicial review doctrine.[95] The early judicial review challenges to screening decisions were primarily concerned with whether forestry activities required an EIS.[96] These cases often involved little in the way of discussion of legal principles and the focus was primarily on interpreting the wording of the legislation, which contained the duty to consider whether an EIA was needed. But while the interpretation of the Act was a matter of law and thus for the court, how discretion was exercised was for the primary decision-maker.[97] Thus a court could interfere if a decision were wrong only if the decision was so unreasonable that no reasonable decision-maker would make it.[98]

By the late 1990s, there emerged another approach to reviewing screening decisions in a judgment of the NSW Court of Appeal.[99] The *Timbarra* case involved a challenge by a local non-governmental organization to a development consent given by a local shire council for the extension and modification of a gold mine. While some form of environmental assessment was prepared, the applicant argued that an SIS should also have been required under the legislation. Spigelman CJ concluded that, as a matter of statutory construction, the question of whether an application was 'likely to significantly affect threatened species' was a question of 'jurisdictional fact' and thus required a judicially reviewing court to review the fact de novo.[100] The concept of 'jurisdictional fact' does exist in other jurisdictions. But it has a particularly prominent role in contemporary Australian doctrine and reflects a commitment to legal formalism.[101]

The transformation of the question whether something was 'likely to significantly affect threatened species' from a discretionary to a jurisdictional fact question had the very important consequence that this was a question that a reviewing court would need to decide itself. It followed that the court could engage in merits review and that it could hear evidence about whether the existence or non-existence of the fact would be admissible. In other words, the effect of this approach was to allow issues about the potential impact of a development to be debated in a judicial forum.

Whether something was a jurisdictional fact was understood as a purely legal question. Spigelman CJ noted:

> The issue of jurisdictional fact turns, and turns only, on the proper construction of the Statute. (See e.g. *Ex parte Redgrave; Re Bennett* (1946) 46 SR (NSW) 122, 125.) The Parliament can make any fact a jurisdictional fact, in the relevant sense: that it must exist in fact ('objectivity') and that the legislature intends that the absence or presence of the fact will invalidate action under the statute ('essentiality'). (*Project Blue Sky Inc v Australian Broadcasting Authority* [1998] HCA 28 at [91]–[93].)
>
> 'Objectivity' and 'essentiality' are two interrelated elements in the determination of whether a factual reference in a statutory formulation is a jurisdictional fact in the relevant sense. They are interrelated because indicators of 'essentiality' will often suggest 'objectivity'.[102]

The inquiry into whether something was a jurisdictional fact was thus largely an inquiry into the nature of the statutory delegation. It was an inquiry underpinned by legal formalism. Spigelman CJ noted:

> Where the process of construction leads to the conclusion that Parliament intended that the factual reference can only be satisfied by the actual existence (or non-existence) of the fact or facts, then the rule of law requires a Court with a judicial review jurisdiction to give effect to that intention by inquiry into the existence of the fact or facts.[103]

The practical implication of this was that a conception that had been understood as discretionary was now being understood not just as factual but as 'super-factual'.[104] This meant that it required particular scrutiny and analysis in the process of judicial review. That super-factual nature is not surprising in light of the 'hot' nature of EIA – facts may be contested but they are also important. Spigelman CJ in the *Timbarra* case reinforced the super-factual nature of jurisdictional facts when he noted that 'jurisdictional fact' was not a doctrine but a conclusion from a process of statutory construction.[105] Essentiality and objectivity were thus place markers for the need for greater accountability. Following this, the NSW Land and Environment Court began to find a number of different statutory provisions giving rise to 'jurisdictional facts'.[106]

However, the application of the doctrine did not prove straightforward. As Pearlman J noted in a case concerning the same statutory provision as in the *Timbarra* case:

> A consequence of the determination being a jurisdictional fact is that the Court is obliged to decide the jurisdictional fact for itself (*Timbarra* at par 94) and evidence is admissible as to the existence or non-existence of the jurisdictional fact (*Timbarra* at par 36). But this case throws into stark relief the consequential difficulty involved. A decision as to whether or not a development is likely to significantly affect threatened species can never truly be an objective fact – it must always be a matter of opinion. That is because it involves 'likelihood', that is, the future possibility of the occurrence of an event, and, as to that, it depends upon expert scientific opinion. In this case, as I shall presently outline, the expert opinion is divided. All five experts who gave evidence are eminent in their field, and yet two consider that the development is likely to significantly affect CPW and three consider that it is not.[107]

Pearlman J's decision thus saw her engaging in an assessment of these different experts. In other cases, judges can be seen to doubt whether a provision creates a jurisdictional fact because of its discretionary nature but they assess the provision on the basis that it is a jurisdictional fact anyway.[108]

Judges in federal courts have also expressed concern about EIA decisions being about 'jurisdictional facts'.[109] So have academic commentators.[110] Turning the questions from screening into 'jurisdictional facts' is not just making them 'super-facts' but is also turning judges into 'judicial ecologists'.[111] The 'hot' nature of EIA law can be seen once more. The doctrinal and conceptual reframing necessary to respond to these developments relates, first, to the different ways decision-making can be characterized and, second, to how the role of the court is understood. Moreover, this process of reframing is embedded in a particular legal culture.

(c) The 'hard look' approach in the US

The above discussion has focused on screening but it needs to be noted that judicial review of the substance of an EIS process has also raised questions for courts – with judges often taking different approaches. Thus in the *Belize Alliance* case[112] Lords Hoffmann and Walker differed in their approach to reviewing the adequacy of an EIA process. Lord Hoffmann focused on the procedural aspects and Lord Walker on more substantive aspects.

That echoes the debate in the US in the 1970s about the nature of 'hard look review'. The concept of hard look review was developed in the late 1960s in the DC Circuit of the Federal Court of Appeals as an interpretation of the nature of scope of review in relation to the arbitrary and capricious standard as set out in US administrative law doctrine.[113] Its central idea was that the courts should ensure that the agency had taken a 'hard look' at the issue before them. The hard look concept was a way of dealing with the institutional competence problem created by a generalist court reviewing a specialist administrator.

Different approaches emerged under the hard look doctrine. Thus, Judge Leventhal's approach to 'hard look' focused on substantive reasoning.[114] He saw it as a particularly important approach to apply in environmental cases. Thus he noted, in commenting on a NEPA case:

> In my view, the 'hard look' metaphor requires more than subjective good faith, which would be essentially untestable; it requires an analysis of the environmental consequences sufficient to convince a court that they have been considered.[115]

In contrast, a judge of the same court, Chief Judge Bazelon, focused on the process aspects of a decision.[116] The hard look doctrine applied in a range of different legal contexts. One of the most interesting lines of litigation concerned a Nuclear Regulatory Commission (NRC)'s consideration of a nuclear power licence in which the licencing process involved rulemaking where the environmental impacts were assessed.[117]

While not a NEPA case, it involved the three hallmarks of EIA: procedure, classification and administrative process.

The purpose of the rulemaking was to consider the environmental effects of the nuclear fuel cycle. The NRC had concluded that nuclear waste presented only an 'insignificant' environmental effect and the Commission developed a series of formulae and numerical tables for cost-benefit analysis that rested on this assumption.[118] The evidence on which the NRC based this conclusion was a 20-page statement of an expert from the Atomic Energy Commission. The statement was submitted in oral hearings. The expert concluded that technology would be found to solve the problem of nuclear waste disposal and that the 'bugaboo' of waste disposal should not hold up development of the nuclear industry even though no reliable techniques for disposal had yet been established.[119]

Judge Bazelon, in the DC Circuit, characterized the role of the courts as being one to ensure that 'genuine opportunities to participate in a meaningful way were provided' and that there was a 'thorough ventilation of issues' through dialogue.[120] He stated that:

> A reviewing court must assure itself not only that a diversity of informed opinion was heard, but that it was genuinely considered. 'The dialogue that the APA's rulemaking section contemplates cannot be a sham.'[121]

Procedure should focus not only on the facts but on a whole range of issues.[122] Likewise the respective role of policy and fact would depend on the issue at hand.[123] In the case before him Judge Bazelon concluded that such dialogue had not taken place and that, because the issue of nuclear waste would be such a long-term problem, this was clearly not appropriate.[124] The conclusions of the NRC had been based on 'conclusory' statements and this was not acceptable where expert administration was leading the community in highly technical and weighty decisions with long-term consequences.[125] Moreover, the expert who had given the advice had acknowledged at a later date that there were serious long-term problems with nuclear waste disposal.[126]

Judge Bazelon stressed that there were many different 'procedural devices' which the NRC could have used, including:

> formal conferences between intervenors and staff, document discovery, interrogatories, technical advisory committees comprised of outside experts with differing perspectives, limited cross examination, funding independent research by intervenors, detailed annotation of technical reports, surveys of existing literature, memoranda explaining methodology.[127]

These procedures were directed at the more technical aspects of decision-making but Judge Bazelon also stressed in his analysis of the record (much of this in footnotes) the failure of the NRC to deal with the complex nature of the problems involved.[128]

The case was appealed to the US Supreme Court and Judge Bazelon's view of hard look review was rejected in the *Vermont Yankee* case,[129] where it was held that courts should not, save in limited circumstances,[130] impose extra procedural requirements, particularly of an adjudicative nature, on agencies above and beyond statutory requirements.[131] The logic behind this decision was twofold: first, the de-shackling of administrative procedure from adjudicative method[132] and, second, to stop judicially imposed procedural requirements being a form of 'Monday morning quarterbacking'[133] in that petitioners could always argue that more procedural requirements should have been required. In rejecting Judge Bazelon's approach this case was an implicit confirmation of Judge Leventhal's more substantive approach.[134] As Edley noted in regards to the hard look review debate: 'Bazelon and Leventhal were talking about two sides of the same coin, that coin being judicial activism motivated by a concern for sound governance'.[135]

The point of all of this analysis is that the concern for sound governance was catalyzed by EIA and similar legal obligations. Moreover, the end result was a readjustment to judicial review that encompassed not only environmental law but also all of US administrative law. 'Hot' law rarely remains contained.

CONCLUSION

What is striking about the foregoing analysis is that in the last 20 years, while much has been written about EIA from a social science or a regulatory theory perspective, the complex doctrinal questions to which EIA has given rise have tended to be overlooked. Part of that, it is suggested, is due to the fact that there is a perception that these cases are beside the point in discussions of EIA as a mode of environmental governance. Nevertheless, what this brief analysis shows is that a study of this case law can provide an insight into the nature of EIA and its legal significance. These cases are not just technical detail – they do illuminate the complexities and challenges involved in EIA.

This chapter has also been about methodological approaches to the study of environmental law.[136] Specifically, this chapter has emphasized the importance of taking the law of environmental law seriously and in this regard I want to end this chapter by explaining the inspiration behind it.

Shortly after finishing my undergraduate law degree I was browsing in a bookshop and came across the recently published *Environmental Law: Text and Materials* by Douglas Fisher (the editor of this collection).[137] Rather than trotting through different regimes, Fisher structured the analysis around the different types of legal obligations and procedures that environmental legislation created at that time. Thus there was a section on EIA that compared the different state and federal EIA obligations as set out in the legislation. It perhaps sounds like dry stuff, but that book has been a navigational point of reference for me ever since. It made clear to me the importance of taking environmental law seriously – not just seeing it as a tool but as a complex legal culture that lawyers and scholars must scrutinize with care. It taught me how to think about doctrine and legislation and how to analyze detail.

I am sure that this explanation will make the editor of this collection blush (and make others think that I am engaging in some form of sycophancy) but it is important to provide such an explanation because it highlights that how scholars write about the legal world and chart it is influential because these writings frame the world for others and provide them with an intellectual agenda. In regards to EIA, that agenda is a significant and challenging one.

NOTES

* Elizabeth Fisher is not related to the editor of this volume, Douglas Fisher.
1. Rodgers (2000, p. 31).
2. O'Riordan (1990).
3. Yang and Percival (2009, p. 623).
4. Ibid. (p. 627).
5. For an overview of it as a process, see Glasson, Therivel and Chadwick (2011).
6. Leventhal (1974, pp. 509–10).
7. Fisher (2013).
8. Eg Holder (2005); Ladeur and Prelle (2001); and Lawrence (1997).
9. Fisher, Lange and Scotford (2013, pp. 848–50).
10. Kahn-Freund (1974).
11. A longer overview can be found at Fisher, Lange and Scotford (2013, ch.19).
12. Holder and McGillivray (2007).
13. Wood (2003).
14. Now Directive 2011/92/EU.
15. Espoo Convention 1991.
16. Rio Declaration 1992.
17. Eg World Bank (2015).
18. 42 USC 4332(2)(C).

19. Directive 2011/92/EU, art.2(1).
20. Eg Sadler et al. (2011).
21. For a more in-depth discussion of the process, see Glasson, Therivel and Chadwick (2011).
22. Eg Directive 2011/92/EU, art.5(2); as amended by Directive 2014/52/EU. In the US, see 40 CFR 1508.8.
23. Eg *Center for Biological Diversity* case (2008).
24. *Berkeley* case (2001, p. 615).
25. For a further discussion on the nature of public participation, see Steele (2001).
26. Sax (1973, p. 239).
27. Hart Ely (1980); and Galligan (1996).
28. 42 USC 4332.
29. Environment Protection and Biodiversity Conservation Act 1999 (Cth), s.3(1)(b).
30. Eg Directive 2011/92/EU splits projects into Annex I projects (which by their very nature require an EIA) and Annex II projects (where an assessment needs to be made as to whether an EIA is required).
31. Breay and Harrison (2015).
32. Star and Griesemer (1989).
33. Star (2010).
34. Town and Country Planning (Environmental Impact Assessment) Regulations 2011, reg.3(4).
35. Cook (1996).
36. This tension is explored in detail in Fisher (2007).
37. Ibid. (chs 3 and 4).
38. See Fisher, Lange and Scotford (2013, chs 7 and 19).
39. Leventhal (1974).
40. I discuss this at greater length in Fisher (2013).
41. Callon (1998, p. 261).
42. Ibid. (pp. 255, 259, 261).
43. Ibid. (pp. 248–50).
44. Ibid. (p. 260).
45. For problems of scientific uncertainty and assessment, see *Leatch* case (1993) and *Waddenzee* case (2004).
46. For a discussion of polycentricity in the context of merits review, see *Bulga Milbrodale* case (2013, paras 31–43).
47. National Research Council (1996, ch.2).
48. Scotford and Walsh (2013).
49. Knox (2002).
50. Craig (2014).
51. Fisher (2016, forthcoming).
52. D.E. Fisher (1993).
53. Sunstein (1988).
54. Mashaw (1983, p. 1129).
55. This is a description that McGarity has given to NEPA. See McGarity (1977, p. 803).
56. Sunstein (1988); and Edgar (2011, p. 436); but see Cane's discussion of the dangers of the over simplification of the public private rights model: Cane (1999).
57. *Australian Conservation Foundation* case (1980, p. 526).
58. Ibid.
59. Eg *Onus* case (1981). Note also the approach under the 'person aggrieved' test under s.13 of the Administrative Decisions (Judicial Review) Act 1977. See the EIA case of *North Coast Environment Council* (1994).
60. Australian Law Reform Commission (1996); and Fisher and Kirk (1997).

61. Cane (1999).
62. Eg Environmental Protection and Biodiversity Conservation Act 1999 (Cth), s.487 and Environmental and Planning Assessment Act (NSW) 1979, s.123. See Edgar (2011).
63. Directive 2011/92/EU, art.11.
64. Aarhus Convention 1998.
65. *Swedish NGO* case (2009, para.59).
66. *Sierra Club* case (1972).
67. *SCRAP* case (1973); and *Monsanto* case (2010).
68. *Walton* case (2012).
69. SEA Directive (Directive 2001/42/EC).
70. *Walton* case (2012, para.88).
71. Ibid. (para.152).
72. Stone (1972), which was argued without success in the *Sierra Club* case (1972).
73. Harlow (2002).
74. Cane (1999).
75. Ibid.; and Australian Law Reform Commission (1996).
76. Fisher and Kirk (1997).
77. In the UK compare Lord Hoffmann in the *Berkeley* case (2001) and Lord Carnwath in the *Walton* case (2012). In the US, see *Winter* case (2008).
78. *Van Gend en Loos* case (1963).
79. *Becker* case (1982).
80. *Kraaijeveld* case (1996).
81. Wyatt (1998, p. 18).
82. Jans (2000, p. 174).
83. Edward (1997, p. xiv).
84. *Linster* case (2000); *Wells* case (2004); Edward (2002).
85. *HS2* case (2014).
86. Craig (2014). The case also concerned the SEA Directive. For a discussion of this, see Fisher (2016, forthcoming).
87. Directive 2014/52/EU has deleted art.1(4) which gave rise to the legal question; but see art.2(4).
88. Jowell (2000).
89. National Research Council (1996).
90. Edgar (2011, p. 436).
91. *Goodman* case (2003).
92. *Jones* case (2003).
93. *Gillespie* case (2003) and *Champion* case (2013), which concern the review of screening decisions where there are mitigation measures.
94. Preston (1986).
95. Fisher (2015).
96. *Prineas* case (1983); *Kivi* case (1982). Note that *Prineas* involved review of an EIS.
97. *Leichhardt* case (1985).
98. *Drummoyne* case (1989); and *Bailey* case (1989).
99. *Timbarra* case (1999).
100. Ibid.
101. Fisher (2015) and Aronson (2001), discussing *Enfield City Corporation* (2000), a case concerning an assessment of environmental effects in planning law.
102. *Timbarra* case (1999, paras 37–38).
103. Ibid. (para.40).
104. I am grateful to Corin Bagshaw for this characterization of jurisdictional facts.
105. *Timbarra* case (1999, para.39).

106. *Gales Holdings* case (1999); *Donnelly* case (2001); and most significantly *Fullerton Cove (No.2)* case (2013).
107. *Plumb* case (2002, para.16).
108. *Smith* case (2002, paras 135–136).
109. *Anvil Hill* case (2008); and see general discussion in Fisher (2015).
110. Aronson and Groves (2013, para.4.510).
111. *Nambucca Valley* case (2010, para.78).
112. *Belize Alliance* case (2004).
113. *Greater Boston Television* case (1970, pp. 850–51).
114. *Ruckelshaus* case (1973).
115. Leventhal (1974, p. 528).
116. See Fisher (2007) for a longer discussion.
117. *Natural Resources* case (1976).
118. Ibid. (pp. 637–8).
119. Ibid. (pp. 648–9).
120. Ibid. (p. 644).
121. Ibid. (p. 646), quoting from an article by Judge Skelly Wright.
122. Ibid. (p. 645).
123. Ibid. (p. 656).
124. Ibid. (p. 652).
125. Ibid. (p. 651).
126. Ibid. (p. 650).
127. Ibid. (p. 653).
128. Ibid. (pp. 650–1). See also Bazelon (1977, pp. 827, 831) discussing why technical procedures are not enough.
129. *Vermont Yankee* case (1978).
130. Where the court were required to afford constitutional due process or where there had been a 'totally unjustified' departure from normal agency procedure. See ibid (p. 542).
131. Ibid. (p. 543).
132. Scalia (1978, p. 378); and Shapiro (1988, p. 164).
133. *Vermont Yankee* case (1978, p. 547).
134. Scalia (1978, p. 354). Leventhal's approach was confirmed in the *Motor Vehicles Manufacturers* case (1983).
135. Edley (1990, p. 227).
136. Fisher et al. (2009).
137. D.E. Fisher (1993).

REFERENCES

Aronson, Mark (2001), 'The Resurgence of Jurisdictional Fact', *Public Law Review* 12, 17.

Aronson, Mark and Matthew Groves (2013), *Judicial Review of Administrative Action* (5th edn, Pyrmont, NSW, Thomson Reuters).

Australian Law Reform Commission (1996), *Beyond the Doorkeeper – Standing to Sue for Public Remedies* (ALRC Report 78).

Bazelon, David (1977), 'Coping with Technology Through the Legal Process', *Cornell Law Review* 62, 817.

Breay, Claire and Julian Harrison (eds) (2015), *Magna Carta: Law, Liberty, Legacy* (London, British Library Publishing).

Callon, Michel (1998), 'An Essay on Framing and Overflowing: Economic Externalities Revisited by Sociology', in Michel Callon (ed.), *The Laws of the Markets* (Oxford, Blackwell).
Cane, Peter (1999), 'Open Standing and the Role of the Courts in a Democratic Society', *Singapore Law Review* 20, 23.
Cook, Brian (1996), *Bureaucracy and Self Government: Reconsidering the Role of Public Administration in American Government* (Baltimore, MD, John Hopkins University Press).
Craig, Paul (2014), 'Constitutionalizing Constitutional Law: HS2', *Public Law* 373.
Edgar, Andrew (2011), 'Extended Standing – Enhanced Accountability?: Judicial Review of Commonwealth Environmental Decisions', *Federal Law Review* 39, 435.
Edley, Christopher (1990), *Administrative Law: Rethinking Judicial Control of Bureaucracy* (New Haven, Yale University Press).
Edward, David (1997), 'Foreword', in Jane Holder (ed.), *The Impact of EC Environmental Law in the United Kingdom* (London, Kluwer International).
Edward, David (2002), 'Direct Effect: Myth, Mess or Mystery?', in Jolande Prinssen and Annette Schrauwen (eds), *Direct Effect: Rethinking a Classic of EC Legal Doctrine* (Groningen, Europa Law Publishing).
Fisher, D.E. (1993), *Environmental Law: Text, Cases and Materials* (Sydney, Law Book Company).
Fisher, Elizabeth (2007), *Risk Regulation and Administrative Constitutionalism* (Oxford, Hart Publishing).
Fisher, Elizabeth (2013), 'Environmental Law as "Hot" Law', *Journal of Environmental Law* 25, 347.
Fisher, Elizabeth (2015), '"Jurisdictional" Facts and "Hot" Facts: Legal Formalism, Legal Pluralism and the Nature of Australian Administrative Law', *Melbourne University Law Review* 38, 968.
Fisher, Elizabeth (2016, forthcoming), 'Blazing Upstream? Strategic Environmental Assessment as "Hot" Law', in Gregory Jones and Eloise Scotford (eds), *The Strategic Environmental Assessment Directive: A Plan for Success?* (Oxford, Hart Publishing).
Fisher, Elizabeth and Jeremy Kirk (1997), 'Still Standing: An Argument for Open Standing in Australia and England', *Australian Law Journal* 71, 370.
Fisher, Elizabeth, Bettina Lange and Eloise Scotford (2013), *Environmental Law: Text, Cases and Materials* (Oxford, Oxford University Press).
Fisher, Elizabeth, Bettina Lange, Eloise Scotford and Cinnamon Carlarne (2009), 'Maturity and Methodology: Starting a Debate about Environmental Law Scholarship', *Journal of Environmental Law* 21, 213.
Galligan, Denis (1996), *Due Process and Fair Procedures* (Oxford, Clarendon Press).
Glasson, John, Riki Therivel and Andrew Chadwick (2011), *Introduction to Environmental Impact Assessment* (Oxford, Routledge).
Harlow, Carol (2002), 'Public Law and Popular Justice', *Modern Law Review* 65, 1.
Hart Ely, John (1980), *Democracy and Distrust: A Theory of Judicial Review* (Cambridge, MA, Harvard University Press).
Holder, Jane (2005), *Environmental Assessment: The Regulation of Decision-Making* (Oxford, Oxford University Press).
Holder, Jane and Donald McGillivray (eds) (2007), *Taking Stock of Environmental Assessment: Law, Policy and Practice* (Oxford, Routledge-Cavendish).
Jans, Jan (2000), *European Environmental Law* (Groningen, Europa Law Publishing).
Jowell, Jeffrey (2000), 'Of Vires or Vacuums: The Constitutional Context of Judicial Review', in Christopher Forsyth (ed.), *Judicial Review and the Constitution* (Oxford, Hart Publishing).
Kahn-Freund, Otto (1974), 'On Uses and Misuses of Comparative Law', *Modern Law Review* 37, 1.

Knox, John (2002), 'The Myth and Reality of Transboundary Environmental Impact Assessment', *American Journal of International Law* 96, 291.
Ladeur, Karl-Heinz and Rebecca Prelle (2001), 'Environmental Assessment and Judicial Approaches to Procedural Errors – A European and Comparative Law Analysis', *Journal of Environmental Law* 13, 185.
Lawrence, David (1997), 'The Need for EIA Theory-Building', *Environmental Impact Assessment Review* 17, 79.
Leventhal, Harold (1974), 'Environmental Decision Making and the Role of the Courts', *University of Pennsylvania Law Review* 122, 509.
Marshaw, Jerry (1983), '"Rights" in the Federal Administrative State', *Yale Law Journal* 92, 1129.
McGarity, Thomas (1977), 'The Courts and the Agencies – NEPA Threshold Issues', *Texas Law Review* 55, 801.
National Research Council (1996), *Understanding Risk: Informing Decisions in a Democratic Society* (Washington, DC, National Academy Press).
O'Riordan, Timothy (1990), 'EIA from the Environmentalist's Perspective', *March VIA* 4, 13.
Preston, Brian (1986), 'Adequacy of Environmental Impact Statements in New South Wales', *Environmental and Planning Law Journal* 3, 194.
Rodgers, William (2000), 'The Most Creative Moments in the History of US Environmental Law: "The Whats"', *University of Illinois Law Review* 1, 31.
Sadler, Barry et al. (eds) (2011), *Handbook of Strategic Environmental Assessment* (Oxford, Earthscan).
Sax, Joseph (1973), 'The (Unhappy) Truth About NEPA', *Oklahoma Law Review* 26, 239.
Scalia, Antonin (1978), '*Vermont Yankee*: The APA, the DC Circuit, and the Supreme Court', *Supreme Court Review* 345.
Scotford, Eloise and Rachael Walsh (2013), 'The Symbiosis of Property and English Environmental Law – Property Rights in a Public Law Context', *Modern Law Review* 76, 1010.
Shapiro, Martin (1988), *Who Guards the Guardians?: Judicial Control of Administration* (Athens, GA, University of Georgia Press).
Star, Susan Leigh (2010), 'This is Not a Boundary Object', *Science, Technology and Human Values* 35, 601.
Star, Susan Leigh and James Griesemer (1989), 'Institutional Ecology, "Translations" and Boundary Objects: Amateurs and Professionals in Berkeley's Museum of Vertebrate Zoology, 1907–1939', *Social Studies of Science* 19, 387.
Steele, Jenny (2001), 'Participation and Deliberation in Environmental Law: A Problem Solving Approach', *Oxford Journal of Legal Studies* 21, 415.
Stone, Christopher (1972), 'Should Trees Have Standing?: Towards Legal Rights for Natural Objects', *Southern California Law Review* 450.
Sunstein, Cass (1988), 'Standing on the Privatization of Public Law', *Columbia Law Review* 88, 1432.
Wood, Christopher (2003), *Environmental Impact Assessment: A Comparative Review* (2nd edn, Harlow, Prentice Hall).
World Bank (2015), 'Environmental Assessment Sourcebook and Update'; http://web.worldbank.org/WBSITE/EXTERNAL/TOPICS/ENVIRONMENT/EXTENVASS/0,,contentMDK:20282864~pagePK:148956~piPK:216618~theSitePK:407988,00.html.
Wyatt, Derrick (1998), 'Litigating Community Environmental Law – Thoughts On the Direct Effect Doctrine', *Journal of Environmental Law* 10, 8.
Yang, Tseming and Robert Percival (2009), 'The Emergence of Global Environmental Law', *Ecology Law Quarterly* 36, 615.

INSTRUMENTS

Aarhus Convention 1998: Aarhus Convention on Access to Information, Public Participation in Decision-Making and Access to Justice in Environmental Matters 1998, (1999) *International Legal Materials* 38, 517.

Administrative Decisions (Judicial Review) Act 1977.

Directive 2011/92/EU of the European Parliament and of the Council of 13 December 2011 on the assessment of the effects of certain public and private projects on the environment (as amended) [2012] OJ L26/1.

Directive 2014/52/EU of the European Parliament and of the Council of 16 April 2014 amending Directive 2011/92/EU on the assessment of the effects of certain public and private projects on the environment [2014] OJ L124/1.

Environment Protection and Biodiversity Conservation Act 1999 (Cth).

Environmental and Planning Assessment Act 1979 (NSW).

Espoo Convention 1991: Convention on Environmental Impact Assessment in a Transboundary Context 1991, (1991) *International Legal Materials* 30, 800.

NEPA: National Environmental Policy Act 1969.

Rio Declaration 1992: Declaration of the United Nations Conference on Environment and Development 1992, (1992) *International Legal Materials* 31, 874.

SEA Directive: Directive 2001/42/EC of the European Parliament and of the Council of 27 June 2001 on the assessment of the effects of certain plans and programmes on the environment [2001] OJ L197/30.

Town and Country Planning (Environmental Impact Assessment) Regulations 2011 (SI 2011/1824).

CASES

Anvil Hill case: *Anvil Hill Project Watch Association Inc v Minister for the Environment and Water Resources* [2008] FCAFC 3.

Australian Conservation Foundation case: *Australian Conservation Foundation v Commonwealth* (1980) 146 CLR 493.

Bailey case: *Bailey v Forestry Commission (NSW)* (1989) 67 LGRA 200.

Becker case: Case 8/81 *Becker v Finanzamt Munster-Innenstadt* [1982] ECR 53.

Belize Alliance case: *Belize Alliance of Conservation Non-Governmental Organizations v Department of the Environment, Belize Electric Company Limited* [2004] UKPC 6.

Berkeley case: *Berkeley v Secretary of State for the Environment* [2000] UKHL 36, [2001] 2 AC 603.

Bulga Milbrodale case: *Bulga Milbrodale Progress Association Inc v Minister for Planning and Infrastructure and Warkworth Mining Limited* [2013] NSWLEC 48.

Center for Biological Diversity case: *Center for Biological Diversity v National Highway Traffic Safety Administration* 538 F 3d 1172 (9th Cir 2008).

Champion case: *R (Champion) v North Norfolk District Council* [2013] EWCA Civ 1657.

Donnelly case: *Donnelly v Delta Gold Pty Ltd* [2001] NSWLEC 55.

Drummoyne case: *Drummoyne Municipal Council v Roads & Traffic Authority of New South Wales* (1989) 67 LGRA 155.

Enfield City Corporation case: *Enfield City Corporation v Development Assessment Commission* (2000) 199 CLR 135.

Fullerton Cove (No.2) case: *Fullerton Cove Residents Action Group v Dart Energy (No.2)* [2013] NSWLEC 38.

Gales Holding case: *Gales Holdings Pty Ltd v Tweed Shire Council* [1999] NSWLEC 195.

Gillespie case: *Gillespie v First Secretary of State* [2003] EWCA Civ 400, [2003] Env LR 30.
Goodman case: *R (Goodman) v London Borough of Lewisham* [2003] EWCA Civ 140, [2003] Env LR 28.
Greater Boston Television case: *Greater Boston Television Corp v FCC* 444 F 2d 841 (DC Cir 1970).
HS2 case: *R (HS2 Action Alliance Ltd) v Secretary of State for Transport* [2014] UKSC 3.
Jones case: *R (Jones) v Mansfield District Council* [2003] EWCA Civ 1408, [2004] Env LR 21.
Kivi case: *Kivi v Forestry Commission of New South Wales* (1982) 47 LGRA 38.
Kraaijeveld case: Case C-72/95 *Aannemersbedrijf PK Kraaijeveld BV and others v Gedeputeerde Staten Van Zuid-Holland* [1996] ECR I-5403.
Leatch case: *Leatch v National Parks and Wildlife Service* (1993) 81 LGERA 270.
Leichhardt case: *Leichhardt Municipal Council v Maritime Services Board (NSW)* (1985) 57 LGRA 169.
Linster case: Case C-287/98 *Luxembourg v Linster* [2000] ECR I-6917.
Monsanto case: *Monsanto Co v Geerston Seed Farms* 561 US 139 (2010).
Motor Vehicles Manufacturers case: *Motor Vehicles Manufacturers Association v State Farm Mutual Automobile Insurance Company* 463 US 29 (1983).
Nambucca Valley case: *Nambucca Valley Conservation Association v Nambucca Shire Council* [2010] NSWLEC 38.
Natural Resources case: *Natural Resources Defense Council v Nuclear Regulatory Commission* 547 F 2d 633 (DC Cir 1976).
North Coast Environmental Council case: *North Coast Environment Council Inc v Minister for Resources* (1994) 55 FCR 492.
Onus case: *Onus v Alcoa of Australia Ltd* (1981) 149 CLR 27.
Plumb case: *Plumb v Penrith City Council* [2002] NSWLEC 223.
Prineas case: *Prineas v Forestry Commission of New South Wales* (1983) 49 LGRA 402.
Ruckelshaus case: *International Harvester v Ruckelshaus* 478 F 2d 615 (DC Cir 1973).
SCRAP case: *United States v Students Challenging Regulatory Agency Procedures (SCRAP)* 412 US 669 (1973).
Sierra Club case: *Sierra Club v Morton* 405 US 727 (1972).
Smith case: *Smith v Wyong Shire Council and another* [2002] NSWLEC 173.
Swedish NGO case: Case C-263/08 *Djurgården-Lilla Värtans Miljöskyddsförening v Stockholms kommun genom dess marknämnd* [2009] ECR I-9967.
Timbarra case: *Timbarra Protection Coalition Inc v Ross Mining NL* [1999] NSWCA 8, (1999) 46 NSWLR 55 .
Van Gend en Loos case: Case 26/62 *NV Algemene Transport en Expeditie Onderneming van Gend en Loos v Netherlands Inland Revenue Administration* [1963] ECR 1.
Vermont Yankee case: *Vermont Yankee Nuclear Power Corp v Natural Resources Defense Council* 435 US 519 (1978).
Waddenzee case: Case C-127/02 *Landelijke Vereniging tot Behoud van de Waddenzee v Staatssecretaris van Landbouw, Natuurbeheer en Visserij* [2004] ECR I-9405.
Walton case: *Walton v Scottish Ministers* [2012] UKSC 44.
Wells case: Case C-201/02 *R (Wells) v Secretary of State for Transport Local Government and the Regions* [2004] ECR I-723.
Winter case: *Winter v Natrual Resources Defense Council* 555 US 7 (2008).

17. The precautionary principle in environmental governance

Annecoos Wiersema

INTRODUCTION

The precautionary principle or a precautionary approach is an important part of environmental decision-making in many legal systems. It emerged on to the international law scene in the later decades of the twentieth century, invoked at the North Sea Ministerial Conferences in the 1980s and adopted on a global level as principle 15 of the Rio Declaration on Environment and Development.[1] The precautionary principle acknowledges the limits of scientific knowledge and states that decision-makers can act in the face of scientific uncertainty where there are serious risks involved in not acting. As principle 15 says, 'where there are threats of serious or irreversible damage, lack of full scientific certainty shall not be used as a reason for postponing cost-effective measures to prevent environmental degradation'.[2] Its adoption was motivated by recognition that society does not always have full knowledge of the risks involved in an activity and that decision-makers may need to act without full knowledge in order to guard against serious or irreversible harm.

The idea of precaution or caution was not new in 1992 with principle 15 of the Rio Declaration. Rather, it has implicitly and explicitly infused legal action in many parts of the world for far longer.[3] In Germany, for example, it was specifically articulated in the 1970s as the *Versorgeprinzip.*[4] Nevertheless, principle 15 set the stage for far broader adoption of the precautionary principle. It now has a pervasive presence in international environmental law and many domestic legal systems.[5]

At the same time, since 1992, debates about the meaning and scope of the precautionary principle, its status in international law, and its usefulness have been ongoing and sometimes fierce. It has often been criticized. Application of a precautionary approach can result in restrictions on products and activities that in turn can have significant financial consequences. Its scope and application, therefore, are no trivial matter. Because the principle specifically authorizes action in the face of scientific uncertainty, it leaves open tricky questions about its relationship to science. Critics have charged that the principle is unnecessary and allows excessive discretion on the part of decision-makers to deviate from scientific assessments of risk.[6] They have also charged that it paralyzes decision making.[7]

This chapter discusses the range of questions that have surrounded the precautionary principle since 1992 and the ways in which those questions play out in the different settings in which precaution is operationalized in order to shed light on the role of precaution in environmental decision-making. It is not an exhaustive discussion of all jurisdictions that have adopted or applied the principle. It focuses on a few key examples that demonstrate general trends. The phrases 'precautionary principle' and 'precautionary approach' are used interchangeably, although, as discussed below, there may be differences in the meaning of these two phrases.

PRECAUTION, RISK AND UNCERTAINTY

1. Precaution

In a broad sense, precaution has been part of environmental law from the beginning. Environmental law is intended to prevent harm. So at minimum a preventive approach is called for. And in order to prevent harm, one must frequently be cautious. More generally, the idea of providing a kind of cushion to ensure prevention of undesired harms or to account for unforeseen or unforeseeable effects is not new to legal systems. For example, when a policy-maker or legislator acts to protect the environment, it is often an acknowledgement that environmental degradation has implications beyond what is immediately visible, foreseen and fixable. Thus, legislation that limits species killing or habitat destruction for identified endangered species or that limits what can be put into water recognizes not only that not every consequence of an action will be immediately identifiable but also that broad consequences could ensue from a failure to regulate certain types of activity. These consequences include direct harms, for example extinction of a species, and indirect harms, such as the overall implications of loss of biodiversity on the planet and human well being. This kind of protective action can provide an efficiency gain here as well. For policy-makers to evaluate every individual activity is in itself unwieldy. Some regulation therefore categorizes activities and creates a framework against which they can be evaluated.

This idea of taking care is still essentially preventive in nature. In a world of complete information and knowledge and infinite administrative resources, this preventive approach might be sufficient. However, no such world exists. This is where the precautionary approach is intended to help. Precaution can marry the prevention goal with the recognition that full scientific certainty does not always exist. At its core, then, precaution comes into play where there is uncertainty. In fact, uncertainty abounds and it abounds for many reasons.

First and most immediately, uncertainty arises from current information gaps. These information gaps in turn exist as a result of many factors. Information gaps in their purest form arise from the introduction of new technologies, such as genetic modification techniques, or changes in natural or human behavior that result in new interactions, such as the effects of human encroachment on forests. In the case of new technologies or products, like new chemicals and genetically modified organisms, even if some studies have been performed, studies will not have been done for the effects of those technologies or products over a long period of time.

Some current information gaps arise not because technologies are new but because scientific study has never focused on that issue. For example, data is missing for many species. Even species subject to regulation can be the subject of insufficient study.[8] This highlights not only that not every species is studied to the same extent, but also that, even if efforts are made to study a wider range of species, choices may have to be made as to which species to prioritize. This in turn means that species not currently part of a regulatory regime may simply not be beneficiaries of time and research resources.

Second, uncertainty also arises from a second source: historical data gaps. Even where current information gaps can be or are being corrected, lack of historical data can lead to difficulties because it leaves researchers without baselines against which to assess current information. These baselines are important to help understand possible patterns and also to determine whether change is occurring, as well as to understand whether that change is likely to be long term or short term and significant. Historical data gaps can lead to different interpretations of current data. For example, lack of historical data about polar bears led to some commentators in the 1960s arguing that polar bear numbers were increasing. These claims have since been discounted.[9]

Third, uncertainty arises from the complexity of ecological systems. Complexity leads to uncertainty because complex systems are connected in myriad ways and their functioning is affected by sometimes unknowable variables. It is difficult to know how any single component of these complex systems will respond to a particular stimulus or change.[10] Further, because humans are part of ecological systems, the variables that contribute to complexity are not limited to apparently natural phenomena. They include socio-economic variables, such as the behaviour of consumers and the effects of war or economic recessions.

Fourth, and related, uncertainty arises from the indeterminacy of ecological systems, which are in a constant state of flux and are considered to be stochastic systems. This means that they are subject to randomness.[11] Further, there is no one state of equilibrium to which an ecological system will inevitably return if humans do not interfere with it.[12] Without this equilibrium, systems may be operating along non-linear paths. That in turn adds to the complexity of the systems, since prediction is harder with non-linear systems.

2. Overcoming Uncertainty

Overcoming uncertainty is not simple. Even the most straightforward source of uncertainty, current information gaps, is not always easy to address. Current information gaps giving rise to uncertainty are, in theory, temporary. But this assumes that society has adequate resources to conduct the necessary studies and to do the necessary research. In practice, these capacity problems are significant. Even where species are the subject of priority for research, structural barriers can limit our ability to learn what we need to learn. Again, thinking about species and biodiversity, some species are simply harder to study. Our knowledge about oceanic species is particularly limited because of some of these barriers. Even large mammals in open terrain can present difficulties. For example, counting polar bears is difficult simply because it entails counting white mammals against a white background.

In addition, since the middle part of the twentieth century, ecologists have emphasized the need to focus on the connections among species and biological processes.[13] This presents particular challenges to our ability to fill in information gaps, because it requires a far more complex set of research methods than traditional methods. Nor are the data gaps limited to biological aspects of individual species. For example, researchers' ability to track the extent of trade in species is limited by whether they have access to full information about the extent of illegal trade as well as about legal trade in that species, which is unlikely. Researchers may also not be able to identify the actual species being traded. For example, in the shark fin trade, once a fin has been separated from the body of the shark, it becomes significantly harder to determine the species of that shark. Historical data gaps can become less critical over time, just as, over time, longitudinal studies can be performed regarding new technologies. Ecologists may still be hampered, however, by not knowing what exactly to study.

Complexity and indeterminacy are inherently difficult to address as sources of uncertainty. Indeed, sometimes more information can exacerbate uncertainty because it can add to complexity.[14] Modeling is a tool frequently used to simplify complex problems, just as a map can provide simplified information about a geographical space. However, modeling operates with scientists determining how to simplify a problem, by making certain assumptions, and by extrapolating for results. These results may be helpful, but they are not certain. When coupled with randomness and indeterminacy, non-linear projections may not be accurate.

In the absence of complete certainty, risk regulation forms the backbone of societies' attempt to navigate uncertainty. Risk assessment processes use scientific methodologies to assign probabilities to both the likely harm and the likely degree of that harm. Risk assessment can provide information about risks. This allows risk managers to make decisions about how to manage those risks, based on considerations that are primarily value-driven, such as the degree of risk a particular society wishes to live with. For some this process of risk assessment, with the added process of risk management, is sufficient to accommodate uncertainty. Alternatively, some commentators are willing to put their faith in cost-benefit analysis, rather than in the precautionary principle, by assigning values to the costs and benefits of a regulatory choice.

3. Risk Assessment and Precaution

Risk and uncertainty are certainly related, since risk assessments themselves are assessments in probability.[15] Risk assessment is critical to navigating our world. Without it, decision-makers would be truly paralyzed. However, risk assessment alone cannot do all the work of accounting for uncertainty, and this opens the door for a greater role for precaution. Precaution has the potential to go further than risk assessment, because it adds a recognition that risk assessment may not always fully anticipate the full range of risks or the degree of risk.[16] Indeed, the precautionary principle is intended to deal with the type of uncertainty that would not always be addressed by standard risk assessment. Some risks, including many contemporary risks, are 'serious, complex, uncertain and socio-politically ambiguous', making them difficult to quantify and distinct from more standard risks.[17] As van Asselt and Vos put it, the principle 'pertains to uncertain risks which are not, or at least not fully, calculable and controllable, because the probability of occurrence or the effect in terms of damage cannot be estimated, and even the potential danger and the relevant causalities may not be established, although there are suspicions of danger'.[18] Certain types of risk are also likely to be under-valued in traditional processes like risk assessment or cost-benefit analysis.[19]

Thus, decision-makers who view risk assessment or cost-benefit analysis as sufficient to provide an objective basis for policy may not be accounting for the range of uncertainty involved. Indeed, reliance on cost-benefit analysis may simply hide the kind of value decisions that critics of the precautionary principle fear: that is, by producing an apparently objective result through processes that can never be entirely objective.[20] Similarly, decision-making that is based on the results of scientific method may not account for the assumptions and choices made during the scientific process. This may mean that the outcomes are not objective.[21] Critics of the precautionary principle have suggested that its proponents are postmodernists. The argument is that proponents of the principle do not believe in the objectivity of science.[22] While this claim is overstated, endorsement of the need for the precautionary principle is in itself an endorsement of the idea that there is always some uncertainty and that scientific processes cannot be entirely objective. Yet proponents of the precautionary principle in some form may still not agree on the source and degree of uncertainty. Even these slight variations lead in turn to important questions about how to operationalize the precautionary principle.

PUZZLES OF INTERPRETATION

1. Introduction

The idea of adding a margin of safety or taking care not to cause harm is uncontentious. Yet the extent to which precaution can or should do more than represent that commonsense idea depends on how it is operationalized. This question arises largely because of the open-endedness of most formulations of the precautionary principle. This leaves puzzles of interpretation that have led commentators to question the usefulness of talking about a precautionary principle for fear of the level of discretion it appears to give to decision-makers.

Principle 15 of the Rio Declaration demonstrates this open-endedness. It states that 'where there are threats of serious or irreversible damage, lack of full scientific certainty shall not be used as a reason for postponing cost-effective measures to prevent environmental degradation'.[23] The generalized definition in principle 15 of the precautionary principle leaves many questions open. Commentators often refer to the overarching question of whether a strong or weak version of the principle is preferable. Several questions are implicit. What are environmental harms? Does the precautionary principle *require* action in the face of uncertainty? Does the principle *require* a reversal of the burden of proof, so that products and activities must be banned unless they can be proven to be safe? Is there a threshold level of identified harm that is required before the principle will apply? Does the principle operate as a sword or a shield for decision-makers? What is the principle's relationship to proportionality or cost-effectiveness? Is there room for risk-risk comparisons? And all of these questions are in some ways tied to questions about the principle's relationship to science because the principle is formulated as a response to the 'lack of full scientific certainty'.

The open-endedness of general formulations of the precautionary principle does not just leave puzzles of interpretation. It is also the source of much criticism of the principle for two primary reasons. First, leaving discretion to policy-makers where they are specifically being asked to act without complete scientific support appears to allow policy-makers to make decisions that are uninformed by science.[24] The precautionary principle then appears anti-scientific and may lead to over-regulation. Second, the lack of clear articulation about how the principle should be operationalized also means that critics can interpret it in different ways and find fault with certain of those interpretations. For example, Cass Sunstein's critical book, *The Laws of Fear* (2005), actually concedes that weak interpretations of the precautionary principle are unproblematic. Yet, his text criticizes the principle as paralyzing decision-making and he is widely seen as having been critical of the principle as a whole. Majone, often cited as a critic of the principle, acknowledges a role for some version of precaution.[25] As Pereira Di Salvo and Raymond's work suggests, the data 'confirm that [precautionary principle] opponents offer a more radical, hazard-oriented version of the principle than supporters'.[26]

This section discusses the main puzzles of interpretation, the criticisms they can lead to, and the ways in which those puzzles have been addressed. It is becoming apparent that, although the puzzles remain important and the criticisms have likely shaped operationalization of the principle, these criticisms lose some force when examples of how the principle has actually been operationalized are analyzed.

2. Binding or Non-binding: Principle or Approach

Commentators and legal instruments use both the phrases 'precautionary principle' and 'principle approach'. The different terminology does not seem to have a significant impact on interpretation. Many commentators use the terms interchangeably.[27] For some, however, the different terminology relates to one of our puzzles: whether the precautionary principle *requires* policy-makers to act in the face of uncertainty or *allows* them to do so, and how clear is the content of any obligation.

The idea of a principle rather than an approach may have legal implications – for example by suggesting that it could be binding in a way that may be unpalatable to decision-makers.[28] When accompanied by the lack of clarity about the principle's scope and meaning, making precaution mandatory means that policy-makers could face having to apply a principle whose exact requirements are unclear. In addition, describing precaution as involving a principle suggests that there is a need for a single definition of the phrase, something that is unlikely and almost certainly unworkable.[29]

By contrast, referring to a precautionary approach softens its import. It suggests that policy-makers can apply precaution to a situation but may not be bound to do so.[30] It also suggests a degree of flexibility in content that a principle may not have.[31] This degree of flexibility could then minimize the concerns of some of precaution's critics.

When precaution is explicitly articulated in a legal instrument, the problem of terminology diminishes because the legal instrument that embodies precaution will generally indicate what the constraints are for the decision-maker and whether the precautionary principle requires them to act in a certain way or simply allows them to do so. However, in the absence of clarification in a legal instrument, the courts may end up as the decision-makers. In international law, this is particularly significant, because an international tribunal would be called on to decide whether the principle is binding on a sovereign state and what kind of action it requires. To date, international tribunals have been willing to refer to the principle and even to acknowledge that it might play a role as a defense to action. But they have shied away from imposing precaution as a concrete obligation in the absence of some other textual basis for that obligation. This is discussed below.

3. Requirement of a Trigger or Threshold

Does the principle require a threshold showing of harm before precautionary measures can be considered appropriate? While 'lack of full scientific certainty' should not prevent regulatory action, principle 15 limits itself to situations where there are 'threats of serious or irreversible damage'. Thus, the implication is that, at minimum, a decision-maker should be able to demonstrate that threat before acting without full scientific certainty. Failure to require a threshold raises the concern that decision-makers could be acting without any basis in science. Courts, particularly, seem wary of allowing decision-makers to act without any threshold showing of harm. As the European Union's Court of First Instance put it in the *Pfizer* case, a:

> preventive measure may be taken only if the risk, although the reality and extent thereof have not been 'fully' demonstrated by conclusive scientific evidence, appears nevertheless to be adequately backed up by the scientific data available at the time when the measure was taken.[32]

The court continued that:

> the precautionary principle can … apply only in situations in which there is a risk, notably to human health, which, although it is not founded on mere hypotheses that have not been scientifically confirmed, has not yet been fully demonstrated.[33]

Indeed, imagine an application of the precautionary approach without any kind of principle limiting when it will apply. In this case it seems that decision-makers could be paralyzed, as some commentators have suggested.[34] Any activity, new or otherwise, entails risk. In the absence of some kind of limiting principle, regulators might be paralyzed for fear of causing harm and for fear of considering that they need to regulate without even having a sense of how likely risks might materialize or how serious those risks are. Requiring a limiting principle has an additional benefit for judges. Once judges look for a threshold, they are either explicitly or implicitly endorsing the need for a decision-maker to have complied with certain procedural obligations. The court can then refer to those procedural obligations to determine the validity of a decision-maker's conclusion that the threshold has been met. Thus, requiring a threshold can lead to procedural obligations that provide an additional check on decision-makers' discretion.

The court's statement in the *Pfizer* case demonstrates, however, that the requirement of some kind of threshold is problematic because it puts arguments based on uncertainty into a strange relationship with these very procedures like risk assessment and environmental impact assessment. As van Asselt and Vos have argued, the approach adopted by the court in the *Pfizer* case is confusing and demonstrates the difficulty with the 'uncertainty paradox' created by this threshold requirement. The paradox arises because precaution itself is premised on uncertainty and on the need to question scientific outputs, while the requirement for a trigger or threshold showing of harm in turn requires reliance on those scientific outputs.[35] At minimum, it seems, decision-makers would have to rely on those scientific outputs to indicate the appropriateness of acting in a precautionary manner. Similarly, for Peel, who is particularly concerned with uncertainties that arise in scientific processes, the requirement of a threshold is problematic.[36] Despite the paradox, courts seem unwilling to leave agencies with an unfettered discretion to apply precaution without some initial threshold showing of harm, even at the risk of limiting the principle's impact.[37] Yet relying on the courts to police the boundaries of uncertainty is an uneasy solution. Courts and science rarely mix well.

The threshold can be set independently of a court by being established in relation to the goal of a particular legal regime. In these scenarios, the legal instrument provides the criteria or trigger for precautionary regulatory action. For example, although the text of the Convention on International Trade in Endangered Species (CITES) does not explicitly refer to the precautionary principle, the regime itself is intended to ensure that species do not go extinct as a result of international trade in those species.[38] The Convention achieves this by listing species in various appendices. The parties have agreed to criteria for the states party to the treaty to apply to listing decisions.[39] In CITES, then, it is not surprising that the precautionary approach is mentioned only in the listing criteria.[40] It seems that the trigger for action is set by the criteria, and the adoption of a precautionary approach would, in theory, be connected to those criteria.

Yet even this approach can lead to over-reliance on scientific output, without questioning scientific methodology. In practice, the parties to CITES have been unwilling to invoke precaution for listing purposes. This suggests that once parties perceive the criteria as a threshold to be met, it is hard for them to perceive uncertainty in the scientific output determining whether or not the species is an appropriate candidate for listing.[41]

Ultimately, the desire for a threshold demonstrates the desire to link precaution to science in order to limit decision-makers' discretion and to ensure that decisions are not made without any objective basis. Yet, the threshold may not be the best way to achieve this because it may undermine the role of the principle. Interestingly, commentators expressing concern about this paradox argue that its resolution is more transparency and additional processes that allow for the questioning of scientific method.[42] Thus, even those commentators concerned with the threshold requirement do not discount the importance of science in the decision-making process. They argue instead for more openness about its limits.

4. Burden of Proof

One important point of contention is whether the precautionary principle reverses the burden of proof for decision-makers in the sense that the decision principle would require regulation unless the activity or product could be proven to be safe. For some, this reversal of the burden of proof is the principle's strength, by changing a business-as-usual approach. It could even affect the starting hypotheses used when conducting scientific study.[43] For others, a principle that would reverse the burden of proof is too strong a version of the principle. Taken out of context, there is reason to be wary of a principle that would completely reverse the burden of proof for decision-makers because it is impossible to prove that something is completely safe. In context, however, the question of where to allocate the burden of proof is not a simple binary question.

First, the particular context can help determine whether or at what point the burden of proof shifts. For example, early applications of the precautionary approach in fisheries law to create a moratorium on high seas driftnet fishing shifted the burden of proof so that fishing could only occur on proof of the viability or sustainability of the fishing.[44] In this context, where over-fishing was of particular concern, shifting the burden of proof made sense. For a general definition of the precautionary principle, a presumption of a shift in the burden of proof may not be as appropriate in the same way.[45] In the later United Nations Convention on the Law of the Sea Relating to the Conservation and Management of Straddling Fish Stocks and Highly Migratory Fish Stocks, the parties chose not to incorporate a reversal of the burden of proof.[46] The European Union Commission's Communication on the Precautionary Principle, issued in 2000, indicated that although in some instances a legislator might choose to reverse the burden of proof for certain products – in the form of a prior approval process – this reversal of the burden of proof would not be of general application.[47]

Second, this also highlights a further important limitation on the impact of a reversal of the burden of proof. The context in which the principle is being applied often indicates that a certain threshold showing of harm has been met and a reversal of the burden of proof is necessary. Thus, when a treaty includes a particular formulation of the principle, it is often because a certain risk of harm or actual harm has already been identified. At that point a threshold showing of a risk of serious or irreversible harm has been made and the burden of proof may be reversed so that greater harm does not materialize.

Thus, the reversal of the burden of proof in most formulations does not occur until the threshold showing has been met. Acknowledging that the burden of proof *may* shift, however, demonstrates an important role that the precautionary principle can play in decision-making. It can provide a basis for decision-makers to question conventional wisdom or scientific outputs without having to demonstrate that those outputs are wrong. Without the precautionary principle, decision-makers may have the burden of proving that the science is incomplete and that safety cannot be fully demonstrated. With the principle, these same decision-makers have a basis for challenging assumptions of safety. This is the principle's strength. But it is also a ground for the suggestion that the principle allows for unprincipled and unscientific decision-making. Here again, however, linking operation of the principle to risk assessment or environmental impact assessment would make a decision-maker more likely to succeed in a challenge to their exercise of discretion. If a decision-maker can show, through compliance with these procedures, that there is a likelihood of harm, the burden of proof may then shift to the other side.[48]

5. Temporary or Indefinite

When the principle is applied, is it meant to be temporary or indefinite? The question of whether the precautionary principle is to be applied on an indefinite basis raises once again a fear of over-regulation and policy paralysis because it might allow decision-makers to put in place bans on products without ever revisiting them in the light of new information. Perhaps for this reason, formulations of the precautionary principle often treat the principle either explicitly or implicitly as temporary. The assumption behind this approach is that precaution should be applied as a stop-gap measure where there is uncertainty until more scientific research has been done and the uncertainty is resolved or at least minimized.[49] Indeed, where the principle is treated as a temporary stop-gap measure, reliance can also be placed on risk assessment or environmental impact assessment as a means of generating the information that will ultimately fill in the gaps.

For example, according to the Agreement on the Application of Sanitary and Phytosanitary Measures of the World Trade Organisation (WTO) ('SPS Agreement'), countries can act in a precautionary manner providing that they are following the risk assessment procedures set out in the Agreement. Under article 5.1, members 'shall ensure that their sanitary or phytosanitary measures are based on an assessment, as appropriate to the circumstances, of the risks to human, animal or plant life or health'. Under article 5.7, an element of precaution is permitted for situations of uncertainty:

> In cases where relevant scientific evidence is insufficient, a Member may provisionally adopt sanitary or phytosanitary measures on the basis of available pertinent information, including that from the relevant international organizations as well as from sanitary or phytosanitary measures applied by other Members. In such circumstances, Members shall seek to obtain the additional information necessary for a more objective assessment of risk and review the sanitary or phytosanitary measure accordingly within a reasonable period of time.[50]

The WTO Appellate Body has confirmed that this article is the sole reflection of the precautionary principle within the SPS Agreement.[51] The text indicates that the precautionary measures are intended to be temporary and revisited and that ultimately the risk assessment is considered 'objective'. A view that the precautionary principle would be applied as a temporary measure, therefore, seems to highlight the uncertainty that stems from current information gaps.

Treating the precautionary principle as temporary again creates tension with those who see the principle as a response to uncertainty that goes beyond current information gaps. It threatens to ignore other sources of uncertainty and tie decision-making once again to the very scientific processes that are being questioned.[52] The result is that treating the principle as temporary suggests that it will be applied only where uncertainty is obvious, rather than when uncertainty either is somehow hidden by the scientific process itself or is unperceived.

6. Conclusion

As the discussion above demonstrates, the open-endedness of the precautionary principle can lead to fears that the principle allows unfettered decision-making that can be anti-scientific and over-reaching. Yet in most instances, the solution has been to tie the principle to certain scientific processes that appear to be rational and objective, such as risk assessment and environmental impact assessment. This has the potential to undermine the very basis for the principle's existence. It also demonstrates that fears that the precautionary principle has or will lead to unfettered decision-making are unfounded. Instead, when viewed in context, the precautionary principle has generally been applied in relatively moderate ways.

INSTITUTIONAL CONTEXT

1. Introduction

This section moves away from looking at puzzles of interpretation and at examples of the substantive context in which the principle has been introduced. It focuses on a few institutional contexts where decisions about the precautionary principle are made. The institutional context is critical. The precautionary principle plays a different role depending on the part of the decision-making process for which it is being invoked. For example, in international negotiations for a multilateral environmental treaty, states are not *required* to apply the precautionary principle. Even if the principle were considered a principle of customary international law, states could only be required not to undermine it if it were to become a *jus cogens* norm. As Birnie, Boyle and Redgwell have written, '[i]n this context the role of the precautionary principle is essentially rhetorical rather than normative'.[53]

The principle, however, can play a very different role in legal settings where it can have a degree of normative force. First, it might be entrenched in law that is binding on legislatures or implementing agencies. To be binding on a domestic legislature, it would have to be enacted as a constitutional provision or as part of a treaty with binding obligations. Some domestic jurisdictions might recognize the principle as binding on domestic institutions if it were considered part of the common law or if it were to be considered a customary international obligation in a jurisdiction that automatically incorporates international law into its domestic law. The most likely scenario in both domestic and international law settings, however, is that the principle is included in legislation or a treaty in a way that imposes obligations on implementing agencies – whether they are domestic agencies or international institutions.

Second, this in turn leads to another institutional context where the precautionary principle can appear – judicial or arbitral proceedings in a court or tribunal. When the precautionary principle is incorporated into law, whether it is customary international law, a treaty or domestic legislation, the court or tribunal will often be called on to be the arbiter of its function for the relevant decision-makers. This in turn means that understanding the precautionary principle requires acknowledgment that these are, as Fisher has said, issues of administrative constitutionalism and constitutional sovereignty.[54] The institution's source of authority and legitimacy and the form of incorporation will make a significant difference in this context.[55] An international tribunal asked to apply the precautionary principle because of an argument that the principle is part of customary international law will be in a very different position from a domestic tribunal asked to apply the precautionary principle because it has been incorporated into domestic law as a required part of an agency's decision-making process.

2. The Role of Regional Courts

The role of the courts in operationalizing the precautionary principle is not only significant but also inherently limited. In a judicial context the principle can be used as a sword or as a shield.[56] As a sword, it is used by someone challenging a decision by arguing that the decision failed to implement the precautionary principle. When used as a shield, it can be raised as a defense by a decision-maker to a challenge that argues that a decision was unlawful.

Whether the principle is invoked as a sword or a shield, the court will be bound in its decision-making by its own rules regarding review. The European Union (EU) provides an interesting case study here because there are so many ways in which the precautionary principle can be invoked and different rules are applicable in the different contexts.[57] Thus, in the EU, the European Court of Justice (ECJ) and the Court of First Instance are bound to apply whatever rules of EU law are applicable for that type of case. This means that when the principle is raised as a shield by a member state invoking the precautionary principle as a defence to a challenge that it is violating the EU's free trade rules, the courts will apply the rules governing free trade as well as the rules stating derogations from these commitments. When the principle is raised as a defence to a challenge against a community institution, the court will be bound to apply its standard of review for community institutional action, which takes into account the degree of discretion available to those institutions. In the EU, this standard of review may well be the reason that cases where the principle is invoked as a shield by a community institution are more likely to be dismissed.[58] The institutional setting also compounds the difficult question of whether the principle requires action by decision-makers or permits action, as discussed above. A few key examples illustrate the effects of institutional context.

The precautionary principle has been enshrined in the text of the EU treaties since 1992 when it was included in the Treaty of Maastricht. The EU courts have been willing to allow its application in a wide-ranging set of substantive areas.[59] For cases in the EU where a community institution is relying on the precautionary principle as a shield to defend a regulatory decision on the basis of the precautionary principle, the courts have acknowledged that the Treaty itself allows application of the precautionary principle by community institutions. The action of the community institution is then subject to a fairly deferential standard of review: that is one based only on 'manifest error or a misuse of powers or whether the Community institutions clearly exceeded the bounds of their discretion'.[60] The courts will not substitute their judgment for the judgment of the institution, although the courts in the EU do seem to require some kind of threshold showing of harm.[61] Because of the degree of deference applied by the court, applicants in these cases are less likely to be successful in their challenge to community institutional action.

On the other hand, the fact that the court is willing to endorse precautionary action taken by community institutions does not mean that applicants seeking to invoke the principle as a sword against a community institution will have more success. Indeed, they are unlikely to be successful because the same degree of judicial deference will mean that the institution's decision-making may well survive the court's review. In a different set of 'sword' cases, where the principle is invoked as a sword against a member state, applicants are also likely to fail. This time, however, it is not because of a deferential standard of review but because the principle is not binding on member states unless a community rule specifically requires it.[62]

EU community institutions and agencies in domestic jurisdictions around the world can, therefore, frequently rely on the precautionary principle as a shield where they have legal authority to apply the principle. However, it is generally more difficult to invoke the principle as a sword against EU community institutions and domestic agencies. The reason is the deference courts frequently give to those institutions and agencies. The deciding factor in these cases is not the precautionary principle itself. Rather it is the status of the parties, the legal basis for the claim, and the factual record. Analysis of the decisions of the EU courts indicates that support for the precautionary principle or for its particular interpretation would have to take these contextual factors into account.[63]

3. The Role of International Tribunals

The degree of deference a court is willing to give can change when the setting changes. When the EU courts are reviewing the actions of community institutions for compliance with the treaty, they behave more like a domestic court or a constitutional court. When the EU courts are deciding cases involving a member state's attempted derogation from a treaty obligation, their role changes. In this setting, the court is acting more like an international tribunal which is bound by the terms of the treaty that has created it and whose function is to ensure compliance with that treaty. The court will ensure that the member state follows certain detailed requirements if its decisions are to survive judicial scrutiny.[64] In particular, a sovereign state seeking to invoke the precautionary principle as a shield to justify trade restrictive measures is likely to be subjected to more judicial scrutiny.[65] How do international tribunals approach this issue?

Consider the way in which the WTO tribunals seem to approach the invocation of precaution as a defence to derogation from free trade principles. The decisions of the Appellate Body have made it clear that any reflection of the precautionary principle in the SPS Agreement – discussed above – is through article 5.7. This allows measures to be adopted provisionally where relevant scientific evidence is insufficient for a risk assessment under article 5.1 of the SPS Agreement. The Appellate Body has not been willing to address the precautionary principle as a separate principle in customary international law. Panel and Appellate Body decisions have similarly not deferred to states' invocation of insufficient scientific evidence to satisfy article 5.7. They have instead applied scrutiny to determine whether there was truly insufficient scientific evidence.[66]

The courts of the EU and the tribunals of the WTO appear willing to condone some trade restrictive activity if it complies with the procedures required. Indeed these judicial institutions seem to have been willing to recognize qualitative as well as quantitative risk assessments as satisfying the requirements. Thus they are not overly scrutinizing the scientific method. But they do require some scientific method. It is not surprising that these judicial institutions would be more wary of allowing an expansive approach to the precautionary principle in the context of sovereign states invoking it to justify trade restrictive measures. This context involves these institutions being asked to apply treaty provisions to sovereign states that have agreed to those provisions in a reciprocal arrangement among states. This context is therefore different from a domestic tribunal whose authority may be clearer.

A range of international tribunals operate in a number of very different settings. They walk a fine line. Like all judicial institutions, they cannot exceed their mandate. Because they are international tribunals, however, their mandate and the sources of law they apply may well be more limited than that of domestic courts. While this limitation is appropriate, it also means that the way in which the precautionary principle is treated will be a consequence of the jurisdiction conferred upon the tribunal.

The International Tribunal for the Law of the Sea (ITLOS), for example, has been more willing to acknowledge a role for precaution than the WTO. However, even the tribunal itself has grounded decisions that invoke the principle in the language of the treaties that suggests the need for precaution or that explicitly invokes precaution. It has not relied on a distinct customary rule of international law requiring precaution.

An example is ITLOS's Order for Provisional Measures in the *Southern Bluefin Tuna* cases. The tribunal did not explicitly invoke the precautionary principle, but grounded its order on the need for prudence and caution. Although Judge Treves, in his separate opinion, would have preferred an explicit reference to precaution in the tribunal's Order for Provisional Measures, he argued that a precautionary approach was inherent in the idea of provisional measures. In other words he did not push for acceptance of the precautionary principle as a principle of customary international law.[67] ITLOS did not go beyond the scope of its mandate under the United Nations Convention on the Law of the Sea (UNCLOS), particularly since the parties had already agreed that fish stocks were at a historic low. Accordingly there was no dispute that the threshold had been met. Provisional measures could then be seen as an appropriate way to ensure no further decline while the parties determined the best way forward.

ITLOS also referred to prudence and caution in the *Mox Plant* cases but in this case the tribunal was unwilling to endorse Ireland's request for provisional measures.[68] Ireland had not presented sufficient proof of the harm it claimed would occur without the provisional measures. Thus, the tribunal was unwilling to go beyond textual mandates to apply a broad interpretation of the precautionary principle. In its 2015 opinion on the Request for an Advisory Opinion Submitted by the Sub-Regional Fisheries Commission, the tribunal referred to the precautionary principle only to the extent that, where the best scientific evidence was insufficient, coastal states would be bound to apply the precautionary principle pursuant to article 2, paragraph 2 of the Convention that the tribunal was dealing with in this case.[69] The precautionary principle was supported by the text of the relevant treaty. There was no further elaboration.

It seems that, although ITLOS has implicitly or explicitly acknowledged a role for the precautionary principle, it has not explicitly endorsed the principle as a principle independent of the treaties that the tribunal is bound to apply. It has not taken opportunities to elaborate strongly on the content of the principle. Instead, the tribunal has tended to spend more intellectual energy on obligations to cooperate, on due diligence, and on environmental impact assessment. These aspects of international law can be more firmly grounded in the text of the relevant treaties. This is consistent with the International Court of Justice's response to the precautionary principle. It has not explicitly endorsed the principle, although it has been willing to articulate certain procedural obligations on the part of sovereign states to undertake environmental impact assessments.[70]

4. Conclusion

The role of a judicial institution will be significant in indicating the approach it is likely to adopt with regard to the precautionary principle. Where the institution has explicit textual support to apply the principle, it can be bolder. Even in those cases, however, the principle's application will be affected by the status of the parties in the case and the nature of the case. Where it does not have textual support, and particularly where its status is dependent on one or more treaties, precaution may still be relevant, but it is less likely to receive elaboration beyond what can be provided in those treaties.

This is not to suggest that judicial institutions should go beyond the scope of their authority to implement precaution. However, it does demonstrate the significance of having precautionary principle questions decided in the forensic context. Because of the institutional setting, with limits of varying degrees on judicial competence and authority, the parameters of the precautionary principle shaped by these institutions are unlikely to be broad.

LOOKING FORWARD

Despite criticisms of the precautionary principle, it appears increasingly entrenched in many domestic jurisdictions and international settings. The content of the principle is highly context-dependent. But even across contexts, there is evidence that the criticisms and concerns about the principle – because it may be anti-scientific and allow too much discretion on the part of decision-makers – have affected the way in which it is operationalized.

Precaution lends itself to thinking about procedural ways to implement or apply it because it does not actually require a particular outcome.[71] The earlier discussion in this chapter about the puzzles of interpretation indicates that the trend is shifting the precautionary principle towards operationalization through procedural requirements, such as risk assessment and environmental impact assessment. These procedures can anchor discretionary decision-making and link it to science, while they continue to appear to acknowledge uncertainty. For judicial institutions, this approach is particularly helpful because it can provide more objective measures for compliance.

However, as has already been suggested, these procedural requirements also create the potential for an 'uncertainty paradox'[72] or over-reliance on the output of these scientific processes.[73] If so, this may ultimately undermine the very reason to invoke the precautionary principle in the first place. What, then, is the future for the precautionary principle so that its application is connected to science but not in a way that adopts a view of that science as the product of pure objectivity?

For many, the answer is more transparency and a need for increased democracy and public participation. Believers in rational science would not accept this approach. The idea that democratic processes should somehow dictate risk management decisions is anathema to the notion of objective risk assessment. However, transparency and democracy do have the potential to save the precautionary principle from procedural quagmire without undermining scientific process. This can happen when scientists are more open about uncertainty and the assumptions they rely on for their risk assessment.[74]

While these would be important steps, they may not be sufficient. Even with enough transparency to challenge the purported objectivity of these procedural provisions, the precautionary principle needs something more. Precaution also signals the need to make value decisions because uncertainty means that there is no known correct answer about how to proceed. Decision-makers acting with a political mandate should, in addition to following procedural requirements, be permitted to use the precautionary principle as a protective tool that can sway a decision one way over another. This is embodied in some of the earliest uses of the precautionary principle in international law, for example in relation to climate change, ozone-depleting substances, and fisheries and whaling moratoria.

Yet, increasingly, adoption of procedural approaches may hint at a lack of desire to confront the difficult value decisions at play. Evidence from the Deep Seabed Mining Authority suggests that decision-makers in that setting have been gradually minimizing the role of the precautionary principle, for example by relegating precaution to environmental impact assessments[75] Yet deep seabed mining presents an example of multiple uncertainties. Is procedure a smokescreen for the fact that too many interests would like to mine the deep seabed? If so, the principle's future looks less promising. It may be here to stay, but its role may be weakened significantly.

Further, the question remains whether the precautionary principle as procedure can fully deal with the full range of uncertainties. If it is treated as temporary and tied solely to procedures, its application may not account for the full range of uncertainties, and some serious or irreversible harm may occur. If, however, those procedures are informed by transparency, and if the role of precaution as a deciding factor in certain decisions is acknowledged as necessary because of inherent uncertainty, then its future looks far brighter.

CONCLUSION

In the face of uncertainty from multiple sources, the precautionary principle is intended to allow decision-makers to take protective action. The foregoing discussion makes clear that, although the original formulation of the precautionary principle in principle 15 of the Rio Declaration left many questions about its interpretation and operation undecided, many of the puzzles of interpretation have been resolved over time. Focusing on the context in which the precautionary principle is being applied, both substantive and institutional, provides insight into the operation of the principle.

The conclusion is that, over time, and perhaps in response to criticisms, the principle has been closely tied to procedural obligations that focus on scientific output. While this has the benefit of limiting the exercise of discretion by decision-makers and of countering arguments that the principle is anti-scientific, this trend also comes with the risk that reliance on procedures that appear to demonstrate objective rationality will undermine the very purpose underlying the precautionary principle.[76]

Ultimately, although the precautionary principle is here to stay, the question of how far it can actually assist decision-makers to limit serious or irreversible harm depends on whether decision-makers and judicial institutions can reconcile the need to link the principle to science and contain discretion with the need to acknowledge the range of uncertainty. If transparency is increased in the procedural mechanisms, and if decision-makers are willing to acknowledge that the application of precaution sometimes requires value-based decisions, the principle's future may serve its original function.

NOTES

1. Freestone and Hey (1996a, pp. 3, 5); Trouwborst (2002, pp. 24, 28); Rio Declaration (1992, principle 15).
2. Rio Declaration (1992, principle 15).
3. Trouwborst (2002, pp. 16, 20); Wiener (2010, pp. 9–10).
4. Trouwborst (2002, p. 17).

5. Fainisi, Ilie and Artene (2012); Zander (2010); Fisher (2002, pp. 10, 13); Trouwborst (2002, pp. 29–30); Freestone and Hey (1996a, pp. 3–4).
6. Bergkamp and Kogan (2013, p. 499); Majone (2002, p. 89).
7. Sunstein (2005, pp. 26–33).
8. Smith et al. (2011, p. 85).
9. Dykstra (2008).
10. Stevens (2009, p. 4); Peel (2005, p. 37).
11. Holling (1995, pp. 3, 19).
12. Ibid.
13. Walters (1986).
14. Van Asselt and Vos (2006, p. 316).
15. Ibid. (p. 315).
16. Ibid. (p. 316).
17. Vlek (2010, pp. 520–21).
18. Van Asselt and Vos (2006, p. 316).
19. Clarke (2010, pp. 167–8); Dana (2009).
20. Rose-Ackerman (2013, p. 286); Clarke (2010).
21. Peel (2005, pp. 42–7).
22. Bergkamp and Kogan (2013, p. 501).
23. Rio Declaration (1992, principle 15).
24. Bergkamp and Kogan (2013, p. 499).
25. Majone (2002, p. 106).
26. Pereira Di Salvo and Raymond (2010, p. 102).
27. Wagner (2012, p. 719).
28. Peel (2004).
29. Hartzell-Nichols (2013, p. 318).
30. *Southern Bluefin Tuna* case (1999, Separate Opinion of Judge Shearer).
31. Peel (2004).
32. *Pfizer* case (2002, paras 144, 146).
33. Ibid. (para.146).
34. Sunstein (2005).
35. Van Asselt and Vos (2006, p. 317).
36. Peel (2005, pp. 221–2).
37. Heyvaert (2006, p. 202).
38. Convention on International Trade in Endangered Species of Wild Fauna and Flora (Washington, DC, 3 March 1973) ('CITES').
39. CITES, 'Criteria for Amendment of Appendices I and II, in Resolutions of the Conference of the Parties', Conf. 9.24 (Rev. CoP15).
40. Wiersema (2015).
41. Ibid.
42. Van Asselt and Vos (2006, p. 332); Peel (2005); Heyvaert (2006, p. 202).
43. Vecchione (2011).
44. Freestone and Hey (1996b, p. 260).
45. Birnie, Boyle and Redgwell (2009, p. 159).
46. United Nations Convention on the Law of the Sea Relating to the Conservation and Management of Straddling Fish Stocks and Highly Migratory Fish Stocks (New York, 4 December 1995).
47. Commission of the European Communities (2000, p. 21).
48. Birnie, Boyle and Redgwell (2009, p. 159). See also Ambrus (2009); Foster (2011, pp. 240–77).
49. Gillespie (2011, p. 466).
50. World Trade Organisation Agreement on Sanitary and Phytosanitary Measures (Marrakesh, 15 April 1994), art.5(7) ('SPS Agreement').

51. *EC-Beef Hormones* case (1998).
52. Wiersema (2015); Van Asselt and Vos (2006, p. 316).
53. Birnie, Boyle and Redgwell (2009, p. 164); von Schomberg (2012, p. 147).
54. Fisher (2002, p. 26).
55. Fisher (2001, pp. 324–5).
56. Ibid. (p. 332).
57. Fisher describes five spheres of operation for the principle within the EU: Fisher (2002, p. 24). See also Heyvaert (2006).
58. Heyvaert (2006, p. 200).
59. Craig (2012, pp. 642–3).
60. *Pfizer* case (para.166).
61. Craig (2012, p. 645).
62. Fisher (2001, pp. 325–6); *Ministero dell'Ambiente e della Tutela del Territorio e del Mare v Fipa Group Srl* (2015, para.40).
63. Fisher (2002).
64. Craig (2012, p. 656).
65. De Sadeleer (2009, p. 6); Fisher (2001, p. 324).
66. Foster (2009).
67. *Southern Bluefin Tuna* cases (1999, Separate Opinion of Judge Treves).
68. *Mox Plant* cases (2001).
69. Request for an Advisory Opinion Submitted by the Sub-Regional Fisheries Commission (2015, para.208(ii)).
70. *Pulp Mills* case (2010).
71. Fisher (2001, p. 319).
72. Van Asselt and Vos (2006).
73. Peel (2005).
74. Van Asselt and Vos (2006); Peel (2005).
75. Rayfuse (2012, p. 781).
76. Rose-Ackerman (2013, p. 286).

REFERENCES

Ambrus, Monika (2009), 'The Precautionary Principle and a Fair Allocation of the Burden of Proof in International Environmental Law', *Review of European, Comparative and International Environmental Law* **21**, 259–70.

Bergkamp, Lucas and Lawrence Kogan (2013), 'Trade, the Precautionary Principle, and Post-Modern Regulatory Process: Regulatory Convergence in the Transatlantic Trade and Investment Partnership', *European Journal of Risk* **4**, 493–507.

Birnie, Patricia, Alan Boyle and Catherine Redgwell (2009), *International Law and the Environment* (Oxford, Oxford University Press).

Clarke, Steve (2010), 'Cognitive Bias and the Precautionary Principle: What's Wrong with the Core Argument in Sunstein's *Laws of Fear* and a Way to Fix It', *Journal of Risk Research* **13**, 163–74.

Craig, Paul (2012), *EU Administrative Law* (Oxford, Oxford University Press).

Dana, David (2009), 'The Contextual Rationality of the Precautionary Principle', *Queen's Law Journal* **35**, 67–96.

de Sadeleer, Nicolas (2009), 'The Precautionary Principle as a Device for Greater Environmental Protection: Lessons from EC Courts', *Review of European, Comparative and International Environmental Law* **18**, 3–10.

Dykstra, Peter (2008), 'Magic Number: A Sketchy "Fact" About Polar Bears Keeps Going … and Going … and Going', *Society of Environmental Journalists*; http://.sejarchive.org//_Excerpts_Su08.htm.

Fainisi, Florin, Marian Ilie and Diana Anca Artene (2012), 'The Insertion of the Precautionary Principle in the Environment: Protection as a Legal Norm in the European Union Countries', *Contemporary Readings in Law and Social Justice* **4**, 489–508.

Fisher, Elizabeth (2001), 'Is the Precautionary Principle Justiciable?', *Journal of Environmental Law* **13**, 315–34.

Fisher, Elizabeth (2002), 'Precaution, Precaution Everywhere: Developing a "Common Understanding" of the Precautionary Principle in the European Community', *Maastricht Journal of European and Comparative Law* **9**, 7–28.

Foster, Caroline E. (2009), 'Precaution, Scientific Development and Scientific Uncertainty under the WTO Agreement on Sanitary and Phytosanitary Measures', *Review of European, Comparative and International Environmental Law* **18**, 50–58.

Foster, Caroline E. (2011), *Science and the Precautionary Principle in International Courts and Tribunals* (Cambridge, Cambridge University Press).

Freestone, David and Ellen Hey (1996a), 'Origins and Development of the Precautionary Principle', in David Freestone and Ellen Hey (eds), *The Precautionary Principle and International Law: The Challenge of Implementation* (The Hague, Kluwer Law International), pp. 3–15.

Freestone, David and Ellen Hey (1996b), 'Implementing the Precautionary Principle: Challenges and Opportunities', in David Freestone and Ellen Hey (eds), *The Precautionary Principle and International Law: The Challenge of Implementation* (The Hague, Kluwer Law International), pp. 249–68.

Gillespie, Alexander (2011), *Conservation, Biodiversity and International Law* (Cheltenham, Edward Elgar).

Hartzell-Nichols, Lauren (2013), 'From "the" Precautionary Principle to Precautionary Principles', *Ethics, Policy and Environment* **16**, 308–20.

Heyvaert, Veerle (2006), 'Facing the Consequences of the Precautionary Principle in European Community Law', *European Law Review* **31**, 185–206.

Holling, C.S. (1995), 'What Barriers? What Bridges?', in Lance H. Gunderson, C.S. Holling and Stephen S. Light, *Barriers and Bridges to the Renewal of Ecosystems and Institutions* (New York, Columbia University Press), pp. 3–34.

Majone, Giandomenico (2002), 'What Price Safety? The Precautionary Principle and its Policy Implications', *Journal of Common Market Studies* **40**, 89–109.

Peel, Jacqueline (2004), 'Precaution – A Matter of Principle, Approach, or Process?', *Melbourne Journal of International Law* **5**, 483–501.

Peel, Jacqueline (2005), *The Precautionary Principle in Practice: Environmental Decision-Making and Scientific Uncertainty* (Sydney, Federation Press).

Pereira Di Salvo, C.J. and Leigh Raymond (2010), 'Defining the Precautionary Principle: an Empirical Analysis of Elite Discourse', *Environmental Politics* **19**, 86–106.

Rayfuse, Rosemary (2012), 'Precaution and the Protection of Marine Biodiversity in Areas Beyond National Jurisdiction', *The International Journal of Marine and Coastal Law* **27**, 773–81.

Rose-Ackerman, Susan (2013), 'Precaution, Proportionality, and Cost/Benefit Analysis: False Analogies', *European Journal of Risk Regulation* **4**, 281–6.

Smith, Matthew J., Hesiquio Benítez-Díaz, Margarita Africa Clemente-Muñoz, John Donaldson, Jon M. Hutton, H. Noel McGough, David H.W. Morgan, Colman O'Criodain, Thomasina E.E. Oldfield, Uwe Schippmann and Richard J. Williams (2011), 'Assessing the Impacts of International Trade on CITES-Listed Species: Current Practices and Opportunities for Scientific Research', *Biological Conservation* **144**, 82–91.

Stevens, M. Henry H. (2009), *A Primer of Ecology with R 3–4* (New York, Springer).
Sunstein, Cass R. (2005), *Laws of Fear: Beyond the Precautionary Principle* (Cambridge, Cambridge University Press).
Trouwborst, Arie (2002), *Evolution and Status of the Precautionary Principle in International Law* (The Hague, Kluwer Law International).
van Asselt, Marjolein B.A. and Ellen Vos (2006), 'The Precautionary Principle and the Uncertainty Paradox', *Journal of Risk Research* **9**, 313–36.
Vecchione, Elisa (2011), 'Science for the Environment: Examining the Allocation of the Burden of Uncertainty', *European Journal of Risk Regulation* **2**, 227–39.
Vlek, Charles (2010), 'Judicious Management of Uncertain Risks: I. Developments and Criticisms of Risk Analysis and Precautionary Reasoning', *Journal of Risk Research* **13**, 517–43.
von Schomberg, René (2012), 'The Precautionary Principle: Its Use within Hard and Soft Law', *European Journal of Risk Regulation* **3**, 147–56.
Wagner, Markus (2012), 'Taking Interdependence Seriously: The Need for a Reassessment of the Precautionary Principle in International Trade Law', *Cardozo Journal of International and Comparative Law* **20**, 713–69.
Walters, Carl (1986), *Adaptive Management of Renewable Resources* (New York, Macmillan).
Wiener, Jonathan B. (2010), 'The Rhetoric of Precaution', in Jonathan B. Wiener, Michael D. Rogers, James K. Hammitt and Peter H. Sand (eds), *The Reality of Precaution: Comparing Risk Regulation in the United States and Europe* (London, Earthscan), pp. 3–35.
Wiersema, Annecoos (2015), 'Uncertainty, Precaution, and Adaptive Management in Wildlife Trade', *Michigan Journal of International Law* **36**, 375–424.
Zander, Joakim (2010), *The Application of the Precautionary Principle in Practice, Comparative Dimensions* (Leiden, Cambridge University Press).
Zander, Joakim (2011), 'Risk Versus Hazard Before the EU Courts – A Comment', *European Journal of Risk Regulation* **2**, 205–208.

INSTRUMENTS

CITES: Ninth Meeting of the Conference of the Parties, Ft. Lauderdale, US, 7–18 November 1994, 'Criteria for Amendment of Appendices I and II, in Resolutions of the Conference of the Parties', Conf. 9.24 (Rev. CoP15).
Commission of the European Communities (2000): Communication from the Commission on the Precautionary Principle, Brussels, 2 February 2000, COM(2000) 1.
Convention on International Trade in Endangered Species of Wild Fauna and Flora 1973 (Washington, DC, 3 March 1973) (CITES) (1973) *International Legal Materials* **12**, 1055.
Rio Declaraton 1992: Declaration of the United Nations Conference on Environment and Development (1992) *International Legal Materials* **31**, 874.
SPS Agreement 1994: World Trade Organization Agreement on Sanitary and Phytosanitary Measures (Marrakesh, 15 April 1994) (1995) *United Nations Treaty Series* **1867**, 154.
United Nations Convention on the Law of the Sea Relating to the Conservation and Management of Straddling Fish Stocks and Highly Migratory Fish Stocks 1995: New York, 4 December 1995 (1995) *International Legal Materials* **24**, 1542.

CASES

EC Beef Hormones case: *EC-Hormones* (1998), WTO AB 16 January 1998, European Communities – Measures Concerning Meat and Meat Products, WT/DS26/AB/R WT/DS48/AB/R.

Ministero dell'Ambiente e della Tutela del Territorio e del Mare v Fipa Group Srl (2015), EU: Case C-534/13.

Mox Plant cases: *Ireland v United Kingdom* (2001) *International Legal Materials* **41**, 405.

Pfizer case: *Pfizer Animal Health SA v Council of the European Union* (2002), EU: Case T-13/99.

Pulp Mills case: *Case Concerning Pulp Mills and the River Uruguay (Argentina v Uruguay)* (2010) *International Legal Materials* **49**, 1123.

Request for an Advisory Opinion Submitted by the Sub-fisheries Commission (2015); https:www.itlos.org/fileadmin/itlos/documents/cases/case_no.21/advisory_opinion/C21.AdvOp_02.04.pdf.

Southern Bluefin Tuna case: *Australia and New Zealand v Japan* (1999) *International Legal Materials* **38**, 1624.

18. The judicial development of ecologically sustainable development

Brian J. Preston

THE ROLE OF THE JUDICIARY

1. Introduction

The concept of ecologically sustainable development (ESD) or sustainable development has been around for at least three decades. In the international arena, the concept has appeared, under various names, in multilateral environmental agreements, soft law instruments, and international policies, plans and programs. Nation states have incorporated the concept into domestic legislation and articulated some of its constituent principles. Executive governments have applied the concept and its principles in decision-making concerning the environment. Notwithstanding this recognition, the concept of ESD still remains elusive. Many questions remain unanswered by the actions of nation states, and of their legislatures and executives.

The judiciaries of the world have, through their decisions, cast some light on the concept and have answered to varying degrees some of the questions about the concept and principles of ESD and how and when they should be applied. These judicial decisions have explicated the spare skeleton of ESD, filled the interstices, and put flesh on the skeleton. In these ways, judicial decisions are developing a body of jurisprudence on ESD.

The development of a body of ESD jurisprudence is the product of judicial decision-making. It was not its purpose. Courts have neither a policy agenda nor a legislative rule-making function. Courts are reactive not proactive institutions. Courts ordinarily do not seek out disputes to resolve. They await and resolve only disputes that parties elect to bring to the court. Their function is adjudication.

2. The Process of Adjudication

The process of adjudication of disputes can result in the development of the law, including jurisprudence on ESD. This can occur at each of the three steps involved in the adjudication of a dispute according to law: finding the law, interpreting the law and applying the law. Finding the law involves ascertaining which of the many rules in the legal system is to be applied or, if none is applicable, reaching a rule for the case on the basis of existing materials in the legal system. Interpreting the law involves interpreting the rule so found, by determining its meaning as it was framed and with respect to its intended scope. Applying the law involves the application of the rule so found and interpreted to the dispute at hand.[1] These three steps interrelate. The functions of finding the law, interpreting the law and applying the law cannot be separated.[2]

Through the first two steps of the adjudicative process of finding and interpreting the law, courts have developed the concepts and principles of ESD. The jurisprudential explanation by which this occurs differs. Positivistic jurisprudence, such as that espoused by H.L.A. Hart, accepts that judges may legitimately fill in the gaps left by rules by using their discretion. In any legal system, there will always be unregulated cases in which, on some issue, no decision either way is dictated by the pre-existing settled law. If in such cases the judge is to make a decision, the judge must exercise discretion and make law for the case instead of merely applying pre-existing settled law that does not fit the facts and circumstances of the case.[3] These law-making powers are interstitial and subject to many constraints.[4]

The distinction is between legislative and adjudicative decision-making. Courts are not legislative rule makers. However, courts do engage in rule making by adjudication. When courts are faced with a dispute over the identification and application of a legislative rule, they may generate a rule to resolve the dispute and this adjudicative rule may modify the operation of the legislative rule.[5]

This positivist approach has been challenged. Dworkin, for instance, argues that judges do not make law because all of the resources for their proper decisions are provided by the existing law as correctly understood. These resources include the explicit settled law – the rules – as well as the implicit legal principles which underlie and are embedded in the settled law. Together, these existing legal resources should be treated as making up a 'seamless web'.[6] The task of judges is to understand the content of the legal system and give effect to it in their judgments to the best of their ability.[7] This task is 'interpretative' but it is also partly evaluative. It involves identification of the principles which both best 'fit' or cohere with the settled law and legal practices of the legal system and also provide the best moral justification for them, thus showing the law in its best light.[8]

3. Developing ESD through Adjudication

(a) Ascertaining the rules

Irrespective of the jurisprudential debate about whether judges interstitially make law by adjudication or find the settled legal rules and implicit legal principles within the legal system, the result is the same. By their decisions, judges identify and interpret the rules and principles that are to be applied to resolve the dispute at hand. This judicial combination of the identification and interpretation of legal rules and principles has resulted in the development of the jurisprudence on ESD.

Sometimes, the concept of ESD and its constituent principles are stated explicitly in legislation. Often, however, they are expressed in vague and open-textured language. Judicial decisions interpret this open-textured language and thereby give more certainty to the concept and principles of ESD. Legislation that prescribes strategic and regulatory rules that govern an application for the approval and undertaking of activities likely to affect the environment may incorporate the concept and principles of ESD. However, they may provide little guidance on the methodology of how and when the concept and principles are to be applied. Judicial decisions can assist in explaining how and when the concepts and principles of ESD are to be applied.

Alternatively, the legislation may not explicitly refer to the concept and principles of ESD. Courts, nevertheless, have found that the concept and principles of ESD underlie and are implicit in the language of the legislation. For example, courts have interpreted the statutory consideration of the 'public interest' to include the principles of ESD.[9] Whether the references to the concept and the principles are explicit or implicit, judicial decisions thereby make or declare – depending on one's jurisprudential viewpoint – the concept and principles of ESD to be part of the law to be applied to the dispute.

(b) Applying the rules

Apart from the two steps of finding and interpreting the law, adjudication involves the third step of applying the law found and interpreted to the dispute at hand. This third step of application of the law encompasses two stages. The first stage is to find the facts relevant to the identified rules of law. The duty of the court in determining questions of fact 'is to exercise its intellectual judgment on the evidence submitted to it in order to ascertain the truth'.[10] The second stage is to apply the identified rule of law to the facts as found. In this way 'a determination of the existence or non-existence of rights, obligations and liabilities emerges to support the award or refusal of remedies as the case may be'.[11]

At the second stage, consideration needs to be given to whether the applicable law accords a judicial discretion as to the remedy, relief or punishment – if any – to be granted by the court if, upon application of the law to the facts of the matter, a breach of the law were to be found. Judicial discretion may have its source in statute, the common law or equity. The duty of the court in matters of judicial discretion is to exercise its moral judgment as to what is right, just, equitable or reasonable in the case.[12] The exercise of a judicial discretion permits individualisation in the application of the law.[13]

(c) Providing a remedy

In the environmental law context, legislation commonly permits a court that has found a breach of the statute to make such order as it thinks fit 'to remedy or restrain the breach'.[14] Such a phrase empowers the court 'to mould the manner of its intervention in such a way as will best meet the practicalities as well as the justice of the situation before it'.[15] The discretion extends to withholding relief if the court does not think that any order is fit to remedy or restrain the breach.[16]

The court may take into account a range of considerations that pertain not only to the private interests of the parties and third parties but also to the public interest. A breach of a planning or environmental law involves a breach of a public duty because the orderly development of the use of the environment is in the public interest.[17] Obligations imposed on public authorities to assess and approve applications under a planning or environmental law impose public duties and are important in the public interest.[18] The subject matter of the litigation may also raise issues concerning the public interest. Natural resources such as the air, waterways, forests and parks can be seen, to use the language of the Roman law, as *res communis* and *res publicae*. As such they are held by the government in trust for the benefit of present and future generations.[19] The notion of the public interest includes ESD. In addition, in awarding or refusing remedies, courts can, and have, applied the concept and principles of ESD through the application of the law. In each case, courts have explained and shown how ESD works in practice.

4. The Structure of this Chapter

This chapter sketches some of the ways in which judicial decisions have found, interpreted and applied the concepts and principles of ESD in adjudicating disputes according to law. The first concerns the meaning of the concept and the principles of ESD. Do they set substantive outcomes or only processes, or both? The second concerns the interrelationship between the concepts and principles of ESD, in particular how ESD is to be achieved through application of its principles. The third concerns the interpretation and explanation of the principles of ESD. The fourth concerns application of the concept and principles of ESD to differing types of disputes. In these ways, the chapter explains the judicial development of ESD and its principles.

THE MEANING OF ESD

1. The Importance of the Language of ESD

(a) The variety of terminology

The meaning of ESD depends on the specific legislation that incorporates it. Judicial interpretation of ESD is, therefore, very dependent on the statutory language in both the provisions defining ESD and those establishing the strategic rules and liability rules that utilise ESD. It is difficult, therefore, to generalise about the meaning given to ESD by the courts.

Legislation that incorporates ESD typically describes it in general terms. Sometimes, the actual concept of ESD is not defined at all, although its principles may be defined.[20] Some legislation simply refers to the object of 'the need to maintain ecologically sustainable development'[21] or to 'promote ecologically sustainable development'[22] but leaves unspecified what it is that is to be maintained or promoted.

Alternatively, there may be a definition of ESD but the definition speaks in general terms of what ESD requires or how it is to be achieved, without actually defining what it is. Consider three examples. First, there are legislative and policy instruments that define ESD in the terms used by the World Commission on Environment and Development (WCED) in its report *Our Common Future* as 'development that meets the needs of the present without compromising the ability of future generations to meet their own needs'.[23] Second, there is legislation that says that ESD requires the effective integration of economic and environmental considerations in decision-making processes.[24] Third, there is legislation that says that ESD can be achieved through the implementation of specified principles which may be defined to be principles of ESD. These include the principle of sustainable use; the principle of integration of economic, environmental and social considerations; the precautionary principle; the principle of intergenerational equity; the principle of conservation of biological diversity and ecological integrity; and the promotion of improved valuation, pricing and incentive mechanisms, including the polluter pays principle and the user pays principle.[25]

(b) The language of process and outcome

It is suggested that these legislative and policy approaches point to a degree of means-ends fluidity. Legislation is traditionally more concerned with means than ends. Hence, environmental legislation characteristically leaves unspecified what the end or outcome of decision-making under the legislation should be. It will, however, prescribe the process and the methodology that decision-making should follow. The end or outcome becomes clear only as a result of going through the prescribed process.[26]

Notwithstanding this means-ends fluidity, there would appear to be a common thread that the concept of ESD does embody an outcome and this is to be achieved through implementation of the various principles of ESD.[27] ESD operates in legislation as 'a standard of conduct or behaviour, as a standard of methodology of decision-making or as a standard of outcome or result'.[28] ESD, therefore, involves both a substantive outcome as well as a process to achieve that outcome. Indeed, ESD has been described as being 'all about integrating process and substance with a view to achieving a single, unified objective'.[29]

But what is the substantive outcome that ESD requires? The WCED definition in *Our Common Future* calls for development that meets the needs of the present without compromising the ability of future generations to meet their own needs. These needs of present and future generations are economic, environmental and social. However, economic and social needs cannot be met continuously in a deteriorating environment. Any further degradation of the earth's natural capital must be prevented for the sake of future generations. Hence, at the core of ESD is ecological sustainability. This is the outcome that ESD demands. It requires living within the planet's ecological limits.[30] It involves development that improves the total quality of life both now and in the future, in a way that maintains the ecological processes upon which life depends.[31]

2. Judicial Analysis of the Language of ESD as Requiring an Outcome

(a) South Africa and India

The Constitutional Court of South Africa recognised the need to protect the environment in order to achieve economic and social development:

> Economic and social development is essential to the well-being of human beings. This Court has recognised that socio-economic rights that are set out in the Constitution are indeed vital to the enjoyment of other human rights guaranteed in the Constitution. But development cannot subsist upon a deteriorating environmental base. Unlimited development is detrimental to the environment and the destruction of the environment is detrimental to development. Promotion of development requires the protection of the environment, yet the environment cannot be protected if development does not pay attention to the costs of environmental destruction. The environment and development are thus inexorably linked.[32]

Bosselmann has argued that ESD involves 'the obligation to promote long-term economic prosperity and social justice within the limits of ecological sustainability'. The principle of sustainability is defined as 'the duty to protect and restore the integrity of the Earth's ecological systems'.[33] Echoing the land ethic of Aldo Leopold, Bosselmann suggests that 'development is sustainable if it tends to preserve the integrity and continued existence of ecological systems; it is unsustainable if it tends to do otherwise'.[34]

This need for maintenance of 'ecological balance' led the High Court of Calcutta to issue an injunction restraining reclamation of wetlands in East Kolkata for development activities. The court recognised that sustainable development requires there to be 'a proper balance between the development and the environment so that both can co-exist without affecting the other'.[35] The goal is 'maintenance of ecological balance'. If development leads to ecological imbalance, the function of the court is to intervene.[36]

Similarly, the Supreme Court of India held that sustainable development ensures that 'mitigative steps are and can be taken to preserve the ecological balance. Sustainable development means what type or extent of development can take place which can be sustained by nature/ecology with or without mitigation'.[37] This ecological core of ESD places a first claim on the earth's natural resources. Only when ecological needs are met should the remaining natural resources be available to supply and meet economic and social needs.[38]

(b) New Zealand

The ecological core of ESD also sets an environmental bottom line that needs to be met. The Supreme Court of New Zealand held that the Resource Management Act 1991 (NZ) (RMA) and the New Zealand Coastal Policy Statement (NZCPS) made under the Act established an environmental bottom line of preservation and protection of the coastal environment as part of the concept of sustainable management.[39] The core purpose of the RMA is to promote sustainable management of natural and physical resources.[40] 'Sustainable management' is defined to mean:

> managing the use, development, and protection of natural and physical resources in a way, or at a rate, which enables people and communities to provide for their social, economic and cultural well-being and for their health and safety while –
>
> (a) sustaining the potential of natural and physical resources (excluding minerals) to meet the reasonably foreseeable needs of future generations; and
> (b) safeguarding the life-supporting capacity of air, water, soil, and ecosystems; and
> (c) avoiding, remedying, or mitigating any adverse effects of activities on the environment.[41]

Section 5 of the RMA is 'a carefully formulated statement of principle intended to guide those who make decisions under the RMA'.[42] It is given further elaboration by section 6.

The RMA envisages the formulation and promulgation of planning documents to give effect to the core purpose. One of the documents made to achieve the purpose of the RMA in relation to the coastal environment of New Zealand is the NZCPS.[43] One of the principal objectives of the NZCPS is 'to preserve the natural character of the coastal environment and protect natural features and landscape values' through specified means, including identifying those areas where various forms of development would be inappropriate and protecting them from such activities.[44]

This objective and these policies of the NZCPS set an environmental bottom line.[45] The NZCPS gives primacy to protecting areas of the coastal environment with outstanding natural features from the adverse effects of development, in order to promote sustainable management.[46] Any regional plan is required to 'give effect to' the NZCPS[47] and any decision to change a regional plan must also give effect to the NZCPS. Hence, it was an error, in considering a plan change, to adopt an 'overall judgment' approach – balancing conflicting environmental, economic and social considerations – rather than the 'environmental bottom line' approach which means giving effect to the NZCPS policy of preserving the coastal environment and protecting it from inappropriate development.[48]

3. Conclusion

It was suggested earlier in this chapter that the concept of ESD involves a substantive outcome that is to be achieved through the implementation of the principles of ESD. The implementation of these principles achieves different aspects of the substantive outcome. Each of the principles should not be viewed in isolation but rather as part of a package. Sometimes the principles reinforce each other and strengthen the case for taking some particular action. At other times they tug in different directions and may need to be weighed against one another to determine the appropriate action to be taken. Courts have emphasised the need to consider all of the principles of ESD that are relevant to the decision to be made.[49]

THE PRINCIPLE OF SUSTAINABLE USE

1. The Language of Sustainable Use

One of the principles of ESD is the principle of sustainable use – the aim of exploiting natural resources in a manner which is 'sustainable' or 'prudent' or 'rational' or 'wise' or 'appropriate'.[50] This principle also has an ecological core: use of natural resources needs to be within ecological limits.

Consider some examples from Australia. The statement of the objects of the Environment Protection and Biodiversity Conservation Act 1999 (Cth) includes 'to promote ecologically sustainable development through the conservation and ecologically sustainable use of natural resources'.[51] Although ESD is the desired end, it is to be achieved through the means of conservation and ecologically sustainable use of natural resources. 'Ecologically sustainable use' of natural resources is defined to mean:

> use of the natural resources … within their capacity to sustain natural processes while maintaining the life-support systems of nature and ensuring that the benefit of the use to the present generation does not diminish the potential to meet the needs and aspirations of future generations.[52]

This definition of ecologically sustainable use sets outcomes, including that the use of natural resources is to be within their capacity to sustain natural processes while maintaining the life-support systems of nature.

In Queensland, the purpose of the Sustainable Planning Act 2009 is 'to seek to achieve ecological sustainability' by, amongst other things, managing the process by which development takes place, including ensuring that the process 'delivers sustainable outcomes'.[53] One of the ways in which this purpose is to be advanced is by:

> ensuring the sustainable use of renewable natural resources and the prudent use of non-renewable natural resources by, for example, considering alternatives to the use of non-renewable natural resources.[54]

The objective of 'ecological sustainability' is defined to involve a balance that integrates 'protection of ecological processes and natural systems' with economic development and social development.[55] Ecological processes and natural systems will be protected if:

(i) the life-supporting capacities of air, ecosystems, soil and water are conserved, enhanced or restored for present and future generations; and
(ii) biological diversity is protected.[56]

If a particular proposed use of natural resources cannot be shown to achieve this outcome of ecological sustainability, it should not be approved.

2. Judicial Analysis of the Language of Sustainable Use

In South Australia, the Environment, Resources and Development Court refused consent to a proposal to establish tuna farms in the waters of Louth Bay in Spencer Gulf because it could not be shown that it could be carried out in an ecologically sustainable way.[57] The development was required to be assessed against the provisions of the applicable development plan made under the Development Act 1993 (SA). One of the provisions was that development of the marine environment, and in particular the marine aquaculture industry, had to be carried out 'in an ecologically sustainable way'.

The court held that 'an adaptive management approach, implemented by way of licence conditions to achieve ecologically sustainable development which could be varied in response to new knowledge, was one means by which the development could proceed in an ecologically sustainable manner'.[58] However, the court found that an appropriate adaptive management regime could not be implemented. It could not be achieved by imposing conditions of development consent because the Development Act did not give the relevant authority power to vary the conditions.[59] Similarly, it could not be achieved by way of a lease or licence under the Fisheries Act 1982 (SA). In circumstances where a lease or licence issued under the Fisheries Act could be for a term as long as ten years, there would be no scope for an adaptive management approach to fish farming, because the terms and conditions of the lease or licence would be fixed for that period and could not be varied.[60] Without implementation of an adaptive management regime, the development could not be carried out in an ecologically sustainable way. The court therefore set aside the original governmental decision to grant development consent.[61]

The Land and Environment Court of New South Wales (NSW) applied the principle of sustainable use in overturning a development consent that had been granted to a waste disposal facility on prime agricultural land.[62] Two adjacent local councils sought development consent to construct and operate a waste disposal facility on land in one council's area. That council granted development consent to the development application. The applicable local environmental plan zoned the land on which the waste disposal facility was proposed as Zone 1(a) General Rural. The objective of the zone was to promote the proper management and utilisation of resources by:

(a) protecting, enhancing and conserving:
   (i) agricultural land in a manner which sustains its efficient and effective agricultural production potential, …
(b) preventing the unjustified development of prime crop and pasture land for purposes other than agriculture.[63]

Clause 10 of the local environment plan provided the mechanism for determining whether or not a proposed development complied with objective (b) of the zone. The clause provided that the council was not to consent to an application to carry out development within Zone 1(a) unless two conditions were satisfied: first, that the council had made an assessment of the effect of the carrying out of the development on, amongst other matters, the present and potential use of the land for the purposes of agriculture; second, that the council was satisfied that the development would not have an adverse effect on the long-term use, for sustained agricultural production, of any prime crop and pasture land.[64]

'Prime crop and pasture land' was defined to mean land identified on a map prepared by the relevant Department of Agriculture as Class 1, Class 2 or Class 3 or as land of merit for special agricultural uses.[65] The land proposed for the waste disposal facility was mapped as Class 3 and thus fell within the definition of prime crop and pasture land.

The court found that the waste disposal facility would have an effect on the long-term use, for sustained agricultural production, of this prime crop and pasture land. The court held:

> The principle of good governance is essential to sustainable development. It requires the enactment and enforcement of clear and effective laws that support sustainable development. The provisions of the LEP relating to the 1(a) zone, including cl 10(1), are part of a law supporting sustainable development, by protecting, enhancing and conserving the valuable resource of agricultural land and in particular prime crop and pasture land in a manner which ensures its use for sustained agricultural production. The upholding and enforcement of that law promotes good governance.
>
> The principle of sustained use of natural resources involves the exploitation of natural resources in a way which is sustainable in the long-term and which reduces environmental harm. It involves consideration of the effects of use on all natural resources, certainly the effect of the use on the resources the intended subject of the activity but also the effect that the use of those resources might have on the sustainable use of other resources.
>
> In this case, whilst adoption of a waste minimisation strategy and operation of a waste disposal facility with a resource recovery facility is beneficial in promoting sustainability, by such means as encouraging more efficient use of resources, reducing unnecessary resource consumption, improving resource recovery and reducing waste generation, by siting the waste disposal facility on prime crop and pasture land, the proposed development impedes achieving sustainability by adversely affecting the long-term use, for sustained agricultural production, of that land.[66]

THE PRINCIPLE OF INTEGRATION

1. The Concept of Integration

The principle of integration requires the effective integration of both long-term and short-term economic, environmental and social considerations in decision-making processes.[67] It was the philosophical underpinning of the WCED's report, *Our Common Future*. That report recognised that the ecologically harmful cycle caused by economic development without regard to and at the cost of the environment could only be broken by integrating environmental concerns with economic goals.[68]

The principle of integration ensures respect and reciprocity between economic development, social development and environmental protection. The Plan of Implementation of the World Summit on Sustainable

Development held in Johannesburg in 2002 noted that efforts needed to be taken to:

> promote the integration of the three components of sustainable development – economic development, social development and environmental protection – as interdependent and mutually reinforcing pillars. Poverty eradication, changing unsustainable patterns of production and consumption and protecting and managing the natural resource base of economic and social development are overarching objectives of, and essential requirements for, sustainable development.[69]

At its simplest, the principle of integration requires that each of the three components of sustainable development – economic development, social development and environmental protection – is taken into account in development decision-making. It requires that decision-makers 'ensure that social and economic development decisions do not disregard environmental considerations, and not undertake environmental protection without taking into account relevant social and economic implications'.[70]

Procedurally, such integration can be facilitated by conducting environmental impact assessments for proposed projects and strategic environmental assessments for proposed policies, plans and programs.[71] As the Land and Environment Court of NSW has noted:

> Requiring prior environmental impact assessment and approval is a key means of achieving ecologically sustainable development. It facilitates the achievement of the principle of integration ('ecologically sustainable development requires the effective integration of economic and environmental considerations in decision-making processes' …). If environmental considerations are to be an integral part of decision-making processes, it is necessary to assess the environmental impacts and risks associated with proposed activities. Environmental impact assessment is widely applied to predict the impacts of proposed activities on the environment.[72]

Integration of economic, environmental and social considerations is assisted by environmental impact assessment addressing both the concept of ESD and all of the principles of ESD of relevance to the decision to be made.

The Land and Environment Court held that the environmental impact assessment for a large coal mine in the Hunter Valley of NSW was inadequate in law in failing to consider the downstream effects of greenhouse gas emissions, known as scope 3 emissions, by the burning of coal mined from the project. The court held that the decision-maker was bound to take into account the principles of ESD, including the principle of intergenerational equity and the precautionary principle. The decision-maker had decided that the environmental impact assessment for the project was adequate. The court held that, in making that decision, the decision-maker failed to take into account the principle of intergenerational equity and the precautionary principle.[73] The court also held that the environmental impact assessment needed to consider the principles of ESD.[74]

2. The Achievement of Integration

Whilst environmental impact assessment is a procedural means of implementing the principle of integration, it still leaves unanswered how integration of the three components of ESD is to be achieved. The principles of ESD require decision-making that integrates and weighs up potentially conflicting economic, social and environmental considerations.[75] What balance is to be struck between these three, often conflicting, needs? As Bosselmann observes, 'if sustainable development would be used merely for integrating and balancing conflicting interests, nothing would be achieved. Without a benchmark, we are left at a guess *how* environmental, social and economic interests should be balanced'.[76]

What benchmark has been suggested? A common view is that the three pillars of economic development, social development and environmental protection supporting ESD are of equal height and standing and should be given equal weight and importance in decision-making processes. This view might be seen to reflect a three scales model of ESD: the environment sits in one scale, economic development sits in a second scale and social development sits in a third scale. The aim for decision-making is to keep all of the scales balanced at the same level. This view, however, is incorrect for at least three reasons.

First, the three scales model assumes a separation between the environmental, developmental and social spheres that does not exist in reality. They are interrelated and interdependent, now and in the future. The pursuit of one affects the ability to pursue the others. The aim of sustainable development is to bring the three together, not to balance them as independent entities.[77] As Bosselmann notes, 'the key element of sustainable development is the recognition that economic and environmental goals are inextricably linked'.[78] Indeed, the Sustainable Planning Act 2009 (Qld) defines 'ecological sustainability' to be a balance that integrates:

(a) protection of ecological processes and natural systems at local, regional, State and wider levels; and
(b) economic development; and

(c) maintenance of the cultural, economic, physical and social well-being of people and communities.[79]

As this definition shows, balancing involves integration but integration does not necessarily require balancing. The balance referred to is a balance that relates to each of the ecological, economic and social limbs and integrating them.[80] Balance can be achieved by integrating the three limbs differentially, but not necessarily equally.

Second, to accord equal weight to economic development, social development and environmental protection may be self-defeating – the environment may deteriorate and hence ecological sustainability cannot be achieved. Bosselmann argues that 'to perceive environmental, economic and social as equally important components of sustainable development is arguably the greatest misconception of sustainable development and the greatest obstacle to achieving social and economic justice'.[81] He continues that 'the concept of sustainable development can only perform its normative functions in so far as it incorporates the idea of ecological sustainability'.[82]

Third, it is unrealistic to expect that all of the ecological, economic and social goals can be equally balanced in every decision made. For example, an equal balance of environmental protection, economic development and social development may not be able to be achieved by every development on every parcel of land. As the Planning and Environment Court of Queensland has noted:

> In assessing the extent to which a proposal advances ecological sustainability, it is appropriate to have regard not just to the subject site but to its context. Ecological sustainability is not necessarily advanced if every parcel of land is, in part, used for economic development of a kind which advances the wellbeing of people and communities and, in part, for the protection of ecological processes. Sometimes the promotion of ecological sustainability, at a broader level, will require, for example, a particular area or site to be entirely preserved from development for the protection of ecological processes while another site or area is given over to intense economic development.[83]

THE PRECAUTIONARY PRINCIPLE

1. The Concept of Precaution

One of the best known principles of ESD is the precautionary principle. There are numerous formulations of the precautionary principle but the most widely employed formulation is based on principle 15 of the Rio Declaration on Environment and Development which states:

> In order to protect the environment, the precautionary approach shall be widely applied by States according to their capabilities. Where there are threats of serious or irreversible damage, lack of full scientific certainty shall not be used as a reason for postponing cost-effective measures to prevent environmental degradation.[84]

An example of a domestic statutory incorporation of the precautionary principle is section 6(2)(a) of the Protection of the Environment Administration Act 1991 (NSW):

> the precautionary principle – namely, that if there are threats of serious or irreversible environmental damage, lack of full scientific certainty should not be used as a reason for postponing measures to prevent environmental degradation.
>
> In the application of the precautionary principle, public and private decisions should be guided by:
>
> (i) careful evaluation to avoid, wherever practicable, serious or irreversible damage to the environment, and
> (ii) an assessment of the risk-weighted consequences of various options ...[85]

The precautionary principle is the principle of ESD that has been the subject of the most judicial consideration by courts throughout the world.[86] Difficulties in its application flow from the 'the indifference of the precautionary approach, both in terms of *when* and *what* action is required'.[87] The courts, by their decisions, have assisted in elucidating the meaning and scope of the precautionary principle in three ways.

First, courts have recognised the precautionary principle to be part of the law of the land. The precautionary principle might not have been expressly incorporated in legislation. Courts have nevertheless found that the precautionary principle is to be implied in the legislation or the common law. The Supreme Court of India has held that 'the precautionary principle and the polluter pays principle are part of the environmental law of the country', notwithstanding that neither was expressly incorporated in constitutional or statutory law.[88] Similarly, the Land and Environment Court of NSW has held that decision-makers who are required to have regard to the public interest in development decision-making are obliged to have regard to the principles of ESD, including the precautionary principle, where issues relevant to those principles arise.[89]

Second, courts have explained when the precautionary principle will apply. Formulations of the precautionary principle based on principle 15 of the Rio Declaration refer to two matters for its application. The first is in the opening phrase 'if there are threats of serious or irreversible environmental damage'. The second is in the statement as to what should not be done: namely 'lack of full scientific certainty should not be used as a reason for postponing measures to prevent environmental degradation'. The Land and Environment Court of NSW has held that satisfaction of these two matters is necessary to trigger the application of the precautionary principle:

> The application of the precautionary principle and the concomitant need to take precautionary measures is triggered by the satisfaction of two conditions precedent or thresholds: a threat of serious or irreversible environmental damage and scientific uncertainty as to the environmental damage. These conditions or thresholds are cumulative. Once both of these conditions or thresholds are satisfied, a precautionary measure may be taken to avert the anticipated threat of environmental damage, but it should be proportionate.[90]

Third, it is clear that the two conditions interrelate. This is because the degree of scientific uncertainty that needs to be established varies depending upon the magnitude of the environmental damage. Nevertheless, it assists explanation of the application of the precautionary principle to address the two conditions separately.[91] The following paragraphs address the two conditions separately before considering the application of the principle.

2. A Threat of Serious or Irreversible Environmental Damage

The existence of a threat is critical. It is not necessary that serious or irreversible environmental damage has actually occurred. It is the *threat* of such damage that is required.[92] The concept of a 'threat' has been taken by the Environment, Resources and Development Court of SA to mean 'likelihood' or 'probability'.[93] However, the Supreme Court of Victoria has held that, in speaking of a threat of environmental damage, the precautionary principle is not making any statement as to the likelihood or probability of its occurrence, except for asserting that the risk is not one that is far-fetched or fanciful. Instead, a threat of environmental damage refers to the foreseeability of the risk of environmental damage. A risk of environmental damage which is remote, in the sense that it is extremely unlikely to occur, may nevertheless constitute a foreseeable risk: 'A risk which is not far-fetched or fanciful is real and therefore foreseeable'.[94]

The threats to the environment that should be considered have been held to include:

> direct and indirect threats, secondary and long-term threats and the incremental or cumulative impacts of multiple or repeated actions or decisions. Where threats may interact or be interrelated (for example where action against one threat may exacerbate another threat) they should not be addressed in isolation.[95]

The environmental damage threatened must attain the threshold of being *serious or irreversible*. Assessing the seriousness or irreversibility of environmental damage involves consideration of many factors. These include:

(a) the spatial scale of the threat – for example, local, regional, statewide, national, international;
(b) the magnitude of possible impacts on both natural and human systems;
(c) the perceived value of the threatened environment;
(d) the temporal scale of possible impacts in terms of both the timing and the longevity – or persistence – of the impacts;
(e) the complexity and connectivity of the possible impacts;
(f) the manageability of possible impacts, having regard to the availability and acceptability of means;
(g) the level of public concern, and the rationality of and scientific or other evidentiary basis for the public concern; and
(h) the reversibility of the possible impacts and, if reversible, the time frame for reversing the impacts, and the difficulty and expense of reversing the impacts.[96]

If there is not a threat of serious or irreversible environmental damage, there is no basis upon which the precautionary principle can operate. The precautionary principle does not apply.[97] This was the conclusion reached by a number of courts in relation to proposed telecommunications developments that, by reason of compliance by a significant margin with relevant standards for the protection of public health and safety, there was no threat of serious or irreversible damage to public health and safety from the developments.[98] Similarly, courts have held that, by reason of the measures taken to protect threatened species of fauna in native forests, logging would not constitute a real threat of serious or irreversible damage.[99]

3. The Lack of Scientific Certainty

In the context of the lack of scientific certainty, the uncertainty is in relation to the nature and scope of the threat of environmental damage.[100] Assessing the degree of scientific uncertainty involves a process of analysis of many factors. These include:

(a) the sufficiency of the evidence that there might be serious or irreversible environmental harm caused by the development plan, programme or project;
(b) the level of uncertainty, including the kind of uncertainty – such as technical, methodological or epistemological uncertainty; and
(c) the potential to reduce uncertainty having regard to what is possible in principle, economically and within a reasonable time frame.[101]

The degree of scientific uncertainty that needs to exist in order to trigger application of the precautionary principle varies depending on the magnitude of environmental damage used in the formulation of the first condition of the precautionary principle. For the formulation of 'serious or irreversible environmental damage', the correlative degree of uncertainty about the threat of environmental damage has been held to be 'highly uncertain of threat' or 'considerable scientific uncertainty'[102] or 'substantial uncertainty'.[103]

Then there is the relationship between the two conditions. If there is an absence of considerable or substantial scientific uncertainty – that is that the second condition is not satisfied – while at the same time there is a threat of serious or irreversible environmental damage – that is that the first condition is satisfied – then the precautionary principle will not apply. The threat of serious or irreversible environmental damage can be classified as relatively certain because it is possible to establish a causal link between the action or event and any environmental damage, to calculate the probability of their occurrence and to insure against them. Measures will still need to be taken but these will need to be preventative measures to control the relatively certain threat of serious or irreversible damage rather than precautionary measures that are appropriate in relation to uncertain threats of environmental damage.[104]

4. A Shift of the Burden of Proof

If each of the conditions is satisfied – there is a threat of serious or irreversible damage and there is the requisite degree of scientific uncertainty about that environmental damage – the precautionary principle will be activated. Courts have held that, at this point of activation of the precautionary principle, there is a shifting of the burden of proof. A decision-maker must assume that the threat of serious or irreversible environmental damage is no longer uncertain but is instead certain and real. The burden of showing that the threat does not in fact exist or is negligible effectively reverts to the proponent of the development plan, program or project.[105] The Land and Environment Court of NSW explained:

> The rationale for requiring this shift of the burden of proof is to ensure preventative anticipation; to act before scientific certainty of cause and effect is established. It may be too late, or too difficult and costly, to change a course of action once it is proven to be harmful. The preference is to prevent environmental damage, rather than remediate it. The benefit of the doubt is given to environmental protection when there is scientific uncertainty. To avoid environmental harm, it is better to err on the side of caution.
>
> The function of the precautionary principle is, therefore, to require the decision-maker to assume that there is, or will be, a serious or irreversible threat of environmental damage and to take this into account, notwithstanding that there is a degree of scientific uncertainty about whether the threat really exists …[106]

5. Application of the Precautionary Principle

(a) Types of precautionary measures

It is important to note that courts have explained what actions are required when the precautionary principle does apply. The Land and Environment Court of NSW has said:

> The type and level of precautionary measures that will be appropriate will depend on the combined effect of the degree of seriousness and irreversibility of the threat and the degree of uncertainty. This involves assessment of risk in its usual formulation, namely the probability of the event occurring and the seriousness of the consequences should it occur. The more significant and the more uncertain the threat, the greater the degree of precaution required.[107]

(b) Obtaining further information to reduce uncertainty

Where there is still considerable scientific uncertainty, prudence may require that the development plan, program or project not proceed until further information is obtained in order to reduce the uncertainty. Thus, the Supreme Court of Pakistan appointed an expert commissioner to examine and study the scheme and the planning used by a government agency for an electricity grid station and to report whether there was any likelihood that the electromagnetic fields that radiated from the grid station might cause a hazard to the health of residents in the locality.[108]

(c) Allowing margin for error

Prudence would also suggest that some margin for error should be retained until all the consequences of the decision to proceed with the development plan, program or project are known. This allows for potential errors in risk assessment and cost benefit analysis. Potential errors are weighted in favour of environmental protection. Weighting the risk of error in favour of the environment safeguards ecological space or environmental room for manoeuvre.[109]

Illustrations of weighting the risk of error in favour of the environment can be found in decisions of the Land and Environment Court of NSW directed at the avoidance of a risk of serious or irreversible environmental damage to endangered species and ecological communities. This is achieved, first, by resolving scientific uncertainty as to whether an endangered ecological community was widely distributed over a development site by assuming the existence of the wide distribution of the endangered ecological community[110] and, second, by determining that proposed developments were likely to significantly affect endangered species and ecological communities so as to trigger the statutory requirement to prepare a detailed environmental assessment in the form of a species impact statement.[111]

(d) An adaptive management approach

One means of retaining a margin for error is to implement a step-wise or adaptive management approach, whereby uncertainties are acknowledged and the area affected by the development plan, program or project is expanded as the extent of uncertainty is reduced.[112] The Land and Environment Court of NSW has held that an adaptive management approach might involve the following core elements:

- monitoring of impacts of management or decisions based on agreed indicators;
- promoting research, to reduce key uncertainties;
- ensuring periodic evaluation of the outcomes of implementation, drawing of lessons, and review and adjustment, as necessary, of the measures or decisions adopted; and
- establishing an efficient and effective compliance system.[113]

The court found that the appropriate and proportionate response to the threat of environmental damage to stygofauna within a limestone formation proposed to be quarried was to implement a step-wise or adaptive management approach. This involved the imposition of conditions of development consent requiring monitoring linked to adaptive management.[114] The court stated:

> Adaptive management is a concept which is frequently invoked but less often implemented in practice. Adaptive management is not a 'suck it and see', trial and error approach to management, but it is an iterative approach involving explicit testing of the achievement of defined goals. Through feedback to the management process, the management procedures are changed in steps until monitoring shows that the desired outcome is obtained. The monitoring program has to be designed so that there is statistical confidence in the outcome. In adaptive management the goal to be achieved is set, so there is no uncertainty as to the outcome and conditions requiring adaptive management do not lack certainty, but rather they establish a regime which would permit changes, within defined parameters, to the way the outcome is achieved …
>
> The conditions of consent requiring monitoring and adaptive management would operate over the life of a project (and, in the case of rehabilitation, beyond it). Over this period there are likely to be changes in technology, understanding of issues and the environment (for example in 30 years' time climatic conditions might be different from those currently prevailing). An adaptive management regime provides the potential for addressing changes without creating a requirement to seek formal amendment of conditions.[115]

The Supreme Court of New Zealand has held that such an adaptive management approach was available and consistent with a proper precautionary approach for managing salmon farms in coastal marine areas.[116] Three adaptive management approaches had been proposed: staged development, tiered approach to monitoring and ongoing adaptive management.[117] The court considered the threshold question of what must be present before an adaptive management approach can even be considered and responded:

> there must be an adequate evidential foundation to have reasonable assurance that the adaptive management approach will achieve its goals of sufficiently reducing uncertainty and adequately managing any remaining risk. The threshold question is an important step and must always be considered. As Preston CJ said in *Newcastle*, adaptive management is not a 'suck it and see' approach.[118]

The court considered the secondary question of what an adaptive management regime must contain in any particular case before it is legitimate to use such an approach rather than prohibiting the development until further information becomes available. The court stated that this will depend on an assessment of a combination of factors:

> (a) the extent of the environmental risk including the gravity of the consequences if the risk is realised;
> (b) the importance of the activity – which could in some circumstances be an activity it is hoped will protect the environment;
> (c) the degree of uncertainty; and
> (d) the extent to which an adaptive management approach will sufficiently diminish the risk and the uncertainty.[119]

The Land and Environment Court of NSW has found on a number of occasions that, consistent with the precautionary principle, an adaptive management approach could be implemented for proposed developments. These included a pearl farm in the waters of Port Stephens;[120] open cut and underground coal mines that might have insufficient water supply for operations;[121] longwall coal mining that might affect hydrological regimes and dependent ecosystems;[122] and a limestone quarry that might affect stygofauna.[123]

(e) Prohibiting the development

Where precautionary measures cannot reduce the threat of serious or irreversible environmental damage to acceptable levels, the appropriate action may be to prohibit the carrying out of the environmentally damaging activity. The Supreme Court of New Zealand has noted that this may be the case 'where urgent measures are needed to avert imminent potential threats, where the potential damage is likely to be irreversible and where particularly vulnerable species or ecosystems are concerned'.[124]

The Environment, Resources and Development Court of SA has found that a proposed tuna farm would be ecologically sustainable only if an adaptive management regime could be implemented but, because a regime could not be implemented, consent for the development should be refused.[125]

The Land and Environment Court of NSW has held that the scarcity of scientific knowledge about the population, habitat and behavioural patterns of two threatened fauna species and the impacts of a proposed road on the species justified the refusal of a licence to take or kill the species.[126] Similarly, the Land and Environment Court has refused development consent to an open cut coal mine, finding that the precautionary measures proposed, including compensatory biodiversity offsets, were unlikely to prevent serious and irreversible harm to an endangered ecological community.[127]

The Victorian Civil and Administrative Tribunal has held, applying the precautionary principle, that because of, first, the uncertainties associated with the potential effects on aquifers from changes in rainfall and associated recharge by reason of climate change, second, the potential seriousness of permanently depleting the groundwater storage and, third, the risk of irreversible damage to the environment, it was inappropriate to grant water extraction licences.[128]

THE PRINCIPLES OF INTERGENERATIONAL AND INTRAGENERATIONAL EQUITY

1. Introduction

The definition of ESD in WCED's report, *Our Common Future*,[129] and principle 3 of the Rio Declaration on Environment and Development[130] contain two ethical elements: concern for the poor – intragenerational justice or equity; and concern for the future – intergenerational justice or equity. Intragenerational equity describes equity within the present generation, while intergenerational equity describes equity between the present and future generations. The needs that are to be equitably shared relate to the three components of ESD: economic development, social development and environmental protection. Equity is not limited to the use or exploitation of natural resources. It extends to maintenance and enhancement of the environment. The Supreme Court of Canada referred to:

> the growing concern on the part of legislatures and of society about the safeguarding of the environment. That concern does not reflect only the collective desire to protect it in the interests of the people who live and work in it, and exploit its resources, today. It may also be evidence of an emerging sense of intergenerational solidarity and acknowledgement of an environmental debt to humanity and to the world of tomorrow.[131]

The importance to ESD of the component of environmental protection is made clear in Australia where intergenerational equity is legislatively defined to require 'that the present generation should ensure that the health, diversity and productivity of the environment are maintained or enhanced for the benefit of future generations'.[132] Similarly, intragenerational equity has been judicially recognised as involving 'people within the present generation having equal rights to benefit from the exploitation of resources and from the enjoyment of a clean and healthy environment'.[133]

2. The Concepts of Intergenerational, Intragenerational and Interspecies Equity

Brown Weiss suggests that there are three fundamental principles forming the basis of intergenerational equity.[134] First, the 'conservation of options principle' requires each generation to conserve the diversity of the natural and cultural resource base in order to ensure that options are available to future generations in solving their problems and satisfying their needs.[135] This principle rests on the premise that diversity contributes to robustness. It is argued that, while diversity may lead to change in the biological population, biodiverse ecosystems will remain robust. Thus, destructive activities – such as clear felling of tropical forests, developing crop monocultures and exhausting non-renewable resources such as fossil fuels – must be avoided to ensure that future generations have a diverse, natural and cultural base comparable to the status quo. Future generations are more likely to survive, attain their goals and be capable of solving problems as they arise if they have a variety of options available.[136]

Second, the 'conservation of quality principle' holds that each generation must maintain the quality of the natural and cultural environments such that they are passed on in no worse condition than they are received.[137] Bosselmann argues that this principle requires the preservation of the integrity of the planetary ecosystem – the natural stock – as well as of knowledge about natural resources and ways to use them – the capital stock.[138]

Third, the 'conservation of access' principle requires that each generation should give its members equitable rights of access to the legacy of past generations and should conserve this access for future generations.[139] This principle holds that the present generation should have a reasonable and equitable right of access to the natural and cultural resources of the earth. Provided the present generation upholds its duties to the future generations, each member of the present generation ought to be entitled to the resources that could improve their own economic and social wellbeing. In this way, this principle of intergenerational equity encompasses the concept of intragenerational equity.[140]

Bosselmann argues that a third element needs to be added to the two elements of intergenerational equity and intragenerational equity: namely concern for the nonhuman world – interspecies justice or equality.[141] He argues that this element is necessary to ensure ecological sustainability and ecological justice.[142]

These three principles of equity – intergenerational, intragenerational and interspecies justice – fix not only the process of consideration in decision-making but also the outcomes or results of decision-making. These include maintaining a healthy, diverse and productive environment now and in the future.[143] The three principles of equity call for distributive justice which is to be achieved by according procedural justice: a fair result reached by a fair process. How have these principles been developed by the judiciary?

3. Judicial Analysis of the Principles of Equity

(a) Intergenerational equity and environmental sustainability

The principle of intergenerational equity and the sub-principle of conservation of options underpinned the Land and Environment Court's decision to refuse development consent for a waste disposal facility on prime agricultural land.[144] The development would have precluded an area of prime crop and pasture land from being able to be used sustainably now and in the future for agricultural production. The court noted:

> The principle of intergenerational equity involves the right of the present generation to use and enjoy the resources of the earth but without compromising the ability of future generations to do likewise. The present generation needs to ensure that the health, diversity and productivity of the environment are maintained and enhanced for the benefit of future generations. This obligation of intergenerational equity would be breached by the carrying out of development which has an adverse effect on the long-term use, for sustainable agricultural production, of prime crop and pasture land. Such development compromises future generations' ability to use and enjoy to the same degree as the present generation the prime crop and agricultural land.[145]

Similarly, the Land and Environment Court, in deciding to approve a large wind farm, recognised that achieving intergenerational equity involved a consideration of the conservation of options sub-principle:

> The attainment of intergenerational equity in the production of energy involves meeting at least two requirements. The first requirement is that the mining of and the subsequent use in the production of energy of finite, fossil fuel resources needs to be sustainable. Sustainability refers not only to the exploitation and use of the resource (including rational and prudent use and the elimination of waste) but also to the environment in which the exploitation and use takes place and which may be affected. The objective is not only to extend the life of the finite resources and the benefits yielded by exploitation

> and use of the resources to future generations, but also to maintain the environment, including the ecological processes upon which life depends, for the benefit of future generations. The second requirement is, as far as is practicable, to increasingly substitute energy sources that result in less greenhouse gas emissions for energy sources that result in more greenhouse gas emissions, thereby reducing the cumulative and long-term effects caused by anthropogenic climate change. In this way, the present generation reduces the adverse consequences for future generations.[146]

The principle of intergenerational equity and the conservation of quality sub-principle have underpinned many judicial decisions in cases where development would significantly impair the quality of the environment, particularly the clearing of forests. The Supreme Court of the Philippines upheld the right of children to bring judicial review proceedings that challenged governmental decisions to grant and renew timber licences that authorised large scale deforestation and environmental damage.[147] The court held:

> We find no difficulty in ruling that they can, for themselves, for others of their generation and for the succeeding generations, file a class suit. Their personality to sue in behalf of the succeeding generations can only be based on the concept of intergenerational responsibility insofar as the right to a balanced and healthful ecology is concerned. Such a right, as hereinafter expounded, considers the 'rhythm and harmony' of nature. Nature means the created world in its entirety. Such rhythm and harmony indispensably include, inter alia, the judicious disposition, utilization, management, renewal and conservation of the country's forest, mineral, land, waters, fisheries, wildlife, off-shore areas and other natural resources to the end that their exploration, development and utilization be equitably accessible to the present as well as future generations. Needless to say, every generation has a responsibility to the next to preserve that rhythm and harmony for the full enjoyment of a balanced and healthful ecology. Put a little differently, the minors' assertion of their right to a sound environment constitutes, at the same time, the performance of their obligation to ensure the protection of that right for the generations to come.[148]

Similarly, the Supreme Court of India has set aside governmental decisions to approve factories for the manufacture of katha that required the cutting down of khair trees. The establishment of katha manufacturing units would have led to 'indiscriminate felling of khair trees which would have a deep and adverse effect upon the environment and ecology of the State' of Himachal Pradesh.[149] The court held that the governmental approval of each proposed manufacturing unit not only violated relevant national and state forest policies, it was also:

> contrary to public interest involved in preserving forest wealth, maintenance of environment and ecology and considerations of sustainable growth and intergenerational equity. After all, the present generation has no right to deplete all the existing forests and leave nothing for the next and future generations. Not keeping the above considerations in mind, it is obvious, has vitiated the approvals granted [by the government] … The obligation of sustainable development requires that a proper assessment should be made of the forest wealth and the establishment of industries based on forest produce should not only be restricted accordingly but their working should also be monitored closely to ensure that the required balance is not disturbed.[150]

The Supreme Court of India has repeatedly held that forests in India are an important part of the environment and constitute a national asset. Consequently, 'if deforestation takes place rampantly, then intergenerational equity would stand violated'.[151] Similarly, the Supreme Court of India ordered the suspension of the illegal mining of iron ore and allied minerals in the State of Karnataka when that was causing loss of scarce natural resources and wide-scale land and environmental degradation. The court found that the environment and ecology are national assets subject to intergenerational equity.[152] In Canada the principle of intergenerational equity has been invoked to declare invalid forest management plans that failed to comply with legal obligations to ensure the sustainability of the forest for future generations.[153]

(b) Intergenerational equity and cultural heritage

Courts have applied the principle of intergenerational equity together with the sub-principle of conservation of quality to cultural heritage. The Land and Environment Court of NSW upheld the principle of intergenerational equity in relation to Aboriginal cultural heritage including Aboriginal objects.[154] The Supreme Court of India has recognised the applicability of the principle of intergenerational equity in relation to two, historical, drinking water tanks that had been used for over 500 years by local villagers and pilgrims.[155] The Supreme Court of Sri Lanka applied the principle of intergenerational equity in restraining the exploration and mining of phosphate and associated minerals at Eppawela. The mining operations were likely adversely to affect monuments and irrigation schemes, including tanks and canals, of great historical and cultural significance.[156]

(c) Intergenerational equity and climate change

Courts have invoked the principle of intergenerational equity in deciding climate change cases. The Land and Environment Court of NSW has held that the failure to consider the greenhouse gas emissions from the mining of coal – that is scope 1 and 2 emissions – and from the burning of coal – that is scope 3 emissions – in the environmental assessment of a proposed open cut coal mine involved a failure to take into account the principle of intergenerational equity.[157] The Land and Environment Court based its decision to impose conditions on an approval of another coal mine to offset greenhouse gas emissions from the mining of the coal on the principle of intergenerational equity.[158] The Hague District Court in the Netherlands found the principle of intergenerational equity relevant in establishing the scope of the duty of care of the Dutch government to take measures to reduce greenhouse gas emissions.[159] In contrast, a majority of the Supreme Court of New Zealand has held that a consent authority does not need to consider the greenhouse gas emissions from the end use of coal mined from a proposed coal mine.[160]

(d) Intragenerational equity

Judicial decisions have also recognised the need for intragenerational justice and have applied the conservation of access sub-principle. The Supreme Court of India ordered a municipal government to abate the nuisance caused by inadequate sewerage and drainage systems that disproportionately affected the poor, thereby causing social injustice.[161] The Supreme Court of India has also taken judicial notice of the intragenerational injustice occasioned by the lack of necessary facilities and essential amenities and of the risk to the lives of pilgrims en route to and around a holy cave. The court gave directions and orders for measures to be undertaken to improve facilities and amenities for pilgrims.[162] Similarly, the Supreme Court of India made various orders restraining and regulating mining of limestone that was adversely affecting the forests and ecology of the Doon Valley area and the health and well-being of rural villagers.[163] The court found that the forests were 'a bequest of the past generations to the present'.[164]

(e) An integrated approach to the principles of equity

The Land and Environment Court of NSW considered each of the three principles of equity – intergenerational, intragenerational and interspecies justice – in refusing approval for a large, open cut coal mine that would have had significant and unacceptable impacts on biological diversity, including endangered ecological communities, noise and social impacts on local villagers. The court found that the economic analyses that justified the project had not considered issues of equity or distributive justice. Rather they were concerned only with the aggregation of costs and benefits and not how or why these were allocated.[165] The court noted that distributive injustice would be caused by the distribution of the burdens of the project in several ways: first, on local villagers by limiting their ability to live in a clean and healthy environment – intragenerational equity; second, on future generations by not maintaining the health, diversity and productivity of the local environment – intergenerational equity; and third, on components of biological diversity, such as endangered ecological communities and threatened fauna, by disturbing the integrity, stability and beauty of the biotic community – interspecies equity.[166]

THE PRINCIPLE OF CONSERVATION OF BIOLOGICAL DIVERSITY AND ECOLOGICAL INTEGRITY

1. The Functions Performed by the Principle

(a) The concepts underlying the principle

One of the principles of ESD concerns the conservation of biological diversity and ecological integrity. In Australia, it is formulated as a fundamental consideration to be taken into account in decision-making processes. For example, 'the conservation of biological diversity and ecological integrity should be a fundamental consideration'.[167]

Biological diversity or biodiversity refers to:

> the variability among living organisms from all sources (including terrestrial, marine and other aquatic ecosystems and the ecological complexes of which they are part) and includes:
>
> (a) diversity within species and between species;
> (b) diversity of ecosystems.[168]

More particularly, biological diversity has been defined to mean:

> the diversity of life and is made up of the following 3 components:
>
> (a) genetic diversity – the variety of genes (or units of heredity) in any population,
> (b) species diversity – the variety of species,
> (c) ecosystem diversity – the variety of communities or ecosystems.[169]

Conservation of biological diversity therefore requires the maintenance of the diversity within species and between species and the diversity of ecosystems and the maintenance of essential ecological processes and life-support systems.[170]

Ecological integrity refers to the earth's life-support systems.[171] The Land and Environment Court of NSW has described ecological integrity in these terms:

> At a macro level, ecological integrity involves conservation of the ecological processes that keep the planet fit for life. They 'shape climate, cleanse air and water, regulate water flow, recycle essential elements, create and recreate soil, and enable ecosystems to renew themselves' …
>
> Maintaining ecological integrity involves maintaining ecosystem health. Ecosystems become unhealthy if their community structure (species richness, species composition or food web architecture) or ecosystem functioning (productivity, nutrient dynamics, decomposition) has been fundamentally upset by human pressures …
>
> Maintaining ecological integrity also involves maintaining ecosystem functioning and ecosystem services. Ecosystem functioning is 'the sum total of processes such as the cycling of matter, energy, and nutrients operating at the ecosystem level' … Ecosystem services are 'the wide array of conditions and processes through which ecosystems, and their biodiversity, confer benefits on humanity; these include the production of goods, life support functions, life-fulfilling conditions, and preservation of options' …
>
> The conservation of threatened species is an essential action in the conservation of species diversity, and hence of biological diversity, and of ecological integrity.[172]

(b) The principle as a process

These formulations of the principle of conservation of biological diversity and ecological integrity describe a process – the consideration of the conservation of biological diversity and ecological integrity in decision-making. Consideration of relevant matters involves more than the matters being adverted to or given mere lip service. The decision-maker has to inform itself sufficiently to be able to take the relevant matters into consideration. For a proposed development for which approval is sought, the decision-maker has to be aware not only of the impacts and the likely harm but also of any protective or mitigative measures. There needs to be an understanding of the relevant matters and their significance to the decision required to be made as well as a process of evaluation sufficient to warrant the description of the matters being taken into consideration.[173]

Where the subject matter of the relevant issue is an outcome or objective, including a performance standard, that is to be achieved, it needs to be considered as a fundamental element in, or a focal point of, the decision-making process.[174] A decision-maker cannot ignore the prescribed standard, outcome or objective, or subvert it by applying some other standard or no standard at all, or by pursuing some other outcome or objective or none at all. A mere perfunctory acknowledgment of the existence of the relevant consideration will not suffice.[175]

(c) The principle as an outcome

The principle, however, is more than a process. Performing the process of consideration of the relevant matter of the conservation of biological diversity and ecological integrity is not an end in itself. Rather it is a means to achieve the end of ecological sustainability that lies at the core of ESD. Implementation of the principle of conservation of biological diversity and ecological integrity is, therefore, not only a process. It may also lead to a substantive outcome. This substantive outcome emerges for three reasons.

First, the subject matter of the consideration that is required is an outcome – the conservation of biological diversity and ecological integrity. This requires maintenance of the diversity within species and between species and the diversity of ecosystems and maintenance of essential ecological processes and life-support systems.

Second, the concept of biological diversity and ecological integrity is not merely a consideration: that is, something to be taken into account in decision-making. It is required to be a 'fundamental' consideration. The adjective 'fundamental' describing the noun 'consideration' means 'essential' or 'primary'. It elevates the weight and priority that must be given to the conservation of biological diversity and ecological integrity relative to any other considerations in the decision-making process.[176] Although it is generally for the decision-maker to accord such weight to relevant considerations as the decision-maker thinks appropriate, a court may set aside a decision where the decision-maker fails to give adequate weight to a relevant consideration of great importance – especially one that is classified as fundamental.[177]

Third, it needs to be remembered that the ultimate objective is to promote and maintain ESD. ESD has at its core the substantive outcome of ecological sustainability – protecting and restoring the earth's ecological systems. This substantive outcome is to be achieved by implementing the various principles of ESD, including the principle of conservation of biological diversity and ecological integrity. Although the principle in terms requires the conservation of biological diversity and ecological integrity to be only a fundamental consideration, if the substantive outcome of ESD as ecological sustainability is to be achieved, so too must the outcome of conservation of biological diversity and ecological integrity. The earth's ecological systems cannot be maintained if the diversity of life on earth and the earth's life-support systems are not protected and maintained.[178]

The consequence is that, in practice, proper consideration of the principle of conservation of biological diversity and ecological integrity ought to result in the making of a decision that promotes rather than demotes the conservation of biological diversity and ecological integrity.

2. Application of the Principle in Practice

(a) Civil proceedings

Has this analysis been supported by the approaches adopted by the courts? In particular, have they upheld the need to afford priority to the conservation of biological diversity and ecological integrity in decision-making? The Land and Environment Court of NSW refused to grant a licence to take or kill two species of endangered fauna – the Giant Burrowing Frog and the Yellow-bellied Glider – for the construction of a proposed road through their habitat.[179] In so doing, the court applied the precautionary principle. There was a scarcity of scientific knowledge about the populations and habitats of the two species and the impacts of the construction of a road on the species. The court held that the applicant for the licence needed to satisfy the court that it was appropriate in all the relevant circumstances to grant the licence to take or kill the endangered species.[180] In circumstances where the court was left in doubt as to the likely adverse effects on the long-term conservation of the two species of endangered fauna, it concluded that a licence to take or kill the species should not be granted.[181]

The Land and Environment Court upheld the need for the conservation of biological diversity and ecological integrity in refusing development consent for an industrial subdivision of land containing an endangered ecological community – the Sydney Freshwater Wetland – and an endangered plant species.[182] Similarly, the Land and Environment Court refused development consent to a large open cut coal mine in the Hunter Valley that would have had significant and unacceptable impacts on endangered ecological communities. These included in particular the Warkworth Sands Woodland, which was an endemic community with a very short range as well as key habitats of fauna species.[183] The mining project proposed no measures to avoid the impacts and few measures to mitigate the impacts. In addition the direct offsets and other compensatory measures proposed would not adequately compensate for the significant impacts on the ecological community. The court held that this was 'a fundamental matter to be considered in the decision-making process, to which significant weight should be assigned'.[184]

Giving priority to the conservation of biological diversity and ecological integrity does not always mean the refusal of approval to a project that is likely to impact on biological diversity and ecological integrity. It may be possible to impose conditions of approval to ensure the conservation of biological diversity and ecological integrity, including by requiring monitoring and adaptive management.[185]

(b) Criminal proceedings

Sentencing decisions for offences against environmental legislation have also recognised the importance of conservation of biological diversity and ecological integrity. A critical factor affecting the objective seriousness of an offence is the harmfulness of the offender's conduct. For environmental offences, the Land and Environment Court of NSW has observed:

> Harmfulness needs to not only be considered in terms of actual harm, the potential or risk of harm should also be taken into account … Harm should not be limited to measurable harm such as actual harm to human health. It can also include a broader notion of the quality of life.
>
> Harm can include harm to the environment and its ecology. Harm to an animal or plant not only adversely affects that animal or plant, it also affects other biota that have ecological relationships to that animal or plant … .
>
> Harm can be direct or indirect, individual or cumulative. Activities that contribute incrementally to the gradual deterioration of the environment, even when they cause no discernible direct harm to human interest, should also be treated seriously.[186]

Sentencing courts have recognised that harm to components of biological diversity and a loss of ecological integrity thwart the achievement of ESD and this includes a failure to apply the principle of conservation of biological diversity and ecological integrity. The culpability of an offender depends on the degree to which the offender's conduct offends against the legislative objectives, including maintenance of ESD and the conservation of biological diversity and ecological integrity.[187]

THE PRINCIPLE OF INTERNALISATION OF ENVIRONMENTAL COSTS AND IMPROVED VALUATION AND PRICING

1. The Concepts Underlying the Principle

(a) Introduction

ESD involves the internalisation of environmental costs into decision-making about economic and other development plans, programs and projects likely to affect the environment. This is the principle of the internalisation of environmental costs. The principle requires accounting for both the short-term and the long-term external and environmental costs. This can be undertaken in a number of ways, including:

(a) environmental factors being included in the valuation of assets and services;
(b) adopting the polluter pays or user pays principle, that is to say, those who generate pollution and waste should bear the cost of containment, avoidance or abatement;
(c) the users of goods and services paying prices based on the full life cycle of the costs of providing goods and services, including the use of natural resources and assets and the ultimate disposal of any waste; and
(d) environmental goals, having been established, being pursued in the most cost effective way, by establishing incentive structures, including market mechanisms, that enable those best placed to maximise benefits or minimise costs to develop their own solutions and responses to environmental problems.[188]

The rationale underlying the internalisation of environmental costs is that if the real value of the environment and of its components is reflected in the costs of using it, the environment will be sustainably used and managed and not exploited wastefully.[189]

(b) Market failure

The concept of internalisation of external costs is an economic rule to address market failure. Market failures occur when markets do not reflect the full social costs or benefits of a good or service. One cause of market failure is externalities. These are uncompensated side effects of human actions. An externality exists whenever an output of one person appears as an input in the consumption or production of another person without accompanying payment of compensation.[190]

An example is where a factory discharges waste into, and thereby pollutes, a stream. The discharged waste is an output of the production at the factory. The factory does not pay the costs of containment, avoidance or abatement of the pollution caused by the waste. Rather, the users downstream experience the negative externality of the pollution of the stream. This is an input in their consumption or production activities. The pollution of the stream has a real economic cost to the users. For example, riparian users such as irrigators may incur input costs in their agricultural production when they treat the polluted water by filtration or chemical treatment. Recreational users may suffer a diminution in the recreational services provided by the stream. The problem with a negative externality is that the people and the environment that are impacted are usually not compensated for the costs they suffer.[191]

Another cause of market failure is government subsidies of infrastructure investment that cause distortions in investment and misallocation of natural resources. Government subsidies to promote the construction of infrastructure distort cost benefit analysis. In most cost benefit analysis, the cost of previous infrastructure investments are regarded as 'sunk' costs to be excluded from the analysis. As history reveals, sunken government subsidies to promote the construction of infrastructure – such as dams, roads, railways and ports – have resulted in significant environmental degradation.[192]

(c) The polluter and user pays principles

The user pays principle and the polluter pays principle are means of dealing with governmental subsidies and negative externalities that lead to market failure. The user pays principle requires that those who benefit from investment should pay for its creation. As Young notes, 'when users have to pay for infrastructure and investment costs there is less risk of poor investments being used as an indirect means to develop marginal resources'.[193]

The polluter pays principle states that the person who causes environmental harm – the polluter – should pay the costs of the environmental harm – the pollution. Under the polluter pays principle, the polluter should pay for the costs of: preventing pollution or reducing pollution to comply with applicable standards and laws; preventing, controlling, abating and mitigating damage to the environment caused by pollution; making good any resultant environmental damage, such as cleaning up pollution and restoring the environment damaged; and making reparation, including compensatory damages and compensatory restoration, for irremediable injury.[194] By requiring the polluter to take responsibility for the external costs arising from its pollution, the principle allocates these costs to the polluter. The polluter must internalise these costs as a cost of doing business. Internalisation will be complete when the polluter takes responsibility for all the costs arising from pollution. It will be incomplete when part of the costs is shifted to society.[195]

The polluter pays principle plays a role in both the prevention of pollution, and the remediation of pollution if it were to occur. The principle plays a role in prevention by justifying decisions either not to approve development that cannot ensure the internalisation of environmental costs or to approve development only on conditions that will ensure the internalisation of environmental costs. Further, the prior knowledge that, if pollution were to occur, the polluter would be responsible for its containment, avoidance and abatement would have a deterrent effect, thereby preventing future pollution.[196] The costs of containment, avoidance and abatement of pollution are usually likely to exceed the costs of its prevention. Acting rationally, a person would undertake the cost of preventative measures rather than the cost of remedial measures.[197]

Application of the polluter pays principle affects market decisions for consumption of goods and services produced by a polluter. As Cordonier Segger and Khalfan observe:

> Instituting the polluter pays principle ensures that the prices of goods reflect the costs of producing that good, including costs associated with pollution, resource degradation, and environmental harm. Environmental costs are reflected (or 'internalized') in the price of every good. The result is that goods that pollute less will cost less, and consumers may switch to less polluting substitutes. This will result in a more efficient use of resources and less pollution.[198]

The polluter pays principle plays a role in the remediation of pollution that has occurred: first, by justifying administrative and judicial orders for clean-up, remediation and rehabilitation of the environment harmed; and, second, by making reparation, including compensation for irremediable injuries.

(d) Conclusion

The concept of internalisation of environmental costs, including the polluter pays principle and user pays principle, is concerned with process by introducing into decision-making by producers and consumers the environmental costs of production and consumption.[199] But this process is only a means to achieve the substantive end of a more sustainable use of resources with less environmental harm including less pollution. Achieving this end furthers the ultimate outcome of ecological sustainability that lies at the core of ESD.

2. Judicial Application of the Polluter and User Pays Principles

To what extent have judicial decisions recognised and applied the concept of internalisation of environmental costs, including the polluter pays principle and the user pays principle? The Supreme Court of India has held that the polluter pays principle is part of the law of the country.[200] The court, by its orders, has applied the polluter pays principle to prevent ongoing pollution, including: to abate the discharge of untreated effluent by tanneries in the State of Tamil Nadu;[201] to relocate tanneries discharging toxic effluent affecting the environment and the health of residents in Calcutta;[202] to order coke- or coal-consuming industries emitting air pollution that was damaging the Taj Mahal in Agra and the residents of the Taj Trapezium to apply for gas connection or, on failing to do so, to relocate;[203] and to order that illegally imported containers of oil, which constituted hazardous waste, lying at Nhava Sheva Port, be re-exported or destroyed at the importers' cost.[204]

The Supreme Court of India has also applied the polluter pays principle to require the polluter to pay the costs of remediation and compensation for loss and damage caused by pollution. The means include requiring chemical factories to pay the costs of carrying out remediation of polluted aquifers and soil;[205] requiring tanneries to pay the costs of removing sludge and other pollutants lying in areas affected by untreated effluent and to compensate for harm caused to the villagers, the soil and the underground water;[206] requiring tanneries to relocate and pay compensation for the loss of the ecological and environmental values of areas affected by toxic effluent and for the suffering of residents;[207] and paying compensation for the costs of restitution of the environment and ecology of a river damaged by construction of a motel.[208]

In Australia, the polluter pays principle has been applied by courts in four situations: in sentencing for environmental crime; in imposing civil orders for statutory breach – both pecuniary penalties and injunctive relief; in reviewing administrative orders imposed by regulatory agencies, including management orders to remediate contaminated land; and in imposing conditions requiring prevention, remediation and compensation in approvals for development in merit review appeals.[209]

The Land and Environment Court of NSW has applied the polluter pays principle in sentencing for environmental crime. The court has stated:

> Courts have repeatedly stated, when sentencing for environmental offences, that the sentence of the court needs to be of such magnitude as to change the economic calculus of persons in determining whether to comply with or contravene environmental laws. It should not be cheaper to offend than to prevent the commission of the offence. Environmental crime will remain profitable until the financial cost to offenders outweighs the likely gains by offending. The amount of any fine needs to be such as will make it worthwhile to incur the costs of complying with the law and undertaking the necessary precautions. The amount of the fine must be substantial enough so as not to appear as a mere licence fee for illegal activity … In this way, the sentence of the court changes the economic calculus of persons who might be tempted not to comply with environmental laws or not to undertake the necessary precautions. Compliance with the law becomes cheaper than offending. Environmental crimes become economically irrational.
>
> Sentences that have this effect result in persons who carry out activities likely to harm the environment, including causing pollution, internalising the costs of preventing and controlling pollution as well as any environmental harm itself. This is the polluter pays principle, one of the principles of ecologically sustainable development. Persons who generate pollution and waste should bear the costs of containment, avoidance or abatement … The sentence of the court should be such as to make it economically rational for such persons to incur the cost of containment, avoidance or abatement of pollution and waste.[210]

In addition, the polluter ought to be required to pay for the costs of remedying any ongoing environmental harm caused by the polluter's conduct. This can be done by ordering the polluter to clean up the pollution and restore the environment as far as practicable to the condition it was in before being polluted. The polluter also ought to be required to make reparation for irremediable harm caused by the polluter's conduct, such as the death of biota and damage to ecosystem structure and functioning.[211]

CONCLUSION

ESD and its principles have been criticised as vague and for being framed appropriately for the purpose of political aspirations but not for implementation as legal standards.[212] This impedes the achievement of ESD. As courts have recognised, in order to achieve sustainability, 'hortatory statements of principle and aspirational goals are insufficient; the grand strategy must be translated into action'. This involves institutionalising ESD and its principles in policies and laws as well as ensuring that functions under those policies and laws are performed in a way that promotes and implements ESD and its principles.[213] It also involves articulating clearly when, how and what action needs to be taken to achieve ESD.

The task of instilling ESD and its principles with legal rigour has generally fallen to the judiciary.[214] The judiciary, through its decisions, has elucidated the meaning of ESD and its principles and how they can be applied meaningfully in decision-making. These judicial pronouncements are neither complete nor comprehensive. More work needs to be done to explain the meaning and application of ESD and its principles. The judiciary has supplied many of the pieces of the 1,000-piece jigsaw puzzle of ESD. Patches of the picture are starting to emerge, but there are gaps. Future judicial decisions need to supply more jigsaw pieces to bring the whole picture of ESD into full view.

NOTES

1. Pound (1954, p. 48). For application of this process of adjudication to environmental disputes, see Preston (2008, p. 103).
2. Pound (1999, p. 179).
3. Hart (1994, p. 272).
4. Ibid. (p. 273).
5. Cane (2000, p. 237).
6. Dworkin (1978, pp. 115–18).
7. Dworkin (1986, ch.5).
8. Dworkin (1998, p. 90).
9. *Telstra Corp Ltd v Hornsby Shire Council* [2006] NSWLEC 133; (2006) 67 NSWLR 256, 268 [121]–[124]; *Minister for Planning v Walker* [2008] NSWCA 224; (2008) 161 LGERA 423, 451 [42], [43]; *Warkworth Mining Ltd v Bulga Milbrodale Progress Association Inc* [2014] NSWCA 105; (2014) 86 NSWLR 527, 587–8 [295]–[296].
10. Fitzgerald (1966, pp. 70, 71).
11. French (2008, p. 328).
12. Fitzgerald (1966, pp. 68–71).
13. Pound (1954, pp. 53, 56, 63).
14. For example, Environmental Planning and Assessment Act 1979 (NSW) s 124(1).
15. *F Hannan Pty Ltd v Electricity Commission (NSW) (No.3)* (1985) 66 LGRA 306, 311.
16. Ibid.; see also *Warringah Shire Council v Sedevcic* (1987) 10 NSWLR 335, 338–41.
17. *Warringah Shire Council v Sedevcic* (1987) 10 NSWLR 335, 339.
18. *Willoughby City Council v Minister Administering the National Parks and Wildlife Act* (1992) 78 LGERA 19, 34.
19. Pound (1999, pp. 202–203); Sax (1970, p. 471).

20. For example, Environment Protection and Biodiversity Conservation Act 1999 (Cth) s 3A.
21. Protection of the Environment Administration Act 1991 (NSW) s 6(1)(a).
22. Threatened Species Conservation Act 1995 (NSW) s 3(a).
23. WCED (1987, p. 44, ch.2, para.1); adopted by the United Nations General Assembly, *Report of the World Commission on Environment and Development* GA Res 42/187, UN GAOR, 2nd Comm, Agenda Item 82e (11 December 1987) A/Res/42/87; included by the UK Department for Communities and Local Government in the *National Planning Policy Framework* (March 2012, p. 2); cited in *Telstra Corp Ltd v Hornsby Shire Council* [2006] NSWLEC 133; (2006) 67 NSWLR 256, 265 [108]; *MC Mehta v Union of India* [2004] INSC 179; AIR 2004 SC 4016, 4044 [46].
24. Protection of the Environment Administration Act 1991 (NSW) s 6(2); adopted by Environmental Planning and Assessment Act 1979 (NSW) s 4(1); Threatened Species Conservation Act 1995 (NSW) s 4(1).
25. For example, Environment Protection and Biodiversity Conservation Act 1999 (Cth) s 3A; Protection of the Environment Administration Act 1991 (NSW) s 6(2); Environmental Planning and Assessment Act 1979 (NSW) s 4(1); Threatened Species Conservation Act 1995 (NSW) s 4(1).
26. Fisher (2014, p. 47).
27. Ibid. (pp. 173, 174, 219, 331, 332).
28. Ibid. (p. 219).
29. Fisher (2013, p. 64).
30. UK Government's Sustainable Development Strategy, *Securing the Future* (The Stationary Office, March 2005) 17.
31. *National Strategy for Ecologically Sustainable Development* (Australian Government Publishing Service, 1992) 8.
32. *Fuel Retailers Association of Southern Africa v Director-General Environmental Management, Department of Agriculture, Conservation and Environment, Mpumalanga Province* [2007] ZACC 13; 2007 (6) SA 4 (CC), 21 [44].
33. Bosselmann (2008, pp. 53, 57).
34. Ibid. (p. 53).
35. *People United for Better Living in Calcutta v State of West Bengal* AIR 1993 Cal 215, 217 [2].
36. Ibid. 227–8 [29]–[30], 231 [40].
37. *Narmada Bachao Andolan v Union of India* [2000] INSC 518; AIR 2000 SC 3751, 3804 [150]; *MC Mehta v Union of India* [2004] INSC 179; AIR 2004 SC 4016, 4044 [46].
38. Mauerhofer, Hubacek and Coleby (2013, p. 43).
39. *Environmental Defence Society Inc v The New Zealand King Salmon Company Ltd* [2014] NZSC 38; [2014] 1 NZLR 593.
40. Resource Management Act 1991 (NZ) s 5(1).
41. Ibid. s 5(2).
42. *Environmental Defence Society Inc v The New Zealand King Salmon Company Ltd* [2014] NZSC 38; [2014] 1 NZLR 593, 618 [25].
43. See Resource Management Act 1991 (NZ) ss 56, 57.
44. New Zealand Coastal Policy Statement 2010, objective 2, policies 13, 15.
45. *Environmental Defence Society Inc v The New Zealand King Salmon Company Ltd* [2014] NZSC 38; [2014] 1 NZLR 593, 651 [132].
46. Ibid. 656 [149].
47. Resource Management Act 1991 (NZ) s 67(3).
48. *Environmental Defence Society Inc v The New Zealand King Salmon Company Ltd* [2014] NZSC 38; [2014] 1 NZLR 593, 657–8 [152]–[154].

49. *Northcompass Inc v Hornsby Shire Council* (1996) 130 LGERA 248, 264–5; *Telstra Corp Ltd v Hornsby Shire Council* [2006] NSWLEC 133; (2006) 67 NSWLR 256, 280 [182]–[183]; *Blue Wedges Inc v Minister for Environment, Heritage and the Arts* [2008] FCA 399; (2008) 167 FCR 463, 480–81 [76]–[78].
50. Sands and Peel (2012, pp. 207, 210–13, 217); cited in *Telstra Corp Ltd v Hornsby Shire Council* [2006] NSWLEC 133; (2006) 67 NSWLR 256, 265 [109]; *BP Southern Africa (Pty) Limited v MEC for Agriculture, Conservation, Environment and Land Affairs* 2004 (5) SA 124 (WLD) 143–4.
51. Environment Protection and Biodiversity Conservation Act 1999 (Cth) s 3(1)(b).
52. Ibid. s 528.
53. Sustainable Planning Act 2009 (Qld) s 3(a).
54. Ibid. s 5(1)(b).
55. Ibid. s 8.
56. Ibid. s 11(a).
57. *Conservation Council of SA Inc v Development Assessment Commission and Tuna Boat Owners Association of SA (No.2)* [1999] SAERDC 86 (16 December 1999).
58. Ibid. [37]; affirmed on appeal in *Tuna Boat Owners Association of SA Inc v Development Assessment Commission* [2000] SASC 238; (2000) 77 SASR 369, 370 [6], 374–5 [32]–[34].
59. *Conservation Council of SA Inc v Development Assessment Commission and Tuna Boat Owners Association of SA (No.2)* [1999] SAERDC 86 (16 December 1999), [35].
60. Ibid. [41].
61. Ibid. [44].
62. *Hub Action Group Inc v Minister for Planning* [2008] NSWLEC 116; (2008) 161 LGERA 136.
63. Ibid. 145 [32].
64. Ibid. 146 [33].
65. Ibid. 147 [36].
66. Ibid. 157–8 [69]–[71].
67. See Environment Protection and Biodiversity Conservation Act 1999 (Cth) s 3A(a); Protection of the Environmental Administration Act 1991 (NSW) s 6(2); Rio Declaration on the Environment and Development 31 ILM 874 (1992) principle 4.
68. As was recognised in *Telstra Corp Ltd v Hornsby Shire Council* [2006] NSWLEC 133; (2006) 67 NSWLR 256, 266 [110].
69. Plan of Implementation of the World Summit on Sustainable Development (Johannesburg 2002), [2]; cited in *Telstra Corp Ltd v Hornsby Shire Council* [2006] NSWLEC 133; (2006) 67 NSWLR 256, 266 [112].
70. Cordonier Segger and Khalfan (2004, p. 104); Sands and Peel (2012, p. 207).
71. Sands and Peel (2012, p. 215).
72. *Bentley v BGP Properties Pty Ltd* [2006] NSWLEC 34; (2006) 145 LGERA 234, 245 [67]; adopted in *Gray v Minister for Planning* [2006] NSWLEC 720; (2006) 152 LGERA 258, 291 [116]; see also *Director-General, Department of Environment and Climate Change v Rae* [2009] NSWLEC 137; (2009) 168 LGERA 121, 129 [17].
73. *Gray v Minister for Planning* [2006] NSWLEC 720; (2006) 152 LGERA 258, 294 [126], 296 [135].
74. Ibid. 293 [118], 294 [127], 295 [131], 296 [133]–[134]; Peel (2008, pp. 17–22).
75. *MyEnvironment Inc v VicForests* [2012] VSC 91, [62]; affirmed on appeal *MyEnvironment Inc v VicForests* [2013] VSCA 356; (2013) 198 LGERA 396, 412 [40], 440 [142].
76. Bosselmann (2008, p. 25).
77. Ibid. (pp. 30–31).

78. Ibid. (p. 31).
79. Sustainable Planning Act 2009 (Qld) s 8.
80. *Chesol Pty Ltd v Logan City Council* [2007] QPEC 1; [2007] QPELR 285, 299–300 [87].
81. Bosselmann (2008, p. 23).
82. Ibid. (p. 41).
83. *Chesol Pty Ltd v Logan City Council* [2007] QPEC 1; [2007] QPELR 285, 300 [90].
84. Rio Declaration on Environment and Development 31 ILM 874 (1992) principle 15.
85. See also Environment Protection and Biodiversity Conservation Act 1999 (Cth) s 3A(b).
86. Godden and Peel (2010, p. 137); Preston (2005, pp. 133–74); Preston (2008, pp. 115–21); Estcourt (2014, p. 288).
87. Bosselmann (2008, p. 60).
88. *Vellore Citizens Welfare Forum v Union of India* AIR 1996 SC 2715, 2721 [13]; *MC Mehta v Kamal Nath* (1997) 1 SCC 388, [37], [38]; *AP Pollution Control Board v Prof MV Nayudu* AIR 1999 SC 812, 818–21; *MC Mehta v Union of India* [2004] INSC 179; AIR 2004 SC 4016, 4045 [48].
89. *BGP Properties v Lake Macquarie City Council* [2004] NSWLEC 399; (2004) 138 LGERA 237, 262 [113]; *Telstra Corp Ltd v Hornsby Shire Council* [2006] NSWLEC 133; (2006) 67 NSWLR 256, 268 [124]; *Minister for Planning v Walker* [2008] NSWCA 224; (2008) 161 LGERA 423, 451 [42]–[43].
90. *Telstra Corp Ltd v Hornsby Shire Council* [2006] NSWLEC 133; (2006) 67 NSWLR 256, 269 [128]; applied in *Environment East Gippsland Inc v VicForests* [2010] VSC 335, [188]; *MyEnvironment Inc v VicForests* [2012] VSC 91, [272].
91. Peel criticises the separation of the threat and uncertainty assessments: Peel (2007, p. 103).
92. *Telstra Corp Ltd v Hornsby Shire Council* [2006] NSWLEC 133; (2006) 67 NSWLR 256, 269 [129].
93. *Conservation Council of South Australia v Development Assessment Committee and Tuna Boat Owners Association (No.2)* [1999] SAERDC 86 (16 December 1999), [24].
94. *Environment East Gippsland Inc v VicForests* [2010] VSC 335; (2010) 30 VR 1, 47 [191]; citing *Wyong Shire Council v Shirt* (1980) 146 CLR 40, 47–8.
95. *Telstra Corp Ltd v Hornsby Shire Council* [2006] NSWLEC 133; (2006) 67 NSWLR 256, 269 [130].
96. Ibid. 269–70 [131]; cited in *Environment East Gippsland Inc v VicForests* [2010] VSC 335; (2010) 30 VR 1, 47 [190]; *MyEnvironment Inc v VicForests* [2012] VSC 91, [274].
97. *Telstra Corp Ltd v Hornsby Shire Council* [2006] NSWLEC 133; (2006) 67 NSWLR 256, 271 [138].
98. For example, *Hutchinson Telecommunications (Australia) Pty Ltd v Baulkham Hills Shire Council* [2004] NSWLEC 104, [27]; *Telstra Corp Ltd v Hornsby Shire Council* [2006] NSWLEC 133; (2006) 67 NSWLR 256, 280 [184]–[185].
99. *MyEnvironment Inc v VicForests* [2012] VSC 91, [277], [341]; upheld on appeal *MyEnvironment Inc v VicForests* [2013] VSCA 356; (2013) 198 LGERA 396.
100. *Leatch v National Parks and Wildlife Service* (1993) 81 LGERA 270, 282; *Telstra Corp Ltd v Hornsby Shire Council* [2006] NSWLEC 133; (2006) 67 NSWLR 256, 271 [140].
101. *Telstra Corp Ltd v Hornsby Shire Council* [2006] NSWLEC 133; (2006) 67 NSWLR 256, 271 [141]; cited in *Environment East Gippsland Inc v VicForests* [2010] VSC 335; (2010) 30 VR 1, 48 [195].

102. *Telstra Corp Ltd v Hornsby Shire Council* [2006] NSWLEC 133; (2006) 67 NSWLR 256, 272 [146]–[147].
103. *Environment East Gippsland Inc v VicForests* [2010] VSC 335; (2010) 30 VR 1, 48 [197].
104. *Telstra Corp Ltd v Hornsby Shire Council* [2006] NSWLEC 133; (2006) 67 NSWLR 256, 273 [149].
105. Ibid. 273 [150].
106. Ibid. 273 [151]–[152]; *Conservation Council of South Australia v Development Assessment Committee and Tuna Boat Owners Association (No.2)* [1999] SAERDC 86 (16 December 1999), [24]–[25]; *Tuna Boat Owners Association of SA Inc v Development Assessment Commission* [2000] SASC 238; (2000) 77 SASR 369, 373–4 [27]–[30]; *Vellore Citizens Welfare Forum v Union of India* AIR 1996 SC 2715, 2720–21 [11]; *AP Pollution Control Board v Prof MV Nayudu* AIR 1999 SC 812, 821 [37]–[39]; *Narmada Bachao Andolan v Union of India* [2000] INSC 518; AIR 2000 SC 3751, 3803–804 [150].
107. *Telstra Corp Ltd v Hornsby Shire Council* [2006] NSWLEC 133; (2006) 67 NSWLR 256, 276 [161].
108. *Zia v WAPDA* PLD 1994 SC 693, [10], [16].
109. *Telstra Corp Ltd v Hornsby Shire Council* [2006] NSWLEC 133; (2006) 67 NSWLR 256, 276 [162].
110. *Providence Projects Pty Ltd v Gosford City Council* [2006] NSWLEC 52; (2006) 147 LGERA 274, 289 [76]–[81].
111. *BT Goldsmith Planning Services Pty Ltd v Blacktown City Council* [2005] NSWLEC 210, [73], [88]; *Gales Holdings Pty Ltd v Tweed Shire Council* [2006] NSWLEC 85; (2006) 146 LGERA 236, 246–8 [56], [60], [66]–[69]; *Gales Holdings Pty Ltd v Tweed Shire Council* [2006] NSWLEC 212, [44]–[47].
112. *Telstra Corp Ltd v Hornsby Shire Council* [2006] NSWLEC 133; (2006) 67 NSWLR 256, 726 [163]; *Environment East Gippsland Inc v VicForest*s [2010] VSC 335; (2010) 30 VR 1, 49 [205].
113. *Telstra Corp Ltd v Hornsby Shire Council* [2006] NSWLEC 133; (2006) 67 NSWLR 256, 276 [164]; see also *Sustain Our Sounds Inc v The New Zealand King Salmon Company Ltd* [2014] NZSC 40; [2014] 1 NZLR 673, 703 [109].
114. *Newcastle and Hunter Valley Speleological Society Inc v Upper Hunter Shire Council and Stoneco Pty Ltd* [2010] NSWLEC 48, [183].
115. Ibid. [184], [187].
116. *Sustain Our Sounds Inc v The New Zealand King Salmon Company Ltd* [2014] NZSC 40; [2014] 1 NZLR 673, 716 [158].
117. Ibid. 702 [104].
118. Ibid. 708 [125].
119. Ibid. 709 [129].
120. *Port Stephens Pearls Pty Ltd v Minister for Infrastructure and Planning* [2005] NSWLEC 426, [56]–[58].
121. *Ulan Coal Mines Ltd v Minister for Planning* [2008] NSWLEC 185; (2008) 160 LGERA 20, 40 [98], [99].
122. *Rivers SOS Inc v Minister for Planning* [2009] NSWLEC 213; (2009) 178 LGERA 347, 379 [131].
123. *Newcastle and Hunter Valley Speleological Society Inc v Upper Hunter Shire Council and Stoneco Pty Ltd* [2010] NSWLEC 48, [187]–[189].
124. *Sustain Our Sounds v The New Zealand King Salmon Company* [2014] NZSC 40; [2014] 1 NZLR 673, 704 [111].
125. *Conservation Council of South Australia v Development Assessment Committee and Tuna Boat Owners Association (No.2)* [1999] SAERDC 86 (16 December 1999);

affirmed on appeal *Tuna Boat Owners Association of SA Inc v Development Assessment Commission* [2000] SASC 238; (2000) 77 SASR 369.
126. *Leatch v National Parks and Wildlife Service* (1993) 81 LGERA 270, 284, 286–7.
127. *Bulga Milbrodale Progress Association Inc v Minister for Planning and Infrastructure and Warkworth Mining Ltd* [2013] NSWLEC 48; (2013) 194 LGERA 347.
128. *Alanvale Pty Ltd v Southern Rural Water* [2010] VCAT 480, [154]–[159], [200].
129. 'Development that meets the needs of the present without compromising the ability of future generations to meet their own needs': WCED (1987, p. 44, ch.2, para.1).
130. 'The right to development must be fulfilled so as to equitably meet developmental and environmental needs of present and future generations': Rio Declaration on Environment and Development 31 ILM 874 (1992).
131. *Imperial Oil Ltd v Quebec (Minister of the Environment)* 2003 SCC 58; [2003] 2 SCR 624, 640 [19].
132. Environment Protection and Biodiversity Conservation Act 1999 (Cth) s 3A(c); Protection of the Environment Administration Act 1991 (NSW) s 6(2)(b).
133. *Telstra Corp Ltd v Hornsby Shire Council* [2006] NSWLEC 133; (2006) 67 NSWLR 256, 267 [117]; citing Boer (1995, p. 320).
134. See discussion in Preston (2005, pp. 176–7); cited in *Gray v Minister for Planning* [2006] NSWLEC 720; (2006) 152 LGERA 258, 293 [119].
135. Brown Weiss (1992, pp. 397, 401); Brown Weiss (1989).
136. Brown Weiss (1992, pp. 402–404).
137. Ibid. (pp. 401, 404–405).
138. Bosselmann (2008, pp. 98–9).
139. Brown Weiss (1992, p. 401).
140. Ibid. (p. 405).
141. Bosselmann (2008, p. 99).
142. Ibid. (pp. 100–101)
143. Fisher (2014, p. 343).
144. *Hub Action Group Inc v Minister for Planning* [2008] NSWLEC 116; (2008) 161 LGERA 136.
145. Ibid. 158 [72].
146. *Taralga Landscape Guardians Inc v Minister for Planning* [2007] NSWLEC 59; (2007) 161 LGERA 1, 12 [74].
147. *Minors Oposa v Secretary of the Department of Environment and Natural Resources* GR No 101083, 30 July 1993; 33 ILM 173 (1994).
148. Ibid. 185.
149. *State of Himachal Pradesh v Ganesh Wood Products* [1995] INSC 482; AIR 1996 SC 149, 152 [10].
150. Ibid. 163 [51].
151. *Glanrock Estate Pvt Ltd v State of Tamil Nadu* [2010] INSC 723; [2010] 12 SCR 597, 624; *Court On Its Own Motion v Union of India* WP (C) 284 of 2012, SC, 13 December 2012; [2012] INSC 783, [1], [14]; see also *TN Godavarman Thirumulpad v Union of India* [2005] INSC 504; AIR 2005 SC 4256, 4259 [1]–[3], 4279–80 [89]–[92] (*Valuation of Forests* case).
152. *Samaj Parivartana Samudaya v State of Karnataka* [2013] INSC 463; AIR 2013 SC 3217, 3237 [31], 3242 [41]; see also *AP Pollution Control Board v Prof MV Nayudu* AIR 1999 SC 812, 824 [51]; *Tirupur Dyeing Factory Owners Association v Noyyal River Ayacutdars Protection Association* [2009] INSC 1624; AIR 2010 SC 3645, 3651 [17].
153. *Algonquin Wildlands League v Ontario (Minister for Natural Resources)* (1998) 110 OAC 201, 26 CELR (NS) 163 (Ontario Divisional Court), [13], [14], [138], [203], [237]; see also De Marco (2004, pp. 22–5).

154. *Anderson v Director General, Department of Environment and Conservation* [2006] NSWLEC 12; (2006) 144 LGERA 43, 91–2 [199]–[200]; *Anderson v Director General, Department of Environment and Climate Change* [2008] NSWCA 337; (2008) 163 LGERA 400, 426–7 [85]–[92].
155. *Intellectuals Forum Tiruphathi v State of Andhra Pradesh* [2006] INSC 86; AIR 2006 SC 1350.
156. *Bulankulama v Secretary, Ministry of Industrial Development* 2000 (3) SLR 243.
157. *Gray v Minister for Planning* [2006] NSWLEC 720; (2006) 152 LGERA 258, 294 [126]; see also *Thornton v Adelaide Hills Council* [2006] SAERDC 41; (2006) 151 LGERA 1, 12–13 [47].
158. *Hunter Environment Lobby Inc v Minister for Planning* [2011] NSWLEC 221, [19]–[21], [100].
159. *Urgenda Foundation v The State of the Netherlands (Ministry of Infrastructure and the Environment)* C/09/456689/HA ZA 13-1396 (Rechtbank Den Haag) (24 June 2015), [4.8], [4.56], [4.57].
160. *West Coast Ent Inc v Buller Coal Ltd* [2013] NZSC 87; [2014] 1 NZLR 32.
161. *Ratlam Municipal Council v Vardhichand* [1980] INSC 138; AIR 1980 SC 1622, 1629 [15]–[16].
162. *Court On Its Own Motion v Union of India*, WP (C) 284 of 2012, SC, 13 December 2012; [2012] INSC 783.
163. *Rural Litigation and Entitlement Kendera v State of Uttar Pradesh* AIR 1988 SC 2187.
164. Ibid. 2196 [21]; see also 2197 [24].
165. *Bulga Milbrodale Progress Association Inc v Minister for Planning and Infrastructure and Warkworth Mining Ltd* [2013] NSWLEC 48; (2013) 194 LGERA 347, 449 [485].
166. Ibid. 449–51 [486]–[494].
167. Environment Protection and Biodiversity Conservation Act 1999 (Cth) s 3A; Protection of the Environment Administration Act 1999 (NSW) s 6(2)(c).
168. Environment Protection Biodiversity and Conservation Act 1999 (Cth) s 528.
169. Threatened Species Conservation Act 1995 (NSW) s 4(1).
170. See *National Strategy for Ecological Sustainable Development* (Australian Government Publishing Service, 1992) 8.
171. Moffet and Bregha (1996, p. 4); Preston (2005, p. 187).
172. *Bentley v BGP Properties Pty Ltd* [2006] NSWLEC 34; (2006) 145 LGERA 234, 243–4 [60]–[63].
173. *Weal v Bathurst City Council* [2000] NSWCA 88; (2000) 111 LGERA 181, 185 [13], 201 [80], 202 [86]; *Anderson v Director General, Department of Environment and Climate Change* [2008] NSWCA 337; (2008) 163 LGERA 400, 421 [58]; *Warkworth Mining Ltd v Bulga Milbrodale Progress Association Inc* [2014] NSWCA 105; (2014) 86 NSWLR 527, 572 [214]–[215].
174. *Zhang v Canterbury City Council* [2001] NSWCA 167; (2001) 51 NSWLR 589, 602 [75].
175. *Warkworth Mining Ltd v Bulga Milbrodale Progress Inc* [2014] NSWCA 105; (2014) 86 NSWLR 527, 572 [215].
176. Fisher (2014, p. 343).
177. *Warkworth Mining Ltd v Bulga Milbrodale Progress Association Inc* [2014] NSWCA 105; (2014) 86 NSWLR 527, 568 [196].
178. Hooper et al. (2012, p. 105); Cardinale (2012, pp. 60–1).
179. *Leatch v National Parks and Wildlife Service and Shoalhaven City Council* (1993) 81 LGERA 270.
180. Ibid. 286–7.
181. Ibid. 284, 286–7.

182. *BGP Properties Pty Ltd v Lake Macquarie City Council* [2004] NSWLEC 399; (2004) 138 LGERA 237, 271 [150].
183. *Bulga Milbrodale Progress Association Inc v Minister for Planning and Infrastructure and Warkworth Mining Ltd* [2013] NSWLEC 48; (2013) 194 LGERA 347.
184. Ibid. 397 [255].
185. *Telstra Corp Ltd v Hornsby Shire Council* [2006] NSWLEC 133; (2006) 67 NSWLR 256, 276–7 [164]–[165]; *Newcastle and Hunter Valley Speleological Society Inc v Upper Hunter Shire Council and Stoneco Pty Ltd* [2010] NSWLEC 48, [183]–[187].
186. *Environment Protection Authority v Waste Recycling and Processing Corporation* [2006] NSWLEC 419; (2006) 148 LGERA 299, 325 [145]–[147]; see also *Bentley v BGP Properties Pty Ltd* [2006] NSWLEC 34; (2006) 145 LGERA 234, 260–61 [173]–[178].
187. *Bentley v BGP Properties Pty Ltd* [2006] NSWLEC 34; (2006) 145 LGERA 234, 260 [170]–[171] (clearing of a threatened plant species); *Garrett v Williams* [2006] NSWLEC 785; (2006) 160 LGERA 115, 133 [89], [90] (clearing of an endangered ecological community); *Director-General, Department of Environment and Climate Change v Rae* [2009] NSWLEC 137; (2009) 168 LGERA 121, 128–9 [15]–[20] (clearing of native vegetation); *Plath v Rawson* [2009] NSWLEC 178; (2009) 170 LGERA 253, 264–6 [49]–[56] (clearing of many threatened plant species).
188. *Telstra Corp Ltd v Hornsby Shire Council* [2006] NSWLEC 133; (2006) 67 NSWLR 256, 267 [119]; see also Protection of the Environment Administration Act 1991 (NSW) s 6(2)(d).
189. Preston (2005, pp. 193–4).
190. Krutilla and Fisher (1975, p. 27).
191. Preston (2015, p. 307).
192. Young (1999, p. 148).
193. Ibid.
194. Preston (2009, p. 259).
195. de Sadeleer (2002, p. 21).
196. ANZECC (1994, pp. 5–6); Kingsbury (1998, p. 41).
197. See *Axer Pty Ltd v Environment Protection Authority* (1993) 113 LGERA 357, 359–60; *Bentley v BGP Properties Pty Ltd* [2006] NSWLEC 34; (2006) 145 LGERA 234, 257–8 [156]–[157].
198. Cordonier Segger and Khalfan (2004, pp. 82–3).
199. Fisher (2014, p. 343).
200. *Indian Council for Enviro-Legal Action v Union of India* AIR 1996 SC 1446, 1466 [67]; *Vellore Citizens Welfare Forum v Union of India* AIR 1996 SC 2715, 2721 [12], [13]; *MC Mehta v Union of India* (1997) 2 SCC 411; 1996 (10) Suppl SCR 383, [18], [19] (*Calcutta Tanneries* case); *MC Mehta v Union of India* AIR 1997 SC 734, 760–61 [26] (*Taj Trapezium* case); *MC Mehta v Kamal Nath* (1997) 1 SCC 388, [37]–[38] (*River Beas* case).
201. *Vellore Citizens Welfare Forum v Union of India* AIR 1996 SC 2715.
202. *MC Mehta v Union of India* (1997) 2 SCC 411; 1996 (10) Suppl SCR 383, [20] (*Calcutta Tanneries* case).
203. *MC Mehta v Union of India* AIR 1997 SC 734 (*Taj Trapezium* case).
204. *Research Foundation for Science Technology and Natural Resources Policy v Union of India* [2005] INSC 14; (2005) 10 SCC 570.
205. *Indian Council for Enviro-Legal Action v Union of India* AIR 1996 SC 1446.
206. *Vellore Citizens Welfare Forum v Union of India* AIR 1996 SC 2715, 2720–21 [11].
207. *MC Mehta v Union of India* (1997) 2 SCC 411; 1996 (10) Suppl SCR 383, [20] (*Calcutta Tanneries* case).

208. *MC Mehta v Kamal Nath* (1997) 1 SCC 388, [39] (*River Beas* case); see also *MC Mehta v Kamal Nath* AIR 2000 SC 1997, [1], [24].
209. Preston (2009, pp. 259–66).
210. *Bankstown City Council v Hanna* [2014] NSWLEC 152; (2014) 205 LGERA 39, 68–9 [152]–[153]; see also *Axer Pty Ltd v Environment Protection Authority* (1993) 113 LGERA 357, 359–60; *Bentley v BGP Properties Pty Ltd* [2006] NSWLEC 34; (2006) 145 LGERA 234, 257–8 [156]–[157]; *Environment Protection Authority v Waste Recycling and Processing Corporation* [2006] NSWLEC 419; (2006) 148 LGERA 299, 341 [229]–[232].
211. *Environment Protection Authority v Waste Recycling and Processing Corporation* [2006] NSWLEC 419; (2006) 148 LGERA 299, 341 [230].
212. *Nicholls v Director-General of National Parks and Wildlife* (1994) 84 LGERA 397, 419.
213. *Hub Action Group Inc v Minister for Planning* [2008] NSWLEC 116; (2008) 161 LGERA 136, 141 [2].
214. Godden and Peel (2010, p. 139).

REFERENCES

ANZECC (1994), Australian and New Zealand Environment Conservation Council, *Financial Liability for Contaminated Site Remediation: A Position Paper.*

Boer, Ben (1995), 'Institutionalising Ecologically Sustainable Development: The Roles of National, State, and Local Governments in Translating Grand Strategy into Action' 31 *Willamette Law Review* 307.

Bosselmann, Klaus (2008), *The Principle of Sustainability: Transforming Law and Governance* (Oxford, Ashgate).

Brown Weiss, Edith (1989), *In Fairness to Future Generations: International Law, Common Patrimony, and Intergenerational Equity* (New York, Transnational Publishers).

Brown Weiss, Edith (1992), 'Intergenerational Equity: A Legal Framework for Global Environmental Change' in Edith Brown Weiss (ed.), *Environmental Change and International Law: New Challenges and Dimensions* (Tokyo, United Nations University Press).

Cane, Peter (2000), 'Merits Review and Judicial Review – the AAT as a Trojan Horse' 28 *Federal Law Review* 213.

Cardinale, Bradley J. (2012), 'Biodiversity Loss and its Impact on Humanity' 486 *Nature* 59.

Cordonier Segger, Marie-Claire and Ashfaq Khalfan (2004), *Sustainable Development Law: Principles, Practices and Prospects* (Oxford, Oxford University Press).

De Marco, Jerry V. (2004), 'Law for Future Generations: The Theory of Intergenerational Equity in Canadian Environmental Law' 15 *Journal of Environmental Law and Practice* 1.

de Sadeleer, Nicolas (2002), *Environmental Principles – From Political Slogans to Legal Rules* (Oxford, Oxford University Press).

Dworkin, Ronald (1978), *Taking Rights Seriously* (Cambridge, Harvard University Press).

Dworkin, Ronald (1986), *A Matter of Principle* (Cambridge, Harvard University Press).

Dworkin, Ronald (1998), *Laws' Empire* (first published 1986, Oxford, Hart Publishing).

Estcourt, Stephen (2014), 'The Precautionary Principle, the Coast and Temwood Holdings' 31 *Environmental and Planning Law Journal* 288.

Fisher, Douglas (2013), *Legal Reasoning in Environmental Law: A Study of Structure, Form and Language* (Cheltenham, Edward Elgar).

Fisher, D.E. (2014), *Australian Environmental Law: Norms, Principles and Rules* (3rd edn, Sydney, Law Book Co).
Fitzgerald, P.J. (1966), *Salmond on Jurisprudence* (12th edn, New York, Sweet & Maxwell).
French, R.S. (2008), 'Dolores Umbridge and Policy as Legal Magic' 82 *Australian Law Journal* 322.
Godden, Lee and Jacqueline Peel (2010), *Environmental Law: Scientific, Policy and Regulatory Dimensions* (Oxford, Oxford University Press).
Hart, H.L.A. (1994), *The Concept of Law* (2nd edn, Oxford, Oxford University Press).
Hooper, David U., E. Carol Adair, Bradley J. Cardinale, Jarrett E.K. Byrnes, Bruce A. Hungate, Kristin L. Matulich, Andrew Gonzalez, J. Emmett Duffy, Lars Gamfeldt and Mary I. O'Connor (2012), 'A Global Synthesis Reveals Biodiversity Loss as a Major Driver of Ecosystem Change' 486 *Nature* 105.
Kingsbury, Anna (1998), 'Funding the Remediation of Contaminated Land in Australia and New Zealand: The Problem of Orphan Sites' 6 *Waikato Law Review* 37.
Krutilla, John V. and Anthony C. Fisher (1975), *The Economics of Natural Environments: Studies in the Valuation of Commodity and Amenity Resources* (Washington DC, Resources for the Future).
Mauerhofer, Volker, Klaus Hubacek and Alastor Coleby (2013), 'From Polluter Pays to Provider Gets: Distribution of Rights and Costs under Payments for Ecosystem Services' 18(4) *Ecology and Society* 41.
Moffet, John and Francois Bregha (1996), 'The Role of Law Reform in the Promotion of Sustainable Development' 6 *Journal of Environmental Law and Practice* 1.
Peel, Jacqueline (2007), 'When (Scientific) Rationality Rules: (Mis)Application of the Precautionary Principle in Australian Mobile Phone Tower Cases' 19 *Journal of Environmental Law* 103.
Peel, Jacqueline (2008), 'Ecologically Sustainable Development: More than Mere Lip Service?' 12 *The Australasian Journal of Natural Resources Law and Policy* 1.
Pound, Roscoe (1954), *An Introduction to the Philosophy of Law* (first published 1922, New Haven, Yale University Press).
Pound, Roscoe (1999), *The Spirit of the Common Law* (first published 1963, New Brunswick, Transaction Publishers).
Preston, Brian J. (2005), 'The Role of the Judiciary in Promoting Sustainable Development: The Experience of Asia and the Pacific' 9 *Asia Pacific Journal of Environmental Law* 109.
Preston, Brian J (2008), 'The Art of Judging Environmental Disputes' 12 *Southern Cross University Law Review* 103.
Preston, Brian J. (2009), 'Sustainable Development Law in the Courts: The Polluter Pays Principle' 26 *Environmental and Planning Law Journal* 257.
Preston, Brian J. (2015), 'Economic Valuation of the Environment' 32 *Environment and Planning Law Journal* 301.
Sands, Philippe and Jacqueline Peel, with Adriana Fabra and Ruth MacKenzie (2012), *Principles of International Environmental Law* (3rd edn, Cambridge, Cambridge University Press).
Sax, Joseph L. (1970), 'The Public Trust Doctrine in Natural Resource Law: Effective Judicial Intervention' 68 *Michigan Law Review* 471.
Young, M.D. (1999), 'The Precautionary Principle as a Key Element of Ecologically Sustainable Development' in Ronnie Harding and Elizabeth Fisher (eds), *Perspectives on the Precautionary Principle* (Sydney, Federation Press).
WCED (1987), World Commission on Environment and Development, *Our Common Future* (Oxford, Oxford University Press).

Index